THE WORLD OF
BUSINESS

THE WORLD OF
BUSINESS

GERALD H. GRAHAM
Wichita State University

ADDISON-WESLEY PUBLISHING COMPANY
Reading, Massachusetts
Menlo Park, California
Don Mills, Ontario
Wokingham, England
Amsterdam
Sydney
Singapore
Tokyo
Mexico City
Bogotá
Santiago
San Juan

Janis Jackson Hill *Acquisitions Editor*

Kristin Belanger *Art Editor*

Hugh Crawford *Manufacturing Supervisor*

Robert Hartwell Fiske *Development Editor*

Hannus Design Associates *Cover Designer*

Lorraine Hodsdon *Design Coordinator*

Intergraphics *Illustrator*

Martha K. Morong *Production Manager*

Margaret Pinette *Production Editor*

Sheila Pulver *Copy Editor*

Margaret Ong Tsao *Text Designer*

Karen Watson *Title Page, Part Opener, and Chapter Opener Artist*

Eric Wurzbacher *Photo Researcher*

Library of Congress Cataloging in Publication Data

Graham, Gerald H.
  The world of business.

  Includes index.
    1. Business.   2. United States — Commerce.
3. Business enterprises — United States.   I. Title.
HF5351.G658   1985   650   84-273
ISBN 0-201-11440-2

ABCDEFGHIJ-DO-898765

PREFACE

In the early 1980s, for the first time in history, three books about business appeared on the best-seller lists at the same time: *In Search of Excellence, Megatrends,* and *The One Minute Manager.* Periodicals about business practices have never been more popular than they are today. Government and community leaders are looking more than ever before to business for answers. Students, also picking up this theme, are enrolling in business courses in record numbers.

With the increasing popularity of business courses, colleges and their instructors and textbook writers and their publishers must assume a greater responsibility for providing the best business education possible. Since the Introduction to Business class is usually the first business course for most college students, it is critical that we do a good job in this area. Of course, the classroom instructor is the most vital ingredient among the total influences on students' learning experiences. A textbook, and the many supplementary materials that accompany it, are simply tools in the hands of a good instructor. Still, the text is an important feature, one that can make the instructor's job easier or more difficult.

All of society is demanding higher quality from businesses and other institutions. No longer can we sell products or services (texts included) simply by providing "balloons and suckers" to would-be purchasers. Like the business world, authors, to be successful, must create texts of outstanding quality. With *The World of Business,* we have responded to this challenge by producing a text for the 1980s, one that carries students to broader and deeper learning experiences.

COMPLETE COVERAGE

"The most complete coverage of any intro to business text on the market," is the way reviewers describe this text. As some critics have pointed out, many introductory texts provide information that is "a mile wide and an inch deep." That is, there is a little information about a lot of different topics but not much about any particular topic. But today's business students are more demanding, wanting solid concepts and comprehensive coverage of relevant topics.

Comprehensive coverage does not, however, mean "dry and dull." After reading the manuscript, one student said, "I found the text to be lively as well as informative." We hope that we have created a comprehensive, yet easy-to-read text. At least, that was our goal.

REAL-WORLD EXAMPLES

Research from communication experiments stresses the importance of tangible, practical examples for increasing interest and learning. After presenting concepts, the text frequently shows several cogent examples to reinforce student learning of the concept. In one of the marketing chapters, after discussing the concept of "pioneering advertising," the text illustrates how Coca-Cola used Hollywood-type hype successfully to launch its Diet Coke. And after presenting "listed securities," in a finance chapter, the text records that Braniff Airlines stock set a record in trades while the company was still in bankruptcy.

Theories of business practices are very important, but nothing happens in a vacuum. Primarily through the use of actual examples, the text shows how businesses translate the theory into practice. For instance, the computer chapter describes electronic mail and then shows how Franson and Associates, a public relations agency, uses electronic mail in their business. Another section shows how Chrysler uses 30 robots, equipped with computer-chip brains, to weld 100 new cars an hour in its Delaware assembly plant. Whenever there is an opportunity, the text describes real-world businesses applying the concepts.

STRONG ISSUES EMPHASIS

The World of Business recognizes the dynamics of the business environment and attempts to capture the ever-changing nature of business by discussing critical, unresolved issues, such as: Should employers be allowed to use lie detector tests? Should insurance rates be the same for men and women? What overall impact will the increasing use of robots have on our economy?

Today's highly competitive business world increasingly demands business people equipped to think clearly about issues and make well-reasoned decisions. Throughout this book, students are presented with current business issues and

asked to take a stand. The "Crossfire" inserts are such a feature; they carefully delineate the pros and cons of issues and can easily be used to generate classroom discussion, mock debates, or student projects.

BACKGROUND FOR THE TEXT

Like most authors, I surveyed the topics considered important for an introduction to business text. And I have used the material in teaching more than 1200 introduction to business students in the last few years. Using the concept of "close to the customer," I've relied heavily on student feedback to tell us what to include and how to present the material. Current business periodicals were examined to get the latest trends and applications of the concepts. I would like to acknowledge the supportive role my publisher played in helping me develop the most effective teaching and learning package for instructors and students. I am greatly indebted to Robert Fiske, developmental editor at Addison-Wesley, for his many original ideas.

STIMULATING PEDAGOGY

The World of Business contains a number of outstanding pedagogical devices that are designed to aid the students' enjoyment in and understanding of the material.

- *Design.* The four-color design of this text is unlike any competing text. The artistic part- and chapter-opener collages, the wealth of photos, the art program, and the magazine-like layout all make this as pleasing a book to look at as it is to read.

- *Writing style.* Great pains have been taken to ensure the readability of this text. An occasional use of humor (quite aside from the *Funny Business* cartoons) also serves to stimulate the students' interest in the book.

- *Realistic examples.* As already mentioned, there is an abundance of up-to-date business examples throughout the text.

- *Part outlines and chapter learning objectives.* These two pedagogical devices help the students grasp the material even before it's presented.

- *Features.* "Business Bulletin" features provide extended real-world illustrations of numerous business areas. "Taking Stock" features assess the current status of specific businesses or various aspects of the business environment. "Crossfire" features present both sides of controversial issues.

- *Enrichment chapters.* There are five supplemental chapters in the text that allow the instructor to tailor the book to student and course needs. Enrichment Chapters A and B are unique to introduction to business books. The five chapters are: A, "Corporate Culture"; B, "Strategic Marketing"; C, "The Uses of Statistical Methods"; D, "Careers in Business"; E, "The Future of Business."

- *Funny Business.* A sprinkling of cartoons occasionally lightens the mood by entertaining the students.

- *End-of-chapter material.* This includes the summary, a synopsis of chapter highlights; "Mind Your Business," a chapter self-quiz for the students (with answers at the back of the book); key terms, bold-faced in the text and listed (with page-number reference) at the end of the chapter; review questions, a chapter test that the instructor may want to assign; and cases, two per chapter, enhance the students' understanding of concepts presented in the chapter.

- *Careerscope.* Following each of the book's six parts is a section on career planning. All six parts have a short vocational aptitude quiz to help the students assess their personality, interests, and values. These quizzes were devised by professional career counselors, Thomas Harrington and Arthur O'Shea of Career Planning Associates, Inc., of Needham, Massachusetts. The "Careerscopes" at the end of Parts II through V also contain a list of job descriptions applicable to the four business areas discussed in the text.

- *Glossary.* Finally, a glossary defines all key terms used in the text. A chapter-number reference accompanies each key term.

COMPREHENSIVE INSTRUCTIONAL/ LEARNING PACKAGE

Accompanying *The World of Business* is a complete, thoroughly integrated package of resource materials designed to assist the instructor in course preparation and management. The components of this instructional package, available to adopters in an attractive resource box, are the following:

- *Course Planner and Film Guide.* This resource is designed to explain the organization and use of the complete text package. A matrix illustrates the interrelationships of the components. Alternative approaches to assigning the text for quarter, semester, or short courses; general strategies for course planning, grading, and administration; and projects and resources are discussed. The extensive Film Guide lists and summarizes films with information on securing and using them in class.

- *Instructor's Resource Manual.* Detailed lecture outlines are presented for each chapter supplemented by teaching strategies for explaining concepts and enrichments materials that summarize recent business events. Student projects and activities; answers to end-of-chapter review questions and cases; and achievement texts, midterms, and final exams are provided.

- *Test Item File and TESTGEN.* Over 2000 test items — multiple choice and true-false — are available. Answers to all questions are key-referenced to chapter and page in the text and identify either factual or applied questions. Test items are available in printed form as well as through TESTGEN, a free computerized testing program available to adopters.

- *Transparencies.* A set of 120 transparencies, mostly original art not appearing in the text, will be available free to adopters. Business documents are included as transparencies.

- *The Career Decision-Making System (CDM).* The CDM is a comprehensive, easily interpreted measure of vocational interests, combining three important elements of effective career counseling — interests, abilities, and values — with extensive interpretive information about 283 occupations that employ the vast majority of the work force. This instrument was developed by Thomas Harrington and Arthur J. O'Shea, professional career counselors, who also prepared the vocational aptitude quizzes appearing in the "Careerscope" sections that follow each part of the textbook. The "Careerscopes," combined with the CDM, offer a well integrated approach to career planning.

- *Businesswise Library.* To enhance your classroom lectures, the Addison-Wesley Businesswise Library offers you a number of timely Addison-Wesley books spanning a variety of business topics: *Theory Z, The Hundred Best Companies to Work for in America,* and *Corporate Cultures,* to name a few. This library is available to adopters.

- *Student Activity Guide.* This useful study aid offers a detailed review of each chapter plus extensive self tests. The innovative aspects of the guide are the numerous involvement exercises that require students to apply information learned from the text to realistic, managerial situations. The exercises can be completed by students on an individual as well as group basis. Features such as "Critics Corner," "Problem Line," "From the Mailroom," "You Are the Manager," and "It's Your Opinion" ask students to assume the role of a manager and make decisions.

- *Bu$iness Sen$e: A Decision-Making Simulation.* A microcomputer simulation specifically designed for this course accompanies the text. Students form companies and make decisions in a competitive environment simulating a business situation. Playing the game gives students a better understanding of the relationship between production and operations management, marketing and finance. The Student Manual explains how to play, supplies worksheets, and provides a case study of the actual industry being simulated. The Instructor's Manual gives numerous options for integrating the simulation into the course.

ACKNOWLEDGMENTS

Many reviewers aided us in the preparation of this text. In recognition and appreciation of their willingness to work with us, we list here their names and affiliations:

Doug Anderson, Marion Technical College

Patti N. Andrews, Boston University

Carol Asplund, College of Lake County

Alec Beaudoin, Triton College

John Beem, College of DuPage

Karen Bessey, Merced College

W. C. Bessey, Golden Gate University

Frank A. Blackwood, Anne Arundel Community College

Robert Boatsman, Seattle Community College

Marvin Burnett, St. Louis Community College at Florissant Valley

William A. Clarey, Bradley University

James Cockrell, Chemeketa Community College

Phyllis Graff Culp, Kansas City Community College

Harris D. Dean, Lansing Community College

Wayne Decker, Memphis State University

Don Freeman, Pikes Peak Community College

Robert W. Harris, Mercer County Community College

Laurence Harvey, DeAnza College

A. C. Hawthorne, Central Piedmont Community College

David Hearn, Jefferson State Junior College

Larry E. Heldreth, Danville Community College

Ron Herrick, Mesa Community College

William Jedlicka, William Rainy Harper College

Tom Johnson, William Rainy Harper College

Gerald W. Jones, Spokane Community College

Elvin E. Kellermeyer, Southwest Texas State University

Francis S. King, Westchester Community College

George Leonard, St. Petersburg Junior College

Chad T. Lewis, Everett Community College

John W. Lloyd, Monroe Community College

Andrew Lonyo, Macomb County Community College

Esther Lowery, Connors State College

James Meszaros, County College of Morris

John Miller, Chabot College

Robert W. Mitchel, Orange Coast College

Bill Motz, Lansing Community College

Bonnie D. Phillips, Casper College

Joseph Platts, Miami-Dade Community College

Paul Plescia, American River College

Kathryn J. Ready, University of Wisconsin/LaCrosse

Edward Rinetti, Los Angeles City College

Robert Rizzo, Indian River Community College

William L. Roach, Washburn University

Gene Schneider, Austin Community College

Dennis Shannon, Belleville Area College

Jack Shapiro, Loop College

Leon Singleton, Santa Monica College

Donald A. Smith, Los Angeles Pierce College

Robert N. Sullivan, Eastern Illinois University

Ray Tewell, American River College

Charles E. Tychsen, Northern Virginia Community College

Pablo Ulloa, Jr., El Paso Community College

Robert Vaughn, Lakeland Community College

Keith Weidkamp, Sierra College

Edward Welsh, Phoenix College

Ralph Wilcox, Kirkwood Community College

Paul Williams, Mott Community College

Ira Wilkser, Lamar University

Martin J. Wise, Harrisburg Area Community College

Heidi Wortzel, Northeastern University

Thomas W. Zimmerer, Clemson University

Wichita, Kansas
November 1984

G. H. G.

ABOUT THE AUTHOR

Gerald H. Graham holds the R. P. Clinton Distinguished Professor of Management Chair at Wichita State University and was recently awarded the Wichita State University Regents' "Excellence in Teaching" award.

The author has more than 20 years of teaching experience at the university level and has taught an introduction to business course during 10 of those years. He received his doctoral degree in business from Louisiana State University. Prior to coming to Wichita State, Dr. Graham taught at Northeast Louisiana University and Nicholls State College, also in Louisiana. He currently teaches in the business area with specific emphasis on introduction to business, management principles, and organizational behavior. Dr. Graham has published dozens of research articles in management and human behavior, which have appeared in such journals as *The Academy of Management Journal*, *Personnel Journal*, and *Personnel Administrator*. He has authored textbooks in management and human relations.

Over the past 15 years, Dr. Graham has conducted management development workshops for more than 75,000 participants from major corporations, such as: American Express, Chase Manhattan Bank, Standard Oil, AT&T, IBM, Bank of America, McDonald's, Wendy's, and Xerox. He has also been a consultant to many other national business organizations and thereby has first-hand experiences with their application of business concepts in their operations. Recently, Dr. Graham has been actively involved in developing and teaching training courses via teleconferencing for managers throughout the country.

Dr. Graham is president of the National Association for Management, which publishes training materials for industry. One of his publications is a monthly *Applied Management Newsletter* that is distributed throughout the United States and other nations to thousands of business managers. He also writes a twice-monthly, nationally syndicated "Management File" column for the Knight-Ridder newspaper chain.

CONTENTS

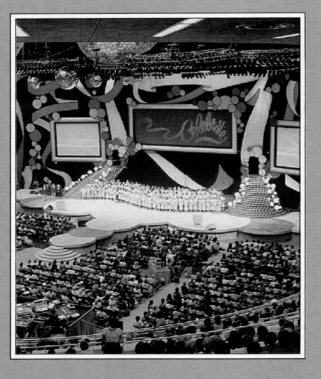

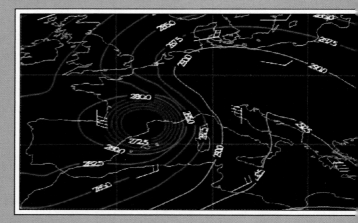

I

THE FOUNDATION OF BUSINESS

LEARNING OBJECTIVES

After studying this chapter, you will be able to:

■ Describe briefly the history of our private enterprise system.

■ List and describe four characteristics of our private enterprise system.

■ Identify four factors necessary to produce goods and services in a private enterprise economy.

■ Analyze five indicators that measure how well our economic system is performing.

1

FOUNDATIONS OF OUR PRIVATE ENTERPRISE SYSTEM

Welcome to the world of business! You could not have picked a more exciting time to study the private enterprise system of the United States. For years, we were content with the fact that our economic system was the strongest and most powerful in the world. And, no doubt, many people took it for granted. In fact, during part of the 1960s and 1970s, some Americans maligned business, blaming our economic system for many of the country's problems.

However, things have changed. We have suddenly awakened to discover that our economy no longer dominates the world in the way that it once did. For instance, some automated factories in Japan can build a car in 9 hours flat; it takes American workers about 31 hours to build a car. In the early 1980s, Japan became the number 1 car producer in the world, exceeding our production by almost 50%. Tokyo, not New York, is the largest city in the world. The economies of many nations, including South Korea, Taiwan, Saudi Arabia, Kuwait, and Japan, are growing at more rapid rates than the U.S. economy. Other nations have greater supplies of global riches than we do; Asia and Australia have far more oil, Russia has more iron ore, Asia and Australia produce more grain, Latin America and Africa have more forests.

How have our nation and private enterprise system reacted to these realizations? Very positively. We still have the largest economy in the world, producing twice as much as our closest rival, the Soviet Union. But we are no longer a sleeping giant. Innovation and change inspire our private enterprise system once again. The evidence is everywhere. Computers are changing everything. "The most dramatic economic change in the next 50 years," according to the editors of *U.S. News & World Report,* "will be the renewal of the private sector as it departs from its manufacturing base and advances further in to the 'Information Age.'" Soon 80% of our employees will be working to provide services and information to society. Robots are taking over many menial tasks. Our large companies are entering into partner-ships with large companies of other nations. And in just 10 years, our businesses, working with government, and perhaps other nations, will have a permanent, manned space station in earth orbit. Shortly after, we will see large-scale commercial manufacturing in space. Yes, this is an exciting time to study business.

But what exactly do we mean by business? In our study we define **business** as any organization — from the largest computer corporation to the corner grocery store — that engages in the creation or sale of goods and services with the goal of earning a profit. The composite of all business firms and their relationships (to one another, the public, and society at large) makes up our **business system.**

We refer to our business system as a private enterprise system. By **private enterprise** (sometimes called **free enterprise**) we mean a system that encourages private choices of individuals and private ownership and operation of businesses. This chapter briefly discusses the evolution of our private enterprise system, defines its components and characteristics, and analyzes just how well the system is doing.

EVOLUTION OF OUR PRIVATE ENTERPRISE SYSTEM

Although it had its beginnings in simple bartering, our current private enterprise system has evolved into an exceedingly complex and dynamic system. In the following pages, we will trace the history of our system and consider the beginning of business, mercantilism, the Industrial Revolution, the consumer era, and the current age of technology.

The Beginning of Business

Cave dwellers engaged in warfare to capture goods and satisfy their needs, but people later learned that the exchange of goods and services was more efficient (and less lethal) than war. The early Greeks and Syrians became especially accomplished in business by founding and developing **trade,** the exchange of goods or services, between countries. They produced fine fabrics and exchanged them for silver and copper from Spain and tin from Britain. Early traders became ship builders and profited from the commerce between countries. By the eleventh century, trade became a source of great wealth. **Barter,** as this process is also called, is still with us in the twentieth century. Though not a common occurrence, it is by no means unheard of for a doctor's or dentist's services to be "paid for" with, perhaps, an original oil painting or an automobile engine tune-up. Recently, in 1983, American Airlines traded eight 747s for fifteen DC-10s from Pan American World Airways. Likewise, some nations barter billions of dollars worth of products with each other.

Mercantilism

Most large European nations developed mercantile policies by the fifteenth century. Under **mercantilism,** these countries established, and controlled, colonies to increase their own wealth. By forcing the colonies to buy products at inflated prices and by capturing their natural resources the European nations prospered. The United States became a colony of Britain in just this way.

Mercantilism provided much of the founda-

---

tion of American business.

Jamestown, for example, provided England with a wealth of raw materials such as tobacco, indigo, ginger, and cotton. At the same time, the colonists were forced to purchase England's surplus goods, such as sugar and tea. Eventually rebelling against the strict rule that controlled their trade, the colonies began trading illegally with other countries and refusing to buy English goods at inflated prices. The Boston Tea Party, where the colonists dumped 342 chests of tea into the harbor, is a famous example of colonial rebellion. Although mercantilism lost its power and popularity by the early 1800s, it provided much of the foundation of American business. It gave a healthy beginning to production and trade and strengthened the settler's desire for independence and private ownership of property.

Industrial Revolution

The **Industrial Revolution,** which was characterized by the substitution of hand tools for power-driven machines, began in England around 1760 and came to the United States some thirty or forty years later. In this country, Alexander Hamilton set the groundwork for expansions in production by encouraging government actions to benefit factories. Eli Whitney's cotton gin (1793) increased the availability of cotton which, along with tobacco, became a valued commodity. What's more, Whitney contracted with the government to deliver 10,000 muskets for the

Established in 1913 by Henry Ford, this movable assembly line could turn out a finished Model T every ten seconds.

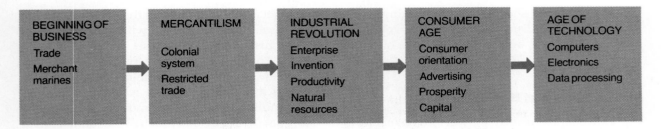

BEGINNING OF BUSINESS	MERCANTILISM	INDUSTRIAL REVOLUTION	CONSUMER AGE	AGE OF TECHNOLOGY
Trade Merchant marines	Colonial system Restricted trade	Enterprise Invention Productivity Natural resources	Consumer orientation Advertising Prosperity Capital	Computers Electronics Data processing

Figure 1.1
Evolution of our private enterprise system.

sum of $134,000 (which at today's prices would probably make it the first million-dollar contract). His concept of interchangeable parts that could be manufactured and assembled by unskilled workers was not only the beginning of mass production, but also the division of labor — the foundation of the factory system.

Other inventions that spurred industry were the steam engine, the steamboat, the telegraph, and the coast-to-coast railroad networks that were completed in 1869. Henry Ford established the first movable assembly line in 1913. This period was also influenced by dynamic business leaders — called **entrepreneurs** — who initiated, organized, and managed resources and workers, reaching record levels of production.

Electronic banking and shopping directly from the home are available to subscribers of this videotex service.

These pioneers included Carnegie (steel), Morgan (banking), Rockefeller (oil), Mellon (aluminum), Ford (automobiles), McCormick (farm equipment), Singer (sewing machines), and Edison (power). This combination of enterprise, invention, natural resources, and productivity quickly made the United States the industrial leader of the world and provided Americans with the highest standard of living.

Consumer Era

With the success of the Industrial Revolution came an adequate supply of products. The next challenge was to sell them. Before the **consumer era,** which began around 1870, the production of goods was determined largely by basic need. There was little regard for color, style, or consumer preference, Ford cars, for example, were available in any color you'd like — as long as it was black. Though stimulated by the prosperous years following World War I and, even more so, following World War II, the consumer era went into full swing when manufacturers became more concerned about the tastes and desires of their customers.

The emergence of General Motors did a lot to spark the flame of the consumer era. With its first cars, GM advertised style and variety. It made a special effort to satisfy consumer needs. Not only did Ford respond in kind, but manufacturers and sellers of most products quickly followed their example. Department stores emerged and began catering to the desires of customers. Montgomery Ward began in 1872. In 1887, Alvah Roebuck, a watchmaker, answered an ad in the *Chicago Daily News* and was hired by Richard Sears. This was the beginning of Sears and Roebuck, one of the most famous partnerships in the business world. The first 5 and 10 cent store was opened by F. W. Woolworth in 1879.

Another feature of the consumer era was the **advertising boom.** Before this time, there was little advertising. Once sellers learned that they could expand their markets and quickly increase sales and profits through advertising, it became a new way of life. Needless to say, it is still with us today and as healthy as ever.

Financial conditions also contributed to the consumer era. Before 1910, banks loaned money mostly to factories and businesses. Even home mortgages were rare. When the Federal Reserve Bank was established in 1913, consumer credit became available for purchases of consumer goods. With healthy supplies of money, products, and advertising, the consumer era thrived.

Age of Technology

Many consider the most recent development in our private enterprise system to be the **age of technology.** While technology was certainly a part of the Industrial Revolution (with its inventions and improvements in productivity), today's business world uses technology to a much greater degree. The age of technology is characterized by the rapid proliferation of electronics in the form of computers, business machines, and household products. Electronic goods of every kind have found their way into America's homes. Electronic technology has revolutionized methods of doing business, both in the factory and in the office. Computers of one sort or another are found in automobiles, stereos, voting booths, video games, and yes, even college testing programs.

BUSINESS BULLETIN

An Example of Evolution in Our Business System

To illustrate the evolution of our business system, let's take a look at agriculture and see how it has changed over the years.

In earlier times, more than 90% of the U.S. population were involved in agriculture. We needed this effort to provide enough food to eat. Still, few nations produce all the food they need or want. As early as 100 A.D., farmers in Italy and France were able to trade their crops through merchant marines for, say, rice from China or olives from Greece.

Mercantilism greatly affected the colonial farmers of the United States. England in essence said to the colonies, ''Grow what we need, and we will pay you what we want to for your crops.'' But the Industrial Revolution, introducing massive machinery and time-saving tools, had probably the greatest impact upon our farming industry. Advanced technology allowed farmers to produce two and three times their previous crop yields.

During the consumer era, farmers were able to produce more and different kinds of crops. Consumers then concerned themselves with agricultural products beyond what they needed to stay alive. Believing there were consumers who desired beer and cigarettes, some farmers plowed under their cotton crops to grow hops and tobacco.

In this advanced technological age, farmers use modern, productive equipment to plant, harvest, process, and transport their crops. Because of the efficiency of today's technology, fewer and fewer farmers are producing more and more food. In fact, less than 10% of our population currently work on the farm, though for all practical purposes, we have the ability to produce enough food to feed the entire world.

OUR PRIVATE ENTERPRISE SYSTEM AT WORK

The qualities of our private enterprise system are the subject of frequent debates among scholars, politicians, business leaders, students, and citizens. Almost every political election, at every level, focuses on issues that affect how our economic system works. Let's take a closer look at the much-discussed characteristics of our system and the factors of production associated with it.

Characteristics of Our Private Enterprise System

In Chapter 2, we shall discuss three economic systems (capitalism, socialism, and communism) with regard to ownership, choice, competition, and profit. Here, we consider each of these qualities as it pertains to our business system.

Ownership and risk. In colonial America, feelings about individual property ownership were so strong that it was protected in the Constitution. Article 5 of the Bill of Rights states that no individual can be deprived of property without due process of law, and no private property can be taken for public use unless individual owners are paid a fair price. Later, the Fourteenth Amendment strengthened this trend by promising the right of private property to all citizens. Thus, our modern business system relies heavily on the right of private property, but we have come to accept more government ownership.

Federal, state, and city governments own parks, lakes, roadways, schools, highway systems, and military bases. Additionally, the govern-ment owns some large enterprises, such as the Tennessee Valley Authority (TVA) utility company. Today, the federal government owns one-third of all the land. This amounts to an area the size of all the states east of the Mississippi River plus Louisiana and Texas, a total of 742 million acres.

Freedom of choice. In our society, individuals can choose to be mechanics, or morticians, or salespeople, scientists, teachers, or tailors, clerks, or welders, or witches. *The Dictionary of Occupational Titles* lists 40,000 different jobs in more than 600 major job groupings. Businesses have almost unlimited freedom to choose a type of business activity, and customers can select from dozens of different product brands, hundreds of automobile models, and thousands of food items.

Our government does limit freedom of choice.

On the other hand, our government does limit freedom of choice. It prevents some mergers in the interest of competition; some states own and control liquor stores; there are several restrictions on cigarette advertising; employers with federal contracts have to follow affirmative action guidelines in hiring; there are many restrictions on pricing; and during some periods, the government imposes rigid price and wage controls.

In our business system, we also have the right to conduct business activities with little restriction. The government does, however, levy some restrictions. Monopolies are limited, and some states have passed laws forbidding pyramid schemes because many unsuspecting people were losing money. While these laws are opposed to the true spirit of capitalism (see Chapter 2), they have been passed to protect the citizens of the country. Most of us have come to accept and even respect these laws.

Our system also offers the freedom to invest our money as we choose. As long as an individual legally acquires capital, the choices of investment are broad. Some restrictions do apply. A person may not invest in illegal activities, such as importing illegal drugs. To sign a contract, one must be of sound mind and at least 18 years of age. To invest

TABLE 1.1 ■ USES OF FEDERALLY OWNED LAND

Predominate Use	Square Miles
Bureau of Land Management	500,000
National Forests	298,437
National Wildlife Refuges	135,937
National Parks and Monuments	115,625
Other (including Indian reservations and military properties)	184,375

Source: General Services Administration.

FUNNY BUSINESS

"How little we really own, Tom, when you consider all there is to own."

by forming a corporation or business requires a license and other approvals. Still, the freedom to invest is probably as great as in any other country.

Markets and competition. Competition was evident in early America, and it is deeply ingrained within our life-style today. We teach competition effectively: Athletic teams compete for victory, churches compete for attendance, students compete for grades, and businesses compete for profits. For our purposes, let us define **competition** as the rivalry between two or more businesses striving for the same customer, market, or resources.

We are quick to praise the benefits of our competitive system. It stimulates development, advancement, and efficiency. To succeed, businesses seek an advantage over their competitors by developing and distributing their products and services more effectively. We give less attention to the potential problems of competition. In efforts to outdo others, managers sometimes resort to cheating, fraud, misleading advertising, and price fixing. For this reason, we have passed many laws to regulate competition. The government does reduce competition by supporting monopolies in utilities, transportation, and communication, and by regulating their prices through commissions.

Contrary to the spirit of true capitalism, the government also has many restrictions with regard to pricing—a most critical aspect of competition. Grocery chains are limited in the degree to which they can take losses in "price leaders." Utilities, such as the phone companies and power companies, must get government approval before raising prices. During the energy crisis, there were numerous restrictions on the prices that could be charged for gasoline. Even a governmental agency like the post office needs approval before raising postage rates. On the other hand, the 1980s has produced many government actions that have deregulated some industries in an effort to stimulate competition.

Economists use the term "competition" in a specialized way. "Pure competition" or "perfect competition" exists when no one seller produces enough of a product to influence the price in the market. Pure competition, in reality, is very limited; but it does occur in some agricultural commodity markets. In wheat, for example, no one farmer produces enough wheat to influence the market price.

More commonly, "imperfect competition" exists when a firm produces a product or service that the consumer considers to be in some way different from other similar products or services. Most companies, through product design and advertising, try to make their product unique, or at least appear to be unique. This allows them some control over the price. Home computer manufacturers, for example, compete more on style, image, and other minor differences than on the basis of price.

The young cable television industry is a highly competitive business, sprung from recent deregulation measures, new technologies, and market demands.

Profits and incentives. Ford Motor Company reported a record $1.87 billion profit in 1983. Chairman Philip Caldwell said that, after three straight years of losses, Ford had become, "profitable at home and abroad." He also added, "Many more good years lie ahead." The 1983 profits broke the previous Ford record of $1.67 billion set in 1977. General Motors also reported a huge profit for 1983, $3.73 billion in fact. The two auto makers, by themselves, earned $5.6 billion for the year, topping the industry record of 5.18 billion in 1977.

Profit, the return received on business activity after all costs and operating expenses have been deducted, is vital to our business system today. Most businesses state that profit is one of their most important objectives, and all recognize that they need profit to survive. Profit, therefore, becomes a driving mixture for businesses to provide goods and services to consumers.

But there is another view. In the 1800s, when many businesses grew very large and some leaders used bribes, price fixing, and other unethical means to reduce competition, many citizens thought businesses were making excess profits at the expense of their employees and customers. The huge profits of oil companies in 1979–1981 created quite a stir. The companies said they needed the increases in profits to promote the risky business of finding oil. But customers, who

Figure 1.2
Profit trends for selected industries:
(a) Corporate profits before and after inflation; (b) earnings of major industries. *Source: U.S. Department of Commerce.*

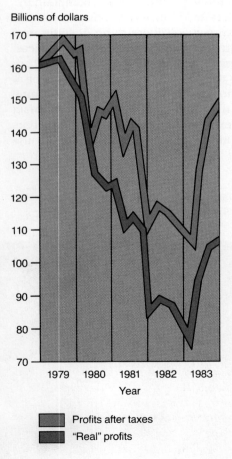

Billions of dollars

Profits after taxes
"Real" profits

(a)

(b)

	4th Quarter, 1983	Percentage Change from Year Ago	4th-Quarter Profits as Percentage of Sales 1982	1983
Aircraft, missiles	$ 451 mil.	Up 32%	3.1%	3.7%
Airlines	$ 112 mil.	Up 15%	3.8%	3.6%
Banks	$2,205 mil.	Up 7%	*	*
Broadcasting	$ 79 mil.	Up 29%	13.3%	13.9%
Brokerage firms	$ 45 mil.	Down 80%	8.5%	1.8%
Building materials	$ 332 mil.	Up 170%	1.8%	4.3%
Chemicals	$ 380 mil.	Up 108%	2.2%	4.1%
Computers, office goods	$2,828 mil.	Up 30%	9.1%	10.1%
Drugs	$ 761 mil.	Up 13%	12.6%	13.1%
Electric utilities	$1,873 mil.	Up 14%	10.4%	11.2%
Food, beverages	$ 573 mil.	Up 37%	4.0%	4.3%
Gas utilities	$ 67 mil.	Down 9%	4.9%	4.9%
Health care, supplies	$ 179 mil.	Up 13%	6.8%	6.9%
Leisure time	$ 25 mil.	Down 19%	8.5%	5.9%
Machinery, electrical	$ 958 mil.	Up 21%	6.0%	7.0%
Machinery, other	$ 10 mil.	*	*	0.3%
Motor vehicles	$ 118 mil.	Up 28%	3.6%	4.4%
Nonferrous metals	$ 206 mil.	*	*	4.9%
Paper	$ 288 mil.	Up 473%	1.0%	4.7%
Petroleum	$5,370 mil.	Up 4%	4.8%	5.2%
Printing, publishing	$ 239 mil.	Up 21%	8.5%	9.2%
Railroads	$ 404 mil.	Down 5%	6.8%	5.2%
Restaurants, lodging	$ 102 mil.	Up 17%	8.1%	8.2%
Retail food stores	$ 43 mil.	Down 1%	1.5%	1.4%
Rubber	$ 41 mil.	Up 239%	1.7%	4.7%
Savings and loans	$ 43 mil.	Up 52%	*	*
Steel	-$ 135 mil.	*	*	*
Telephones	$ 735 mil.	Down 54%	8.9%	3.9%
Textiles, apparel	$ 121 mil.	Up 64%	3.0%	4.4%

were asked to lower their thermostats and drive smaller, more fuel-efficient cars, viewed the oil executives as crooks. Most people felt that big business was taking advantage of a scarce resource and charging excessive prices. Most Americans want fewer restrictions, but will call for them under extreme conditions. Figure 1.2 shows profits for selected major industries.

The purpose of the progressive tax structure is to reallocate income from the wealthy to the less wealthy.

Under pure capitalism, profits determine who will have wealth. In recent times, our government has taken a larger role in allocation by attempting to distribute wealth through such plans as taxation, social security, and welfare programs. The purpose of the progressive tax structure is to reallocate income from the wealthy to the less wealthy by increasing the rate of tax as earnings increase. Social security contributions transfer income to benefit older and less privileged persons. Welfare programs such as food stamps, rent supplements, and housing aid are other means of redistributing income. While these practices have moved us from our earlier free enterprise practices, the world still considers us to be the epitome of a free enterprise nation.

Factors of Production

Factors of production are the elements necessary to produce goods and services; they include (1) natural resources, (2) labor, (3) capital, and (4) management.

Natural resources. In addition to land, we consider oil, coal, gravel, water, and natural gas to be examples of **natural resources.** Natural resources also include items we produce from the land such as cotton, corn, lumber, and hay. As the bases of production, natural resources are used to make other things. Unfortunately, nations eventually deplete their natural resources. As all of us know, we use millions of barrels of oil every day, yet it takes thousands of years for nature to create oil. Motivated by our creative technology that requires us to use oil in hundreds of products, our demand has been greater than our resources. Since we and other nations have a tendency to use our natural resources avariciously, we will probably continue wrangling over shortages.

Labor. **Labor** is the physical and mental effort of people. Factory workers, farmers, doctors, lawyers, and writers are only a few examples of laborers. Although our supply of natural resources is limited, labor expands with the population, but not directly. Certain segments of the population—the very young, the very old, and the handicapped—may not be a part of the labor force. In 1984 there were more than 100 million persons in the labor force. Two specific changes have been occurring within the labor force in the past few decades. First, the labor force has more years of formal education. In 1964, workers averaged 12.2 years of formal education. By 1980, that figure was 12.6. It is expected to be even higher in 1985 when eight out of every ten adults will have completed high school. Second, productivity per person-hour has virtually levelled off. It has been increasing only 2 to 3% during the last 5 years compared to 6 to 8% in earlier years. In 1981, it actually decreased. This compares to increases of 10 to 15% in Japan and Germany. At first, these two trends appear to be contradictory. But the combined desire for higher education and dissatisfaction with highly specialized jobs has resulted in worker apathy and inefficiency in many jobs.

Labor is obtained by wages. If the cost of labor increases the price of a product too much, the demand for the product will fall. In these cases, workers may lose their jobs. What better example exists than the problems facing U.S. auto workers in 1982? Their unions actually gave up increased wages and benefits so that the factories could stay open and workers could keep their jobs.

Capital. The monetary value of machinery, equipment, buildings, and tools, as well as cash investment and reserves, represents **capital.** Capital is essential to all business activity. It is required to start a business as well as to run it. In fact, a common reason for business failure is inadequate capital. The major sources of capital to companies are investors, lenders, and retained earnings. People invest in companies in the hope of earning a reasonable return on their investment; we loan for

High-risk ventures like exploring for oil—a natural resource, one factor of production—bring into play the three other factors: an experienced management, substantial capital investment, and a skilled labor force.

the promise of repayment plus interest; and managers hold onto some of their profits for the purpose of using them to make even greater profits. With technological advances, capital requirements are increasing rapidly. Since most of the capital in the United States is privately owned, firms continuously seek ways to attract capital.

Management. The management skill of successfully utilizing the first three factors of production is called **entrepreneurship.** Entrepreneurs are the people who unite natural resources, labor, and capital within a business to produce and sell goods and services. These entrepreneur–

managers face both opportunities and risks. If they are successful, they are well paid; but a failure may result in the loss of money put up by investors as well as the loss of a job. As a successful entrepreneur–manager put it, "I have been very successful. Last year, I made over a million dollars. But there were times when I thought we were going to lose the whole thing."

Likewise, each factor of production presents additional risks. Natural resources may become scarce or be available at too high a cost; environmentalists may make it difficult to get certain resources. Labor is a constant source of worry. Not only do entrepreneur–managers have to find and

Success and Failure in Computer Manufacturing

Why does one firm succeed mightily and another have less success? For many different reasons, of course. The stories of Three Rivers Corp. and Apollo Computer Inc. provide a vivid contrast in operations and in degree of success.

The firms are similar in that both build supermicrocomputers, and both had emerged as industry leaders in the late 1970s. But in 1983, Apollo's stock had a market value of $365 million and its sales approached $100 million. By contrast, Three Rivers' sales totaled about $10 million, the same as in 1982; what's more, their top management team had just resigned under pressure.

Three differences in strategies apparently account for the success of Apollo: (1) financing methods, (2) marketing strategy, and (3) delivery.

1. Three Rivers' early financing consisted primarily of a quick $5 million investment from two Schlumberger executives. This dried up other financing because venture capitalists were not willing to put up money for additional needs, nor were the original investors willing to ante up more. As one venture capitalist said, "Three Rivers went to amateur investors without staying power." Apollo, however, put togther a very elegant financing scheme, getting venture from The First National Bank of Boston and four other top venture capital firms. Their contacts led to other investment contacts as well as to early customers.

2. The differences in marketing strategies were quite pronounced. Apollo targeted a 50–50 split in sales between end users of their computers and original equipment manufacturers (OEMs). Contact with the end users kept them close to applications, and the OEMs provided a base for long-term purchasing power. Apollo also signed more than 100 companies to write software programs for their computer, making their product more desirable to the end user. Three Rivers was very inconsistent in its marketing. With no well-defined strategy, they were very late to sign software vendors. And they concentrated mostly on sales to OEMs; but there were so many hardware vendors, the OEMs were quite selective and bought only a few computers at the time.

3. Finally, Apollo worked hard to have computers ready when the orders began to roll in; and when they shipped their machines to the users, they worked. There were many reliability problems in Three Rivers' product, and they got behind in shipping their orders. Customers who had prepaid their order were understandably furious about late shipments.

In this comparison, two firms with good technical products performed quite differently, clearly demonstrating that success depends on good management as well as on resources, labor, and capital.

Source: G. Thomas Gibson, "Two Startups, One Winner," *Venture,* August, 1983, pp. 96–98.

develop the proper skills in the work force, they have to worry about labor unions, strikes, turnover, and pressures for higher pay. Capital is a scarce commodity. Companies must attract enough capital to meet the needs of the business at the right time and at a reasonable cost. The entrepreneur – manager is also an element of risk, for he or she must make crucial decisions. Too many wrong choices could mean failure of the business.

HOW WELL IS OUR SYSTEM DOING?

The United States has always taken pride in its stance as the world's symbol of private enterprise opportunity. Yet, there is some question as to how well our system is working, especially in light of the recessions of the 1970s and early 1980s. Let's look at some hard facts about our economy's performance.

① In Satisfying Economic Needs

The 1970s delivered two recessions and the sharpest inflation rates in decades. The early 1980s produced the greatest economic downturn since the Great Depression. Yet, in almost every way, we are better off today than ever before.

The buying power of the average person is almost twice as much today as it was 30 years ago.

Buying power is the money we have left to spend after taxes and after accounting for inflation. Since the hardening experience of World War II, buying power has increased 94%. This means that the average person is able to buy almost twice as much today as 30 years ago. We have also had increases in the number of people who own their own homes, frequency of foreign travel, average life span, and proportion of families owning more than one car. In addition, we are wealthier and better educated than ever before. For heads of families, age 25 or older, who had finished college, the median family income in 1982 was $35,778. For those who had finished high school, the figure

was $23,837. Figure 1.3 illustrates these improvements.

"But," you might ask, "are we happy?" A recent Gallup poll showed that 57% of citizens expressed "a high level of satisfaction" with life in the United States. Gallup pollsters also took samplings in nine democratic countries in the Western world. Citizens of the United States and Denmark showed more satisfaction with their general lot in life than people in other countries.

② In Providing Methods of Production

Productivity rate, the increase or decrease in goods and services produced in an hour of work, measures the effectiveness of our methods of production. **Output** is the annual production per person, adjusted for inflation.

As Figure 1.4 shows, our productivity rates declined the past 10 years. During this time, our productivity growth has trailed that of Japan, France, and Germany. In three years, the productivity rate was negative; and in 1982, it was zero. However, experts are now predicting that annual growth rates in output could run as high as 3.0% a year for the rest of the decade.

Several reasons caused the earlier decline in productivity rates. First, we allowed our plants and equipment to run down because we did not invest enough to keep them modern. Second, many companies did not spend enough in research and development, and they were not able to come forth with new innovations in products and services. Third, some experts believed that management did not do enough to motivate employees effectively. Incentives that management had traditionally relied on — higher pay, bonuses, fringe benefits, and the like — did not seem to work so well during the 1970s and early 1980s. Employees coming into the work force today are more interested in job challenge, advancement, and fulfilling work.

Experts are more optimistic about future productivity growth rates for several reasons. The Economic Recovery Act of 1981 encourages businesses to invest more capital by offering them faster depreciation write-offs. As a result, capital per worker is expected to increase into the 1990s. This will encourage the introduction of more and better technology, especially robots and computers, into the workplace. The government hit commerce and industry with a wave of federal regulations during the 1970s. Now, most people believe that the cost of these regulations has been largely absorbed. Further, the trend has swung toward deregulation, and this is expected to boost productivity even more. Companies have increased their research and development spending, bringing forth a wave of innovations in methods and in products. Finally, stimulated by foreign competition and economic troubles of the early 1980s, a new cooperation has emerged between workers and management. Now, joint labor–management productivity teams are trying to get workers to identify more closely with company goals.

In short, we may still be hard pressed to catch up to the productivity increases of some other nations, especially Japan, but the situation looks better for the remainder of the 1980s.

Figure 1.3
Improvements in our economic need satisfaction. *Source: Compiled from data from U.S. Department of Commerce, Labor, and Health, Education and Welfare; the Federal Reserve Board; the Motor Vehicle Manufacturers Association.*

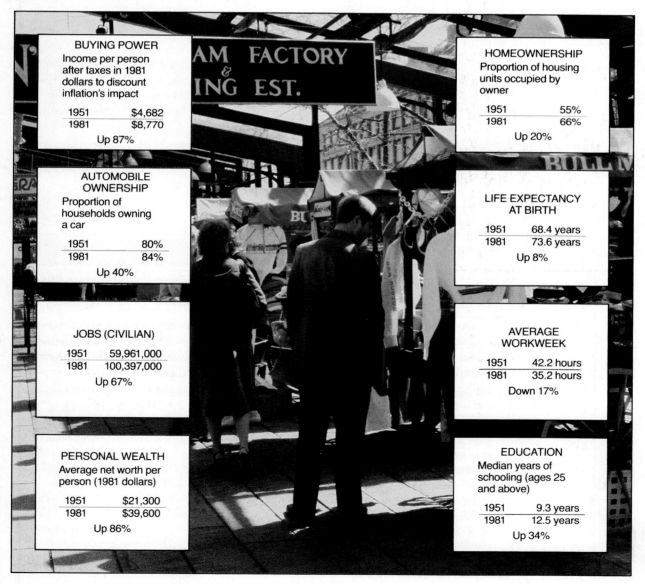

BUYING POWER
Income per person after taxes in 1981 dollars to discount inflation's impact

| 1951 | $4,682 |
| 1981 | $8,770 |

Up 87%

AUTOMOBILE OWNERSHIP
Proportion of households owning a car

| 1951 | 80% |
| 1981 | 84% |

Up 40%

JOBS (CIVILIAN)

| 1951 | 59,961,000 |
| 1981 | 100,397,000 |

Up 67%

PERSONAL WEALTH
Average net worth per person (1981 dollars)

| 1951 | $21,300 |
| 1981 | $39,600 |

Up 86%

HOMEOWNERSHIP
Proportion of housing units occupied by owner

| 1951 | 55% |
| 1981 | 66% |

Up 20%

LIFE EXPECTANCY AT BIRTH

| 1951 | 68.4 years |
| 1981 | 73.6 years |

Up 8%

AVERAGE WORKWEEK

| 1951 | 42.2 hours |
| 1981 | 35.2 hours |

Down 17%

EDUCATION
Median years of schooling (ages 25 and above)

| 1951 | 9.3 years |
| 1981 | 12.5 years |

Up 34%

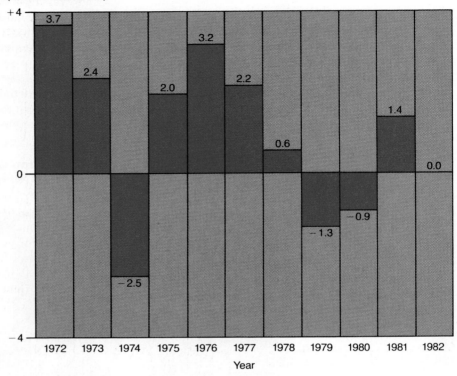

Percentage of change in output per hour (nonfarm businesses)

Figure 1.4
Decline in U.S. productiv-ity. *Source: U.S. Department of Labor.*

Comparing the U.S. and Soviet Economies

In analyzing how well our economy is doing, it is almost impossible to resist comparing the U.S. version of capitalism to that of our major communist rival, Russia. In 1982, comparisons on several key items show that our economic output is still far ahead of Russia's.

	U.S.	U.S.S.R.
Total output	$2.9 trillion	$1.4 trillion
Steel (in metric tons)	100.8 million	148.0 million
Autos produced	6.4 million	1.3 million
Grain produced (per person)	2,552 lbs.	1,571 lbs.
Oil produced (barrels per day)	8.57 million	12.18 million
Population	230 million	268 million
Land area (square miles)	3.6 million	8.6 million

Source: Various government and industry sources.

In Distributing Wealth

Critics might give our system bad marks for the way that we distribute wealth. They would say that we have too many people at the extremes — too many that have accumulated too much wealth and too many that have accumulated too little. The poor and disadvantaged, experts say, account for many of our criminal and social problems. However, proponents point out that we need accumulations of wealth, for that is where much of our investment and growth capital comes from. They also add that accumulation of wealth is the reward for being successful in a capitalistic economy in providing goods and services that others need. Finally, even though we have people who are poor and disadvantaged, this group in our economy is far better off than the poor and disadvantaged in other economies.

There is also evidence that more and more people are entering the wealthy class. There are about 638,000 millionaires in the United States, or 1 out of every 360 Americans. And almost 6000 people make a million dollars or more per year. This is up from only 33 in 1920. Sure, a million dollars today is worth only about $200,000 in 1920 dollars, but there are 167 times as many people making a million dollars annually today as there were in 1920.

 In Providing Growth

In the past, our economic system has provided an excellent growth record. However, because of the decline in productivity and output rates, our overall growth rate has also slowed.

Seven nations met at the annual economic summit in 1983. A comparison of economic growth in six important indicators for the years 1972–1982 ranked the United States third, behind Japan and West Germany. Figure 1.5 totals these

Figure 1.5
A comparison of economic growth.
Changes in six important indicators of economic growth from 1977 to 1982. *Source: U.S. News & World Report, June 6, 1983.*

Output: Production per Person, Adjusted for Inflation

1. Japan	Up	19.4%
2. Italy	Up	12.1%
3. France	Up	8.2%
4. West Germany	Up	8.0%
5. Great Britain	Up	2.8%
6. United States	Up	2.0%
7. Canada	Up	1.3%

Currency: Change in Value

1. Japan	Up	17.0%
2. United States	Up	12.8%
3. Great Britain	Up	11.5%
4. West Germany	Up	10.0%
5. Canada	Down	9.6%
6. France	Down	16.0%
7. Italy	Down	28.6%

Jobs: Persons Employed

1. Canada	Up	9.5%
2. United States	Up	8.0%
3. Japan	Up	5.5%
4. Italy	Up	3.2%
5. West Germany	Up	0.3%
6. France	Down	0.4%
7. Great Britain	Down	5.3%

Exports: Amount per Person

1. West Germany	Up	24.5%
2. Japan	Up	20.2%
3. France	Up	16.5%
4. Italy	Up	14.6%
5. United States	Up	9.4%
6. Great Britain	Up	8.1%
7. Canada	Up	7.4%

Prices: Cost of Living

1. Japan	Up	25.1%
2. West Germany	Up	25.9%
3. United States	Up	59.3%
4. Canada	Up	63.2%
5. France	Up	73.6%
6. Great Britain	Up	76.0%
7. Italy	Up	115.3%

Industrial Production: Output of Factories and Mines

1. Japan	Up	27.7%
2. Italy	Up	9.6%
3. West Germany	Up	3.3%
4. France	Up	2.0%
5. United States	Up	0.3%
6. Canada	Down	2.0%
7. Great Britain	Down	2.9%

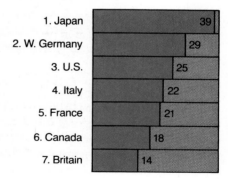

On the basis of 7 points for first place, 6 for second place, and down to 1 for seventh place:

1. Japan	39
2. W. Germany	29
3. U.S.	25
4. Italy	22
5. France	21
6. Canada	18
7. Britain	14

CROSS FIRE

An Industrial Policy? Free Enterprise versus Government Intervention

In recent years, we have seen our nation fall behind Japan, Germany, and some other European countries in economic performance. Because of this, many people are calling for an industrial policy (IP) to help the United States maintain its competitive position in the world. Generally, an IP is an overall, conscious government policy to aid industrial development and growth. Government assistance may come in several forms, for example, subsidies, tariffs, cheap loans, export aid, tax breaks, and research support. The intent would be to identify future growth areas, called "sunrise industries," and help them grow as a part of our overall strategy.

Arguments for an IP

There are many arguments for an IP. Some of the major ones are:

1. A national, coordinated IP will help make the United States more competitive, thereby reducing the odds that we will become a second-rate economic power.
2. Japan and other nations have had success with their IPs.
3. The government currently helps many industries, but there is no thought-out, coordinated plan of assistance. For example, the government now spends five times more on research for commercial fishing than for steel.
4. The government has always aided some industries, so we should quit pretending that we are pure free enterprise.
5. Ad hoc attempts to help industries, such as guaranteed loans to Lockheed, Chrysler, and New York City, are too often politically motivated bail outs; they do not replace a centralized plan.

figures. Since 1975, our growth rate has continued to be sluggish; it looks as though moderate growth will continue into the foreseeable future.

In explaining moderate growth, an economist from the Brookings Institute lists some probable causes: (1) more inexperienced workers in the labor force — more previously unemployed women, more younger workers, (2) the end of the migration from farms to the cities, (3) inflation and high interest rates that scared off some necessary investment and expansion, and (4) the need for more investment to meet the high cost of safety and pollution standards.

Other experts point out that the news may not be as bad as it appears. Many view the 1970s as a period when things did not improve much; still, personal income, after adjusting for inflation, increased 28%; gross national product, after infla-

tion, rose 33%; and the number of workers in the civilian labor force increased 28%.

In Providing Methods of Economic Activity

While our methods of economic activity have been excellent in the past, the 1970s produced some problems in this area as well. Two recessions in the 1970s produced high interest rates — as high as 21% for a period, and unemployment — more than 9% in 1982. It looks as though the high inflation rates — more than 10% for much of the 1970s — have finally been conquered. Now the goal throughout the 1980s will be to stimulate additional growth and increase employment. In late 1983, economists were concerned about eco-

Arguments against an IP

Some of the major arguments against an IP are:

1. An IP is clearly a method of government intervention that reduces the forces that make a private enterprise economy effective.
2. An IP will create additional governmental bureaucratic layers that make for inefficiency.
3. Historically, the bigger the role of the government, the more messed-up things become. For example, the government heavily subsidized both the railroads and interurban transportation, both of which have suffered under heavy regulations.
4. Subsidizing industry increases the cost to the taxpayer; it does not increase the ability of firms to compete.
5. Conditions are not the same as they are in Japan, and success with an IP there does not mean it is the thing for us to do.

How do you feel about government involvement in business via an industrial policy? (Check the following statement that best describes your position.)

_____ A. An IP would be very helpful to the United States.

_____ B. An IP would be somewhat helpful to the United States.

_____ C. An IP would be somewhat harmful to the United States.

_____ D. An IP would be very harmful to the United States.

List three reasons for your position.

A. _____

B. _____

C. _____

nomic growth and increased employment during the last half of the decade.

SUMMARY

The private enterprise system stresses private ownership of business and individual choices in business activities. It is close to the free enterprise system, which gives total power to individuals without government intervention. A business is an organization that engages in the production and sale of goods and services with the goal of making a profit. The business system is the composite of all businesses and their relationships.

Early forms of business included trade and mercantilism. The Industrial Revolution, which was characterized by the replacement of hand tools with power-driven machines, has provided the greatest boom to business and industry. During the consumer era, businesses started to emphasize the tastes and desires of the consumer. The advertising boom took place during this era. The modern age of technology utilizes electronics and computers in business and household products.

Our free enterprise system stresses a limited role of government in business activities. While it is not totally capitalistic, our system encourages a maximum (though not total) role of individual choice within business. It strives for the highest levels of competition, profit, and private ownership. Resources used to produce goods and services are natural resources, labor, capital, and entrepreneurship and are called the factors of production.

In viewing how well our business system is doing, we decided that it provided us with the highest standard of living at one time. Recently, problems with recession, interest rates, unemployment, and decreased productivity have issued challenges to our system.

MIND YOUR BUSINESS

Instructions. Indicate whether you think the following statements are true (T) or false (F).

____ 1. On the average, business profits amount to 25% of their total sales.

____ 2. The real backing of the U.S. dollar is gold.

____ 3. Higher wages is the major cause for an increase in the standard of living.

____ 4. About two-thirds of all civilian workers belong to unions.

____ 5. There are more corporations than individually owned businesses in the United States.

____ 6. The major purpose of the stock market is to increase company profits.

____ 7. The federal government owns less than 5% of all the land in the United States.

____ 8. Fringe benefits such as vacations, insurance, retirement, and sick leave average about 20% of our paychecks.

____ 9. Most of the money spent on advertising goes for television ads.

____ 10. When you buy a company's bonds, you become part of the company.

____ 11. Spending by governments at the federal, state, and local levels is equal to about 20% of the total gross national product.

____ 12. Over the past 25 years, prices have increased more than wages.

____ 13. When the dollar gains value in foreign markets, the cost of living in the United States goes up.

____ 14. It is impossible for a company with a union to fire an employee.

____ 15. There is clear evidence that advertising causes the prices of goods to be higher.

See answers at the back of the book.

KEY TERMS

REVIEW QUESTIONS

1. What was the first business activity? What was business like before mercantilism?

2. What is the difference between business and the business system?

3. What is the difference between the private enterprise system and the free enterprise system?

4. What is the difference between barter and trade?

5. Describe mercantilism and its effects upon our modern business system.

6. What were the characteristics of the Industrial Revolution? Where did it begin? What are some of the events that occurred in the United States during that period?

7. Describe each era within the evolution of our private enterprise system.

8. What prevents our business system from being pure capitalism? Explain.

9. Why was private ownership of property so important to the American colonists? What steps did they take to ensure the private ownership of property?

10. What is competition and what role does it play in our business system? What is profit and what is its relationship to competition? Explain in detail the strengths and weaknesses of our private enterprise system. What are its current challenges?

CASES

Case 1.1: How Are Economic Indicators Related?

Recently, a U.S. congressman said that most of our economic problems were caused by the fact that Americans were just not willing to work as hard as people did in the past. He cited statistics showing high job turnover, changes in attitudes of younger employees, and scant increases in productivity rates. He commented that inflation was too high because we wanted to buy too many things that we did not need, and because we made too many demands on the government. "Everyone," he said, "was looking for a handout, from the largest corporations to the smallest business, as well as most of the individuals in the country." "In short,"

he said, "we were spoiled, pampered, and expected too much without having to work for it."

Questions

1. How do you feel about these statements? _____ generally agree? _____ generally disagree?

2. Why did you answer as you did? List reasons.

Case 1.2: Potential Entrepreneur

Mari Tallinger is a college student with a strong desire to work for a while and then get into a position, either with a large company or on her own, to operate as an entrepreneur. She feels that she has the capability to put together the ingredients necessary to make a business function. However, at this point in her education, she feels a desire for a great deal more information and she has come to you for advice.

Questions

1. What do you think about a college student who has the desire to be an entrepreneur?

2. Make an extensive list of the types of things Mari would have to know to operate effectively as a business entrepreneur.

After studying this chapter, you will be able to:

■ List the goals of an economic system.

■ Describe four characteristics that differentiate between economic systems.

■ Describe and list the main differences between the three major economic systems of the world: capitalism, socialism, and communism.

■ List and interpret ten key indicators of economic activity.

■ Describe economic growth cycles.

BUSINESS AND ECONOMIC SYSTEMS

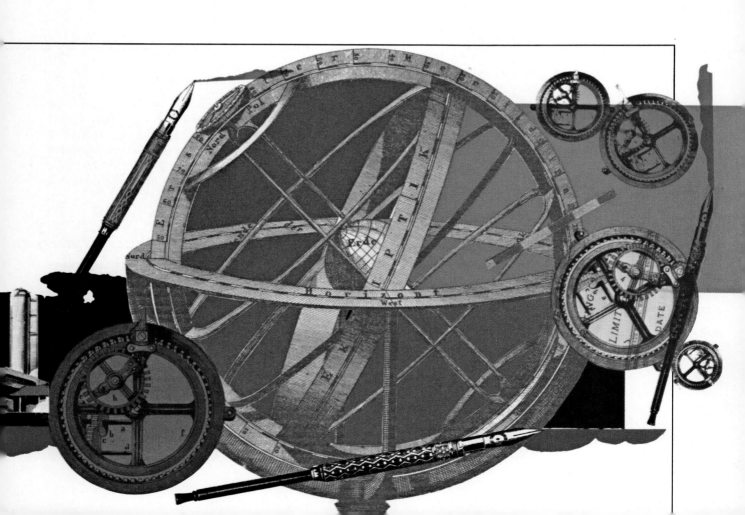

T here is only one free lunch in economics," according to Treasury Department economist Ronald Hoffman, "—an increase in efficiency." And that is just what businesses have been doing. Battered by foreign competition and mounting customer complaints, businesses have worked hard to improve quality and efficiency. In November 1983, production at B. F. Goodrich Tire Company was a full 36% higher than in 1975. Goodrich and other companies have adapted to the pressures within our economic system by eliminating waste, improving scheduling, slimming product lines, and using technology more effectively. And that is the way our economic system is supposed to operate, by providing incentives to reduce waste and be more efficient.

WHAT ARE THE GOALS OF AN ECONOMIC SYSTEM?

Though **economic systems** may differ substantially, they generally have similar goals (see Fig. 2.1):

■ To satisfy the economic needs of people.
■ To provide methods of producing goods and services.
■ To distribute wealth.
■ To stimulate growth.
■ To create economic activity.

Satisfying Economic Needs

If you were to make a list of the things you have used today, what would you mention? Food? Clothes? Transportation? Stereo? Books? Have you ever stopped to think where these came from and how they got to you? Although we tend to take most of our daily necessities and pleasures for

**Figure 2.1
The goals of an economic system.**

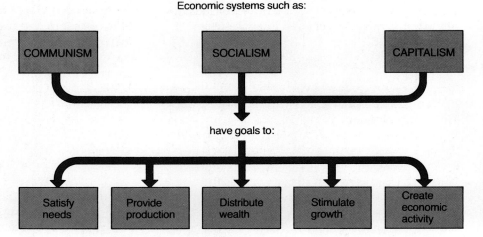

Economic systems such as:

COMMUNISM   SOCIALISM   CAPITALISM

have goals to:

Satisfy needs | Provide production | Distribute wealth | Stimulate growth | Create economic activity

granted, our economic system is usually working overtime to deliver them. The primary goal of an economic system is to satisfy the economic needs of its people. When we are left wanting, we tend to blame **economics;** but when our stomachs are filled, we often forget to credit the system.

Providing the Methods of Production

To satisfy economic needs, an economic system must establish methods for producing goods and services. Sometimes these methods emerge naturally and spontaneously, while at other times, the economic policies of a country attempt to cause certain productions. For instance, although Japan has almost no natural resources relating to steel production, they do have the ability to manufacture automobiles quite efficiently. Japan's economic system assumed the economic responsibility for trading with other countries to acquire much-needed steel so they could produce automobiles. They did this so successfully that they became the number 1 producer of automobiles in the world.

Distributing Wealth

Through economic incentive and reward systems, an economic system tries to provide ways of distributing wealth to its people. As a political candidate recently said, "One of the greatest problems that any economic system has is to distribute the wealth of the country fairly." Different nations handle wealth distribution in various ways. In Mexico, there are both extremely wealthy and extremely poor citizens. Finland, however, has few affluent citizens and very few that are poor.

Stimulating Growth

Economics strives to provide growth in our production and distribution of goods and services. Most countries need growth to continue to satisfy the economic needs of their expanding populations. The economic system spurs growth by identifying needs and finding ways to meet them. Before the end of World War II, the German government decided that more automobiles were needed. To stimulate growth in the automobile industry, the government built factories and man-

Providing and delivering goods and services to consumers is a primary goal of any economic system.

ufactured the Volkswagen, which means "car of the people."

Establishing Methods of Economic Activity

An economic system develops methods, rules, and procedures by which it operates. Businesses then must follow these regulations. As corporations in the United States began to grow very large, there seemed to be a need for an efficient method of investing in and owning them. So our government developed a system of laws for owning and investing in businesses. One of the results is today's stock exchanges where people buy and sell millions of shares of stocks daily.

WHAT ARE THE CHARACTERISTICS OF AN ECONOMIC SYSTEM?

Although the goals of differing economic systems may be similar, characteristics of systems vary greatly. We can differentiate between economic

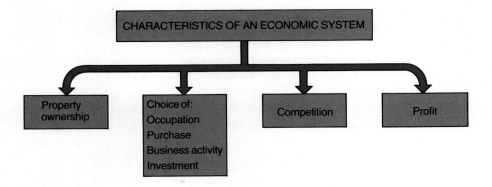

**Figure 2.2
Characteristics of an
economic system.**

systems by looking at how they treat (1) property ownership, (2) freedom of choice, (3) competition, and (4) profit.

Property Ownership

To most readers, individual ownership of property is taken for granted. We buy homes, cars, records, and fishing equipment which we own in our own names. However, this is not the case in all economic systems. In a country without individual ownership, a worker may work in a state-owned factory and live in a state-owned house.

Freedom of Choice

Different economic systems also provide varying degrees of freedom of choice. Citizens of some countries might actually be told where to work, what type of work to do, and they may have few choices regarding goods and services. Likewise, citizens may not have the opportunity to invest in a business, sign a contract, or choose where to take a vacation. While freedoms of working, purchasing, and investing seem basic to us, some systems do not provide such liberties.

Competition

Competition plays a different role in economic systems. Some economic systems, such as ours, stimulate competition in many areas, especially sales of products and services. Yet other countries do not encourage, or even allow, competition. A state-owned factory, for example, might hire workers at a state-determined wage; and the people may buy a product or service at a state-determined price.

Profit

Each system develops policies concerning profits. Will profit be allowed? If so, how much? Some countries operate businesses where the concepts of profits do not really exist. Proceeds from business sales go for the costs of production. If there is an excess, it goes to the state.

There is some correlation among these characteristics within an economic system. A system that encourages private ownership will also encourage freedom, competition, and profit. And systems that discourage one of these factors will also discourage the others. These characteristics are diagrammed in Fig. 2.2.

ECONOMIC PHILOSOPHIES

In the world today, three major economic philosophies exist: capitalism, socialism, and communism. We will see how each of these systems treats property ownership, freedom of choice, competition, and profit. (See Table 2.1 for a capsule comparison of these three economic systems.)

Capitalism

Adam Smith, a Scottish economist, described the foundations of **capitalism** in his book, *The Wealth of Nations*. Ironically, he published the book in 1776—the same year the American colonies stated their feelings in the Declaration of Independence. Smith argued for a policy of **laissez-faire,** meaning that the government should keep its hands off all business activities, letting them function without regulation or restriction. He believed that businesses competing among themselves would produce the most efficient product at the best price. He likened the competition between firms to that of an "invisible hand" that would encourage firms to set prices at their lowest feasible point and thus reward the most efficient. As a store owner explained, "We have to operate as efficiently as we can to keep our costs low. If our costs are not low, we cannot keep our prices low; and if our prices are not low, our competitors will take our customers." If profits become too high in a particular industry, competitors will move in, driving the prices down. Efficient producers with the lowest prices gain the rewards of high sales and increased profits, and inefficient firms would be eliminated.

Though the economic system of the United

States is a good example of capitalism, it is

not purely capitalistic.

While the economic system of the United States may be a good example of capitalism, it is not purely capitalistic. In this section, we present the idea of capitalism.

Property ownership. Maximum ownership of private property is basic to capitalism. It stresses that an individual, with profit as an incentive, will manage the property with maximum efficiency and greatest results. Governments, with their detached motivation and bureaucracy, cannot utilize property with the same zeal and productivity as an individual who stands to gain from the profitable management of property. Consider the situations where one family owns its home and another rents from either a landlord or a government. The first family will care for and improve its home because it will benefit from the increased value when it decides to sell. The second family, because of lack of motivation, may let the property fall into a state of disrepair because only the owner will benefit from its efforts. Under this concept, if all families owned their own

TABLE 2.1 ■ A COMPARISON OF CAPITALISM, SOCIALISM, AND COMMUNISM

Concepts	Capitalist Theory	Socialist Theory	Communist Theory
Property ownership	Privately owned, capital invested by owners.	Mixture of private and public ownership, basic industries owned by state (steel, transportation, utilities, etc.), individuals may own other businesses.	Common ownership through the state which owns all productive capacity.
Freedom of choice	Wide range of choices, workers free to select occupations, consumers face many choices at the marketplace.	Limited range of choices, workers select occupations but state planning influences employment, consumers have some variety in purchases.	Very limited choices, state determines your occupation and where you will work, consumer items are standard.
Competition	Unrestricted competition, owners assume risk of gains and losses, determine prices and wages.	Regulated competition, wages highly regulated by state, citizens assume risks of state-owned companies with losses coming from taxes, private companies may be pressured by state to produce certain things.	No competition, planned economy, state owns markets, state assumes risks, losses reduce living standards, state planning is enforced by law.
Profit	Highly desirable, reward for risk and efficiency, profits and wages are in relation to willingness and ability to contribute.	Profits within boundaries, stresses nonmonetary incentives, privileges and prestige.	No profits, try to get people to produce out of loyalty to the state, medals, state recognition, and fear of legal punishments.

Deregulation and the Airlines

In 1978, the U.S. government ordered an end to government control of airline fares and rates. This allowed carriers to invade each other's markets and compete by offering lower rates. Many fare wars developed, in which bargains and discounts were offered to passengers.

Reacting to these new freedoms, Braniff expanded its routes significantly. However, the airline was unable to attract enough customers at the rates needed to cover its costs, and in the summer of 1982, Braniff declared bankruptcy.

Since 1978, many other airlines have also lost money. In fact, the airline industry did not show a profit between 1979 and 1983. Pan American lost more than $485 million in 1982, more than any U.S. airline in history. After staggering along for several months, Continental Airlines sent shudders through the industry when it became the second major airline to file for bankruptcy within 16 months. Eastern Airlines, apparently on the brink also, threatened to file for bankruptcy before getting their union to agree to a pay cut.

Although adjustments to deregulation, after decades of highly regulated routes and fares, was no doubt the cause of many problems, the airlines also faced other obstacles. The economy was in a recession during the early 1980s, interest rates were high, fuel costs were high, and air traffic controllers had a strike. Any one of these events would have been enough to create shock waves; combined, they created havoc in a once-predictable industry. The accompanying diagram shows the profit picture of airlines since 1975. Experts predicted that other airlines would also suffer bankruptcy, and everyone agreed that it could be many years before the industry stabilized.

Operating income of U.S. scheduled airlines. *Source: Air Transport Association.*

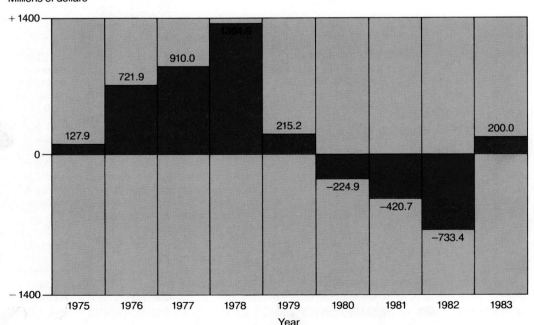

Millions of dollars

homes, all homes would be better cared for and increase in value much faster than properties owned by the state. For another example, consider farmers who own their own land. They will likely be motivated to work hard because they could benefit directly from their labor. If the state owned the land and paid them standard salaries, the assumption is (and the evidence suggests) that they would be less motivated.

Freedom of choice.   Freedom of choice means that individuals can make their own decisions. Believing that freedom of choice increases motivation and productivity, capitalists stress freedoms when choosing occupations, purchases, professions, schools, and the like. Within a capitalist system, a high school senior has the freedom to decide whether or not to go on to college. Because of incentives of higher pay, better working conditions, and more prestige, many students choose to become better educated. The result is more doctors, engineers, and business professionals, which benefit the society as a whole. The front end sacrifice of school, study, and less wealth is made for future goals of wealth, status, and a higher standard of living. In a capitalist system, these choices are made by individuals, whereas in a communistic society, they are made by the state according to need.

Competition.   The capitalist system encourages maximum competition within all business activities. Capitalists believe that increased competition results in better products, greater efficiency, and superior service. Again, the theory is that the rewards gained by outperforming the competition will motivate individuals to greater achievements and benefit the overall society as a result. If competition becomes too great, some businesses will fail, and those people and resources will be directed by the "invisible hand" to enter other industries that are less competitive and more profitable. In a capitalist system, competition is regulated by the choice of individuals rather than restrictions by the state.

For example, if a firm is having difficulty in competing in the minicomputer market, it may choose either to improve its strategies or to switch its resources to another, less competitive industry. If it wants to become more competitive, it must find a way of producing better computers at a lower price. Capitalists view competition to be ad-

A corporate-sponsored careers seminar for students provides information on the wide range of occupational choices available — a characteristic feature of capitalist economies.

vantageous to the society because it creates more effective methods, superior products, and lower prices. A minicomputer produced by a communistic system may be more expensive and less efficient, but, because there is no competition, it continues to be produced and be the only model available. Smith would say that because of lack of competition, the society suffers by having to use an inferior product.

Profit.   After a company pays all its costs and expenses, what remains is profit — the difference between the total income received and total expenditures of operating the business. Under capitalism, we identify winners by the amount of their profits. Because of the incentive of profits, capitalists believe that individuals will work harder and produce more, and that this will thereby benefit the overall society.

Socialism

Socialism is a broad term used almost interchangeably with communism until after the Russian Revolution. The system favors use of property for public welfare and challenges the sanctity of private property. Socialism developed during the Industrial Revolution as an alternative to help poor people who had no choice other than poverty. In socialist countries, governments own and operate much of the property, but there is also individual ownership. Socialist theory stresses limited freedoms of choice, regulated competition, and less emphasis on profits. The United Kingdom, West Germany, Finland, and Norway are some of the best-known examples of socialist countries. In their functioning and characteristics, they are somewhere between the communist and capitalistic countries.

Property ownership. In many socialistic countries, the government owns the basic industries, such as banking, large manufacturing, and mining. Socialists feel that the state can operate these large industries more efficiently than individuals can. However, there is private ownership of smaller companies and shops.

Freedom of choice. The socialist system stresses that a country's resources ought to be allocated according to some master plan that will best serve the needs of the majority. Yet consumers do have some freedom of choice with purchases, and workers can choose among several occupations. However, the state has means of encouraging employees to enter occupations of the greatest need. Investments and business activities are conducted by individuals but are limited and carefully restricted by the state.

Competition. While competition exists within the socialist framework, it is limited and highly regulated by the government. Many of the larger industries are completely owned and controlled by the state, allowing no competition in the key segments of the economy.

BUSINESS BULLETIN

On Adam Smith

Adam Smith, a bachelor with no recorded love affairs, lived the life of the stereotypical absent-minded professor. At social gatherings he might relegate himself to a corner for long periods smiling and talking to himself. In the classroom, he would stutter and stammer for 15 to 20 minutes before getting warmed up for the lecture. One night he awoke from his sleep and walked more than 15 miles in his nightgown, intellectually massaging a theory, before he realized what he was doing. Indeed, few businessmen sought the advice of the quiet, intense scholar on such matters as prices, wages, and profits. Yet his writings, salted with just the right amount of deadpan wit, came alive, breathing his views of the necessity of political and economic liberty. Smith's book *The Wealth of Nations* went through five editions in his lifetime at a price equivalent to $65 per copy, and it still sells several thousand copies annually. Smith's insatiably curious, broad-ranging intellect speculated on the intellectual underpinnings of many aspects of society:

ON COLLEGE RULES: The discipline of colleges and universities is . . . contrived not for the benefit of the students, but for the interest, or more properly speaking, for the ease of the masters.

ON WORK AND LEISURE: Great labor, either of mind or body, continued for several days together . . . requires to be relieved by some indulgence sometimes of ease only, but sometimes too of dissipation and diversion.

ON LOTTERIES: The world neither ever saw, nor ever will see, a perfectly fair lottery . . . because the undertaker would make nothing by it.

ON HAPPINESS: What can be added to the happiness of a man who is in health, who is out of debt, and has a clear conscience?

ON HUMAN EQUALITY: The difference between the most dissimilar characters, between a philosopher and a common street porter, for example, seems to arise not so much from nature, as from habit, custom, and education.

Source: ''The Revolutionary of Economy,'' Time, July 14, 1975, pp. 54–55.

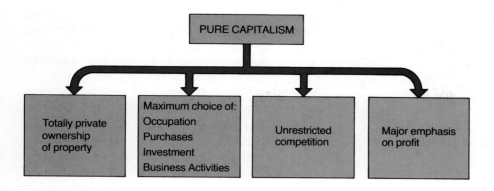

PURE CAPITALISM

- Totally private ownership of property
- Maximum choice of: Occupation Purchases Investment Business Activities
- Unrestricted competition
- Major emphasis on profit

**Figure 2.3
Characteristics of pure capitalism.**

Profit. Profits exist in socialist economies, but they do not carry the importance of capitalist profit. The guiding force of socialism is a carefully planned system that regulates, rather than controls, the production and distribution of goods; however, privately owned businesses do make a profit.

Communism

The basics of communist theory were set forth by **Karl Marx,** a German economist who lived from 1818 to 1883. His major tenets were presented in a work entitled *Das Kapital,* first published in 1867. He predicted that there would be a class struggle and the laboring classes would overthrow the capitalists. Marx believed that the state should own everything. **Communism** stresses centralized management of all production and distribution. It is quite willing to sacrifice freedom for production, distribution, and production efficiency. The best-known examples of communist economics are Russia, Communist China, and Poland.

Property ownership. Communism practices common ownership by all. There is no private property; everything belongs to everyone in the state. Farmers do not own their land, laborers do not own their tools, and doctors do not own their offices. The central government owns all property. The will of the state is of utmost importance. The state not only owns all the factories and businesses but also the homes that people live in. According to Marx and his followers, individuals will be better off if they suppress their desires for individual accumulations of wealth.

Freedom of choice. Communism gives the central government the strongest possible role in all aspects of business and economics. The central party sets the goals and operates the distribution of goods. Individuals have limited choices. The central government carefully plans the careers of its citizens by selecting them for and guiding them into particular jobs. They have little choice regarding the type of work they will do or for whom they will work. Likewise, customers face limited choices in the marketplace: In the extreme, there is only one type of each item that the government deems necessary. This is because the state dictates the type, style, quality, and amount of goods to be produced. Investments and business activities are not conducted by individuals.

The purchase of certain equipment—such as this British Airways Concorde airliner—is often demanded by the government in socialist economies.

Competition. There is little need for competition in a communist society, especially within the business world. The state allocates resources according to its judgment of who is needful of what goods. The government asks individuals to contribute to the production of goods and services according to their abilities. In short, the planners allocate goods according to who needs them, and they demand contributions according to individual capabilities.

Profit. The communist philosophy, through central planning, eliminates the necessity of profits. Goods and services resulting from workers' efforts benefit the state rather than individuals. Individuals' compensation comes from the government as it perceives their needs. All financial resources are managed by the state rather than by business. All proceeds go to the government and are utilized in other forms of business that are managed, owned, and controlled by the state. In this way, communists believe that people will work harder and accomplish more than when there is the potential handsome profit which is basic to the capitalistic system. For example, all grocery store owners in Russia may receive the same compensation regardless of the amount of business or the efficiency of their operations. A capitalist grocer, however, would strive to buy at a lower price, advertise to attract more customers, and carry products that better fulfill the needs of customers in order to realize a greater profit.

INDICATORS OF ECONOMIC ACTIVITY

Now that we understand the goals and characteristics of various economic systems, we can add to our knowledge of economics by discussing some indicators of economic activity and by looking at how our economy tends to go through growth cycles.

Key Economic Indicators

Economists try to identify major changes in our economy that serve as key indicators of how well the economy is doing. Since our economy is so complex, we often look at several indicators of

> **By comparing the key economic indicators with previous periods, we can tell whether our economy is growing or declining.**

economic activity. Some of the key indicators are expressed as indexes, and others are expressed in actual dollar amounts. By comparing current indicators with previous periods, we can tell whether our economy is growing or declining. Many of the more popular key indicators are as follows.

Gross national product. **Gross national product,** or **GNP,** is a measure of the dollar value of the economy's output of goods and services. GNP tells us the value of business activities and is usually presented for a period of a year. For example, the GNP for the United States in 1983 was more than $3 trillion, meaning that business activities produced goods and services worth that amount for the year. The percentage increase (or decrease) in GNP from one period to the next indicates growth or decline. **Real gross national product** is the measure of GNP that removes price changes. If, for example, from one year to the next, GNP rose 5% while prices increased 4%, real GNP would only increase 1%. Figure 2.4 shows the changes in real GNP for 1982, 1983, and 1984.

Consumer price index (inflation). The **consumer price index (CPI)** is an average of the prices of goods and services and is published regularly by the Department of Labor. The number used in the CPI expresses a percentage change over the established costs of a previous year — the current base year is 1967; however, 1977 will soon become the base year. The base year merely represents a year that the Bureau of Labor Statistics chooses to use as a benchmark. For example, the estimated index for the United States in 1983 was 309. That means a sample of goods and services purchased in 1967 would cost 309% more in 1983. **Inflation** simply means "increase in price"; therefore, the increase in the consumer price index is a measure of inflation.

Inflation concerns us because it means that we have to spend more money to buy the same amount of goods and services. Suppose that you

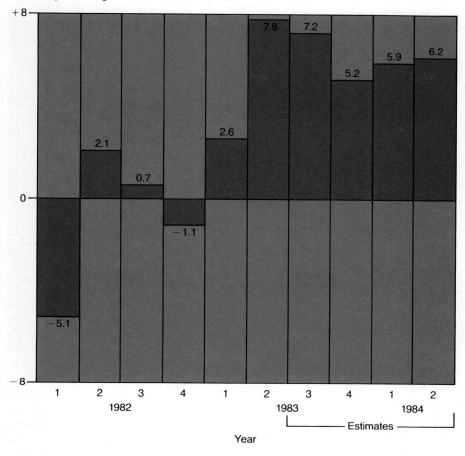

Percentage of change

Year

rent an apartment for $300 per month. After one year, when the lease expires, the landlord increases the rent to $330 per month. This is the same as cutting your income by $30 per month because you have to pay that much more for the same product. While the **inflation rate** caused extreme concern in the early 1970s and during the first part of the 1980s, the mid-1980s indicated that the rate was once again down to a reasonable level. Figure 2.5 shows the increase in prices for selected items during a 5-year period, and Fig. 2.6 shows the average increase in consumer prices from 1973 to 1983.

Unemployment rate. The **unemployment rate** is the percentage of employable persons looking for work that are not employed. During the early 1980s, the employment rate climbed to more than 10%. Historically, this was an excep-

tionally high rate, and it caused hardships for many people in our society. By early 1984, the rate had reduced to 8%, and it was expected to fall slowly during the next few years.

Unemployment causes more trouble in some groups and in some regions of the country than in others. The highest rate of unemployed persons is typically among blacks and especially among black teenagers. Table 2.2 shows the unemployment rate by category and industry for 1982 and the first half of 1983. Figure 2.7 shows swings in the unemployment rate since 1969.

People's incomes. People's incomes represents the total amount of income for all the people in the United States, after taxes. This figure reveals the total amount of money that people are making from all sources, and it suggests their ability to buy products and services and to invest. The figure

Percentage of change

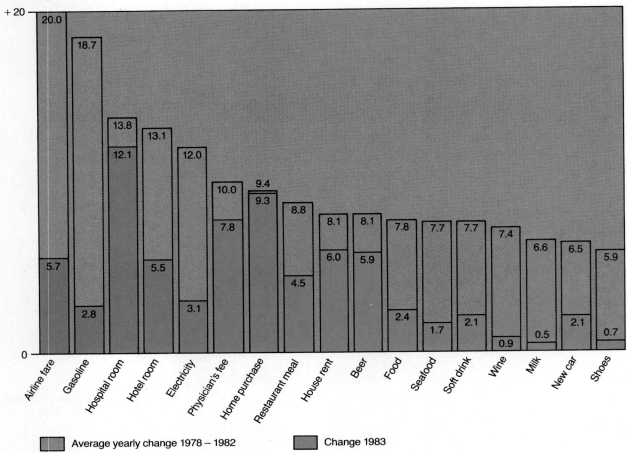

■ Average yearly change 1978 – 1982   ■ Change 1983

Figure 2.5
How inflation in the cost of consumer items has slowed. *Source: Bureau of Labor Statistics.*

Figure 2.6
Average annual increase in consumer prices, 1973–1983. *Source: Bureau of Labor Statistics.*

Percentage of change

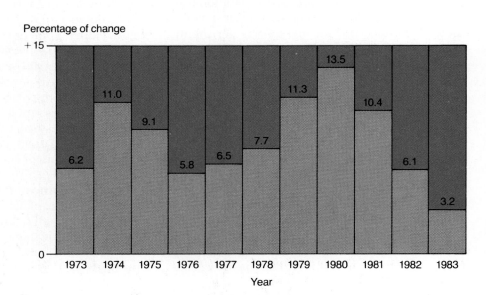

amounted to approximately $2.3 trillion in mid-1983.

Retail sales. Retail sales is the total volume of sales by retail outlets. An increase in retail sales is a healthy sign because it means that more people have confidence in the economy. Also, the increase in retail sales allows retail outlets to buy more inventory, hire more people, and perhaps expand their facilities.

Producer prices, finished goods. This is the price of finished goods at the wholesale level, that is, before the costs of transportation and retailer costs and profits are added to the final price. This price is similar to the consumer price index except it represents wholesale rather than retail prices. Movement of producer price index is important because if it goes up (or down) consumer prices are likely to go up (or down) in the near future.

Corporate profits. Corporate profits is the after-tax profit made by all corporations. Higher profits suggest economic growth because the profits can be used for expansion, increasing employment, and greater distribution of profits to stockholders.

TABLE 2.2 ■ UNEMPLOYMENT RATE BY CATEGORY AND INDUSTRY

	December, 1982 (%)	June, 1983 (%)
By Category		
Adult men	10.1	9.0
Adult women	9.2	8.6
Whites	9.7	8.6
Blacks	20.8	20.6
Hispanics	15.3	14.0
White teenagers	21.6	20.0
Black teenagers	49.5	50.6
By Industry		
Construction	22.0	18.1
Farm employees	16.5	17.0
Manufacturing	14.8	11.5
Trade	11.0	10.2
Transportation	8.0	7.8
Finance	7.9	7.2
Government	5.1	5.1

Source: Department of Labor.

Figure 2.7
Highs and lows in unemployment rate, 1969–1982. *Source: Department of Labor.*

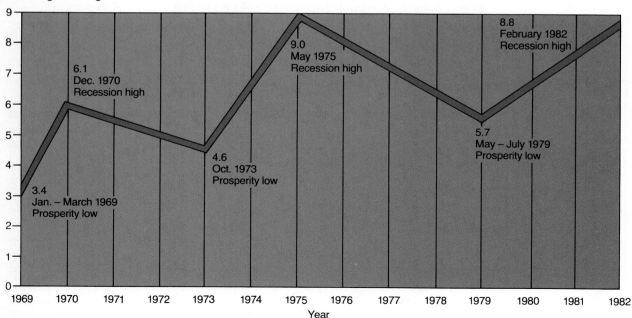

Since new home building represents both employment in several major industries and a general consumer confidence, the number of housing starts serves as a key economic indicator.

Auto production. Auto production measures the total number of cars produced for a period of time. Because auto production is such a large segment of our economy, it influences many other factors. For example, an increase in auto production increases employment significantly, but it also increases the need for many products such as steel, rubber, glass, and the like. Literally thou-sands of companies derive their livelihood from the auto industry.

Home building. Home building figures register the number of private housing starts per year. Similar to auto production, home building is a key indicator because so many other aspects of our economy depend upon it. An increase in home building suggests that people are able and willing to purchase additional homes. In mid-1983, the annual rate of housing starts was running at about 1.7 million units per year, one of the highest levels in recent years.

Interest rates. Interest rates, the amount paid to borrow money, also indicate economic movement. Higher rates slow economic growth because people will borrow less, therefore curtailing expansion. Likewise, lower interest rates spur economic growth because people are willing to borrow more for expansion and growth. Interest rates affect the consumer also; when rates are lower, the consumer typically uses more credit to increase consumption. Interest rates, as an indicator, are a little complicated because there is no single rate that reflects the cost of money. The

BUSINESS BULLETIN

What Key Economic Indicators Are Doing

In mid-1983, the ten key economic indicators discussed in the text showed the following measurements. (You might want to get a comparison by looking up current measures to see how the indicators have changed since mid-1983. The indicators are published regularly by government sources, and you can also find them in many periodicals such as *Business week, U.S. News & World Report*, and the like.)

Key Indicator	Mid–1983	Current
Gross national product (billion 1972 dollars)	$1,477.26	_____
Consumer price index (1967 = 100)	296.9	_____
Unemployment rate	10.2%	_____
Peoples' incomes (billion per year after taxes)	$2,286.5	_____
Retail sales (billion per year)	$1,156.6	_____
Producer prices, finished goods (1967 = 100)	286.0	_____
Corporate profits (billion per year after taxes)	$124.0	_____
Auto production (cars per quarter)	1,800,000.	_____
Home building (private starts per year)	1,632,000.	_____
Interest rates (prime rate)	10.5%	_____

How Reliable Are Economic Indicators?

"In a narrow sense, the statistics are doing the job, but they do not capture the trends as well as they did 5 years ago," says Stephen S. Roach, senior economist at Morgan Stanley & Co. Some critics have always doubted some aspects of our economic indicators, but our economy is now changing at a dizzying pace. Newer industries, the so-called high-tech firms, come and go quickly. And our indicators tend to read activities in the older, more mature industries.

Economists believe that the indicators may be OK for short-term analysis; but if used for long-term policy making, indicators could lead us far astray. If the government intervenes too much in the economy, many economists contend, the mistakes in the data are multiplied.

Look at an example of an out-of-date classification. Decisions about major industry groups were made in the 1930s. Thus, the leather and tobacco industries, which between them account for only 0.4% of total output, are both listed as major industries. Yet, the computer industry, which did not even exist in the 1930s, is not represented accurately in industry figures. The accompanying table is an estimate by *Business Week* of indicator accuracy.

How 15 Key Economic Indicators Rate

On the mark	Understate activity	Unreliable
Employment	Real gross national product	Money supply (weekly M1*)
Consumer price index	Industrial production	Retail sales
Housing starts	Personal income	Inventories
Auto sales	Savings rate	Durable goods orders
Weekly unemployment claims	Capacity utilization	
	Productivity	

* Currency and checking accounts.

Source: "Why Economic Indicators Are Often Wrong," *Business Week*, Oct. 17, 1983, p. 168.

prime rate is the rate that banks will loan to their best customers. New treasury bills, which come due every six months, give an indication of short-term interest rates, whereas the rate for corporate bonds provides a more long-term view of rates. In mid-1983, these rates were as follows: prime rate = 10.5%, new treasury bills = 9.02%, and corporate bonds = 11.34%.

Business Cycles

Economic systems have fluctuations in the degree of business activity, called **business cycles** — periods of growth and declines. **Booms** are periods of prosperity with increased production, employment, profits, and consumption. By contrast, hard times, called **recessions,** occur when the same functions decrease. **Depressions** are periods of severe recession where economic conditions are much worse compared to other periods. These conditions are relative, however. A developing country such as India could be experiencing a boom period under the same conditions in which Japan would be having a depression. Modern business cycles tend to swing through five stages: recovery, heating up, holding the boom, cooling off, and recession.

Stage 1: *Recovery.* The recession is over and business starts picking up. There is a lot of idle capacity and companies are hungry for orders. Many people, unemployed during the recession, are eager to get back to work.

Stage 2: *Heating up.* People gain confidence and are willing to spend more. Companies are getting more orders and are willing to expand and hire more workers. Retailers foresee the need for more products. Profits are increasing, encouraging businesses to expand and invest even more. The recession is over, and people are looking ahead with optimism.

Stage 3: *Holding the boom.* Because of the increased pace of the economy, problems begin to occur. Factories exceed capacity and can-

CROSS FIRE

SUPPLY-SIDE ECONOMICS?

When President Reagan entered office, the economy was in a recession. He and his advisors suggested a new approach to stimulating economic growth which became known as **supply-side economics** because it tended to stimulate the production of goods and services, as opposed to the more traditional attempts to stimulate demand for products and services. Arguments ensued over which was the best way to spur an economy that was in a recession.

A comparison of the supply versus the demand orientations is as follows:

Supply-Side Economics	Demand Stimulation
1. Economy is in a recsssion. Cut taxes on individuals and corporations; also provide other economic incentives for firms to produce more goods and services. Reduce government spending.	1. Economy is in a recession. Increase government spending and cut individual taxes to put more money in consumers' pockets
2. Firms are able to retain more profits which they are able to invest. Investment and expansion creates jobs and, along with individual tax cuts, stimulates consumer buying. These incentives also encourage individuals to work harder and produce goods and services at a cheaper cost.	2. The increased amount of money in consumers' pockets stimulates them to spend more for goods and services.
3. The expansion by businesses combined with increased effort of employees increases output of industry and provides more money for consumer spending.	3. Increased spending and demands of consumers stimulates firms to expand, produce more, and hire more employees.

4. *Desired result by both approaches:*
Economic growth—increased employment, greater consumption, business expansion, inflation held in check, interest rates low, increased tax receipts due to increased profits and incomes.

Which of these two approaches do you think is most effective for stimulating an economy in a recession?

___ A. Supply-side   ___ B. Demand stimulation

List three reasons for your selection.

A. _____

B. _____

C. _____

GNP growth rate

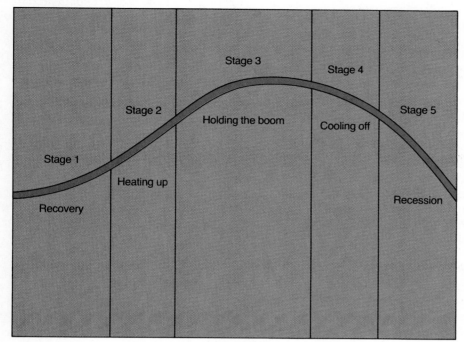

Figure 2.8
The business cycle.

not keep up with the new demand. Shortages develop, prices soar. Demand for credit increases, as do interest rates. Unions strive for higher wages to keep up with higher prices. Consumers have caught up with their demands and increase their spending at slower rates. Merchants have more goods in inventory, so they start to order less. The stage is set for a cooling of the economy.

Stage 4. *Cooling off.* Producers cut their production and lay off some workers. Consumers tighten their belts even more as their income lessens. Prices and interest rates are still high. Confidence drops and the economy moves toward recession.

Stage 5. *Recession.* Businesses cut costs and work their inventories down, and consumers strive to pay their debts. Many companies go bankrupt and some plants close. The government looks for ways to make more money available so that companies can invest and consumers can buy more. Interest rates are lowered and government spending usually increases. Eventually, we will overcome this slowdown, but exactly when is uncertain. If

the recession is severe and lengthy, it becomes a depression. Figure 2.8 illustrates this business cycle.

SUMMARY

An economic system is made up of citizens, businesses, and governments that work together to provide laws and guidelines for business activity. Each economic system has five main goals: satisfying economic needs, providing production, distributing wealth, providing growth, and creating economic activity. Each economic system can be characterized by its views concerning property ownership, freedom of choice, competition, and profit.

There are three major economic systems or philosophies: communism, socialism, and capitalism. There are few, if any, countries that are purely communistic or capitalistic. Communism was founded by Karl Marx, who believed that the state should own everything, that people should have almost no choice in commerce, and that all business activity should benefit the state. Socialism is a blend between communism and capitalism and places somewhat equal emphasis upon the individual and the state with regard to co-ownership and control. Capitalism, founded by Adam Smith, stresses that the individual is paramount and should have total control over all business and economic activities. Smith's doctrine of laissez-faire states that government should not interfere with commerce. His concept of the invisible hand maintains that, if left to its own functions, business will naturally operate within reasonable, acceptable boundaries.

Key economic indicators offer suggestions on how our economy is doing. The ten key indicators discussed in this chapter include GNP, consumer price index, unemployment rate, people's incomes, retail sales, producer prices, corporate profits, auto production, home building, and interest rates.

Business cycles are the fluctuations in the level of business activity where booms are times of prosperity and recessions are the downswings. A depression is a severe recession.

MIND YOUR BUSINESS

Instructions. Match the following descriptions with the proper economic philosophy by placing the appropriate letter in the blank at the left.

A = capitalism   B = communism   C = socialism

_____ 1. State owns the sources of production.

_____ 2. Elected government slowly takes control of nation's key industries.

_____ 3. Government uses taxing power to redistribute the wealth.

_____ 4. Private individuals own land and businesses.

_____ 5. Consumers in the marketplace largely determine at what prices goods will be sold.

_____ 6. Central planners set production quotas.

_____ 7. A government can regulate businesses through laws.

_____ 8. Government sets wages of employees.

_____ 9. Strong unions bargain with management for wages.

_____ 10. Employees and management in individual firms determine wages.

See answers at the back of the book.

KEY TERMS

economic system, 26

economics, 27

Adam Smith, 28

capitalism, 28

laissez-faire, 28

socialism, 31

Karl Marx, 33

communism, 33

gross national product (GNP), 34

real gross national product, 34

consumer price index (CPI), 34

inflation, 34

inflation rate, 35

unemployment rate, 35

interest rate, 38

business cycles, 39

boom, 39

recession, 39

depression, 39

supply-side economics, 40

REVIEW QUESTIONS

1. What is economics? What is an economic system, and how does it function?

2. What are the five major goals of an economic system? Can you give an example of each?

3. What are the three main economic philosophies or systems? What are the differences between them? Who were the founders of communism and capitalism?

4. Who coined the terms "laissez-faire" and "invisible hand"? What do they mean and which system are they a part of?

5. If you were to begin a business, which economic system would you prefer? Why?

6. What reasons would Karl Marx and Adam Smith give for our current economic problems? Would they agree?

7. What are key economic indicators? Identify the ten indicators discussed in this chapter.

8. What does the consumer price index measure, and how is that measurement expressed?

9. What is the difference between inflation and the inflation rate?

10. What is a business cycle? Is our country currently in a business cycle and if so, which one? What is the difference between a boom, recession, and depression? At which stage of the business cycle are economic times the best?

CASES

Case 2.1: Is the United States Going the Way of Britain?

Nobel Prize-winning economist Milton Friedman says, "If we continue down the road that Britain has been following, we shall have much higher inflation than we have yet had; we shall see a larger and larger part of our freedom taken over by the government; our vaunted productivity will go down." Others agree with him, but we still see support for the government taking a larger part in our lives.

If the United States becomes more socialized, we will see some or all of the following happening:

- Government will own and run many of the coal mines, steel mills, and railroads.
- Most sick people's medical and hospital bills will be paid for by the government.
- Much more housing would be subsidized.
- Taxes would go up.

Questions

1. Do you think any of these are likely to happen within the next 5 years?

2. Which would you like to see happen, if any? Which would you argue against?

3. What are the arguments for moving in this direction? Against?

Case 2.2: The Role of Profits

In a talk given to a college class in business, a business leader was asked, "What is the major purpose of your business?" The leader responded, "Profits, the bottom line! That's where it is. If you don't have profits, you don't have anything. You can't grow, you can't expand, you can't progress, you can't even survive."

In response, a student commented, "Yes, but you really seem to be involved in growth and expansion, and you are using your profits for that purpose. Are you really interested in the profits, or only what they can do for you?"

In answering, the businesswoman admitted that she really liked the excitement of growth and expansion—the contest of the game of winning by outdoing competitors. In her words, "It is true profits are the score; they tell you how well you are doing relative to others. I enjoy the game of competition; I just like to win. That's why I like the profits to keep growing."

In further discussion, other students asked what she thought about government regulation, well-being of consumers and employees, and government ownership of property and businesses. In sum, she thought that government should get out of business altogether and should own nothing, and that consumers and workers never had it so good.

Questions

1. Do you find yourself agreeing or disagreeing with the viewpoints of the businesswoman? Why?

2. If you had been a student in the class, what questions would you have asked?

3. If you were in business, how would you have answered these questions?

After completing this chapter, you will be able to:

- List the arguments for and against businesses becoming involved in social responsibilities.

- Define consumerism.

- List the major points of the Consumer Bill of Rights.

- Describe the current state of our pollution problems.

- Provide current data on discrimination and identify business and government responses.

- Describe the four major sources of ethics in our society.

- Comment on ethical behavior in business.

- Describe the energy situation in America.

3

BUSINESS AND
SOCIETY

Pollsters frequently check the attitudes of Americans toward their major institutions. The institution of "big business" has often been ranked at, or near, the unenviable bottom of the heap — below the military, television, organized labor, and Congress. There is today, however, a burgeoning interest in and newfound respect for the field. As evidence, witness the unprecedented success of popular books on business. During 1983, nonfiction bestsellers were *In Search of Excellence, The One Minute Manager,* and *Megatrends.* These three books were also the bestsellers on campuses from coast to coast. Late in 1983, *In Search of Excellence* climbed to number 1 on the Chronicle of Higher Education's campus reading list, making it the first business book to top the list since it was started 13 years ago. When books like these can capture such a large reading audience, we can be fairly sure that a change in attitude is taking place.

Nevertheless, as we've said, big business does often suffer from a bad image. What do you suppose — in this land-rich, career-oriented, and pension-assured society of ours — accounts for this attitude? As one executive commented, "I just cannot understand it. We provide good products, we pay people good wages, give them comfortable jobs, pay enormous taxes, and help with community projects. Yet the public's opinion sours on us." Many business owners and executives share this frustration.

There are three possible explanations why people do not have more confidence in business. First, historically, societies have not viewed business in a positive light. Religions taught against the evils of materialism and usury. Business was a low occupation in Greece. Napoleon slurred the British as "a nation of shopkeepers." No doubt, some of these jaded attitudes are still with us today. Second, some businesses are very big, and people have a tendency to distrust bigness. Some business leaders accuse the media of stirring public anger by spotlighting big business's problems, while failing to mention its contributions. Third,

people in business do make mistakes. Business owners and leaders got their values from our society, which sometimes places too much emphasis on materialism, greed, and intense competition. This chapter presents arguments for and against the involvement of business in social concerns (see Figure 3.1) and outlines what is happening in consumerism, the environment, discrimination, ethics, and energy.

THE SOCIAL RESPONSIBILITY OF BUSINESS

Social responsibility means that decision makers consider the impact of their actions on society's welfare by evaluating the expected social impacts as well as the firm's profits. This contrasts with the traditional role in which they considered only the profits of their business activity. Social responsibility suggests that such narrow interest undermines the overall benefits to society.

Today, social concerns of business are fixtures in the programs of most business schools; novels, movies, and plays reflect the issue; and social concerns are commonly discussed in boardrooms, planning meetings, business flights, shop floors, legislative committees, and production lines. Business leaders cannot escape taking a position on the social responsibilities of their firms.

Arguments for Social Responsibility

Advocates of social concern believe that business should take an active role in improving society and solving social problems. They believe that businesses, by working to improve the overall society, can often improve their operation and profits in the long run.

Society grants businesses the right to exist. One of the strongest arguments for the social concern of business is the premise that society grants organizations the right to exist. Cultural norms — sometimes expressed through legal means — allow businesses to form and function; actions of individuals in society enable them to flourish. Business leaders should not forget that their right to exist carries an obligation to serve society's

goals. Business organizations should serve society rather than society serving business. It is the moral duty of all units of society — including business — to strive for a better world. As overall conditions improve, all the components of society will benefit accordingly.

Social responsibility contributes to business profits. In many cases, a company will make greater profits in the long run if it considers benefits to society. Since cultural norms permit organizations to exist, profits are earned only within cultural limits. When enough people believe a business no longer serves society's best interests, they may pressure the firm into its grave by boycotting its goods or services, influencing officials against it, condemning it in the media, or patronizing other firms.

Social concern can also benefit short-run profits because of current public expectations. Because the public now expects business to benefit society, a firm that maintains a good record will find it easier to hire better employees and win more customers. In the early 1970s, Caesar Chavez and the United Farm Workers called a strike

Figure 3.1
Issues of social responsibility.

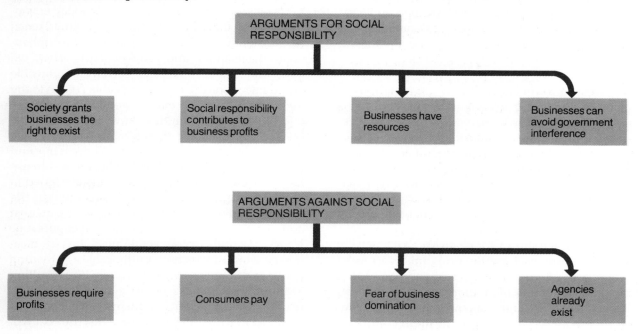

A company's daycare center for its employees' children is one example of how business resources can be used in a socially beneficial manner.

against the Gallo wine company because of alleged abuses in the compensation and working conditions of employees. After much publicity, it was estimated that as many as 20% of consumers boycotted the purchase of Gallo wine. After several years, Gallo came to terms with the farm workers and the boycott was officially cancelled. Sales of Gallo wine improved dramatically. It could be argued that if Gallo had originally invested more in the benefits of its employees, both short-run and long-run profits would have been much better. Also, it is hard to establish just how much the company was hurt by the bad publicity. Possibly, as many as 5 to 10% of consumers still prefer to give their business to other companies as a matter of principle.

Businesses have resources.   Another argument for business involvement in social concerns is that businesses have personnel and capital resources. Businesses, the argument continues, also have years of experience in organizing human, technical, and monetary resources to solve seemingly uncontrollable problems. In this day, when we view government bureaucracy as too big, too costly, and too inefficient, there may be strong reasons for business to do more.

Experience shows, for example, that federally sponsored day-care center programs tend to be quite costly. By contrast, several companies that hire a large number of mothers of young children have established and managed their own company-operated centers. Some of these company-operated centers cost only about 20% as much as the typical, federally sponsored center. Companies offer these centers because they can attract highly motivated and happier employees as a result.

Businesses can avoid government interference.   Businesses can forestall additional government regulations by voluntarily serving some social needs. From management's view, government regulations are undesirable because they limit freedom. Keeping up with social demands may be a small cost to retain flexibility, restrain government growth, and advance both company and society interests. For instance, equal opportunity in hiring and training employees is a major concern of government and society. If a business takes the initiative, provides the necessary programs, and gives more opportunities to the disadvantaged, it may avoid future restrictions levied by government in the way of quotas and hiring requirements.

Arguments against Social Responsibility

Critics of business participation in social responsibility also have valid points to make. Like the pro side, the cons range from philosophical views to everyday pragmatic considerations.

Businesses require profits.   Classical economists argue that business can best fulfill its social responsibilities by maximizing profits through increased efficiency and reduced costs. They believe that business is more socially responsible when trying for the highest possible return to the investors. When the total system operates more effectively, Adam Smith's "invisible hand" disperses improvement throughout. Milton Friedman, a classical economist, says, "There is one and only one social responsibility of business — to use its resources and engage in activities designed to increase its profits so long as it stays within the rules of the game, which is to say, engages in open and free competition, without deception or fraud." Overall, these economists say, if businesses would focus only on its goal of providing goods and services more effectively, the resulting economic advantages would naturally help improve social conditions. If businesses become too involved in providing social benefits, the cost will be a diminished overall economy.

Consumers pay. Critics are quick to add that social benefits provided by business do not come free. Ultimately, consumers pay through higher prices for consumer goods. The private enterprise system motivates managers to operate as efficiently as possible to produce the greatest amount of goods using the fewest resources. If they have to expend part of their income on social needs, managers simply have to charge higher prices, causing this social burden to be borne by consumers. As in the example of day-care centers, the cost in terms of monies spent and employee time expended will be recovered by the higher cost of goods and services provided by the company. Just as government involvement results in higher taxes, company efforts result in higher prices and, possibly, lower profits.

Fear of business domination. Some people fear that business money for social causes will result in solutions that reflect business values. Each institution, such as business, religion, military, government, or education, has values that it imposes upon the society as a whole. If any of these institutions becomes too powerful in its influence, it could negatively affect society. Some social scientists believe that business already has enough social power and that further influence could threaten the balances within our society. They argue that if business becomes too powerful, it might control and dictate to other institutions such as religion and government.

Agencies already exist. Many critics of the business resource argument say that the government has spent billions of dollars on social agencies and programs to solve social problems. Perhaps implying that the government has spent too much on these issues, critics say that it is wasteful duplication for businesses to try to solve the problems. In fact, under the Reagan administration, there were attempts to slow the rate of growth of these government agencies and, in some cases, actually cut back on budget allocations. Still, this argument maintains that, since the agencies exist, let them take responsibility for the problems.

The Reality of Social Responsibility

The case against business's social responsibility is weakened in the face of severe social problems, an oversimplistic concept of profit maximization,

and the force of society's demands. Concerned citizens feel that social problems threaten our culture's supporting foundation. If the system that guards against social problems fails, our entire enterprise system may be in jeopardy.

Peter Drucker, a noted management consultant, observes, "Under any circumstances, we are moving in the direction of demanding that our institutions take responsibility beyond their own performance and beyond their own contribution. We will demand this not only of business enterprise but of all other institutions as well — the university and the hospital, the government agency and the school." Management simply cannot ignore these pressures.

CONSUMERISM

The public demand for more protection of buyer's rights is called **consumerism**. Every day, about 230 million people in our country spend more than $3 billion. We are satisfied with a lot of things: product availability, variety of goods and services, opportunities to work, and a high standard of living. But as consumers deal with business, some serious problems occur. Here are just a few complaints from the files of a consumer protection agency: "A repair person worked on my refrigerator on and off for two years and never got it working properly." "I had my hair colored in a beauty shop; the color was awful, my hair went flat and my scalp burned for a week, and there was nothing I could do but let it grow out." "A washing machine repair person gave me an estimate of $25, but charged $110 for the job." "They were especially nice to me when I applied for the loan, but when I got a little behind in payments, they called me three or four nights a week, threatened to take my furniture and get me fired."

In a recent year, consumers filed more than one million complaints with the Better Business Bureaus around the country.

"When I bought the coffee maker they said 'satisfaction guaranteed,' but I have been trying to return it for three weeks and the company refuses to give me my money back." In a recent year, consumers filed more than one million complaints

TABLE 3.1 ■ THE TEN MOST COMMON CONSUMER COMPLAINTS

Category	Percentage of Complaints
Autos	23
Consumer credit	16
Recreation goods, activities	6
Books, magazines	6
Medical supplies, services	4
Housewares	3
Debt-collection services	3
Appliances	2
Home furnishings	2
Other goods, services	35

Source: The Federal Trade Commission.

with the 143 Better Business Bureaus around the country. **Better Business Bureaus** are nonprofit organizations that businesses organize to monitor and control unethical and illegal practices; most deal with poor service. The ten most common complaints in 1981 appear in Table 3.1.

Consumer Rights

Worried about consumer's rights, President John F. Kennedy established a **Consumer Advisory Council** in 1962. One of the Council's actions included a **Consumer's Bill of Rights** which included:

Safety. When we purchase a product or service, we have a right to expect it to be safe. Because of this, laws have been passed to keep dyes and other chemicals out of foods, to require the warning "may be injurious to your health" to be printed on cigarette and saccharine packages, and to force the recall of automobiles with defective brakes and dangerously located fuel tanks. Perhaps some of the most visible aspects of consumer safety are the recent laws requiring drug manufacturers to be more precise in describing uses and negative side effects of drugs.

Information. We have a right to expect the information given us about products and services to be accurate. The Federal Trade Commission (FTC) oversees advertising to make sure that it is true. In recent years, the FTC has: pressured toy manufacturers to stop showing ads that made toys do things that children at home could not duplicate, prohibited the STP Oil Corporation from saying that its oil treatment prevented friction and engine breakdowns when it did not, ordered Warner-Lambert to admit lying about the effects of Listerine mouthwash against colds and sore throats, and made firms cease claiming that their products were better than competitors', without proof.

Choice. Our society believes that we should have a right to choose from several products and brands. Competition is healthy in our private enterprise system. We encourage several different producers to make similar products under different labels. In 1890, the government passed the Sherman Antitrust Act to prevent monopolies. Today, the FTC and the Justice Department work to prevent companies from restraining competition.

Hearing. Consumers have a right to be heard; thus companies should establish ways to respond to consumer complaints. Surveys show that as many as 70% of customers will return products to retailers in a given year.

Consumer Protection

Because of the interest in consumer welfare, the federal and state governments have created agencies and councils to watch out for consumers' interests. There are several nongovernment agencies that also help. Better Business Bureaus and Chambers of Commerce exist in most cities, and they often hear complaints from customers. These groups may bring a complaint to the attention of the seller, or keep a record so that when others ask about a business's reputation, they can provide the correct information. Several newspapers, radio, and television stations publicize consumers' complaints so that public opinion will act as a pressure to correct problems. The **Consumer Union**, another nongovernment organization, tests and rates products. Results are published in a respected monthly magazine called *Consumer Reports*.

Most states and many cities have consumer agencies that help consumers with reasonable complaints. Most cities operate small claims courts where you can bring lawsuits for small

VDT Safety

Debates abound over the safety of video display terminals (VDTs). Since the early 1970s workers have realized that frequent use of VDTs may cause eye strain and back aches. But now, growing numbers of women who regularly operate VDTs are becoming increasingly concerned that working on them could cause miscarriages, birth defects, or difficulties in conception. Though no conclusive evidence exists that VDTs pose such a hazard, recent reports of pregnancy problems among VDT operators in the United States and Canada are beginning to create widespread fear.

Because of this, researchers at the National Institute of Occupational Safety and Health (NIOSH) are now studying whether VDTs are the cause of these problems. It is known that VDTs do emit tiny amounts of X-ray and microwave radio-frequency radiation, but these emissions are extremely low. NIOSH will look at nearly 4000 women workers—half will use VDTs and half will not—over three years. NIOSH hopes to release its findings by 1987.

What's more, some state legislatures, in response to growing public concern, are beginning to consider rules to limit workers' exposure to VDTs. In at least five states, proposed legislation would allow pregnant workers to transfer from work requiring a VDT. Canada and Sweden are also examining the effects of radiation emitted by VDTs.

The organization for office workers, 9to5, is pushing for legislation to regulate the manufacture of the keyboard and terminal combinations. Critics of the organization say 9to5 is just trying to drum up support and publicity for the union. However, Karen R. Nussbaum, executive director of 9to5, says their toll-free "VDT risks" hotline gets 100 calls a day. "Over the next five years," she predicts, "we'll see serious legislation passed in several states."

Although the radiation hazards of personal computers are still controversial, other physical discomforts are not. This ad illustrates one company's response.

Source: "Pregnancy and VDT Workers: Pressure Leads to a Quest for Hard Facts," *Business Week*, April 23, 1984, pp. 80–82.

amounts (usually under $500) without having to hire a lawyer. You simply fill out a form, appear in court, and present your evidence. The court then decides what should be done.

Businesses have responded to these activities by being more sensitive to consumer complaints. Most larger businesses have created customer service departments whose primary objective is to respond to problems and maintain positive customer relations. Usually, if there is a doubt regarding a customer complaint, most companies decide in favor of the customer. One large department store recently returned money to a customer for a pair of shoes she'd bought there that she said hurt her feet. Since the department manager was not familiar with the style, he researched his files and found that the shoes had been discontinued in 1939.

ENVIRONMENTALISM

Just what is the cost of a dead sea gull? At an oil conference, an economist put the estimate between $1 and $10. "I don't think anyone," he said, "would say they have a value of more than $10 a bird." To this, the environmentalists reacted with pained disbelief. One naturalist commented that economists "know the price of everything and the value of nothing."* In light of the many world problems, such a reaction over one sea gull may seem to be out of place. But it demonstrates the attention we have begun to place on our environment. It also illustrates the conflicts. We need to drill for offshore oil, but who pays when the wells leak and cover our beaches? We need cheaper energy, but do the highly efficient nuclear power plants exact too great a price in terms of safety and pollution of the environment? Chemicals in the streams and air are unsafe, but who pays to clean them up? **Environmentalism** is the movement that tries to protect our resources and our health by keeping the environment clean and safe.

How Serious Is Pollution?

Pollution of the environment has been an issue for centuries, but for the first time, many fear pollution to be a real danger to human survival. Within the past 15 years, we have become aware of many

From 1971 through 1982, chemical spills killed 287 persons and injured 7638 people in 126,622 separate incidents.

dangers. Although air in many major cities is cleaner than it was before the passage of the Clean Air Act in 1970, the Environmental Protection Agency reported in early 1983 that 111 of the nation's 3000 counties (50 million people) failed to meet federal air pollution standards. From 1971 through 1982, chemical spills killed 287 persons and injured 7638 people in 126,622 separate incidents. About one-third of the country's streams and shorelines remain polluted. Many streams and lakes, once sparkling and pure, are now off limits to swimmers; fishermen cannot eat their catch; and water must be purified to be drinkable. Toxic waste disposal has everyone fearful, and acid rain takes the joy out of fresh rainfall. Acid rain is formed when chemicals from burning coal, oil, or gasoline get into the air and mix with rain. The mixture forms a weak sulfuric acid, nitric acid, or nitrous acid. Almost 10,000 lakes in the eastern half of the United States have suffered some acid rain damage, according to the National Wildlife Federation. Once acid rain destroys a lake, there is virtually no way to restore it. Many citizens are subjected to between 50 and 90 decibels of noise pollution; and solid waste threatens to bury us. As the pollution problems have become better known, public sensitivity has increased. In a public opinion survey of environmental and economic issues sponsored by the Continental Group, Inc., 77% of the respondents put a high priority on a clean environment. In July, 1983, William Ruckelshaus, administrator of the Environmental Protection Agency said, "We're just fooling ourselves if we think Americans will let Congress or any administration ease up in any way if it seriously jeopardizes public health or the environment."*

Business and Government Response

There is little doubt that businesses have been a major contributor to our pollution problems; but until recently, accountability had been nil. For in-

---

* *The Wall Street Journal*, September 2, 1975, p. 1.

* "We Must Restore Our Credibility," *U.S. News & World Report*, July 11, 1983, p. 50.

stance, many years ago, Pittsburgh was covered by blankets of steel mill smoke. To complaints, officials responded, "Smoke means jobs." Thirty years ago, the Ford Motor Company, responding to a Los Angeles County official complaining of soot, stated, "The Ford engineering staff, although mindful that automobile engines produce gases, feels that these waste vapors are dissipated in the atmosphere quickly and do not present an air pollution problem." Although environmental decisions today are still controversial, our attitude has changed drastically from these early days. We no longer think of pollution as merely a nuisance; it menaces the survival of many people. Over the years, government and business programs have begun to tackle environmental problems.

Programs. Perhaps the greatest impact upon environmental protection has been made by the **Environmental Protection Agency (EPA),** which formulates and interprets environmental laws. The EPA has assessed penalties against polluters and prompted a number of laws, including the **National Environmental Quality Act of 1970** which regulates air pollution and the **Clean**

BUSINESS BULLETIN

The Dioxin Controversy

In 1983, Times Beach, Missouri, moved—all 2500 residents. The federal government bought most of their 800 homes and 30 businesses. Cost to the government was $36.7 million.

People were moving away because a very toxic substance, known as dioxin, was found in their community. Dioxin, a highly toxic by-product of certain chemical-making processes, is considered dangerous by some experts at one point per billion. Levels many times higher than this were found in people's driveways and yards. The chemical was apparently in waste oil used to spray for dust control on roads in Missouri and in other parts of the country.

Dioxin is not just one chemical; actually, the label refes to any of seventy-five different chemicals in eight different chemical families. One of the most widely known uses of the substance was in Agent Orange, a defoliant used in the Vietnam War. It is also the by-product in many insecticides, herbicides, wood preservatives, coolants, and copy paper.

Even though dioxin has caused quite a scare around the country, the American Medical Association (AMA) claims that the news media have blown the issue completely out of proportion. Their resolution said in part that the "lives and well-being" of people living in areas contaminated by dioxin "have been unnecessarily and ignorantly damaged by this hysterical malreporting."* Doctors, representing the AMA, report that dioxin has been around a long time, yet it has not produced any documented deaths or anything of a serious medical nature. Chemical companies also maintain that fears are exaggerated.

Still, researchers report links between dioxin and many health problems with research animals in the laboratory. And some doctors say that persons exposed to dioxin are much more susceptible to heart attacks, liver problems, and soft-tissue cancer. Finally, more than 16,000 Vietnam veterans have filed disability claims attributing many ailments to the dioxin in Agent Orange. Experts on both sides agree that more study is needed to pinpoint the effect of dioxin on human health.

* "AMA says Dioxin no Imminent Threat," *The Boston Globe*, Associated Press, June 23, 1983.

TABLE 3.2 ■ MAJOR FEDERAL ENVIRONMENTAL LEGISLATION

1899 Refuse Act

Made it unlawful to dump refuse into navigable waters without a permit. A 1966 court decision made all industrial wastes subject to this act.

1947 Federal Insecticide, Fungicide and Rodenticide Act

Enacted to protect farmers from fraudulent claims of salespersons. Required registration of poisons.

1955 Federal Water Pollution Control Act

Set standards for treatment of municipal water waste before discharge. Revisions to this act were passed in 1965 and 1967.

1963 Clean Air Act

Assisted local and state governments in establishing control programs and coordinated research.

1965 Clean Air Act Amendments

Authorized establishment of federal standards for automobile exhaust emissions, beginning with 1968 models.

1965 Solid Waste Disposal Act

Provided assistance to local and state governments for control programs and authorized research in this area.

1965 Water Quality Act

Authorized the setting of standards for discharges into waters.

1967 Air Quality Act

Established air quality regions, with acceptable regional pollution levels. Required local and state governments to implement approved control programs or be subject to federal controls.

1967 Federal Insecticide, Fungicide and Rodenticide Amendments

Provided for licensing of pesticide users. (Further authority granted through 1972 revision.)

1970 National Environmental Quality Act

Established Council for Environmental Quality for the purpose of coordinating all federal pollution control programs. Authorized the establishment of the Environmental Protection Agency to implement CEQ policies on a case-by-case basis.

1970 Clean Air Act Amendments

Authorized the Environmental Protection Agency to set national air pollution standards. Restricted the discharge of six major pollutants into the lower atmosphere. Automobile manufacturers were required to reduce nitrogen oxide, hydrocarbon and carbon monoxide emissions by 90% (in addition to the 1965 requirements) during the 1970s. Set aircraft emission standards. Required states to meet deadline for complying with EPA standards. Authorized legal action by private citizens to require EPA to carry out approved standards against undiscovered offenders.

1970 Resource Recovery Act

Authorized government assistance for the construction of pilot recycling plants. Authorized the development of control programs on national level.

1970 Water Quality and Improvement Act

Required local and state governments to carry out standards under compliance deadlines.

1972 Federal Water Pollution Control Act Amendments

Set national water quality goal of restoring polluted water to swimmable, fishable waters by 1983.

1972 Noise Control Act

Required EPA to establish noise standards for products determined to be major sources of noise. Required EPA to advise the Federal Aviation Administration on acceptable standards for aircraft noise.

1972 Pesticide Control Act

Required that all pesticides used in interstate commerce be approved and certified as effective for their stated purposes. Required certification that they were harmless to humans, animal life, animal feed, and crops.

1974 Clean Water Act

Originally called the Safe Water Drinking Act, this law set (for the first time) federal standards for water suppliers serving more than twenty-five people, having more than fifteen service connections, or operating more than sixty days a year.

1975 Federal Environmental Pesticide Control Act Amendments

Established 1977 as the deadline for registration, classification, and licensing of approximately 50,000 pesticides. This deadline was not met.

1976 Resource Conservation and Recovery Act

Encouraged conservation and the recovery of resources. Put hazardous waste under government control. Disallowed the opening of new dumping sites. Required that all existing open dumps be closed or upgraded to sanitary landfills by 1983. Set standards for providing technical, financial and marketing assistance to encourage solid waste management.

1977 Clean Air Act Amendments

Changed deadline for automobile emission requirements from 1975 and 1978 to 1980–1981.

1977 Amendments to Clean Water Act

Revised list of toxic pollutants and set new policies for review. Required that pollutants be monitored "by best available technology" that is economically feasible.

1977 Federal Water Pollution Control Act Amendments

Authorized extension of the 1972 regulations.

Water Act of 1974 which controls water pollution. In 1980, Congress created a Superfund to deal with toxic waste dumps. The Superfund, containing $1.6 billion in 1983, was being used to help clean up chemical dumps in alleys, backyards, and other places. Additionally, the **Solid Wastes Disposal Act** exercises some control over disposal of solid wastes, and the **Federal Occupational Safety and Health Act** regulates noise levels for manufacturers in interstate commerce. (See Table 3.2 for a list of major federal environmental legislation.) The government has also used financial incentives, zoning restrictions, research grants, and denial of government contracts to enforce pollution control measures.

Prompted by society's concern and Congress's prompting, businesses are now investing billions of dollars to reduce and prevent pollution. In fact, in 1983, government and business's pollution control expenditures amounted to $50 billion a year — $220 for every person in the country. For a power plant, capital costs for pollution control may run as high as 25%. For most other plants, it ranges between 1 and 10%. For example, Mobil Oil engineers have designed many refinery units to minimize emission of mist, sulfur dioxide, petroleum vapor, and other chemical compounds. Georgia Pacific installed a system that recycles and removes all pollutants. Dow pledged, "No plant will be built if there is any waste effluent or air pollution." Another approach by businesses is to design and produce products that improve pollution control. Examples include automobiles that are less polluting, detergents that dissipate more quickly, and recyclable cans and bottles. See Table 3.3 for a listing of the costs of fighting pollution in the 1980s.

Achievements and future problems. Environmentalists show many achievements in their attacks on pollution. Some of them are as follows:

- In the eighteen worst cities, violations of carbon monoxide standards have dropped 66% since 1975.
- Private industry has invested about $60 billion to control air pollution during the past 10 years.
- Smoggy days have dropped 36% during the last decade in the twenty-two cities with the worst smog.

TABLE 3.3 ■ ESTIMATED COSTS OF FIGHTING POLLUTION IN THE 1980s	
Air pollution	$393 billion
Water pollution	$228 billion
Solid waste pollution	$ 22 billion
Land reclamation	$ 19 billion
Noise	$ 11 billion
Toxic substances	$ 11 billion
Drinking water	$ 4 billion
Pesticides	$ 2 billion
Total cost (1980 – 1989)	$690 billion

Source: Environmental Protection Agency.

- Since 1975, sulfur dioxide emissions — from burning coal, oil, and other fossil fuels — have been cut by 5 million tons a year.
- Automobile-produced carbon monoxide is 40% lower than a decade ago.
- The Great Lakes cleanup campaign in the late 1970s has produced increased fish and other marine life once again.

While we appear to be slowly winning the battle against air and water pollution, chemical and radioactive wastes are emerging to provide new threats. Our factories produce between 40 to 60 million tons of contaminated wastes per year. Service stations, dry cleaners, and other small businesses add to this, making the total about a ton a year per person.

Although some firms practice controlled disposal of hazardous chemical wastes, improper disposal and pollution have emerged as major environmental concerns of the 1980s.

CROSS FIRE

Should Pollution Laws Be Tighter or Looser?

The debate over the government's role in fighting pollution is ongoing. In an interview with Gaylord Nelson, Chairman of the Wilderness Society, reported in *U.S. News & World Report,* Nelson makes the following points for not loosening pollution laws.

- Our society cannot last long if we do not fully implement the laws passed by Congress over the past few years.
- Although it is costly to prevent and clean up pollution, cleanup measures save society billions of dollars. In the long run, antipollution measures are cheaper than pollution costs.
- We will not be at a disadvantage in international markets by spending more on pollution control because other countries are going to have to do the same thing.
- If the federal government's role is reduced, you would have fifty states, each with different standards — an unmanageable mess.

A. Alan Hill, chairman of the Council on Environmental Quality, makes the following points for reducing the federal government's role in environmental protection:

- We are already spending a lot of money on pollution control — $50 billion annually. This is much more than the gross domestic product of 141 nations that report such expenditures.
- According to statistics, lower spending levels will not endanger the environment.
- Laws protecting public health should be given top priority.
- Since people throughout the nation demand a clean environment, giving more power to the states would not worsen the problems.
- Experience by 3M, Eastman Kodak, and other companies has shown that pollution control measures can be cost effective; thus, it is reasonable to expect industry to do more voluntarily in the area.

How do you stand? Do you think the federal government should be more or less involved in controlling pollution?

____ A. Much more involved   ____ C. Somewhat less involved

____ B. Somewhat more involved   ____ D. Much less involved

Give three justifications for your position.

A. _____

B. _____

C. _____

Source: "Should Pollution Laws Be Loosened?" *U.S. News & World Report,* April 4, 1983, pp. 51–52.

DISCRIMINATION

Discrimination is unequal treatment of people based on race, sex, religion, age, or national origin. Measurable discriminations against minorities and the disadvantaged, including women, blacks, Mexican-Americans, Indian-Americans, and other ethnic groups, have revealed blatant injustices within our society. These groups have difficulty gaining access to many of the opportunities within business. Furthermore, they are discouraged from pursuing their traditional cultures.

Although law and adjustments are being made in some areas, the actual figures show that discrimination is still widespread. The number of women in the work force is at the highest peak ever, more than 44 million, and that number is expected to top 54 million by 1990. In 1950, only 30% of the total work force consisted of women. The number will be 45% by 1990 (see Figure 3.2). In spite of the influx of women into the work force, a wide disparity in pay exists between jobs dominated by men and those held by women. According to U.S. Department of Commerce, women still earn only 59¢ for each dollar earned by men.

Business Reaction to Discrimination Pressures

As the dire need has become more evident, businesses have tried to deal with discrimination in several ways. Federal and local governments have been active in providing pressures that encourage the support of business in overcoming discrimination.

Although the media have publicized the Reagan administration's hostility toward enforcement of affirmative action laws, two-thirds of the executives in a 1982 Harris poll reported that government pressure for salary equity is as strong as ever.*

Hiring and promotion. The **Civil Rights Act of 1964** prevents employment discrimination based on race, religion, national origin, or sex. The federal government appointed the **Equal Employment Opportunity Commission (EEOC),** a

---

* "How Executives See Women in Management," *Business Week*, June 28, 1982, p. 10.

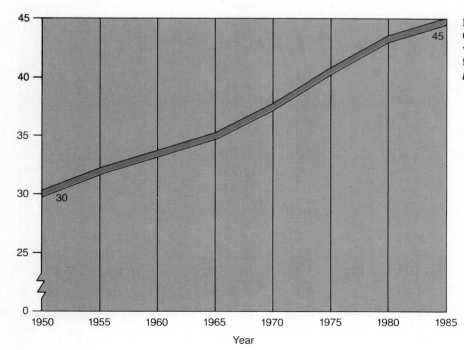

Figure 3.2 Growing percentage of women in the work force. *Source: Department of Labor Statistics.*

More Women in Management

In 1982, about 28% of all managers and administrators were women. This is up from 18% ten years earlier. Though this is a substantial increase, speculation exists that the percentages of women in top and middle level management is lower than it should be. Perhaps because the competition is getting keener, some women wonder if men — holders of nearly all the top jobs, as they are — will instinctively favor other men. Patricia McGrath, a graduate of the Harvard Business School, laments that "in big corporations it's not as easy to promote a woman as a man." Nevertheless, there are women who fervently aspire to becoming their company's CEO (chief executive officer), gaining directorships, or being picked for a plum governmental post. The accompanying chart pictures the growth in percentage of women bosses.

Female managers and administrators
(millions)

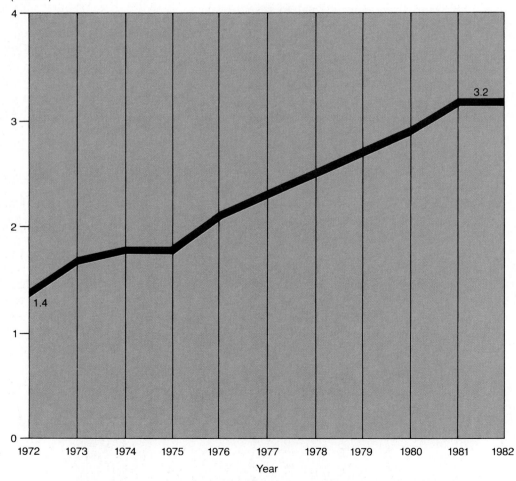

Year

Source: "Women as Bosses: The Problems They Face," *U.S. News & World Report,* July 11, 1983, pp. 56–57, and "How Harvard's Women MBAs Are Managing," *Fortune,* July 11, 1983, pp. 58–72.

federal agency, to enforce the act. Title VII of the Civil Rights Act, strengthened by several executive orders, requires an **Affirmative Action Program** as follows:

> Every company that has 40 or more employees and government contracts of $50,000 or more must develop a detailed plan that identifies weaknesses in hiring and promoting minorities and women, and a specific plan, along with dates, for correcting them.

In 1973, the EEOC won a landmark discrimination settlement against AT&T which required them to pay $15 million in back pay and $23 million a year in raises for discrimination in job assignments, pay, and promotions. However, there is some concern that this requirement places to heavy a burden on small businesses, and in 1983 there were efforts to relax requirements for some small firms.

Even in the face of President Reagan's budget-cutting efforts, the EEOC budget was increased to $150 million for 1983, up $6 million from the year before. About 2800 of the commission's 3100 employees operate in the investigative area. Companies found guilty of job discrimination may be prevented from bidding on government contracts. Also, courts may force a guilty employer to hire an individual, provide back pay, or take other corrective actions.

Prompted by these pressures, companies have become more sensitive in hiring and promoting. While some must try to meet the minimum requirements of hiring and promotion without regard to sex or race, other companies vigorously publicize their openings to minority groups. And some companies give priority to minorities and women, even though doing so makes them susceptible to the charge of reverse discrimination.

According to activity in the EEOC, unlawful job discrimination (including age, racial, and sex discrimination) continues to be a problem in our society (see Figure 3.3). Clarence Thomas, chairman of the Equal Employment Opportunity Commission, says, "It's fair to say that job discrimination is still very, very serious, although it is not nearly as blatant and obvious as it was 20 years ago."

Training programs. Offering a job does not always solve the problem, especially for the underqualified. Again, with some government prompting and assistance, businesses have offered training programs to help train disadvantaged people to perform at required skill levels. In 1984, the Job Training Partnership Act provided federal funds in an effort to unite public and private sectors into a job-producing partnership. Businesses who hire the unemployed and provide on-the-job training receive some reimbursement for their costs and may receive special tax credits. Small business owner John Ringler says the program is very helpful. In his case, government funds pay about 40% of the salary of an employee, allowing him to hire two people instead of one.

Minority enterprise support. **Minority enterprises** are businesses owned by blacks, Spanish-speaking Americans, native Americans, Orientals, and other minority groups. For instance, as a result of the 1971 settlement, enacted by Congress, of the land claims of Alaska's 80,000 Eskimos, Indians, and Aleuts, the natives of Alaska are establishing business empires. The natives were granted 44 million acres to help them enter the

FUNNY BUSINESS

Source: *Stockworth* by permission of Sterling & Selesnick, Inc. and The New York Times Syndication Sales Corp.

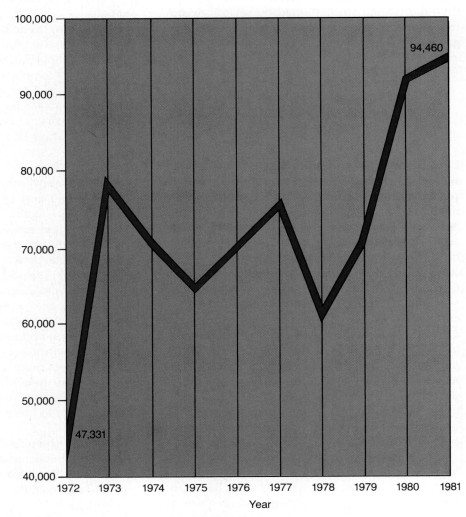

Figure 3.3
Charges found to have merit by the EEOC (1972–1981). *Source: Equal Employment Opportunity Commission.*

capitalist mainstream, and $962.5 million was included to establish 203 village businesses and 12 giant regional corporations (see Figure 3.4). In addition to this and other government-sponsored programs, a number of companies help minority-owned businesses by specifically awarding contracts to them and agreeing to finance some developmental projects. For instance, Southland Corporation, the operator of 7-Eleven convenience stores, pledged a 5-year commitment to raise the level of minority participation in the corporation to 23% by 1988. The percentage goal applies to all levels in the organization, including managers, professionals, technicians, sales workers, office personnel, and clerks. In addition, Southland pledged to expand its college intern

program to include at least 23% minorities; use minority vendors for 23% of its outside purchases; and increase usage of minority companies it does business with in accounting, advertising, banking, insurance, legal services, and real estate.

Corporate charity. Studies show that many companies have voluntarily increased their donations to aid minority causes. These efforts, often not related directly to their businesses, aid in education, drug programs, playing centers, day-care centers, hospitals, career development programs, and help for the elderly.

The United Way is one of the most visibly successful programs where companies and individuals work together to aid the disadvantaged. Companies provide skilled managers to help run the campaigns, and company employees collect and encourage donations from other employees. Many companies match the contributions of their employees. That is, if employees raise $5000 among themselves, the company will contribute another $5000.

Another example of corporate charity to minority groups is Xerox Corporation's recent $6 million gift of talking computers for blind students at various colleges across the country. Two hundred Kurzweil Reading Machines, which convert any kind of printed material into actual spoken English, will be used by an estimated 4600 of the 6000 currently enrolled U.S. college students who have severe visual impairments.

Corporations, needless to say, do not contribute exclusively to minority groups and concerns. Many instances of corporate philanthropy could be listed, but let us mention merely a few:

- IBM recently contributed $40 million in computer-aided manufacturing equipment to twenty universities.

These Native American salmon fishermen are shareholders in their own company, one of many established through Congressional action in 1971.

BUSINESS BULLETIN

The Discrimination Case of Christine Craft

In the summer of 1983, Christine Craft sued her former employer, Metromedia, Inc., for sex discrimination. Craft had been hired as a television anchorwoman by Metromedia to do newscasts.

After a few months on the job, Craft's supervisor demoted her because, as the supervisor said, ". . . audience reaction to her was very negative." The reaction was based on surveys that the station had taken of its viewing audience. An expert witness testified that the survey's findings were based on unscientific data. He commented that the sample of the audience was not a true representation of the station's total audience, and he said that the survey asked questions that were not normally asked about male newscasters.

However, Craft maintained that she was demoted because the news director told her she was, ". . . too old, unattractive, and not deferential enough to men." The news director denied saying this to Craft.

Craft's suit claimed sex discrimination. The federal jury of four men and two women agreed. They recommended awarding $500,000 to Craft — $375,000 for actual damages plus $125,000 in punitive damages. Although Metromedia appealed the decision and got some changes, the courts agreed substantially with Craft's position.

Source: "Jury Awards Craft $500,000 in Suit Against TV Station," Associated Press, *The Wichita Eagle Beacon,* August 9, 1983, p. 1.

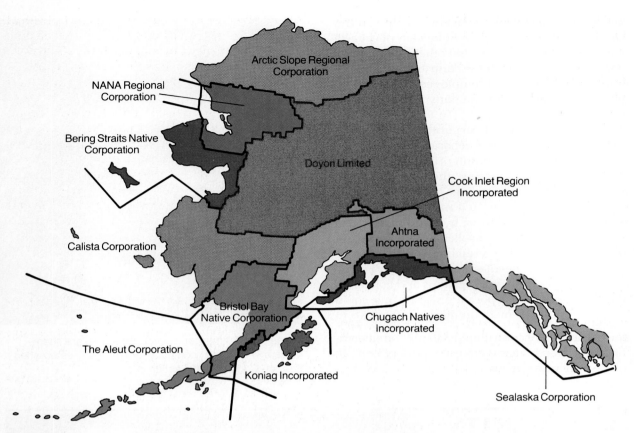

Figure 3.4
The Alaska regional native corporations.

- Wang Laboratories contributed $4 million to the Metropolitan Center in Boston.

- Mainpro, a $2.8 million maker of lubricants and maintenance products, each month gives each of its fifty employees a $24 check to be used for any philanthropic purpose.

ETHICS AND WHITE COLLAR CRIME

Ethics are principles of right or good behaviors. They involve moral values as to what conduct is proper. And business ethics involve other moral values in our society. As one businesswoman said, "Many of our moral decisions are borderline; some people view a certain practice as being unethical, while others think it to be totally proper." Many influences in our society determine which behavior is ethical.

Sources of Ethics

While each individual develops a code of what is ethical, we are influenced by laws, cultural attitudes, professional codes, and individual values.

Influence of law on ethics. Many ethical standards are defined by laws. But the law does not cover all unethical conduct; it merely tries to prevent serious violations. Many laws, especially new ones, are unclear. Since humans make laws, some of them are not perfect and others are later found to be unconstitutional. Still, most authorities agree

Recent surveys by the Cable Channel News indicate that as many as 40% of the population cheated on their income tax returns.

that abiding by the law defines a minimum guide for ethical behavior. For example, the law states that each citizen must be honest in filing tax returns, yet recent surveys done by the Cable Channel News indicate that as many as 40% of the population cheated on their income tax returns. Also, the law states that employees should not steal from their employers, yet many workers see nothing wrong with taking office supplies home for personal use.

Cultural values and ethics. Values are accepted standards of behavior within a given society. All societies develop broad-based values that are generally accepted by most of its members. Communities of people usually share common views. Often, these views affect the values and conduct of businesses in local areas. For example, many communities believe that stores should not sell alcoholic beverages on Sunday. And, in fact, citizens may exert pressure for passages of laws that prohibit doing so. Stores in other areas may remain closed on Sunday mornings, not because of laws, but out of respect for the community's values.

Professional codes and ethics. Many national associations have ethics committees that develop standards for their communities. The purpose is to use group behavior to encourage ethical practices that build goodwill and trust. A good example would be the code of ethics published and enforced by the National Board of Realtors in Fig. 3.5.

Individual values and ethics. Although we may all grow up in the same society, there is a broad range in the values we adopt. Individual values vary with background, family, religion, and environment. Some people think it is all right to mislead customers in order to get a sale. Others may choose to lose the sale rather than misrepresent the product in any way. In one survey of business people, 19% said they had quit a company for ethical reasons. Sometimes a company may try to influence an employee to act against personal values. In the same survey, 87% said it was wrong to compromise personal values even if the success of the company was at stake. While individual values vary, most people agree that it is wrong to lie, cheat, steal, and purposefully misrepresent.

How Ethical Is Business Behavior?

Are business practices becoming more unethical? There is no easy answer. Bribery, profit gouging, price fixing, embezzlement, monopolizing, and other illegal practices cost consumers more than $40 billion a year in higher prices and taxes. A spokesperson for the U.S. Chamber of Commerce says that the extent of bribes, kickbacks, and payoffs is "pervasive." These unethical activities might involve anyone from the janitor to the chairman of the board. A recent study of 3000 executives by the American Management Association found that most employees felt pressure from their companies to compromise their personal values. Another study by the Opinion Research Corporation of 531 top and middle mangers reported that 48% felt that it would be all right to pay bribes to foreign officials if that were an accepted way of doing business in that country. The famous

Figure 3.5
Excerpts from the code of ethics of the National Association of Realtors.
Source: The National Association of Realtors.

Article 1. The Realtor should keep himself informed as to events affecting real estate in his community, the state, and nation so that he may be able to contribute responsibly to public thinking on such matters.

Article 4. The Realtor should seek no unfair advantage over his fellow-Realtors and should conduct his business so as to avoid controversies with his fellow-Realtors.

Article 8. The Realtor shall not accept compensation from more than one party, even if permitted by law, without the full knowledge of all parties to the transaction.

Article 9. The Realtor shall avoid exaggeration, misrepresentation, or concealment of pertinent facts. He has an affirmative obligation to discover adverse factors which a reasonably competent and diligent investigation would disclose.

Article 10. The Realtor shall provide equal professional services to all persons regardless of race, creed, sex, or country of national origin. The Realtor shall not be a party to any plan or agreement to discriminate against a person or persons on the basis of race, creed, sex, or country of national origin.

Article 17. The Realtor shall not engage in activities that constitute the unauthorized practice of law and shall recommend that legal counsel be obtained when the interest of either party requires it.

Watergate caper and the recent ABSCAM scandal, with their resulting public outrage, have increased investigations into the ethical practices of business. To date, almost 450 firms have admitted to secret payments or bribes, both within the United States and to other countries.

Can society thrive without some minimum standards of honesty and ethics? We think not. Since business depends on society's survival, a certain level of honest dealing is necessary. The capitalist system glorifies pursuit of self-interest, but business people understand as never before that they cannot be successful without the trust of others. Bad-mouthing competitors is sometimes considered a valid business strategy, but as Kirk Hanson, a business administration professor at Stanford University, says "There is a growing appreciation for the fact that businesses owe some kind of obligation to competitors and customers. They are realizing they are vulnerable [to each other's] innuendo."

Some business people feel that it is simply good business to be ethical. Ethical behavior stimulates others to be more cooperative and prevents angry behavior by competitors, peer companies, and government agencies. Customers like to trade with honest companies, employees value fair bosses, and investors feel more secure with law-abiding companies. Further, the recent interest in corporate culture (see Enrichment Chapter A) and the realization that successful companies are the ones with good values have helped spotlight corporate ethics still more.

Since the Watergate incident, more than 300 business ethics courses have been added to the curriculums of the nation's colleges and universities. What is more, business ethics is showing up in more sales training classes, boardrooms, and company policy statements. As an indication of the emphasis that some companies have begun to place on ethical behavior, Chemical Bank in New York now includes ethics in a new management training program, and Conoco Inc. publishes an in-house booklet on moral standards.

New ethics issues are always emerging. As some experts see things now, the most important ethics issues during the next decade will be:*

The rights of workers. Do companies owe anything to laid-off workers? Do they owe them training or new jobs? What about the effect of automation on the work force, or company responsibility to the families of working women, or sexual harassment on the job, or minority hiring? The whole issue of hiring and the quality of work life is having, and will continue to have, an immense impact on workers' rights.

The rights of citizens in other countries. Kenneth Goodpaster, a professor at Harvard Business School, believes "there is a globalization of business." Companies will likely have to "look at their values from a transcultural" point of view in order to help ensure their success in the marketplace.

The rights of companies and the public as technology advances. With the change to a society based on information come concerns about the right to privacy. Along with this, there is an increasing concern about people stealing trade secrets and copyrighted material. With the burgeoning field of computers and information processing comes computer crime and the need for computer laws.

The rights of the environment. Only today are we beginning to experience the effects of acid rain and toxic waste dumping. Who has responsibility for cleaning up wastes that were disposed of a decade or two ago? Dow Corning Corporation, a manufacturer of silicones, says in its code of ethics that "Dow Corning will be responsible for the impact of its technology upon the environment."

ENERGY

With only 6% of the world's population, Americans consume over 30% of the world's total energy. And our consumption rate has been rising rapidly during the last few years. In the United States, an average person uses as much energy in a few days — driving a car, mowing the lawn, mixing a cake, cleaning the rug, cooling and heating homes, and enjoying leisure — as most individuals in other countries use in a year.

This hydroelectric facility at a Massachusetts dam and the geothermal steam plant in Utah represent options to meet future energy needs with renewable, regionally distinct, resources.

Where Do We Get Energy?

Energy is the capacity for the action or the ability to do work. Of course, we use physical energy when we run, walk, lift, stand, or even sit. But we have such great demands for energy that it is impossible to satisfy all of our energy needs with physical effort. We can't very well propel a jetliner across the ocean with human energy, can we? Energy comes from many sources, most of which are becoming increasingly expensive.

Oil. Oil is our greatest source of energy, and we are hugely dependent on it. By 1990, we will be using more than 20 million barrels a day, or more than 7 billion barrels annually. Because the United States is not capable of producing all the oil it uses, half of our needs must be imported. (See Figure 3.6 for a graphic of the world's known oil reserves.)

Indeed, our known and proven reserves within the United States amount to only about 28 billion barrels, enough for about 4 more years at our current rate of consumption. If we rely on so much foreign oil, we leave ourselves open for political blackmail and price gouging. And we are trying to become less dependent. We built a pipeline from Alaska, but by 1985, it is expected to supply only about one eighth of the oil we need. Politicians talk about energy savings plans, but oil is so central to our economy, it is hard to reduce our consumption sharply.

Coal. Within our boundaries, we have one of the world's oldest energy sources: coal. And we have a lot of it, about one fifth of the globe's supply. If we mined and used all of it, we could run all our machines and gadgets — to meet all of our energy

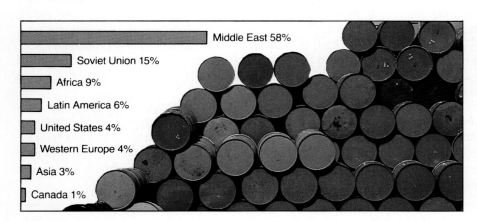

Middle East 58%

Soviet Union 15%

Africa 9%

Latin America 6%

United States 4%

Western Europe 4%

Asia 3%

Canada 1%

**Figure 3.6
The world's supply of known oil reserves.**
Source: American Petroleum Institute, Canadian Petroleum Association, Oil & Gas Journal.

needs—for the next 200 or 300 years. But, although we have the resources, there are problems with using it. It defaces the land when mined and pollutes the air when burned. The EPA (Environmental Protection Agency) and the Clean Air Act of 1970 regulate the burning of coal. Scientists can turn coal into natural gas, which burns cleaner, yet the cost is too great.

Natural gas. As far back as 1950, natural gas supplied about 17% of our energy demands. By 1980, it supplied almost 25% of our energy needs. It has been a less expensive form of energy and we have a lot of gas wells. The Federal Trade Commission has regulated natural gas prices in order to keep them low. In fact, prices have been kept so low that there has been little incentive to undertake the costly exploration of new supplies. In 1981, legislation was passed to deregulate gas prices, allowing gas companies to charge higher prices. This, some experts argue, will provide the push for more discovery and production.

Atomic energy. Nuclear power, which is generated from atomic reactors, is surely the most controversial energy source. Advocates insist that it is the only reasonable and practical source of energy for the future. And they argue that utility companies will have to start expanding their capacities by the mid-1980s to meet expected demands in the 1990s.

Others strongly oppose atomic energy because of the safety hazards in processing it and storing its waste. The Three Mile Island mishap in 1979 was an eye-opener for many people. They realized, perhaps for the first time, that something could go seriously wrong.

We currently generate 12% of our electrical energy from atomic power. But this may grow to 18% over the next 2 years when 33 more reactors begin their operations. Still, because of the heated emotions involved, the nuclear controversy will probably continue for some time.

Other energy sources. Several other possible energy sources for the future include synthetic oil, fusion atomic energy, solar energy, and wind energy. All sources of energy have pluses and minuses, as Table 3.4 indicates.

BUSINESS BULLETIN

Dim Future for Nuclear Plants

On April 20, 1983, the Supreme Court ruled that states may outlaw nuclear plants not yet under construction. The decision upheld California's 1976 moratorium on building new nuclear plants until there was an acceptable method for handling nuclear waste. Several other states have similar moratoriums and others are sure to follow.

Still, according to a Washington think tank, the American Enterprise Institute, business and government leaders have a strong preference for nuclear power. Yet, the American public apparently does not feel the same way, and, in this case, public opinion prevails.

The much-publicized Three Mile Island (TMI) incident is still very much an issue. The problem at TMI occurred in 1979, and cleanup operations began in 1982. Cost of the cleanup is a staggering $1 billion, and experts feel that it will take 4 years to achieve the cleanup.

Currently, 80 nuclear plants are operating, and another 57 are still under construction. The court ruling affects neither the operating plants nor those under construction. But the future for nuclear construction appears dim, considering public desires. As an official of the Nuclear Regulatory Commission said, "A utility executive would be crazy to commit his company to a nuclear power plant in the current political and regulatory climate."

Source: "Nuclear Industry Takes It on the Chin Again," *U.S. News & World Report*, May 2, 1983, p. 8.

TABLE 3.4 ■ SOURCES OF ENERGY

Energy Source	Advantages	Disavantages
Foreign oil	Plentiful, accessible, safe.	Political dependence, high cost, lack of control, outflow of dollars, political problems, transporting cost.
Coal	Plentiful, cost effective, wide usage.	Polluting, defacing in mining, transporting cost, water needed for processing.
Natural gas	Limited, cost effective, clean, efficient, wide usage.	Limited resource, transporting cost, safety hazards.
Atomic energy, fission	Cost effective, plentiful, efficient, accessible, wide usage.	Safety hazards, storage of wastes, polluting, capital investment, political problems, nuclear threats.
Atomic energy, fusion	Plentiful, efficient, clean, unlimited energy with more technology, accessible, wide usage.	Safety hazards, more technology required, capital investment, political problems, nuclear threats.
Solar	Clean, plentiful, safe, accessible.	Limited usage, original cost, not efficient, more technology.
Wind	Clean, plentiful at times, safe, accessible.	Not consistent, limited usage, not efficient, noise and visual pollution.
Synthetic oil	Clean, plentiful, safe, accessible.	Cost, limited usage, more technology required, capital investment, limited usage.

Source: Lester Thurow, *Zero-Sum Society*, New York: Penguin Books, 1980.

What Can Business Do?

No doubt, there is a serious energy shortage facing us. We either need greater, more efficient supplies or we need to consume less energy. Business is responding to both sides of the equation.

Finding new resources. A lot of firms are exploring for new sources of energy. They are discovering new oil, coal, and gas reserves. There are numerous projects underway to advance our technologies for converting coal into gas, sun into energy, synthetics into oil, and wind into power. As in the past, when a need exists, business rises to the challenge of fulfilling that need.

Conserving energy. A lot of energy, as much as half, is actually wasted. We lose some by transmitting it. Electricity may travel thousands of miles from its source to the consumer, resulting in a loss of energy. In research and development departments throughout the country, companies are finding new ways to conserve, produce, and transmit energy. And companies are trying to conserve by lowering their thermostats in the winter and using less air conditioning in the summer. Some large companies are using less energy now than they did 8 years ago. In the manufacture of products, businesses now take energy usage into design considerations. Government encourages consumers to use less energy by such measures as the 55 mile per hour speed limit and gas mileage requirements for new cars.

Attentive energy audits of industrial processes led to reduced energy needs for this steel manufacturer.

There are many solutions to the energy problem, but some choices will have to be made, and some sacrifices will have to be endured. We may choose to conserve, depend on foreign sources, risk safety, harm the environment, tolerate noisy windmills, or install solar receptors. For each choice, there are benefits and resulting costs.

SUMMARY

In recent years, society has applied increased pressure for businesses to become more socially responsible. The major arguments for social responsibility are: (1) Society grants businesses the right to exist, (2) social responsibility contributes to business profits, (3) businesses have resources, and (4) businesses can avoid government interference. Arguments against business participation in social problems are: (1) Businesses require profits, (2) consumers pay, (3) there is fear of business domination, and (4) agencies already exist. Consumerism requires that businesses act in the interest of consumer protection and consumer rights.

In the past, business has been a major polluter of the environment. Although the environment is a continuing concern, environmentalists, working together with business, are preventing some future pollution and cleaning up past mistakes.

Discrimination against employees because of race, religion, sex, age, and national origin continues to be a problem in our society. Business and government agencies are working together in an effort to combat discrimination and provide more equality for the future.

White collar crime continues to be a social ill. Business is working to establish more rules of conduct and educate employees in ethical values.

Because of the severity of the energy crisis, business has become involved in finding new sources of energy, as well as conserving present resources. The energy shortage can be overcome, but some sacrifices will have to be made.

MIND YOUR BUSINESS

Instructions. Business's relationship to social problems provokes many arguments and emotions. To get an idea of where you stand on the major socially related issues, respond to the following questions by using a scale from 7 to 1 to record the intensity of your feelings.

Very strongly   Very strongly
 agree 7 6 5 4 3 2 1 disagree

____ 1. Businesses should contribute time, money, and expertise to solve social problems.

____ 2. Government and business should protect and ensure the rights of consumers.

____ 3. It is the responsibility of government and business to clean up the environment, regardless of the economic cost.

____ 4. Businesses and government should make more effort to ensure that discrimination at work and in the marketplace is eliminated.

____ 5. The ethical behavior of businesses should be improved.

____ 6. We should try to solve future energy problems by government-induced rationing methods, as well as by searching for new energy sources.

See answers at the back of the book.

KEY TERMS

social responsibility, 46
consumerism, 49
Better Business Bureaus, 50
Consumer Advisory Council, 50
Consumer's Bill of Rights, 50
Consumer's Union, 50
***Consumer Reports*, 50**
environmentalism, 52
**Environmental Protection
Agency (EPA), 53**
**National Environmental Quality
Act of 1970, 53**
Clean Water Act of 1974, 55
Solid Wastes Disposal Act, 55
**Federal Occupational Safety and Health
Act of 1970, 55**
discrimination, 57
Civil Rights Act of 1964, 57
**Equal Employment Opportunity
Commission (EEOC), 57**
Affirmative Action Program, 59
minority enterprises, 59
ethics, 62
energy, 65

REVIEW QUESTIONS

1. Define social responsibility. Give an example.
2. List and explain each of the arguments for business becoming more involved in social problems.
3. List and explain the arguments against business becoming more involved in social problems.
4. What is consumerism?
5. What are the provisions of the Consumer's Bill of Rights?
6. Discuss the means by which consumers are protected.
7. What is discrimination?
8. Discuss the ways in which businesses are reacting to discrimination pressures.
9. What is environmentalism?
10. What has the government done to fight environmental problems?
11. What have businesses done to help with environmental problems?
12. Define ethics. What are the major influences of ethics?
13. What are our major sources of energy? What can businesses do to help with the energy problem?

CASES

Case 3.1: Are Businesses Doing Enough to Hire Minorities?

Many women and blacks complain that they are not getting good jobs in business and government. And companies complain that they cannot find enough professional and skilled women and minority workers to meet their affirmative action goals. Business leaders say they are working hard, but competition for hiring women and minorities has increased intensely.

There has been, according to government statistics, a steady but slow gain for women and minorities in higher-paying jobs. But feminist and civil rights leaders do not believe the statements of business leaders that "we just cannot find enough qualified minority and women workers." One industry leader says, "We cannot find enough engineers period, much less women and minority engineers." He makes his point by stating that only about 800 of the 40,000 engineering graduates in a recent year were black.

Labor experts say that businesses are not hiring enough women and minorities for three reasons: (1) Some professions, such as engineering, traditionally attract only a few women and minorities, (2) some businesses do nothing more than skim off the top women and minority professionals, and (3) other businesses simply do not look hard enough.

Questions

1. Whose arguments do you tend to agree with?
   ___ A. Women and minorities
   ___ B. Business executives
2. Why?

Case 3.2: What Can Our Company Do?

A citizens' group in a medium-sized industrial city planned a discussion between city officials and industry representatives. The topic of the discussion concerned industry's responsibilities to the city. The city was having trouble with unemployment, discrimination in employment, traffic congestion, air pollution, pollution in a nearby stream, a rising crime rate, and a deteriorating tax base.

Mr. Appleby is a top official in one of the chemical companies that uses city resources. He is respected by both government and industry as a sincere, concerned citizen. Like many business leaders, he has devoted a considerable amount of time to civic projects. His company has been quite profitable over the years but has spent little money attempting to curb the pollutants it discharges into the river. At the preliminary presentation by representatives of the citizens' committee, Appleby appeared concerned about the problems faced by the city. Upon closer questioning, he seemed somewhat frustrated and curtly responded, "But what can our company do?"

Questions

1. Prepare a position paper for Mr. Appleby, outlining the reasons for and against his company's participation in city problems.
2. What specific actions should the city take to enlist the support of the industrial community?
3. What specific actions do you recommend that Mr. Appleby's company take?

After completing this chapter, you will be able to:

■ Define proprietorship and list the advantages
and disadvantages of this form of ownership.

■ Define partnership and list the advantages and
disadvantages of this form of ownership.

■ Understand partnership modifications that we
call joint ventures, limited partnerships, and
business trusts.

■ Define corporation and list its
major characteristics.

■ List the procedures for creating a corporation.

■ Understand the rights and responsibilities of
owners of corporations.

■ List the advantages and disadvantages of the
corporate form of ownership.

■ Describe the major forms of
business combinations.

FORMS OF
BUSINESS
OWNERSHIP

Businesses that produce Snickers® candy bars and Estee Lauder® cosmetics are both owned by families. When the board of directors of these firms meet, they might start with kissing and hugging among brothers, sisters, cousins, and other relatives. Economists predict that family owned businesses account for about 50% of the gross national product, and they constitute more than 12 million of the approximately 14 million businesses in the United States.

Stroh Brewery Company, also family owned, persuaded its twenty-seven family members to take a lower dividend so they could borrow funds to buy Joseph Schlitz Brewing Company. Peter Stroh says that family sacrifice is one of the major reasons they are successful. Leonard A. Lauder, president of Estee Lauder, says their family name is on every package. This produces a drive to succeed with a high-quality product.

Although most large companies are corporations, many started as sole proprietorships or partnerships. Some companies have a few owners, as in the case of the family-owned businesses mentioned; others have thousands of owners. As we shall see in this chapter, owners face several alternatives when deciding upon a form of ownership, and each form has advantages and disadvantages.

SOLE PROPRIETORSHIPS

A **sole proprietorship** is a form of business that is owned by only one person. Its simplicity makes it by far the most common form of business. Proprietorships in the United States total about 10.9 million companies, or about 78% of our 14 million businesses. However, proprietorships do only about 10% of the total business sales. Most are quite small; their average profits are not much more than $25,000.

Over half of the proprietorships are farms, and many others are part-time, operating out of the owner's spare room, basement, or panel truck. They are also popular in service businesses, such as laundromats, beauty parlors, newsstands, drugstores, liquor stores, repair shops, nightclubs, restaurants, and plumbing services.

Advantages of Proprietorships

Most advantages of single-owned companies stem from their simplicity and relative freedom.

Ease of starting and stopping. In many cases, an individual can form a proprietorship without permission from the city, state, or federal governments, although in some cases, a license is required. Doctors and lawyers usually need state

Convenience shops offering quick-turnover items are a common type of business owned — and often operated — by a single proprietor.

approval to practice. Other businesses, such as restaurants, liquor stores, and bars, may require a special license. But the dream of owning a business is still quite accessible, even today. The new owner can just put up a shingle, rent a building, have stationery printed, and open for business. The company is just as easy to dismantle. The owner merely settles outstanding accounts and agreements and closes the door.

Wide range of freedom. There is no body of law directed at proprietorships: no special tax laws, no unique liability laws, and no ownership agreements. The individual's business activities are not distinguished from personal activities; thus, for all practical purposes, the owner enjoys all rights as an individual citizen in running the business. A versatile owner can expand, apply for a loan, offer new services, alter prices, sell on credit, or engage in a variety of other business activities simply by deciding to do it.

Greater motivation. Single-owned companies appeal to the old-time values of independence and hard work. All the rewards of success and the frustrations of failure rest squarely on the shoulders of the owner. More than in any other form of ownership, the owners can see the results of their work. This motivates many owners to work long hours and endure extreme hardships in order to accomplish the goal of personal success and independence.

Almost unlimited secrecy. Proprietorships do not have to make public reports, and they have no boards or committees with which they have to share information. The owner can make all the decisions and does not have to tell anyone. The only time this prime secrecy might be threatened is during a tax audit. Otherwise, the proprietor can be as secret as he or she wants. This privacy makes it very difficult for competitors to uncover the strategies of a proprietor.

Tax advantages. There are no special taxes on a proprietorship; the owner simply pays personal income tax on profits. However, the tax advantage may not be as great as it was once thought to be. For one thing, small corporations may, in most states, choose to be taxed as a proprietorship. Thus, the proprietorship may have no tax advantage. Second, many owners of smaller corporations take the income out in personal salaries. Although the owners must pay personal income tax on their salaries, it is a nontaxable expense to the company.

Disadvantages of Proprietorships

Like the advantages, most disadvantages of a proprietorship stem from its simplicity.

Unlimited liability. Unlimited liability means that the owner's personal wealth may be used to pay off debts and obligations of the business when the business is unable to do so. Without doubt, this is the most stunning disadvantage. Thousands of small businesses fail each year, and the owners lose many of their personal assets and some of their pride in the process.

Size and capital limitations. Usually, it is hard for an individual owner to acquire the capital necessary for rapid growth. Even if the owner is wealthy, it would be hard to raise the several million dollars needed to develop a new product, expand a new plant, or hire salespeople nationwide. As a small business owner commented, "It is hard for me to spend $40,000 or $50,000 on some risky new idea. The slightest credit squeeze or drop in sales may create a new crisis for the business."

Limited management and employee skills. Since the business usually operates on limited capital, the owner provides most if not all of the management skill. Often, one manager, the owner, makes all decisions on marketing, pricing, financing, taxes, hiring, buying, advertising, and the like. It is hard for one person to have expertise in all these areas, yet the proprietorship must compete with corporations that may have specialists or even departments making these decisions. In a proprietorship, there is little or no opportunity for advancement, pay is usually low, and the fringe benefit package meager. For these reasons, employees are quite often relatives, friends, or individuals with limited skills.

Noncontinuous life. A business that is entirely dependent on the energies and resources of one owner is highly unstable. Sickness or a serious accident to the owner might prove fatal to the business; death of the owner is a legal end to the business. Further, proprietorships are difficult to sell because survival is so dependent upon the owner's reputation. The company may be passed on to a relative upon the owner's death, but when this occurs, a new business is formed. Finally, limited resources render most small proprietorships vulnerable to swings in the economy. About one in five new proprietorships goes out of business during the first year of operation, and only one in ten survives five years or more.

PARTNERSHIPS

A partnership, sometimes referred to as a **general partnership,** is a business with two or more owners and is slightly more complex than a proprietorship. A few partnerships number more than one hundred owners, but more than 80% have only two. A partnership does not necessarily require a written contract, but it is most advisable. Most states require a written contract when real property is transferred to the name of the partnership or when the agreement lasts longer than a year. The **partnership agreement,** sometimes called *articles of co-partnership,* varies from state to state, but usually includes: (1) the name of the company and identity of the owners, (2) arrangements for contributing finances, skills, and management to the company, (3) means for dividing income, (4) method for one or more partners to withdraw, and (5) steps for dissolving the agreement.

We can classify partners according to whether or not they are active in management and known to the public. A **silent partner** takes no active part in management but is known to the public. Usually this occurs when a company takes a well-known personality as a partner for the use of a famous name. In reverse, a **secret partner** actively participates in management but is unknown to the public. A combination of a silent and secret partner is a **dormant** or **sleeping partner.** This owner is not active in management and is not known to the public; he or she merely invests in the business. Last, a **nominal partner** allows, or even encourages, the public to think that he or she is a partner, but is not an owner at all. This rarely occurs because the courts have maintained that this pretender can be held liable in the same sense as a general partner.

Historically, partnerships date back to Roman law, as early as the eleventh century. They are

> **Partnerships are not only few in number, but their total number decreases each year. One million partnerships exist in the United States, and they account for only 4% of total sales.**

almost as old as proprietorships, but they are less common. Their greatest area of concentration is in wholesale and retail trade and professional services such as accounting, medicine, law, and insurance. Partnerships are not only few in number, but their total number decreases each year. One million partnerships exist in the United States, and they account for only 4% of total sales. An analysis of the advantages and disadvantages of partnerships indicates why they have such a small impact on our total business system.

Advantages of Partnerships

The partnership is an extension of a proprietorship, and its advantages overcome some of the major shortcomings of individually owned companies.

More specialized management. A logical reason for two or more persons to own a business is to combine skills and judgment. Two or three people can bring different but complementary skills to an association. One partner might be a specialist in manufacturing, another in marketing, and a third partner might be an accountant. Medical doctors and lawyers often form a partnership so that they can pool their resources and hire specialists to manage the internal affairs of their respective practices. Another seemingly ideal strategy is when one partner is a creative risk taker and the other is a logical, conservative decision maker. Their combined judgment often leads to better decisions than would have been made individually.

Greater source of capital. Partners have the advantage of combined capital resources. The partnership can draw upon the savings of all partners, and their combined personal wealth makes borrowing easier. Many partnerships form

Architectural firms are often partnerships, combining the specialized skills of several professionals to attract and serve clients.

when an individual with an idea or skill lacks the capital to produce and distribute the product or service. This individual may find a financial backer who becomes a partner and supplies the needed capital for a piece of the action (percentage of the profits).

Incentives for key employees. If a partnership wishes to keep a particular employee who contributes a valuable skill, it can make that employee a partner. Many accounting and law firms operate on this principle. When employees realize that it is possible to become part-owner of the company, they have incentive to stay with the company and perform much better on the job.

Legal certainty. Partnerships, though less complicated than corporations, have more legal certainty than proprietorships. The **Uniform Partnership Act** of 1914 established specific guidelines for the function of partnerships. Since then, with more legislation that clearly defines the operation of partnerships, legal arrangements can

be very specific. Specific written agreements at the time of partnership can avoid future problems. A lawyer who deals in partnerships can provide legal advice on most questions quickly at minimal cost.

Wide range of freedom. Like the proprietorship, the partnership is relatively free from government control. Since the partnership is not an entity separate from its owners, it is subject to few reports and taxes. Also, it can conduct business in other states as freely as can an individual.

Disadvantages of Partnerships

The partnership overcomes many disadvantages of proprietorship, but not all.

Unlimited liability. Like the proprietorship, each partner is liable for the obligations of the business. Should the business fail, each partner's personal wealth may be legally taken to fulfill the obligations of the venture. Also, each partner is an agent for the partnership. If one of the partners makes a decision that costs the company a loss, all of the partners are responsible. Such responsibility for the actions of other partners is enough to make a person think twice before entering into a partnership agreement.

Short length of life. There are many situations that can dissolve a partnership. Death, withdrawal, bankruptcy, or insanity of a partner will end the venture. Also, the transfer of one partner's share to someone else or failure of a partner to fulfill contractual agreements can cancel the partnership. Of all the forms of business, partnerships average the shortest life span. When the partnership is terminated, the benefits of long-range planning are often lost.

Owner conflicts. Partners Simon and Blanchard own Kelso Chemical Company. Although the two founders have been in business for ten years, they have not talked with each other for the past three. Blanchard gets to the office before 9:00 A.M.; Simon comes in later to avoid meeting Blanchard. They communicate to each other via memos, which they pass back and forth between their secretaries. The partners have yelled at each other, thrown water on each other, and even got into an old-fashioned fist fight about their differences. Eventually, the business suffered, and a court-appointed receiver now runs the business. Simon and Blanchard are both in their seventies.

Partnership squabbles have become so common—the American Arbitration Association reports a 78% increase in the past two years—that attorneys have developed a new service industry to help partners with their disagreements. Partners must cooperate to run a business effectively. Often, disagreements over decisions, rewards, and business practices create tension between partners. These conflicts can threaten not only the profits but even the existence of the business. Partners may fight over who has the right to enter into a contract, negotiate a loan, hire or fire an employee, or invest in a new product or service. The partnership agreement may have methods for reconciling differences, but it does not prevent them. Unfortunately, partners sometimes dissolve their successful business because of these conflicts.

Difficulties in withdrawing. Unlike a proprietorship, a partnership is not easy to dismantle. As a result, partners may lose control over their investment. For example, a partner may want to sell out, but the other partners may vote against it. If partners want out, they must either find other investors or sell their shares to the remaining partners. Often, this is difficult. Finally, even if the partnership is agreeable to the withdrawal of a partner, it is not legally possible if the partnership is in the middle of a contractual obligation. When a partner insists on withdrawing, the result may be a forced sale at a price less than the value of the business.

Modifications in Partnership Agreements

As partnerships evolved, owners made several adjustments to overcome their limitations. Most changes try to reduce personal liabilities.

Joint venture. In a **joint venture,** a group of people set up a temporary partnership for the purpose of carrying out a single business project. The joint venture lasts for a specified period of time; during the life of the venture, each partner has the same legal obligations as a general partner.

Typically, however, only one person takes responsibility for the management decisions of the project. Historically, joint ventures have been used primarily in real estate developments. For instance, a group may agree to invest money in a project to build and sell six condominiums. If they formed a joint venture, their partnership would last for the time that it took to build and sell the condominiums.

Today, however, joint ventures are becoming increasingly common, especially among high-tech firms. One way that biotechnology firms (those engaging in the new field of genetic engineering) can remain independent and still gain access to marketing and manufacturing expertise that they lack is by forming joint ventures with large drug or chemical companies. Zsolt Harsanyi, an E. F. Hutton vice-president, predicts that at least a dozen joint ventures will be formed this year. Genentech, for example, has set up several joint ventures, the most recent with Baxter Travenol Laboratories, Inc., to develop diagnostic tests.

Limited partnership. In 1822, New York State set the precedent for limited partnerships by passing an act allowing partnerships to limit the liability of one or more of its partners. Many other states soon followed. Sales of limited partnerships were expected to reach a record $18 billion in 1984, up from $14 billion in 1983 and $8 billion in 1982. **Limited partners** have the right to inspect the company's books, receive information from the business, and participate in earnings. If they take an active part in the control of the business, they become liable as general partners. Every partnership must have at least one **general partner** that has unlimited liability and is usually active in management. A business can attract investment dollars by adding limited partners who can invest capital without assuming risks beyond their investment. The law assumes partners to be general partners unless otherwise stated. Oil com-

Major corporations are joining together in limited partnership agreements to cooperate on common research problems and raise money.

panies such as Dyco Petroleum, Sampson Properties, and Saxon Oil have been particularly successful in raising money for investment through limited partnerships. In real estate, another hotbed area for limited partnerships, JMB Realty, Balcor/American Express, and Consolidated Capital have been successful.

Major corporations are also joining together in limited partnership agreements to cooperate on common research problems and raise money. In late 1983, the following firms were talking about limited partnership agreements: National Steel Corp. and Battelle Memorial Institute were looking at a research and development project as a way to finance research on production of steel strips; Semiconductor Research Corp. (SRC) was considering a limited partnership to raise money to develop a 4-million-bit, random-access computer memory; and Boeing, Lockheed, and McDonnell Douglas were looking at the possibility of collaborating in a 10-year program to design and develop the next generation jetliner.

Business trust. The **business trust** is able to limit the liability of its owners by excluding them from control. Typically, a few partners solicit funds from a large number of investors who receive shares in the trust. But the trustee makes all the management decisions, including the distribution of profits. Investors do not even elect the managing group. Investors merely furnish the capital and allow the trustees to speculate with it. A business trust is very similar to a corporation, and it is still rather widely used.

Through these examples of modifications in partnership agreements, we can see the modern corporation emerging. Today's corporations have proven so successful that they have overshadowed proprietorships and replaced nearly all partnerships.

CORPORATIONS

Leonard and Clara Murray have operated a pancake house as partners for 15 years. Recently they decided to incorporate for several reasons: they wanted to get worker's compensation, to be able to deduct the cost of their medical insurance, and to give their son and daughter part ownership of the business. Incorporating made all this possible.

The **corporation** is an actual being in the eyes of the law. It is an intangible person with many of the legal rights, powers, and obligations of an individual. The corporation may make contracts and buy, hold, and sell property; it can sue and be sued in its own name. Chief Justice John Marshall's legal definition of a corporation has become famous. In the case of *Dartmouth College* v. *Woodward* in 1803, Marshall breathed life into the corporate body with a definition that read in part:

> A corporation is an artificial being, invisible, intangible, and existing only in contemplation of law. Being the mere creature of law, it possesses only those properties which the charter of its creation confers upon it, either expressly or an incidental to its very existence. . . . Among the most important are immortality, and, if the expression may be allowed, individuality; properties, by which a perpetual succession of many persons are considered as the same, and may act as a single individual.

Although relatively few in number, corporations dominate today's business world. The two million corporations in the United States account for more than 85% of the total sales of all businesses. Table 4.1 lists the twenty largest corporations, ranked according to sales, in the United States in 1982.

Characteristics of Corporations

Because of their unique legal identity, we create, own, and manage corporations differently from other companies. Since the states define and regulate corporations, the laws may differ slightly from one state to another. Some corporations are owned by individuals; we call these **private corporations.** Most large businesses that you think of — General Motors, the Boeing Company, Sears — are examples. By contrast, **public corporations** are owned by the government, such as the Tennessee Valley Authority (TVA), liquor stores in a few states, park boards, and city governments.

There are several types of private corporations. Some are profit corporations, those organized to make a profit for the owners. Most companies are profit corporations. But some are nonprofit corporations; they may receive and spend money, but their goal is not to make a profit. Nonprofit organizations include charities, churches, public television stations, hospitals, and private schools. An **open corporation** makes its stock available to the public and therefore usually has many owners. Usually a family or only a few people own a **close corporation.** These may also be called privately held companies since they do not offer their stock for public sale, and it is not traded on the stock markets. A company may choose to remain closed for several reasons, including:

■ They do not have to produce a lot of financial reports to the public.

■ They can make decisions with less red tape.

TABLE 4.1 ■ THE TWENTY-FIVE LARGEST U.S. INDUSTRIAL CORPORATIONS IN 1983

Rank 1983	Rank 1982	Company	Sales $ Thousands	Assets $ Thousands	Rank	Net Income $ Thousands	Rank	Stockholders' Equity $ Thousands	Rank
1	1	Exxon (New York)	88,561,134	62,962,990	1	4,977,957	2	29,443,095	1
2	2	General Motors (Detroit)	74,581,600	45,694,500	2	3,730,200	3	20,766,600	3
3	3	Mobil (New York)	54,607,000	35,072,000	4	1,503,000	11	13,952,000	6
4	5	Ford Motor (Dearborn, Mich.)	44,454,600	23,868,900	9	1,866,900	6	7,545,300	14
5	6	International Business Machines (Armonk, N.Y.)	40,180,000	37,243,000	3	5,485,000	1	23,219,000	2
6	4	Texaco (Harrison, N.Y.)	40,068,000	27,199,000	5	1,233,000	12	14,726,000	4
7	8	E. I. du Pont de Nemours (Wilmington, Del.)	35,378,000	24,432,000	7	1,127,000	13	11,472,000	8
8	10	Standard Oil (Indiana) (Chicago)	27,635,000	25,805,000	6	1,868,000	5	12,440,000	7
9	7	Standard Oil of California (San Francisco)	27,342,000	24,010,000	8	1,590,000	8	14,106,000	5
10	11	General Electric (Fairfield, Conn.)	26,797,000	23,288,000	10	2,024,000	4	11,270,000	10
11	9	Gulf Oil (Pittsburgh)	26,581,000	20,964,000	13	978,000	14	10,128,000	12
12	12	Atlantic Richfield (Los Angeles)	25,147,036	23,282,307	11	1,547,875	9	10,888,138	11
13	13	Shell Oil (Houston)	19,678,000	22,169,000	12	1,633,000	7	11,359,000	9
14	15	Occidental Petroleum (Los Angeles)	19,115,700	11,775,400	21	566,700	25	2,640,900	50
15	14	U.S. Steel (Pittsburgh)	16,869,000	19,314,000	14	(1,161,000)	489	5,355,000	20
16	17	Phillips Petroleum (Bartlesville, Okla.)	15,249,000	13,094,000	18	721,000	18	6,149,000	16
17	18	Sun (Radnor, Pa.)	14,730,000	12,466,000	19	453,000	34	5,236,000	21
18	20	United Technologies (Hartford)	14,669,265	8,720,059	32	509,173	28	3,783,755	31
19	19	Tenneco (Houston)	14,353,000	17,994,000	15	716,000	19	5,822,000	18
20	16	ITT (New York)	14,155,408	13,966,744	17	674,510	21	6,106,084	17
21	29	Chrysler (Highland Park, Mich.)	13,240,399	6,772,300	38	700,900	20	1,143,058	126
22	23	Procter & Gamble (Cincinnati)	12,452,000	8,135,000	34	866,000	17	4,601,000	27
23	25	R. J. Reynolds Industries (Winston-Salem, N.C.)	11,957,000	9,874,000	26	881,000	16	5,223,000	22
24	24	Getty Oil (Los Angeles)	11,600,024	10,385,050	23	494,314	29	5,402,707	19
25	21	Standard Oil (Ohio) (Cleveland)	11,599,000	16,362,000	16	1,512,000	10	8,094,000	13

The Most Admired Corporations

Fortune polled over 7000 corporate executives, outside directors, and financial analysts; half responded. Those surveyed were asked to rate only the ten largest companies in their own industry, using a scale of 0 (poor) to 10 (excellent), on eight key attributes of reputation: quality of management; quality of products or services; innovativeness; long-term investment value; financial soundness; ability to attract, develop, and keep talented people; community and environmental responsibility; and use of corporate assets.

RATINGS ON EIGHT KEY ATTRIBUTES OF REPUTATION

Most Admired	Score	Most Admired	Score
Quality of management		*Financial soundness*	
IBM	9.16	IBM	9.45
Hewlett-Packard	8.75	General Electric	8.88
Dow Jones	8.70	Dow Jones	8.80
		Ability to attract, develop, and keep talented people	
Quality of products or services			
Dow Jones	9.06	Hewlett-Packard	8.42
Boeing	9.02	IBM	8.39
Anheuser-Busch	8.64	Merck	8.29
Innovativeness		*Community and environmental responsibility*	
Citicorp	8.69	Johnson & Johnson	8.44
Merrill Lynch	8.35	Eastman Kodak	8.26
Time Inc.	8.26	IBM	7.95
Long-term investment value		*Use of corporate assets*	
IBM	8.88	IBM	8.47
Dow Jones	8.39	Dow Jones	8.26
Hewlett-Packard	8.08	Hewlett-Packard	8.01

OVERALL RATINGS

Rank	Company	Industry Group	Score
1	IBM	Office equipment, computers	8.53
2	Dow Jones	Publishing, printing	8.35
3	Hewlett-Packard	Office equipment, computers	8.24
4	Merck	Pharmaceuticals	8.17
5	Johnson & Johnson	Pharmaceuticals	8.15
6	Time Inc.	Publishing, printing	7.99
7	General Electric	Electronics, appliances	7.96
8	Anheuser-Busch	Beverages	7.91
9	Coca-Cola	Beverages	7.87
10	Boeing	Aerospace	7.79

TABLE 4.2 ■ EXAMPLES OF SOME LARGE, CLOSE CORPORATIONS

Company	Business
Koch Industries	Crude oil marketing
Hughes Aircraft	Aerospace products
United Parcel Service	Parcel delivery
Reader's Digest	Publishing
Gates Rubber	Rubber, aviation
S. C. Johnson and Sons	Household products
Hallmark cards	Cards, novelties

■ They do not have to hold public stockholder meetings.

Some very large companies remain privately held. Table 4.2 lists several of the largest. We also classify corporations according to where they were organized. A business is a **domestic corporation** in the state in which it is incorporated. To do business in other states, it must register as a **foreign corporation. Alien corporations** have been organized in other countries, but they have received permission to do business in the United States. Figure 4.1 illustrates the various types of corporations.

How to Create a Corporation

The first step in the birth of a corporation is the promotion of the proposed company. Somebody, usually the owner, sees an advantage in creating a new corporation or incorporating a proprietorship or partnership. The promoter must then convince others that they stand to benefit by investing in the venture (by the purchase of stock). The pro-

moter usually prepares a prospectus outlining the potential of the proposed concern, and he or she may enter into certain preincorporation contracts. Professional promoters usually handle the task of selling the new corporation, especially for the larger ventures.

The second step is the filing of the **articles of incorporation** with the appropriate state office, usually the secretary of state. Promoters and lawyers often help in this step. The content of the articles will vary according to state laws, but they generally include:

■ Name and purpose of the corporation.

■ Address of the main office.

■ Number of shares of stock of all classes, and restrictions on transferability of shares, if any.

■ Number of directors and perhaps their names.

■ Names and addresses of the incorporators.

■ Amount of paid-in-stock with which the business will begin.

Once the articles are consistent with the law, the state will grant a charter that gives the company permission to operate as a corporation.

Ownership of Corporations

An owner of a corporation is called a **stockholder.** A **stock certificate** is evidence of ownership (see the example in Figure 4.2). Stockholders are of two major types: common and preferred. **Common stockholders** are owners who have a right to vote on the corporation's board of directors. **Preferred stockholders** are also owners, but they usually do not have voting

Figure 4.1
Kinds of corporations.

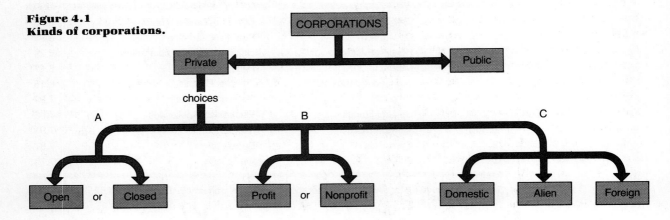

Figure 4.2
A sample stock certificate. *Courtesy of the Coca-Cola Company.*

rights. They do, however, usually have first claim on profits — the reason they are called preferred. The main rights of common stockholders are to:

- Elect the board of directors.
- Receive a share of the profits in the form of dividends.
- Sell and purchase stock on the open market.

Once a year, common stockholders vote on members of the **board of directors,** a group charged with the responsibility of managing the company. Since the owners are usually scattered throughout the country, it would be difficult to get them all together for voting. So owners may sign a **proxy,** a document transferring their voting rights to someone else, and mail it in. Figure 4.3 is an example of a proxy. The board of directors, at the company's expense, mails proxy forms to all owners and asks them to sign and return the forms. By so doing, the owner transfers his or her right to vote to someone else. In large corporations with many stockholders, the owners seldom keep tabs on the board's decisions. So, unless the company has grave problems, the board members usually vote themselves in. Owners often have the right to vote on amendments to the charter, pension and bonus plans for the officers, acceptance of a merger, and other major issues.

The owners receive profits in the form of dividends. **Dividends** are payments to the stock-holders over a given period of time, at a given amount per share. Directors usually decide quarterly how much, if any, of the profits they wish to distribute to the owners. The profits are either distributed to the owners in dividends or they are reinvested back into the company in the form of **retained earnings.** If the company decides to keep the profits, the company may become more valuable and the price of the stock usually goes up. Some investors prefer profit in the way of dividends while others speculate for an increase in the price of stock.

How Corporations Are Managed

In smaller corporations, the major owners may also be the managers. But in larger corporations, the thousands of owners could not possibly manage the daily activities. So the elected board of directors is responsible for running the business. Members of the board are not only principal officers and employees of the company but also some specialists with legal and financial expertise from outside the company. Although stockholders have the right to draw up the bylaws, they usually delegate this task to the board of directors.

The bylaws cover such activities as:

- Time and place of meetings.
- Method of calling meetings.
- Pay for the directors.

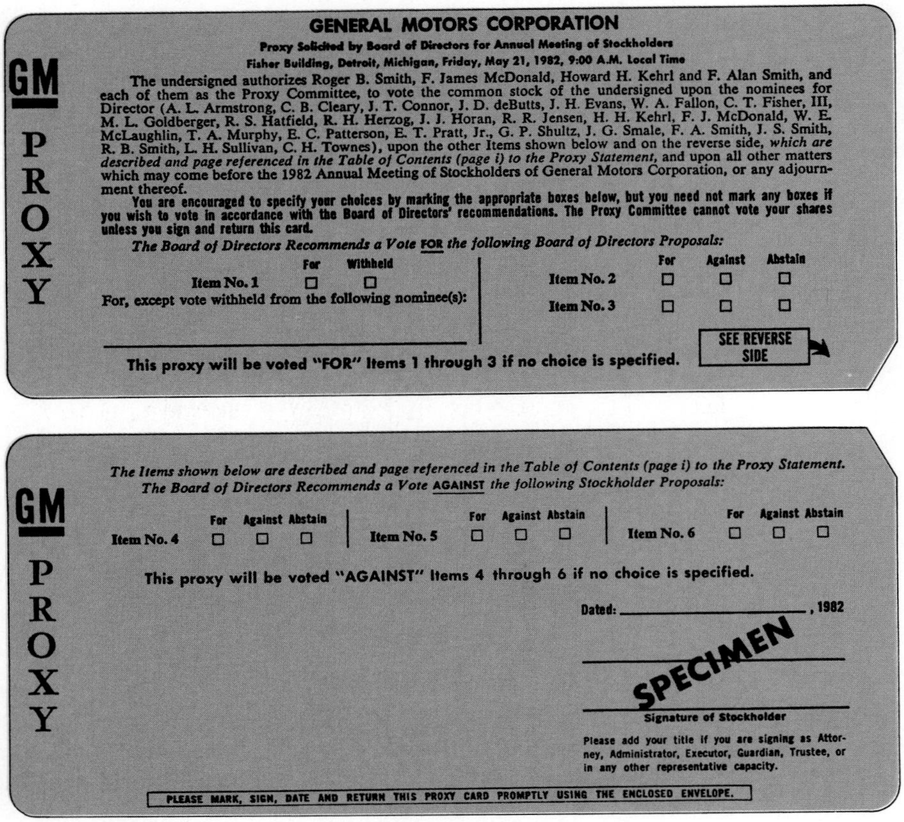

GM PROXY

GENERAL MOTORS CORPORATION

Proxy Solicited by Board of Directors for Annual Meeting of Stockholders
Fisher Building, Detroit, Michigan, Friday, May 21, 1982, 9:00 A.M. Local Time

The undersigned authorizes Roger B. Smith, F. James McDonald, Howard H. Kehrl and F. Alan Smith, and each of them as the Proxy Committee, to vote the common stock of the undersigned upon the nominees for Director (A. L. Armstrong, C. B. Cleary, J. T. Connor, J. D. deButts, J. H. Evans, W. A. Fallon, C. T. Fisher, III, M. L. Goldberger, R. S. Hatfield, R. H. Herzog, J. J. Horan, R. R. Jensen, H. H. Kehrl, F. J. McDonald, W. E. McLaughlin, T. A. Murphy, E. C. Patterson, E. T. Pratt, Jr., G. P. Shultz, J. G. Smale, F. A. Smith, J. S. Smith, R. B. Smith, L. H. Sullivan, C. H. Townes), upon the other Items shown below and on the reverse side, *which are described and page referenced in the Table of Contents (page i) to the Proxy Statement,* and upon all other matters which may come before the 1982 Annual Meeting of Stockholders of General Motors Corporation, or any adjournment thereof.

You are encouraged to specify your choices by marking the appropriate boxes below, but you need not mark any boxes if you wish to vote in accordance with the Board of Directors' recommendations. The Proxy Committee cannot vote your shares unless you sign and return this card.

The Board of Directors Recommends a Vote FOR *the following Board of Directors Proposals:*

	For	Withheld
Item No. 1	☐	☐

For, except vote withheld from the following nominee(s):

____

	For	Against	Abstain
Item No. 2	☐	☐	☐
Item No. 3	☐	☐	☐

This proxy will be voted "FOR" Items 1 through 3 if no choice is specified.

SEE REVERSE SIDE

GM PROXY

The Items shown below are described and page referenced in the Table of Contents (page i) to the Proxy Statement.
The Board of Directors Recommends a Vote AGAINST *the following Stockholder Proposals:*

	For	Against	Abstain
Item No. 4	☐	☐	☐
Item No. 5	☐	☐	☐
Item No. 6	☐	☐	☐

This proxy will be voted "AGAINST" Items 4 through 6 if no choice is specified.

Dated: ______________________, 1982

SPECIMEN

____
Signature of Stockholder

Please add your title if you are signing as Attorney, Administrator, Executor, Guardian, Trustee, or in any other representative capacity.

PLEASE MARK, SIGN, DATE AND RETURN THIS PROXY CARD PROMPTLY USING THE ENCLOSED ENVELOPE.

Figure 4.3 A proxy statement for General Motors stockholders. *Reprinted by permission.*

BUSINESS BULLETIN

Will There Be More Women on Boards of Directors?

In 1976, there were only 147 women directors in the United States, a remarkably small number. By 1979, the number had more than doubled to 300. In 1979, there were more than 16,000 men on these same boards. While there is no legal penalty for not having women on boards, there are pressures to recruit more women for these positions.

Still, the facts show that most board members, of both sexes, are more than 50 years of age. They grew up in a period where women stayed at home or worked as volunteers to improve the community. For most male directors, this value imprinting has remained strong, and they do not automatically accept women in the boardroom. A major problem is finding women that can make the transition to board membership. To facilitate this, an organization called Catalyst began in 1977. Its purpose is to bring potential women board members and organizations together through the use of files, information, and other data on qualifications and positions.

Source: Felice N. Schwartz, "'Invisible' Resource: Women for Boards," *Harvard Business Review,* March–April, 1980, pp. 6–8, ff.

TABLE 4.3 ■ REVIEW OF THE FEATURES WITHIN THE FORMS OF OWNERSHIP

Features	Sole Proprietorship	Partnership	Corporation
Creation	Easy; no legal requirement	Relatively easy; incorporated by law	Difficult; incorporated by law
Ownership	Single owner	Few or many owners	Few or many owners
Liability	Unlimited	Unlimited	Limited
Freedom	Wide range	Wide range	More limited
Motivation	Strong for owner, weaker for employees	Fairly strong for owners and key employees	Weak for lower level employees, strong for management
Tax	No special income tax	No special income tax	Heavily taxed, and income is double taxed
Size	Limited	Limited	Unlimited
Stability	Unstable	Unstable	Stable
Capital	Hard to attract	Relatively hard to attract	Easier to attract
Ownership transfer	Relatively easy	Difficult	Easy
Government regulations	Fewer by comparison	Fewer by comparison	Many by comparison

- Identification of management positions.
- Duties of the major officers.
- Ways of filling vacancies.
- Regulations for issuing stock.
- Methods of altering the bylaws.

The appointment of the principal officers is another responsibility of the board. The charter defines principal officers; they typically include the president, secretary, treasurer, and several vice-presidents. Normally, the board will elect the president, who then chooses the other officers.

A final responsibility of the board is to serve as a watchdog for the owners. Board members should evaluate the performance of the company's officers, and they usually have authority to accept or reject major decisions of the officers. In this role, they often give "rubber-stamp" approval to the plans of the chief officer, resulting in little protection for the owners.

Board members are liable for illegal decisions and fraud. But they are not liable for decisions of poor judgment unless the court decides the actions were blatantly irresponsible. Recently, courts have toughened their stand and, in a few cases, board members have been held personally liable for their "bad judgment." Table 4.3 reviews the features of different ownership forms, and Figure 4.4 summarizes how corporations are managed.

Advantages of Corporations

We have personalized corporations by creating legal advantages that deal with the legal being concept. The major advantages are as follows.

Limited liability. Unlike partners and proprietors, owners in a corporation have **limited liability.** They stand to lose only what they have invested. Suppose you invest $20,000 in the stock of a company and that company goes bankrupt and is left owing a half million dollars. You can lose — because of limited liability — only your investment, even if you have enough wealth to pay the debt. Since the corporation is a legal being, it sues and is sued in its own name.

Ease of transferring ownership. You can withdraw your investment in a corporation simply by selling your stock to someone else. Major stock exchanges list the latest selling price for thousands of stocks by the minute, and they pro-

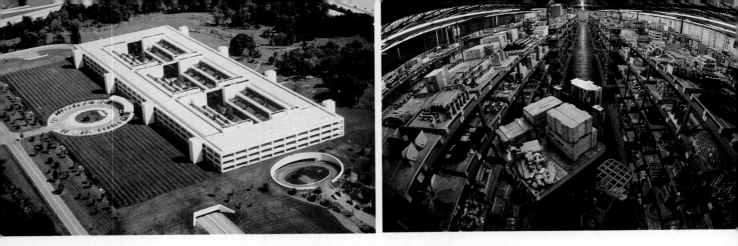

The relative ease with which corporations attract large amounts of capital is one of the advantages of this form of business ownership.

vide a ready market for buyers and sellers. Many corporations are not listed on the exchanges. And those owners may have more difficulty finding buyers and sellers. But the withdrawal is still easy compared to the other forms of ownership because the sale of an owner's stock does not dissolve the corporation. An owner can usually sell stock to anyone at any time, but the corporation must keep records of who owns its shares.

Continuous life. Unlike proprietorships and partnerships, a corporation can last indefinitely. While some charters specify the length of life of the company, most assume an indefinite life span.

The corporation overcomes the instability caused by change of ownership and also provides management separate from the owners. For these reasons, the corporation has a form of eternal life.

Ease of attracting capital. How can a business get more money for expansion? Proprietorships are limited by the owner's ability to borrow or supply capital. Partnerships have a small advantage; they are limited by their few owners' abilities to raise money or to draw from their personal assets. Corporations have a large advantage. They can raise money by selling shares of stock, and investors know that they cannot lose more than

**Figure 4.4
How corporations are managed.**

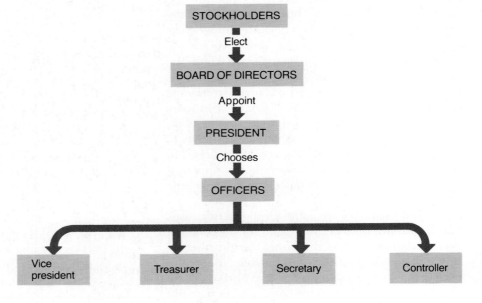

the price of the stock. Thus, it is easier for corporations to become large.

Large size. While all corporations are not large, most large businesses are corporations. Large size offers the advantage of economical production methods: Large companies can buy materials, manufacture products, and ship finished goods in bulk. But even more important is the ability to specialize. In a large company, managers can specialize in financing, production, marketing, legal assistance, and the like. Employees can specialize in their areas of interest and have more opportunity for advancement than in most small companies. This potential, combined with the ability to pay higher salaries and offer attractive fringe benefits, gives the corporation an advantage in hiring and keeping top-rate employees.

Disadvantages of Corporations

On the one hand, we have supported the corporate form of ownership by legally promoting size and continuous life. At the same time, we are concerned about its control over our lives. Some of the disadvantages of corporation ownership stem from fears associated with its enormous size and vast power.

Government regulations. The government created the corporation as an artificial being and feeds its offspring with dozens of rules and regulations. State governments begin by reserving the authority to approve each charter before a corporation can exist. The federal government gets into the act with regulations on retirement plans, procedures for hiring and paying employees, safety programs, control of mergers, pricing arrangements, and taxes. Many of these regulations apply to all organizations, but enforcement is focused on the larger corporations. In order to comply with all the regulations, corporations spend a good deal interpreting laws, maintaining records, and reporting to government agencies.

Higher taxes. Owners pay taxes twice on corporate profits. The corporation pays corporate taxes, and then the owners pay personal income tax on dividends (distributed profits). Corporate taxes vary, but in recent years they have fluctuated between 22 and 30% on the first $25,000 of income and hovered around 50% on profits above $50,000. In addition, corporations pay many fees and special taxes that do not apply to other organizations.

Corporations with fewer than ten shareholders that meet certain legal requirements may elect to be taxed as a **Subchapter S corporation,** meaning that the corporation is taxed like a partnership. If you owned a small business, for example, you might want to incorporate to limit your liabilities to the amount you have invested in the business. In all probability, you could qualify under Subchapter S of the Internal Revenue Code. This would allow you to take advantage of the corporate form of ownership, while avoiding the double taxation on your profits.

Lack of personal interest. Many employees lose their ability to identify with a giant company. They begin to feel like computer punch cards, cogs in the machine, and six-digit payroll numbers. Many employees do not even know the name of the company president and couldn't care less. This vast gap between managers, owners, and employees leads to many communication problems, indifference, and reduced employee motivation.

Lack of secrecy. Because corporations have to report so many of their activities and because many government agencies scrutinize their activities, corporations often lose the competitive advantage of secrecy. Corporations must make public reports on profits, total sales, and research expenditures. Competitors can learn much about each other by reading reports and studying the reports from hearings. A competitor can even buy a nominal ownership in the company and receive, by law, information intended especially for the owners. Of course, corporations realize how much of their information is public knowledge. It is common for them to disguise the information reported.

Rigid structure. A proprietor can have a brainstorm over a ham sandwich at lunch, make a decision, and act on it before the end of the day. But corporations have many departments, committees, and boards that must approve major projects before action can be taken.

Difficulty in creating. A corporation is more costly and difficult to create than other forms of ownership. Preparing the articles of incorporation, developing a prospectus for potential owners, complying with regulations on stock issues, and registering in other states is costly and time consuming. Filing fees, lawyer expenses, and promotion costs can be expensive.

Modifications of the Corporate Form of Ownership

Cooperatives and mutual companies are two modifications of the corporation that have become popular. Special needs have created both of these forms.

Cooperatives. A **cooperative (co-op)** is a business, owned and operated by the people it serves — mainly for their benefit. They are nonprofit. If, at the end of the year, they have received more money than they have spent, they might distribute these "savings" to their members. The savings are not taxed as business income to the co-op, and this, as you might expect, results in protest from competing corporations. Co-ops organize under state charters and elect a board of directors to manage the business. Each member has one vote.

Co-ops began in the United States with farmers who grouped together to sell their products and make purchases such as feed and seed. Today, co-ops operate retail outlets and provide services such as electricity, telephone service, housing, health care, and credit. Co-ops vary in size from thousands of members to a few families who pool their resources. **Buying co-ops** buy products such as fuel, feed, groceries, and electricity in volume at low cost for the benefit of the members. **Consumer co-ops** are retail outlets owned by the customers. Farmers may organize a gasoline consumer co-op (nonprofit) in order to make purchases at more reasonable costs. **Producer co-ops** market products for its members. Here, crafts people may form a co-op to retail their pottery, clothing, and jewelry. Being nonprofit, they can market the products more efficiently, leaving more profits for the members. A prime example comes from Detroit where a housing co-op for the elderly charges its tenants an average of $40 per month less than other apartments. A member of a California health co-op says, "We have reduced the cost of health care to our members by 50 to 60%."

Still, there have been some problems. Critics say that members are usually surprised by the amount of time and effort required to make the co-op successful. Members become dissatisfied and drop out, and the venture fails. Also, some co-ops, intent on serving more people effectively, invest their profits in new services. The result is loss of savings to members. In these cases, the goal of the co-op saving money for its members is not met.

Farm and electrical co-ops have been the most successful. **Credit unions,** another popular form of co-op, are groups of people who accumulate their savings and loan them to other members at interest. Here, owners buy shares in the credit union as an investment, and they receive interest that is usually higher than bank savings accounts. If you wish to borrow from the credit union, you can make a small investment by purchasing one share, and then get a loan at competitive rates. Most credit unions are quite successful; many are tied into companies as fringe benefits for employees.

Mutual companies. **Mutual companies** are similar to cooperatives in that the users are also the owners. Although mutual companies have a board of directors, they do not normally send out proxies, and most members do not vote. Mutual companies are popular as life insurance companies, savings banks, and savings and loan associations. When consumers purchase policies from a mutual company, they automatically become owners. When people deposit money in mutual savings banks or savings and loan companies, they automatically become owners. Currently, mutual life insurance companies control about two-thirds of the total assets of all life insurance companies; mutual savings banks hold about 12% of all the savings of individuals; and almost nine out of ten savings and loan associations are organized on a mutual basis.

While mutual companies have most of the advantages of corporations, they have a different tax status. Companies return "savings" to their members in the form of dividends. Mutual life insurance policyholders do not have to pay taxes on their dividends. But money returned to owner-members of savings banks and loan associations is regarded as interest and therefore is taxable to its members.

Business Combinations, Breakups, and Buyouts

Many businesses combine with othes to form larger businesses. They do this to take advantage of size, add expertise and extra money, spread operating expenses over a larger base, and fill out the product offerings. Mergers and holding companies are the two most popular combination forms.

Mergers. A **merger** is the joining of two or more companies to operate as one. Typically, a larger firm buys enough interest in a smaller one to con-

Should Mergers Be Encouraged or Discouraged?

Traditionally, we have worried when a business such as General Motors or IBM gets too large. We also get a little concerned when the number of firms in a particular industry shrink to four. (Four is no magic number; it just seems to have arisen as subjective benchmark.)

People who wish to discourage mergers argue that large business, or few businesses within an industry, can have unhealthy effects on competition. For instance, it is easier for a few larger firms to get together to fix prices than it is for many smaller firms to do so. Also, one large firm can enter into long-term contracts with suppliers or buyers with the result of driving out smaller competitors. A large producer might also agree to sell only to retailers who do not discount the prices of its product. And we do have examples of such illegal activities. In December 1983, there were seventeen prosecutions in process against thirty-seven construction companies for entering into big-rigging practices.

People who encourage more mergers and cooperative practices between companies say that we need increased size for several reasons. First, we have to compete in the world market, and other governments subsidize and assist large companies. The Japanese government, for example, gives its cement industry special loans and other financial aids to help them compete with the American market. Second, many research and development projects require millions of dollars of investments. This is just too much risk for even our largest firms. Third, companies in ailing industries such as steel need to be able to merge so they can preserve jobs. If a company goes bankrupt, it will disappear from competition. Why not let this firm merge with another rather than go under?

Currently, merger activity has increased. Many firms in basic industries such as steel, railroads, and banks and financial services are consolidating at record rates. Santa Fe and Southern Pacific railroads, two giants in the rail industry, backed off from a proposed merger in 1980 because they feared government disapproval. However, at this writing, they were planning a $6.3 billion merger, leaving just six major railroads in the United States.

Are you concerned about the increasing rate of mergers in the United States?

___ A. Very concerned   ___ C. Somewhat unconcerned

___ B. Somewhat concerned   ___ D. Very unconcerned

Do you think that our Justice Department should encourage or discourage mergers, joint research and development projects, and other consolidated efforts by large businesses in the United States?

___ A. Encourage strongly   ___ C. Discourage

___ B. Encourage   ___ D. Discourage strongly

Give three reasons for your position:

A. _____

B. _____

C. _____

trol it. Stockholders of both companies have to approve this, usually by a two-thirds vote. When two or more firms producing the same type of product or service combine, it is a **horizontal merger**. An example of a horizontal merger was the purchase of Gulf Oil by Standard Oil Co. of California (Socal) for $13.4 billion in 1984, the largest corporate takeover to date. This merger created the third largest oil company in the United States, exceeded in sales only by Exxon Corp. and Mobil Corp.

A **vertical merger** brings under one roof several different firms involved in different stages of the production and distribution process. A manufacturing company might buy a wholesale firm. Or a wholesale company might buy retail outlets. The firms are usually not competing, but the merger links up customer-supplier relationships into one company. If enough firms combine into a vertical merger, they can control the product or service from the point of production to the end user.

Conglomerates, a third type of merger, join two or more companies that offer unrelated products or services, as when Mobil Oil Company bought Montgomery Ward. Most of the world's largest companies grew through conglomerate mergers. In 1982, both Mobil Oil and U.S. Steel tried to buy Marathon Oil Company. Had Mobil bought Marathon, the merger would have been horizontal since both were oil companies. But because U.S. Steel ultimately bought Marathon for more than $5 billion, the merger formed a conglomerate. Had Goodyear Tire Company purchased Marathon, the merger would have been vertical. Figure 4.5 diagrams these three merger types.

Holding companies. Technically, **holding companies** are any firms that own stock in other companies. However, the term is more frequently used to describe companies that own enough voting stock in other companies to have control over them. In this way, one firm combines several different operations under a single policymaking structure. Some holding companies exist only for that purpose.

Traditionally, holding companies have been popular in the utility industry. Before its breakup, American Telephone & Telegraph (AT&T), owned all the stock in at least ten companies and part of

The merger of Marathon Oil with U.S. Steel elicited strong opinions all around. Here, Marathon employees rally in support of U.S. Steel's takeover bid.

the stock of many others. Holding companies may own stock in companies which also own stock in other firms. Figure 4.6 shows the makeup of the Ravelston Corporation, an example of a holding company.

Divestitures. During recent years, at the same time that many firms have been joining ranks through mergers, other large corporations have been selling off many of their holdings, a process called **divestiture**.

Perhaps the most newsworthy divestiture was the federal government's forced breakup of AT&T. In January 1984, AT&T released control of its twenty-two local operating companies, which were formed into seven regional companies. The seven holding companies will retain use of the Bell name, and they will receive about two-thirds of AT&T's $153 billion in switching equipment. This will allow, probably within a 3-year period, competitors such as MCI, Sprint, Longer Distance, Metrofone, and Skyline access to most customers. AT&T will retain Western Electric and Bell Laboratories, and it will be able to enter the data processing and computer markets through a new subsidiary, AT&T Information Systems.

Leveraged buyouts. Another form of breaking up larger companies comes through **leveraged buyout (LBO)**, where investors buy the shares of a company using a lot of debt relative to the equity they have invested. Typically, investors finance leveraged buyouts by big chunks of money that they borrow against the company's assets; then,

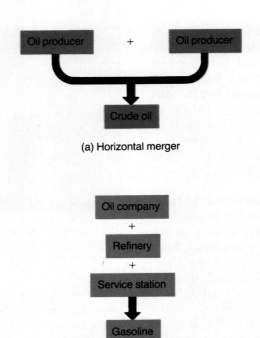

(a) Horizontal merger

(b) Vertical merger

Figure 4.5
Different types of mergers.

(c) Conglomerate

Figure 4.6
An example of a holding company.

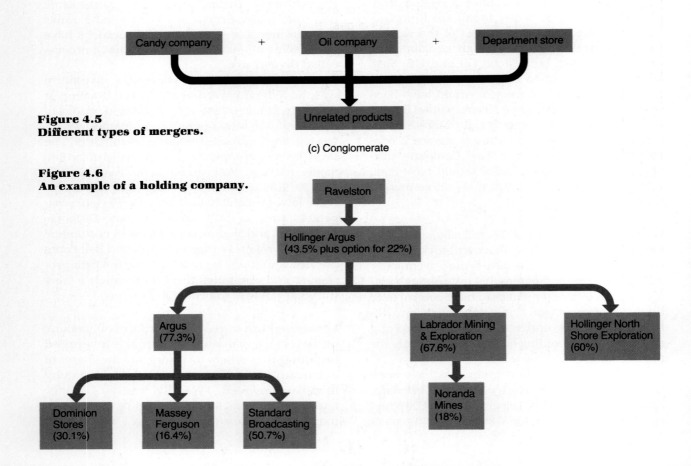

Corporate Sell-Offs

While corporate mergers attract a lot of attention, many companies are actually doing the reverse (that is, they are selling many of their holdings). This process, called divestiture, increased in the early 1980s, while the rate of mergers actually decreased.

There appeared to be several reasons for the wave of demergers, including:

- Some companies wanted to sell losing operations during the recession before the operations created too much drag.
- Cash-starved companies sold some of their holdings to get money to invest in better growth prospects.
- Other companies suffering under high-interest loans and declining sales needed cash.
- Unions accused some firms of spinning off subsidiaries so they could renegotiate less costly wage contracts.
- And many experts feel that diversification has just gone too far.

Companies are in so many unrelated ventures producing unrelated products that customers have a hard time identifying with what they stand for.

The accompanying charts show the number of divestitures and mergers from 1978 to 1982 and the ten largest spinoffs in 1982.

Number of divestitures and mergers and acquisitions

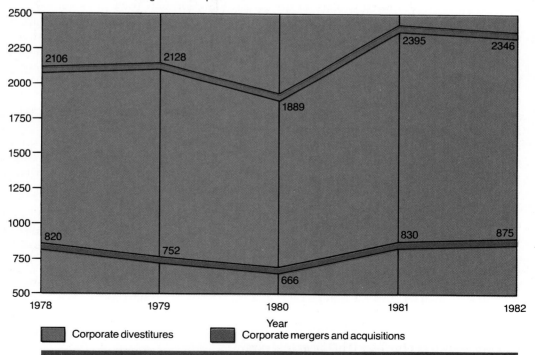

Corporate divestitures   Corporate mergers and acquisitions

Source: W. T. Grimm and Company, "The Merger Drive Goes Into Reverse," *U. S. News & World Report,* May 2, 1983, pp. 55–56.

they repay the loan out of the company's cash flow. Often, managers of a division of a larger company will use the LBO to buy the division themselves, thus establishing the division as a privately owned company. Some have called this technique "management buybacks" and "deconglomeration."

Partly because of the lower interest rates and liberalized tax rules of today, the trend toward LBOs is increasing. According to W. T. Grimm & Co., a merger brokerage firm, 6% of all divestitures in 1978 used LBOs, and by 1982, the figure had increased to 13%. In 1983, LBOs amounted to more than half of all corporate acquisitions.

SUMMARY

Three basic forms of business ownership have evolved: sole proprietorship, partnership, and corporation.

The proprietorship is ownership by only one person and has the advantages of: (1) being easy to start and to dissolve, (2) a wide range of freedom, (3) strong motivation of the owner, (4) high degree of secrecy, and (5) tax simplicity. Its major disadvantages are: (1) unlimited liability of the owner, (2) limitations on size and capital accumulation, (3) lack of management and employee skills, and (4) instability.

The partnership is an association of two or more owners. It was formed to offset some of the disadvantages of the proprietroship. Advantages of the partnership are: (1) more specialized management, (2) more sources of capital, (3) greater incentives for key employees, (4) more legal certainty, and (5) a wide range of freedom. Because of the following disadvantages, the partnership has very little impact in our current business: (1) unlimited liability, (2) short length of life, (3) potential owner conflicts, and (4) difficulties in withdrawing investment.

The corporation is an artificial being in the eyes of the law. To create a corporation, its promoters must file articles of incorporation indicating what its major purposes will be and identifying owners, addresses, and so on. Owners of a corporation are called stockholders or shareholders; they elect the board of directors, receive a share of the profits in the form of dividends, and buy and sell their stock on the open market. In large corporations, management of the corporation is in the hands of the board of directors who appoint the principal officers of the company. The principal officers manage the day-to-day operations.

The corporation has the advantages of: (1) limited liability, (2) ease of transferring ownership, (3) continuous life, (4) attracting capital, and (5) large size. The disadvantages are: (1) increased government regulations, (2) higher taxes, (3) lack of personal interest, (4) little secrecy, (5) rigidity, and (6) difficulty in starting. Modifications in the corporation include cooperatives and mutual companies. Cooperatives receive a charter from the state and elect a board of directors to run the company. Rather than seeking a profit in the traditional sense, they try to accumulate savings to distribute to their members. Many credit unions make use of this form of ownership today. Mutual companies, like cooperatives, are owned by their users. Life insurance companies, savings banks, and savings and loan associations make extensive use of the mutual form of ownership.

Many businesses combine with other companies through mergers or holding companies. A merger occurs when a larger company buys controlling interest in a smaller company, and they combine their managements. A holding company is one that owns stock in another company, usually enough to control it. Large businesses also break up into smaller ones, primarily through divestitures and leveraged buyouts.

MIND YOUR BUSINESS

Instructions. Check your understanding of the forms of business ownership by matching the items in the right column with those in the left column.

___	1. Has only one owner.	A. Proprietorship
___	2. Noncontinuous life is a major disadvantage.	B. Partnership
		C. Corporation
___	3. Owner conflicts are a disadvantage.	D. Joint venture
___	4. An actual being in the eyes of the law.	E. Limited partnership
		F. Business trust
___	5. Common stockholders are owners	G. Cooperative
		H. Mutual company

of this type of business.

____ 6. Proxy is associated with this form of ownership.

____ 7. This form of ownership has the most difficulty attracting capital.

____ 8. Income of this ownership is said to be double taxed.

____ 9. Limited liability is a major advantage.

____ 10. Ease in transferring ownership is an advantage.

____ 11. Government regulations are a disadvantage.

____ 12. A nonprofit organization owned and operated by the people it serves.

____ 13. A popular form of ownership for many financial organizations.

____ 14. There are more organizations of this type than any other.

____ 15. This owner's personal assets may be taken to pay business debts of another owner.

____ 16. A temporary partnership set up for a specified time period.

____ 17. A type of partnership that limits the liabilities of some of its partners.

____ 18. Limits the liability of owners by excluding them from control.

____ 19. Boards of directors are associated with this form of organization.

____ 20. This form of ownership tends to encourage businesses to grow large.

See answers at the back of the book.

KEY TERMS

REVIEW QUESTIONS

1. What is a sole proprietorship? Discuss its impact on our economy.

2. List and discuss the advantages of a sole proprietorship.

3. List and discuss the disadvantages of a sole proprietorship.

4. What is a partnership? Discuss the impact of partnerships on the economy.

5. What does the partnership agreement contain?

6. Distinguish between silent, secret, dormant, and nominal partners.

7. List and discuss the advantages of a partnership.

8. List and discuss the disadvantages of a partnership.

9. Distinguish between limited partnerships, business trusts, and partnerships.

10. What is a corporation? Discuss the impact of corporations on our economy.

11. Identify the various kinds of corporations.

12. Trace the process of creating a corporation.

13. How is the management of a corporation set up?

14. List and discuss the advantages of a corporation.

15. List and discuss the disadvantages of a corporation.

16. What are cooperatives? How do they differ from corporations?

17. What are mutual companies? How do they differ from corporations?

18. What is a merger? Describe the different kinds of mergers.

19. What are holding companies? How do they differ from mergers?

20. Explain what a divestiture is. Explain leveraged buyout.

CASES

Case 4.1: A Ban on Mergers?

Some critics argue that the government should place a ban on mergers. They argue that mergers allow companies to become too powerful and that they reduce competition in the following ways: (1) There are a reduced number of competing companies; (2) with the power in fewer hands, there are greater opportunities for cooperation among the company leaders; and (3) some mergers place barriers for firms wanting to enter the market.

Others believe that mergers are healthy for our economy. They argue that mergers: (1) help firms grow so they can compete better in world markets, (2) increase a firm's efficiency and stability, (3) should be judged by the quality of its product or service, not by whether it is large or small.

Questions

1. Which side of the argument do you agree with? Why?

2. Are there other things to consider concerning mergers?

3. Do you think mergers will increase or decrease in the future?

Case 4.2: Ownership Choices

Assume that you and a close friend have the opportunity to buy a locally owned ice cream store. In the past few years, the store has been deteriorating and business has fallen off rapidly to the point that the store is no longer profitable. The owner is ready to retire and has not been doing a very good job of management for the last four years. Yet, the store is in a good location, on a business corner across from the college, and you think that it has good possibilities of becoming a hang out for the college kids. The owner wants to sell both the store and the land. You will need about $20,000 cash to get into the business and carry you the first couple of months while you are rebuilding the ice cream store's image. You have $8000 available from savings and a "friendly loan" from your father. Your friend has the ability to raise another $8000 but this leaves you about $4000 short. There is a possibility of skimping by with only $16,000, but if your first month is bad, you don't know how you will pay your bills.

In discussing the situation with your friend, you consider several alternatives for ownership.

- You can buy the business, borrow $8000 from your friend, and hire her as one of your key employees.

- You and your friend can form a partnership with each person putting up $8000 and manage the business jointly.

- You and your friend can look for a third person who has $4000 to contribute to the business in return for less involvement in management.

- You and your friend can form a corporation and become the major stockholders. You would then try to sell enough stock to raise the remaining $4000.

Questions

1. What other alternatives can you list?
2. The first two alternatives have the disadvantage of going into ownership with very little cash in case something goes wrong. The second two alternatives have the disadvantage of bringing in other people and having to share the decision making and control.

After completing this chapter, you will be able to:

■ **Describe the role of small businesses in our society.**

■ **List the Small Business Administration's five categories of small business.**

■ **List four contributions of small businesses to our society.**

■ **Describe the major sources of financing for new businesses.**

■ **List four reasons why small businesses succeed and three reasons why they fail.**

■ **Identify the sources of help for small businesses.**

■ **Describe the services of the Small Business Administration.**

■ **List four advantages and four disadvantages of franchising to the owner.**

5

SMALL BUSINESS, ENTREPRENEURSHIP, AND FRANCHISING

Allen E. Paulson, 61, grew up in Iowa during the depression. He sold newspapers and cleaned hotel bathrooms to support himself. After graduating from high school, he went to work for TWA as a mechanic. Eventually, he began advising TWA and other airlines on engine design. He started his own business in 1951, converting surplus passenger planes into cargo aircraft. In 1978, he bought Grummann's corporate aircraft division in Georgia and began making the plush Gulfstream corporate jets. In 1983, Gulfstream went public and Paulson collected cash and stock worth more than half a billion dollars.

"I was an average kid; I was an average student," is the way Neil Hirsch, founder of Telerate Systems, an electronic financial information service, describes himself. Hirsch, whose father ran the buying office of a family-owned department store chain, studied business in college for two years. He dropped out and began hanging around stockbrokerage offices. Hirsch formed Telerate in 1969 to keep track of commercial paper prices. He sent the prices electronically to customers' video terminals. Today, 11,000 subscribers pay an average of $700 per month for the service. When Telerate went public in 1983, Hirsch held shares valued at $67.5 million.

Practically all large businesses start small; usually they begin as these two examples illustrate, with one person's idea. Of course, the vast majority of new businesses stay small; only a fraction grow to be giants. This chapter explores the nature of small business, identifies the characteristics of entrepreneurs, and explains franchising.

WHAT IS A SMALL BUSINESS?

More than 98% of all businesses in the United States have fewer than fifty employees. Because small businesses make up such a vital part of our business system, we are devoting this chapter to small business ownership and management. Before we begin, we need to decide "What is a small business?" The answer to this question has to do with type of industry, number of employees, and annual sales. The Small Business Administration

(SBA) offers us a technical definition of a **small business:**

- Manufacturers who have fewer than 250 employees.
- Retailers with annual sales of less than $1 million.
- Wholesalers with annual sales of less than $5 million.

The Committee for Economic Development (CED) classifies a business as small if it exhibits the following characteristics:

- Independent management.
- Owner-supplied capital.
- Mainly local area of operations.
- Relatively small size within industry.

Owners usually manage their small businesses, and they make all the decisions without boards, committees, stockholders, or partners. They finance the operation out of their personal wealth and their ability to borrow; they often restrict their operations to the local community; and they have little influence in their industry. The SBA and CED definitions combined form our concept of a small business.

The Role of Small Business

Almost 97% (about 10.2 million companies) of all nonfarm businesses are small. Employing almost 60% of all the private, nonfarm workers in the United States, their output makes up 43% of the gross national product. More than 70% of all retail sales are made by small businesses; in the construction industry the figure is 80%.

Despite the recent rise of mammoth businesses, small business remains a mainstay of our economic system. Although writers have, for years, predicted that we would soon see the end of small business, this hearty breed endures. In fact, in percentage of the total assets and income, small businesses have remained fairly steadfast since 1900.

Popular Types of Small Businesses

The SBA suggests that there are five categories of small businesses.

1. *Service businesses*, meaning businesses that provide services to consumers and to other businesses, are a most popular form of small business. Management consultants, printers, graphic shops, janitorial services, CPAs, and computer time sales companies are examples of service companies that deal with other businesses. Personal service businesses include barbers, theaters, restaurants, gas stations, and film developing shops. Agents, people who are commissioned to perform a future service, are also popular small businesses. There are sales, real estate, and travel agents — all usually small businesses.

2. *Retail businesses* sell goods directly to consumers and are another popular form of small business. Small neighborhood shops are everywhere — bakeries, liquor stores, card shops, and record and stereo stores are good examples. Unless part of a larger chain, these types of stores are almost always small businesses.

3. *Wholesalers* are called the middlemen between the producer of goods and the retailer. Here again, local wholesalers tend to be small businesses. They deal in products such as books, records, foods, furniture, clothing, building materials — just about all products.

4. *General construction* firms deal locally and are usually small businesses. They typically agree to build homes, apartments, office buildings, roads, or schools at given prices.

5. *Manufacturing firms* produce actual goods out of raw materials. Because of large costs, most of these firms are big businesses. But some small manufacturing businesses may deal in crafts, tee shirts, posters, custom clothing and jewelry, and specialized home products.

Contributions of Small Business

Small businesses contribute many valuable qualities to our economic system by providing jobs, stimulating competition, creating new ideas, and supplying goods and services to larger companies.

Provide jobs. During the past 10 years, we have created 20 million jobs in this country. But during the same period, the *Fortune 500* companies have lost 4 to 5 million jobs. Thus, most of the 20 million jobs are in new, small enterprises. The Small Business Administration reports that 60% of the people employed in the United States work for small businesses. This provides livelihood, either directly or indirectly, for approximately 100 million Americans. Small businesses provide jobs and lots of them.

Stimulate competition. Because our leaders have understood the value of small businesses in our competitive system, they have passed many laws to protect them. For instance, laws prevent sellers from charging higher prices to smaller companies than they do to larger companies. And larger companies cannot conspire — say, through pricing or altering supplies — to put smaller competitors out of business. Competition from many thousands of small businesses helps keep larger businesses in check by keeping prices down, encouraging better service, stimulating new product development, and the like.

Consider gasoline sales. Without strict laws, the corporate giants could alter supplies and prices to drive smaller competitors out of business within months. However, the smaller companies, through competition, help keep prices down, provide more specialized and personal service, and cause larger businesses to be more sensitive to competition.

Birth of new ideas. We mistakenly think that all of our important products and services come from large companies. They do not. Small, enterprising businesses have been responsible for the develop-

Several small firms in the early 1980s developed ultra-light aircraft for the home consumer market.

ment of insulin, power steering, ballpoint pens, self-winding watches, strained baby foods, frozen peas, and zippers. Henry Ford struggled as a small businessman while developing an automobile. Just two individuals — the Wright brothers — created the airplane. Remember Alexander Graham Bell, Samuel Morse, and Thomas Edison? According to a study by the Office of Management and Budget, firms with fewer than 1000 employees have come up with almost half of the industrial innovations since 1953. *The Wall Street Journal* got attention when it predicted that the infant Elite Corp. would beat both IBM and Hewlett-Packard into the market of high-performance desktop computers for engineers and scientists. Because of smaller staff, less overhead, and heightened innovation, Elite's lead system, the Consultant, is between one-sixth and one-half the cost of its competitors. Sales for 1985 were predicted to top $10 million, up from $3 million in 1983.

Smaller businesses often serve as a proving ground for new ideas because they have greater freedom to experiment.

Smaller businesses often serve as a proving ground for new ideas because they have greater freedom to experiment. The bureaucratic approval machinery of big business — committees, boards, staff experts, research departments, and complex decision methods — usually causes them to be less innovative and flexible.

Suppliers to large companies. Large companies rely heavily upon smaller businesses to furnish parts, subassemblies, and specialized services. Costly overhead and lack of flexibility make it difficult for large businesses to produce these parts or services. For example, General Motors may include a motorized sunroof in less than 5% of their cars. Rather than go to the expense of manufacturing the electric motor themselves, they will contract with a specialized smaller firm to provide the motors they require. The result is lower costs and lower prices. In fact, General Motors relies on thousands of smaller firms to provide specialized parts. During the 1982 recession, when American car manufacturers were forced to cut back drastically, many of these smaller firms went out of business.

In a similar vein, many of the large chain stores find it too costly to build in small communities. Thus, the corner department store steps in to fill these needs. Small businesses remain important in filling the gaps by providing goods and services that the large corporations cannot.

Small Business Trends

How are small businesses adapting to changing needs? One trend is an increase in support of big business. Huge corporations are relying more and more on small businesses in supplying parts, goods of all kinds, and services. Ford Motor Corporation, for example, may rely on as many as 30,000 smaller companies to provide goods and services for their operation.

A second trend shows small retailers and wholesalers holding their own against competition from giant chain stores and mail-order houses. Still, 95% of retail firms hire fewer than twenty employees. Opportunities in wholesaling for small business have diminished. Large manufacturers and retailers have taken over many of those functions. However, the small business wholesaler still provides many valuable services.

Finally, the most noticeable trend is the increase in small businesses in the service industry. Smallness is a distinct advantage in service firms because, through small size, they can offer a high degree of personal contact. Examples of thriving small service businesses include hair styling salons, repair shops of all types, storage companies, and food outlets.

STARTING A SMALL BUSINESS

What happens when skilled white-collar workers lose their jobs? Many of them decide to start their own businesses. In all, people started more than 581,000 new businesses in 1983. Not including farmers, almost 8 million people own their own businesses, and practically all these businesses are small.

Most small businesses that fail are either poorly planned or inadequately financed. The first step in starting a business is a specific, realistic plan. Other arrangements include financing, legal requirements, taxes, and insurance.

The Business Plan

A **business plan** is a method of projecting income, expenses, and expected profit of a venture. It is a road map or blueprint for the small businessperson. It not only reveals the success possibilities of the venture, but sets goals. After the business has begun, the plan provides a yardstick to measure how well the venture is doing. A well-conceived business plan may also help the owner obtain financing. A business plan offers at least four benefits:

1. The most important benefit is that a plan gives you a path to follow. A plan helps make the future what you want it to be.

2. A plan makes it easy to let your banker in on the action. By seeing the details of your plan, your banker will have valuable insight into your situation.

3. A plan can be a communications tool to orient sales personnel, suppliers, and others about your operations and goals.

4. A plan can help you develop as a manager. It can give you practice in thinking about competitive conditions, promotional opportunities, and situations that seem to be advantageous to your business.

Although there are abbreviated forms of business plans, many plans are more than 100 pages long. A detailed example of a proper business plan can be obtained from the SBA, or seen at the Center for Entrepreneurial Management in New York, where a library has been started of original plans for some of the country's well-known and not so well-known companies. The library already includes the original plans of Federal Express and Pizza Time Theatre, both of which weigh nearly half a pound.

Financing

According to the Small Business Administration, inadequate financing is the major reason for small business failure. Successful owners secure adequate financial arrangements before they begin their business. As one owner who had started several successful businesses said, "It is best to have capital resources well beyond your needs. Something always happens that you did not anticipate. If you are on a shoestring, the slightest mishap can put you under."

In any new venture, the cost of capital to the owner is directly related to the risk of the business. That is, if the business is one where the failure rates are high, the owner will have to pay more interest for money borrowed. Conversely, if the chances of failure are low, the owner can get

Whether money is borrowed from an institution or an individual, the prospective small business owner must convince the lender of the soundness of the investment.

money more easily and more cheaply. The following are eight possible sources of capital for a new business venture.

Owner investment. "I scraped and saved and finally decided to put up my money in a new business" is a typical statement of an owner. The majority of all new businesses start with the owner's personal savings. Eager proprietors have been known to sell their cars, stocks, interests in family estates, and even their homes to finance a venture. It is usually better for the owner to put up as much of the original investment as possible. This allows a return of maximum profits, while avoiding high interest payments and dividing profits (and decision making powers) with other investors.

Investment from family and friends. Wealthy relatives or friends are a popular capital source for new ventures. However, a prospective owner should be careful to keep money and personal matters separate. Failed investments have destroyed valuable personal relationships many times in the past.

Commercial banks. Although it may be hard to get venture money from banks, they do have the advantage of charging the lowest interest rates (among capital suppliers). Banks usually want to see a sound investment plan and a substantial owner investment, and they also like to use your tangible assets as security for loans. Before a bank approves a loan, bank personel will need to be convinced that there is little risk of losing the bank's money. In fact, the bank might even insist that the owner repay bank loans before dividing profits among investors.

Mortgage loans. A mortgage loan is when the lender loans money and the borrower pledges property as security. The lender likes this arrangement, because he or she can take the property if the business fails and the owner cannot repay the loan. Examples of mortgage loans are second mortgage on a house, a lien on equipment or other company assets, or even using a car as collateral. Again, interest rates are usually reasonable because the lender faces little risk.

Government agencies. Many government agencies will help small business owners secure money. (See page 110 for further discussion of these sources.)

Credit from suppliers. Suppliers may agree to sell supplies or perhaps even inventory to you on credit for as much as 30, 60, or in a few cases, 90 days. They do this to get your business. It helps if you can sell the inventory within the credit period and repay the supplier from the proceeds of the sale. In the case of equipment or supplies, the seller may allow you several months to pay off the debt. For instance, a new restaurant may be able to purchase an expensive walk-in cooler and pay for it over several years, or a clothing boutique may be able to pay for its inventory 30 to 60 days after purchase.

Finance companies. Finance companies make loans in somewhat the same way that banks do. However, because they take riskier projects than banks, they may charge interest rates 5 to 6% higher than banks.

Venture capital companies. Venture capital companies organize investors who are willing to take higher risks for a much higher return on their investment. Venture capitalists usually are not interested in a project unless it promises a sparkling tenfold return within a five-year period. Venture companies need this type of heady potential to return to their investors the 35 to 60% annual returns they require. Venture capital companies usually specialize in investments such as real estate, banking, manufacturing, and retailing. In the early 1980s, high-technology companies were the darlings of venture capitalists. In 1982, the 100 most active venture capital companies launched a blur of new businesses by investing $1.38 billion in entrepreneurial companies. Table 5.1 shows the top ten venture capital companies of 1982.

Legal Arrangements

Obtaining financing is the hardest part, but a new owner must clear other hurdles. For instance, most cities and states require a license to do business. The owner must secure the license before opening a business. Licensing allows local governments to keep track of business activity. It also clears the use of business names so that they will not conflict with other local businesses.

Some businesses also need permits. A restaurant or food manufacturer may need food handler permits for its employees. Businesses dealing out of state may require a special permit. A business that serves or sells alcohol typically needs a permit; retailers may require a vendor's permit; and a manufacturing firm may need a permit so agencies can check on employee safety.

Since requirements for licenses and permits vary, it is helpful to visit a local attorney who specializes in small businesses. City governmental offices and Chambers of Commerce may also help.

Taxes

There are always taxes. Each new business must collect and pay several kinds of taxes. A retail firm must collect sales taxes; an employer may have to collect and pay various taxes on employees' wages; and the owner may have to pay a self-employment tax. The Internal Revenue Service has two publications that help: *Mr. Businessmen's Kit* and *Tax Guide for Small Business.* An owner might also want to call state and local tax revenue departments for information.

TABLE 5.1 ■ THE TEN TOP VENTURE CAPITAL COMPANIES OF 1982

		1982 Investments (in millions)								
Rank (Last Year)	Firm Name	Total ($) Invested	No. of Deals	Startups ($)	Deals	Buyouts, Others (Buyouts Alone) ($)	Deals	Follow-On Investments ($)	Deals	General Partners
1 (1)	The Hillman Co. Pittsburgh, Pa.	101.5	39	NA	14	NA (17.5)	11 (5)	NA	14	Henry L. Hillman, president Carl G. Grefenstette, Senior VP
2 (9)	Allstate Insurance Co. Venture Capital Div. Northbrook, Ill.	64.2	30	8.8	7	36 (25)	9 (2)	19.4	14	Charles Rees, director
3 (2)	First Chicago Investment Corp. Chicago, Ill. (First Nat'l Bank of Chicago)	48.5	45	5.4	5	27.7 (13.5)	14 (5)	15.4	26	John A. Canning Jr., president
4 (27)	General Electric Venture Capital Corp. Fairfield, Conn. (GE Corp.)	41.6	20	NA	4	11.4*	4	30.2	12	Terence E. McClary, president
5 (10)	Brentwood Associates Los Angeles, Calif.	35	20	10	8	20	7	5	5	Frederick J. Warren, B. Kipling Hagopian, Timothy Pennington, George M. Crandell, Roger C. Divisson
6 (12)	E. M. Warburg Pincus & Co. New York, N.Y.	33.9	30	3.5	6	22.9 (10.7)	10 (2)	7.5	14	Lionel I. Pincus, chairman; John L. Vogelstein, president
7 (4)	TA Associates Boston, Mass. (Tucker Anthony & R. L. Day)	32.3	21	8.3	7	20.5	9	3.5	5	Peter A. Brooks, David B. Croll, C. Kevin Landry, managing partners
8 (8)	Security Pacific Capital Corp. Newport Beach, Calif.	32.25	11	.94	1	30.7 28.7	6 (4)	.6	4	Timothy Hay, president
9 (3)	Citicorp. Venture Capital Ltd. New York, N.Y.	30.5	54	8.0	12	12.0 (6)	13 (4)	10.5	29	William T. Comfort, president
10 (45)	BT Capital Corp. New York, N.Y. (Bankers Trust N.Y.)	26	16	—	—	26 (20)	16 (9)	—	—	James G. Hellmuth, president

NA = Not available.
* = estimate.
Source: Reprinted from the June, 1983, issue of *Venture, The Magazine for Entrepreneurs,* by special permission. © 1983 Venture Magazine, Inc., 35 West 45th St., New York, N.Y. 10036.

TABLE 5.2 ■ KINDS OF INSURANCE COVERAGE

Fire insurance
Liability insurance
Automobile insurance
Worker's compensation
Business interruption insurance
Crime insurance
Glass insurance
Rent insurance
Group life insurance
Group health insurance
Disability insurance
Retirement income
Key-man insurance

Insurance

A business needs several kinds of insurance. If customers come into a place of business, the owner will need liability insurance. If you serve food, you will need additional insurance. Should the business hire employees, you will need insurance — both mandatory and optional — to protect both yourself and the employees. Employees may also require accident or disability insurance as well. Again, a small business lawyer and local government agencies can be very helpful. See Table 5.2 for a listing of the kinds of insurance coverage (and see Chapter 19 for more discussion of insurance).

THE SUCCESS OF SMALL BUSINESS

Although they have been called an endangered species, the traditional, small, mom-and-pop businesses are still around. Businesses with fewer than ten people, according to government statis-

---

After one year of operation, about one-third of all new small businesses discontinue; about half close after two years; and only one-third make it as long as five years.

---

tics, make up 70% of all businesses. Not that they have an easy time. By percentages, the success rate is not very high. After one year of operation, about one-third of all new small businesses discontinue; about half close after two years, and only one-third make it as long as five years. Even against these odds, about 5 million small businesses start up each year. These businesses can increase their chances for survival if they maximize their advantages and guard against the causes of failure.

Why Small Businesses Succeed

Flexibility, personal touch, lower overhead, and owner motivation are natural strengths of small business. And these are the reasons that the successful ones make it.

Greater flexibility. Surveys show flexibility to be an important benefit of being small. Small firms have more informal organization and, likewise, more efficient communication. Within minutes, they can create, alter, implement, and terminate a plan. This allows the small company to take advantage of fleeting opportunities and to avoid bad situations. Systems, approval procedures, and communication channels of larger companies cause them to adapt with dinosauric clumsiness, while small firms deftly outmaneuver them.

More personal service. Small business owners usually have a rather close personal relationship with their customers and employees. Personal friendships encourage trust and understanding between owner and customer. Owners who know their patrons take more pride in customer satisfaction, which in turn enhances old-time client loyalty. Small business owners may also be more intimately involved with the community, and they get an understanding about consumer needs and wishes that sophisticated market research could never uncover. Friendly relationships with employees improve communication, commitment to owners' objectives, and responsibility. Employees of small businesses are much less prone to organize unions or develop adversary relationships with the owner. These first-hand relationships reveal the owner as more human and understanding than distantly removed owners and managers of larger companies.

Small business operations often can generate close relationships between owner and employees, resulting in a deeply committed work force.

Low overhead. Small companies have less capital tied up in costly investments such as building, machinery and equipment, executive salaries, fringe benefit programs, and research departments. Therefore, small companies can take on ventures of only a moderate return. Smallness is less expensive. A look at the minicomputer industry provides an example. Most of the early innovations in minicomputers were made by small business owners. They had much more to gain personally, and their risk of failure was much less. The development of the Apple computer may have cost as little as 5% of IBM's similar product. Because the IBM venture was on a much larger scale and because IBM had much more to lose by any mistakes, their investment was massive by comparison.

High motivation of owners. Horace and Joan Gimbell work in their small grocery store from 8:00 A.M. until 7:00 P.M., six days a week. Many nights after they close the doors, they stay around to clean up, keep records, and stock shelves. For this, they earn about $20,000 per year. Yet, in

BUSINESS BULLETIN

Things You Might Want to Check in Starting Your Own Business

Though many small businesses are easy to start, some require licenses, permits, and other approvals. The following list is a reminder of a few things that you probably should check:

1. Check with the city to see if you need a local business license.
2. Check to see if you need a special license if you plan to sell such items as cigarettes, alcohol, drugs, firearms, real estate, insurance, and vending machine goods.
3. Check with the Internal Revenue Service to see if you need an Employer's Identification Number.
4. Check with the state about the Tax Identification Number.
5. Check with the state, county, or city (or all) to see if you need permits from the health department.
6. Check with the local fire department to see if you need a permit.
7. Check with the Federal Occupational Safety Office to see if you comply with the Occupational Safety and Health Act.
8. Check with the city or county (or both) to see if you need a building permit or a certificate of occupancy.

order to be independent and free, they are willing to work harder for less income. The most outstanding quality of a small business owner is an untiring dedication to work. This allows smaller businesses to overcome many of the disadvantages of small size.

Why Small Businesses Fail

Although different sources will show slightly different figures, small businesses have high failure rates, and they do not make their owners worshipful of wealth. Of the 5 million sole proprietorships that form every year, nearly 50% of them fail within two years. What's more, 40% of small business owners earn less than $15,000 per year.

According to *Dun & Bradstreet*, 90% of all business failures are due to poor management.

According to **Dun & Bradstreet,** a financial credit rating organization for businesses, 90% of all business failures are due to poor management. And James D. McKevitt, director and chief lobbyist of the National Federation of Independent Business (NFIB), says that small business owners often have only themselves to blame for their failures. More specifically, lack of experience and aptitude, improper record keeping, and unwise handling of money usually account for small businesses not lasting.

Limited experience and aptitude. Research shows that the combination of formal education and experience offers the highest probability of success. Also, experience with ownership itself seems to be more important than expertise in a particular line of business. Similarly, much of the owner's formal education does not necessarily have to relate to his or her line of business in order to be helpful.

In failure, many small business owners state that they had little control over their problems. Economic recessions, rising interest costs, street relocations, labor situations, changes in laws, and sudden style changes can cause failure of a small business. Yet, successful owners find ways to soften these blows and even turn them into oppor-

tunities. Large corporations, with special research departments, tend to be more aware of these problems. The successful small businessperson makes every effort to keep informed of potential problems.

Inadequate record keeping and planning. Failing small business owners are not aware of how they jeopardize their venture by not keeping proper records. These records may well detect poor business practices. Poor records are either outdated or deficient in such key areas as sales volume, accounts receivable, assets, inventory, expenses, and employment records. Too many owners are content to drop their income into a cigar box and take the money out as needed or as bills become due. In fact, they may not even know if they are making a profit until the end of the year when their accountant files their income tax.

Too many owners let wholesalers, brokers, and suppliers suggest what they ought to buy. As a result, they find their money is tied up in some merchandise while they are out of stock in other items. Some owners may keep a record of gross sales, but few know how many of each item they are selling, and they cannot distinguish between high-profit and low-profit goods. Records on costs associated with accounts receivable are valuable, but seldom available.

Planning beyond a day or two seldom occurs. Intuition and hazy judgment serve in lieu of reasonable forecasts of cash, supply, and capital needs. Many small companies let tremendous opportunities for growth slip away because they do not adjust their capacity to manufacture more goods, sell more products, or furnish more services. Often, small business owners fail to plan for employment needs. Finally, they only lightly consider economic situations. Failure to consider an economic boom or recession can be costly.

Unwise handling of money matters. Ultimately, most businesses fail because they cannot pay their bills. Most businesses feel the pinch of money problems now and then. At no time is awareness of money needs more important than during start-up. It is important to consider and properly forecast all expenses and cash requirements. Even after a successful start, money problems are more acute for smaller businesses. Generally, they face a limited source of funds. It is

Small Business Failures

The early 1980s, with high interest rates, slow-paying customers, and sluggish orders, took the zest out of many small businesses. Nineteen eighty-two saw more than 25,000 business failures, most of which were small businesses.

However, it now appears that the economic turnaround has arrived just in time for many small businesses. The chief economist for the National Federation of Independent Business (NFIB) says that demand is increasing, employment is improving, and companies are adding to their inventories. Experts say that small businesses are being helped primarily by interest rate declines. Not only do lower interests reduce borrowing costs to customers, they allow the small business owner to borrow for expansion. The accompanying chart shows business failures from 1973 through 1982.

Number of business failures

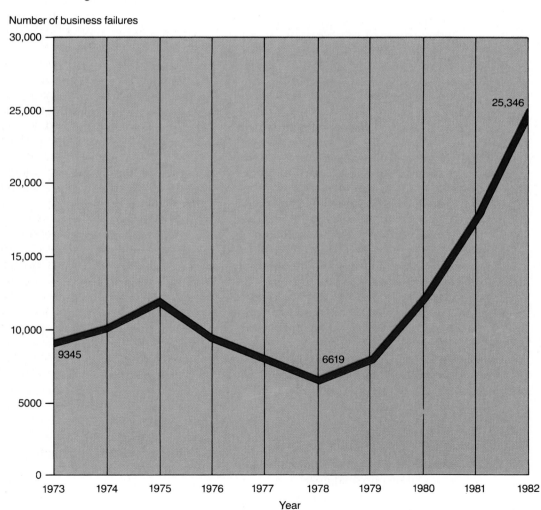

Year

Source: "The Famine is Over for Small Businesses," *U.S. News & World Report,* July 4, 1983, p. 55.

hard to get additional money for working capital or long-term expansion, especially when interest rates are high. Insufficient cash flow, uncollected accounts, and high debt are usually serious blows for the small business owner.

THE ENTREPRENEUR

"Give me enough Swedes and snuff and I'll build a railroad to hell," the entrepreneur James J. Hill is supposed to have said before he built the Great Northern Railway across the plains in the 1880s. An entrepreneur is one who takes the risks of starting and managing a business. Many an everyday citizen envies this hard-driving, risk-taking independent of the business world. Entrepreneurs have the nerve to put their money and skill on the line. If they succeed, life is glamorous and independent. Fear of failure, however, is a constant companion. Millions of Americans take the risk and start their own businesses; most of the rest of us flirt with the idea at some time during our careers.

Some entrepreneurs are visionary dreamers. Carter Canada, a successful real estate developer, has spent eight years trying to raise money to develop huge pyramids to house a resort hotel complex in Nevada. William Kumm wants to start a company to transport oil via a fuel-driven cell underneath Alaska's North Slope to the East Coast. While these two visions may have long odds against them, Alan Boyd and Lawrence Gilson, two former Amtrak executives, might see their dream realized. In 1987, their dream project, the first "bullet" train in America, is scheduled to begin whisking passengers between Los Angeles and San Diego. Most entrepreneurs, however, are much more practical.

Purdue University professors Arnold C. Cooper and William C. Dunkelberg, after studying 890 business founders, identified three basic types of people that start their own businesses:

1. Crafts people who exploit a personal skill (mechanics, hair stylists, and plumbers).
2. Growth-oriented people who start a business to seek financial or personal goals.
3. People who start their own businesses to avoid working for others.*

---

* "Small Business," *The Wall Street Journal*, July 15, 1983.

Ted Turner, a well-known example of the successful entrepreneurial personality, has become a major force in the telecommunications industry.

Businesses started by crafts people, according to the study, tended to have a slower growth rate than other types of businesses. Even though each entrepreneur is unique, there are some common traits found in successful entrepreneurs.

Personal background. The entrepreneur is likely to be the first or oldest child in the family. His or her parents are usually not involved in any kind of corporate bureaucracy. In a study of eighty people who started their own businesses, only 3% had parents who were managers in large or medium-sized organizations. Sixteen percent of the entrepreneurs' parents were professionals, clerks, or salespeople. Nineteen percent had parents who were farmers, and 25% of the parents were independent business owners. The largest group, 30%, had fathers who worked as skilled or unskilled laborers. Almost 79% of the owners described their family as poor, while less than 30% came from affluent backgrounds. This study suggests that dire childhood circumstances serve as the primary catalyst for the entrepreneur in starting a business. Although few independents go from rags to riches, their alternatives are often less promising.

Studies have shown that self-employeds have more education than average students but less than corporate executives. Learning from "the school of hard knocks" is common. More current research shows that, for self-employeds, a master's degree in business management or some technical field is quite common.

Independence

The cherished values of independence and self-sufficiency radiate from small business owners. They toss aside the selection and promotion practices of large organizations for the right to be their own bosses. The enterpriser resists being pigeonholed or following routine habits. In fact, entrepreneurs become frustrated when they have to follow someone else's direction. They have to be the boss. They like to be in control. They find it difficult to work under the direction of others.

High Achievement

People who operate their own businesses have a great need to achieve. They strive to take personal responsibility for finding their own solutions to problems. And they crave tangible, measurable feedback on their accomplishments. They like specific answers to the question, "How am I doing?" Contrary to popular opinion, achievers are not long-shot gamblers who stake their life savings on hundred-to-one odds. They are moderate risk takers. Typically, their choice is a calculated risk that can be achieved by their labor and devotion. While their careers are much less secure than a nine-to-five job, their risks are still somewhat moderate.

Hard Work

Willingness to work — and work hard — is an outstanding trait of entrepreneurs. They seem able to work endless, 12-hour days. You can bet that the successful business owner has paid with tedious, sweat-filled hours, emotional stress, and perseverance. Most likely, the business verged on failure many times in the beginning, but the owner simply would not let it die. A successful entrepreneur described his early experiences: "When I started, may workday began at 6:00 A.M. and often lasted until 8:00 or 9:00 P.M., sometimes later. I worked this pace at least 6 and sometimes 7 days a week. You might say it was my whole life."

BUSINESS BULLETIN

Characteristics of Entrepreneurs

In 1983, *Inc.* magazine published findings of their study of the chief executive officers of America's 100 fastest growing companies. Some of the characteristics of these people are:

Parents who were entrepreneurs	43%
Would like to see children become entrepreneurs	75%
Between the age of 25 and 35 when they started the company	41%
Initial source of capital — personal savings	69%
Initial source of capital — outside investors	39%
Initial source of capital — banks	28%
Share equity with key employees	96%
Undergraduate degrees in engineering	30%
Graduate degrees	46%
Worked in a Fortune 500 company	49%
Started the business with one or more partners	67%

Source: Curtis Hartman, "Who's Running America's Fastest Growing Companies," *Inc.*, August, 1983, pp. 41–47.

WHERE SMALL BUSINESS OWNERS CAN GET HELP

To stimulate the important role that small businesses play in our business system, we have devised several sources of aid. Some banks have advisors who specialize in small business. And suppliers can be a prime source of information.

The Small Business Administration remains

---

the major source of organized assistance

---

for small business owners.

Many books and articles are written on the subject, and colleges and universities offer courses, workshops and seminars on small business ownership. But the Small Business Administration remains the major source of organized assistance. Other resources include the Department of Commerce and professional organizations.

The Small Business Administration

The federal government established the **Small Business Administration (SBA)** with the *Small Business Act of 1953*. The SBA helps small businesses to secure funds, find management assistance, and bid for government contracts. Since its origin, the Small Business Administration has:

- Made or guaranteed loans for 461,000 businesses.
- Attracted more than 300,000 people per year to seminars and workshops.
- Provided 905,000 disaster loans totaling $12.2 billion.
- Created 33.4 million person-hours of work.
- Created $468 billion of additional gross national products.
- Provided $67.3 billion of income tax revenue.

Source of funds. The SBA helps small businesses secure funds by helping to provide three kinds of loans:

1. **SBA direct loans** are made by funds directly from the SBA. These are made only in special circumstances, where the SBA feels that the enterprise has merit and where the owner is not able to get financing from other sources.

2. **SBA participating loans** are situations where the SBA supplements the required funds from loans from banks or other investors.

3. In an **SBA guaranteed loan,** the funds come totally from a bank, while the SBA guarantees that 90% of the loan will be paid. Should the venture fail, the SBA will pay the bill. Because this loan is much more secure, the owner may not only get the loan, but usually, because of the guarantee, it is at a lower rate of interest.

However, the SBA is limited to a commitment of $350,000 in guaranteeing and sharing loans. Also, the SBA can commit for capital funds up to 15 years and working capital loans for up to 6 years.

Disaster loans. To businesses that suffer losses from floods, storms, or earthquakes, the SBA can make **disaster loans** of up to a half million dollars for 30 years. To qualify, the business must be in a presidentially declared disaster area.

Low-income loans. Since 1964, the SBA has been able to make loans to low-income individuals who exhibit potential for running a business but do not qualify under the standard program. It may loan up to $50,000 for 15 years and usually relaxes credit standards, looking instead at managerial ability and financial responsibility.

Small business investment companies. Finally, the SBA regulates some 500 privately owned **small business investment companies (SBIC).** These SBICs are organized specifically for the purpose of helping small businesses with their long-term capital needs. An SBIC helps finance firms by direct loans and equity investments. In the direct loans, the SBIC will provide funds and accept collateral when banks will not. As this is a private transaction, the interest rate is usually negotiable. However, the transaction must be regulated by the SBA. With equity loans, the SBICs usually share in the growth and profit of the venture. Sometimes, the SBIC will purchase common stock in the firm. Because these ventures are usually high-risk, they demand a high rate of interest. The owner usually must pay a high percentage of the profits and increased value of the company back to the private investors. The SBICs are similar to venture capital companies, except that they operate within the framework of the SBA.

In 1983, the nation's SBICs were seeking to sever their ties to Congress and the Small Business Administration, which polices and doles out funds to them. Walter Stults, president of the National Association of Small Business Investment Companies, says that by taking the program out of government hands and putting it in the private sector much more money could be provided for SBICs, which would mean more money for small business loans and investments.

Management assistance. A variety of management help, from direct counseling to advising and training programs, is available to proprietors. First, the SBA assists owners in locating sources of funds through regular lending agencies. It assists them in preparing their financial statements, shows them how to approach lenders, and helps them evaluate the proposal. Also, it gives specific guidance to entrepreneurs in competing for government contracts.

Small Business Institute (SBI) programs sponsor student-faculty teams from universities to provide consulting help with decisions such as seeking loans, collecting debts, hiring and supervising employees, improving records, managing cash, selecting location sites, controlling inventory, and increasing sales. Student-faculty teams serve only as staff advisors; the decisions remain with the owners.

Finally, the SBA provides management assistance through Small Business Development Centers (SBDC). Although not available in all states, the program organizes the resources of the community, university, and state government to offer management help to small businesses.

Service Corps of Retired Executives. The SBA also sponsors a group of about 5000 retired executives who volunteer their time to serve as part-time consultants for small business owners **(the Service Corps of Retired Executives (SCORE))**. A small business owner can usually get assistance from SCORE by calling the nearest SBA office. These consultants are usually free for the first 90 days, although they do ask the owner to cover out-of-pocket expenses. After 90 days, some compensation is established between the owner and the consultant.

Small business owners can call on the experience of retired executives who serve as consultants for SCORE.

Active Corps of Executives. ACE is organized and sponsored in much the same way as SCORE, yet it involves executives that are still active in business management **(Active Corps of Executives (ACE))**. They can provide valuable counseling for the small business owner.

Small business innovation research program. Under an act of Congress, the SBA in 1982 established a research program that makes eleven federal agencies set aside 1% of their research funds for small businesses. In 1983, more than 1700 proposals were submitted by small businesses hoping for further research funding. This source was expected to provide $50 million in 1984 for new companies developing products for government use.

Information. A wealth of information is provided for the new business entrepreneur. The Small Business Administration publishes many booklets, pamphlets, and research reports on starting and managing a small business. Some of these are specifically focused on particular types of business, such as restaurants, services, and manufacturing firms. Commercial publications, such as *Entrepreneur Magazine, Inc., Venture,* and *Money* magazines can provide valuable information. Standard business publications such as *The Wall Street Journal, Forbes, Business Week,* and *Fortune* can also provide crucial information to keep the small business owner aware of current events.

Too Much Help for Small Businesses?

Some argue that small businesses actually receive too much help from the government and other sources. These critics say that small businesses should succeed or fail on their own merits, and aiding them actually encourages inefficiencies in our system. They point to the money and time invested in the Small Business Administration and suggest that this should not really be a government effort. They further argue that many of the most successful small businesses made it without government help.

However, others say that small businesses are vital to our economy for both practical and psychological reasons. Practically, they provide most of the new jobs in our economy; they provide products and services that would not be available otherwise; and they are more creative than larger businesses. Psychologically, they make it possible for people to have the freedom to ''chase the American dream'' by starting a business, be their own boss, and perhaps become wealthy. Finally, this side says that the actual amount of government aid is really not all that great in the first place.

Do you believe that the government offers too much assistance to small businesses?

___ A. Offers way too much   ___ C. Offers too little

___ B. Offers too much   ___ D. Offers way too little

List three reasons for your position:

A. _____

B. _____

C. _____

Minority Business Development Agency. Since 1969, the federal government has made some special attempts to help small minority enterprises. These programs try to provide financial, technical, and management assistance to blacks, Puerto Ricans, Mexican Americans, native Americans, and other minorities. In 1969, the Department of Commerce established the **Minority Business Development Agency (MBDA)** (formerly the Office of Minority Business Enterprise or OMBE). Also, there are two agencies within the MBDA that assist minority enterprises.

Minority Business Opportunity Committee. The Minority Business Development Agency created the **Minority Business Opportunity Committee (MBOC)** to help coordinate programs from over sixteen different federal agencies that serve minority businesses. MBOC promotes opportunities for minority enterprises, helps them find risk capital, and serves as a watchdog to ensure that funds and assistance get to the people who need it.

Minority Enterprise Small Business Investment Company. This agency works much the same way as the SBICs yet they specialize in raising money for minority ventures. The **Minority Enterprise Small Business Investment Company (MESBIC)** aids in securing starting and long-term capital requirements.

Professional Organizations

Small business owners have been especially difficult to organize in lobbying for laws and in resisting regulations unfavorable to them. This type of group activity goes against their independence. Proprietors tend to want to take care of themselves. However, two groups have emerged and have gained some impact. The **Junior Chamber of Commerce** organized the **National Small Business Association** in 1937, and the **National Federation of Independent Businesses** in 1943. These groups represent small business owners' interests in Washington. They strive to improve the competitive position of small businesses by opposing monopolistic practices, reducing government burdens on small businesses, and helping small companies get their share of government business. **Better Business Bureaus** are local nonprofit organizations that help police the activities of businesses. They protect consumers and businesses against unfair and unethical business practices.

FRANCHISING

In 1984, the third largest pizza franchise, Godfather's, opened war on the two leaders, Pizza Hut and Domino's, by entering its deep-dish pizza into the market. Deep-dish pie now accounts for about two-thirds of all pizza sales. Godfather's has taken the offensive in their promotion with a slogan that says, "We'll get very specific about our pan pizza versus their pan pizza." Even though both Pizza Hut and Domino's continued to rock along quite successfully, Godfather's aimed to open 200 to 300

TAKING STOCK

Aggressive Management Plus Speed Equals Success

Domino's Pizza, with estimated sales of $400 million in 1983, is one of the fastest-growing companies in a rapidly expanding fast-food industry. Key executive and founder Thomas Monaghan says that his success is due to speedy delivery and aggressive management.

Domino's Pizza, Inc., is a home delivery chain, and he promises to get a pizza to customers within 30 minutes. Monaghan says he can make a pizza in 11 seconds flat.

Although there are a few large pizza chains, local chains and mom-and-pop stores tend to dominate. However, Monaghan felt that there was a market for a chain that delivers, and he aggressively set out to capture it. His strategy paid off; in 1982, pizza sales hit $250 million ($76 million from owned units, and the rest from franchises), and his total number of outlets ranked second only to Pizza Hut's. By 1988, according to current projections, Domino's and Pizza Hut will be neck and neck with about 5000 stores each.

Showing a strong preference for growth over profits, Domino's earned only $3 million last year. Investment bankers say Domino's could easily raise $150 million with a public stock sell, but Monaghan prefers to keep control of the firm himself. He has a $52 million revolving loan which he can use for expansion, and the company has little debt. Monaghan says, "My competitors want a return on investment. I don't care about that, I just want to be No. 1 in every market we're in."

Source: "Domino's Pizza: How It Became the No. 2 Chain," *Business Week,* August 15, 1983, p. 114.

TABLE 5.3 ■ PROFILE OF A FRANCHISE

Name of franchise	Kentucky Fried Chicken
Address	P.O. Box 32070, M-680, Louisville, Kentucky
Product or service	Fried chicken
Year business began	1930
Franchising since	1952
1980—Number of franchises	4928
Company owned	1198
1981—Number of franchises	5146
Company owned	1203
1982—Number of franchises	5200
Company owned	1286
Range of capital needed	$385,000–486,000
Franchise fee	$10,000
Royalty	4%
Advertising royalty	5%
Financing provided	No
Industrial rank	12

stores a year until they reached about 4000 stores. At the end of 1983, Pizza Hut had a little over 4000 stores.

A few examples of franchise arrangements are McDonald's, Walgreen's, Kentucky Fried Chicken, and H & R Block.

Franchising has been around for some time, but it has undergone a whirlwind growth since the middle 1950s. A **franchise** is an exclusive arrangement between a manufacturer or operating company and a private owner. Franchise arrangements can be divided into two broad classes: (1) product distribution arrangements in which the dealer is to some degree, but not entirely, identified with the manufacturer/supplier, and (2) entire business franchising, in which there is complete identification of the dealer with the buyer. A few examples of franchise arrangement are McDonald's, Western Auto, Walgreen's, Kentucky Fried Chicken (see Table 5.3), Coca-Cola distributorships, and H & R Block. The parent company gives an individual or group the right or privilege to do business. These rights, provided in a written contract, usually establish the method of business, the period of time, and the location. The parent company is called a **franchisor**, the privilege is a franchise, and the private owner is called the **franchisee**. The franchisee is an independent owner tied to the parent company by the contractual agreements.

The franchise method provides several advantages to the small business owner. There are also some disadvantages.

Advantages to the Owner

Why would an individual owner prefer a franchise to the more independent form of ownership? Franchising allows small business owners to enjoy the advantages of smallness while offsetting many of the disadvantages. The major advantages include instant recognition, management assistance, financing assistance, and reduced failure rates.

Instant recognition. The franchisor develops a highly visible trade name, usually through flashy national advertising that is easily recognized by the public. The positive image created through national promotion is transferred to franchisees. When they first open the new business, the company name and product is already familiar to most customers. This helps franchisees compete with the nationwide advertising of larger businesses. While traveling, for example, most consumers would prefer stopping at McDonald's over the local hamburger stand. This is because they are familiar with the quality, prices, and types of food available.

Management assistance. Many franchisors have gathered specific information on the location, design, and management of their outlets. They have important data on store layout, methods of hiring and training employees, pricing policies, preparation of the product or delivery of the service. They provide continuing advice on markets, prices, and changes in the economy. Through mass purchasing and production, they can provide better supplies at less cost. The franchisor's prior experience with the products and services is a great advantage. Their expertise helps prevent failures; the small business owner does not have to learn about them the hard way. Finally, the franchisor will often counsel the owner on unusual problems.

One young, fast-growing series of franchising operations actually specializes in management assistance for dentists. The franchise company offers to oversee all the details of managing the dentist's office — choosing and leasing the site, hiring the staff, and marketing the dentist's services. The dentist merely buys the franchise and shows up for work. The franchisor does all the rest. United Dental Network, one of the largest such franchisors, has sixty-two franchisee offices.

Service stations have long been franchised operations, the owners benefiting from the financial, marketing, and management assistance provided by the franchisor.

Financial assistance. Franchisors may aid the franchisee with direct loans or leasing agreements. Or franchisors can help the owners prepare their loan applications and even use their influence with lending agencies. While financing is still the responsibility of the owners, they receive expert help and get to trade on the reputation of the franchisor.

Reduced failure rates. Some estimates on the odds for success favor a franchise over a privately owned small business by 20 to 1. While this figure may be exaggerated, there is no doubt that the help provided by the franchisor greatly reduces the risk of business failure by the owner.

Disadvantages to the Owner

While the advantages are the reason for the rapid growth rate of franchising, there are some disadvantages: franchises are becoming rather expensive; their reputation has been tainted by a few fly-by-night outfits; some owners resent the control of the franchisor; sometimes the quality and personalized services are lacking; and legal confusion may become a problem.

Increasing expense of franchising. In addition to the initial fee, most franchisors have ongoing charges for their services. The fee may range from $3000 to over $1 million, but most fall between $20,000 and $50,000. And their continuing services can be expensive. More than 90% of all franchisors charge a royalty fee ranging from 3 to 20% of sales. Also, about 70% assess owners for advertising services. New franchises tend to be less expensive. Here, there may also be an advantage to the franchisor. If the owner buys in early and the franchise becomes unusually successful, the franchise may be sold for considerable profit.

Fraudulent practices. The aura of success in franchising has been somewhat dimmed by fly-by-night operators. An owner who put a hard-earned $20,000 into a new franchise explained his feeling, "When they came in, it looked like they were going to start a massive advertising campaign within the week. I gave them my money, they sent me some materials, and kept promising a lot of results. As my patience wore thin, I found it harder and harder to get them to respond to my questions. Finally, they seemed to disappear into thin air." New franchises, like new businesses, have a greater threat of failure.

Silk-tongued opportunists capitalize on success stories by promoting nonexistent trade names, peddling undeliverable services, and selling illegal pyramid schemes. They make numerous blue-sky promises, most of which they never intend to fulfill, take their franchise fee, and go out of business, leaving the owner on his own. Others have been known to raise their fees or change their practices, resulting in great pressures on the profits of the business. Sometimes, they charge exorbitant prices for goods and equipment, and the franchisor has no choice other than to pay those prices.

Franchisor control. The benefits of standardized practices are diminished when the owner loses control over the management of the business. A major benefit of small business — independence and autonomy — is often lost in the regimen of a franchise. Franchisors usually insist on a particular layout, set procedures for processing customers, and may even dicatate store hours, methods of hiring, employee salaries, and prices.

BUSINESS BULLETIN

A Checklist for Evaluating Franchise Opportunities

In checking out franchises, you will want to get "yes" answers to most of the questions in this list.

check if yes

I.   Is the franchisor successful?
  1.   Has the franchisor been in business for more than five years? _____
  2.   Does the franchisor have a good reputation and credit rating? _____
  3.   Have you found out how many franchises are operating? _____
  4.   Is the failure rate small? _____
  5.   What assistance will the franchisor offer you? _____

II. What about the product or service?
  6.   Has it been on the market long enough to gain acceptance? _____
  7.   Is it priced competitively? _____
  8.   Is it a staple product, not a fad? _____
  9.   Would you buy it on its merits? _____
  10. If product and supplies must be purchased exclusively from the franchisor, are prices competitive? _____

III. What do you know about the franchise contract?
  11. Does the fee seem reasonable? _____
  12. Do continuing royalties appear reasonable? _____
  13. Does the cash investment include payment for fixtures and equipment? _____
  14. Can you, as the franchisee, return merchandise for credit? _____
  15. If there is an annual sales quota, can you retain your franchise if it is not met? _____

The potential conflict becomes clear: the highly valued independence of the enterpriser versus the rigid rule of the franchisor. For example, a successful owner of a national fast-food restaurant that was located in a Mexican American neighborhood wanted to add four Mexican dishes to the menu. The request was strictly forbidden by the franchisor.

Legal confusion. The growth of franchising raced ahead of legislation governing its practices. In order to control illegal and unethical practices, some states passed laws regarding franchising.

The more respectable franchises encouraged these laws. Still, there were variations between state laws, and some states had no laws whatsoever. In 1971, the Federal Trade Commission, recognizing this problem, proposed a trade regulation requiring full disclosure of all facts to prospective investors. The law requires a **uniform offering circular**, with a disclosure of all financial information and details regarding the specific arrangements between the franchisor and the franchisee. It is now more difficult for the franchisor to make promises that are left unfulfilled.

16. Do you have an exclusive, protected territory? _____

17. Can you terminate your agreement if you are not happy? _____

18. May you sell your business to whomever you please? _____

19. Did you have a lawyer study each paragraph of the contract and approve it? _____

20. Does the contract cover all aspects of your agreement with the franchisor? _____

IV. What about your market?

21. Are your boundaries completely and understandably defined? _____

22. Does your product or service have a market in your territory? _____

23. Does your territory provide an adequate sales potential? _____

24. Is the existing competition not too well entrenched? _____

V. What about you, the franchisee?

25. Do you know where you are going to get the money to invest? _____

26. Have you compared the costs to starting other similar businesses? _____

27. Are you prepared to give up some of your independence? _____

28. Are you prepared to accept rules and regulations you may disagree with? _____

29. Are you capable of accepting some supervision from the franchisor? _____

30. Are you ready to spend much or all of your remaining life with this franchisor? _____

Source: Adapted from Wendell O. Metcalf, *Starting and Managing a Small Business of Your Own*, Washington, D.C.: Small Business Administration, 1973.

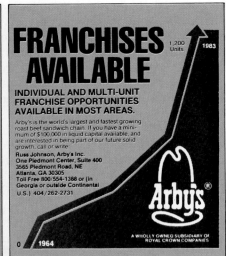

Figure 5.1
Franchise ads that appeared in *The Wall Street Journal*.

State laws governing pricing and territorial arrangements may conflict with those of the franchisor. There exists a legal question as to whether territorial agreements are anticompetitive. These unsettled laws may create problems for franchising. They may also mean numerous reports for both franchisor and franchisee.

Future of Franchising

While the rapid-paced growth of franchising may not continue indefinitely, the immediate future of franchising looks rosy. Fast-foods have been booming for the last few years and seem likely to continue thriving. Restaurants now capture 37% of the family food dollar, and projections aim at 50% by 1990. Fast-food franchises, buoyed by past successes, are continuing rapid expansion. Table 5.4 lists the top ten franchises of 1982.

Convenience food stores are surviving their hot competition with supermarkets by locating close to residential areas and staying open at odd hours. Thanks to shorter work weeks, longer vacations, rising incomes, and early retirements, leisure and travel businesses continue to thrive. But while new franchising fields offer greater growth opportunities, the traditional franchises—fast-food restaurants, automobile dealers, gasoline stations, soft drink companies, and retailing outlets — continue to dominate (see Figure 5.1).

TABLE 5.4 ■ THE TOP TEN FRANCHISES OF 1982

1. McDonald's
2. One Hour Martinizing
3. Hanna Car Wash
4. Parts Plus
5. Domino's Pizza
6. Diet Center
7. Wendy's Old-Fashioned Hamburgers
8. Burger King
9. American International Rent A Car
10. Nutri/System Weight Loss Medical Center

SUMMARY

Small businesses make up the vast majority of our enterprises. The Small Business Administration (SBA) defines a small business as:

1. Manufacturers who have less than 250 employees.
2. Retailers with annual sales of less than $1 million.
3. Wholesalers with annual sales of less than $5 million.

The SBA also defines the five general types of small businesses: service, retail, wholesale, general construction, and manufacturing.

Even though we are increasingly dominated by large corporations, small businesses still thrive because of their unique contributions. They are adaptable and flexible. Smallness allows the firm to make decisions much more quickly than the bureaucratic giants. Because of less overhead costs, small firms can take risks that larger companies cannot. Smaller businesses are better able to serve local needs, and they can offer more specialized goods and services. Also, small business owners are usually more motivated and have more control than do corporate employees. However, small companies have problems in raising capital and attracting key employees. Because of their small size, their costs are often greater due to economies of operation. Finally, small firms do not usually have the recognition enjoyed by larger companies.

Small businesses contribute to our business system by stimulating competition, providing new ideas, and serving larger companies. In starting a small business, the first step is a specific business plan. Other early considerations are financing, legal arrangements, taxes, and insurance. Sources of small business financing are owner investment, investment from family and friends, commercial banks, mortgage loans, government agencies, credit from suppliers, finance companies, and venture capital companies.

Small companies succeed when they capitalize on their flexibility, personal contacts, low overhead, and strong owner motivation. However, small businesses have a high failure rate, which can be attributed to the owner's lack of education and experience, inadequate record keeping and planning, and improper handling of finances. According to Dun & Bradstreet, 90% of all business failures are due to poor management.

Entrepreneurs — owners and managers of small businesses — have unique characteristics. Thirty percent have parents who work in skilled or unskilled labor; another 25% have parents who also owned businesses. Enterprisers retain strong values of independence. They demonstrate high achievement needs and prefer to take moderate, calculated risks that they can influence. Finally, independents are motivated to work harder than most people.

The primary source of help for small businesses is the Small Business Administration (SBA), which was created by the federal government with the Small Business Act of 1953. Its main contribution is helping the small business obtain financing, both for start-up and working capital. It also provides management assistance and valuable information for the entrepreneur. Minority businesses get special help from the Office of Minority Business Enterprise (OMBE), created by the Department of Commerce in 1969. Also, professional organizations, such as the Junior Chamber of Commerce, offer crucial assistance.

A franchise is an exclusive agreement between a manufacturing or operating company and independent owners; the franchisor gives the owner (or franchisee) specified privileges to operate in a particular territory, and the owner handles only the franchisor's products. The advantages to the owner are recognition, management assistance, financial assistance, and reduced failure rates. The major disadvantages of franchising are the increasing expense, potential fraudulent practices, reduced independence, and legal confusion. The recent growth rate of franchising has been phenomenal and the future looks bright.

MIND YOUR BUSINESS

Instructions. Indicate whether each statement is true (T) or false (F).

____ 1. An entrepreneur is most commonly the oldest child of the family.

____ 2. Most entrepreneurs are men.

____ 3. Most entrepreneurs are not married.

____ 4. Most entrepreneurs start their first company in their twenties.

____ 5. The entrepreneurial tendency first appears when an individual is between 30 and 40 years of age.

____ 6. When beginning a first business, an entrepreneur typically has a master's degree.

____ 7. The major reason entrepreneurs start their own business is to make money.

____ 8. An entrepreneur typically starts only one business in his or her life.

____ 9. The entrepreneur's high need for achievement is based on his or her relationship with his or her father. .

_____ 10. To be successful in a new venture, the entrepreneur needs an abundance of luck.

_____ 11. Entrepreneurs are frequently in conflict with financers.

_____ 12. A successful entrepreneur relies on no one but himself or herself for critical advice on how to run the company.

_____ 13. Entrepreneurs are excellent planners.

_____ 14. Entrepreneurs are high risk takers (big gamblers).

_____ 15. The only really necessary ingredient for a successful business is money.

See answers at the back of the book.

Source: Adapted from Joseph R. Mancuso, *How To Start, Finance, and Manage Your Own Business*, Englewood Cliffs, New Jersey: Prentice-Hall Publishing Co., 1978.

KEY TERMS

REVIEW QUESTIONS

1. What is a small business? How are the SBA and the CED definitions of small business similar? Different?

2. What are the most popular types of small businesses? Give some local examples of each.

3. Discuss the advantages and disadvantages of small business. What businesses do you know of that provide examples of these?

4. Nationally, what role do small businesses play in terms of: (a) number or percentage of all businesses, (b) percentage of all sales, and (c) percentage of all employees?

5. What specific contributions do small businesses make to our economic system?

6. List the steps that should be taken in starting a small business. What should the business plan include and why is it important? List the sources of business financing with the advantages of each.

7. What factors most contribute to the success of a small business? Discuss the major reasons for small business failure.

8. Define entrepreneur. List and discuss the ways that entrepreneurs differ from most people.

9. What is the SBA and how can it help small business owners?

10. What are the three major types of SBA loans and how do they differ?

11. What are the three major organizations that operate within the SBA? Name each, along with the specific services they provide.

12. What are the three major organizations that assist minority business owners and how, specifically, can they help?

13. What are the four professional organizations, as discussed in the text, that work in the interest of small business?

14. What is a franchise? How does it work? Name at least ten examples of franchises. What franchises have you recently patronized?

15. List and discuss the specific advantages and disadvantages that a franchise offers an owner.

16. What is the future of franchising?

17. What specific questions would you ask before buying a franchise?

CASES

Case 5.1: When Do You Quit?

Jack Hand has owned his own small appliance repair shop for over 23 years. With help from his wife, he has managed to raise three children and get them through college. While he has always worked long hours, he does enjoy being his own boss.

But problems are mounting, and his wife has asked him the very reasonable question, "What is going to happen in the future?" Jack is 49 years old, but his business income has been dropping during the past 5 years until it now averages less than $20,000 per year. They have some savings and they own a couple of small apartments which they rent. The area where the business is located has changed so that the income level of those that live in the area is less than half of what it was a few years ago. Many of his regular customers have moved away, and he has not received enough additional customers to replace a lot of tools and buy some additional equipment. He talked with his banker, who discouraged additional investment at his current location. Jack and his wife have talked seriously about their future, and they have considered several options:

1. They could move. They have found a possible location, and they could also arrange the financing.

2. They could stay where they are and try to hold on until retirement.

3. They could retire now, sell their properties, and invest in blue chip securities. This, along with social security and his retirement fund which he has been carefully building for years, would allow them to maintain their standard of living at close to their current level.

Questions

1. Which alternative do you think they should take? Why?

2. What other alternatives can you think of? Are these better or worse than what they were considering?

Case 5.2: A Fabulous Franchise

Fabulous Franchise Company has approached you about buying a franchise to sell their product in your city. They promote high-cost candies and cakes that appeal primarily to the "gift for the person who has everything" market. Assume that you have funds for the purchase. You are considering the merits of purchasing the franchise and hiring someone else to manage it for you. The owners of Fabulous Franchise say that they expect to lay out several hundred thousand dollars during the next couple of years to build product identity and create a demand for their confections. Since they are just beginning, their products are not yet known in your city.

Questions

1. Make a detailed list of the information that you would require from the company to help you make your decision. Do you think you would be able to obtain all of this information? Explain.

2. Other than the company, where else would you go to look for information? What type of information would you look for?

3. Set the criteria that you think would be necessary for you to reach a decision to buy the franchise.

This is the first of six sections in this book that we have prepared hoping to involve you in a process of career planning. You will be examining yourself and your interest in four different business specializations: management, marketing, finance, and data processing. You will be trying to find out if the business world is appropriate for you and how you can fit into it in the most satisfying way possible.

Career decision making is a long process. You may change your mind often. Our purpose in writing these Careerscopes is to help you to organize your thinking about topics that are important in choosing a career. We will not tell you which specific career you should choose. Instead, we will suggest careers for you to explore, and some guidelines will be provided to help you narrow your choices. **Thomas F. Harrington, Ph.D.** *(Professor of Counselor Education, Northeastern University)* **Arthur J. O'Shea, Ph.D.** *(Professor of Psychology, Boston State College)*

PERSONALITY AND CAREER SATISFACTION

Many psychologists believe there are six basic kinds of people — scientific, artistic, crafts, social, clerical, and business. They also tell us that there are six basic kinds of work environments — the same six — and that you are more likely to find satisfaction if you go into a job that matches your personality.

What kind of person are you? Finding out may help you to develop a career plan that will lead to job satisfaction.

Which one of the following personality types is most like you? Put a check mark in front of those adjectives and statements that most closely describe you. (Obviously, we don't mean to suggest that these descriptions are absolutely accurate, but they should give you a good sense of each personality type.)

Under each personality type, you will find two lists. The one on the left has jobs that provide a work environment that is usually distinctively reflective of the type. To the right, jobs are listed that reflect the type in question and also include a strong business component. Psychological research shows that most of us possess personalities that are a combination of types.

The Scientific Person

___ Analytical

___ Curious

___ Likes science

___ Creative

___ Likes math

___ Intellectual

___ Independent

___ Studious

___ Theoretical

___ Precise

___ Enjoys working alone

___ Organized

___ Philosophical

___ Persevering

___ Enjoys solving problems

The Scientific Worker

Chemist
Physicist
Biologist
Engineer
Mathematician
Physician

The Scientific-Business Worker

Programmer
Sales engineer
Electrical engineer
Systems analyst
Actuary
Technical sales worker

The Artistic Person

____ Imaginative
____ Nonconforming
____ Enjoys music
____ Introspective
____ Sensitive
____ Independent
____ Creative
____ Enjoys writing

____ Impractical
____ Uninhibited
____ Enjoys painting
____ Expressive
____ Unsystematic
____ Critical
____ Complex

The Artistic Worker

Singer
Dancer
Actor/actress
Novelist
Artist
Musician

The Artistic-Business Worker

Industrial designer
Advertising worker
Public relations representative
Advertising copywriter
Radio-TV announcer
Movie-TV producer

The Crafts Person

____ Uncomplicated
____ Conforming
____ Likes to work with hands
____ Practical
____ Prefers the outdoors
____ Mechanical
____ Predictable
____ Shy

____ Unassuming
____ Unphilosophical
____ Detached
____ Blunt
____ Persistent
____ Materialistic
____ Conservative

The Crafts Worker

Carpenter
Auto mechanic
Plumber (pipefitter)
Farmer
Sewing machine operator
Long-distance truck driver

The Crafts-Business Worker

Buyer
Blue-collar worker supervisor
Computer service technician
Warehouse manager
Optician
Agribusiness manager

The Social Person

___ Friendly
___ Trustworthy
___ Helpful
___ Genuine
___ Understanding
___ Open
___ Tolerant
___ Idealistic

___ Kindly
___ Skilled in teaching
___ Sharing
___ Sympathetic
___ Verbal
___ Compassionate
___ Cooperative

The Social Worker

Counselor
Nurse
Secondary school teacher
Social worker
Clinical psychologist
Clergy

The Social-Business Worker

Human resources manager
Labor relations specialist
Employment interviewer
Social service director
Training and development worker
Community recreation director

The Clerical Person

___ Conscientious
___ Organized
___ Likes well-structured tasks
___ Persistent
___ Conventional
___ Efficient
___ Precise
___ Conservative

___ Systematic
___ Orderly
___ Stable
___ Enjoys office work
___ Practical
___ Submissive
___ Conforming

The Clerical Worker

Secretary
Bookkeeper
Bank teller
File clerk
Typist
Receptionist

The Clerical-Business Worker

Credit manager
Accountant
Market researcher
Insurance underwriter
Bank officer
Real estate appraiser

The Business Person

___ Aggressive
___ Energetic
___ Willing to take risks
___ Social
___ Eager to lead
___ Persuasive
___ Ambitious
___ Confident

___ Outgoing
___ Status-seeking
___ Exhibitionistic
___ Daring
___ Personable
___ Materialistic
___ Verbal

The Business Worker

Insurance agent
Investment fund manager
Government administrator

Stockbroker
Real estate agent
Business executive

The lists above show how the business personality combines with the other five types.

You have had a brief introduction to the broad range of occupations within the world of work, with particular emphasis on the business world. A more careful examination of yourself and your vocational future is essential.

In the remaining Careerscopes of this book you will find exercises designed for you to explore your interest in major business areas: the Careerscope in Part II focuses on management; the Careerscope in Part III on marketing; the Careerscope in Part IV on finance; and the Careerscope in Part V on data processing. The Careerscope in Part VI discusses work values commonly associated with the business field.

II

1234567890

1111222333344455566677888 9

THE MANAGING
OF BUSINESS

After completing this chapter, you will be able to:

■ Identify the four basic functions of management.

■ Describe the planning function and give examples of common types of plans.

■ Describe the organizing function.

■ Describe the directing function.

■ Discuss leadership and leadership styles.

■ Distinguish between Theories X, Y, and Z.

■ Describe how the controlling function works and identify four typical problems with controlling.

THE PROCESS
OF MANAGEMENT

Peter Drucker, a $1500-a-day consultant, says that management ability is the most important ingredient in the success of a business or a nation. Regardless of how wealthy a company is, how smart its people are, and how good their intentions, it will soon be turning out bleak status reports unless staffed by capable managers.

Management is the process of accomplishing group objectives through the functions of planning, organizing, directing, and controlling human activities.* **Managers** help accomplish these group objectives by performing the functions of management to get the work done through others. Managers do not actually perform the work themselves; the president of General Motors surely could not single-handedly assemble a Corvette. Like chemical catalysts, managers cause things to happen. When the catalyst is too strong, it becomes a monster to the other elements; when it is too weak, desired actions never happen.

The manager's job is to plan what employees are supposed to do, organize them to do it, direct the employees, and check to see that the work is properly done. Some management positions, especially at lower levels, may include actual work assignments as well as management responsibilities. Figure 6.1 is a diagram of the four management functions.

THE PLANNING FUNCTION

Planning involves establishing objectives and deciding on the strategies and tasks necessary to accomplish the objectives. Planning is primary to the other management functions; it is impossible to organize, direct, and control effectively without proper plans. And planning is demanding. As an experienced manager commented, ''Planning re-

---

* Traditionally, writers of business books also considered staffing as a management function. However, we include staffing in *Human Resources Management* (Chapter 9), as do most current business writers.

quires the accumulation of intricate details, the discipline of highly structured thinking, and the persistence of Sherlock Holmes.'' After discussing planning time periods and offering examples of plans, we will examine the planning process.

The Planning Time Period

Plans may be either short-range or long-range.

Short-range planning. Normally, **short-range plans** cover a period of a year or less. Some people refer to short-range planning as **tactical planning;** that is, they represent tactics for

**Figure 6.1
Functions of management.**

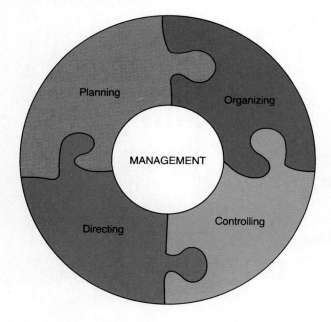

reaching longer-range goals. It should be obvious that short-range plans need to be integrated with long-range plans. But experience shows that too often managers do not attain this coordination. As a result, some short-range plans contribute little or nothing to long-range purposes. A middle manager discusses this hitch: "Our long-range plans called for an ability to increase sales by 40% over a 5-year period. However, we found that budgets had been cut in recruiting and training to meet some temporary, short-term financial projections. This really unraveled our long-range hopes, and we had to alter them."

Long-range planning. Since planning concerns the future, this spurs the question, "How far into the future should managers plan?" In actual practice, planning periods vary widely. But to be long-range, by most definitions, plans must cover more than 1 year into the future. Some companies have **long-range plans** of only 2 years, while others devise 20- or 30-year plans. But the most

The most common form of long-range planning is strategic planning.

common long-range planning period seems to be from 3 to 5 years, and almost all organizations plan for at least 1 year.

The most common form of long-range planning is strategic planning. Typically, **strategic planning** includes (1) determining the major mission of the organization, (2) analyzing the organization's environment, (3) analyzing the organization's internal strengths and weaknesses, (4) setting 5-year targets of accomplishment, and (5) developing strategies for implementing the plans.

Common Types of Plans

In the broadest sense, any provision for the future is a plan. Most plans include objectives, policies, procedures, rules, and budgets.

BUSINESS BULLETIN

Managerial Skills

Managers are responsible for seeing that others (their subordinates) perform the work. To do this effectively, managers must become skilled in the four functions of management discussed in this chapter. And to be successful in a particular position, managers need to develop competencies along three dimensions:

1. *Technical skills.* While it is not necessary for managers to know all the technical aspects of the work they are managing, they must have enough technical knowledge to communicate effectively with their subordinates and superiors. And they must have enough technical knowledge to gain some credibility with their subordinates.

2. *Human skills.* As one writer put it, "Good managers must have a way with people." Managers need to practice good, sincere human relations with their people. A manager can be a technical expert, but if he or she does not generate confidence and commitment from his or her subordinates, the group will be ineffective.

3. *Conceptual skills.* Finally, managers need to be able to think of problems and solutions in a logical and systematic way. Rather than concentrating solely on a short-term solution to an immediate crisis, good managers put all of their smaller decisions in a broader, long-term perspective that benefits the total organization.

Objectives. Objectives, sometimes called goals, are the end result of our efforts. An objective is where we want to be or what we want to have accomplished when finished. While profit is the most frequently mentioned objective, businesses also have objectives of growth, efficiency, increased market share, resource attraction, employee development, public responsibility, and customer service. Well-defined organizational objectives serve managers by (1) establishing priorities, (2) serving as standards against which results are measured, and (3) unifying management-employee efforts.

Many organizations do not get the maximum impact from their objectives because they are improperly conceived and stated. To be effective, objectives should be:

- Challenging yet realistic.
- Stated in specific, measurable terms.
- Strongly supported by superiors.
- Able to generate enthusiasm and commitment from subordinates.
- Communicated to all subordinates involved in attaining the objectives.
- Put in writing.
- Regularly discussed at departmental meetings.

Policies. Policies are plans that guide thinking. They create boundaries that encourage consistent decisions throughout the many facets of the company. Firms create policies in nearly all areas, including employee relations, financial commitments, profit, growth, community relations, and sales. Policies may be broad as "satisfaction guaranteed," for example. They may be more specific, such as "satisfaction guaranteed or money refunded in full if returned within 10 days." Either way, managers use some discretion in interpreting the policy. They do not decide, in this example, whether the company sells on credit, but they may have to determine what "satisfaction guaranteed" means.

Procedures. More limiting than policies, **procedures** are specific guides to action. They outline steps for such activities as hiring, requesting capital equipment, accounting for inventory, re-

Companywide procedures provide guidelines for action at all levels of large firms.

questing transfers, returning merchandise, utilizing scrap, and the like. An example of a purchasing procedure reads, "To purchase supplies, you must complete four copies of Purchase Requisition Form PR-3A. The yellow copy goes to your manager, the green copy to purchasing, and the pink copy to the business office. Keep the white copy for your files."

Critics complain that procedures are bureaucratic and time-wasting red tape. Employees may become impatient with procedures they do not understand and usually feel that they create unnecessary paperwork. The purpose of procedures, however, is to help managers and employees complete their work efficiently.

Rules. Narrowing still further, **rules** are specific guides to action. Rules tell people what they can and cannot do in well-defined situations. Rules need no interpretation and allow no exceptions. "Hard hats must be worn in this area" and "An employee will be given a three-day layoff for his/her third absence in a six-month period" are examples of rules.

Budgets. Budgets express future expectations in numbers. Cash budgets predict the need for

TABLE 6.1 ■ EXAMPLES OF COMMON PLANS FOR AN ACTUAL ORGANIZATION

Objectives	1.	To gain a reputation as the most reputable and innovative firm in the industry within 10 years.
	2.	To earn an annual rate of 10% on investment.
	3.	To improve sales by 15% each year for the next 3 years.
Policies	1.	We promote employees on the basis of skill value, performance, and tenure.
	2.	We extend credit to customers with good ratings.
	3.	Our product standards exceed those of our major competitors.
Procedures	1.	To purchase capital equipment, three copies of Form 304-B must be prepared, showing justifications for the purchase. The original and one copy go to purchasing; retain one copy for your files. Requests above $2000 must be approved by the finance manager.
	2.	On customer complaints, salespeople must make a record of the complaint on Form 601, including the specific reason for the complaint. Unless the item shows obvious customer abuse, the customer must be allowed to exchange the item or receive a cash refund. If there is customer abuse, refer the customer to the sales manager.
Rules	1.	Lunch breaks will be from 12:00 P.M. to 1:00 P.M. for all employees.
	2.	All employees in the assembly area must wear steel shoes, protective clothing, and goggles.
	3.	Employee theft will result in automatic termination.

cash; operating and expense budgets show profit expectations; and sales forecasts estimate future sales. But budgets need not be financial. Labor budgets, for instance, are expressed in hours. Tables 6.1 and 6.2 show common examples of plans.

The Planning Process

Effective managers follow a logical, well-developed approach to planning, similar to the steps in scientific decision making.

Recognize opportunities. Certainly, good planning requires awareness of opportunities. Can we offer a desirable service? Is there any historical evidence of a contrary need? What does our market research tell us? Are our competitors doing anything of concern? Can we obtain additional resources? Can we produce or market additional but similar lines? Great successes occur when a manager has the insight to recognize an opportunity.

Select planning objectives. Each plan must have a purpose. Where is it leading us? What is the target? Without a clear, measurable objective, a plan will fail. Conversely, a precise goal gives direction and meaning to the planning steps.

Identify and create alternatives. Effective planners try to identify several alternatives for reaching and planning objectives. At this stage, creative thinking is important because some of the best alternatives may not be immediately obvious.

Evaluate alternatives. Precise evaluation of alternatives is crucial. Each alternative must be judged in light of the objectives. Success requires a careful study of the advantages and disadvantages of each plausible alternative. What are the costs? What are the probable outcomes? Do we

TABLE 6.2 ■ EXAMPLE OF BUDGET PLANNING

Projected Labor Budget for Project 29			
Work Station	*Hours*	*Rate*	*Estimated Cost*
Cutting	500	$7.00	$3500
Lathes	100	8.50	850
Assembly	230	8.20	1886
Finishing	80	8.40	672
Shipping	100	7.00	700
TOTALS	1010		$7608

have the necessary resources? How much time will it take?

Select an alternative. If we have performed the previous steps carefully, we can be more confident of our selection. However, the pros and cons of each alternative may be unclear. Managers never have all information they would like and they cannot be sure they have chosen the correct alternative; still, they have to make a selection.

Follow-up. Because of uncertainties and imperfect decision makers, even the best plans need to be checked. Follow-up continually checks the plan and helps a manager decide whether it is best to switch to other alternatives.

THE ORGANIZING FUNCTION

While the planning function provides purpose and direction to the company, the **organizing** function makes it possible to pursue these plans collectively. Because organization structure is so important and rather complex, we devote Chapter 7 to this topic. In this section, we will discuss the purposes of organization, how managers relate to the organization's structure, and the benefits of an effective organization.

The Purpose of Business Organization

The theory of business organization presents five major purposes:

1. To provide the structure for defining job functions, descriptions, and relationships.
2. To establish lines of authority and responsibility. Organization makes clear who is in charge and who is responsible for what tasks.
3. To create communication channels. The organizational structure establishes channels for upward, downward, and interdepartmental communication.
4. To establish methods for reaching organizational objectives.
5. To provide for hiring and placement of human resources. As a company hires employees, the employees join a department, branch, or division with specific duties.

How Levels of Management Differ

Within complex organizations, there exist various levels of management. We can divide managers into three levels: top management, middle management, and operating management (see Fig. 6.2).

**Figure 6.2
Pyramid of management levels with examples of responsibilities.**

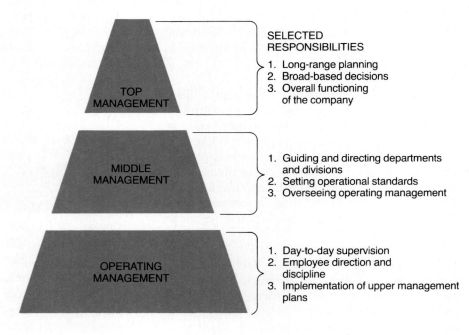

SELECTED RESPONSIBILITIES

TOP MANAGEMENT
1. Long-range planning
2. Broad-based decisions
3. Overall functioning of the company

MIDDLE MANAGEMENT
1. Guiding and directing departments and divisions
2. Setting operational standards
3. Overseeing operating management

OPERATING MANAGEMENT
1. Day-to-day supervision
2. Employee direction and discipline
3. Implementation of upper management plans

TABLE 6.3 ■ TOP PAY FOR TOP MANAGEMENT

	Salary	Bonus	Total
John H. Gutfreund, *cochairman,* Phibro-Salomon	$344,495	$2,200,000	$2,544,495
Robert Anderson, *chairman,* Rockwell International	$977,083	$1,340,560	$2,317,643
Steven J. Ross, *chairman,* Warner Communications	$350,000	$1,951,497	$2,301,497
Henry Kaufman, *vice president,* Phibro-Salomon	$264,495	$1,880,000	$2,144,495
Gedale Horowitz, *vice president,* Phibro-Salomon	$264,495	$1,880,000	$2,144,495
Donald R. Beall, *president,* Rockwell International	$668,333	$ 804,336	$1,472,669
Fred Hartley, *chairman,* Union Oil Co. of California	$561,667	$ 838,675	$1,400,342
Rawleigh Warner, Jr., *chairman,* Mobil	—	—	$1,388,072
Clifton C. Garvin, Jr., *chairman,* Exxon	$800,000	$ 536,350	$1,336,250
Harry J. Gray, *chairman,* United Technologies	$760,350	$ 520,000	$1,280,350

Source: Company proxy statements.

Top management. Top management develops the broad plans for the company and makes decisions that shape the direction 2 to 10 years or more into the future. Through careful analysis, top managers establish major objectives of the firm, based upon the resources and capabilities of the company. While they spend a lot of time planning, they must also guide their team through effective organizing, directing, and controlling. Top managers usually go by such titles as chairman, president, vice-president, treasurer, and secretary (see Table 6.3).

Middle management. Middle management, including levels below top management and above operating management, does the tasks of top management but on a more specialized level. Middle managers are usually responsible for certain areas, departments, divisions, or subdepartments of the team. They make decisions and carry out plans within the broad guidelines set by top management. Titles may include department head, divisional manager, head buyer, chief engineer, plant manager, regional manager, and so on.

FUNNY BUSINESS

Drawing by Saxon; © 1982 The New Yorker Magazine, Inc.

"I suggest you take your proposition to Mr. Hodkiss at the office. He may send you to Sam Watson or Bob Exum. Eventually, of course, you will have to talk to me."

Operating management. At the lowest management level, **operating management** is re-

Most authorities believe that operating management is the hardest of all management positions because they have to get employees to do what upper-level management has planned.

sponsible for putting into operation the plans of higher and middle management. On the firing line, operating managers direct their people to get the work out. Most authorities believe that this is the hardest of all management positions because operating managers have to get employees to do what upper-level management has planned. Supervisor and foreman are the most common titles of operating managers. While all these managers perform the functions of management, they do not spend the same amount of time and energy in each function. Figure 6.3 shows how management effort at differing levels relate to function.

TAKING STOCK

Educational Backgrounds of Successful Managers

Psychologists Douglas Bray and Ann Howard have for more than 25 years been studying college graduates in entry-level management ranks for AT&T. Here are some of their findings:

1. Master's degrees can be helpful. Howard says of master's degree holders, "They bring us greater administrative and interpersonal skills and more motivation for status and money, but they're not any smarter." This applied equally to holders of an M.A., M.S., and M.B.A.

2. There are key differences between technical and nontechnical majors. Business majors led the pack in organizing, planning, and decision-making skills. Humanities and social science graduates also scored high. Math, science, and engineering majors scored much lower in these skills. Technical majors did have higher general mental ability, but they were not as creative or as good at interpersonal skills. As you might expect, social science majors were quite low on quantitative skills. Business majors were the ones most eager to get ahead.

For future managers, AT&T is still looking for about a third each of business, technical, and liberal arts majors. While they are still looking for master's degrees, some firms say the era of the M.B.A. has passed. Many companies offer the same management training programs for their new people, whether or not they have a master's degree.

Regardless of the success/failure studies of managers, educational background is probably less important than the actual skills that people develop. Leo J. Corbett, vice-president of sales management for Salomon Brothers, says, "We're really looking for a particular kind of person, rather than a particular degree."

Source: Peter Hall, "Surprise! Liberal Arts Students Make the Best Managers," *Business Week's Guide to Careers,* Fall/Winter, 1983, pp. 16–19.

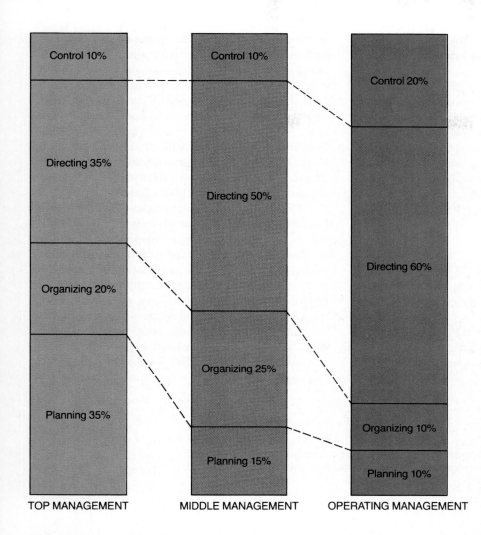

Control 10%

Control 10%

Control 20%

Directing 35%

Directing 50%

Directing 60%

Organizing 20%

Planning 35%

Organizing 25%

Organizing 10%

Planning 15%

Planning 10%

TOP MANAGEMENT

MIDDLE MANAGEMENT

OPERATING MANAGEMENT

**Figure 6.3
Distribution of a
manager's time.** *Source:
Adapted from H. Mintzberg,*
The Nature of Managerial
Work, *New York: Harper &
Row, 1975.*

THE DIRECTING FUNCTION

After we have planned where the company is going and organized people to accomplish goals, we push the starter button. **Directing** leads employees to carry out company objectives by performing their duties. **Leadership,** the exercise of influence and power, is necessary to perform the directing function. Without leadership, the department or company drifts aimlessly, but effective leaders give form and purpose to the group. They seek out, identify, and articulate group objectives and influence subordinates to work toward these objectives. Communicating and motivating are also important to the directing function; we cover these topics in detail in Chapter 10.

Theories of Leadership

The study of leadership has travelled many paths. One of the earliest ideas of leadership was the **traitist theory,** a belief that capable leaders have personality traits that differentiate them from ineffectual leaders. This theory specifies personality criteria such as intelligence, initiative, tenacity, fairness, and creativity. A few traitists still exist, but this approach lost much of its thrust because researchers could not agree on a list of traits.

Later, the **situationalist theory** developed, which states that traits necessary for leadership vary according to the situation. A construction crew foreman might require different leadership traits than a manager of a shoe department. Situationalists do not believe in absolute leaders who emerge in any situation; rather, they say the situation dictates the leader. The same group might prefer one individual for its work supervisor, another to captain its softball team, and still another to plan the office party. The situational approach switched the emphasis from leaders to situations.

More recently, theorists have been considering both traits and situations, and they add a relational dimension. These comprehensive theories consider such variables as leadership personality, nature of the job, characteristics of the employees, and the relationship between leaders and followers.

Leadership Styles

To the practicing manager, leadership styles are more important than theory. There are three predominate leadership styles: autocratic, democratic, and free-rein (laissez faire). **Autocratic leaders** make decisions without consulting their subordinates. Autocrats tend to be dogmatic and task-oriented, and they fully expect subordinates to heed their commands. **Democratic leaders,** by contrast, involve their subordinates in decision making. Before making a major decision, a democratic leader will get opinions and ideas from staff. Democratic leaders, though they may hold high expectations, tend to be more open, cooperative, and supportive than autocrats. **Free-rein leaders** provide very little, if any, direction to their subordinates. Rather, they leave their subordinates to figure things out for themselves. Figure 6.4 shows this range of leadership styles.

Some assume that one style of leadership is best for all situations, that there is an "ideal" style. However, the **contingency approach** to leadership assumes that different situations require different leadership styles. For instance, if a leader were in charge of a group of immature employees performing routine tasks, an autocratic style might be more effective. By contrast, a very mature and responsible work group would probably respond better to a more democratic or even free-rein style. **Style flexibility** is the ability of leaders to adapt their style to the situation.

Figure 6.4
Range of leadership styles. *Source: Adapted from Robert Tannenbaum and Warren H. Schmidt, "How to Choose a Leadership Pattern,"* Harvard Business Review, *March– April, 1958, p. 96.*

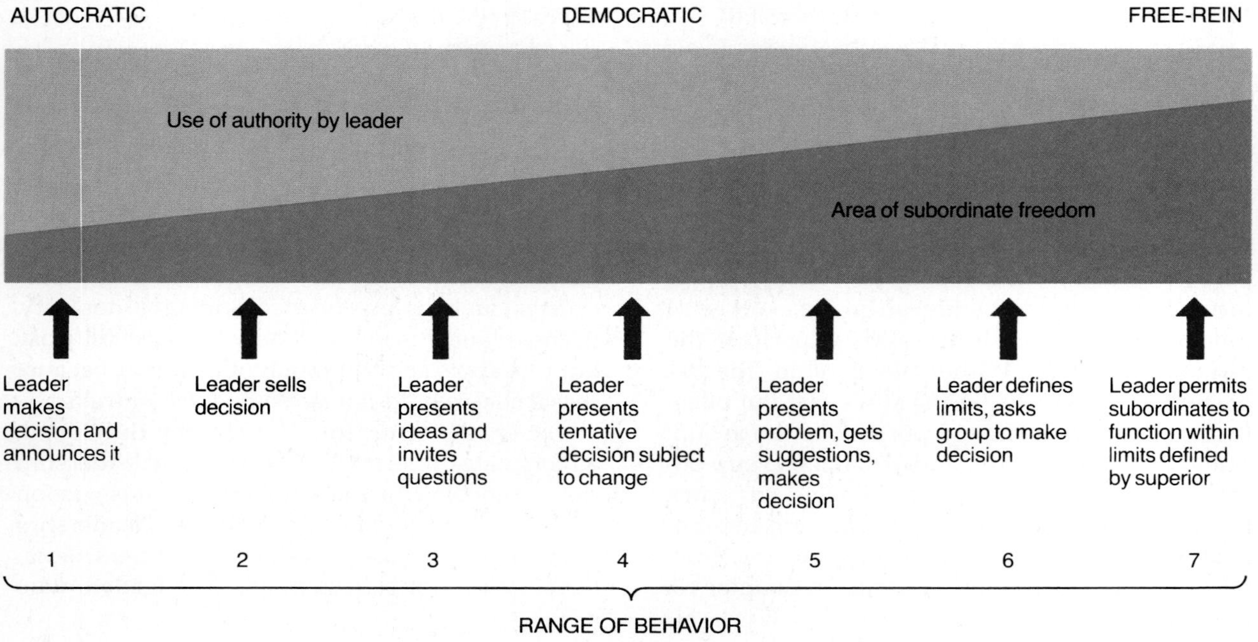

AUTOCRATIC			DEMOCRATIC			FREE-REIN
Use of authority by leader						
					Area of subordinate freedom	
Leader makes decision and announces it	Leader sells decision	Leader presents ideas and invites questions	Leader presents tentative decision subject to change	Leader presents problem, gets suggestions, makes decision	Leader defines limits, asks group to make decision	Leader permits subordinates to function within limits defined by superior
1	2	3	4	5	6	7

RANGE OF BEHAVIOR

THEORY X ASSUMPTIONS	THEORY Y ASSUMPTIONS
1. Most people work as little as possible.	1. It is as natural to work as it is to play.
2. Most people lack ambition.	2. Most people exercise self-direction toward the objectives to which they are committed.
3. Most people avoid responsibility.	3. Most people seek responsibility under the proper conditions.
4. Most people prefer to be led.	4. Imagination and creativity are widespread throughout the population.
5. By nature, most people resist change.	5. Motivation and desire for improving are widespread throughout the population.
6. Most people are rather gullible and uninformed.	6. People will be committed to objectives if they receive rewards for attaining them.
7. Without management direction, most subordinates would do very little to serve the organization.	

Figure 6.5
Theory X and Theory Y leadership assumptions.

Theory X and Theory Y

Noted researcher Douglas McGregor, recognizing that leaders could choose from wide ranges of behavior, said that much leader behavior is the result of how the leader views people. To make this point, McGregor identified two opposing sets of assumptions that leaders make about people. He labelled these assumptions **Theory X** and **Theory Y** (see Fig. 6.5).

CROSS FIRE

Do We Have a Shortage of Executive Leaders?

"Wanted: corporate leaders. Mere managers need not apply," is the title of an article in the May 30, 1983 issue of *Fortune* magazine. Warren Bennis, Professor of Management at the University of Southern California School of Business Administration, says, "Business schools are training people who are good staff members but not good leaders." Do we have, as Bennis and others suggest, a shortage of effective leadership in our corporations?

Whereas managers focus on doing things right, leaders focus on doing the right things. Critics suggest that we have lost some of the fabric for creating leaders. Parents, because their children are involved in so many activities outside the home, no longer pass along strong values needed for success in leadership. Companies, because they want to maintain good images, do not allow subordinates and others to diagnose their failures, a necessary ingredient for building leaders. Bureaucratic organizations encourage teamwork and harmony at the expense of experimentation and failure. Business schools, with their emphasis on logical, rational, financial analysis, reduce risk taking, also a necessity of leadership.

Others suggest that the critics are being too harsh. At any time in history, we can make a case for producing more and better leadership in our corporations and in society. However, this does not mean that our current approach is ineffective in producing good leaders.

Do you think that we have a severe shortage of leaders running our business corporations today? Why?

___ A. Definitely, yes

___ B. Probably, yes

___ C. Probably, no

___ D. Definitely, yes

Noted researcher Douglas McGregor argued that the assumptions leaders had about their employees actually had a lot to do with how subordinates behaved; the assumptions became self-fulfilling.

McGregor argued that the assumptions of the leader had a lot to do with how subordinates actually behaved. In other words, the assumptions became a self-fulfilling prophecy. That is, if you believe something to be true, you act as if it were true, and your actions make your belief come true.

To illustrate, suppose a leader believes that most of her subordinates are hard-bitten Theory Xs. Because the leader assumes that employees

BULLETIN

BUSINESS

In Search of Excellence

Professional managers have forgotten how sloppy, irrational, and spontaneous the real world can be. Rather, they have come to think of organizations as rational, scientific devices. At least, this is the contention of Thomas J. Peters and Robert H. Waterman, Jr. In their *New York Times* number 1 best-seller, *In Search of Excellence,* the authors contend that successful businesses pay attention to the basics: customer service, concern for employees, low-cost manufacturing, innovation, and risk taking. Their book has been so successful that each day brings ten to fifteen mail requests for speeches and consulting work, and the phone rings constantly.

Through extensive research, the authors identified America's best-run companies. Their question was, "How do the most successful companies differ from other organizations?" Their answer lists eight characteristics that make the best-run companies excellent.

1. *Bias for action.* "Do it, fix it, try it" is the motto of successful companies. These companies had many small groups of people informally trying new things, working on new products, and in general doing something. "The most important and visible outcropping of the action bias in excellent companies," write Peters and Waterman, "is their willingness to try things out, to experiment." McDonald's, one of the successful companies, has more experimental menu items, store formats, and pricing plans than any of its competition.

2. *Close to the customer.* In well-managed companies, the most important element is the customer — more important than technology, more important than product, and more important than strategy. IBM, as an example, is fanatical about customer service. They promote some of their best salespeople to assistants for top officers. While in this position, typically 3 years, they do only one thing — answer every customer complaint within a 24-hour period. Excellent companies also want to give their customers the best quality possible. The major objective at Maytag is "ten years trouble-free operation" from any machine.

3. *Autonomy and entrepreneurship.* Small firms produce about twenty-four times as many creations as large firms, according to a National Science Foundation study. Successful large firms also encourage this innovation. In many excellent companies, bands of eight to ten people work in corners, hallways, conference rooms, and any place they can find, energetically creating new products.

are lazy and gullible, the leader will employ a directive, autocratic leadership style. After a period of time, most employees will rebel against this smothering direction by doing only what they have to, resisting management, avoiding responsibility, and calling in sick at the first sniffle. Then the leader will say, "See there, I was right. They will not do anything unless you make them." But suppose the leader assumes that most employees are Theory Ys. This leader, believing that subordinates are mature and responsible, will tend to use a more democratic, supportive leadership style. Employees, after a period, will respond by taking responsibility, acting maturely, and not calling in sick even when feeling badly. This leader is likely to brag that "I have a good group of employees. They're cooperative, motivated, and work themselves to a frazzle on tough projects."

Are most subordinates like Theory Y, or is this just wishful thinking? In reality, few of us are pure

4. *Productivity through people.* Managers of effective organizations really do believe that people will respond well if you treat them as adults. A researcher in one study asked twenty Hewlett-Packard executives why their company was successful. Eighteen of the twenty spontaneously said, "It is our people-oriented philosophy." Founder Bill Hewlett puts it this way, "It is the tradition of treating every individual with consideration and respect and recognizing personal achievements." They call it "The HP way."

5. *Hands-on, value-driven.* To the authors, this means good companies pay a lot of attention to values. Founders and executives spend a lot of time encouraging and reinforcing their key values. The shared values create teamwork. For instance, an executive at Delta Airlines explains, "There is a special relationship between Delta and its personnel that is rarely found in any firm, generating a team spirit that is evident in the individual's cooperative attitude . . . , cheerful outlook on life, and pride in a job well done."

6. *Stick to the knitting.* This simply means keep doing what you do best, what has made you successful. Former University of Texas football coach Darrel Royal put it this way, "We are going to dance with the people that brung us." Many firms make a mistake by diversifying into too many areas. Sooner or later, they get into trouble.

7. *Simple form, lean staff.* Bigness tends to create complexity. Not so with effective organizations. They want to keep their structure simple, clear, and autonomous. They also want a lean staff, that is, too few rather than too many assistants. One official said, "I believe management is more effective when they cannot control everything."

8. *Simultaneous loose-tight properties.* The excellent companies believe in freedom to fail, experimentation, risk taking, room to perform, and the like; but every one of them was also a stern disciplinarian. Employees could do many things on their own, but if they violated a key value like customer service, they were out of a job.

Source: Thomas J. Peters and Robert H. Waterman, Jr., *In Search of Excellence,* New York: Harper & Row Publishers, 1982.

Theory X or Theory Y. But we tend to lean in one direction or the other. Because some people had Theory X parents, teachers, or previous employers, they may have become a Theory X before they ever went to work. And if a leader tries to treat a Theory X employee with a Theory Y management style, the results are often plainly disastrous. If an employee insists on being a Theory X, leaders would probably be more effective in getting their attention by presenting the work in a tougher style. Then after the leader has the confidence of the employee, he can try to bring him along toward a Theory Y by using a more democratic, supportive approach.

Theory Z

Theory Z management emerged in the 1970s, primarily as a result of the Japanese influence on our markets. Professor William Ouchi, in his best-selling book, *Theory Z*, described the principles of **Theory Z.** In essence, Theory Z includes the following:

1. *Commitment to lifetime employment.* For all practical purposes, when a company hires an employee, the company commits to employing the person until retirement.

2. *Slow evaluation and promotion.* Evaluations occur over a relatively long period of time, and promotions come very slowly.

3. *Consensus decision making.* Managers encourage input into decisions by all who will be affected by the decision. Also, they try to reach a consensus; that is, everyone agrees, at least to some extent, with the decision.

4. *Collective responsibility.* Responsibility for success or failure of the organization is shared by the group as a whole. One individual is not necessarily responsible for more productivity than another.

5. *Informal, implicit control.* Within the formal organization, younger employees are not expected to disagree with or rebel against their superior managers. However, managers are expected to take their employees out for frequent social gatherings. In these settings, employees can make their disagreements known in a subtle, kidding way.

6. *Wholistic concern for employees.* The company's influence extends into almost all aspects of their employees' lives. The company sponsors many group vacations and social outings, and it may subsidize their employees' housing and transportation.

While most of these ideas may have emerged from the Japanese culture, Ouchi's description of Theory Z management was largely derived from the practices of American companies.

THE CONTROLLING FUNCTION

After charting the course, organizing the members, and directing employees, managers complete their duties by making periodic readings and corrections. The word "control" evokes a host of meanings, many of which are negative. But the essence of **controlling** is adjustment—checking actual events against plans and reconciling the differences. More specifically, controlling involves the following: (1) management sets standards of performance covering some future time period, (2) they measure the actual performance during the period, (3) they compare actual to expected performance, and (4) they reconcile the difference between the actual and the expected performance. Sometimes this means finding out why things did not go right and figuring out what to change in the future. Other times, it might mean reexamining plans to see if they were off base. A manager described his controlling function in this way, "I keep a constant check on how well we are doing by looking at weekly and monthly reports. Since we plan our work well in advance, I know where we are supposed to be each week. When we are behind or ahead of our plans, I have to find out why. If something unusual happened, I probably will not make any changes. But if we fall behind consistently, I have to find out why and make some changes."

How Controlling Works

Controlling begins with plans. As you recall from the earlier part of the chapter, objectives tell us where we are going. Policies, procedures, rules, and budgets offer guidelines as to how to get there. We begin controlling by communicating these plans to all the people involved in the effort.

Communicating expectations. Managers begin the controlling process by communicating plans to all the people involved. People should know exactly what is expected of them. And they should know what is expected of the group effort. Good communication helps prevent problems and provides a benchmark by which to judge performance.

Getting feedback. After we develop and communicate plans, we need information on the progress of actual events. This is the role of feedback. Feedback may vary from simple observations such as taking a look now and then to very complex, computer-based monitoring techniques.

BUSINESS BULLETIN

Better Communication

On the average, 25% of all management messages are lost at each organizational level. There is little doubt that effective management communications can improve productivity, employee commitment, and morale.

Most managers can significantly improve their communications and productivity by following five basic guidelines:

1. Communicate your overall purpose. To help ensure top performance, high morale, and low turnover, and to make your employees feel wanted, needed, indeed, indispensable to the success of the organization, it is important that they have a good sense of their job and just how it relates to the company as a whole.

2. Communicate your expectations. Effective communicators tell their people exactly what they expect, and they provide tangible performance standards to subordinates. It is better to say, "We need the entire report completed by Tuesday the 10th, with no errors," than to say, "We'd like to have this as quickly as possible." The first request is specific; the second is vague.

3. Provide feedback on performance. People need and want to know how they are doing. No communication responsibility is more important than this. Annual performance reviews are the most common ways of providing feedback, but they are frequently ineffective because (1) the manager does not honestly tell the subordinate what he or she needs to improve upon, and (2) subordinates need much more information than what is in the annual review.

4. Communicate all changes. People do not like to be surprised, and when they are, they usually act with distrust. Subordinates react much better to change when they know in advance that change is coming. Also, if at all possible, let the people affected by the change have a chance to comment upon the proposed change before it actually occurs.

5. Communicate face to face. Effective communicators get out of their office to spend time with their people where the people work. It is much better for a manager to go to an employee's work station than to call employees into the manager's office for discussion. During these personal contacts, it is important that managers communicate openly and directly. Do not hold back information; rather, share it naturally and easily.

Exchanging information and ideas is vital to fulfilling management's controlling function.

Some examples of feedback include such historical information as financial records, turnover reports, sales figures, and quality control records. Other data are more immediate, for example, supervisors watching and checking employees' work methods. Whatever its form, to be useful, feedback must allow us to compare the actual with the expected.

Evaluating results. When activities compare favorably to plans, we assume things are going well. But suppose events do not match exactly (and they hardly ever do) with what we expected. To evaluate the difference, we raise the questions: How much deviation is allowed? What caused the deviation? Are events out of line, or were the plans off? The analysis of these questions may come in rule-of-thumb judgments or through complex cause-and-effect formulas.

Reconciling the differences. When deviations fall outside an allowed limit, we want to correct them. If some unusual event caused the deviation—the salesperson was ill and did not work 3 days—we probably would let it go without making any changes. But if the difference becomes consistent, we need to fix it. Correcting actual events may require training, improved procedures, reassigning or adding personnel, using different types of people, managing more effectively, getting more information, using different equipment, and so on. But improperly set plans can also cause deviations. If the objective is far too high, we are not likely to achieve it consistently, regardless of how determined our efforts are at plucking the prize. In this case, management needs to restudy its information and set more realistic goals.

Major Problems in Controlling

Control methods are an attempt to prevent and correct problems, but they sometimes create problems of their own.

High cost of control. Control costs money. Quality control departments in some companies have budgets running into hundreds of thousands of dollars. If we compute the hours managers spend in everyday control functions—budgeting, performance appraisal, correcting mistakes, and constructive criticism—the total cost mounts.

Repressive control. Sometimes managers place so many demands on their employees, trying to control their behavior, the controls become repressive. This overcontrol may gain observable compliance, but employees become frustrated, tense, and anxiety-ridden. They express their resistance in creating alibis, slanting the truth, passing the buck, and undercutting the boss's wishes. At the same time, job satisfaction and morale go down, while absenteeism and turnover go up.

Objective displacement. Displacement occurs when policies, procedures, and rules become more important than objectives. Guidelines are necessary, but their only purpose is to help people achieve the organization's objectives more effectively. Too often, policies, procedures, and rules outlive their usefulness, yet someone in the organization may insist on following them.

Feedback problems. Control relies on feedback as a measure of success, but some managers get so involved with the numbers that they forget other important issues. And sometimes employees and managers try to manipulate measurement data just to make the numbers look good. In fact, overemphasis on numbers may lead employees to inaccurate reporting, distrust, and hostility.

THE MANAGEMENT PROCESS AND THE ENTREPRENEUR

This chapter has presented management in the context of large organizations. While these concepts do apply to small business entrepreneurs, applications may differ. Entrepreneurs still plan, organize, direct, and control their organizations, but they do it on a smaller scale and with fewer people. Typically, this means that the manager is unable to specialize. For instance, large organizations will likely have different managers for sales, finance, production, and so on. Each of these managers is specialized. However, in smaller organizations, one manager may be responsible for sales, finance, hiring, discipline, customer service, inventory control, and sweeping up after closing the doors.

Lack of specialization may be a drawback, but small business managers also have some advantages over larger companies. For instance, employees today insist on participation in decision making. Larger companies are trying to do this, but smaller companies can probably do it more effectively. Because smaller companies are more informal and spontaneous, it is easier for the manager to seek input from employees in decision making. Further, participation requires a lot of

A computer game under development receives an impromptu staff appraisal. Such informality is often the rule in the small startup companies of this growth industry.

information. Again, smaller companies, with their informal associations between manager and employee, can more easily communicate information to the employees. Small companies also are better able to get their people to think about themselves as a total group, as a team. Smaller companies are less likely to have separate dining and parking privileges for management and employees, and this makes it more comfortable for them to work together as a team. Finally, smaller organizations can be more flexible in dealing with their employees. If, for example, a single parent needs to schedule unique working hours, the small business manager is more likely to be aware of this and more likely to be able to accommodate the worker.

SUMMARY

Management functions include planning, organizing, directing, and controlling. Planning is deciding in advance the objectives to be accomplished and developing guidelines for reaching them. Nearly all companies have monthly and yearly plans; many plan for 5 years and some plan for 20 or 30 years.

Examples of common plans are objectives, policies, procedures, rules, and budgets. Effective planners follow a sequential, rational approach to the planning process, including the following steps: recognize opportunities, select planning objectives, identify and create alternatives, and follow up.

Organizing is the management process of arranging employees of a business so that they can best accomplish the organization's objectives. Lines of authority and channels of communication are established. Organizing is most often accomplished by means of an organization chart. Such a chart also provides structure for the organization and methods for hiring and training employees.

There are three basic levels of management: top management, middle management, and operations management. At each of these levels, the manager's time is divided into a different combination of management processes. Effective organization provides many worthwhile benefits to a company.

Directing involves leading, motivating, and aiding employees toward the accomplishment of the firm's objectives. It ensures that tasks are performed properly. The process of control includes communicating plans, checking actual events against plans, and correcting the differences. While there are some negative effects of control, it is necessary to be certain that efforts are successful and effective.

MIND YOUR BUSINESS

Instructions. Check your knowledge of the management process by answering true (T) or false (F) to the following questions.

____ 1. When you get into management, success depends only upon human, interpersonal skills; technical skills are not needed.

____ 2. To be effective, objectives need to meet all of the following requirements: challenging but realistic, specific and measurable, supported by superiors, and communicated to all people in the organization.

____ 3. Procedures are guides to thinking, while policies are specific guides to action.

____ 4. One purpose of organizing is to define job functions, descriptions, and relationships.

____ 5. "Most people work as little as possible," is a Theory Y assumption.

____ 6. "Commitment to lifetime employment," is an aspect of Theory Y.

____ 7. Excellently managed organizations tend to have a strong bias for action, that is, doing something.

____ 8. High cost is a problem with most control systems.

____ 9. It is easier to get employee participation in smaller organizations than it is in larger ones.

____ 10. Research clearly shows that a business or M.B.A. degree will more likely lead to managerial success than a liberal arts degree.

See answers at the back of the book.

KEY TERMS

management, 130
manager, 130
planning, 130
short-range planning, 130
tactical planning, 130
long-range planning, 131
strategic planning, 131
objective, 132
policy, 132
procedure, 132
rule, 132
budget, 132
organizing, 134
top management, 135
middle management, 135
operating management, 136
directing, 137
leadership, 137
traitist theory, 137
situationalist theory, 137
autocratic leadership, 138
democratic leadership, 138
free-rein leadership, 138
contingency leadership, 138
style flexibility, 138
Theory X, 139
Theory Y, 139
Theory Z, 142
controlling, 142

REVIEW QUESTIONS

1. What is a manager? What do managers do?

2. Define planning. How far into the future do managers plan? Explain. Distinguish between strategic planning and tactical planning.

3. Identify and describe the most common types of plans.

4. Explain the planning process and identify the six major steps to planning.

5. Define organizing. What is involved in the organizing process?

6. Identify the levels of management with examples of job titles for each.

7. How do the levels of management differ?

8. Explain the differences of duties for each of the three levels of managers.

9. What are the benefits of good organization?

10. Define directing. What does it involve?

11. Discuss the theories of leadership.

12. What is the difference between a Theory X and a Theory Y manager? How does Theory Z differ?

13. Define controlling. How does an organizational control system work?

14. Explain the four major steps in the controlling process.

15. Describe the four major problems of the controlling process.

CASES

Case 6.1: A Tough Leader?

Phil Drew is the supervisor of a construction crew. He often argues with his people, berates them, and curses when they make mistakes. Turnover is high, but Phil can always hire additional people because the pay is good and unemployment is high in the local area. The workers despise Phil, but they work pretty hard because they do not want him on their backs all day. They are actually afraid of Phil, who has been known to become violent from time to time. The crew seldom talks back and they stay out of his way as much as possible. Phil can never leave, even for a few minutes, because the crew will loaf around or ruin a job.

Phil is known by contractors as a very responsible supervisor who gets the job done on time and in the manner planned. They know that once Phil agrees to do a job they can depend upon him.

Questions

1. How would you analyze Phil's leadership style?

2. Would you like to work for Phil? Why?

3. Would you like Phil to work for you? Why?

4. Would you regard Phil as a good leader? Explain.

Case 6.2: A Business Failure

As director of marketing for the Sony Corporation, manufacturers of stereo equipment, Roberta had her hands full. Because she felt the need for more control over her forty-five sales representatives, she quickly designed a complex form that they were to complete after each work day. Because the form took about one hour to complete — mostly on their own time after the day's work — the sales force was up in arms. Roberta insisted upon receiving the forms and has four months' worth on her desk. Roberta has had three secretaries in the past six months. They say they leave because there is not enough flexibility and freedom on the job. They had to deliver coffee to her at precisely the same time, four times a day. If their work was not completed at the end of the day, they stayed late regardless.

Roberta has three regional sales managers, yet she works and communicates directly with each representative whenever possible. She spends most of her time directing her forty-eight salespeople and staff of five. Because of morale problems, turnover, and lack of results, Roberta was put on probation three months ago. Last week she was fired.

Questions

1. Of the six steps of the planning process, which did Roberta fail?

2. Why was Roberta unsuccessful as a leader? What style of leader was she? How could she have changed her tactics and become a more successful leader?

3. What was the one glaring mistake she made with regard to the organizing process? How could better organizing practices have benefited her?

4. Which steps of the control process were ignored by Roberta? What should she have done in order to have been successful?

After completing this chapter, you will be able to:

■ Define the term "corporate culture."

■ Identify and describe the four elements of corporate culture.

■ Describe how heroes, storytellers, and priests help create and promote corporate culture.

■ Relate the importance of rites and rituals to corporate culture.

■ Compare and contrast the four generic corporate cultures.

■ Explain why corporate culture must sometimes be changed.

■ Relate some of the most successful ways of managing corporate culture change.

A
CORPORATE
CULTURE

Every company has a culture. Sometimes we are given insights into this culture by the organizational motto or the things we hear others say about it. For example, General Electric's motto is "Progress is our most important product." From this, we are led to believe that this firm strives to recruit and keep personnel who are highly educated, innovative, creative, and hardworking. Would someone who enjoys working in a stuffy bureaucracy consider applying for a job at GE? Probably not. The corporate culture would be viewed as too threatening to such an individual. Or consider IBM. This company's image is one of quality products and timely service. It is a no-nonsense firm in which people work hard and are well rewarded, but there is no place for laggards or goldbricks.

Corporate culture is the norms, beliefs, attitudes, and philosophies of the organization. Organizational culture is shaped by the values of the people who start the organization and those who carry on its leadership. In successful firms, these managers actually shape and encourage the "right" types of personnel values. In fact, most of these companies share three common organizational culture characteristics: (1) they stand for something, that is, they have a clear and explicit philosophy about how they should conduct their business; (2) management pays a lot of attention to shaping and encouraging values so that they conform to the environment in which the company operates; and (3) these values are both known and shared by the personnel. These characteristics create a sense of identity for the people who work there. The personnel feel special. And this sense of togetherness helps build and maintain high esprit de corps.

Organizations with a strong culture also have an informal system of rules. The personnel know how they are supposed to behave most of the time. A strong culture also helps the personnel feel better about what they are doing. For example, an IBM salesperson can proudly say, "I'm with IBM. It's a great firm!" And the individual means it. He or she feels a commitment to the organization, and this translates into greater efficiency and higher sales.

ELEMENTS OF CULTURE

How does a company create an organizational culture that encourages high productivity, efficiency, and esprit de corps? Often it does so by consciously fashioning a specific value system. For example, during his early years at IBM, Thomas Watson, Jr., taught the salespeople his own personal philosophy of work and life. By putting strong emphasis on selling, urging them not to waste time, and encouraging them always to think, he built the company into the premier office equipment corporation in the world. Today he is gone, but his values live on because the three

The major elements of culture are heroes, rites and rituals, and a communication network.

major elements of culture are still present at IBM: heroes, rites and rituals, and a communication network that conveys Watson's values to every part of the corporation.

Heroes

Heroes are an integral element of corporate culture. They serve as role models for the personnel. People identify with them and attempt to emulate them. Every company has its heroes. Watson was a hero at IBM. Edwin Land, founder of the Polaroid Corporation, has been a hero there for years; young employees are continually encouraged to follow his examples of innovativeness and hard work. Yet it is not necessary to be a giant in the field to serve as a hero or role model in the organization. Consider the following two cases:

> Richard A. Drew, a banjo-playing college dropout working in 3M's research lab in the 1920s, promised to help some colleagues solve a problem they had with masking tape. Soon thereafter, DuPont came out with cellophane. Drew decided he could go DuPont one better and coated the cellophane with a colorless adhesive to bind things together — and Scotch tape was born. In the 3M tradition, Drew carried the ball himself by managing the development up through the ranks; he went on to become technical director of the company and showed other employees just how they could succeed in a similar fashion at 3M.

> Mary Kay Ash, founder of Mary Kay Cosmetics, believes in offering herself as a visible role model to her employees. She trains saleswomen not simply to represent her but to believe that they *are* Mary Kay. To inspire them with her own confidence, she awards diamond bumblebee pins and explains that, according to aerodynamic engineers, the wings of the bumblebee are too weak and the body is too heavy for the insect to fly. But bumblebees don't know this, and so they fly anyway. The message is clear: anyone can be a hero who has the confidence and persistence to try.*

Heroes play a very important role in promoting corporate culture. First, they symbolize the organization to the outside world. Consider some of the popular top managers who do their own commercials, like Lee Iacocca of Chrysler Corporation. These people, heroes in their organization,

convey an image to the TV viewer of the type of company they represent. A second important role played by heroes is preserving what makes the corporation special. The values that have helped bring the company to its current position are maintained, thanks to the hero's ability to inspire emulation by the personnel. Third, the hero helps set a standard of performance in the organization. The hero represents the very best, and, as other employees attempt to emulate this person, they achieve higher standards of performance than would be the case otherwise. Heroes serve to motivate employees.

Rites and Rituals

Rites and rituals are important to corporate culture because they help reinforce desired behavior. For example, when someone does something well, like sell $1 million of insurance, the company will often award the individual a plaque. This is just a token; however, it serves as a way of saying thank you. In many instances, these plaques or awards are given at a dinner or special ceremony. For example, at Mary Kay there is an awards night in which the spotlight is placed on those who have done well. There is an extravaganza in which the leading saleswoman of the year is crowned. Diamonds, minks, and cars are given to those who have done well. At the end of the ceremony, it is

The annual awards presentation of Mary Kay Cosmetics is a distinctive ritual in this company's culture.

* Terrence E. Deal and Allan A. Kennedy, *Corporate Cultures* © 1982 Addison-Wesley Publishing Company, Inc., Reading, Mass., pp. 39–40. Reprinted by permission.

obvious to all that the number 1 rule in the firm is to sell.

Yet these rituals need not be so elaborate. In hospitals, it is common for surgeons to scrub down for about 7 minutes before an operation. In fact, most germs are destroyed within 30 seconds. However, the 7-minute scrub-down time is a ritual and to stop before this time is to break the ritual — a signal that the surgeon is ill-prepared. Other rituals are geared more for recognition. Consider the following.

At Intel, when someone does something well, the founder calls him or her in, reaches in his desk, and produces a handful of M&Ms as a sign of recognition. The ceremony began years ago, and now everyone keeps a supply of these candies ready.

The giving and receiving makes everyone feel good.

At Addison-Wesley Publishing Company, a bronze star is passed from one achiever to the next. At the same time, a "Martyr of the Week" award consoles the person having the roughest time. The point here is the recognition that even a good worker can have a bad time.*

Rites and rituals are important because they reinforce the actions of those who are doing well. Others in the organization who want to be rewarded need to emulate the behavior of these individuals. Additionally, rites and rituals legitimatize the reward process. They say, "Here is

* *Ibid.*, p. 72.

Example of a Hero

"He has been compared to an evangelist, a football coach, and all sorts of things. He gives chances to people who would never have had it," is the way Judge William Enfield describes Sam Walton, the founder and "hero" of the very successful Wal-Mart Discount City Stores.

Sam Walton has made Wal-Mart successful by locating stores in smaller communities, hiring rural strivers with a strong work ethic, and living the simple, small-town philosophy. He also makes a strong effort to infuse enthusiasm and pride in their work. On most Saturday mornings, Sam Walton will be in Bentonville, Arkansas, leading cheers for his buyers, truckers, clerks, warehouse workers, and other executives.

Many storytellers relate incidents that perpetuate the Walton value system. John Jeffers, president of the Bentonville Chamber of Commerce, says, "The Waltons are givers, not takers. They don't live in a mansion in the center of town and try to run everything." The community banker said, "I am totally convinced that if a petition was passed around, you could legally change the name of the town to Waltonville. They're super great people."

Sam Walton appreciates small-town values, and small-town consumers appreciate him. He still starts each day with a predawn breakfast at the Bentonville Holiday Inn. And he holds the annual stockholder's meeting in the high school gym. People say he likes to hunt quail and he likes to work. He named his line of dog food after his favorite bird dog, "Old Roy, 1970–1981. Gone but not forgotten."

According to former Wal-Mart president, Ferold Arend, Sam's philosophy is simple: "You treat your people right, pay 'em right and listen to them, and you can't go wrong." These values lived out by this corporate hero have made consumers and employees happy, stockholders wealthy (if you had bought a thousand shares in 1970 for $2000, you would be worth $2.5 million today), the community prosperous, and Sam Walton the second-richest man in the United States.

someone who did an outstanding job. This is the reward we gave that person. Do the same and you will be rewarded."

Communication Network

While rites and rituals help communicate desired behaviors, effective organizations try to influence the behavior of personnel from the moment they begin working for the company. These firms tell their people what they expect of them and try to guide them along the desired paths. In this regard, it is common to find heavy reliance being made on "storytellers" and "priests."

The storyteller's basic theme always remains the same: Work hard and you will succeed.

A **storyteller** is an individual who has been around the organization a long time and has done an outstanding job. The individual is someone whom the organization would like its personnel to emulate. One way of achieving this is by having the old-timer share some stories with the new people. The exact story will differ from storyteller to storyteller, however, the basic theme always remains the same: Work hard and you will succeed.

The following is a typical example of what a storyteller might relate.

When I was just starting out with this firm back in 1946 I was given three western states and told "get out there and sell our new calculators." Well, I had never been to Utah before so when I got there in mid-December I couldn't believe how cold it was. Coming from Alabama, I was unaccustomed to this weather. Nevertheless, I checked into the biggest hotel in Salt Lake City and turned in early so that I'd be up on time for my 9 A.M. meeting with the president of the largest bank in the city. When I awoke, it was snowing hard. I couldn't believe my eyes. I got dressed and ran out in front of the hotel. The flakes were coming down so fast, I couldn't see 10 feet ahead of me. Nevertheless, I knew where the bank was and figured I could walk over there in a few minutes. First, however, I ran back inside and asked the desk clerk where the nearest hardware

store was. He told me and I walked over there. When the store opened at 8:30 A.M. I went in and bought a snow shovel. I then went over to the bank and positioned myself outside the main door. I knew the president would be showing up early because he wanted to talk to me before starting business for the day. As soon as I saw a car drive up at 8:45 I knew it was him. I shoveled a path from the bank door to his car. When he got out, I said, "Hi. I'm Bob Petersen. I think we have a 9 A.M. meeting. I thought I'd get here early and help you get through all of this snow." He was impressed by my initiative and assistance. And later in the bank when I made my sales presentation to him, I continually stressed that our business sells products and stands behind them. I told him, "You can rely on us." He smiled and told me, "If you take as good care of me as you did this morning, I know I'll be in good hands." He then gave me a large order for calculators. We won't leave you out in the snow. We shovel a path for you and make sure that you stay on it. If you have a problem, we're there to pick you up.

This type of story is typical of those told by storytellers. It is particularly effective when employed by old-timers around the corporation who can recall the early days when things were difficult. Young people joining the firm identify with these stories and those who tell them. It is not uncommon to hear these stories repeated over and over again. It becomes part of the folklore of the firm.

Quite often the storyteller will enhance the tale by showing some type of physical evidence related to the episode. For example, the individual in the preceding story might have a snow shovel mounted on the wall of his office. Everyone dropping by sees the shovel and is reminded of the story. New employees who see the shovel but have not heard the story will undoubtedly ask questions. So they too will learn what happened. The shovel story serves to reinforce certain values that the organizaton wants its people to accept: work hard, be prepared for any eventuality, and show the customers that they can count on us.

Priests in the corporation are very much like clerical priests. They try to guard the congregation's values and keep the flock together. They also, in their own way, listen to confessions and offer recommendations for action.

In organizatonal culture terms, priests are those who have been around the firm for a long time and have seen a lot of things happen. They are very familiar with the past history of the organization, and, while a priest in a religious order might respond to a question by citing the Bible, an organizational culture priest will cite a past event in the firm's history. For example, a young manager might ask an older one about a recommended plan of action she is considering, involving special price discounts to large-quantity buyers. The older one might reply, "We suggested that same plan to the board of directors back in 1963. They rejected it because they felt this firm sells quality. They don't want us to get a reputation as a discounter. No one has ever again suggested discounting." Result? The young manager

CROSS FIRE

Are the Skills of Managing Different from the Skills of Leading?

With the new emphasis on heroes, storytellers, and corporate culture, an old debate is emerging, "What skills or abilities are necessary for effective leadership?"

For some time now, we have been teaching that a good manager needs to be skilled at planning, organizing, directing, and controlling an organization. This typically requires skills in financial analysis, long-range planning, structural design, and control systems. Managers, to be effective, must be rational, logical, controlled, and able to take the initiative in problem solving. The image of a good manager, oversimplified of course, is one who can use intelligence to analyze a problem, discover the most reasonable alternative, and execute the decision.

However, Dr. Abraham Zaleznik, endowed chairholder at the Harvard Business School, says that the psychology of leaders differs dramatically from that of managers. He says that managers, without much emotion, get things done through contractual relationships within an organization. But leaders, often with much emotion and perhaps even irrational thinking, change the course of events.

A typical manager might try to get people to do things for money or other rewards, or out of fear. For instance, a manager might communicate, "We need to work hard to reach our quarterly projections of 5% increase in return on investment." But a leader, relying upon more intuitive "gut feeling," might passionately exhort his group to, "Apply yourselves to the highest task of all, providing our customers with satisfaction and joy."

Typical Freudian managers have strong consciences that keep them feeling guilty with low self-confidence. Their aggressive tendencies will then result in attacks on themselves and others. The result will likely be distrust of subordinates and peers, overuse of corporate policies, battles over turf, win–lose confrontations, and demoralizing of others.

Leaders, because they do not have such strong consciences, are more secure and look for help from others. They are more willing to turn people loose, but at the same time, more forthright. Leaders might bluntly tell people when they are not performing up to the mark and they may even fire people and worry about it less than managers. The manager tends to be a worrier, the leader a doer. The manager says, "How well am I doing?" The leader says, "Are we getting the job done?"

Do you believe that managers and leaders are psychologically different? Why?

___ A. Yes   ___ B. No

Given the preceding descriptions of managers and leaders, which do you think would be most effective guiding an organization over the long term? Why?

___ A. A manager   ___ B. A leader

scraps her plan. She knows from past history that it won't work. It flies in the face of the company's values. Thanks to the priest, she has saved herself from making a proposal that will be turned down. Deal and Kennedy offer additional insights of priests in action.

> Priests also aid people in event of defeat, frustration, and disappointment. The person who handles worldwide assignments of managers is one company's favorite priest. A young manager will walk into his office and say, "My God, I've been assigned 18 months with our South American divisions. I'll be away from the heart of the action, and I came here to get a lot of experience. What's the use?" By the time he leaves the priest's office, he will have been told indirectly about how the company's chief executive officer spent 10 years working in Brazil. The manager won't know what's happened to him because of the meandering, eccentric way storytellers work, yet he'll trudge off feeling, "Maybe I can spend 10 years with this division and wind up as CEO." Stories are parables that motivate others and extend the power of the effective storyteller.*

IDENTIFYING CULTURES

The easiest way to examine a particular organization's culture is in terms of risk and feedback. What kinds of risk does the firm take? How much time elapses before the organization finds out if it made the right or wrong decision? Risks can be classified into two categories: high or low. Feedback can be classified into two categories: fast or slow. The result is four generic cultures. These cultures are briefly sketched out in Table A.1.

Tough-Guy, Macho

The **tough-guy, macho culture** is typical in organizations where people make high-risk decisions. For example, a person producing a Broadway play may invest $10 million (along with other backers, of course) and spend three months in rehearsal and on the road before bringing the play to New York City. There, after opening night, the individual learns whether the play will be a success or not. The risk is great, and within 24 hours of the Broadway opening there is feedback.

Ibid., p. 89.

Tough-guy, macho types are opportunistic, individualistic, and enjoy winning.

People who function well in this environment are often young and stress speed over endurance. The entrepreneur who makes $1 million before the age of 21 is an example. Tough-guy, macho types like the fast-paced environment. They are opportunistic, individualistic, and enjoy winning. They are also creative both in terms of their work (they look for unique solutions) and their life-style (they wear designer clothing, drive expensive sports cars, and live in one-of-a-kind houses).

Work Hard/Play Hard

The **work hard/play hard culture** is typified by individuals who are successful in a low-risk, fast feedback environment. Sales organizations typically fall into this category. If the salesperson does not make a sale, it usually is not the end of the world. However, the individual often finds out very quickly if the sale is made. Some of the firms that fall into this category include Mary Kay Cosmetics, IBM, Bloomingdale's, Xerox, and Digital Equipment.

Survivors in this environment tend to be supersalespeople. They are also team players, knowing that the success of the enterprise depends on their ability to work in unison with one another. For example, the people in sales know the importance of coordinating their efforts with production so that delivery promises can be kept.

Survivors in the work hard/play hard environment tend to be very high achievers, but they do not go to extremes.

Research and development knows the value of its input to new product lines and the importance of having these products ready for manufacturing at the agreed-upon time. Survivors in this environment also like feedback on how well they are doing and tend to be very high achievers. They dress well and often live in nice houses. However, in contrast to the tough-guy, macho types, they do not go to extremes.

TABLE A.1 ■ ORGANIZATIONAL CULTURE PROFILES

	Tough-Guy, Macho	Work Hard/Play Hard
Type of risks that are assumed	High	Low
Type of feedback from decisions	Fast	Fast
Typical kinds of organizations that use this culture	Construction, cosmetics, TV, radio, venture capitalism, management consulting.	Real estate, computer firms, auto distributors, door-to-door sales operations, retail stores, mass consumer sales.
Ways survivors and/or heroes in this culture behave	Have a tough attitude. Are individualistic. Can tolerate all-or-nothing risks. Are superstitious.	Are supersalespeople. Often are friendly, hail-fellow-well-met types. Use a team approach to problem solving. Are nonsuperstitious.
Strengths of the personnel/culture	They can get things done in short order.	They are able to produce a high volume of work quickly.
Weaknesses of the personnel/culture	They do not learn from past mistakes. Everything tends to be short-term in orientation. The virtues of cooperation are ignored.	They look for quick-fix solutions. They have a short-term time perspective. They are more committed to action than to problem-solving.
Habits of the survivors and/or heroes	They dress in fashion. They live in "in" places. They like one-on-one sports such as tennis. They enjoy scoring points off one another in verbal interaction.	They avoid extremes in dress. They live in tract houses. They prefer team sports such as touch football. They like to drink together.

Source: Adapted from Terrence E. Deal and Allan A. Kennedy, *Corporate Cultures: The Rites and Rituals of Corporate Life,* Reading, Mass.: Addison-Wesley Publishing, 1982, Chapter 6.

Bet Your Company

The **bet-your-company culture** is characterized by high risk and slow feedback. There are many examples of organizations that fit into this

Oil exploration firms typify the high-risk, slow-feedback nature of the bet-your-company culture.

category. Banks, aerospace firms, oil exploration firms, capital goods manufacturers, and the military are examples. People in these organizations often put their careers on the line by risking the future of their entire enterprise. Michael Murphy, an investment analyst for Venture Capital Management, says that Apple Computer is "betting the whole company on the Macintosh," their new personal computer that is competing head to head with IBM's PC. "If Mac is a flop," says Murphy, "Apple doesn't stand a chance. It will just disappear."

Consider oil explorers. It may cost $5 million and a year's time from when a firm decides where to look for oil until it finds out whether there is oil in that location. If the company is right, it stands to make a lot of money. If it is wrong, the entire investment is lost. Or consider the military. If the navy builds a superaircraft carrier but sea power over the next 10 years is decided by submarines, the organization has made a serious mistake. Any time a decision is made regarding defense spending, whether it be for a new fighter aircraft or an MX missile system, a mistake can be detrimental to

TABLE A.1 ■ (Continued)

Bet Your Company	Process
High	Low
Slow	Slow
Oil, aerospace, capital goods manufacturers, architectural firms, investment banks, mining and smelting firms, military.	Banks, insurance companies, utilities, pharmaceuticals, financial service organizations, many agencies of the government.
Can endure long-term ambiguity. Always double-check their decisions. Are technically competent. Have a strong respect for authority.	Are very cautious and protective of their own flank. Are orderly and punctual. Are good at attending to detail. Always follow established procedures.
They can generate high-quality inventions and major scientific breakthroughs.	They bring order and system to the work place.
They are extremely slow in getting things done. Their organizations are vulnerable to short-term economic fluctuations. Their organizations often face cash-flow problems.	There is lots of red tape. Initiative is downplayed. They face long hours and boring work.
They dress according to their organizational rank. Their housing matches their hierarchical position. They like sports where the outcome is unclear until the end such as golf. The older members serve as mentors for the younger ones.	They dress according to hierarchical rank. They live in apartments, or no-frills homes. They enjoy process sports like jogging and swimming. They like discussing memos.

the interests of the country. There is a lot at risk in bet-your-company cultures, but the participants only find out if they were right or wrong after a number of months or years have elapsed.

Survivors in this environment need to have the stamina to endure the long-run ambiguity and lack of feedback. For this reason, it is common to find them checking and double-checking their decisions. They don't want to make a mistake. These individuals also respect authority and technical competence since they are so important to success in this environment. Their life-style is much more sedate than the tough-guy, macho people. For example, their housing tends to fit with their rank in the organizational hierarchy.

Process

The **process culture** environment is characterized by low risk and low feedback. Typical examples operating in this culture include banks, insurance companies, utilities, and governmental agencies. Consider banks. Customers are judged

on the basis of their credit worthiness. Does the person have collateral to back up the loan? Can the individual repay the principal and the interest? If so, the person usually is judged a good risk and given the money. The risk is (or at least is supposed to be) low. How does the bank know it will get back its money? Only time will tell. However, given the fact that the applicant has been checked out, the loan should be safe. Of course, it does not always turn out that way. For example, in the last couple of years, many banks that have loaned money to South American governments have found the latter unable to repay. Mexico and Poland are other examples. Unfortunately, the banks were unable to forecast economic problems in these countries. So only after a nation announced that it was unable to meet debt obligations did it become evident that the loan was much higher risk than was initially believed.

Survivors in the process culture tend to be very cautious and protective. They follow the rules, write memos on everything, and observe all procedures. Titles and formalities are very important. Bureaucratic behavior is commonplace. It even affects life-style. For example, when it comes to athletics, personnel like process sports like jogging and swimming.

RESHAPING CULTURES

Corporate culture is an important area in business today because it helps dictate how people in the structure will behave. However, this behavior is not fixed; it can be changed through a reshaping process should this be necessary.

When Change Is Necessary

Change in corporate culture can become necessary in certain instances. One instance is when the environment in which the firm is operating undergoes fundamental change. The culture may have to be altered. For example, in the case of AT&T, there have been significant changes over the last 5 years. Local operating companies have been taken away, and the firm now consists of but three major parts: Bell Laboratories (research and development), Western Electric (manufacturing equipment) and long lines (long distance). AT&T used to have no competition. Now it must vie with a host of competitors. In the case of manufactured equipment, there are many companies currently offering telephones to the general public. It is no longer necessary to get a phone from Ma Bell. In the case of long distance calls, MCI, Sprint, and a host of others offer reduced long-distance rates. How is all this affecting AT&T? While it is still too early to tell, there must be a tremendous internal change taking place.

Second, when an industry is highly competitive and the environment changes quickly, the

TAKING STOCK

Creating a Corporate Culture

Harry V. Quadracci, president of Quad/Graphics, has been very successful in creating a strong work-oriented culture among his employees. His firm, employing about 700 people, is a printing company with customers like *Newsweek, Harper's,* and *U.S. News & World Report.*

Like most companies that have a strong culture, the president, Quadracci in this case, takes a significant role in establishing shared values. He personally instructs the beginning printing course that all new employees must take. And he says that he does not automatically trust new employees to be responsible. New hires cannot even wear the company uniform until they have served a rigorous 2-month probation period. He believes that most of his new people are "kids," and "they don't all have their heads screwed on right." Half are under 24, and most have never had a full-time job.

Quadracci admits, "They get indoctrinated, brainwashed. . . . They're raw recruits, and as far as we're concerned, they're in boot camp for about 2 years," he adds. The values most cherished by Quadracci, and therefore spread to the work force, appear to be:

- Performance is everything.
- Nobody gets points for seniority.
- Absenteeism and sloth will not be tolerated.
- Most important is pride and exacting standards in the work they turn out.

However, the company also encourages participation and freedom among its people, after they have served their proving period, of course. Each year, the entire

Organizational changes in AT&T after the 1983 divestiture ruling no doubt have altered its culture as well.

culture may have to change as well. For example, the Digital Equipment Corporation (DEC) has always been very competitive in the computer field. Every time there has been a change in customer needs, the firm has adapted to that end of the market and succeeded. However, in recent years, DEC has not moved into the microcomputer field quickly enough. For whatever reason, the firm allowed Apple and IBM to get a big jump on them. The DEC personal computer (PC) does not appear to be a serious challenge to IBM's PC. DEC's culture has not changed fast enough to keep it strong in this part of the computer market.

Third, when a firm is mediocre or worse, a change in culture is needed. Eastern Airlines is a good example. Before Frank Borman took over, the firm was in terrible shape. Although Borman has not managed to turn the airline into one of the big money makers, he has prevented collapse.

top management team leaves the workers in charge of everything while they retreat to do their planning. The early cultural indoctrination process apparently develops employees management can trust. Quadracci says, ''Our people shouldn't need me or anybody else to tell them what to do.'' When the firm was growing and adding new operations, he tapped people with expertise — both internal and external — and told them they were entrepreneurs and turned them loose. They were very successful; some of the groups won awards for innovations and many sell some of the products to others — including competitors.

On the one hand, Quad/Graphics is very demanding; and on the other hand, people have a lot of freedom and participate significantly in major company decisions. The company also appreciates its employees by providing:

- An employee stock ownership plan.
- A profit-sharing program.
- An extensive list of benefits.
- Numerous employee education and training programs.
- Luxurious working facilities.
- A $3 million sports center.
- Original art, even in the locker room.

All this is apparently working; 1983 sales volume for the 11-year-old company was $75 million.

Source: Ellen Wojahn, ''Management by Walking Away,'' *Inc.,* Oct. 1983, pp. 68–76.

This was done by changing the culture to an over-riding orientation toward customer service, coupled with a sense of shared commitment to the firm's welfare by both management and employees.

Fourth, when a firm is on the threshold of becoming a large company, a change in culture is often required. Things cannot go along as before. There has to be greater attention to building teamwork, as opposed to encouraging everyone to go their own way as they did when the firm was small and growing.

Managing Cultural Change Successfully

Cultural change has to be managed skillfully. While there are a number of ways of doing this, most are complementary. Some of the most useful successful steps have been the following:

1. Put a hero in charge of the process. Many people in the organization already identify with this person. When he or she encourages them to change, do things a different way, accept a new approach to their jobs, etc., they are likely to listen and respond accordingly.

2. Use transition rituals to bring about change. By setting up meetings in which people can talk about their concerns and learn how the company is changing and why, there is the opportunity to win personnel support for the new cultural values.

3. Bring in outside assistance. Where useful, consultants should be brought in from outside to discuss necessary changes and make useful recommendations regarding how these changes should be implemented.

4. Ensure security during the transition. A company must ensure that no one is arbitrarily fired along the way. Otherwise these people become martyrs, and the change process breaks down. Keeping people around is an important ingredient of successful change.

Steps such as these are vital in helping reshape corporate culture. They also assist in seeing that the new values result in the desired behaviors.

SUMMARY

Corporate culture is the beliefs, attitudes, values, and philosophies of an organization. This culture helps dictate what personnel will do and how they will do it. There are three elements of corporate culture: heroes, rites and rituals, and communication of the culture. Heroes are individuals who symbolize the company to the outside world and set standards of performance. They also serve as a role model for other personnel. Rites and rituals are behaviors and ceremonies that are carried out in support of the desired culture. Typical examples include monetary rewards, plaques, vacation trips, etc., which are given out at recognition dinners. The culture itself is communicated through these formal recognition procedures. However, there are additional ways of communicating culture including the use of storytellers and

priests. Both use past company history and experience to guide and shape the thinking of personnel, reinforcing the culture in the process.

There are four basic types of corporate culture: tough-guy, macho; work hard/play hard; bet your company; and process. There are certain types of industries or environments in which one culture is much more prevalent than the others. Those who survive in their respective culture tend to adopt the values and behaviors that allow them to adjust most effectively to their environment.

Sometimes it is necessary to reshape a corporate culture. This can occur when the environment undergoes a fundamental change, when the industry is highly competitive and the environment changes quickly, when the firm is mediocre, or when the firm is on the threshold of becoming a large company. In successfully managing cultural change, there are a number of things managers should consider doing. Four of the most helpful include: (1) put a hero in charge of the process; (2) use transition rituals to bring about the change; (3) bring in outside assistance; and (4) ensure personnel security during the transition.

MIND YOUR BUSINESS

Instructions. Answer each of the following questions with a Y (yes) or N (no).

_____ 1. Is organization culture something that can be defined?

_____ 2. Are heroes important to the organization's culture?

_____ 3. Are storytellers harmful to the organization's culture?

_____ 4. Are priests in the organization culture much like clerical priests?

_____ 5. Is the tough-guy, macho culture one that is likely to take a long-term view of things?

_____ 6. Would supersalespeople likely be associated with the work hard/play hard culture?

_____ 7. Are order and slow response to change characteristic of the bet-your-company culture?

_____ 8. Would executives of the process culture be likely to enjoy jogging and swimming?

_____ 9. If you wanted to change the organization culture, would you be likely to put a hero in charge of the process?

_____ 10. Are outside consultants considered helpful when trying to change an organizaton culture?

See answers at the back of the book.

KEY TERMS

corporate culture, 150
hero, 151
storyteller, 153
priest, 153
tough-guy, macho culture, 155
work-hard/play hard culture, 155
bet-your-company culture, 156
process culture, 157

REVIEW QUESTIONS

1. In your own words, what is meant by the term "corporate culture"?

2. How can a hero help a company develop a corporate culture? Give an example.

3. How do rites and rituals help develop corporate culture?

4. What role is played by storytellers to help develop a corporate culture? Explain.

5. What role is played by priests in developing a corporate culture? Explain.

6. How does a survivor in a tough-guy, macho culture behave?

7. In what kinds of businesses are we likely to find a work hard/play hard corporate culture? Cite at least two examples and explain each.

8. How do survivors in a bet-your-company culture behave?

9. What types of people would do best in a process culture? Why?

10. When it comes to reshaping corporate culture, what are some of the most useful guidelines for the manager to keep in mind? Identify and discuss three.

CASES

Case A.1: The Bardell Way

The Bardell Corporation is a very successful construction firm. During the last 12 months, the company has won a series of state and local contracts for major building projects. It has also bid successfully on seven new office buildings located from New York to Los Angeles.

Many of the people who work on these construction projects are union laborers who are hired from the local area. However, the company maintains a solid core of management staff. Some of the staff work out of the home office in Chicago. The rest are in management positions in the field.

Because of the large increase in business over the past year, Bardell has found it necessary to recruit more managerial personnel. Some of these people have been hired right out of engineering programs. Others are M.B.A. graduates. Still others have been hired away from competitive firms. In all cases, they know very little about Bardell and its operating philosophy.

The head of the personnel department has suggested that each of these new people be put through a 3-day in-house seminar in which they are taught the history, values, and operating philosophy of the firm. In particular, the personnel manager would like to see some of the top staff and up-and-coming middle managers take 15 to 30 minutes to talk to these new people about the company. "We've got to get these new personnel thinking the Bardell way," the manager told the company president. "If we start them out right, they'll be more effective as members of our management team." The president agreed, and the first 3-day seminar is scheduled to begin next week.

Questions

1. In scheduling people to talk at her seminar, how likely is it that the personnel manager will use some heroes? Why? Explain.

2. What type of corporate culture best describes Bardell? (Use Table A.1 to help you.) Defend your answer.

3. How valuable will this 3-day seminar be? Why? Defend your answer.

Case A.2: Bob's Choice

When Robert Flaherty decided to retire from the military, he was already under consideration for promotion to general. Nevertheless, he decided to get out and enter industry. "I want to start a new career, and, if I am promoted to general, I know I'll stay in at least another five years," he told his wife. "I've enjoyed my military career, but I'm now ready to move on."

Bob already had his eye on a job with a large computer firm. The company has been very prominent in the industry for over 30 years and the individual who recruited him told him, "Bob, you're used to taking charge. You know the importance of assuming responsibility and getting things done. You'll fit in well with us. We think it's a natural step from a military career to one in the world of business, especially computers." Bob

agreed with the recruiter and is scheduled to start his new job in five weeks.

He will be vice-president of sales for western operation. In this capacity, Bob will be responsible for directing the sales force in a ten-state area. He will have five people reporting directly to him and a total of 375 people in the entire region. In addition to handling the management side of the job, Bob will be expected to pitch in and help out with sales to large business and military customers. "I'm really looking forward to getting started," he told the president of the firm yesterday. "Well, we're glad to have you with us, Bob," the CEO told him.

Questions

1. In your own words, describe the organization culture of the military.

2. What does the organizational culture of a successful computer sales organization look like? Compare it with your answer to the preceding question.

3. Are there any particular problems Bob is likely to have in adjusting to this new job? What are they? Be complete in your answer.

LEARNING OBJECTIVES

After completing this chapter, you will be able to:

- Define the function of organization.

- Describe five means for subdividing work in organizations.

- Draw three kinds of organizational charts.

- Define authority, responsibility, chain of command, delegation, accountability, and span of control.

- Distinguish between line and staff authority.

- Distinguish between centralized and decentralized authority.

- Define and describe the key aspects of the informal organization.

- Draw and explain five alternate forms of organization structure.

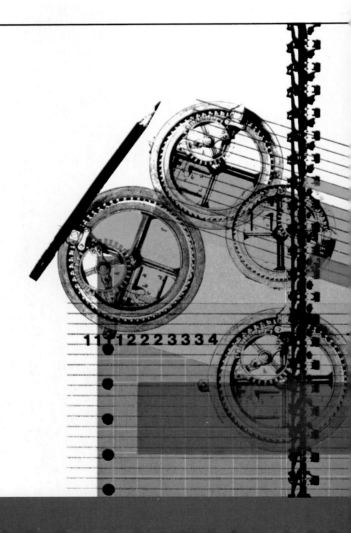

7

BUSINESS
ORGANIZATION
AND STRUCTURE

Suppose you recruited twenty people to accomplish a task; for example, you might want to produce a new piece of furniture that you designed. What would happen if you hired the people, explained that you wanted to manufacture your uniquely designed furniture, and told them to go to work? No doubt, the result would be confusion. Your employees would not know what you expected them to do and they would not know where to start. In fact, there is a strong likelihood that several employees would soon become frustrated and begin arguing about who should be doing what. Chances are slim that any useful product would result, even though the effort of the people might be quite serious.

To reduce such chaos, a manager could organize the work groups by:

- Determining what tasks are necessary.
- Dividing tasks into work groups.
- Assigning managers to be responsible for each group's tasks.
- Giving each manager the authority to complete the tasks.

For instance, the manager might organize as follows:

- Determine the tasks to be cutting, sanding, polishing, sewing, assembling, and painting.
- Group the tasks according to ordering the materials, producing the product, and selling the furniture.
- Select a manager for each grouping of tasks, that is, a manager for purchasing, production, and sales.
- Give each manager the authority to complete the tasks, for example, buying materials, supervising employees, and making the sales.

In complex organizations, it is impossible for one person to do everything. To produce airplanes, automobiles, or windows requires thousands of varied jobs.

As discussed in Chapter 6, the four basic functions of management are (1) planning, (2) organizing, (3) directing, and (4) controlling. Organizing, because of its complexity, is covered in greater detail in this chapter. Topics include formal organization, authority and responsibility, informal organization, and alternative forms of organization.

FORMAL ORGANIZATION

The underlying purpose of organization is to divide, and subdivide if necessary, the work into groupings. We call this process departmentation. Organization charts show us the relationships between departments.

Departmentation

To organize, we divide the work into large groups (divisions, regions, plants, etc.); then we divide into smaller groups (departments, shifts); and finally, we have a job description for each employee. By dividing work into small units, we benefit from specialization. The process of creating these divisions of work is called **departmentation,** and we call the divisions **departments.**

Departmentation by function. A functional division of work separates tasks into the company's major activities such as manufacturing, sales, finance, and personnel. Everything related to manufacturing goes into the manufacturing department, everything related to sales comes under the sales department, and so on. For instance, the function chart in Fig. 7.1 shows marketing, human resources, finance, and production to be the four major company divisions. The work of each major division is further divided into subdepartments. Advertising and promotion departments are under marketing, personnel is under human resources, and the like. Division by function is popular at top organizatonal levels.

Departmentation by territory. Division by geographic location (territory) is popular in marketing departments. When a company promotes its products or services over large territories, it is effective to divide the work according to these territories. Then each manager can make decisions that take into account the unique characteristics of that particular territory.

A company with only twenty salespeople may have only four sales managers, with each responsible for five salespeople. However, if a firm has one hundred salespeople, each of the four regional managers may supervise three or four district managers. District managers would then be in charge of salespeople for their own districts.

Departmentation by product. Companies that produce varied products often organize their work by product or class of product. General Motors, for example, has Cadillac, Chevrolet, and Buick divisions. A clothing manufacturer may have divisions such as boys' wear, junior miss, men's wear, and women's wear.

Departmentation by process. Creating departments by process is popular, especially in manufacturing companies. Division of labor by process creates departments for each step of what is usually a continuous process. Consider a shoe manufacturer which may organize into departments of design, cutting, sewing, gluing, and finishing. Employees in each department could specialize in the activities of the department.

Final testing, the responsibility of this department, marks the end of the manufacturing process for these copying machines.

Departmentation by client. When a company departmentalizes by client, it groups its activities by customer. For instance, a major producer such as Crown-Zellerbach might produce nonbrand-labeled products for several different types of customers. The company may have special departments for major clients, such as Safeway, Luckies, Sears, and the like. Or a publishing company might divide its activities according to its reading markets — trade, textbooks, reference books, children's books.

In reality, companies usually employ a combination of these departmentation schemes. At one level, they may organize by function; they may choose territorial departmentation for another level; and they might departmentalize by product at another level. See Fig. 7.1 for examples of the various methods of departmentation.

Organization Charts

An **organization chart** is a diagram of the departments and their relationships to each other. There are three major types of organization charts: (1) vertical, (2) pyramid, and (3) horizontal.

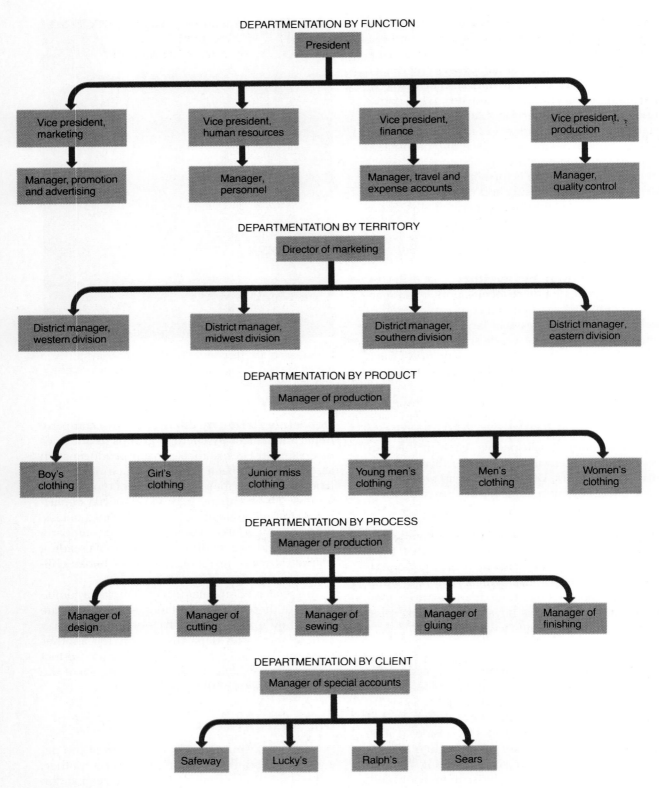

Figure 7.1
Various methods of departmentation.

The vertical chart. An example of a vertical organization chart appears in Fig. 7.2. As you can see, the power positions appear at the top levels of the chart, and the subordinate positions would be at the lower levels. The lines show the relationships of the departments to each other. For exam-ple, in the **vertical chart** in Fig. 7.2, the manager of advertising reports to the director of marketing who, in turn, reports to the president.

The pyramid chart. The **pyramid chart,** al-though much like the vertical chart, is usually ex-

Figure 7.2
Various types of organization charts.

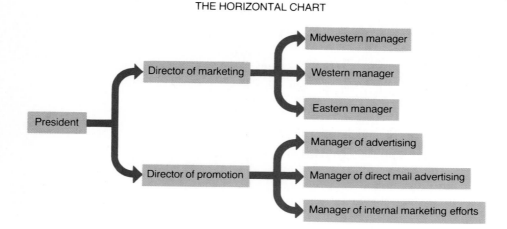

THE VERTICAL CHART

President

Director of marketing

Manager of advertising

Manager of direct mail sales

Manager of the sales force

Manager of internal marketing efforts

THE PYRAMID CHART

President

Director of marketing

Director of promotion

Midwestern manager

Western manager

Eastern manager

Manager of advertising

Manager of direct mail advertising

Manager of internal marketing efforts

THE HORIZONTAL CHART

President

Director of marketing

Midwestern manager

Western manager

Eastern manager

Director of promotion

Manager of advertising

Manager of direct mail advertising

Manager of internal marketing efforts

panded to show more detail. Like the concept of a pyramid, it reflects power at the top and lower management levels at the bottom (or the base) (see Fig. 7.2).

The horizontal chart. Although not so frequently used as the vertical and pyramid charts, the **horizontal chart** shows the higher levels of management at the left with the lower management levels extending to the right. Some companies developed the horizontal chart because they did not want to emphasize the fact that the higher positions were on top and the lower positions were on the bottom. Figure 7.2 shows an example.

AUTHORITY AND RESPONSIBILITY

The organization chart is useful because it shows relationships between departments, but it does not show precisely just how much power one department has over another. This aspect of the relationship involves the concepts of authority and responsibility. **Authority** is the organization's right to do something, to make decisions regarding the tasks of the department. **Responsibility,** on the other hand, is an individual's personal obligation to carry out the activities assigned.

Let us consider the example of a community hospital located in a small midwestern community. The hospital administrator has the right to make decisions necessary to manage the hospital. Her job description states that she has the authority to purchase supplies and equipment; hire, assign, and terminate personnel; engage in fundraising; appoint and delegate appropriate authority to departmental executives; make decisions regarding financial control; and develop and maintain a sound organization. And, although it is not specifically stated, she also has the responsibility to carry out these duties to the best of her ability. Even if she delegates some of her authority to her department heads, she still remains responsible for the overall operation of the hospital.

A serious problem occurs when authority and responsibility are not equal. Suppose the board of trustees of the hospital told the administrator that they would hold her responsible for running the hospital. But if the trustees did not give the admin-

istrator the authority to make decisions regarding subordinates, finances, purchasing, and the like, the administrator would be unable to fulfill her responsibilities.

To fully understand authority and responsibility, we need to know something about the chain of command, authority delegation, accountability, span of control, line and staff authority, centralization, and decentralization.

Chain of Command

The **chain of command** is the established set of authority relationships between the departments. It shows who reports to whom. The hospital administrator mentioned previously reports to the board of trustees; and her assistant director, a director of nursing, and other staff department directors report to her. Figure 7.3 traces this chain of command.

To illustrate how the chain of command works, let us suppose one of the nurses complains, ''I don't like my work assignment. I always get scheduled at the most undesirable hours.'' To complain through the chain of command, the nurse should talk to the director of nursing. If

Figure 7.3
Chain of command at a community hospital.

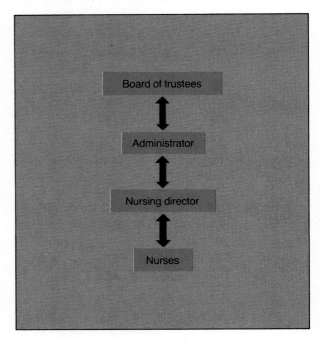

things are beyond the director's immediate control, both the nurse and his director might visit with the administrator. Likewise, the administrator should not make work assignments directly to the nurse. Rather the administrator, through authority delegation, asks the nursing director to run the nursing department. The nursing director then makes work assignments to the nurses.

Authority Delegation

Authority delegation means (1) assigning a task to a subordinate, (2) granting the rights and freedom to accomplish the task, and (3) checking to see that the subordinate performs the task properly.

Effective managers learn to delegate, but many managers insist on making all decisions themselves.

Effective managers learn to delegate, but many managers insist on making all decisions themselves. By adopting the idea "If you want something done right, you have to do it yourself," they spread themselves too thin. This creates stress for the manager and frustrates subordinates. Typically, managers who refuse to delegate use excuses such as that subordinates will not do a task correctly, there is not enough time to delegate, this is too important to delegate, the employees have not been trained well enough, or they just do not feel comfortable letting someone else do this. These excuses often signify that the manager is not secure enough or does not have enough self-confidence to delegate properly to subordinates.

Accountability

Once subordinates accept the authority to do a job, they should be held accountable for its accomplishment. **Accountability** is the liability of subordinates to accomplish tasks and objectives as agreed upon. Accountability is more narrow in scope than responsibility. Responsibility is an assumed obligation to do the best that one can in performing one's duties. Accountability is that part of the job that higher authorities will evaluate

to determine whether they should reward or punish the subordinate. For example, the nursing director is in a general way responsible for doing the best that she can. But she can be held accountable only for the specific aspects of the job that can be evaluated.

Span of Control

Span of control refers to the number of employees reporting to a manager. Authorities debate the proper span of control, but most agree that it varies with different situations. Lower-level supervisors who manage employees completing routine, stable tasks may manage as many as forty employees. However, at upper levels where jobs are complex and constantly changing, the span of control may be as few as three or four subordinates.

C. Northcote Parkinson, in *Parkinson's Law*, reasoned that (1) officials want to multiply subordinates, not rivals; (2) therefore, top officials have a tendency to add staff; (3) the added staff make work for one another; and (4) this results in the need for more staff.

C. Northcote Parkinson in *Parkinson's Law* says that the number of subordinates that a manager can control reduces as you move up the organizational hierarchy. He believed, for example, that presidents could effectively control fewer subordinates than first-line supervisors. Drawing upon his experiences, Parkinson, somewhat tongue-in-cheek, offered an explanation for why organizations add more staff at the management level. His reasoning, known as **Parkinson's law,** goes like this: (1) officials want to multiply subordinates, not rivals, (2) therefore top officials have a tendency to add staff, (3) the added staff make work for one another, and (4) this results in the need for more staff. When a department gets too large, the top official divides the department and

The M-Form Structure

In his latest book, *The M-Form Society,* professor and writer William Ouchi prescribes a way for American companies to increase their teamwork and recapture their competitive edge.

Ouchi identifies three structural forms of large companies: the U-form structure, the H-form structure, and the M-form structure.

The U-form structure, the most common, is simply a functional organizational structure. As the drawing below suggests, a chief executive officer (CEO) oversees functional divisions. In the U-form, all departments must exist alongside one another. Sales would have nothing to sell unless production produced a product or service. No subunit can exist by itself and no subunit can measure its performance independently of the other units. Because the subunits are dependent on each other and because there is no simple measure of performance for each unit, the decisions tend to be highly centralized. Such organizations typically do not develop a long-term view.

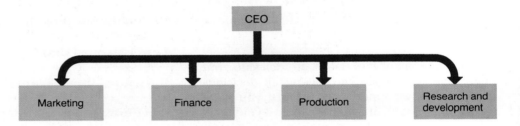

The H-form structure identifies a holding company, typically with a small central staff that keeps financial controls over separate operating units. Each unit stands alone, independent from all other aspects of the business. The top management of the holding company knows very little about the separate units but can evaluate each one independently by using profits as a guideline. Since top management has a simple measure (profits) of each unit, decisions are usually very decentralized. The corporate management team does get to know quite a bit about the top managers of each unit, and the home office financial people are usually well-versed in the financial affairs of each unit. The drawing below shows a hypothetical example of an H-form structure.

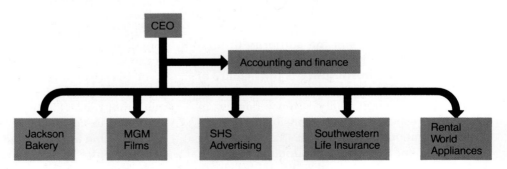

Existing between the U-form and the H-form, the M-form structure (or multidivisional organizaton) is the high-performing type, with partially independent operating units. Each operating unit makes a product or creates a service that is independent from the other units, but they all draw from some common pool such as technology, skill, or other features. Hewlett-Packard is an example of an M-form structure. H-P has nearly fifty semiautonomous divisions. One division manufactures oscilloscopes; another produces computers; another makes hand-held calculators; and so on. Each sells to a slightly different market, and each may use different methods of production. But they all draw from a common base of electrical engineering expertise, and they depend to some extent on the inventions from their central laboratories to supplement their own research. In short, subunits of the M-form structure are both partially independent and partially dependent upon the overall organization.

Top management may ask each division to maximize its profits, and it can measure this easily enough. However, managers of each division usually have to draw on central office skill, technology, marketing ability, and the like. And each divisional manager is concerned about the performance of the division as well as the performance of the overall operation. The success comes from providing a proper balance of independence and teamwork. The drawing below shows an M-form structure.

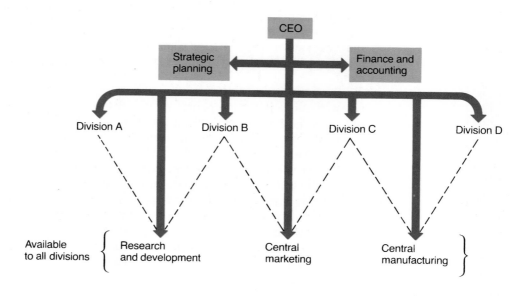

Summarized from William Ouchi, *The M-Form Society,* Reading, Massachusetts: Addison-Wesley Publishing Co., 1984.

creates two department heads. These two department heads, both of whom are subordinate to the top official, also create work for each other. In fact, Parkinson said that the number of people in any working group tends to increase regardless of the amount of work to be done. In reality, until very recently, organizations in both England and the United States have shown a tendency to increase their management positions at a much faster rate than their employee positions.

Wide spans of control tend to produce a **flat organization;** that is, a manager has large departments, and there are fewer managerial levels. By contrast, narrow spans produce a **tall organization,** the result of small departments and many management levels. Figure 7.4 diagrams examples of spans of control.

Research suggests some advantages to both wide and narrow spans of control. Some advantages of wide spans are:

- Communication is better because of fewer levels.
- Subordinate initiative is encouraged.
- Employees feel closer to top management.
- Lower-level employees have more responsibility.

Some advantages of narrow spans are:

CROSS FIRE

The Authority Dilemma

The vice-president of an information processing firm, concerned about cutting costs, issued an unconditional order forbidding managers and supervisors to authorize overtime under any circumstances. On a Thursday morning, the data processing manager called the vice-president's assistant and explained that water damage from the recent storm had damaged some of their records and equipment. They called the repair service, but they do not expect to get the equipment running until late Friday night.

A systems supervisor, a subordinate of the data processing manager, has requested overtime for ten people so that they can get the monthly dividend statements mailed on time. When the dividend checks are late, owners become angry and complain. The data processing manager forwarded the overtime request to the vice-president's assistant, but he said he could not authorize the overtime. He tried to get in touch with the vice-president, but he was out of town and could not be reached. Finally, the vice-president's assistant told the data processing manager to use his own discretion in the matter. The data processing manager explained to the systems supervisor, ''I could not get in touch with the vice-president. The vice-president's assistant told to us to use our own judgment. So I guess you will just have to use your own discretion about whether you ask your people to come in this weekend.''

What decision do you think the systems supervisor made?

___ A. Told his people to come in and turn in the overtime.

___ B. Did nothing over the weekend; reported to work Monday as usual.

Explain the reasoning behind your choice.

A. _____

B. _____

C. _____

D. _____

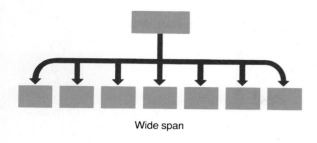

Wide span

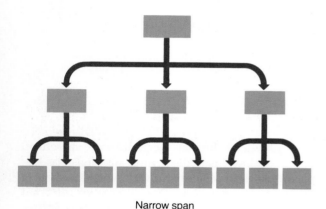

Narrow span

Figure 7.4
Examples of wide and narrow spans.

- More levels of management are created, providing more promotion opportunities to quality employees.
- Each manager is allowed to specialize more narrowly.
- More control over employee behavior is provided.

Line and Staff Authority

Thus far, we have been discussing **line authority,** the formal right to tell others what to do. However, because of increasing complexities in organizations, a more elaborate system has developed. **Staff authority** supplements line authority by providing specialized advice. Staff managers can only make recommendations to other departments. As one manager put it, "The line tells, the staff sells."

In many organizations, the human resources department has staff authority with other departments. Human resources people might, for exam-

ple, interview people and make recommendations for hiring; nevertheless, the line manager of the department probably has the final say on hiring. Or, computer specialists might develop a new system for recording costs in a department, and they may recommend this new system to the manager of the department. The department manager then can accept or reject the plan.

In practice, line and staff relationships are often major sources of conflict. In looking for better methods, improved procedures, or greater efficiency, staff people usually initiate changes. And staff people may even specify certain procedures and actually control the line manager's resources to some extent. It is easy for a line manager to think that a staff person is infringing upon his territory. For instance, staff engineers may specify what materials will be used in making a product and how the product is to be manufactured. But line managers are responsible for the output of their production subordinates. Understandably, a line manager might feel a little resistant when staff people begin suggesting to—often telling—the line manager's subordinates how they ought to perform part of their production jobs. In such situations, a line manager frequently thinks, "I do not have complete authority to tell my subordinates what to do, but I am still responsible for the output."

To compound this dilemma, line and staff managers usually have different personal backgrounds. Staff people tend to have more formal education, they come from different social backgrounds, and they tend to be younger than line managers. Staff managers, because of their specialized knowledge and frequent association with upper-level management, are also closer to the power structure. All these things cause line managers to worry about staff people usurping some of their influence. Figure 7.5 diagrams line and staff relationships.

Centralization and Decentralization

Managers must decide how much authority to vest in each managerial position. **Centralization** occurs when a few managers at the top reserve most of the important decisions for themselves. By contrast, **decentralization** of authority means that employees at lower organizational levels

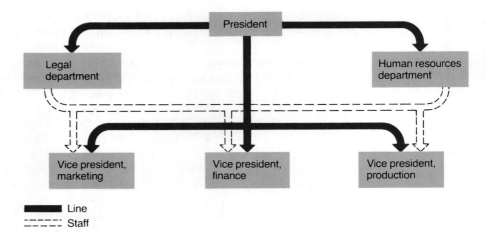

**Figure 7.5
Line and staff
organization chart.**

━━━ Line
----- Staff

Routine, recurring decisions are generally decentralized; less routine, critical decisions are usually centralized.

have more power to make decisions. Generally, routine, recurring decisions are decentralized, whereas decisions that are less routine and more critical are centralized.

Which is better: centralization or decentralization? Many feel it is better to decentralize whenever possible. By giving lower-level managers and employees more authority, you create initiative and develop better-trained managers for the future. Centralization tends to frustrate many employees. Suppose the mailroom manager had to get permission to buy stamps. Perhaps she is even required to submit a daily report on postage costs. This could become tedious and frustrating. In a decentralized firm, upper-level management would likely give departments a postage budget. Department managers could spend their postage as they wished so long as they stayed within the budget. Upper-level managers would want to look only at special problems. However, if decisions have a great impact on the firm, they are likely to be centralized. Or if lower-level managers and employees are not responsible enough to make proper decisions, upper-level management may need to centralize more of the decisions. IBM, General Motors, and Kodak are a few examples of decentralized companies.

INFORMAL ORGANIZATION

The planned, formal organization structure, which we have been discussing, has divisions, departments, and relationships. However, members of a working group develop their own informal relationships as they work together. This **informal organization** involves group norms, roles, status, personality traits, and the grapevine. The impact of the informal organization upon the goals and policies of the formal organization depends upon management's approval of the informal groups.

Group Norms

Group norms are standards that the group informally sets for themselves. Norms may involve performance standards, ways of relating to managers, and ways of interacting within the group. An observer reported, "I found three major norms to exist within my group: (1) you should not produce more than to 70% of your capabilities, (2) you should avoid brownnosing the manager, and (3) you should share gossip with the other employees."

Often the social pressures of the group may overpower the authority of the manager. Suppose an individual in the preceding example decided to break with the group and begin producing to 100% of her ability. This rate buster may become such an outcast with the department that the manager may have to let her go even though her performance is superior.

Characters in the Informal Organization

According to writers Deal and Kennedy, 90% of what goes on in an organization has nothing to do with formal events. Rather, the informal network, the ''hidden hierarchy,'' is in reality how an organization operates. They describe several characters in the informal culture. In addition to the storytellers and priests discussed in Enrichment Chapter A, several other roles emerge in the informal culture.

Whisperers

Whisperers are the powers behind the throne. They are the movers and shakers, but they do not hold formal authority. They get their power because people know that they are doing the boss's dealings. No one wants to cross whisperers because of the influence they have with Mr. Big.

Gossips

Gossips pass the latest ''Have you heard . . . ?'' like lightning throughout the organization. They are not always taken seriously, and they do not have to always be right; but they entertain and the organization tolerates them. They also reinforce the informal culture.

Secretarial sources

A knowledgeable person who wants to tap into the power network goes to the clerical people. They know what the organization is really like. Acting in a noninvolved role, they can tell you about the argument in the boardroom, a memo the vice-president's secretary is about to send, and who is about to do what to whom.

Spies

Every good manager has spies. Good spies are well-liked; people trust them enough to confide in them. They know all of the stories and the names that go with them. Cultural spies do not work with cloak and dagger; they seldom say a bad word about anyone, and most people like them. They know what is going on because they keep their fingers on the pulse of the organization.

Cabals

Two or more people who secretly join together for a common purpose form a cabal. The common purpose is usually to advance themselves. Two junior officers in the Dutch navy made a pact. They decided that, at cocktail parties and other social gatherings, each would go out of his way to tell people what a great guy the other was. One might say, ''Charlie is the best man in the navy. I can't believe how good he is with people.'' Or, ''Did you hear about the brilliant idea that Dave had?'' These two revealed their deal the day they were promoted to admiral — the two youngest ever appointed in the Dutch navy.

Source: Terrence E. Deal and Allan A. Kennedy, *Corporate Cultures,* Reading, Mass.: Addison-Wesley Publishing Co., 1982, pp. 85–97.

Effective managers are sensitive to informal norms and can even make them work in their favor.

Effective managers are sensitive to informal norms and can even make them work in their favor. The manager may create a norm of "employees liking their boss," and this can create better communication and cooperation.

Role

A **role** is a set of expected behaviors. Job descriptions outline formal work expectations, but the group may develop other views. Few job descriptions, for example, dictate that bank officers get involved with community projects. Yet, as one officer said, "I soon learned that the top managers expected you to help the bank's image by doing visible things to help the community." This was an informal role or expected behavior that came with the position.

Status

Status is the way that other people perceive an individual's prestige. The formal chain of command defines the authority ranking, but informal, social opinions may alter the manager's actual prestige and power.

Sometimes a manager or employee with low formal authority may attain high status with other employees. This might frustrate higher-level managers, causing conflict and disruption. For example, suppose the office manager has formal authority over the receptionist. Because the latter is outgoing, sociable, and well-liked by everyone in the office, she may have a higher status than the manager. Feeling the loss of power, the manager might decide to reassign the receptionist to a lesser position, claiming that the receptionist wasted too much time talking. However, the receptionist, with the strong support of the remainder of the office staff, might balk at the move and perhaps actually cause the manager to change her mind.

High-status managers sometimes use their power to build an empire and gain even more status, often at the expense of the organization's objectives. Many such managers become very ineffective while chasing fancy titles, hiring excessive subordinates, requesting oversized desks, and wearing $700 suits.

Personality Traits

Ways of acting socially—**personality traits**—also affect the informal organization. Employees may be outgoing or shy, active or docile, wild or straight, naive or informed. Employees make social connections with other employees according to their tastes, and some of these relationships can cause problems. Information meant to be confidential may be passed along among friends. And interoffice dating might create awkward and uncomfortable situations. Effective departments achieve a balance of personality traits where peo-

FUNNY BUSINESS

Stockworth by permission of Sterling & Selesnick, Inc., and The New York Times Syndication Sales Corp.

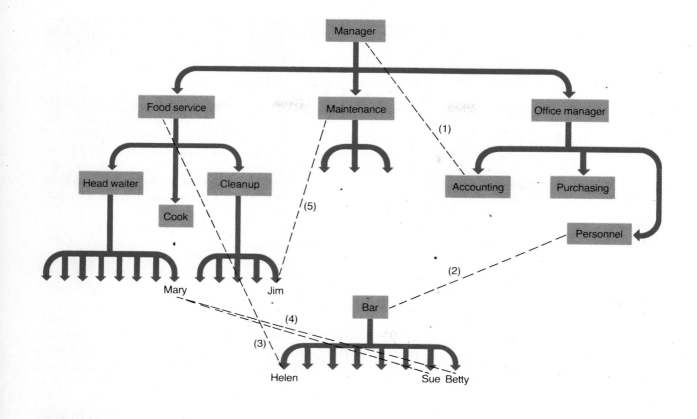

Formal relationships
---- Informal relationships

Figure 7.6
An organization chart showing informal relationships.

The Grapevine

Much information passes around the formal chain of command. In fact, rather stable networks develop and spread information informally. This informal communication network is a **grapevine.** While the grapevine often carries accurate information, it also carries rumors, exaggerations, and gossip. Some employees, wanting to be "in the know" spend a lot of their time gossiping about company business and employees. Sometimes rumors and exaggerations carried along the grapevine can seriously damage an organization. As a manager explained, "We had a rumor that the plant was closing down. Before we could get it stopped, we lost some of our best people and created so much confusion that it was 3 months be-

ple can accept, although not necessarily like and respect, each other's personality.

fore things got back to normal." Figure 7.6 diagrams part of an informal organization in a restaurant.

Management and the Informal Organization

Whether or not the informal organization works for or against management depends upon management's approach. Managers who effectively deal with the informal organization both recognize and accept its existence. They do not send informal networks underground with their policies or actions. Effective managers also identify informal leaders and try to get them to support the department's goals. As a manager who took over a group commented, "The previous supervisor tried to control all the informal discussions among the people. He even posted rules against rumors, discussing salary schedules, and the like. He

Sex in the Office: Changing Norms and Roles

In a 1976 survey by *Redbook* magazine, 90% of those questioned said that they had experienced some form of sexual harassment on the job. Phyllis Schlafy, an antifeminist crusader, says, "Sexual harassment on the job is not a problem for virtuous women." More and more women are entering the work force, and the norms governing relationships between the sexes appear to be unclear. In a recent, *Redbook-Harvard Business Review* study, nearly two-thirds of the respondents felt that their company should issue formal statements decrying sexual harassments. But only one-third said their companies had done so.

Historically, the role of women in business has been to work in low-power, serving jobs — secretaries, clerks, receptionists, and the like. And the norms regarding sexual behavior were more clearly defined. Certainly, there always have been and always will be office romances, but the traditional norm was to avoid them. The male adage expressed it as, "Don't fish off the company pier," or "Don't play where you work and don't work where you play."

However, the woman in business today is clearly creating new roles. Better educated and more ambitious, she is vying with males, often on equal terms, for power positions. It should be no surprise that this is straining traditional sexual norms at work. Working in close contact for long periods makes it possible to develop trust and affection for each other. And working on a risky venture with an attractive partner can create romantic, exciting feelings: adrenalin pumps, you feel nervous, elements of success create confidence. For many, this high-wire balancing act quite easily translates into sexual attraction.

In fact, the *Redbook* survey showed that more than half of the working women in their late thirties admitted to having affairs, compared to only 24% of housewives. Twenty-six percent of the readers of *Self* magazine admitted to having an "office affair."

Both men and women agree that working in offices with the opposite sex is both more exciting and enjoyable than working with a group of the same sex. A woman editor said, "Men make me feel good. I'm funnier, sharper, and feel more competent with them around." A male engineer agreed, ". . . we tend to show off a little more, to be at the top of our form when there are women around. It just makes work more fun, less rigid and demanding."

During this evolution of roles and norms, people differ about what the most effective relationships should be. Some say that office romance should be avoided by both sexes, that it is too risky on both a personal and professional level. Yet some say that the office is the best place to meet people and learn to trust them. This state of flux creates problems. Some women are bright, intelligent, and sexually emancipated, looking for action. Others are bright, intelligent, and equally appealing, but will not tolerate sexist remarks. And it is sometimes hard for men to tell the difference until they embarrass themselves and create an uncomfortable relationship. And women have to face the dilemma of wondering whether a potential relationship is sincere or a male power trip by an aggressive executive. While these informal relationships may be confusing, they can have just as much impact upon the organization as the formal relationships.

Source: Patrice D. and Jack C. Horn, *Sex in the Office,* Reading, Mass.: Addison-Wesley Publishing Company, 1982.

treated the informal association like a weed, and all he succeeded in doing was driving it underground."

In any formal organization, there are numerous informal relationships. The dotted lines in Fig. 7.6 show a few of the informal relationships between people in a large restaurant.

1. The manager is having an affair with the accounting manager.
2. The bar manager and the personnel manager are good friends. Both attended the same college for a short period, and their wives are good friends.
3. The food service manager is recently divorced, and he has been spending some time talking with Helen, a cocktail waitress.
4. Mary, a waitress, and Sue and Betty, both cocktail waitresses, are very good friends. They carpool to work and take most of their breaks together. This group is also one of the first to hear company gossip.
5. The maintenance manager has three part-time employees, but he is something of a loner. About the only person that he gets along well with is Jim in food service. Both worked together at another restaurant, and they developed a trust in each other.

ALTERNATIVE FORMS OF ORGANIZATION

Organizational critics suggest that the traditional structure is too inflexible to meet the fast-paced changes of today's modern business world. They criticize the formal structure for thwarting individual autonomy and development. Modern theorists suggest some new forms of structure that are more fluid.

The Matrix Organization

While the formal structure builds on power centers, the **matrix organization** identifies a project and puts together a team based on what members can contribute. Both the aerospace industry and the high-tech industry, recognizing the inflexibility and inappropriateness of a traditional structure, have adopted matrix forms of organization. Rather than being strictly divided by

Complex aerospace projects (such as the engines of the Space Shuttle) often require the flexibility of a matrix organization.

functions, project members may come from marketing, finance, production, and personnel departments. A **project manager** with line authority takes charge for the duration of the project. After completing the project, members return to their respective departments.

Figure 7.7(a) shows a matrix structure. It has the flexibility of temporarily drawing resources to various projects. But uncertainties and vague relationships sometimes result in confusion over authority. Suppose an employee leaves the marketing department and works for a project manager for 8 weeks. The project requires him to do things that his regular boss would not OK. He gets confused and a little insecure. Also, permanent managers may disagree with project managers over merit ratings, raises, promotions, and the amount of employee time that goes into the special project.

The Xerox Corporation's market share in copy machines fell to 45% in the early 1980s, down from a high of 96% in 1970. Although foreign competition accounted for a lot of the market share loss, Xerox executives freely admit that they strangled themselves with a matrix organization. While the heads of such groups as product planning, design, service, and manufacturing were based in Rochester, New York, they reported to separate executives at their Stamford, Connecticut, headquarters. Insiders admit that the groups had endless debates over features and design trade-offs. Many of the debates ran all the way to the president's office. It seemed that no one had the responsibility for getting the products out the door. Xerox redesigned its structure to set up four

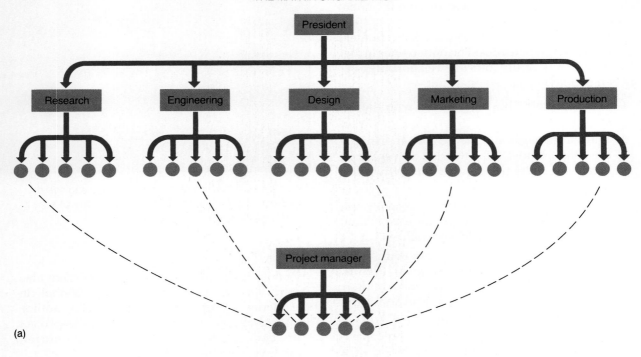

THE MATRIX ORGANIZATION

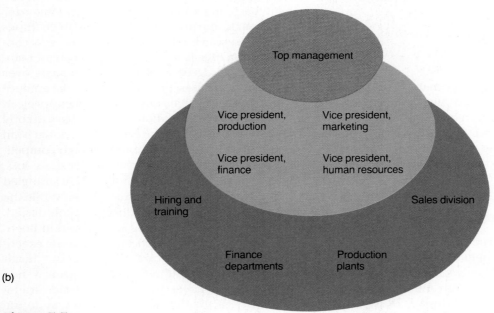

THE BEEHIVE ORGANIZATION

Figure 7.7
Organization charts for alternative forms of organization.

TABLE 7.1 ■ ADVANTAGES AND DISADVANTAGES OF ALTERNATIVE ORGANIZATIONAL FORMS

	Advantages	Disadvantages
Matrix	Flexibility Pooling talents More interaction Reduces boredom Employee participation	Confusion over authority Disagreement over merit ratings, promotions, pay raises
Beehive	Encourages communication More freedom Less structure	Confusion in authority and responsibility relationships Less clear evaluation and promotion channels
Doughnut	More interaction More freedom	Uncertainty Some confusion over formal relationships
Ladder	Specifies staff function Clarity More certainty	Less flexible More rigid Slower to change
Pyramid	Clarifies relationships and incentives in sales departments	Not adaptable to most functions

The Pyramid Organization

Direct sales firms sometimes use a unique organizational form called the **pyramid organization.** Some people are sensitive to the term "pyramid" because there are pyramid structures that are illegal. Under this organizational form, each salesperson usually gets a percentage or bonus, based on the sales of the employees that work under him or her. Employees' positions on the chart are determined by the date they were hired and by the number of people they hire to work for them. Companies selling health foods, household products, and lingerie are most likely to use a pyramid organization. The pyramid provides clear relationships for sales groupings, but it is not readily adaptable to all functional areas. For example, see Fig. 7.7(e). (And see Table 7.1 for a listing of the advantages and disadvantages of these five alternative organizational forms.)

SUMMARY

Organizations are given structure through departmentation. These departments are created by function, territory, product, process, or client. Organization charts are used to illustrate graphically each department and its relationship to other segments of the company. The three major types of charts are vertical, pyramid, and horizontal.

The major purpose of business organization is to establish channels of authority and responsibility. It also helps define job functions. Channels of authority are referred to as the chain of command. Delegation is when authority is passed on from one level of management to another. When a manager or employee accepts authority, there is a corresponding responsibility to be certain that tasks are accomplished as agreed. The acceptance of authority implies accountability.

The span of control refers to the number of employees responsible to any one manager. When a manager has authority over many employees, it is called a flat organization. A tall organization is where the manager has authority over only a few employees. Depending upon the situation, there are advantages to both a wide and a narrow span of control. Line authority is the right to direct the work of others, while staff authority is usually advisory and outside direct authority relationships. While conflicts often occur between line and staff employees, most firms have found this form of organization useful.

Centralization is a term that refers to authority and decision making being at the top or upper levels of the organization. When much of the authority is delegated to lower levels, it is called decentralization.

The informal organization refers to relationships and events that occur as people interact within the firm. This less structured behavior creates group norms, roles, status, friendships, and informal means of communication. These all have an impact upon workers and managers.

Alternatives to the line and staff forms of organization are the matrix, the beehive, the doughnut, the ladder, and the pyramid types of organization.

MIND YOUR BUSINESS

Instructions. The following are statements of managers describing their relationships with their subordinates. Check the statements that you believe describe ineffective relationships.

____ 1. I watch over my subordinates very closely at all times.

____ 2. I am aware that my subordinates will make some mistakes.

____ 3. I believe that a subordinate should be held responsible for everything that has been assigned to him or her.

____ 4. I perform many jobs that my subordinates could do because I enjoy the job very much myself.

____ 5. I ignore many mistakes that my subordinates make.

____ 6. I insist that subordinates check with me before they try anything that I have not previously approved.

____ 7. I like to have only a very few subordinates reporting to me at any one time.

____ 8. I have a firm policy against employees discussing rumors and grapevine information among themselves.

____ 9. I ask my subordinates to make an appointment when they wish to visit with me; this allows me to plan my day better.

____ 10. I do not allow my subordinates to go around me to a higher level of management.

See answers at the back of the book.

REVIEW QUESTIONS

1. Discuss the benefits of effective organization within a business. Why should a manager be concerned with organization?

2. What is departmentation? List the five major methods, with examples of each.

3. Why do managers create organization charts? What benefits do they provide? Describe the three major types of organization charts.

4. Define authority and responsibility. Explain the relationship between the two and give examples. What is the most common mistake that managers make with regard to these two concepts?

5. Explain chain of command; give an example.

6. What is delegation? What are the advantages and disadvantages of delegation within an organization?

7. Explain the concept of accountability. While it is similar to that of responsibility, what is the difference between the two terms?

8. What is meant by the span of control? How are the two extremes termed? What are the advantages of each?

9. Define both line and staff authority. How do they differ? Discuss the problems that tend to occur between the two.

10. Explain the difference between centralization and decentralization. How do these concepts affect the span of control? What is the major misconception regarding centralization?

11. What is meant by informal organization? In what specific ways does it affect the formal organization discussed earlier? Discuss the formal organization with regard to: (1) group standards, (2) expected behavior, (3) prestige, (4) friendships, and (5) communication.

12. The text covers five alternative forms of organization. Explain each of them and discuss their similarities and differences. What are some of the advantages of each?

CASES

Case 7.1: The Whole Earth Bakery, Part I

Esther Chavez owns and manages a bakery called the Whole Earth Bakery. The bakery makes health foods and sells them in local grocery and health food stores in Syracuse, New York. The enterprise employs sixty people: twenty-five in production, fifteen in marketing, two in finance, three in management, seven in maintenance, three in promotion and advertising, one general manager (Esther), two in purchasing and inventory control, and two in personnel. Esther also has a lawyer and a CPA on retainer.

Questions

1. Create an organization chart for the Whole Earth Bakery. Be sure to consider departmentation, authority and responsibility, chain of command, span of management, line and staff authority, and centralization. Explain the rationale behind your organization chart.

2. Consider modifying your chart to include some of the optional organizational forms (matrix, beehive, doughnut, ladder, and pyramid) presented in the latter part of the chapter.

Case 7.2: The Whole Earth Bakery, Part II

Several interesting conditions exist within the Whole Earth Bakery, which Esther Chavez owns and manages. For example: (1) Only five employees smoke. Many of the other employees are applying considerable pressure to prevent smoking on the work premises. The smokers feel repressed, and they think their rights are being violated. They only smoke in the areas designated for smoking. (2) Although Maria, one of the cooks who works in the kitchen, has no official management position, she exerts a lot of influence. She has been with the company a long time, and most employees hold her opinions in high regard. (3) Three employees, known as the "wild ones," are always throwing parties. They invite most of the firm's employees, but few attend. The parties sometimes get out of hand, and there is a feeling that the group attending the parties is immature and a bit irresponsible. (4) The kitchen employees work, by their own admission, at about 70% of their capacity. Individuals who try to be more productive are sure to feel the scorn of the group. (5) Roberta, a secretary, is the company gossip. She is always talking about personal and professional information that, as the secretary, she is privy to.

Questions

1. Analyze the case in terms of group norms, roles, status, personality traits, and the grapevine.

2. Explain how each of the five conditions in the case could be either beneficial or harmful to the company.

3. If you were the general manager, what would you do to ensure that each of the situations was as beneficial as possible?

After completing this chapter, you will be able to:

■ Describe the purpose of production management.

■ Discuss seven criteria that firms evaluate when deciding where to locate a plant.

■ Explain four different kinds of plant layout designs.

■ Identify the following production scheduling techniques: program evaluation and review technique (PERT), critical path method (CPM), and materials requirements planning (MRP).

■ Describe standard purchasing policies and procedures.

■ Explain the benefits and drawbacks of just-in-time inventories.

■ Explain the production process and production control.

■ Explain computer-aided design/computer-aided manufacturing (CAD/CAM) and flexible manufacturing systems (FMS) production.

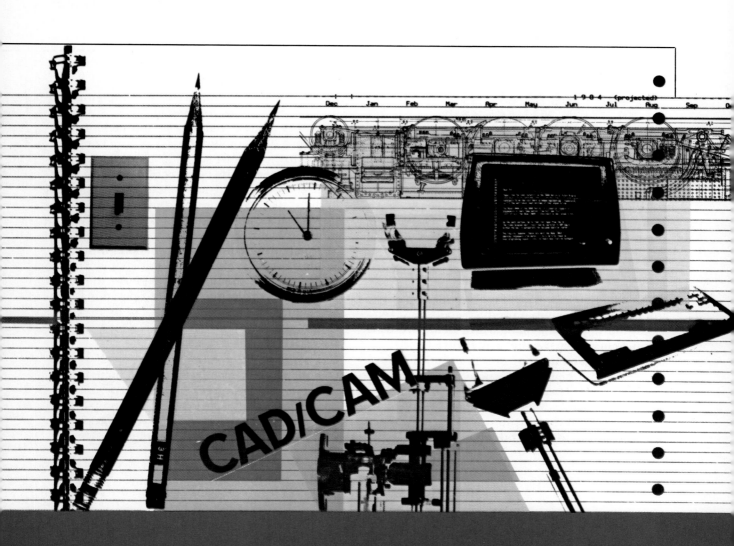

8

PRODUCTION AND
OPERATIONS
MANAGEMENT

During the 1981–1982 recession, many companies became very much concerned about productivity, a measure of goods produced in consideration of resources used. For many years, the United States had led the world in increased productivity rates and innovative productivity methods. However, in the past few years, the United States has lagged behind while other nations, especially Japan, have continued to increase their productivity rates. In 1981, Japan replaced the United States as the number 1 automobile producer in the world. Why has the United States fallen behind? Many reasons are given. While productivity methods is only one ingredient in the overall productivity rates, this chapter aids our understanding of production and operations management by exploring (1) the purpose of production management, (2) product planning, (3) materials management, and (4) the plant in operation.

THE PURPOSE OF PRODUCTION MANAGEMENT

A bicycle is produced by molding metal, rubber, plastic, and paint into a frame with wheels, spokes, handlebars, and a seat. We buy bicycles for fun, exercise, and transportation; but the scattered raw materials would not do us much good. **Production,** the process of creating goods and services, creates value by converting raw materials into finished forms. Conceptually, production includes: (1) input, (2) processing, and (3) outputs.

Production is crucial to the overall economy; the more effectively we produce goods and services, the higher the standard of living we can attain. Economists use the term **utility** to refer to the extent to which a good or service satisfies consumers. Thus, the major purpose of **production management** is to increase utility by better satisfying consumers' wants and needs.

Traditionally, production concepts have been applied strictly to the production process. More recently, however, managers are applying production techniques to other business functions, including finance, marketing, and general management. The application of production techniques to the broader scope of business operations is called **operations research** (OR). Using scientific, computer, and mathematical systems, OR implies that accounting firms, police departments, banks, and repair shops face many of the same problems in delivering their services as do manufacturing companies in making a product. While most of the examples in this chapter refer to manufacturing methods, we endorse the broad perspective of production and operations management.

PRODUCTION PLANNING

Like all areas of management, production management requires good planning. For our purposes, important aspects of production planning include plant location, plant layout, production scheduling, and capital requirements.

Plant Location

One of the first crucial decisions in establishing a production facility is location. Plant location decisions include where to place new facilities, as well as continuing evaluations of current facilities. Location decisions move through three phases. First, management selects the region of the country (the South, West, East, Midwest) it wants to build in. Second, choices narrow to cities and communities within the region. And third, they must select a specific site, a spot where they will build. These decisions usually hinge on a set of rather standard factors.

Labor supply. Any plant requires labor. Highly automated factories need few employees, but some plants employ thousands of people. Such companies try to determine if the community has a large enough labor force; then they check for skills. If the local labor force does not have the skills, the company considers the feasibility of training programs. A successful firm built a branch plant in another city. The executive explained, ''We like the city we are in, but the labor market is so tight, we can't hire the right people.

Other things being equal, a company would prefer to locate where labor unions are weak or nonexistent.

We had to build our branch where workers are available.'' Labor costs were once a significant concern, but geographic wage differentials have become smaller than in the past. Like wages, labor

---

BUSINESS BULLETIN

Modern Production Characteristics

Several terms characterize modern production methods.

1. **Mechanization** is the replacement of human labor with machines. While this process was popular during the Industrial Revolution (Chapter 1), it is becoming even more popular today. We are using machines and robots to perform many routine, diverse, and complex functions. Companies like machines because they do not join unions, demand higher wages, go on strike, need rest breaks, argue with each other, or call in sick. As one manager commented, ''Machines can often work 24 hours a day while performing tasks consistently and accurately.''

2. **Standardization** is the production of uniform and interchangeable parts. Via standardization, we can produce parts that can be used in many different kinds of products. For example, because of standardization, we can interchange many of the parts in cassette tapes, tape decks, and recorders.

3. **Automation** occurs when managers divide the production process into routine, standard (automatic) functions. This clear definition of tasks makes it easier for machines to perform the work.

4. An **assembly line** is a production process whereby an item moves along a designated route, sometimes on a conveyor belt, and people or machines perform specific operations at various stages along the line.

5. Because of mechanization, standardization, automation, and the assembly line, we are able to manufacture products in great quantities, that is, by **mass production.** Mass production, in turn, results in lower per unit costs, which makes the product affordable to more people, thereby raising the standard of living.

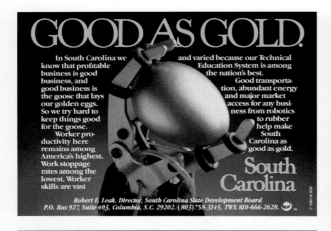

Although bidding for high-technology companies, these ads cite several of the location factors that any business must consider in production planning.

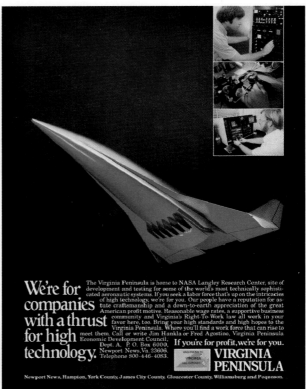
union strength is less of an issue than it was in the past. Other things being equal, a company would prefer to locate where labor unions are weak or nonexistent. Traditionally, unions have been stronger in the East, North, and West, than in the South and Midwest.

Raw materials. A skilled and plentiful labor force may be useless without raw materials. Many production companies require a plentiful supply of raw materials — unprocessed resources such as oil, coal, minerals, and agricultural products. A component part or semifinished product might also be a raw material: tires are finished goods for a tire manufacturer, but they are raw materials for automobile producers. To avoid prohibitive transportation costs, plants are located near weighty and bulky raw materials. For example, chemical companies select the Mississippi riverbanks of Louisiana to be near sulfur, salt, limestone, and oil deposits. Likewise, brick manufacturers locate near clay deposits, and lumber mills operate near forests. Firms that depend on highly perishable

> **"Market proximity is particularly important where customers require quick delivery, flexibility, and fast service."**

resources, such as the fishing industry, try to locate close to the source. Canning operations choose to locate in agricultural areas so they can reduce spoilage losses. Some products use raw materials that are geographically dispersed and their manufacturers locate nearby in order to reduce transportation costs; for example, a brewery may choose to locate in Oregon rather than Arizona.

Markets. If firms can transport raw materials economically, then they like to locate near their markets. As an analyst commented, "Market proximity is particularly important where customers require quick delivery, flexibility, and fast service." For example, many subcontractors for airframe manufacturers locate in Wichita, Kansas, where Beech, Cessna, and Gates Lear jet, the largest producers of small aircraft, are situated. For national markets, branch plants and warehouses enhance customer contact and service. However, when raw materials are costly to transport and finished products can be moved cheaply, it is better to be located near the input source rather than the prime consumers.

Power and water. Power and water are costly to store or transport. And both may be crucial to a manufacturer. Companies that need reasonable power sources or large quantities of water may be forced to locate near these resources. Chemical companies require a lot of power, whereas textile and furniture manufacturers are more concerned with labor resources. Major sources of power are electricity produced from dams, natural gas, coal, and more recently, nuclear energy. These power sources are limited, and prices vary widely within different locations.

A few companies choose to generate their own power, but for most this is an expensive venture. Similarly, steel mills and pulpwood plants are thirsty operations: They seek out rivers and lakes. The Coors brewery has been considering a plant in California, the state drinks 40% of its product. But Rocky Mountain spring water, an essential ingredient, anchors the company in Golden, Colorado.

Transportation. Except in very localized operations, either the raw materials or the finished products must be moved. Speed, flexibility, and cost considerations underlie most transportation decisions. Airplanes transport products rapidly, but the high cost may be prohibitive. Truck deliveries are flexible enough to alter days, hours, and routes to fit almost any schedule. The slower means of water and rail transporting are less expensive, but they are inflexible, both in terms of source and destination. And because of building and maintenance expenses, pipelines usually have to be in service for several years to justify their costs.

> **Rails still carry most of the freight in this country — several billion tons per year.**

Rails still carry most of the freight in this country — several billion tons per year. Trucks are becoming more popular because of flexibility and the vast network of highways. Waterways are prime movers of grain, gravel, coal, lumber, and other massive materials. Air transportation is used for small, expensive items such as computer parts. Because the cost of transportation varies within locations, these cost factors are considered in the plant location decision.

Community inducements. Communities, cities, and states have been recruiting industry for years. Recently, most states have greatly increased their efforts to attract new industry. They offer lavish, well-organized proposals. The wide variety of lures includes tax-free bonds, low-cost financing, easing of local zoning laws and even pollution standards, and free or nominal land cost. City and state officials say they need new industry to widen their tax bases and reduce unemployment. Texas officials persuaded Diawa Spinning Company of Osaka, Japan, to build a $20 million

COST FACTORS	SITE FACTORS	COMMUNITY FACTORS
Energy	Accessibility (roads, rails, airports)	Educational systems
Labor	Availability of goods and materials	Fire and police protection
Construction	Location of markets	Medical services
Taxes		Zoning laws
Real estate	**LOCAL BUSINESS FACTORS**	Legal restrictions
Rent		Cultural opportunities
	Related business activities	Political environment
RESOURCE FACTORS	Service businesses	Crime rate
	Available transportation	Tax rates and regulations
Manual labor	Subcontracting firms	Public services (business)
Skilled personnel	Vendor resources	
Natural resources		**EMPLOYEE CONSIDERATIONS**
Energy		
Land		Shopping facilities
		Housing costs
		Religious facilities
		Cost of living
		Public facilities and services

Figure 8.1
Considerations of plant locations.

cotton spinning mill in Leveland, Texas. Japanese textile companies are the biggest importers of Texas cotton. The state agency spent 3 years convincing Diawa to locate in Texas. Japanese officials inspected 32 possible sites, and each community submitted a bid for the plant. Leveland won by offering land and water rights for a mere $10. In explaining their decision, the city officials said, ''The cotton plant will mean 120 new jobs, and as many as 1000 in the near future. It was worth the cost of the land and water to have the plant in our community.''

While the factors described here are the major considerations for plant location, there are many others. Some of these appear in Fig. 8.1. Of course, not all these factors are equally important to all types of companies. For example, an oil refinery must be near a source of oil, regardless of other issues.

Evaluating location factors. Where a company locates is usually a compromise between several factors. One site has a more desirable labor supply, but another has better transportation facilities. One community offers an outstanding incentive package, but it would place the company in an inaccessible location. In almost all decisions,

key managers visit several sites, study the variables, and make individual evaluations. They may prepare elaborate estimates of total costs and expected returns at various volume levels for each

TABLE 8.1 ■ COMPANY LOCATION FACTORS

	Value 1–10	Relative Importance to Company 1–10	Total Points
Labor supply	6	10	60
Raw materials	8	9	72
Power and water	7	7	49
Transportation	8	9	72
Markets	4	4	16
Community inducements	9	3	27
Site factors	3	7	21
Cost factors	7	8	56
Community factors	9	5	45
Employee considerations	4	4	16
TOTAL POINTS (This Location)			454

location. Some use a point-rating system by which they list and assign points to the important factors. The list of factors and point values might appear as shown in Table 8.1.

This point system helps managers clearly evaluate the alternatives as they apply to their company. The site with the highest rating may not automatically be the final choice, but this system certainly helps in making an informed decision.

Plant Layout

Once plant location has been settled, the next planning task is plant layout. If all the plant location factors did not give you a headache, consider-ing all the criteria for plant layout may. **Plant layout** refers to the physical positioning of machines, work space, storage, shelving, and equipment within the building. First, we have to decide how big a plant we are going to build.

Plant capacity. The sales forecast is the major determinant of **plant capacity.** But sales in most industries fluctuate. So managers have to consider the cost of both unused space during slack times and lost orders due to shortages in peak periods. Size and number of machines also influence plant capacity. Larger and faster machines may produce lower per-unit costs, but higher sales volume is needed to justify them. Shift work also has an

TAKING STOCK

Auto Producers Come Back

After a deep recession in the auto industry, manufacturers of automobiles in the United States staged a strong comeback in 1983. In the second quarter of 1983, quarterly earnings rose 86% for General Motors, 165% for Ford, and 190% for Chrysler.

The auto comeback also means good news for suppliers, many of which have been operating below 50% capacity since 1979. The Eaton Corporation, which sells engine components to auto producers, says that both sales and profits are up. National Steel, which lost $52 million in the second quarter of 1982, made a $9.3 million profit in the second quarter of 1983. They credited the turnaround to increases in auto-related orders.

Machine tools, which are also very dependent upon the auto industry, are also beginning to fare better. "When the auto industry reaches 80% capacity, machine tools take off," a spokesperson said.

As a nation, we are very much concerned about what happens to the auto industry because it has such a tremendous impact upon our economy. For example, the auto industry:

- Provides, directly and indirectly, about 12 million jobs.
- Generates about $25.8 billion taxes annually.
- Uses about 15% of U.S. steel.
- Uses 60% of U.S. rubber.
- Uses 62% of U.S. lead.
- Totals about one-fourth of all retail sales.

Therefore, success among auto producers usually means success in many other aspects of our economy.

Source: "Spreading Impact of Auto Comeback," *U.S. News & World Report,* Aug. 8, 1983, p. 44.

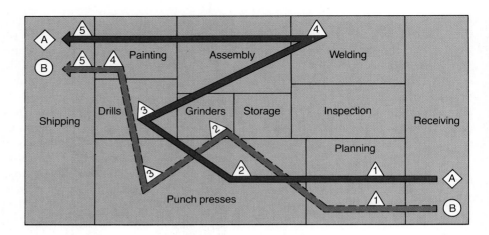

**Figure 8.2
Example of a process layout.**

impact on plant size. If an around-the-clock, three-shift operation is practical, a smaller plant is adequate. A one-shift plant would require a much larger plant for the same output.

Manufacturing processes. As plant capacity affects layout, so does the type of manufacturing process. An **intermittent process** has periodic starting and stopping points. Product #612 may appear on the production schedule for 25 days, be off the schedule for 13 days, and back on again for 22 days. The schedule may change often, according to the demand of that product. Intermittent processes turn out products in small volumes and use easily adaptable, general-purpose equipment. A **continuous process** operates for long, uninterrupted periods—months or even years. But "continuous" does not mean "indefinite." New developments and style changes may cause changes in the process. Continuous operations employ specialized, highly efficient equipment to create large volumes of standardized output. **Custom manufacturing,** or producing to special customer specifications, has declined in popularity because it is so expensive. Standardized, mass-produced products are much less expensive. Some clothes, a few automobiles, and some homes are still custom-made, primarily for status-seeking and wealthy customers.

Examples of plant layouts. Used primarily for intermittent manufacturing, the **process layout** clusters all functions of a particular type. Processes such as welding, painting, assembly, drilling, and finishing are all done in specific, prees-

tablished sections of the plant. Processes such as inspecting, planning, and receiving also have their designated areas. The more dangerous operations are often grouped and separated. Each product may flow through the plant in a different path; flexibility is necessary because one piece of equipment is used for several different products. However, having a different flow pattern for each product reduces operating efficiency. And it requires careful planning. See Fig. 8.2 for an example of a process layout. Note how the products follow different routes. Product A comes into receiving and moves to the planning department, is routed through punching, drilling, and welding, then shipped. Product B is received and goes from planning to grinding, punching, painting, and shipping.

In a **product layout,** operators and equipment are stationed in one spot; assembly line conveyer belts move materials and semifinished products through each station. Unlike a process layout, the same types of processing equipment

**Figure 8.3
Example of a product layout.**

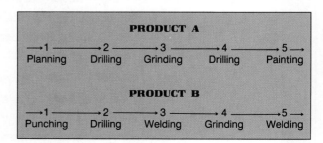

are frequently located in different parts of the plant. Product layouts that are more adaptable to continuous operations are desirable where a company produces a few highly standardized products in large volume. Straight-line flows that require minimum movement in transporting parts between operations are most common. Raw materials enter one end, flow straight through, and come out the other end as finished products (see Fig. 8.3). Other product layouts may utilize U-shaped, circular, or S-shaped flow patterns as shown in Fig. 8.4. The U-flow is convenient when construction requires shipping and receiving at the same end of the building. A circular flow also permits shipping and receiving at the same end of the building. When operations are physically crowded, the serpentine or S-flow lends efficiency. With each method, the type of production process also affects the type of flow pattern.

Fixed-position layouts move employees, equipment and even machinery around the stationary product. It is impractical to circulate large products such as some airplanes, ships, and bridges. Fixed layouts are flexible, but because they are slow, tend to be more expensive. Many plants use **combination layouts** — utilizing elements of all three layout types. Here, combinations of the process and product layouts and flow patterns are essential. Wrong choices can result in the failure of the venture.

Production Scheduling

After the plant location and layout have been settled, the next production planning step is scheduling. **Scheduling** identifies the sequence and timing of each step in the production process. By scheduling, a planner can forecast the time of each production process and project costs, sales, and profits. Each of the several methods of scheduling usually includes:

- A listing of all things that have to be done.
- An estimate of the time each operation will take.
- Which operations have to come before others.
- An estimate of the total time required for each project.

Control charts are used to illustrate the production processes and chart the time required for

U-flow   S-shaped   Circular

**Figure 8.4
Basic flow patterns for product layouts.**

each step. Many scheduling techniques use control charts. We describe three popular scheduling techniques here.

Program evaluation and review technique. One of the most popular scheduling techniques is **program evaluation and review technique (PERT).** Originally developed by the U.S. Navy, PERT identifies each job that makes up the project and details the time required for each step. It also recognizes that some jobs are dependent upon other jobs and that some jobs must be completed before others. Planners estimate the time for each task and identify a sequence of operations that requires the longest time period. This becomes

Fixed-position layouts are employed in jet aircraft production, bringing workers, machinery, and pre-assembled parts to the stationary product.

the critical path, that is, the sequence of processes that takes the longest to complete.

The longest path through the diagram is the critical path; it is the quickest the job can be completed.

To illustrate how PERT works, consider the process of manufacturing shoes. In a much-simplified example (see Table 8.2), we can divide the process into ten different tasks, each requiring a given number of time units. Now, look at the PERT diagram in Fig. 8.5. Notice that Tasks #4, #5, and #8 must be completed before Task #9, as must Tasks #2, #6, and #7. The longest path through the diagram, represented by the heavy line, is the critical path; it is the quickest the job can be completed. The circles indicate the completion of a task. Often, the length of the lines indicates the time required for each task.

Critical path method. When planners use the longest process within a task to estimate production completion times, it is called **CPM (critical path method).** In the shoe manufacturing example, the critical path is sixty-two time units (which

could be hours, days, weeks, or months). The total for all processes is eighty-eight time units. Once the critical path is determined, other processes are planned around it. For example, the work on heels and soles takes less time; fewer employees will be required to complete those tasks. Scheduling will allow for the proper number of soles, heels, and tops to be completed and received for the next process of sewing them together.

Materials requirements planning. In planning, managers need to get the proper number of products or the right amount of materials to a specific place at a certain time. The method of accomplishing this task is called **materials requirements planning (MRP).** Looking again at the shoe example, notice how heels (eighteen time units), soles (twelve time units), and tops (thirty-three time units) must arrive at the same point for assembly. If too few parts arrive, it will stop the rest of the operation. If too many are completed, storage and stockpiling problems occur. MRP allows for the exact number to arrive at the proper place and time.

Of course, these methods can be used in other functions of production management. PERT charts, for example, are used in plant operation as well as production control. These methods are critical in production scheduling, however. Like the other aspects of production planning, scheduling can make the difference between success and failure.

TABLE 8.2 ■ THE TASKS AND TIME UNITS REQUIRED TO MANUFACTURE SHOES

Task No.	Task	Number of Time Units
1	Receiving	1
2	Cutting heels	8
3	Cutting soles	8
4	Cutting pattern	12
5	Dyeing leather	8
6	Glueing heels	4
7	Glueing heels to soles	6
8	Sewing tops	13
9	Sewing tops to heels and soles	14
10	Finishing	10
11	Packaging	2
12	Shipping	2

Capital Requirements

While capital or finance topics are covered in several other places within the text, some discussion is fitting here because of the tremendous investment required for modern production plants. As costs of equipment may change rapidly, accurate forecasts are difficult. Too often, investment is much greater than anticipated. The U.S. government's planning of the B-1 bomber is a prime example, as are many atomic energy plants. Large businesses, especially production companies, have the same problems. Consider the costs of land, buildings, technical equipment and machinery, design and engineering costs, storage facilities, and transportation. Many of these are difficult to forecast 5 years into the future, not to mention the cost of capital itself. The cost of spe-

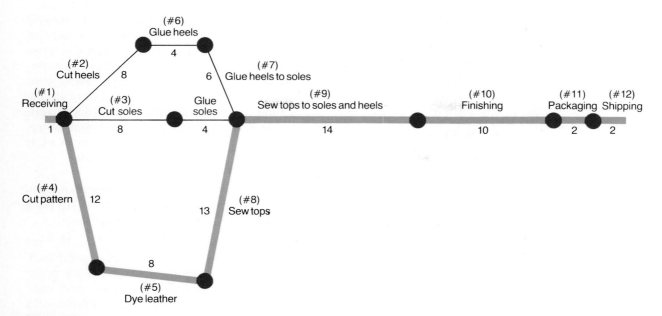

Figure 8.5
PERT chart for the manufacture of shoes.

cialized manufacturing equipment and machines is staggering. For these reasons, planners need not only adequate financing but large funds for unexpected costs.

MATERIALS MANAGEMENT

Once the specifics of product planning have been established, the next function is materials management. Effective plant management requires proper handling of materials used in the production process, including purchasing and inventory control.

Purchasing

Have you ever purchased a car, a suit, a pair of shoes, or an electric blender? Think of all the decisions you had to make. "What model, brand, or size should I get? How much should I pay? Does the seller have a good reputation? When will the product be available? What is a reasonable price?"

Since few businesses exist entirely on their own, thousands of purchasing decisions must be made. To make a large product, a company might purchase from as many as 14,000 different suppliers located throughout the United States and other parts of the world. Purchases include raw materials for products, supplies, services from other companies, land, buildings, and even automobiles and insurance. The aim of purchasing is to get the right amount, quality, and price from the right place at the right time.

Purchasing policies. Large and medium-size firms devote a department to the purchasing function. The department head is called an agent or general purchasing agent. This manager may supervise a staff of buying specialists. A company establishes policies on exactly how the purchasing will be done. These policies assign the buying authority and responsibility to certain departments and individuals. Policies also set limits on what can be purchased. For example, the personnel department may be in charge of the purchasing office, but only up to certain quantities and amounts. The mailroom manager may purchase postage and mailing supplies. Different people in production may be responsible for purchasing raw materials, semifinished products, production supplies, and various services. The purchasing authority may vary, according to budget, need, and company projections. This authority may be centralized, with the decision making in the higher levels of the organization. Other firms decentralize this authority, giving it to various departments or local branches.

In establishing purchasing policies, managers have to resolve several issues, including the following:

1. *Make-or-buy decisions.* **Make-or-buy decisions** involve a firm deciding whether they should make a part or buy it from another firm. Sometimes a larger company may produce many of its own needs; other times, the company may choose to buy many things. Should a car manufacturer purchase tires or create its own department to produce them? Should a winery grow or purchase its grapes? A cheese producer may have a large farm operation or purchase milk from a local farmers co-op.

2. *Hand-to-mouth buying vs. forward buying.* In **hand-to-mouth buying,** a company places orders frequently and usually in small amounts. This style of buying is popular when products are perishable, needs vary, or storage is a problem. In **forward buying,** a company usually purchases large quantities less frequently. For example, a winery may purchase vast amounts of grapes only once a year, whereas a cheese producer may purchase varying amounts of milk daily.

3. *Contract buying.* Producers may enter into contracts with suppliers, or **vendors,** to purchase goods of certain quantities over several years. A contract may be necessary because both the buyer and seller must be certain of the deal. The producer needs the materials to ensure smooth running of the plant, and the vendor needs to know that the products will be purchased. **Contract buying** is popular in heavy industries, such as automobiles, electronics, construction, and transportation.

4. *Bidding.* Often a producer will resort to **bidding** from vendors. Vendors are told the quantities and specifications of a certain good and then submit bids on what they will charge for a good or service. In large purchases, it benefits the buyer by creating competition between the vendors. Usually, the lowest bid will result in business for the supplier.

5. *Reciprocal buying.* Sometimes companies will agree to buy from each other. This form of **reciprocal buying** is popular in some types of business. However, both illegal and unethical practices may result unless this type of agreement is carefully guarded. For example, a computer company and a television manufacturer may become vendors for each other. But if the arrangement is too restrictive, each may lose business to other companies.

Purchasing goods. To help understand the kinds of goods that companies purchase, we have divided them into four general catagories.

1. *Raw materials.* Raw materials are the resources from which a product is produced. These include lumber, iron, oil, dairy products, rubber, plastics, chemicals, and minerals. These raw materials are combined in the production process to create the finished products that we buy in the stores.

2. *Semifinished goods.* Sometimes production companies purchase goods that are already partially manufactured. These are called semifinished or semimanufactured products.

3. *Supplies.* Supplies do not go into the actual product, but they assist in its production. Examples include cleaning materials, sandpaper, saw blades, and office supplies.

4. *Capital items.* Machinery and major equipment used to produce the product are called capital items. Examples are robots, finishing machines, drill presses, saws, lifts, trucks, and conveyors.

Purchasing services. In addition to goods, production companies also purchase a wide range of services, such as the following:

1. *Industrial services.* Firms may hire other companies to clean their shops, building, and machines, remove their waste products, protect against theft, or provide food for employees. Outside companies can often provide these industrial services more efficiently than the company itself.

2. *Professional services.* Companies may also hire outside professionals to perform a variety of services including advertising, printing,

These fibers being readied for shipment are semifinished goods, the material basis for a variety of finished products.

data processing, accounting, legal assistance, and management consulting.

3. *Subcontracting work.* Sometimes a firm will hire other companies to complete all parts of a particular job. The original company is called the prime contractor, and the firms doing the work are called subcontractors. This arrangement is most common in the construction business. A contractor may hire or subcontract other companies to complete the electrical, plumbing, paint, glass, or insulation aspects of a job. Manufacturing companies often subcontract parts of their work on a permanent or part-time basis to other companies.

Purchasing procedures. The actual purchase usually follows a plan with well-established steps. While these procedures vary from firm to firm, they usually include describing specifications, completing a purchase requisition, selecting a supplier, placing the order, and receiving the goods.

1. *Specifications.* Various departments within the company usually cooperate in creating the specifications (specs) of the goods to be puchased. Engineering, production, quality control, and sales departments may all contribute to the desired specifications. For example, an office might require a calculator to compute square roots, have a certain storage capacity, and perform so many calculations per minute. For repetitive purchases such as nuts, bolts, and screws, there are industry-wide standards that are usually graded; establishing specs in this case simply means identifying the grade.

2. *Purchase requisition.* The need for materials, supplies, or services is recognized either by the people who use them or by someone in a materials management department. When inventories run below the desired level, they indicate the need to reorder with a **purchase requisition** — a form listing the quantities, specifications, and date needed. Usually, this form is routed to the proper department for approval and then to the purchasing department to initiate the buying process.

3. *Supplier selection.* Where does a company buy? From the vendor with the lowest price? Not always. While price is important, there are other considerations: Speed of delivery, dependability, quality of product, the sales-person, reputation of the firm, and previous experiences with the vendor all affect the final decision.

4. *Order placement.* When agents select a supplier, they complete a **purchase order.** This, in effect, is a contract to buy. If the purchase is large, agents will probably make frequent follow-ups to see how the order is progressing and make sure that the delivery is on time.

5. *Receiving.* Upon delivery, a receiving clerk checks the quantity, price, and other qualities against the purchase order to be certain that they fit the specs. If the shipment is correct, the clerk makes a note on the supplier's invoice and sends it to the purchasing department where it is approved for payment. If the

Production Techniques in Service Organizations

Unlike a product, a service is intangible and perishable. Services are usually used at the time they are created; and, for the most part, they cannot be stored.

How services differ from products

Services differ from products in at least four ways. One, services are intangible. When producing a product, employees can see, touch, and perhaps taste and smell the item. But since services are intangible, neither employees nor customers can touch or taste them. Further, producers cannot get a patent on services. When Hertz, the car rental company, created the Hertz #1 Club to make it possible for customers to get a car without filling out all the forms, Avis and other competitors were quick to copy this service.

Two, services are perishable. Nothing is more perishable than an airline seat, a hotel room, or an hour of a consultant's time. If these are not used at the time they are available, you cannot inventory them. Three, services are heterogeneous. Holiday Inn may train all of their reservation clerks in the same way, but there is no way they can ensure that service in Los Angeles will be the same as service in New York. The same services will differ among locations and from hour to hour, depending upon the mood and motivation of the clerk. Four, we typically produce and use services at the same time. While we design manufacturing facilities with employees and products in mind, we design service facilities with the customer in mind.

Applying production techniques to service operations

Even with these differences, we can apply many production techniques to service operations. Here are three examples of plant layout applied to the creation of services.

- *Straight-line flow.* In straight-line flow layouts, products move from one station to another through the production process in a straight line (for example, an assembly line). A cafeteria is an example of a straight-line flow for service operations. Customers move in a straight line through the process as they are ''served'' with food of their choice.

- *Job shop.* In a job shop, employees may produce many different types of products by using different sequences and combinations of activities. A job shop usually produces custom-made products for customers. An example of a service job shop is the more traditional restaurant, which provides meals to order. Medical doctors who are general practitioners are another example of a service job shop.

- *Intermittent processes.* While both line and job shop processes provide a continuous flow of products, some require intermittent processes. For instance, service firms have to manage the periodic task of introducing new services to their customers. Further, architects and movie studios often find themselves managing the services of projects. They have to concern themselves with the starting and stopping of operations as well as with their integration.

Thus even though the creation of services differs from production of a product, production techniques are still useful to service companies.

order is deficient, the purchasing agent usually works out the difference with the supplier.

Inventory Control

Purchasing policies and procedures are influenced by how much inventory a company maintains and the size of the order. When the plant runs out of materials, production stops, resulting in costly waste. Too much inventory can result in storage costs, bottlenecks, obsolescence, insurance, theft, deterioration, and waste. While inventory control is important to all companies, it is crucial to a production company.

Small inventories require frequent, small orders. They result in increased ordering costs and paperwork. But small inventories reduce storage and handling costs. Larger inventories allow for volume discounts, ensure necessary levels, and incur less ordering costs. But they require the necessary inventory and handling costs. Many techniques are used to balance these storage and ordering costs. One popular method is called **economic order quantity (EOQ).** Assume that a plant annually uses 10,000 units of Part 40B. Placing an order costs $20, and the annual inventory costs average $.10 per unit. Economic order quantity is obtained by determining the point at which the combined costs are the least. EOQ is illustrated in Fig. 8.6.

This is the most economic order size because it balances the inventory and ordering costs. While other technical methods provide guidelines for ordering quantities, additional practical reasons also affect the decision. **Anticipation inventories** exist because of some planned future need. Model changeovers, anticipated strikes, vacation shutdowns, recessions, or intensive sales

Annual cost (in thousands of dollars)

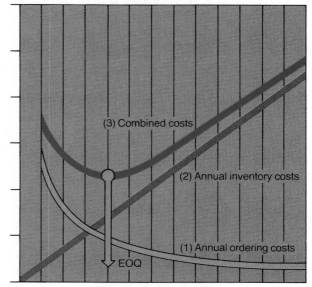

Order quantity (in number of units ordered at one time)

Figure 8.6
A chart for determining economic order quantity (EOQ).
(1) The annual costs of ordering; this cost decreases as the size of the order increases. (2) Annual inventory costs; this cost increases as larger quantities are ordered. (3) This is the combination of ordering costs and inventory costs.

campaigns are factors that affect future needs. **Buffer inventories** are additional orders that serve as safety measures against unforeseen events; demands may exceed forecasts, or output may deviate from plans. Figure 8.7 lists factors favoring large and small inventories.

Finally, to keep an accurate record of inventory on hand, people actually count the materials and supplies at scheduled times. **Materials in-**

Figure 8.7
Factors that favor large or small inventories.

MAINTAIN LARGER INVENTORIES WHEN:	MAINTAIN SMALLER INVENTORIES WHEN:
1. Cost of placing an order is great	1. Inventory costs are high
2. Storage is inexpensive	2. Goods deteriorate rapidly
3. Quantity discounts are substantial	3. Storage costs are expensive
4. Prices are expected to rise	4. Goods are easy to get
5. Shortages are anticipated	5. Cash is hard to get or in short supply
	6. Prices are expected to drop

ventories record the materials that go into the finished product; **supplies inventories** register the supplies on hand; and **merchandise inventories** count the finished products.

To cut inventory costs, many firms are switching to the just-in-time method popularized by Japan.

To cut inventory costs as much as possible, many firms are switching to the just-in-time method popularized by Japan. **Just-in-time inventory** means ordering smaller quantities more frequently and receiving them as close to their use as possible. This drastically reduces the need for large shipments that have to be stored and controlled on the premises. At Apple Computer's new Macintosh plant in Fremont, California, no more than 5 days' worth of supplies for any one component are kept at the site, reducing inventory costs and the possibility of damage in storage. When large purchasers convert to such a system, suppliers often have to move closer to their customer. When General Motors modernized its plant in Baltimore, many suppliers called to ask about sites nearby.

Apart from cost reduction, other benefits develop when suppliers cluster near the producer. Because deliveries and contacts occur more frequently, engineers from both supplier and purchaser get together more often and help solve common problems. However, there is a disadvantage to the supplier because they have to depend rather heavily upon one outlet for their products.

THE PLANT IN OPERATION

Now that the plant has been located, the layout established, and all materials arranged for, the stage is set for plant operation: production processes and production control.

Production Processes

Routing specifies the particular path through which a production process will take place. While it is planned for in, say, a PERT chart, those plans have to be put into effect within the plant. Back to the shoe example. At #9 on the assembly line, sewn tops arrive at the same place as the glued soles and heels. Routing allows not only for the separate process, but also for the right number to arrive at the proper place for the next step of the production process.

Dispatching provides work orders to managers and supervisors, allows for the resources of labor and materials, and outlines the schedule of completion for the specific task. It activates all the resources necessary for the actual performance of production, the next step of the process. **Performance** is, simply, the action of machines and labor in the actual production process. It requires supervisors to be certain that each step is completed properly and to solve any problems or interruptions. The finished product now comes off the production line.

There are two major types of production processes: the analytic and the synthetic processes. The **analytic process** is the breaking down of raw materials into one or more products. The final product may or may not resemble the raw materials. A good example would be the making of records out of plastic products. The **synthetic**

Inventory control functions for Apple Computer's production of the Macintosh personal computer are handled by a single Macintosh.

process is the combining of two or more materials in the production of one final product. Cleaning fluid, for example, may contain several raw materials that are combined in special quantities in order to produce the final product.

Production Control

Even with the most careful plans and execution, results often fall short of the goal. Production control compares production progress to plans and checks for proper product quality. Quality control reflects deviations in schedule, quantity, and quality of the finished product.

Progress control. With **progress control,** managers compare actual production time to the schedule. An individual or a department may have responsibility for production control, and there are a number of ways to check actual progress. For an intermittent process, each department's foreman may prepare daily reports listing work ordered, work completed, and work still in progress. Another method is to issue job tickets that go to production control, signifying that the job is completed. Also, standard forms may be filled out as each job is completed. Production control receives these reports to get an accurate progress status.

The **Gantt chart,** developed by Henry Gantt, uses a bar graph to compare what was planned to what remains to be done. Figure 8.8 is an example. Order numbers are listed in the left column. Solid bars show planned starting and stopping times,

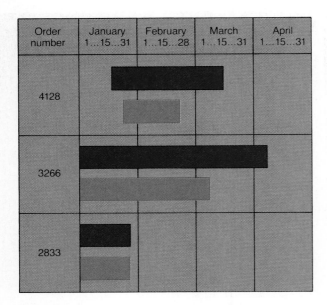

Order number	January 1...15...31	February 1...15...28	March 1...15...31	April 1...15...31
4128				
3266				
2833				

Figure 8.8
A Gantt chart.

and light bars represent actual progress. The Gantt chart is simple and revealing, but it is used less frequently today because of the time required to keep its data current. Much of this same information is recorded and displayed by modern computers.

The basics of progress control are similar for continuous manufacturing. They begin with the authorization to produce. Planning issues a production schedule with quantities and dates. A tally, comparing the actual number produced with that planned, is kept at regular intervals. Production control then uses a variety of charts such as the one in Fig. 8.9 to compare actual and scheduled output.

Production that is behind schedule usually adds to the costs and may delay delivery dates, so production control tries to detect problems early. Lags result from breakdowns, improper planning, poor material handling, supervisory errors, employee disturbances, or strikes. The plant tries to catch up by working overtime, adding shifts, pressuring suppliers, and hiring additional or part-time people. Ahead-of-schedule problems are less serious, but production control must find out why there is a variance. They may put other items into production sooner than expected, build up inventories, or cut back production as a result.

Computer-aided design and computer-aided manufacturing. Of course, more recently, companies have been using computers quite extensively in all aspects of their manufacturing processes. In **computer-aided design (CAD)** systems, designs can be sketched on an electronic drafting board or directly on a computer screen, thereby allowing the operator to view from any angle or modify in any way a stored design. CAD systems are typically used by aerospace, automotive, and manufacturing companies for mechanical design and drafting; by electronics firms for printed circuit and integrated circuit design; by architectural and construction organizations for structural design; by energy companies and utilities for plant design and layout; and by government agencies and private companies for various mapping applications. General Motors, for instance, uses a CAD system to help with complicated engine and chassis design problems.

Computervision Corporation, the industry leader in CAD/CAM products, says that the 1970s was the decade of CAD and that the 1980s will be the decade of **computer-aided manufacturing**

Figure 8.9
A control chart.

Cumulative output

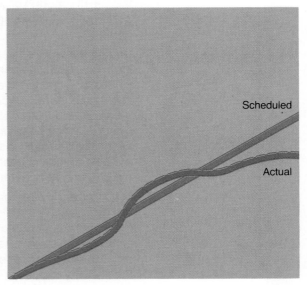

Days

Using a CAD/CAM system, a small firm like Compo Industries can quickly and cost-efficiently design and manufacture a variety of their product-molds for shoe soles.

(CAM). It is not unusual, during batch manufacturing, for a part to stand idle for weeks, waiting at each step of the manufacturing process for a machine tool to become available. About 95% of the time required to manufacture a typical part is spent waiting for machines; 3.5% is devoted to setup; and only 1.5% of the time is actual machining. By intelligently collecting, integrating, and using information, CAM systems can increase productivity and cut manufacturing costs. Compo Industries, a firm that designs and fabricates injection molds for shoe manufacturers, uses a CAD system to design shoe molds and a CAM system to machine the finished mold designs.

The next step in industry automation, in realizing the fully automated factory of the future, is **computer-integrated manufacturing (CIM),** the integration of design and manufacturing activities and of all ancillary elements of manufacturing operations. Electronic manufacturing is an important and growing segment of CIM. Automated numerical control drilling for printed circuit boards, automatic component insertion, and automatic testing are a few examples of CIM technologies.

Flexible manufacturing systems. Flexible **manufacturing systems (FMS),** the newest thing in production, integrate all the elements in the production process. Computer-driven systems control practically everything, including machine shop operations, transporting parts and products within the plant, and even replacing worn-out or broken drill bits.

A flexible manufacturing system can cost $25 million or more, but it is infinitely more flexible than conventional, numerically controlled operations. For instance, designers can instantly reprogram an FMS to make new parts or products. Thus, one machine can replace several conventional lines and save in capital investment. General Electric uses an FMS to produce 2000 different versions of an electric meter, and IBM was able to shorten the time needed to introduce new products by adopting an FMS that made it possible to build several successive models on the same production line.

To date, one of the largest FMSs exists near Mount Fuji in Japan's Fanuc Ltd.'s plant, which produces machine tools and parts for robots. The part of the plant that produces machine tools covers 54,000 square feet, and a single controller supervises the whole area via closed-circuit television. If something goes wrong, the controller can shut down the part of the operation with the problem and reroute the work to other stations.

Robots versus Jobs

Every time a nation steps up its automation efforts, people debate whether the overall impact will be positive or negative. Today, the concern centers around the increasing use of robots. About 15,000 robots were in use in the United States in 1983. By 1993, the figure is expected to balloon to 268,000.

Industry sees these "smart" machines as a blessing because they expect them to cut labor costs while, at the same time, increasing both quality and productivity. However, labor fears that the machines will take away jobs. An Arthur D. Little, Inc., expert says that three jobs will be taken over by every two robots installed by 1993. Other experts place the displacement figure even higher; maybe as many as 3.8 million jobs will be affected. However, some of the displaced workers will be transferred or retained within the company, maybe as many as 85% in some cases.

Donald Smith, director of the University of Michigan's industrial development division, says that if firms do not use robots, "silent firings"—loss of jobs because industries cannot compete—may reduce the jobs available. General Motors contends that, with almost 2000 robots in place, workers have not lost jobs. Another company says that robots will result in net additions to the work force because they will create jobs in the "care and feeding" of robots.

Still, Harley Shaiken, labor analyst at MIT, asks, "What of the welder in Flint, Michigan? He's being asked to commit economic suicide so GM can return to profitability."

Briggs & Stratton Corporation, however, resists robots. As the world's leading producer of low-cost engines, used mostly in lawn mowers and garden tractors, they have been profitable for years. What's more, they maintain that human skill and agility, not automation, are responsible for their high-quality, successful products. Briggs & Stratton, which may put as many as 500 parts into one of its machines, emphasizes effective management, good communication, worker participation, and a piecework incentive payment system. Some workers earn as much as $30,000 per year; one visitor said, "They even run to and from the bathrooms." The company says they will consider automation whenever practical, but they do not believe they will ever go to a completely automated, unmanned plant.

What overall impact do you think the increasing use of robots will have upon our economy? Do you believe we will be:

____ A. Much better off   ____ D. Somewhat worse off
____ B. Somewhat better off   ____ E. Much worse off
____ C. No significant change

Give reasons for your response.

A. _____
B. _____
C. _____

Sources: "Will Robots Bring More Jobs—or Less?" *U.S. News & World Report,* September 5, 1983, p. 25; "Where Robots Can't Compete," *Fortune,* February 21, 1983, p. 64.

Abusing Products before Using Them

United Laboratories (UL), a nonprofit organization that tests products strictly for safety, burned and bashed, torched and trashed, sank and smashed nearly 60,000 products in 1982 in their testing procedures. Firms are willing to pay $2000 and more to UL to test their products. Consumers look to the UL label as proof of a product's safety, and the imprimatur may even help a manufacturer defend itself against product liability suits since it proves the manufacturer sought independent evaluation. Here are a few examples of their testing methods:

- UL, with a machine, opened and closed a waffle iron 6000 times. They opened refrigerator doors 30,000 times and microwave ovens 100,000 times. Technicians then examined the wiring and other parts for possible danger.

- A 150-pound technician (the likely maximum weight of a child) rode and bucked for 25 minutes on a coin-operated toy elephant while observers checked volts, watts, amperes, and motor temperature.

- To test an electric sander, technicians dropped it three times from a 6-foot height onto a concrete floor. Then they looked for cracks and exposed wires that might be dangerous to an operator.

- UL staff drilled holes in the bottom of a fiberglass skiff, slashed the seats, and held it submerged for 18 hours. If the boat got back to the surface horizontally, they declared it seaworthy.

A safe is tested for resilience to a cutting torch in the burglary-proofing section of Underwriters Laboratories.

Source: ''The Lively Art of Product Abuse,'' *Fortune,* May, 1983, pp. 93–98.

Although there were about thirty FMS in the United States in early 1983, Japan had as many as thirty in one large company.

Once again, Japan seems to be leading the world in a manufacturing advancement. Although there were only about thirty flexible manufacturing systems in place in the United States in early 1983, Japan had as many as thirty in one large company.

Quality control. As it is necessary for products to be completed on time, so it is necessary for products to be of a certain quality. Perfection is not essential for all products, but some must be exactly according to the specs. So what if we produce 5000 calendars a day, if 2000 have October missing? Poor quality might reduce sales, waste materials and labor, and even cause a repeat of the same process. A given product may have many different attributes. Some must be precise in the production process, others may not be so crucial. As in progress control, records are kept to compare the actual quality with that planned. Most products have acceptable ranges of deviance. Figure 8.10 shows a control chart for measuring the deviations in the weight of manufactured hot dogs. If periodic checks show that some of the weights are beyond the upper or lower control limits, production is usually stopped and adjustments are made.

In **quality control,** there are periodic checks of products to test their standards. A natural question regarding this process is "How many of the items do we actually check?" For large volumes of standard-sized products, quality control may decide that a 10% sample is enough to make predictions about the remaining products. Larger sample sizes ensure less chance of error, but they are more costly. For grander, more expensive products, a 100% sampling may be used, which means a quality check of each item. Manned space rockets might require 400 or 500% inspection — meaning each item is checked four or five times. The actual test might require simple operations such as weighing, measuring, or testing function, for example, screwing a light bulb into a socket.

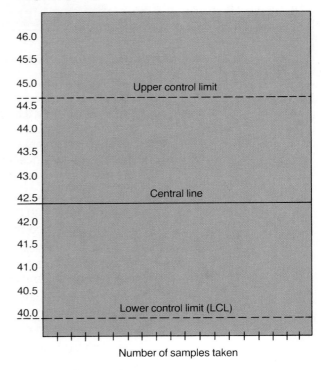

Weight (in grams)

Figure 8.10
Control chart for acceptable weight ranges in the manufacture of hot dogs.

More complex tests employ highly sensitive measuring instruments such as x-rays or electron microscopes. And some testing requires destroying the product, as with shotgun shells.

SUMMARY

The purpose of production management is to manufacture the best possible products at the lowest possible cost. Production provides utility for businesses and countries alike. Operations management is like production management, but is a broader term that applies some of the same concepts to the running of the entire company. Production management utilizes many of the concepts of mass production in order to accomplish its goals.

In planning the production plant of the future, location and layout are two of the main considerations. Production scheduling, also part of planning, plans the exact process whereby the product will be produced. Arranging for the capital requirements is another function of production planning.

Materials management includes purchasing and inventory control. Purchasing procedures and policies help implement the acquisition of goods and services. Inventory level and order size are the primary concern of inventory control. Just-in-time inventory, a relatively new policy in the United States, means ordering smaller quantities more frequently.

The six major steps within the production process are planning, scheduling, routing, dispatching, performance, and control. The two most common types of production processes are called the analytic and the synthetic processes. A Gantt chart is used for progress control, and various charts and methods are used in quality control. CAD/CAM and FMS are both recent developments that use computers to increase manufacturing efficiency. Increased productivity is the goal of every plant, and it will become an even more important issue in the future.

MIND YOUR BUSINESS

Instructions. Answer each of the following statements with true (T) or false (F).

___ 1. For the past 10 years, the United States has led the world in productivity rates.

___ 2. Communities, cities, and states may offer tax-free bonds, low-cost financing, and free or nominal land costs to attract plants.

___ 3. An intermittent manufacturing process operates continuously for long, uninterrupted periods of time.

___ 4. PERT is a scheduling technique.

___ 5. A firm that practices buying materials and supplies from one of its customers is practicing reciprocal buying.

___ 6. Just-in-time inventory refers to the practice of buying inventories in large quantities so they will be available when they are needed.

___ 7. An analytic production process involves breaking down raw materials into one or more products.

___ 8. By 1990, robots will be operating 90% of the manufacturing functions of our plants.

___ 9. The United States leads the world in the design and use of flexible manufacturing systems (FMS).

___ 10. Authorities agree that, during the next 10 years, robots will increase unemployment by more than 30%.

See answers at the back of the book.

KEY TERMS

productivity, 190
production, 190
utility, 190
production management, 190
operations management, 190
mechanization, 191
standardization, 191
automation, 191
assembly line, 191
mass production, 191
plant layout, 195
plant capacity, 195
intermittent process, 196
continuous process, 196
custom manufacturing, 196
process layout, 196
product layout, 196
fixed-position layout, 197
combination layout, 197
scheduling, 197
control chart, 197
program evaluation and review technique (PERT), 197
critical path, 198
critical path method (CPM), 198
materials requirements planning (MRP), 198

layout, what two types of manufacturing process have impact on the choice of a particular plant layout?

5. Describe the three major methods of production scheduling as discussed in the text.

6. How are PERT and CPM used together?

7. What is MRP? Why is it important in running a production plant?

8. What are five issues that managers have to resolve in establishing purchasing policies?

9. Discuss the four types of goods and three services that a production may require.

10. What is the purpose of inventory control? What happens when inventory control is not done properly?

11. Define and describe just-in-time inventory.

12. What are the six major steps within the production process? Describe and differentiate between each of them.

13. Scheduling and routing are quite similar. Exactly how do they differ?

14. What is the difference between progress and quality control?

15. Exactly what is productivity? How is it measured? How is productivity important to a business? To a country?

16. Discuss the three recent developments in production management as they are mentioned in the text.

17. Briefly describe CAD/CAM. Describe FMS. How are these systems similar? Different?

REVIEW QUESTIONS

1. What is the purpose of production management? Describe the five methods used to accomplish this purpose.

2. What are the four major steps in production planning? How is each important to the production process?

3. Describe the factors in choosing a plant location. When are more or fewer of these factors considered? Give an example.

4. What factors affect plant layout? Discuss the five major types of plant layout. In terms of

CASES

Case 8.1: How Far Should the Community Go?

A large manufacturing company was considering locating a branch plant in a small community of about 25,000 people. Supposedly, the plant would create about 250 jobs initially and add another 500 jobs over the first 5 years of operation. The community had a relatively low unemployment rate, about 5%, but the wage level for the community was lower than the national average. Many people thought that the plant would help in getting wage rates up. There was a bit of a problem with pollution from the new plant, and there was some concern about taxes. The company was looking at several locations, and some communities had offered tax exemptions and even agreed to help raise money for building the plant.

Many people were a little concerned about bringing in the new facility. Since it is mostly a farming community, some thought that the factory, the first in the area, would change their lifestyles. The local chamber of commerce was in favor of attracting the new plant to their community, but its leaders were aware of community concerns.

Questions

1. What are the major advantages of a new plant to such a community? Disadvantages?

2. How could such a community attract the new plant? What are the disadvantages to the company of locating in such a community?

3. If you lived in the community, what would you recommend? Why?

Case 8.2: Cost versus Safety in Product Manufacturing

Each year, 50,000 people die in auto accidents. And people continue to argue about how to make this vital product more safe. Most deaths occur upon impact when the driver is thrown against some part of the auto's interior. Thus, most testing and design changes attempt to protect the driver and passengers from these impacts.

Auto engineers say that the cheapest way to reduce injuries and deaths is to pass a federal law requiring seat belt usage. Critics say that the federal government has no business requiring people to do such things against their will, and there is no way to prevent the determined driver from removing his or her seat belt. Some people say that the law should require air bags that inflate upon impact. Still others add that manufacturers should put more padding around the dashboard instruments.

Manufacturers are using computer-aided design systems to come up with more effective means of preventing auto injury. However, practically every possible protection design has one or more drawbacks: it adds to the cost of the auto, people will not use it, or people do not like the design changes necessary to accommodate the protection.

Questions

1. Who has the major responsibility for reducing auto-related injuries and deaths? Why?

    ____ A. The manufacturer

    ____ B. The government

    ____ C. Drivers

2. How would you like to see manufacturers design cars differently to reduce injuries and deaths?

3. How much more would you be willing to pay for a car that is substantially safer? Why?

    ____ A. Much more

    ____ B. A little more

    ____ C. No more

After completing this chapter, you will be able to:

■ Identify the functions of a human resources
   department.

■ Discuss major laws affecting human resources
   and personnel matters.

■ Distinguish between a job analysis, a job
   description, and a job specification.

■ Identify ten external sources for recruiting
   employees.

■ Explain the seven steps in the employee
   selection process.

■ Discuss the training and development function.

■ Explain the nature and purpose of performance
   evaluations.

■ Describe the major types of wage payment plans.

INCENTIVE COM
L. PURPOSES

9

HUMAN
RESOURCES
MANAGEMENT

People are our most important assets," is the watchword of many organizations today. More and more, we are realizing that we cannot have a long-term successful firm without selecting, training, and treating our people properly. Of course, it is the responsibility of all managers to treat their people with dignity and respect, but people in the human resources area devote all, or most, of their time to people.

Have you ever wondered how organizations select people to work for them? What they do to train and develop their people? How they evaluate employees' performances? How they decide what to pay their people? These are the concerns of human resources management. After a brief description of human resources administration, this chapter deals with these topics.

WHAT IS HUMAN RESOURCES ADMINISTRATION?

Human resources tries to develop a zestful, highly motivated work force. They want employees to be happy and to experience high levels of job satisfaction. Although this is the responsibility of all managers, human resources specializes in matching people with jobs and providing a good reward system. **Human resources management,** a modern term that replaces "personnel management," is usually a staff position responsible for staffing, training, compensating, and providing services for the entire company.

The Functions of Human Resources

From its humble clerical beginnings in the early 1900s, the human resources profession has grown to include more than 170,000 specialists working in government and industry. Though human resources departments still keep numerous employee records, they now participate with top management in diagnostic and policy-making functions. Like any other department in the organization, human resources now administers programs that directly affect profitability. In small companies, human resources shares more of these responsibilities with line managers. Human resources departments expend considerable effort in advertising job openings, recruiting, and selecting the right people. Selecting also implies training, and human resources is usually responsible for training. In addition to in-house programs, training specialists investigate and sponsor general education and employee development programs with universities, professional associations, and workshop consultants. Human resources specialists also analyze jobs according to skill level and contribution to objectives before recommending wage and salary systems. Table 9.1 lists twenty-four critical issues (or pressure points) ranked by priority that human resource managers identified in a recent survey.

As companies grow, the human resources department tends to receive those duties that really don't fit anyplace else. Human resources carries out a wide range of employee services from company parties to managing benefits, from providing information about the company to producing the company newsletter. Other human resources functions often include labor relations, conducting research, maintaining records, providing supplies, and implementing safety programs. Figure 9.1 profiles some of the typical responsibilities of human resources administrators.

Human Resources Department Structure

Structural relationships of the human resources department depend somewhat upon the size of the company, but management philosophy and practical concerns have the greatest influence on structure. As the need for human resources services has grown, human resources departments have become more visible and influential.

In smaller companies, the human resources department may consist of an assistant to the president or may report directly to the operations manager. In about 15% of the departments, the head administrator has the title of vice-president of human resources. Other common titles are personnel administrator, industrial relations manager, head of employee relations, manager of labor relations, director of personnel administration, and human resources manager. Although more than 80% of human resources administra-

tors have college degrees, many have not been formally trained in human resources. More recently, larger departments have begun to hire trained specialists. Entry-level jobs include interviewers, training specialists, analysts, counselors, and labor negotiators.

The human resources department does not exist in isolation; its major purpose is to help other departments handle employees through service, control, and advisory relationships.

Service relationships.   Specialists provide many services to other departments. Record keeping is paramount, but other services include issuing the company newspaper, managing the

TABLE 9.1 ■ HOW 309 HUMAN RESOURCE EXECUTIVES RANKED THE IMPORTANCE OF 24 HUMAN RESOURCE ISSUES

Ranking	Pressure Point	Average Critical Value (on a scale of 10)	Ranking	Pressure Point	Average Critical Value (on a scale of 10)
1	Productivity improvement programs	7.74	13	Promotional opportunities for female and minority employees	5.76
2	Controlling costs of employee benefits	7.72	14	Employee relocation costs	5.61
3	Compensation planning and administration	7.57	15	Recruitment of mid-level and senior technical and/or engineering personnel	5.42
4	Employee communications	7.38	16	Labor relations and contract negotiations	5.23
5	Upgrading management training development programs	7.16	17	Improvements to employee benefits program	5.07
6	Organizational development programs	7.13	18	Compliance with OSHA/ EEOC and other governmental regulations	5.01
7	Management succession planning	7.12	19	Administering health and accident prevention programs	4.88
8	Improving employee morale	6.80	20	Reducing employee turnover	4.82
9	Human resource information systems	6.47	21	Employee willingness to relocate	4.81
10	Quality improvement programs	6.22	22	Recruitment of entry-level management talent	4.76
11	Recruitment of mid-level and senior management talent	6.12	23	Outplacement counseling	4.37
12	Union avoidance programs	5.85	24	Union decertification programs	2.59

Source: Jack Herring, "Human Resource Managers Rank Their Pressure Points," *Personnel Administrator*, June, 1983, pp. 113–116, 137.

SELECTION	TRAINING	WAGES AND SALARIES	SERVICES
Recruiting	Technical training	Job analysis	Pensions
Interviewing	Supervisory training	Job descriptions	Life insurance
Testing	Management development	Job specifications	Retirement
Evaluating	General education	Job grades	Profit sharing
Placing	Correspondence programs	Wage standards	Recreation
Orienting	Off-campus programs	Wage surveys	Health facilities
Promoting	Company library	Employee classifications	Credit union
Transferring			Cafeteria
			Newspaper
LABOR RELATIONS	SAFETY	RESEARCH AND RECORDS	Parking
			Medical insurance
Grievances	Standards	Personnel records	Legal aid
Labor contracts	Inspection	Personnel audits	
Collective bargaining	Contests	Labor market surveys	
Hours overtime	Safety engineering	Organizational analysis	
Work conditions	Rules	Design of reports	
Suggestion plans	Accident investigation	Manuals	
Affirmative action	Prevention	Policies	
		Statistical analysis	
		Turnover studies	

Figure 9.1
Examples of human resources functions.

cafeteria, planning the company picnic, scheduling vacations, and keeping the inventory on such items as table tennis balls. Specialists also write job descriptions, place recruiting ads, perform preliminary interviewing, and handle employee testing for the departments. Line departments are usually quite willing for human resources to take over these headache-producing activities, but there are a few friction points. For example:

■ Line and human resources managers sometimes disagree over how well a service fulfills a need.

■ Line departments may resist directions from human resources services.

■ The line may make requests that human resources thinks are the responsibility of line managers.

■ Conflicts sometimes exist over who has the right to do what.

Control relationships. Although service activities were the first concerns of human resources work, now human resources departments are becoming responsible for controlling company policies and procedures. Increased government regulation stimulates the need to control hiring, firing, wage administration, and safety practices. In a typical control relationship, line management has to clear certain decisions with the human resources director. For example, suppose a middle manager in the line wants to promote a subordinate into a supervisory position. Before he or she can implement the decisions, the line has to check with human resources to see if all the affirmative action guidelines are being followed.

Advisory relationships. Perhaps the most significant role for modern human resources departments is developing recommendations and providing advice for line managers. Human resources members work on policies for promoting managers, improving hiring, building better union relationships, designing modifications in organizational structure, and incorporating the newest ideas of employee motivation. This advisory relationship is usually tricky because the human resources manager has to persuade line managers to accept advice. Line managers resist the inconveniences of change and often perceive the recommendations as a threat to their authority. Human resources advisors must spend time developing the trust and confidence of line managers before identifying problems and offering assistance.

Legal Considerations

Human resources managers are concerned about some legal aspects of their work. Even when there is a separate legal department, human resources oversees some company activities to ensure legality in several areas, especially in the areas of safety, hiring, and firing. Safety has long been a human resources concern, and the passage of **Occupational Safety and Health Act (OSHA),** which sets safety standards for industry, has drastically increased the need for safety administration. Human resources is still charged with the all-important but tedious task of record keeping on almost all facets of the employee's work life. And human resources departments conduct internal surveys on attitudes, morale, employee feelings, and audits of skills and talent.

The **Civil Rights Act of 1964** prohibits discrimination in all phases of the job. And the government appointed an Equal Employment Opportunity Commission (EEOC), a federal agency to enforce the civil rights act. By law, companies cannot make selection decisions on the basis of race, color, national origin, religion, or sex. The only exceptions are very small companies (employing fewer than 15 employees for less than 20 weeks per year), religious organizations, and private clubs exempt from paying income taxes.

In 1973, the EEOC got the attention of the nation and most large companies when it won a pay discrimination suit against AT&T. The suit forced AT&T to pay $15 million in back pay and $23 million a year in raises for discriminatory practices in job assignments, pay, and promotion. This judgment was based on the premise that people doing the same jobs should be paid equally.

More recently, some groups have tried to replace the concept of equal pay for equal work, with comparable worth. Under **comparable worth,** dissimilar jobs would be paid at the same rate if the content of the work — the skills, responsibility, hazards, and mental and physical effort — is similar. According to job evaluators in Illinois, for example, the predominantly female job of secretary is roughly comparable in value to the predominantly male job of electrician. However, the average monthly salary for electricians in Illinois is $2826 while the average monthly salary of a secretary is only $1486. The Equal Pay Act of 1963 requires equal pay for equal work, but unions and women's groups say that equal pay for comparable work is needed to fully eliminate sex discrimination in employment compensation. Worried about the wide disparity in pay between male- and female-dominated jobs, the city of Spokane, Washington, recently granted $200 pay equity increases for lower-paid women office workers. In past negotiations, the city had given the same percentage increase to all of its workers. However, the city agreed to recognize the comparable worth concept and grant raises on the content of the work rather than trying to ensure that all people doing similar jobs get equal pay.

In mid-1984, the U.S. Equal Employment Opportunity Commission had 250 wage discrimination complaints pending. If the comparable worth notion is applied to these cases, it could dramatically restructure wages and salaries for women and men in organizations. Employers and conservatives are fighting the issue, saying that the marketplace should determine the value of jobs.

Executive Order 11246 created the Office of Federal Contract Compliance Program (OFCCP).

These power company engineers are testimony to the success of affirmative action programs.

Every company that has forty or more employees and government contracts of $50,000 or more is subject to affirmative action policies.

Among other things, this order requires an **affirmative action** program which states in part:

Every company that has forty or more employees and government contracts of $50,000 or more must develop a detailed plan that identifies weaknesses in hiring and promoting minorities and women, and a specific plan, along with dates, for correcting them. In short, affirmative action requires an effort by employers to:

- Identify barriers of race, sex, religion, national origin, and other factors that keep employees from reaching their full potential.

- Eliminate barriers quickly.

- Set up special programs to speed corrections.

Affirmative action also guides recruiting and selection policies. Recruiters, for instance, cannot legally ask questions that allow management to make prejudiced decisions. Questions such as, "How do you plan to combine marriage and a career?" "Where were you born?" and "Do you have an honorable discharge?" are examples of discriminatory questions. Figure 9.2 shows a list of

**Figure 9.2
Examples of interview questions that would be likely to be judged discriminatory.**

1. Are you married?
2. How do you plan to take care of your children?
3. Have you changed your name recently?
4. Do you have any handicaps?
5. What is your religious affiliation?
6. How many times have you been arrested?
7. What is your draft classification?
8. What is the date of your military discharge?
9. What were the conditions of your military discharge?
10. Where were you born?
11. What is your nationality?
12. What is your mother tongue?

interview queries that are discriminatory and therefore illegal.

As an example of affirmative action, the courts recently ordered General Motors to contribute $42 million to programs to correct for past pay discriminations. The cases had been in the courts for 10 years, but there was evidence that the company had paid different wages to people doing similar jobs. In another case, Lockheed California Co., a division of Lockheed Corp., agreed to hire and promote several hundred women over the next few years to settle a sex discrimination suit. Since the company just received a $2 billion contract from NASA, it appears that they will create between 1500 and 2000 new jobs in the next few years. Women will probably get half of them.

The **Age Discrimination in Employment Act of 1967** outlaws discrimination against candidates between the ages of 40 and 65. The law does not prevent a company from asking a candidate's age on an application blank, but the company cannot legally use age as a reason for not hiring. In 1979, Congress amended this act to prohibit mandatory retirement before the age of 70.

Are quotas necessary for affirmative action programs? Most people automatically associate hiring and promoting quotas with affirmative action. However, there has been a continuing debate about whether companies need to develop hiring quotas for women and minorities in order to fulfill affirmative action requirements.

Some experts contend that affirmative action was never intended to require quotas. They say it was to prevent discrimination against certain groups of employees. Further, advocates of this view add that Labor Department regulations say that hiring goals should not be used to discriminate against any applicant because of race, color, religion, sex, or national origin. Goals, they say, are just that: goals. They are not intended to be strict quotas. Finally, the use of goals is just one aspect of a company's total effort to reduce discrimination.

The other view says this may sound good in theory; in actual practice, however, hiring quotas are often necessary to meet affirmative action guidelines. For example, suppose an employer has ten jobs to fill and a goal of hiring two minorities. If the first eight people the company hires are white, in reality, the next two hires will have to be minorities. Thus, the goal turns into a quota. This side also quotes court decisions and practices to support their conviction, for instance: (1) a court ordered the Boston Police Department to hire a fixed number of minorities until the work force reached roughly the community percentage of minorities, and (2) Kaiser Aluminum reserved 50% of all openings in its craft apprenticeship program for minorities until their percentages were equal to the percentage of minorities in the local work force.

What is reverse discrimination? Reverse discrimination occurs when companies give hiring and promotional preferences to women and minorities who are less qualified than whites. Congress says they never intended to promote reverse discrimination with the law; rather, they were just trying to make sure women and minorities got an equal chance. However, critics say that some companies have overreacted and actually hired and promoted some women and minorities who were less qualified than white, male applicants.

In the *Bakke* decision of 1978, a highly publicized reverse discrimination case, the U.S. Supreme Court ruled that Allan Bakke, a white male, had been the victim of reverse discrimination. Bakke applied to the University of California School of Medicine at Davis but was not admitted.

It will probably be some time before there is a clear understanding of just what constitutes reverse discrimination.

He sued, saying the university had admitted less-qualified minority applicants. The university agreed that they had admitted some minorities under "special admissions programs" to get a more equal minority representation. The Supreme Court said the school's special admissions program was unconstitutional because its quota system amounted to discrimination against whites. In a confusing statement, though, the court said that schools wanting a more diverse student body could use race as a factor in determining admission standards. Many other reverse discrimination cases are still in the courts, and it will probably be some time before there is a clear

understanding of just what constitutes reverse discrimination.

STAFFING

As a human resources specialist described part of her job, "I spend a lot of time recruiting and selecting employees. I also have to determine how many employees are needed and what kinds of skills the company requires." The staffing function includes planning employment needs, recruiting prospective employees, selecting the best candidate, and finally, hiring the employee.

Planning Employment Needs

Employment planning forecasts the future needs of the company's human resources. These employment forecasts are determined, in part, by sales forecasts, budgets, and growth estimates. Of course, planners must also consider employee turnover in the planning. Employment planners try to meet the challenge of hiring top-flight employees, ideally qualified for the tasks, at exactly the right time.

Forecasting needs. Planners consider the company's growth plans and anticipated turnover when projecting employment needs. **Turnover** is the number of employees that leave a company over a period of time — typically a year. Turnover occurs when employees quit, retire, die, or are terminated. By considering the company's turnover history and allowing for situations such as retirements, possible layoffs, transfers, and probations, managers can project the future turnover rate.

After projecting turnover, specialists consider growth projections of the firm. Is a new department planned? What will production requirements be? Are sales expected to increase? While these methods of projecting employment needs may, in some cases, be quite accurate, most human resources managers get some real surprises. And quick action is often required to fill positions that suddenly become vacant.

Accurate employee forecasting is very important to the company's profitability. Should a forecast provide too few employees, the company will likely lose sales because it will not be able to deliver the needed goods or services on time. And if the firm hires too many employees, the result will be higher-than-necessary labor costs.

Defining the job. The staffing task would be easier if all jobs in a firm were similar. However, the best salesperson could probably not replace the controller, and the ace producer probably could not substitute for the sales manager. Planners use job analysis and job descriptions to help them identify the particular skills that the firm will need.

Job analysis determines the exact tasks that make up a job. By detailing the precise requirements of the job, recruiters can find potential employees with necessary skills and aptitudes. Figure 9.3 shows a sample checklist for job analysis.

Information gathered from the job analysis is used to write a **job description,** a summary of the employee's job duties and responsibilities. A good manager will be certain that these job descriptions are kept up to date. Incomplete or inaccurate job descriptions result in criticism by employees and make it difficult to match the employee to the task. Highly technical or rapidly growing departments require job descriptions to be revised at regular intervals—say, every six months. Figure 9.4 shows an example of a job description.

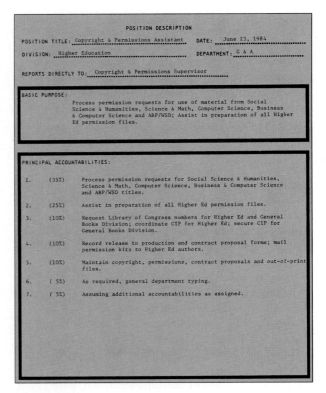

Figure 9.4
An example of a job description.

Figure 9.3
A sample checklist for job analysis.

TASKS PERFORMED

1. What is actually done?
2. How is it done?
3. Why is it done?
4. How much time is required to do it?
5. What tools are used?
6. Where is the work accomplished?
7. What is the employee's responsibility?

REQUIRED PHYSICAL AND MENTAL SKILLS

1. What technical skills are required?
2. What kinds of job knowledge are needed?
3. Does it require special training?
4. Will employees have to cooperate with other employees?
5. What personality characteristics are desirable?
6. What are the intelligence requirements?

Job specifications list the physical, mental, and emotional requirements of a job. Physical specifications are usually the easiest to identify. In minute detail, they list the job demands for walking, lifting, crouching, climbing, grasping, sitting, and the like. Mental specifications set minimum requirements for mental capabilities, and they may be defined by indirect means such as a high school degree, two years of college, a certificate of accomplishment, or a college degree. Other, more direct examples of mental specifications spell out standards for general intelligence, memory, planning ability, reading proficiency, abstract reasoning capability, and judgment. Although not as precise as physical or mental specifications, there is a trend among analysts to look more closely at emotional and social requirements.

For jobs that require working with the public or with other groups, social skills may be more important to success than technical or mental aptitudes. Difficulty of measurement causes the same conflict over emotional specifications. How can you predict when an employee will behave immaturely? Some companies rely upon testing to judge emotional stability and social skills; other submit their people to examinations by psychologists. Still another input is recommendations from prior employers on the prospective employee's ability to work cooperatively with others, react objectively under stress, and handle personal problems. Figure 9.5 is an example of job specifications for a particular job.

Recruiting

It is one thing to know labor needs. It is quite another to recruit people with the necessary skills. Companies begin recruiting by projecting a public reputation that attracts qualified employees. Everything that the company does reflects upon this image and thereby influences the success of recruiting. Recruiters select from internal and external sources, making their decisions after following a systematic screening process.

Internal sources. Internal sources are the present work force, and there are two good reasons to fill vacancies with current employees. Present employees are easier to find and evaluate, and human resources already has records on their backgrounds, education, experience, skills, mental abilities, attitudes, and work habits. The second advantage of replacing from within is the effect on morale and motivation. Internal transfers and promotions are concrete evidence that the company is concerned about employee development and loyalty.

Of course, internal sources pose potential problems. A major barrier is inbreeding. Employees, being aware of current policies and pro-

Figure 9.5
An example of a set of job specifications.

> **QUALIFICATIONS:**
>
> Minimum of 45–50 wpm accurate typing.
> Knowledge and use of CRT.
> Knowledge and understanding of manufacturing process and terminology.
> Good organizational skills and an aptitude for figures.
> Effective communication and interpersonal skills.
> Minimum of two years of college.

cedures, understand the company much better than outsiders, but insiders have more trouble seeing and judging improved methods. If companies *only* promote from within, they may become stagnant. Industry analysts say a large part of the operational problems that Digital Equipment Corporation was wrestling with recently was due to President Kenneth Olsen's tradition of promoting from within, which, these critics feel, has created an insular management team. "Top management is not open to new ideas, and the atmosphere is stifling," complained one observer.

Availability of supply is another limitation of internal sources. It is unlikely that expanding companies can find all the skills they need within their present work force. Current employees can often be retrained to meet changing labor needs, but not all workers are both willing and able to make adjustments.

External sources. To fulfill all a firm's employment needs from internal sources is virtually impossible. But where can the company go for people? It is not practical to kidnap drunks as shipping companies used to do. Nor can human resources lay back and wait for the employees to scamper enthusiastically to their world of opportunity. Effective recruiters go outside to several standard sources.

1. *Walk-ins.* Most companies regularly receive unsolicited applications, especially when the unemployment rate increases. Walk-ins usually find their way to the human resources office where someone records preliminary information in recruiting files. Periodically, a staff member scans the information to determine whether any of the walk-ins' skills match company needs. Although the source is unpredictable—companies never know the number of applicants or variety of skills that may come in—it is inexpensive and good for public relations.

2. *Public employment agencies.* The U.S. Employment Service was created as a subunit of the Labor Department during World War I to recruit civilian workers into war industries. To combat the depression ills of the 1930s, states added their own public employment offices, and they became more important with the passage of the Social Security Act,

which requires unemployed workers to register at state agencies before they can receive benefits. Today, public agencies are funded by employer contributions to unemployment compensation funds, and they are clearing-houses for jobs and information. Additionally, many agencies have expanded their services to include counseling, psychological testing, aiding handicapped workers, and giving special attention to war veterans. Many public agencies have recently become heavily involved in helping disadvantaged and minority employees overcome their unique problems in finding work.

3. *Private employment agencies.* Private employment agencies have grown along with public services. But private agencies specialize more in registering technical or professional personnel such as typists, programmers, engineers, and salespeople. Some private placement groups specialize in low-skilled labor, but they are generally inadequate sources for most blue-collar workers. To improve their services, private agencies have joined forces to exchange computerized lists of talent. Many have added sophisticated testing procedures, counseling services, and vocational guidance programs. Employers say the major advantages of private agencies are their more specialized human resources services. A disadvantage of private agencies is

High-technology professionals are often recruited through specialized private employment agencies.

the cost; they charge a percentage of the newly hired employee's salary. Most often, this fee is paid by the hiring company, but for some types of jobs, the employee must pay the agency for securing employment.

4. *Employee referrals.* An RCA Corporation facility pays $1000 to its current employees for recommendations that result in hiring new people. In three years, they have hired at least 100 employees through the program. Several divisions of Wang Laboratories, Inc., pay from $300 to $500 each for employee referrals that result in the right person for the right job. During a recent six-month period, one Wang division hired 43 employees, all of whom passed the 90-day probationary period. Company officials say the program boosts the self-esteem of their current employees and saves a lot of money in recruiting expenses. Recruiting expenses for a new engineer or scientist, including advertisement, employment agency fees, relocation expenses, and visits, may go as high as $9000 for a single hiree. Some human resources officers fear that extensive use of employee referrals could possibly throw the workforce out of balance in the eyes of the EEOC. For instance, a predominantly white group might tend to refer other whites, thereby causing this composition of the work group to be unrepresentative of the community. While new, employee referral has gained a lot of popularity, and more companies are likely to use this method.

5. *Labor unions.* Labor unions, with their hiring halls and job listings, are a source of unskilled and skilled labor for certain industries. Through apprenticeship programs and labor agreements, some unions have maintained firm control over labor supplies. It is illegal for unions to insist that employers hire only union members, but this law has not been vigorously enforced in some industries. Union referrals are particularly important in industries with small companies where demand for unskilled labor fluctuates erratically. Examples include construction, trucking, printing, maritime, and Saturday-night dance bands.

6. *Professional associations.* Many professional societies and trade associations operate placement services for their members. At regional and national meetings, special recruiting

Figure 9.6
Examples of services offered by college placement centers.

rooms are set up where recruiters meet with prospective employees. In conjunction with the formal procedures, recruiters flush out hot prospects through informal meetings at dinner, cocktail gatherings, and hallway conversations. A few associations regularly publicize lists of openings and applicants in their newsletters and journals.

7. *Educational institutions.* Almost all colleges and universities operate placement or career development centers that assist graduates in their job search. A few centers screen applicants, but most concentrate on coordinating information and securing physical arrangements for bringing recruiters and prospective employees together. Typically, placement directors attract recruiters to the campus, publicize the visits to graduating students, and make appointments between interested students and company recruiters. Placement offices may also compile folders on student qualifications and distribute brochures, pamphlets, and other recruiting literature. After a preliminary on-campus interview, the recruiter normally invites the best candidates to additional interviews on the company's premises. Most companies visit university campuses to seek professional, managerial, and technical talent. Figure 9.6 lists examples of services offered by college placement centers.

8. *Advertising.* Companies have long used advertisements in newspapers, trade journals, posters, billboards, radio, television, and roving sound trucks to attract employees. Advertisements have the advantage of attracting a lot of attention about job openings, but their disadvantage is they produce an uncertain range of candidates. Even with properly written and well-timed ads, employers attract many unqualified applicants. Companies increase their advertising efforts when labor supplies are scarce and reduce them during periods of plenty.

9. *Computer matching.* Although not widely used as yet, computers are very adept at gathering and distributing information in quantity. IBM, Western Union, the U.S. Employment Service, and the College Placement Council operate computer-oriented job banks, which they hope will eventually match skilled applicants and openings nationwide. The computer is best suited for handling jobs with tangible specifications; it is less effective for filling professional and managerial needs.

10. *Job fairs.* Some organizations promote job fairs where several potential employers gather for a day, rent booths, and offer literature on available jobs. They invite people to attend the fairs and talk with representatives of the firms who might ask applicants to fill in applications. And they might conduct some preliminary interviewing with prospects.

11. *Pirating.* Many companies are not beyond pirating employees from other employers. For instance, at professional meetings, representatives from Company A might informally talk with a top-notch professional from Company B about the prospect of changing jobs. Pursuing specific employees from another company may be a quick way to get high-level executives at a modest recruiting cost, but pirated employees may be as disloyal to their new firm as they were to their old.

The Selection Process

True, many organizations, especially smaller ones, observe a candidate's hairstyle, mannerisms, and personality and hire on the basis of some mysterious chemistry. As one president put it, "I look for a prospect that turns me on." No selection procedures entirely eliminate subjective judgments, but good procedures assist the "gut feelings" in two ways. One, they reinforce the positive or negative feelings of company officials. Two, they may ascertain information contradictory to the subjective feelings and cause an executive to reconsider. The selection decision usually moves through several steps, with each step narrowing the field of applicants until only one person is left. Some organizations find the total process to be too expensive and time-consuming, and they skip some of the steps.

1. *Preliminary screening interview.* The preliminary screening interview determines whether the candidate is in the ballpark. Receptionists usually accomplish the preliminary interview with a few questions such as: "How many years of college do you have?" "Can you type and take shorthand?" "Do you have welding experience?" The interviewer also observes the candidate for dress style and general appearance if these are important to the job. If the employee is clearly unqualified, the process ends here. If there is a reasonable chance of qualifying, the interviewer asks the prospect to complete an application blank.
2. *Application blanks.* Practically all companies require candidates to complete an application blank because it is an efficient instrument for gathering data on education, experience, location, achievements, and personal references. See Fig. 9.7 for an example of an application blank.
3. *Testing.* Companies have been using employment tests for more than 50 years, but they are still controversial. Tests may attempt to determine an employee's skill, aptitude, knowledge, personality, and the like. Objectivity is the primary purpose of testing, but some administrators use the scores as a peg to hang the entire selection decision on. Interviewers' subjective judgments are good selection inputs, but there is a tendency to suppress judgments in favor of test scores. Sometimes, when testing for middle- or upper-level management positions, a company may test both the applicant and the manager for whom the applicant would work. This, ideally, would reduce potential personality conflicts. To improve testing validity, companies can compare test scores to employee performance to see if good performers actually outscore low achievers. This is called validity, a determination of whether the test truly measures what it is supposed to measure. Obviously, tests should be reliable; that is, they should unfailingly measure the same thing every time. Although test publishers supply national norms, it is misleading for companies to apply the norms indiscriminately.

   Tests may not be used as often today as they were a few years ago. Now, you have to be sure that the test does not discriminate between sexes and races and that it does not invade a person's privacy. All applicants must have an equal opportunity for the job. A human resources manager of a smaller firm who had quit testing said, "It just got to be so much trouble that it was not worth it. The cost in time and effort was too great to justify the results. And we had to worry that we did not violate some of the newer legal requirements."

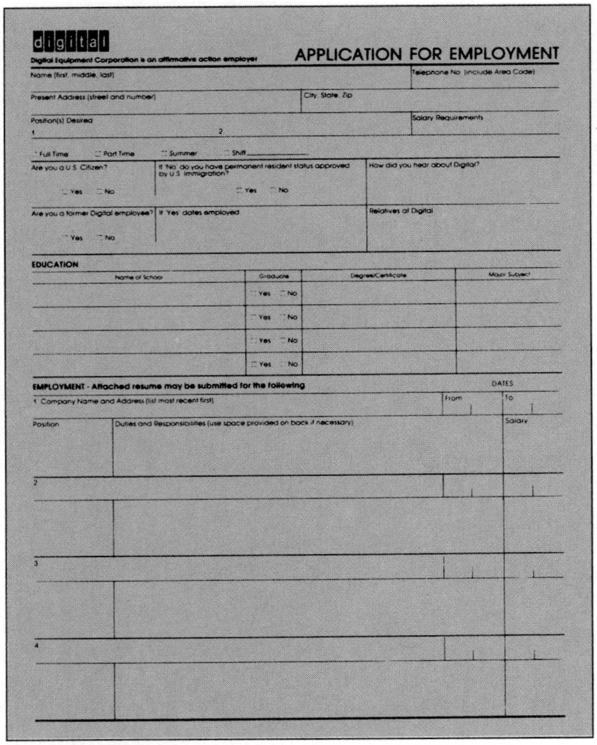
digital
Digital Equipment Corporation is an affirmative action employer
APPLICATION FOR EMPLOYMENT
Name (first, middle, last) | Telephone No. (include Area Code)
Present Address (street and number) | City, State, Zip
Position(s) Desired 1 2 | Salary Requirements
Full Time | Part Time | Summer | Shift
Are you a U.S. Citizen? Yes No | If 'No' do you have permanent resident status approved by U.S. Immigration? Yes No | How did you hear about Digital?
Are you a former Digital employee? Yes No | If 'Yes' dates employed | Relatives at Digital

EDUCATION

Name of School	Graduate	Degree/Certificate	Major Subject
	Yes No		
	Yes No		
	Yes No		
	Yes No		

EMPLOYMENT - Attached resume may be submitted for the following
DATES
1. Company Name and Address (list most recent first) | From | To
Position | Duties and Responsibilities (use space provided on back if necessary) | Salary
2
3
4

Figure 9.7
An employment application form. *Courtesy Digital Equipment Corporation.*

However, **bona fide occupational qualification (bfoq)** testing — determining if someone can meet specific, tangible requirements of the job — may not cause the concern of other types of testing. For instance, if you need an employee to lift 50-pound boxes as part of the job, you could, through strength tests, determine with precision whether the person could lift the weight.

4. *Reference checks.* For those candidates who make it through testing, firms contact references either before or after the interview stage to check on background. Although some firms check personal and school references, previous employers are the most preferred references. Recruiters want to know the applicant's title, nature of work, quality of work, length of experience, and reason for leaving. Recommendation letters are usually required, but they rarely turn up negative information because candidates select references who are likely to write favorable evaluations. Previous employers are reluctant to criticize because of concerns over the individual's right to privacy and lawsuits arising from derogatory evaluations. Personal interviews or telephone calls to former employers are more likely to elicit candid comments, and the interviewer can probe questionable areas.

5. *Employment interviews.* According to surveys, more than 98% of companies use interviews to judge candidates. Opinions vary about whether interviews should be structured or unstructured. Structured interviews follow a predeveloped format. Interviewers ask questions from a checklist and record responses on the space allotted. Unstructured or nondirective interviews are more spontaneous. The interviewer probes with a few general questions such as: "What do you think about your future employment?" "Will you tell me more about that?" The purpose is to get the candidates to do most of the talking on the assumption that they will reveal many things about themselves.

6. *Physical examination.* Responding to increasing emphasis on employee health and safety, almost all firms require applicants to pass a physical examination. Since physical exams are expensive, they are used toward the end of the selection procedure when the field has

narrowed. The physical exam tries to accomplish three purposes. First, the company wants to protect itself against paying workmen's compensation claims for health problems the employee had at the time of hiring. Second, managers wish to determine that the employee is physically capable of performing the job. Third, the organization is obligated to avoid hiring someone with a serious communicable disease. While effective for detecting current health problems, physical exams have been poor at predicting future ailments.

7. *The employment decision.* All the preliminary steps lead to the crucial question: to hire or not to hire? Employment decisions have far-reaching implications for training, discipline, and turnover. Even the best training programs do not overcome all hiring mistakes. Assigning an unsuitable person to a job is sure to cause troubles. Replacement costs range from $1000 for unskilled positions to $7000 for semiskilled positions; for specialists and management, human resources hiring expenses might zoom to $25,000 or more.

Hiring Employees

After making the employment decision through the selecting process, the actual hiring takes place. But it cannot be assumed that the employee will accept the job when offered. Prime applicants usually interview with several companies. Also, the candidate may have become less enthusiastic about the job during the screening process. Good human resources management requires a talent for "closing the deal." Often, salary and benefits are negotiated. Enticements, such as a research budget, additional equipment, or tempting bonus plans, are offered to hire the ideal prospect. The hiring process begins with a formal offer from the company. It includes the salary, benefits, and conditions. Usually, the candidate has a short period to consider the offer. Hiring the best candidate may be as important to the company as closing a large sales contract.

Terminating Employees

Because of many potential legal liabilities, human resources managers usually get involved when employees are **terminated,** that is, leave the company. In most cases, the human resources department conducts an **exit interview** with the person to try to determine the specific reasons for leaving. Frequently, an interviewer will ask, in an exit interview, such questions as: "Do you have any suggestions that could help us improve?" "What was your relationship with your supervisor?" "What frustrations did you experience while you worked here?" Employees typically leave a company in one of four ways: (1) retirement, (2) resignation, (3) layoff, and (4) firing (terminating).

CROSS FIRE

Should Employers Be Allowed to Use Lie Detector Tests?

The use of polygraph (lie detector) tests is increasing rapidly. About 1 million Americans take polygraph exams each year. There are approximately 5000 polygraph examiners in the United States today, about twice the number 10 years ago. Firms such as Montgomery Ward, Coors brewery, Zale's jewelers, and 7-Eleven stores use them regularly. However, there is a hot debate over polygraph use, centering around validity.

Points in favor of the use of polygraph testing include:

1. It reduces theft. The Jack Eckerd Corporation tests each of its 30,000 employees annually. An official says, "It's a good tool in maintaining an honest corps of employees. We have one of the lowest levels of internal theft in the chain drug industry."
2. It helps eliminate "bad apple" job applicants. "If an applicant knows that he or she is going to have to undergo a polygraph," says an examiner, "unethical applicants will be less likely to apply."
3. It is more accurate than most people think. The technology has been available for 60 years.

Points against the use of polygraph exams include:

1. The exams are not always accurate. People frequently "fail" not because they have lied but because they get nervous during the exam.
2. The questions many examiners ask are an invasion of a person's privacy— questions on sex habits, drug abuse, and personal relationships.
3. Courts agree that many who failed exams have been wronged. For example, a Florida man won a $250,000 suit against a company who dismissed him on the basis of a polygraph test concerning missing cash. A Connecticut jury awarded $219,000 to 22 persons who were wrongly dismissed for failing a lie detector test.

To what extent do you agree or disagree with the following statement: "Employers should not be allowed to require employees to take polygraph exams for any reasons." Why?

____ A. Strongly agree   ____ C. Disagree somewhat

____ B. Agree somewhat   ____ D. Strongly disagree

How accurate do you think polygraph exams are? Answer by circling the appropriate number on the following scale:

Very accurate   7 6 5 4 3 2 1   Very inaccurate

The Age Discrimination in Employment Act makes it illegal for companies to force people out of work strictly because of their age.

Retirement.   Employees retire at different ages and for different reasons. Ill health, boredom with the work, or attractive retirement benefits may cause an employee to retire early. In some cases, a manager may want an employee to retire early to replace him or her with a more specialized or up-to-date person. The Age Discrimination in Employment Act makes it illegal for companies to force people out of work strictly because of their age. Sometimes retirement is negotiated, just like hiring is negotiated. Many companies now make both early and late retirement available to their employees. It is human resources' responsibility to make sure that retirement situations go as smoothly as possible for both the retiree and the firm.

Resignation.   Employees often decide to leave a company voluntarily. Sometimes they leave because they obtain a more attractive position with another firm. Other times they leave because they are dissatisfied with their current jobs. Here again, human resources personnel, through exit interviews and other means, try to find the real reason for a person's resignation.

Layoffs.   Sometimes downturns in economic conditions require a company to reduce its work force through layoffs. Human resources personnel may be responsible for seeing that the layoffs occur in an orderly and rational fashion. They may also try to reduce the ill feelings of layoffs by providing severance pay or by helping employees find positions with other companies. Some human resources departments have developed extensive programs, called **outplacement,** for finding work for employees that they have to lay off.

Less serious economic conditions may result in temporary layoffs where employees lose their jobs for a temporary time period, say 6 weeks, or 3 months. If conditions improve during the temporary layoff, many or all of the employees may be called back to work. But if economic conditions worsen, the company may have to extend the layoff period. Layoffs challenge the human resources department to be as fair as possible because they create a lot of stress and potential ill will for employees and the firms.

Firing.   The most delicate human relations task of a firm is firing an employee. Usually, the company will put an employee on probation and give him or her several chances to improve before they actually terminate the employee through firing. During the probation period, progressive managers ask such questions as: "Has the employee been properly trained?" "Is there a way to improve the employee's attitude?" "Would a transfer solve the problem?" "Are there legal implications involved?" Termination usually occurs for one of two reasons: The employee does not perform up to a minimum level of expectations, or the employee continues to violate some of the company's policies such as attendance, safety regulations, tardiness, and the like.

Recently, there has been an erosion of the "employment at will" idea. **Employment at will** is a legal doctrine, accepted by the courts, which says an employer or an employee can terminate a relationship at will. That is, an employee can quit at any time and an employer can terminate at any time. However, some union contracts now guarantee employment for some workers. Further, consider the salesperson in one large company who made a large sale to a customer. The company, rather than pay the commission to the salesperson, terminated the employee. The courts, though, said the company could not legally do this because the termination was based on malice. In another case, a company fired an employee because he refused to testify for the company in a price-fixing case. Again, the courts said that the company could not legally do this. These, and similar cases, have demonstrated that there are limits to the employer's ability to terminate a relationship with an employee.

Before terminating an employee, it is very important to document, in writing, the evidence against him or her.

Before terminating an employee, it is very important to document, in writing, the evidence against him or her. For instance, a company had to

Late Retirement

Many U.S. companies are altering the usual pattern of employee retirement. They are keeping some older workers on the job by offering inducements such as reduced hours, job changes, and job sharing.

Changing demographics are responsible for many of these new corporate responses to retirement. Largely because of the "baby bust" that started during the 1960s, businesses see a relative shortage of young people entering the work force. The problem, says Lawrence Olson of Sage Associates, a Washington management consulting firm, is that the work force will increase by only 1.2% a year from 1985 to 1990 and grow by no more than a mere 0.8% a year in the 1990s. Therefore, says Olson, there must be a reversal of the early retirement option for the elderly and increased incentives for voluntary delays in retirement.

A number of companies have varied retirement options available for their employees. For example, Polaroid Corporation, in Cambridge, Massachusetts, uses "retirement rehearsal" and "phased retirement" to ease the anxieties of their workers who want to test the water before retiring. Rehearsal retirement allows older employees a 3-month, unpaid leave of absence with all benefits. Phased retirement allows them to cut back to 4 days a week or less at reduced pay. Polaroid's hope is that some workers will feel so good after a leave or a shortened week that they will want to extend their working life beyond the traditional retirement age of 65 or the legal retirement age of 70.

Source: "Why Late Retirement Is Getting a Corporate Blessing," *Business Week*, January 16, 1984, p. 69.

---

terminate a minority employee. He refused to follow company rules and policies, caused major disruptions, and called in sick about 20% of the time. After termination, the employee filed suit against the company for discrimination. A series of carefully worded memos and documentation from managers and other employees allowed the company to uphold the termination.

TRAINING AND DEVELOPMENT

Training and development occurs after an employee has been hired. Training includes teaching an employee to perform specific skills, whereas development includes more general education about such things as leadership, communication, economic understanding, and the like. Some companies offer extensive training and development; others offer little or none.

New Employee Orientation

Most companies offer some type of orientation for new employees. The **orientation program** introduces new employees to the company and explains corporate policies to them. A larger company may have a formal, classroom-type training session for new employees. Smaller organizations may use the first line supervisor to orient the new employee to the company. Studies show that orientation is important to both the company and the employee. A good orientation program increases the likelihood of training the employee effectively and helps the employee become productive more quickly. Figure 9.8 offers a checklist of topics to consider including an orientation program.

Training and Development Programs

Regardless of the experience level of an employee, some training is almost always necessary. Some

ORIENTATION CHECKLIST

Informal relations		parking	insurance
____ name	____ greatest hopes	____ rest breaks	____ vacation
____ introduction	____ biggest problems	____ smoking areas	____ payday
____ sponsor	**The job**	____ coffee	____ incentive plans
____ prepare other employees	____ training	____ lunch facilities	____ promotions
____ your leadership style	____ help	____ chain of command	____ sick pay
____ group norms	____ learning period	____ forms, paperwork	____ payroll deductions
	____ standards	____ grievance procedure	____ pay increases
Organizational objectives	____ common mistakes	____ suggestions	____ work stability
____ departmental objectives	____ quality	____ transfers	____ athletic activities
____ employee contribution	____ quantity	____ performance appraisals	____ social activities
____ major product/service		____ first aid	____ hobbies
____ growth	**Policies and procedures**		____ clubs
____ major competitors	____ check-in, check-out	**Rewards**	____ security
____ position in industry	____ discipline	____ pay	____ pride
____ deadlines	____ safety	____ benefits	____ prestige

Figure 9.8
Items typically covered by employee orientation programs.

companies conduct their training in-house; that is, their own staff, usually from human resources, conducts the training. Other companies encourage their employees to attend programs at universities or other training centers at company expense. Of course, many companies use a combination of these two approaches.

Some examples of typical types of training and development programs are:

1. *On-the-job training (OJT).* The supervisor or an experienced co-worker has the responsibility of teaching the employee skills on the job.

2. *Job instruction training (JIT).* This instruction method breaks a job into logical steps and lists them in a sequence. The trainer, perhaps a supervisor or someone from human resources, teaches the employee how to perform the steps.

3. *Apprenticeship training.* A new employee is given a temporary, lower-status position to

In-house classroom training is one way to upgrade employees' value to a company.

learn basic skills of a job. Once he or she attains the necessary expertise, the **apprenticeship** title is dropped, and the employee moves up in status and pay.

4. *Vestibule training.* **Vestibule training** creates a simulation of a working situation so an employee can sharpen his or her skills in a mock experience. An early part of flight training, for example, may include learning in a flight simulator that simulates actual flying.

5. *Job rotation.* Job rotation provides a series of assignments, moving trainees from one job to another on a planned basis. Normally, the trainee receives coaching from individuals in each assignment, as well as from the training specialist in charge of the program.

6. *In-basket training.* Usually reserved for management development, in-basket training begins with a series of written materials describing the background of a firm and the job the trainee is assumed to perform. An instructor presents memos, letters, notes, phone calls, and typical problems. The trainee has to react to the situation as he or she might in an actual situation.

7. *Films.* Some firms put certain skills on films or slide-tape presentations. An employee watches the film or tape to attain a set of skills.

TAKING STOCK

Emerging Roles of the Human Resources Manager

Patricia McLagan, chairperson of the 1981 Competency Task Force of the American Society for Training and Development, has identified several new activities that are emerging as having a major role within the profession of human resources management:

■ Strategist: the role of projecting what human resources management will be in the future.

■ Policymaker: the role of determining broad values or principles that will guide human resources managers.

■ Researcher: the role of developing theories that verify, advance, or change human resources views of the alternatives available in human resources work.

■ Evaluator: the role of identifying to what extent a curriculum, program, product, or service is achieving or has achieved its stated goals within the mission, strategy, and policy framework of the human resources department and the overall organization.

■ Transfer agent: the role of ensuring that competencies learned in education, training, and self-development are remembered, reinforced, and used in the appropriate contexts.

These new roles imply a shift in two directions. There will be a need for human resources specialists to have a more significant influence on top management concerning the use and development of human resources. What's more, human resources specialists will have to become more adept at utilizing the sophisticated techniques of research, evaluation, and maintenance and reinforcement of learning.

Source: Neal Chalofsky and Carnie Ives Lincoln, *Up the HRD Ladder: A Guide for Professional Growth,* Reading, Mass.: Addison-Wesley, 1983, pp. 74–75.

8. *Classroom training.* Many firms also conduct traditional classroom training for their employees. Such training may consist of information about company policies, plans, and history, as well as management and supervisory development programs. Sometimes company trainers instruct the sessions; other times, the firm hires an outside trainer to teach the classes.

9. *Off-site seminars.* Many firms take management retreats periodically where they may conduct management development training for their middle- and upper-level managers. Typically, a selected group of managers meets at a resort area for 2 to 3 days to attend a program conducted by an outside expert. Additionally, many consulting firms conduct seminars throughout the country on management topics. Firms may select one or a few of their management people to attend these programs. Most programs are 1-day events, but some continue for 2 or 3 days.

PERFORMANCE EVALUATION

Performance evaluation is the activity that the firm uses to judge whether employees are performing their jobs effectively. Most companies require managers to appraise their subordinates formally and periodically, typically once a year. While evaluation programs vary, some objectives and techniques tend to be common.

Evaluation Objectives

The most obvious and most common reason for formal evaluations is to determine rewards for productivity. So they can "water where the flowers grow," managers wish to distinguish between employees who do a lot and those who do a little. Merit ratings justify granting one employee a 12% increase in wages or salary, while another employee gets only 4%. Superiors use rating results to back up their decision when subordinates dispute their raises. Managers also rely upon performance evaluations to select employees for promotions.

Employee improvement is the second objective of evaluations. In the review, supervisors can

On-the-job evaluations help assess an employee's job skills. Here, a manager listens in on a customer service situation.

point out weaknesses that could be overcome with training. Honest progress reviews, although potentially painful, help employees and managers isolate behaviors that need correcting or work habits that need improving. In this way, the evaluation develops data for counseling, coaching, and attitude change to help employees overcome barriers to their development. Properly done, the review also motivates employees because they receive continuous feedback on how well they are doing. Reviews also assist with transfers. If an otherwise good worker experiences problems because of a personality conflict with a superior or unique circumstances surrounding peer relationships, the review folder can help determine if a transfer would solve the problem.

Third, evaluation can help justify disciplinary action. If, after training and counseling, employees do not perform to a minimum standard, dismissal or discipline for poor performance may be necessary. The review can be solid documentation for the company that is called upon to defend its decision before union committees or in court.

Employee Evaluation Form

Employee's Name _____ Classification _____

Division/Branch _____

Period Covered by Report: From _____ To _____

Circle the appropriate score for each factor and write a short statement explaining why the employee was rated at the particular level.

I. **Output:** Ability of the unit supervised to meet required standards as to quality and quantity.

1	2	3	4	5
Unsatisfactory	Needs improvement	Satisfactory	Above average	Outstanding

Why _____

II. **Job knowledge:** Clear understanding of the facts or factors pertinent to the job.

1	2	3	4	5
Unsatisfactory	Needs improvement	Satisfactory	Above average	Outstanding

Why _____

III. **Organization and planning:** Ability to devise work methods and anticipate needs; Systematic, etc.

1	2	3	4	5
Unsatisfactory	Needs improvement	Satisfactory	Above average	Outstanding

Why _____

IV. **Judgment:** Ability to make effective decisions without undue delay, etc.

1	2	3	4	5
Unsatisfactory	Needs improvement	Satisfactory	Above average	Outstanding

Why _____

V. **Work relations:** Builds morale; public relations; personal relations; leadership qualities, etc.

1	2	3	4	5
Unsatisfactory	Needs improvement	Satisfactory	Above average	Outstanding

Why _____

VI. **Delegation of authority and responsibility:** Frees self of details; Unit continues to function in absence, etc.

1	2	3	4	5
Unsatisfactory	Needs improvement	Satisfactory	Above average	Outstanding

Why _____

VII. **Initiative:** Earnestness in seeking increased responsibilities; Self starting; Unafraid to proceed alone.

1	2	3	4	5
Unsatisfactory	Needs improvement	Satisfactory	Above average	Outstanding

Why _____

VIII. **Capacity for advancement:** Can assume additional responsibility; Understands related functions, etc.

1	2	3	4	5
Unsatisfactory	Needs improvement	Satisfactory	Above average	Outstanding

Why _____

IX. **Personal qualities:** Personality; appearance; sociability; integrity.

1	2	3	4	5
Unsatisfactory	Needs improvement	Satisfactory	Above average	Outstanding

Why _____

X. **Overall performance:** Consider all factors.

1	2	3	4	5
Unsatisfactory	Needs improvement	Satisfactory	Above average	Outstanding

Why _____

Figure 9.9
A sample employee evaluation form. *Reprinted from the June 1983 issue of* Personnel Administrator, *copyright, 1983, The American Society for Personnel Administration, 606 North Washington Street, Alexandria, VA 22314, $30 per year.*

Merit reviews also help to prevent indiscriminate, personalized discipline.

Evaluation Techniques

What should be evaluated? To this question, most managers will answer, "We look first for results. How well did the employee accomplish the tasks as assigned?" Firms use a variety of indicators to focus on results. Surveys of actual practices show that quality of work, quantity of work, job knowledge, and obedience are the most popular.

A second quality to evaluate is personality. A worker's personality may detract from the overall group performance if he or she does not fit in. Or some personality factors may keep the employee from performing up to potential. A supervisor describes this dilemma, "Henry was one of the most promising employees we had in the department. He had all the skills and was most capable. But he just could not get along with the other workers. He was always arguing and would not cooperate." Surveys of actual practices show that initiative, cooperation, and dependability are the personality factors most popular for evaluation.

There are many techniques for rating job performance. Sometimes called a checklist, the graphic rating scale is the oldest and most widely used technique. The evaluator rates each employee on several qualities that relate to the job. The rating scale is simple to construct, easy to understand, and convenient to use (see Fig. 9.9). But, like grades in school, the evaluation is often judged to be unfair by the employee. With the ranking method, a supervisor lists employees from the highest to the lowest on performance. This overcomes the problem of rating everyone high. But managers do not like to rank anyone toward the bottom of the scale. It does, however, give the evaluator some idea of the relative performance of the workers.

Another increasingly popular method of evaluation is setting objectives. At the beginning of the period — usually six months or a year — the manager and employee jointly set performance goals. These may be for measurable performance or subjective evaluations by the manager. At the end of the period, the evaluation is based on how well the objectives were met. Whatever method of evaluation is used, the goal is generally the same: to give the company an accurate idea of job performance and to help the employee improve.

WAGE AND SALARY ADMINISTRATION

Employee evaluation dovetails with wage and salary administration. The reward system should pay employees according to their contribution to departmental and company objectives. This requires not only evaluating employee performances, but also determining how important each job is relative to all other positions. Why do secretaries earn less than engineers? Why do some engineers earn more than others? Why do medical doctors earn more than doctors of philosophy?

While there is little argument that clerks, salespeople, research chemists, maintenance mechanics, and computer programmers should receive different salaries, there is little agreement on what the differences should be. Specialists debate job evaluation methods and the best procedure for paying wages to employees.

Evaluating Jobs

Before compensation can be determined, the relative worth of each job needs to be considered. While many methods are used to determine the value of each position, the following factors are a prime consideration:

- Degree of expertise required. This includes education, experience, aptitude, physical ability, and social skills.

- Availability of qualified applicants. Is there a shortage of people with the necessary skills?

- Relative contribution to the company's success.

- Available resources in terms of budgets for compensation.

- Current success in the operation of the business.

- Economic conditions.

- Growth plans for the company.

Once these factors are considered, a compensation level can be set.

Wage Payment Plans

After determining the appropriate pay range for each job, managers turn to the riddle of pay method. How should the company pay? By the hour? By the day? By the week?

By far the most widely used pay plan is **day work,** where the company simply pays according to the hours worked. To compute wages, payroll accountants multiply the number of hours each employee works by the hourly rate. Employees know exactly how their salaries are determined, but this method has received criticism for not providing an incentive to produce. **Straight salary,** a variation of day work, also pays according to time worked. But the method is figured by week, month, or year, rather than hours. Straight salary is quoted in such terms as $250 per week, $900 a month, or $13,500 annually.

A second grouping of pay plans bases payment on worker performance in an effort to use money as an incentive. Although relatively popular 30 to 40 years ago, the use of incentive plans is declining. **Piecework,** the most widely used incentive plan, pays according to units produced. If the piece rate for a certain part is $0.03 and a worker produces 1800 parts in a day, his wage for the day would be $54 ($0.03 × 1800). **Group incentive plans** operate on a similar premise to piecework, but they pay according to a group rather than an individual effort. Supervisors keep records of group performance when the group achieves above the standard. Many firms pay a percentage, called a commission, of the value of the sale. Although commissions are not referred to as piecework plans, they are quite similar to them. **Profit sharing,** a modified group incentive plan, pays employees a percentage of the profits each year. Percentages vary, but 25% is typical. Companies frequently pay upper-level managers a bonus — extra pay related to the performance of their companies or divisions. For large companies, the total annual salary of a key executive may contain more than 50% bonus pay.

Which is the best method of wage payment? At this point, there is no clearly superior plan. Companies have experienced success and failure with all the approaches. Piecework and other incentive plans are more conducive to job stability and the ability to measure output. Where change and improvement are important to the company, day work and straight-salary methods are more appropriate.

Some firms, usually because of a union-negotiated agreement, provide **guaranteed annual wages (GAW)** or guaranteed annual employment. These plans typically guarantee an identified group of employees a certain amount of wages or a certain amount of work during the year. Employees like it because it gives them some degree of economic security; however, companies usually resist because these plans create a built-in cost that is hard to reduce should sales tailspin. Procter & Gamble, Hormel, Nunn-Bush, and some automotive plants are examples of firms that have GAW plans.

Regardless of the plan in effect, a number of uncontrollable factors also affect the company's compensation system. For example, local wage rates, supply and demand for labor, a firm's financial condition, laws, and union agreements are a few phenomena that influence pay.

Promotions

A promotion is a type of compensation that results in greater status and responsibility and higher salary. Human resources works with managers in making promotion decisions. While most companies like to reward their employees with promotions, care must also be taken. Mistakes can be serious. Employees placed improperly may cause turnover, inefficiency, and poor morale.

Some executives may also feel hurt or rejected when they have been passed over for promotions. Graber Industries of Wisconsin tries to provide counseling for those who are passed over because they want to keep them in the organization. Garber's president, James Sheridan, says, "It [the counseling] has been highly successful in every case." Most workers feel thankful for the counseling, and they especially like to know what they can do to improve their chances for future promotions.

Fringe Benefits

According to Hewitt Associates, a nationwide consulting firm, fringe benefits account for 41% of salary costs. Fringe benefits are company-sponsored programs that take care of employee needs. While employees have received nonpay benefits for years, complex benefit packages have been evolving in the last few years.

According to a survey of 1507 companies in 1982 by the Chamber of Commerce of the U.S., fringe benefits averaged $7187 per worker. The fringes were divided as shown in Table 9.2. Richard L. Adams, director of employee benefits for Reynolds Metals Company, says, "Our benefits have grown like mad. It's amazing to look at old

TABLE 9.2 ■ FRINGE BENEFITS PER WORKER

Social Security (employer's share)	$1274	Paid rest periods	$523
		Unemployment compensation	269
Life, health insurance	1274	Workers' compensation	258
Pensions	1040	Sick leave	244
Paid vacations	902	Profit sharing	218
Paid holidays	553	Other fringe benefits	632

Source: Chamber of Commerce of the U.S.

BUSINESS BULLETIN

How to Communicate Employees' True Earnings

Research shows that many employees are not fully aware of their total earnings, that is, they do not know what they are being paid. Some firms try to communicate to employees what they are making by sending out information at least once a year on their total pay package. Here is an example of a letter that communicates this information:

Dear _____ :

We thought you might be interested in knowing the total you earned this year, including salary, fringe benefits, and bonuses. Your annual salary was _____, plus benefits totaling _____ and bonuses of _____, for a total of _____.

The breakdown of your fringe benefit package includes:

1. Life insurance   _____
2. FICA (Social Security)   _____
3. Worker's compensation   _____
4. Entertainment   _____
5. Counseling services   _____
6. Medical/dental insurance   _____
7. Value of vacation time   _____
8. Sick leave value   _____
9. Contribution to pension plan   _____
10. Company's sponsorship of clubs   _____
    Total Benefits Paid   _____

We are pleased that we could provide you with these rewards, and we appreciate the contribution that you made to our organization.

Sincerely yours,

Companies report that they have had good experiences in communicating the total pay package to their employees.

documents from the early days of our program in the 1940s to see how far we have come." Much of the expansion has come in health and welfare coverage. U.S. Steel, as an example, now covers workers' hospital stays of up to 2 years per illness; the limit was 120 days 10 years ago. Fringe benefit programs have been expanding in other areas also. However, the economic recession of the early 1980s considerably slowed the expansion of fringe benefit programs.

Many companies today are offering their employees **"cafeteria-style" benefits.** Instead of providing fixed programs to everyone on the payroll, a number of major firms are offering flexible programs that allow employees to pick and choose their benefits. For example, employees whose spouses already have family medical coverage might prefer added vacation time or child-care coverage to a second medical coverage program.

Proponents of fringe benefits argue that these indirect incentives build employee loyalty, commitment, and satisfaction, while reducing absenteeism and turnover. Others counter that since most of the benefits automatically apply to all employees, few workers actually understand what they are and how much they cost. Thus, benefits have little of the hoped-for impact. According to a spokesperson, "We are in a delicate trap; we spend billions of dollars on fringes with few positive results, yet we must continue to add to these packages or face the wrath of disgruntled employees and upset labor unions."

To help identify the skills the company will need, experts study jobs in the company. Job analysis determines the tasks that make up a job, the job description summarizes the employees' duties and responsibilities, and job specifications list physical, mental, and emotional qualifications required by the job. Companies recruit internally and externally. Major external sources include walk-ins, public and private employment agencies, employee referrals, labor unions, professional associations, educational institutions, advertising, and computer matching. In selecting employees for jobs, effective recruiters follow a systematic process involving (1) a preliminary screening interview, (2) an application blank, (3) testing, (4) reference checks, (5) employment interviews, (6) physical examination, and (7) the employment decision.

Companies formally evaluate their employees in order to reward employees according to their contributions to company objectives. Other reasons for evaluations are to obtain data for counseling and training employees and to justify disciplinary action. Five evaluation techniques are graphic rating scales, ranking, paired comparisons, forced choice, and field reviews.

Wage and salary administration begins with job evaluations. Job evaluation is the process of determining the relative worth of different jobs. After jobs are evaluated, managers must choose to pay employees according to a day work or the incentive-based method. Rewards, in addition to money, include a host of fringe benefits.

SUMMARY

Human resources departments concentrate on developing a motivated and fulfilled work force. In its beginnings, human resources was mostly a clerical function, but recently it has broadened to include employee selection, training, wages and salaries, services, labor relations, safety, and research and records. For other departments, human resources provides services, control, and advice.

A major function of the human resources department is to assist with recruiting and selecting employees. This begins with planning the work force. Planners try to project how many employees the company will need by analyzing turnover records and sales and production forecasts.

MIND YOUR BUSINESS

Instructions. Select the correct answer for each of the following by placing the appropriate letter in the blank at the left.

_____ 1. All the following would likely be considered functions, or responsibilities, of human resources personnel except:
   a. Productivity improvement programs
   b. Market segment analysis
   c. Compensation planning and administration
   d. Training and development programs

_____ 2. Which of the following best illustrates the concept of comparable worth?
   a. Equal pay for equal work

b. Equal pay for equal experience

c. Equal pay for equal skills, responsibility, and effort

d. Across-the-board pay increases

_____ 3. All the following are part of defining the job except:

a. Job history

b. Job analysis

c. Job description

d. Job specifications

_____ 4. Which of the following selection techniques is the most controversial?

a. Application blanks

b. Testing

c. Reference checks

d. Physical examinations

_____ 5. Which of the following training methods depends upon creating a simulated work environment?

a. On-the-job training

b. Job instruction training

c. Apprenticeship training

d. Vestibule training

_____ 6. Which of the following pay plans pays according to the number of hours worked?

a. Day work

b. Straight salary

c. Piecework

d. Group incentive plans

See answers at the back of the book.

KEY TERMS

human resources management, 216

Occupational Safety and Health Act (OSHA), 219

Civil Rights Act of 1964, 219

comparable worth, 219

affirmative action, 220

Age Discrimination in Employment Act of 1967, 220

reverse discrimination, 221

turnover, 221

job analysis, 222

job description, 222

job specifications, 222

bona fide occupational qualification (bfoq), 227

termination, 227

exit interview, 228

outplacement, 229

employment at will, 229

orientation program, 230

apprenticeship training, 232

vestibule training, 232

performance evaluation, 233

day work, 236

straight salary, 236

piecework, 236

group incentive plan, 236

profit sharing, 236

guaranteed annual wage (GAW), 236

cafeteria-style benefits, 238

REVIEW QUESTIONS

1. Describe the characteristics of today's workers.

2. What are the major functions of human resources departments? Who performs these functions in small companies without human resources departments?

3. How are human resources departments in larger companies organized?

4. Explain the service, control, and advisory relationships between human resources departments and other departments.

5. Explain the laws discussed in the chapter that influence the legal aspects of human resources.

6. Discuss affirmative action and comparable worth.

7. What is reverse discrimination?

8. What does employment planning involve? How do companies forecast their needs for employees?

9. Distinguish between a job description, job analysis, and job specification. How are they used in employment planning?

10. What are the advantages of recruiting internally? Externally? What are the disadvantages of recruiting internally? Externally?

11. Identify the standard external sources of recruiting. Briefly describe each.

12. Explain the selection process for making an employment decision. Which steps in the process are most critical? Which steps could a company eliminate?

13. Explain employment at will.

14. What is employee evaluation? What purposes does evaluation serve?

15. Why is documentation so important in the evaluation process?

16. Identify and briefly describe the more popular techniques for evaluating employees.

17. What is job evaluation?

18. How are day work and incentive pay systems alike? Different? Identify and describe examples of each method. Which is the most common? Why?

19. Analyze the role of fringe benefits in the reward system.

CASES

Case 9.1: A Contrast in Attitudes

The following are comments from two employees relating their differing attitudes toward their organizations.

A younger employee describes his first few years of experience:

"I was really excited when I first took the job. I thought I would advance fast. But after a few months, I began to feel like I was just going to be doing the same routine things for a long time. I had finished high school, but an eighth grader could do what I was doing. The pay was good, better than I expected, but I just wasn't able to do very much. I could see that they were doing a lot of things that could be improved. I tried to make a few suggestions for improvement. They didn't really listen. There was always some reason why they could not take my ideas. I suspect they just did not want to go to the trouble to make the changes. Finally, I just seemed to lose interest. Now, it's just a job. I do my work, at least most of the time. I'm not too happy; I'll probably start looking around for a new job in a few months."

An older employee describes her many years of experience:

"I've been around for a long time. I see the new people coming in, and they want to change things overnight. If things do not go right, they get upset. Most don't seem to worry if they lose their job, and they are sure not as loyal as people were 30 years ago. At one time, I was unhappy with my job also, but after awhile, you realize that the world is not perfect. I take my job seriously; I know some things could be changed. And we *have* changed a lot of things. But many of the things younger people want to change have served us well. They are into so many things, a job is sometimes just another hobby for them. It seems that their job is not central to their lives."

Questions

1. Discuss some possible reasons why these two employees see things differently.

2. Which set of attitudes is more helpful to the organization? To the employee?

Case 9.2: The Employment Decision

You are considering two applicants for a management trainee position in your sales department. For the first two years, the trainee will work in several different jobs in the department to learn how your company does things. Then the employee will be assigned a position as assistant to one of your department managers. The trainee's progress thereafter will depend upon how well he or she performs. You have interviewed several applicants and have narrowed your choice to two people. Both are young college graduates with little or no experience.

Wally Hendrich is a bright young graduate with a B+ average and a major in business. He scored very well on your tests and has excellent references from his professors and from an employer for whom he worked part-time while attending school. Other people in your company have been somewhat impressed by Wally, but not as much as you have been. They feel that he has done all the "right" things, but they worry that he does not have the ambition to be a successful sales manager. Wally places high priorities on getting married, raising a family, being at home, and living a "normal" life. You are aware of this, but since

Wally has been successful at everything he has done, you feel that he will be successful in his work.

Sally DeWolf is also a college graduate with above-average grades in business. She has an outgoing personality, dresses attractively, and communicates a feeling of confidence. She has worked part-time at several different jobs, never staying in one job for very long. When asked why she changed jobs so often, she said she got bored. Her test scores are a little below Wally's but still above average. Others in the organization really like her and think that she has the personality and drive to be a success. You also think she is a good prospect, but you feel that she is too self-centered. You get the impression that she will put her personal growth and advancement ahead of her de-sire to make the department look good. Also you have a slight fear that she will try shortcuts and might leave if the company does not "take care of her."

Questions

1. Analyze the strengths and weaknesses of Wally; of Sally.

2. How will you consider the opinions of others in relation to yours? Which will you give the most attention to? Why?

3. On the basis of this information, which candidate would you select? Why? What are the potential problems with your selection? What would you do to prevent or reduce these problems?

After completing this chapter, you should be able to:

■ **Discuss Maslow's hierarchy of needs theory of motivation.**

■ **Diagram and explain Herzberg's motivation-hygiene theory.**

■ **Explain the role of money in employee motivation.**

■ **Describe job enrichment.**

■ **Explain management by objectives (MBO).**

■ **Discuss the history and process of quality circles.**

■ **Describe quality of work life (QWL) programs.**

■ **Identify eight practical ways managers can motivate today's employees.**

10

UNDERSTANDING

AND

MOTIVATING

EMPLOYEES

I n a recent survey by the Public Agenda Foundation of New York, only 23% of the respondents told interviewers they were working as hard as they could in their jobs. Management expert Peter Drucker says, "The quickest way to quench motivation is not to allow people to do what they've been trained to do. In other words, take the nurse in the hospital and make her spend 80% of her time on paperwork that has nothing to do with patient care."

The management at Owens-Illinois, in an effort to restore employee confidence and build employee commitment, holds periodic meetings with employees to report on company performance and to answer questions. Management says they are trying to motivate employees through terms and concepts they can understand; they do not want to rely strictly upon financial objectives. Their program also wants to show a close link between individual prosperity and company success.

At a time when technology and robotics seem to be dominating management decisions, Owens-Illinois and many other companies are making special efforts to understand and motivate their people. A researcher asked twenty Hewlett-Packard executives why their company was success-

On their own initiative, active and retired employees of Delta Airlines purchased this 767 airliner and presented it to the company.

ful. Eighteen of the twenty spontaneously said, "It is our people-oriented philosophy." Explaining the reasons behind their long-term success, an executive at Delta Airlines said, "There is a special relationship between Delta and its personnel that is rarely found in any firm, generating a team spirit that is evident in the individual's cooperative attitude . . . , cheerful outlook on life, and pride in a job well done." Hideo Sugiura, chairman of Honda Motor Company, explains their people-oriented philosophy: "Our workers are not tools of production. We never say we want to hire welders, or lathe operators, or whatever." Sugiura further explained that if you hired a welder and found a robot to replace him, there is nothing you can do with the welder. But if you hire someone and train him in all the skills of assembling a motorcycle, to him a robot is just another machine to make his work easier.

This chapter examines major motivational theories, practical applications of the theories, and methods of motivating employees.

MAJOR MOTIVATIONAL THEORIES

Two theories of motivation, Maslow's hierarchy of needs and Herzberg's motivation-hygiene theory, have stood the test of time.

Maslow's Hierarchy of Needs

Maslow, a well-known psychologist, believed that needs were the underlying causes of all behavior. The only reason a person does anything is to satisfy **needs.** Thus, we can understand human **motivation** if we understand needs.

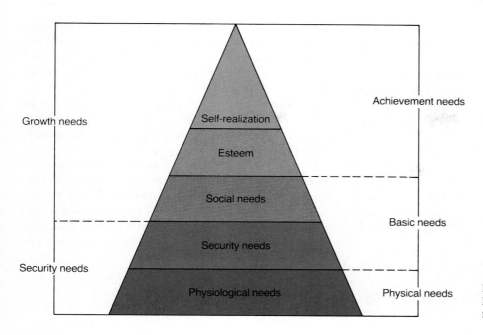

**Figure 10.1
Maslow's hierarchy of
needs.**

Based on his research and experience, Maslow divided human needs into five levels: physiological, safety, social, esteem, and self-realization. These needs are arranged in **Maslow's hierarchy** as shown in Fig. 10.1 and Table 10.1.

Physiological needs include the basic needs necessary for survival. Examples are oxygen, food, rest, sex, and water. We have to satisfy these needs regularly to keep ourselves alive. The next higher level is security needs, originally called

safety needs by Maslow. **Security needs** reflect the desire for certainty, predictability, safety, and stability in our lives. We like to believe that some things will remain the same tomorrow as they are today. We try to satisfy these needs through such activities as fringe benefit programs, hospitalization insurance, retirement programs, life insurance, savings, and the like. The need to love and be loved, to have friends and be a friend, to enjoy the companionship of other humans is a **social need.**

TABLE 10.1 ■ MASLOW'S NEEDS: PERSONAL, SOCIAL, AND PHYSICAL ASPECTS

Maslow's Needs	Personal Aspects	Social Aspects	Physical Aspects
Physiological needs	Personal, physical comfort		Food, water, oxygen, sex, rest, temperature
Security needs	Personal safety, continuity, comfort, no future threats		Security of a continuance of physiological needs without threat of loss in future
Social needs	Acceptance, friends, a feeling of belonging	Acceptance by others, prestige and value acknowledged by peers	Feeling comfortable, accepted, and secure in social situations
Esteem needs	Respect for self, pride, achievement	Evident respect from others, professional accomplishment acknowledged by peers	More basic needs fulfilled; threats to safety, comfort, and social acceptance overcome
Self-realization needs	Total self-development, fulfillment, maximum personal growth	Unusual accomplishment acknowledged by peers	Concern about basic needs seems petty; of course, basic needs will be met

And these social needs form the third level in Maslow's hierarchy. We try to satisfy these through marriage, parties, office groups, coffee breaks, fraternities, and clubs. At the fourth level is esteem needs. **Esteem needs** mean respect from others and respect for one's self. We want to feel that we are doing something that is worthwhile, and we want others to respect us for it. The need for esteem is the need for our peers to say, "You are a person of value, of worth." "You are doing something we respect." "You are good at what you are doing." We try to satisfy this need through reputation and expertise gained through knowledge, preparation, experience, and accomplishments.

Maslow said a housewife could achieve self-realization by creatively preparing a bowl of soup.

Finally, at the apex, is the need for **self-realization,** the need to do the very best that we are capable of doing. We do not have to be corporation presidents or world-renowned artists to satisfy these needs. Maslow said that a housewife showed him that she could achieve self-realization by creatively preparing a bowl of soup, a football player by executing a block to perfection, and a high school janitor by expertly performing his duties. We achieve some degree of self-realization when we do a task or create an idea that utilizes all, or practically all, of our abilities. See Fig. 10.2 for characteristics of people who operate at the self-realization level.

Maslow also agreed that some people were out of sync with his theory. Some artists, religious leaders, and creative people seek to satisfy higher-level needs without first fulfilling lower-level needs. Without sufficient shelter, security, or social life, they toil away, driven by their quest for self-realization. Maslow explained this by saying they were exceptions to his general theory. Numerous research studies have shown that this theory helps to explain the behavior of most people in our culture.

Herzberg's Motivation-Hygiene Theory

Like Maslow, Frederick Herzberg, a psychology professor and world-famous management consultant, used needs as the basis of his theory of motivation. As seen in Fig. 10.3, **Herzberg's motivation-hygiene theory** divides our needs into two categories: (1) hygiene and (2) motivational.

Hygiene needs. The group of needs outside the circle, Herzberg called hygiene needs. Generally, **hygiene needs** represent factors that are peripheral to the job itself (that is, they are job-context

Figure 10.2
Characteristics of people who operate at the self-realization level. *Source: Adapted from Abraham H. Maslow,* Toward a Psychology of Being, *Litton Educational Publishing, Inc., 1968.*

Evaluate yourself on the following scales by selecting the number that describes how you see yourself.

Clear perception of reality	1 2 3 4 5 6 7 8 9 10	Unclear perception of reality
Open to different experiences	1 2 3 4 5 6 7 8 9 10	Closed to different experiences
Spontaneous	1 2 3 4 5 6 7 8 9 10	Guarded
Autonomous	1 2 3 4 5 6 7 8 9 10	Dependent
Objective	1 2 3 4 5 6 7 8 9 10	Subjective
More creative	1 2 3 4 5 6 7 8 9 10	Less creative
Democratic	1 2 3 4 5 6 7 8 9 10	Autocratic
Great ability to love others	1 2 3 4 5 6 7 8 9 10	Limited ability to love others

The values on the left of this scale are characteristics of people operating at the self-realization level. Thus, if you total your points on all the scales, a score of 49 or less indicates greater tendencies toward self-realization. A score of 51 or more indicates lesser tendencies toward self-realization.

Figure 10.3
Herbzerg's motivation and hygiene needs.
Source: Adapted from M. Scott Myers, "Who Are Your Motivated Workers?" Harvard Business Review, *January/February 1964, p. 86.*

oriented). Examples include company policy, administration, supervision, work conditions, salary, relationships with peers, personal life, relationships with subordinates, status, and security.

Herzberg says, "Hygiene factors do not motivate employees to perform." Does this mean they are not important? No! While hygiene needs may not motivate performance, they do cause people to be upset when they are unfulfilled. We must satisfy hygiene needs of employees or they will get frustrated and quit, work slowly, be absent, form a union, or express their displeasure in other ways. On the other hand, when we do satisfy employees' hygiene needs, we cannot necessarily expect them to show their gratefulness by working hard. In a sense we only come out even, because we have merely prevented unhappiness; we have not created a desire to perform.

As you study Fig. 10.3, you will see many ways that organizations motivate their people. A skeptic usually remarks, "I know that money is motivating. That is the reason a lot of people work." Before you concur too strongly with these skeptical supervisors, think about what would happen if an organization doubled the salary (or status, or working conditions) of its employees. Would they work twice as hard? Probably not. Would they be 50% more productive? Probably not. Would they work any harder? Probably, but only for a few weeks. People surely want to satisfy their hygiene needs. And organizations have done a very good job of providing these satisfactions. But if we are to motivate today's employees, we must appeal to their motivational needs.

Motivational needs. While hygiene factors are peripheral to the work, **motivational needs** are associated directly with the work itself (that is, they are job-content oriented). Figure 10.3 contains examples of these needs, including the work

What People Want from Their Work

Motivation, in reality, is an exchange process. The organization wants employees to apply their physical and mental efforts toward reaching the objectives of the department. For this, the organization must give their workers what they want. However, many managers try to give employees what they think they want from their work without really trying to find out their real aspirations. A survey conducted by the Labor Relations Institute of New York some years back, and repeated many times since then, reveals the differences between what employees actually want from their work and what managers think they want. Rankings of ten things employees wanted from their work are listed here. The left column shows how the employees ranked these items, and the right column shows how managers ranked them.

Employees' Rankings		Managers' Rankings
1	Full appreciation for work done	8
2	Feeling of being "in" on things	9
3	Sympathetic help on personal problems	10
4	Job security	2
5	Good wages	1
6	Interesting work	5
7	Promotion and growth in the organization	3
8	Personal loyalty to employees	6
9	Good working conditions	4
10	Tactful disciplining	7

Note the vast differences on the first three items. What employees ranked 1, 2, 3, the managers ranked 8, 9, and 10. Do you see why we have motivational problems?

itself: individual growth, recognition, advancement, responsibility, achievement, and individual development. According to Herzberg's research, and hundreds of others that have replicated his studies, people are moved to perform by the satisfaction of these higher-level needs.

PRACTICAL APPLICATIONS OF THEORIES

Theory is necessary because it gives us a good understanding of why things happen. But knowing theory does not automatically guarantee that we can practice it. So, we will now dwell on the practical ways to apply these theories. After a discussion of the role of money in motivation, we will examine the techniques of job enrichment, management by objectives, quality circles, and quality of work life.

The Role of Money in Employee Motivation

Compare the following comments of two managers.

"I just don't understand people today. We try to pay according to performance, but they just don't seem to be interested in money. Many seem to do their jobs poorly even when they know it will be reflected in their paychecks."

"That's not true of our employees. Money is all they want to talk about. In fact, a lot of our people say they enjoy working for us, but they quit to take higher-paying jobs."

Such comments underline the confusion over money as a motivator. To motivate, money must fulfill some of the needs that we discussed earlier. From experience and research, we see that money can in some way apply to both higher- and lower-level needs.

Surely, money is necessary to help satisfy the basic needs of life. While we cannot eat, drink, or clothe ourselves in money, we use it to purchase food, water, clothing, and shelter. Money also helps to satisfy security needs. We save it, invest it, build retirement programs with it, and buy insurance with it. All these purchases help to satisfy our need for security and safety.

In our culture, money is also a great help in satisfying social needs. We may have friends without much money. But, money makes it easier to socialize with others at the movies, parties, or clubs. We also use it to entertain in our homes, join fancy clubs, and travel with family and friends.

But as a once-popular song put it, "Money talks, but it can't dance and it can't sing." Few people would say that money equals respect and dignity. Still, money can be a sign of respect. Salaries represent the worth of an individual to the organization. Therefore, high salaries and good pay increases show that the organization respects the individual's contribution. And this can be used to communicate to others outside the company how much their organization respects them. "If you really want to show me how much you appreciate my work, put it in my paycheck."

So we see that money satisfies need levels from the tangible to the intangible. We feel insecure when we do not have enough money for life's basics. And we may feel a lack of respect when our companies do not pay us what they are paying our peers or what we feel we deserve.

Because money applies to so many different need levels, it would appear to be an excellent motivator. But practice suggests that money does not have nearly the motivational impact it once had. Compared to 20 or 30 years ago, real wages and incomes are much higher. Yet, employees do not seem to be as motivated by wages. As a speaker in a recent training session put it, "If we could solve our motivational problems with money,

they would be solved. Employees receive much more pay today than they did in 'the good old days.' Yet, we have more apathy, absenteeism, theft, and general unconcern for the work output than ever before."

In fact, we probably rely too much on money. Although monetary incentive plans were quite effective 40 or 50 years ago, most are not producing the desired results today.

Job Enrichment

While pay is an attempt to reward zestful employees, job enrichment is an effort to motivate via the work itself. **Job enrichment** is the process of changing the job so that the work will appeal to employees' higher-level needs. Its aim is to make the work itself more meaningful. If people get enjoyment and need fulfillment from doing their tasks, the job will motivate them to work.

First, job enrichment is not asking people to produce more, or sell more, or get through their work more quickly. This is merely speeding up, working harder at what you are doing. Second, it is not **job enlargement,** merely adding another meaningless task to an already meaningless job. Washing knives and forks is not a lot more fulfilling than washing just knives. Some managers assume they are enriching subordinates' work lives by adding other duties, but the duties must make the job more whole or more meaningful in order to be enriching. Third, rotating meaningless tasks does not help, at least not very much. To say that you can wash knives in the morning, but you get to wash forks in the afternoon will cause few, if any, employees to shout and sing. Fourth, job enrichment does not mean taking away all the hard parts and making the task more routine. Such a change takes fulfillment out of the job rather than putting it in.

Job enrichment means checking less frequently on your employees, giving them more responsibility, and making them more accountable for their work.

Then what is job enrichment? Here are a few pointers. Remove some of the controls. If you have been checking on employees every hour, start checking only every two hours, then every three. Place more responsibility on people. Make people accountable for their work. If they do not do it, the work does not get done. If there are problems, the employee should correct them, not the supervisor. An older employee relates an example, "I've had this scheduling job for years. It is tough; hard to get everything right. There are always conflicts. The boss got a new assistant. I guess she wants to impress someone, so she has started double-checking everything I turn in. Now, when I get the schedule down to two or three conflicts, I turn it in. She finds the problems, then takes whatever time is necessary to straighten them out. It was fun doing this at first, watching her scurry around. But I've lost a little respect and the scheduling is not as satisfying. I don't get the satisfaction of knowing that I did a good job."

There are many other ways to broaden and enrich a task. Give an employee a complete natural work unit and more authority to make decisions. Rather than instructing a secretary to "fill in Part A of Form 1098," let him complete the entire

Does New Role of Father Reduce Motivation?

In the 1960s, the role of parents was well established. Typically, the role of the mother was to raise the children, and the father's responsibility was to provide financial support for the family and be a caretaker for the mother. While this is surely oversimplifying the situation, these father-mother roles were quite recognizable in the 1960s.

However, the changing roles of mothers in society have also brought about a changing role for fathers. A father, today, is more likely to share the domestic role with the mother, especially the role of child care. Simultaneously, the mother is more likely to take some responsibility for "bringing home the bread."

Some psychologists say the father's increased role in child care has significantly reduced the motivation to succeed in business. A study by American Telephone & Telegraph Co. of ten major industries found that the younger employees had less motivation and interest in getting ahead, and they were less concerned about their organization than were their older counterparts.

Reporting at the American Psychological Association conference in 1983, Professor Philip Cowen said that fathers who were more involved in the family were more likely to feel better about themselves and have wives that were less depressed, regardless of whether the mother worked. Cowen further said that industries should adapt their working hours so that fathers can assume more of the child care role.

Other studies also indicate that younger managers have less drive for leadership and accomplishment than their counterparts did 20 years ago, but some of these studies attribute the difference to the "generation gap" rather than changing roles. What do you think?

Do you think that the increased role of a father in child care reduces the father's desire to succeed in the company? Why?

____ A. Yes   ____ B. No

Do you think that companies should try to adapt their working hours to family needs, regardless of whether it affects productivity at work? Respond on a scale from 7 to 1, with 7 indicating companies should "try hard to adapt" and 1 indicating they should adapt "no more than at present." Why?

Try hard to adapt   7 6 5 4 3 2 1   No more than at present

Honda Plants in the United States

Honda built its first manufacturing facility in the United States in Marysville, Ohio — a $35 million motorcycle plant. The first motorcycle came off the sparkling new assembly line in 1979. A couple of years later, Honda started building a $250 million car plant, and the first Honda Accord car was produced in 1982.

One reason Honda located in Marysville is that they wanted to find a relatively homogeneous work group without previous assembly-line experience. Unlike most American auto companies, Honda trains their people in all aspects of the work, not to do just a narrow job. Honda management also spends a lot of time communicating with people in the plant. They have short meetings every morning to talk about any problems that might have arisen the previous day. And the top executives spend a lot of time in the field. An official says that none of top management's desks is very comfortable. This goes back to an early tradition established by Mr. Honda. He believed that managers would more likely be out and available to employees if their desks and offices were not too comfortable.

So far, the employees and the community have responded well to the new Honda plants. "We could not ask for any finer or any fairer relationship than with Honda," said Marysville's mayor, Tom Nuckles.

The big question is, "Can the Japanese be as successful producing products in the United States as they were in Japan?" Although it is too early to tell whether they will be successful, the early signs look good. As one of the plant coordinators admitted, when dealers find out that a Honda product was produced in the United States, "they will be looking for a flaw." Management says it is up to the employees to make sure that the cars produced here are of the same outstanding quality as those produced in Japan.

project and carry it through. Rather than having the receptionist refer every call to the boss, train her to answer many of the callers' questions. Then try to give employees direct feedback on how well they are doing. If there are computer printouts on costs, scrap, hours, and the like, teach the employees to read them. Seeing direct feedback themselves is more powerful than having a leader interpret progress, or lack of it, to them. Occasionally, introduce new and harder tasks to employees. They really want to do more, not less. Learning is a form of growth; it awakens and refreshes us. Finally, it is very enticing to become known as a person who is an expert. So give people specific areas of responsibility. When things go well, everyone will know who gets the credit.

Most readers have work experience. Can you think of some changes that would cause a job to be more exciting? Figure 10.4 contains a checklist that can be used to evaluate the meaningfulness of work.

Management by Objectives

Like job enrichment, **management by objectives,** often called **MBO,** is a program that tries to increase motivation by appealing to higher-level needs. Basically, management by objectives involves a supervisor and subordinate agreeing upon what the subordinate is to accomplish in the immediate future, say 3 to 6 months. Rather than describing activities of a job, MBO concentrates on the results of the job. For example, the traditional job description of a service department manager might include such things as supervising service employees, maintaining accurate service records, training employees, establishing relationships with customers, and the like. Under MBO, the service manager might have four to seven specific objectives to accomplish such as: (1) design a new maintenance contract program by June 14, (2) reduce the absentee rate in the department from 4% to 2% within the next 6 months, (3) select at least

PLANNING: Can the individual or group . . .	no	sometimes	yes
1. Set goals and standards of performance?	—	—	—
2. State the product quality and quantity commitments?	—	—	—
3. Organize the work layout and influence personnel assignments?	—	—	—
4. Name customers and state delivery dates for products and services?	—	—	—
5. State the sources of their materials and problems in obtaining them?	—	—	—
6. List direct and overhead costs, selling price, and other profit and loss information?	—	—	—

DOING: Does the job . . .	no	sometimes	yes
1. Utilize peoples' talents and require their attention?	—	—	—
2. Enable people to see the relationship of their work to other operations?	—	—	—
3. Provide access to all the information they need to do their work?	—	—	—
4. Have a satisfactory work cycle—neither too long nor too short?	—	—	—
5. Give people feedback on how well they are doing?	—	—	—
6. Enable them to see how they contribute to the usefulness of the product or service to the customer?	—	—	—

CONTROLLING: Can the individual or group . . .	no	sometimes	yes
1. State customer quality requirements and reasons for these standards?	—	—	—
2. Keep their own records of quality and quantity?	—	—	—
3. Check quality and quantity of work and revise procedures?	—	—	—
4. Evaluate and modify work layout on their own initiative?	—	—	—
5. Identify and correct unsafe working conditions?	—	—	—
6. Obtain information from people outside the group as a means of evaluating performance?	—	—	—

Figure 10.4
Sample items from supervisory worksheet for analyzing meaningfulness of work. *Source: Adapted from M. Scott Myers, "Every Employee a Manager,"* California Management Review, *1968, pp. 9–20.*

four employees to attend technical training schools within the year, and (4) handle 3000 projected service calls during the year within 24 hours after each call is placed. Once they agree on the objectives, the supervisor more or less gets out of the way and lets the employee work toward the objectives in his or her own way. At the end of the period, the supervisor and employee get together to measure progress. If the employee has reached the objectives, they set others for the next period and repeat the process. If the employee came up short of some objectives, they try to find out why and improve during the next period. Figure 10.5 diagrams the concept of MBO.

MBO has several sweet-sounding benefits. It gives employees specific targets (objectives) to work toward. It goes beyond the specifics of tasks they are supposed to perform to what they should be accomplishing. And once objectives are set,

employees can monitor their own progress on a daily or weekly basis. They get feedback on whether they are ahead or behind or on schedule. Such feedback on progress helps to satisfy higher level needs of growth, improvement, and autonomy. It also allows the employees to work more on their own because they know where they are and where they are going. Supervisors do not have to look over their shoulders all the time, checking on progress. Research also shows that when people are involved to some degree in setting their own objectives, they are more committed to reaching them. The objectives are no longer something that the impersonal organization requires of them; they are, at least partly, their own ideas. In these ways, MBO appeals to higher-level needs.

MBO has not been equally successful in all organizations. In fact, research reports numerous failures and partial successes of MBO in organizations. Organizations that have maintained successful MBO programs tend to:

1. State in specific, measurable terms four to seven objectives for each manager's job.
2. Ask each subordinate manager or employee to report his or her objectives to superiors in writing. Both superior and subordinate must come to agreement on the objectives.
3. Include methods to measure results and steps that are necessary to accomplish the objectives.
4. Systematically gather data on the progress toward the objectives and regularly report this to subordinates.
5. Engage managers and subordinates in supportive, problem-solving discussions to improve performance when progress falls behind.
6. Concentrate on using MBO at management levels.

Quality Circles

A **quality circle (QC)** is a group of workers in the same area who meet together voluntarily on a regular basis to try to solve problems and reduce costs in their departments. The early 1980s saw U.S. organizations placing a tremendous emphasis on using quality circles to motivate their employees to produce better-quality products and services.

Authorities estimated that more than 400 organizations had some type of quality control system in 1983.

In fact, authorities estimated that more than 400 organizations had some type of quality circle system in 1983.

Dr. W. E. Deming, an American consultant, introduced QCs in Japan, probably around 1961. QCs spread throughout most of Japanese industry; and in 1974, Lockheed introduced them into the United States. After Lockheed reported savings of $2.8 million in the first 2 years of using QCs, other companies became interested. Companies provide many instances of how their circles have benefited them, for example:

Keithley Instruments, Inc., a manufacturer of electronics measuring equipment, using the quality circle concept in the form of product-oriented work teams, reports that:

■ Inventory costs were reduced $550,000 from 1981 to 1982.

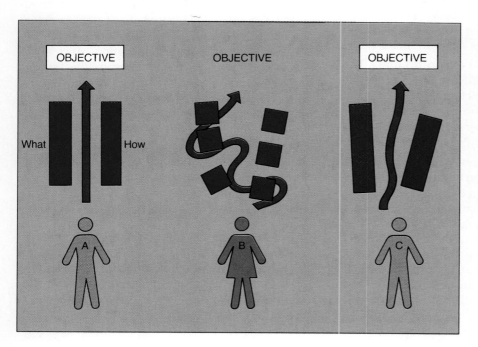

Figure 10.5
The concept of MBO.
Employee A is told exactly what to do and how to do it. He is too closely supervised. Employee B is neither told what to do nor how to do it. She is too loosely supervised. Employee C and supervisor agree on what to do, and Employee C has some latitude as to how he will do it. This is management by objectives.

- Inventory turnover was increased from 1.8 to 2.14 per year.
- Increase in productivity was 21 percent.
- Improvement in the company's quality audit rating went from the low 80s to 95.5%.

How quality circles typically operate. While there is variation among circle operations, most follow a pattern that includes five themes:

1. *Regular meetings.* Circles typically have between five and ten members, and they meet on a regular basis. Effective QCs set a schedule and stick by it. Usually, they meet once a week, for an average of 45 minutes to an hour per meeting. Most meetings occur on company time, but some occur before work, during lunch, or after work.

2. *Problems within their departments.* QCs tackle problems within their areas of expertise, usually within their departments. They try to solve only those problems they have control over. Many of the problems they deal with, especially when a circle is new, may seem insignificant. But effective circles do not try to tell other departments how they should operate, nor do they try to tell the president how to run the company.

3. *Participation by all members.* Circle leaders encourage participation by all members. When deciding what problems to work on and when searching for solutions, effective leaders encourage ideas from all members.

4. *Training.* Circles receive a lot of training. Experts, usually from outside the company, train the leaders on topics ranging from leadership to statistical techniques. Leaders then train their circle members. Training may be a part of the circle meetings for 15 to 20 weeks.

5. *Management presentation.* When QCs identify significant problems and solutions, they may present these to a group of higher-level managers. This is called a "management presentation." Using charts, visuals, slides, and other analytical devices, circle members try to persuade management that they have found a way to solve a problem. Of course, the circle members must understand that management has the final say on whether the solution will be adopted.

Organization of quality circles. In addition to the QC members and leader, circle structures typically include facilitators, coordinators, and a steering committee. The facilitator helps the leader coordinate the circle activities, provides training when needed, and aids the circle in whatever way is necessary. The coordinator oversees the overall company program, and policies are set by the steering committee. Figure 10.6 diagrams a typical organization structure of a QC program.

Potential problems with quality circles. Since U.S. culture differs from Japanese culture, many authorities have warned that we simply cannot adapt circles easily into our work force. And while there have been many successes, there is also evidence that some circles also have problems. In fact, after about a year's operation, it is not uncommon for a circle to show signs of burnout. Some members stop attending meetings, both members and leaders get frustrated and lose patience with the process, the group runs out of problems, and upper management loses interest. Our work force is also much less stable than Japan's. Turnover and layoffs make it hard to maintain continuity in circle meetings.

Dr. Matthew Goodfellow of University Research Center studied quality circle programs in twenty-nine companies and found that in twenty-one companies the quality circles produced measurable results totaling less than their cost. Westinghouse, which established about 1000 circles at 200 locations, has been disappointed, primarily because of poor union cooperation. And North American Phillips Corp. in Jefferson City, Tennessee, developed a quality circle program that did not succeed. Again, failure to gain union commitment, as well as lack of preparation for the circles, probably led to the failure. While there are many reported successes with circles, managers should be aware that they require large investments in time and energy to make them successful.

Quality of Work Life Programs

In an effort to improve both employee satisfaction and productivity, General Motors in 1973 incorporated **quality of work life (QWL)** activities into its collective bargaining agreement with the United Auto Workers. Work teams of sixteen persons at GM's Cadillac plant in Livonia, Michigan,

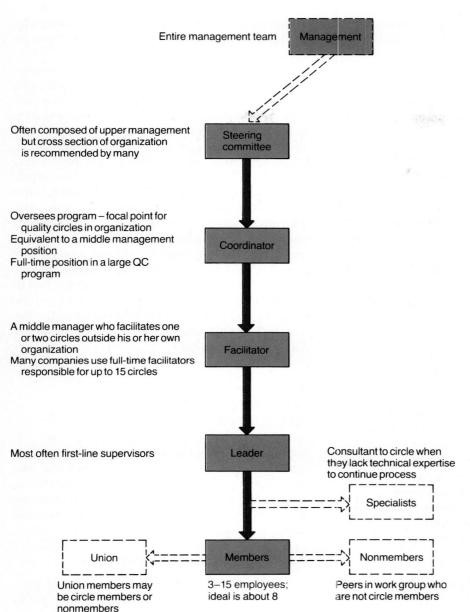

Entire management team — Management

Often composed of upper management but cross section of organization is recommended by many — Steering committee

Oversees program – focal point for quality circles in organization
Equivalent to a middle management position
Full-time position in a large QC program — Coordinator

A middle manager who facilitates one or two circles outside his or her own organization
Many companies use full-time facilitators responsible for up to 15 circles — Facilitator

Most often first-line supervisors — Leader

Consultant to circle when they lack technical expertise to continue process — Specialists

Union members may be circle members or nonmembers — Union

3–15 employees; ideal is about 8 — Members

Peers in work group who are not circle members — Nonmembers

Figure 10.6
Example of a quality circle structure. *Source: William L. and Harriet Mohr, Quality Circles, Reading, Mass.: Addison-Wesley Publishing Co., 1983, p. 78.*

QWL activities saved General Motors $440,000 in 1982.

---

set their own work rules, production levels, and were responsible for quality of their output. Suggestions from the workers saved GM $440,000 in 1982, and outside auditors rated their engines as the best or among the best produced by the company. Because of the success at General Motors, many other corporations have introduced some type of QWL program into its management.

Quality of work life programs are efforts by companies and employees to increase employee participation, democratic processes, and improved working conditions in the company. The programs usually consist of employee problem-solving groups and gain-sharing plans. Employees, through group discussion and other means, try to develop ideas that will improve productivity and employee contentment. And when these programs result in improved productivity, the company usually shares the savings through some type of bonus system for the employees and managers.

Results of quality of work life programs. As you might expect, some QWL programs are successful and some are not. In a coal mining company, QWL programs have introduced additional job training, supervisory training, some pay changes, and better communications between shifts. These efforts resulted in slight productivity increases. An auto parts factory gained significant productivity increases by making the following changes through their QWL program:

- Time-off bonus incentives.
- Increased training.
- A safety program.
- A plant newsletter.

Other examples of changes by QWL programs in companies include: (1) four-day work weeks, (2) communication programs, (3) better equipment, (4) improved parking facilities, (5) staff meetings, (6) management development activities, (7) attitude surveys, (8) job assignment systems, and the like. Many of these changes improve the working life of employees; some improve both working life and productivity; and others improve neither.

Conditions for success. Companies that have improved both productivity and employee satisfaction with their QWL programs meet the following conditions:

- There is an apparent need for change.
- There is a strong commitment from higher management.
- There is sufficient time and budget to effect changes.
- The firms have a reputation for being well managed.
- Employee-management trust is high.
- Changes occur only after adequate planning and preparation.

When these conditions are not met, the company likely will be disappointed in the results of its QWL programs.

When these conditions are present, however, a QWL program can have very positive benefits for both employees and the company. The production department of a large chemical plant remained dissatisfied with its production performance even after repeated efforts to increase it. They formed a QWL program and held many meetings with hourly workers and other appropriate groups throughout the company. After much discussion and a long time lapse, employees, working with their supervisors, created many new work plans and projects for improvement. As a result, production rose from 90% of capacity to 106%, the packaging department produced 125% of its goal, the lab consistently met its turnaround target of 3 hours, and cooperation and employee morale increased significantly. Figure 10.7 lists the problem-solving process used in QC and QWL groups.

MOTIVATING EMPLOYEES THROUGH EFFECTIVE SUPERVISION

In addition to the suggestions for applying motivational theories, managers can increase employee motivation through more effective day-to-day supervision. Here are some guidelines for improving motivation through effective supervision.

Increasing Authority Delegation

Authority delegation includes (1) assigning work to people, (2) getting out of their way while they perform it, and (3) checking when the job is finished. As individuals become proficient at their current jobs, managers can encourage them to take on even more responsibilities. Some employees may resist this process at first, but both theory and practice suggest that they really want to progress to more responsible tasks.

Communicating Expectations

It is surprising how many employees do not know what is expected of them, that is, do not understand their goals. A research experiment with second-grade school children illustrates the power of

1. Identify a list of problems.
2. Select one problem to solve.
3. Clarify the problem.
4. Identify and evaluate causes.
5. Identify and evaluate solutions.
6. Decide on a solution.
7. Develop an implementation plan.
8. Present the plan to management.
9. Implement the plan.
10. Monitor the solution.
11. Think ahead.

Figure 10.7
The problem-solving process. *Source: William L. and Harriet Mohr,* Quality Circles, *Reading, Mass: Addison-Wesley Publishing Co., 1983, p. 82.*

expectations. Researchers tested the children at the beginning of the year. One of the tests was an intelligence test. At the end of the semester, researchers compared the teacher's grades to the test scores. Sure enough, the kids with higher intelligence scores also had higher grades. This does not surprise you, right? But the reported intelligence test scores were not that at all: They were the kids' locker numbers, which had been randomly assigned.

The kids with higher locker numbers responded to teacher expectations. Suppose you were the teacher. A student with a locker number of 120 turns in ten arithmetic problems and gets only five right. You are disappointed. You ask the child, "What is wrong? Why did you miss five? What can I do to help you?" But suppose locker number 65 turns in five correct problems. You say, "That's good! You got five right. Now don't get discouraged." You expect more from the higher locker numbers and you get more.

If you expect employees to be at work on time every day, tell them. If you expect employees to finish a job in a specific time, let them know. Goals are important and should be made known.

Giving Earned Recognition and Praise

Employees want to please their superiors, and they want them to appreciate what they do for them. In a survey, a researcher asked supervisors,

Flextime and Job Sharing

Two trends have emerged in recent years to try to accommodate more of employees' special needs: flextime and job sharing.

Flextime means letting employees have some flexibility in choosing their working hours. Typically, employees have a choice about what hours they will work, within limits set by the company. For instance, employees might be able to choose to come to work between the hours of 6:00 to 9:00 A.M. Of course, they would have to work their normal number of hours.

To the employer, flextime often reduces tardiness, absenteeism, and time lost due to sick leave. It can create some scheduling and record keeping problems, however. For the employee, flextime provides an opportunity to gain some control over the work day and to accomplish errands and keep doctor's appointments, for example, that must be done during usual working hours.

Job sharing allows two employees, each of whom works part-time, to share a job. Typically, one employee will work in the morning and another employee will work in the afternoon. Firms encourage job sharing to accommodate parents who want to work part, but not all, of the day. By doing this, companies have been able to acquire better-qualified people than they could otherwise find.

Both flextime and job sharing are attempts to attract and retain a more highly motivated work force.

"How many of you give your employees a pat on the back when they do a good job?" Eighty-two percent said they did. But when subordinates were asked the same question, only 12% said they received a pat on the back for good work. A simple but sincere "thank you" is a powerful motivator.

After attending a seminar on motivation, a supervisor was determined to put some of the ideas into practice. She called one of her maintenance helpers over. The helper, probably thinking that he was going to be criticized, was a little frightened and slowly walked over, shoulders slumped and head slightly bowed. The supervisor placed her hand on the helper's shoulder and commented, "I want to thank you for the job you did on the machine yesterday. We really needed you and you sure came through." The helper gradu-

With one balloon marking each of a succession of accident-free days, a unique ceremony recognizes work well done.

The One Minute Manager

Kenneth Blanchard and Spencer Johnson are the authors of a small book called *The One Minute Manager.* They believe that the quickest way to increase productivity, profits, job satisfaction, and personal prosperity is to follow their three-step management method: one minute goal setting, one minute praising, and one minute reprimanding. (The authors contend that not one of these three processes takes more than one minute to do; indeed, so manic about minutes are they, the book scarcely takes more than a minute to read.)

One-minute goal setting works well when you:

- Agree on your goals.
- See what good behavior looks like.
- Write out each of your goals on a single sheet of paper, using fewer than 250 words.
- Read and reread each goal.
- Take a minute every once in a while to look at your performance.
- See whether your behavior matches your goal.

One-minute praising works well when you:

- Tell people up front that you are going to let them know how they are doing.
- Praise people immediately.
- Tell people specifically what they did right.
- Tell people how good you feel about what they did right, and how it helps the organization and the other people who work there.

ally straightened, and when he walked back to his work place, he was almost beaming.

Giving Feedback on Progress

An experiment divided employees into two groups. Group A was told to work as well as they could and to finish as quickly as they could. During the week, they were never told how well they were doing. Group B received different instructions: They discussed and set specific weekly targets and were also issued weekly progress reports, so they could easily tell if they were ahead or behind. Group A, working on the same kind of tasks, knew nothing of Group B's arrangement. As you probably have guessed, Group B outperformed Group A by about 40%. Employees seek specific, tangible feedback on how well they are doing.

Involving Employees in Decision Making

People like to feel that they have some degree of control over their destinies. Although they may resist management's first efforts, employees do want to be more involved in their work. They want to use their intelligence and experience as well as their muscles. If employees are not in the habit of offering suggestions, managers should take it easy at first. Managers might tell them something like, "I want to allow you more involvement in your work. In the next three months, I will gradually broaden your responsibility, and I will

- Stop for a moment of silence to let them feel how good you feel.
- Encourage them to do more of the same.
- Shake hands or touch people in a way that makes it clear that you support their success in the organization.

One-minute reprimanding works well when you:

- Tell people beforehand that you are going to let them know how they are doing and in no uncertain terms.
- Reprimand people immediately.
- Tell people specifically what they did wrong.
- Tell people how you feel about what they did wrong — in no uncertain terms.
- Stop for a few seconds of uncomfortable silence to let them feel how you feel.
- Then, shake hands or touch them in a way that lets them know you are honestly on their side.
- Remind them how much you value them.
- Reaffirm that you think well of them but not of their performance in this instance.
- Realize that when the reprimand is over, it's over.

Applying these practices to daily management, the authors say, will result in healthier, happier, more productive lives for managers and minions.

Source: Kenneth Blanchard and Spencer Johnson, *The One Minute Manager,* New York: William Morrow and Co., Inc., 1982, pp. 34, 44, and 59.

expect more inputs from you." Patience is necessary. Five or six months should be allowed for employees to change. When people are involved in decisions that affect their work, they are much more likely to accept, and become committed to, those decisions. By contrast, people who are not involved in decision making often resist decisions involving them.

Encouraging Learning and Growing

Learning is a powerful motivator. Almost any educational program improves morale and productivity. But a training program need not be big and fancy to be effective. Supervisors should look around to see what training employees can benefit from.

Managers can make suggestions for improvement and teach employees new skills. More communication on the department's objectives involves employees, as does additional information about products and services. Supervisors can share with employees criteria the organization evaluates for promotions. It is a good idea to pick out something new to teach employees each week and do it!

Giving Salary Increases on Merit

Most supervisors are not honest in their employee reviews. They do not tell employees their weaknesses and how to improve. Sometimes a manager has to say to an employee something like, "Frankly, I'm disappointed that you have not been able to do your job as expected. Here is what I expect of you during the next three months. If you perform properly, I will be eager to give you a good salary recommendation. What can I do to help?" Even though the employee may get angry, such an approach will be appreciated by most people.

Stimulating Creativity in Employees

Since the 1960s, a number of firms have been buying works of fine art to display in their corporate corridors and offices. Though the art may be bought because the chief executive officer is a collector, it does seem to stimulate employees to be more creative. The Business Committee for the Arts estimates that more than 500 corporations now have art collections. Atlantic Richfield Company, for instance, has a 9000-piece collection of contemporary works with which they ornament their offices throughout the world.

Aside from such purely atmospheric concessions to stimulating creativity, a number of firms are hiring creativity consultants who provide consultations, seminars, and publications to stimulate creativity and innovation in business and industry. Roger von Oech, founder and president of Creative Think, specializes in unlocking the minds of his clients so they may become more receptive to new ideas. He has identified ten mental attitudes that keep people thinking the same old things:

- Believing there is only one right answer.
- Being forever logical.
- Always following the rules.
- Being practical.
- Avoiding ambiguity.
- Believing to err is bad.
- Believing play is frivolous.
- Shunning a topic if it's not in your area.

A painting from Atlantic Richfield's large contemporary art collection adorns a new West Coast office.

- Not wanting to appear foolish.
- Believing you're not creative.

By overcoming these attitudes, von Oech believes, business people will find it far easier to generate new ideas and be creative. John Opel, CEO of IBM, says that to its motto "Think," IBM has appended the word "differently." "Too many people in business are binary," he laments. "It's either left or right, on or off" — right or wrong.

SUMMARY

Motivation is the use of physical or mental effort, resulting from unfilled needs. A need is a tension or state of discomfort that exists within people. The two major theories of motivation are Maslow's need hierarchy and Herzberg's motivation-hygiene theory. Maslow identified five needs, existing in a hierarchy, that people strive to satisfy: physiological, safety, social, esteem, and self-realization. Herzberg said we can divide needs into two categories: hygiene and motivational. Hygiene needs represent factors peripheral to the job itself. Although they will not motivate people to higher performance, they will cause people to be unhappy if they are not fulfilled. Motivational needs are associated directly with the work itself and include the need for growth, recognition, praise, advancement, and the like.

We use money, job enrichment, management by objectives, quality circles, quality of work life programs, flextime, job sharing, and management practices to implement these theories. Research shows that money can help to satisfy employees' needs, but to motivate, it must be directly related to employees' unfulfilled needs. Job enrichment is the process of changing the job so that the work will be more appealing to employees. Management by objectives tries to accomplish similar goals by asking managers and employees to agree on what each employee is to accomplish in the near future. Both quality circles and quality of work life programs encourage employee participation in decision making and problem solving. Flextime allows employees discretion about the hours they will work, and job sharing makes it possible for two part-time employees to fill one job.

Managers can help motivate employees by the way they supervise them. Suggested practices for improving employee motivation are to increase authority delegation, communicate what you expect from employees, give praise and recognition when earned, give feedback on progress, involve employees in decision making, encourage learning and growing, base salary increases on merit, and encourage innovativeness in employees.

MIND YOUR BUSINESS

Instructions. In the list below, mark a Y (yes) beside those items you believe people are motivated to work for and N (no) beside those items you believe people are not, or are no longer, motivated to work for.

—— 1. Lighting
—— 2. Employee handbooks
—— 3. Praise
—— 4. Coffee groups
—— 5. Promotions
—— 6. Goal setting
—— 7. Job title
—— 8. Delegation
—— 9. Fringe benefits
—— 10. Company newspapers
—— 11. Unemployment compensation
—— 12. Increased knowledge
—— 13. Recognition
—— 14. Office furnishings
—— 15. Work layout
—— 16. Feedback
—— 17. Bulletin boards
—— 18. Bowling teams
—— 19. Sense of accomplishment
—— 20. Work status
—— 21. Christmas turkey
—— 22. Social security
—— 23. Merit increases
—— 24. Paid leave
—— 25. Access to information
—— 26. Freedom to fail
—— 27. Challenge
—— 28. Seniority rights

____ 29. Office parties

____ 30. Wages and salaries

____ 31. Company growth

____ 32. Sympathetic help

See answers at the back of the book.

KEY TERMS

needs, 244

motivation, 244

Maslow's hierarchy of needs, 245

physiological needs, 245

security needs, 245

social needs, 245

esteem needs, 246

self-realization, 246

Herzberg's motivation-hygiene theory, 246

hygiene needs, 246

motivational needs, 247

job enrichment, 249

job enlargement, 249

management by objectives (MBO), 251

quality circles (QC), 253

quality of work life (QWL), 254

flextime, 257

job sharing, 257

REVIEW QUESTIONS

1. Define motivation. Define needs. How are they related?

2. Describe Maslow's need hierarchy theory of motivation.

3. In Herzberg's motivation-hygiene theory, distinguish between hygiene needs and motivational needs. Give some examples of each.

4. Does money motivate employees to perform better? Explain.

5. What is job enrichment? Give some examples. How does it differ from job enlargement? Identify some factors that are not enriching to jobs.

6. What is management by objectives? What are the problems with MBO? Benefits?

7. Define quality circles. How do quality circles typically operate? Identify potential problems with them.

8. Define quality of work life programs. Discuss the results of QWL programs and identify the conditions for success.

9. Describe flextime and job sharing.

10. List and describe some practical ways supervisors can motivate their employees.

11. Discuss the impact of feedback on employee performance.

CASES

Case 10.1: New Leader of a Demoralized Marketing Department

To say that the marketing department of Hybrith Company, a manufacturer of auto parts, was demoralized is an understatement. The morale decline started about a year ago when their sales began falling off. Their previous manager had not kept up the sales organization, and with increasing competition, their sales began to slide. She was terminated because of declining sales.

Morton Williams, a long-time and well-liked employee in the department, got the job as marketing manager. Williams soon became an unimaginative paper shuffler, and sales declined further. Muddled and confused, the morale of the entire department worsened. Reacting to pressure from top management, Williams resigned after a few months and went back to his previous job.

Today was the big day. Mervin Hopson, the president, had called the staff together to introduce their new marketing manager, Susan Blanchard. After a brief introduction, Hopson turned the meeting over to Blanchard.

"Men and women," Blanchard began, "I want to get better acquainted with you as quickly as possible. Together, we have to work Hybrith back to the top. I am new to Hybrith and unknown to you, so I would like to give you an idea about my way of working, my style, so to speak."

Blanchard continued, "There is an old legend about a small Greek village that was constantly under attack. Their problem was leadership. One year, a stranger by the name of Gordias came into the village and provided leadership when they were attacked. The people supported him, and they were successful in warding off their attackers. Gordias was wise, and in his old age, he tied a large knot around the yoke of a chariot at the edge of the village. Gordias said, 'This knot, which is the most complex knot in the universe, will be your symbol of strength. Until someone who can untie this knot comes along, you will never have to worry.'

"The village remained safe for years until one day Alexander the Great marched by. Upon seeing the knot and hearing the legend, Alexander took out his sword and slashed through the knot. His army then stormed the village, which put up no defense against the attack." Blanchard finished with, "Symbols of strength will not stop us. Together, we will slash our competition and move on."

Questions

1. Do you think this approach would motivate you?

2. Do you think this was an effective approach?

3. What would you suggest that Blanchard do to improve her first impression?

Case 10.2: Where Do You Draw the Line on Sympathetic Help?

Betty Hart has been supervisor for three years. She has nineteen people in her department and is respected for being a very good supervisor.

One of her employees, William Wentz, is 24 years old and his wife is expecting their first child. Wentz has been in the department for a year and is an above-average worker. During the last couple of months, he has been bringing many of his personal problems to Hart. He has asked her advice about purchasing a car, how to prepare for the baby's arrival, whether he should take out more life insurance, how to humor his wife during her pregnancy, and many other such personal questions. It has come to the point where Wentz seems to want to talk about his personal situation every chance he gets. Hart suspected that Wentz needed to feel appreciated, and she was careful to listen and pay a lot of attention to him at first.

Now, Hart feels uncomfortable in her role as counselor. She worries that other employees might think she is spending too much time with Wentz. She also thinks that Wentz is leaning too much on her, asking her to make decisions that he really should be making. Wentz shows a lot of promise, and Hart wants to do what she can to help him.

At a recent meeting with her boss, she summed up her feelings, "I want to help Wentz, but I think I must discourage him from bringing all of his personal problems to me. I would like to do this without hurting his feelings."

Questions

1. Does a supervisor have a responsibility to talk with employees about their off-the-job, personal problems? Why?

2. If you were Hart, what would you do?

After completing this chapter, you should be able to:

■ Describe three things unions do for their members.

■ Identify three types of unions.

■ Discuss the implications for business and labor of the four most significant labor laws of this half-century.

■ Discuss the pros and cons of right-to-work laws.

■ Outline and identify the steps in the collective bargaining process.

■ List key factors typically covered in labor-management contracts.

■ Diagram and explain a typical method for handling employee grievances.

■ Speculate on the future of union-management relations.

11

MANAGEMENT
AND LABOR

The early 1980s were hard times for unions. The country was in an economic recession, unemployment was high, and sentiment shifted away from unions. Still, some of the largest unions and some of the largest companies were squaring off with each other. The Teamsters, by a 45 to 41 vote, won the right to represent characters like Mickey Mouse, Donald Duck, and Goofy at Disney World in Florida. The Communication Workers of America struck American Telephone & Telegraph Company for both pay increases and job security. The United Auto Workers, which had given up more than $4 billion in wage and benefit concessions, increased their expectations of getting additional benefits as the auto industry began showing profits.

Arguments about the value of unions, such as the one that follows, will no doubt continue to be part of management-labor relations for many more years.

"Would you join a union if we had one?"

"No."

"Why not?"

"Because I don't need them. I want to do my best. If you do your work and give an honest day's labor, management will treat you fairly."

"But unions can get you more money. My cousin belongs to a union, and his pay scale is much higher than ours."

"But he lives in a large city where the cost of living is much higher than it is for us."

"Why do you think management cares about us? All they want from us is production. If they could find a robot to do our work, we'd be out of here in a second."

"Well, I don't think so. Look at the pension plan they have set up for us, and you can't knock our benefits either."

"But who is going to protect you if you get a supervisor you don't like?"

"I'll just go to the big boss. He said anyone can stop by to see him if we're having a problem. Anyway, I couldn't go on a strike against this company; I've worked for them for over 12 years."

"Maybe you couldn't, but I could. I've been here for 2 years, and I can't see any hope for advancement unless we bring some pressure to bear on management. All they seem to be interested in is cutting costs, and that might mean my job."

"I know what you're saying, but I'll take my chances without the union. I'm voting against them."

"Well, I'm voting for them."

This argument between a procompany and a prounion employee poses some good questions concerning labor-management relations. **Labor unions** were formed so that workers could increase their bargaining power. They felt that, with larger numbers, employees would have more say in their jobs and gain a larger piece of the reward pie. Now, we have two large structures in many organizations: union and management. The competition and cooperation of these two groups have brought about a body of labor law to govern their relationship. The contracts between labor and management have become so entangled that many labor specialists work full time on ensuring that the company does not accidentally or purposefully violate the agreement.

Labor relations are also important to nonunion companies. Responding to indirect pressures, many managers have set up procedures for dealing with employees much like those of unionized companies. And more than one manager has said, "We purposefully keep our salaries higher than those of unionized companies to show our employees how much better off they are without a union." Because they are so important in business, this chapter focuses on labor relations by discussing unions, labor legislation, collective bargaining, and grievance procedures.

UNIONS

Unions are highly visible in today's industrial world, but just a few years ago, unions were struggling to become accepted. Amidst antiunion sentiment, big business power, and government indifference, employees banded together to present a counterforce to the all-powerful owners. In the last 50 years, unions have emerged as a powerful force.

The Birth of Unions

The early 1800s marked the beginning of union activity in the United States. Printers, carpenters, shoemakers, and other skilled trades grouped to-

Though an early force in the union movement, the Knights of Labor lost much of their influence after 1886, when a rally in Chicago's Haymarket Square exploded into a riot.

gether to bargain collectively with their respective employers. Goals of these early unions were higher wages and better working conditions. Following the introduction of factories, many employees were forced to work long hours under hazardous conditions with little pay. This prompted the development of larger unions to deal with the growing power of large management. The **Knights of Labor** exercised its influence during the 1870s and grew to more than

700,000 members by 1885. But its ambitions out-reached its resources by the late 1880s, and it began to fade. The next year, however, during a labor rally in Chicago's Haymarket Square, some-one threw a bomb, killing a number of policemen and workers. The riot that resulted did as much as anything to turn public opinion against the labor movement in general and the Knights of Labor in particular, whose influence quickly began to wane.

In the early 1900s, the International Workers of the World (IWW, or Wobblies), a group modeled after the Knights of Labor, grew by seeking to organize all industrial workers into one huge union. The Wobblies, however, had difficulty holding onto their members, perhaps partly because of the violent activities of some of its leadership. With the one exception of the Knights of Labor, unions had only nominal influence on management until the 1930s. Unions were unable to muster much support for several reasons:

1. Most manufacturing companies were small and did not have enough employees to make organization worthwhile.

2. Employees feared economic recession and retaliatory actions by business owners.

3. Employers made it hard for union leaders to get work by circulating a **blacklist** of activists.

4. At hiring, companies required employees to sign a **yellow-dog contract,** an agreement that they would not join a union. (The implication was that the employees would be "yellow dogs" if they joined.)

5. Because owners received sympathy from the courts, they were able to stop strikes under a **conspiracy doctrine,** a doctrine stating that it was an illegal act of conspiracy for unions to bring economic pressure on employers.

6. Many companies merely refused to deal with the unions.

Nevertheless, several unions originated during these years. The most significant was the **American Federation of Labor (AFL),** which was formed in 1886 and flourished under the leadership of Samuel Gompers. By the 1930s, the AFL was a major force in the work world. In 1935, a group of unhappy members, under the leadership of John L. Lewis, split off to form the **Congress of Industrial Organizations (CIO).** The

two organizations competed with each other for many years before rejoining in 1955 to create the AFL-CIO and become the largest federation of unions in the United States, with a membership of about 16 million.

What Unions Do for Their Members

Just what do unions do for their membership? In trying to improve the lot of workers, they perform three major functions: collective bargaining, political lobbying, and employee care and fringe benefits.

Collective bargaining. By far the most important union function is collective representation of employees to management. Individually, workers exert almost no power over an owner's ability to withhold wages, terminate or discipline employees, and otherwise make life miserable. So unions balance management power with organized collective bargaining. Union representatives meet with management to negotiate wages, fringe benefits, working conditions, discipline, safety, work hours, job design, and the like. These agreed-upon conditions form the labor contract and become binding to both labor and management. During the contract period, unions monitor its implementation and provide a channel of appeal.

Political lobbying. A second union function is to lobby with politicians, legislators, government agencies, and the public to gain advantages favorable to their membership. Unions give financial support, offer organizational expertise, and volunteer individual effort to their legal and public causes.

Employee care and fringe benefits. Third, unions offer avenues for their members to satisfy security, social, recognition, and leadership needs. Some unions offer fringe benefits very similar to company fringes, and some organize consumer watchdog groups to protect their membership in the marketplace. Larger unions offer such services as medical and dental assistance, scholarships for employees' children, vacation retreats, recreational facilities, hobby groups, and strike benefits. Union leaders say that members become more closely identified with their peers, which leads to more recognition and a sense of belonging. Finally, the organization structure provides some employees with leadership opportunities that would not be available through company involvement.

Types of Unions

Four types of unions have developed: craft unions, industrial unions, independent unions, and associations.

Craft unions. Craft unions such as the International Brotherhood of Electrical Workers, restrict their membership to employees of a certain trade (craft) regardless of company affiliation, and they represent the unique interests of similar employees. Within a community, there might be a craft union for carpenters, another for meat cutters, and still another for painters. Each union has members who work for competing firms. Local

CROSS FIRE

Should There Be a Lower Minimum Wage for Teenagers?

For years, the business community and labor leaders have been divided over whether Congress should lower the minimum wage for teenagers. The basic arguments for lowering the minimum wage are:

1. Employers would hire more teenagers at the lower wage rates, thereby reducing unemployment among teenagers. Robert Thompson, Chairman of the Board, U.S. Chamber of Commerce, estimates that a lower wage could create several hundred thousand jobs.

2. The program should be limited to newly hired teenagers so as not to reduce the wages of teenagers currently working year round.

3. As a concession to labor, the plan would only take effect during the summer months.

4. Adding workers under reduced wage plans would be creating new jobs; therefore, it would not jeopardize the jobs of older people in the work force.

Arguments against plans to reduce minimum wages for teenagers include:

1. Subminimum wages do not provide new jobs; they only displace current workers. Thus, such a program would simply mean a wage cut for many people currently employed at the minimum wage level.

2. Many employers such as mom-and-pop stores are already exempt from minimum wage standards.

3. There is already a provision for full-time students to be paid 85% of the minimum wage, and Labor Department studies show that this has caused no appreciable increase in the number of jobs available.

What is your position?

Do you believe that lowering the minimum wage for teenage employees in the summer will create new jobs or displace current workers at a lower wage rate?

____ A. Create new jobs   ____ B. Displace current workers

How do you feel about lowering the minimum wage rate for teenage employees?

____ A. It should be lowered significantly.   ____ B. It should be lowered only slightly.

____ C. It should not be lowered.

TABLE 11.1 ■ PRINCIPAL U.S. LABOR UNIONS AND EMPLOYEE ASSOCIATIONS, 1980

Labor Union	Membership
International Brotherhood of Teamsters, Chauffeurs, Warehousemen, and Helpers of America	1,891,000
International Union, United Automobile, Aerospace and Agricultural Implement Workers of America	1,357,000
United Food and Commercial Workers Union	1,300,000
United Steelworkers of America	1,238,000
American Federation of State, County and Municipal Employees	1,238,000
International Brotherhood of Electrical Workers	1,041,000
International Association of Machinists and Aerospace Workers	745,000
Service Employees' International Union	650,000
Laborers' International Union of North America	608,000
Communications Workers of America	551,000
American Federation of Teachers	502,000
Amalgamated Clothing and Textile Workers of America	455,000
Hotel and Restaurant Employees and Bartenders International Union	400,000
United Association of Journeymen and Apprentices of the Plumbing and Pipefitting Industry of the United States and Canada	352,000
International Ladies' Garment Workers Union	323,000
American Federation of Musicians	299,000
American Federation of Government Employees	255,000
American Postal Workers Union	251,000
United Mine Workers of America	245,000
International Union of Electrical, Radio and Machine Workers	233,000
National Association of Letter Carriers	230,000
United Paperworkers International Union	219,000
Retail, Wholesale, and Department Store Union	215,000
National Association of Government Employees	200,000

craft unions have considerable power relative to their national unions, which they use primarily as a servicing agency.

Industrial unions. Unlike craft unions, **industrial unions** cut across trade lines to represent a wide variety of occupations. Industrials criticize the crafts for being elitist, worrying only about the highly skilled laborers, and ignoring the masses. But in reality, few crafts or industrials exist in pure form. Some crafts accept a mix of trades, and industrials may be organized around a particular trade. The United Mine Workers, made famous by John L. Lewis, illustrates the overlap. Although it is a mine workers' union, its membership includes several types of industrial workers.

Independent unions. A third group, **independent unions,** are not associated with any national organization. Being local in nature, many independents take their total membership from one company or include members from companies within a narrow region. Independents retain complete control and concentrate on the specific needs of their communities; they also do all the bargaining, watchdogging, and public relations. The Teamsters Union, one of the largest independents, was originally affiliated with the AFL-CIO, but the association ruptured because of disagreements over ethical standards.

Associations. Some groups, employees in the public sector and white-collar, professional em-

TABLE 11.1 ■ (continued)

Labor Union	Membership
United Transportation Union	190,000
International Association of Bridge and Structural Iron Workers	184,000
American Nurses Association	180,000
Brotherhood of Railway, Airline, and Steamship Clerks, Freight Handlers, Express and Station Employees	180,000
International Association of Firefighters	178,000
International Brotherhood of Painters and Allied Trades of the United States and Canada	164,000
Amalgamated Transit Union	162,000
United Electrical, Radio, and Machine Workers of America	162,000
Bakery, Confectionary, and Tobacco Workers International Unions of America	160,000
Oil, Chemical, and Atomic Workers International Union	154,000
Sheet Metal Workers International Association	154,000
United Rubber, Cork, Linoleum, and Plastic Workers of America	151,000
Fraternal Order of Police	150,000
International Brotherhood of Boilermakers, Iron Ship Builders, Blacksmiths, Forgers, and Helpers	145,000
International Union of Bricklayers and Allied Craftsmen	135,000
Transport Workers Union of America	130,000
National Alliance of Postal and Federal Employees	125,000
International Printing and Graphic Communications Union	122,000
International Woodworkers of America	112,000
Office and Professional Employees International Union	107,000
California State Employees Association	105,000
Brotherhood of Maintenance of Way Employees	102,000

Source: U.S. Department of Labor, Bureau of Labor Statistics.

Although they do not refer to themselves as unions, associations behave much like unions and represent their members collectively to higher management.

ployees, form **associations** that tend to operate much like unions. Although they typically do not refer to themselves as unions, they behave much like unions and they represent their members collectively to higher management. Some examples include American Federation of State, County, and Municipal Employees (AFSCME) and 9to5, the

National Association of Working Women. See Table 11.1 for a list of principal labor unions and employee associations.

LABOR LEGISLATION

The greatest single influence on union strength has been labor legislation. Laws have changed from preventing collective bargaining to guaranteeing it. We can relate union strength directly to key legislation.

Although a few labor laws of minor impact existed earlier, the **Railway Labor Act of 1926** was the first significant piece of legislation. This act gave railroad employees the right to organize and bargain collectively and established an independent mediation board to assist unions and managers in settling their differences. The **Norris-La Guardia Act of 1932** made the controversial yellow-dog contract illegal and severely reduced the conditions under which courts could issue injunctions preventing work stoppages. But the landmark law that gave unions a big boost was the Wagner Act of 1935.

The National Labor Relations Act (Wagner Act), 1935

The **National Labor Relations Act (Wagner Act),** giving workers the legal rights to organize and join unions of their choice, made the following five practices unlawful for employers:

1. Employers may not interfere with an employee's right to join a labor organization or engage in union activities.

2. Employers may not interfere with an employee's right to recruit new members on their own free time.

3. Employers may not dominate or interfere with any labor organization or contribute to its support in any way.

4. Employers may not hire, fire, or discriminate against employees because of their attitudes toward unions.

TAKING STOCK

Rights and Respect for Office Workers

In 1973, Karen Nussbaum, at the time a clerk-typist at the Harvard Graduate School of Education, founded an organization of female clerical workers known as 9to5. Starting with only ten women, the group, by 1983, had more than 12,000 members in 22 chapters across the country. On their tenth anniversary, 9to5 was able to proclaim the following victories:

1973	First edition of the *9to5 News* leads to the first Bill of Rights for office workers.
1973	Formation of Local 925 of the Service Employees' International Union, a union for office workers.
1975	9to5 forces investigations into employment practices of major banks and insurance companies, leading to hiring, training, and promotion programs for women.
1975–1978	9to5 National Association of Working Women becomes a national organization.
1976–1978	First working women's convention brought together by 9to5.
1976–1978	9to5 targets three book publishers and files three sex discrimination suits resulting in $1.5 million in back pay for women employees, job-posting procedures, tuition reimbursement for training, and written job descriptions for all employees.
1979–1980	9to5 targets a large national bank and wins a 10% across-the-board pay increase for nonmanagement employees and a job-posting program.
1979–1980	SEIU District 925, a national union for office workers, is established.
1979–1980	9to5 won an age discrimination suit resulting in $¼ million in back pay for dismissed "over 40" employees.
1981	Pressured by 9to5, a large insurance company granted 10.5% pay increase to nonmanagement personnel, established a complaint-review process, granted $19,000 in back pay to word processing personnel, and donated $100,000 to area child-care centers.
1982–1983	9to5 hosted the International Conference on Office Automation.
1982–1983	9to5 published "The Human Factor," the first consumer guide to office automation.
1982–1983	Tenth Anniversary of 9to5.

5. Employers may not refuse to bargain collectively with union representatives.

The Wagner Act also established the **National Labor Relations Board (NLRB)** and gave the board the power to determine which workers are in a bargaining unit, to conduct secret union elections, and to prosecute those who commit unfair labor practices.

It has been said that, "The Wagner Act was labor's Magna Carta." For the first time, employees who wished to organize were legally protected, and union growth started a surge that lasted for 10 years.

The Fair Labor Standards Act, 1938

Aimed at ensuring minimum pay levels, the **Fair Labor Standards Act (Minimum Wage Law)** made it illegal for most companies to pay wages below a fixed level. The minimum wage began at 25¢ per hour in 1938, but quickly moved upward. Since 1946, Congress has upped the minimum wage 625%, while the cost of living has climbed only 277%. (See Fig. 11.1.) Although the law first covered only industries engaged in interstate commerce, it has been broadened until the vast majority of today's workers are covered. While this is not a union law *per se,* it helped unions by applying pressures for higher pay.

Despite these victories, there were, at the tenth anniversary celebration of 9to5, some "horror stories" told as well:

- An employer in Minneapolis still refers to his secretary as his "squaw."

- A woman reported that she still has "to take the seeds out of her boss's watermelon and the stems off his grapes."

- Another woman, who had to take time off from work to care for a sick child, was told by her boss she "had to choose between her family and her job."

9to5 Tenth Anniversary Poster.

Source: By permission of 9to5 Organization for Women Office Workers.

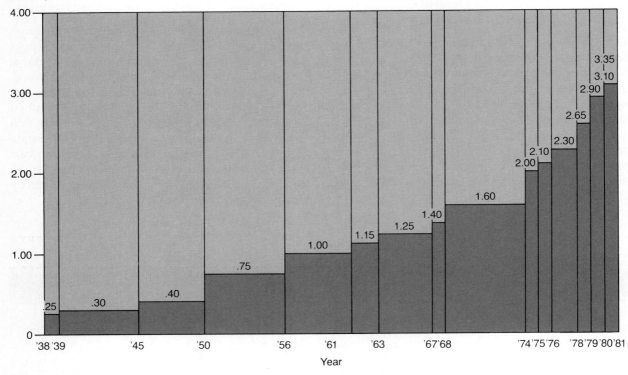

Dollars per hour

Figure 11.1
Federal minimum wage per hour over the years. *Source: U.S. Department of Labor.*

The Labor-Management Relations Act (Taft-Hartley Act), 1947

Many people thought the Wagner Act had swung the pendulum of power too much in favor of the unions. Reacting to this feeling, Senators Taft and Hartley authorized the **Labor-Management Relations Act (Taft-Hartley Act)** to more nearly equalize management and labor. Labor strongly opposed the law. When the law finally emerged from Congress, President Truman vetoed it, and Congress squared off in another confrontation. They finally mustered the support to override the president's veto. In amending and supplementing the Wagner Act, the Taft-Hartley Act defined unfair labor practices of both employers and unions.

Unfair employer practices. As of 1947, the following activities by employers were defined as unfair and therefore illegal:

1. Employers may not interfere, restrain, or coerce employees in their exercise of the right to organize freely.

2. Employers may not dominate or interfere with the information or administration of any labor organization, or contribute financial or other support for it.

3. Employers may not discriminate in hiring, tenure, or in conditions of employment for the purpose of encouraging or discouraging membership in any labor organization.

4. Employers may not discharge or otherwise discriminate against employees who filed charges or gave testimony under this act.

5. Employers may not refuse to bargain collectively with the duly chosen representative of the company's employees.

Unfair union practices. The Taft-Hartley Act also defined many union practices as unfair and illegal, for example:

1. Unions may not restrain or coerce employers in the exercise of their rights under the Wagner Act.

2. Unions may not restrain or coerce an employer in the selection of parties to bargain on management's behalf.

3. Unions may not persuade an employer to discriminate against any employees.

4. Unions may not refuse to bargain collectively with an employer.

5. Unions may not participate in secondary boycotts and jurisdictional disputes.

6. Unions may not attempt to force recognition of a union when another union is already certified as the employees' representative.

7. Unions may not charge excessive initiation fees.

8. Unions may not require wage payments for services not performed (a practice frequently referred to as **featherbedding**).

The act also permitted employers to express their feelings more freely about labor matters as long as they did not threaten employees. What's more, companies could fire employees who engaged in illegal strikes. To smooth jangled nerves, the act provided for an 80-day cooling-off period before a strike becomes legal (a provision that is also used by the president of the United States

Organized labor's opposition to the Taft-Hartley Act centered on restrictions the bill placed on union practices.

when he feels the nation's safety or health is being put in danger by a strike). During the first 60 days, management and labor unions are permitted to reach an agreement on their own. During the next 20 days, the NLRB conducts a secret ballot among workers to see if they will accept their employer's final offer.

Landrum-Griffin Act (1959)

After a few years of experience with the Taft-Hartley Act, several abuses began to leak through legal loopholes. Many felt a need to protect the rights of individual employees through better supervision of money in union welfare and pension funds and by curbing racketeering by union officers and company managers. Because of these concerns, Congress passed the Labor-Management Reporting and Disclosure Act in 1959, more widely known as the **Landrum-Griffin Act.** Most provisions of this complicated act try to regulate internal union affairs with a bill of rights and detailed reporting requirements.

Union members' bill of rights. A major section of the Landrum-Griffin Act identifies specific rights of all union members, including the right to:

■ Nominate candidates for union offices.

■ Vote in union elections.

■ Attend union meetings.

■ Participate in union meetings.

■ Vote on union business.

■ Examine union records and accounts.

If members were denied these rights, they could seek relief in federal courts.

Reporting regulations. The act also spelled out specific procedures for both union officers and company managers to protect employees' money in welfare and pension funds. Unions are required to submit annual financial statements to the Secretary of Labor. They must also report any loans to union officers in excess of $250 and all conflicts of interest by union officers. Company managers must report money spent and any agreements made between the company and labor consultants in their attempts at persuading employees to exercise their bargaining rights. While these laws did not eliminate all the undesirable conflict in union-management struggles, they illustrate the increasing concern for the individual caught between two bureaucratic forces.

Right-to-Work Laws

Section 14-B of the Taft-Hartley Act allows states to pass laws prohibiting the union shop. A **union shop,** sometimes called a **closed shop,** means that, if workers vote to have a union, all employees must join the union, and future employees who come to work for the company must eventually join the union. An **open shop** means that individual employees may choose not to join the union. Obviously, unions prefer states that permit union shops, and the repeal of Section 14-B has long been a goal of organized labor. Unions maintain that all employees benefit from their activities and benefits. Thus it is unfair for employees to come to work, receive the same pay, fringe benefits, and other union-won privileges without sharing the costs by paying union dues. However, many states, arguing that it is morally improper to require workers to join unions to get and hold a job, have passed laws making the union shop illegal.

By 1980, twenty-one states had passed right-to-work laws.

Some arguments provide for an **agency shop** where all employees pay dues to the union whether they join or not. By 1980, twenty-one states had such laws, which are referred to as **right-to-work laws.** The vast majority of these states are nonindustrial and heavily agricultural. The industrial states, where the bulk of union members reside, are nowhere close to passing right-to-work laws.

COLLECTIVE BARGAINING

Most labor legislation aims at refining collective bargaining, the key ingredient in labor-management relations. **Collective bargaining** is the process of negotiating the labor contract, which spells out the working conditions and relationships between employees and employer in a unionized company. Union representatives speak for their membership in an adversary struggle with company representatives. Because the labor contract legally binds both parties for at least a year (more commonly, three years), detailed procedures are followed in preparing and negotiating the contract. There are also well-defined alternatives for handling bargaining deadlocks.

Preparing for Negotiation

The thoroughness of preparations varies with company size and union strength. Where the company is small or union strength is nominal, preparations may be skimpy, but in larger companies or where unions are powerful, they are extensive. Both parties begin preparing for the next negotiation immediately after they agree to the current contract.

Company personnel specialists chart the day-to-day disturbances in employee relations by studying grievances, turnover, layoffs, overtime, transfers, and all disciplinary problems. The company continuously studies the contract for mistakes and unforeseen occurrences, while remaining alert to rumors about what the union will ask for in the next negotiation, and what they will settle for. Company fact-finding groups survey prevailing wage rates in the community and record setlements of similar companies in the industry. Experts also study business literature on economic conditions and analyze industry and company forecasts to build their case for the company's limitations in meeting union demands.

In matching company preparations, union officials also study the contract continuously and analyze grievances, turnover, and related disciplinary problems for clues as to what they can do to serve employee needs. Union experts also gather their version of economic conditions, community wage rates, industry trends, and the company's financial health. Many unions periodically poll their membership to find out what members would like to see changed in the current contract and what they would like to bargain for in the upcoming contract. Even though both sides prepare for negotiations by analyzing similar information, no one is surprised when wide gaps occur in data interpretation.

As the end of the current contract period nears, both union and management begin shaping their bargaining strategy by preparing lists and cost estimates of preliminary demands. Before negotiations begin, companies may try to gain public

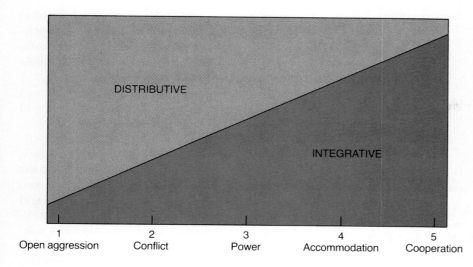

DISTRIBUTIVE

INTEGRATIVE

1	2	3	4	5
Open aggression	Conflict	Power	Accommodation	Cooperation

Figure 11.2
Bargaining strategies.

favor by publicizing their positions through newsletters and press releases. Unions also seek public support by inviting the press to their meetings and circulating information to their memberships.

Negotiating the Contract

After the spring training of preparations, the season begins as both sides battle for an advantage in the negotiation contest. Management's team usually consists of three to five members, including such specialists as lawyers, economists, engineers, and personnel experts. The union team is usually larger because it includes local officers, **shop stewards** (elected union officials who represent union members' interests), committee regional and national representatives, and (more and more frequently) legal counsel. Both sides approach the bargaining table to fight for specific issues with cloak-and-dagger strategies.

Bargaining strategies. The strategies range from open hostility to enlightened cooperation (see Figure 11.2). **Distributive bargaining** describes confrontations in which one party wins points at the direct expense of the other. **Integrative bargaining** assumes that both union and company officials work cooperatively. The distributive extreme is open aggression: a hungry, hostile management attempts to choke the union, while the equally aggressive union fights to take over all management's prerogatives. Conflict strat-

egies are used in those situations in which management tries to get rid of the union, and the union fights for the right to represent employees. More common is power bargaining: union and management struggle to win as many concessions from the other as possible. Accommodation strategies reflect a more realistic live-and-let-live attitude. Company officials might prefer not to deal with a union, but they accept their role as a fact of life.

Cooperative bargaining strategies assume that both sides are working for the betterment of employees and the company, but collective strategies are rarely seen.

Union leaders are more educated to management's pressures and try to analyze the issues from both perspectives. Cooperative strategies assume that both sides are working jointly for the betterment of employees and the company. Bargaining strategies appear to be more cooperative than in the past. American Can shares with their union just about any piece of information that the union wants, including income, capital plans, and profit margins on customer contracts. And the United Steelworkers union is experimenting with agreements that have no seniority provisions or grievance procedures. About 4% of union contracts have cooperation between labor and man-

The signing of a new contract satisfactory to both labor and management is the goal of collective bargaining. (Seated from left are United Auto Workers executives Owen Bieber and Douglas Fraser and General Motors Chairman Roger Smith in March, 1982.)

agement built into the provisions. The steps of negotiating a contract appear in Fig. 11.3.

The union contract. If the bargaining is successful, the result is a **union contract** (or agreement): a legal document spelling out the conditions of employment. Both employees and management are bound by this contract for the

specified period, usually one to three years. However, for all practical purposes, collective bargaining is now a year-round activity. Tony Verdream, vice president for American Can, says, "Changes are occurring too rapidly to wait three years." A few contracts, called evergreen pacts, are subject to near-constant revisions. While these are still few in number, labor experts predict that they will become more common in the future.

Since the contracts are usually quite complex, both union and management make special efforts to be sure the terms are communicated to employees and supervisors. Many companies hold training programs for their supervisors, identifying what they can and cannot do under the contract terms. Union leaders communicate in writing and through meetings what employees can expect under the new contract and what to do if their rights are violated. Table 11.2 summarizes some of the factors generally covered in the labor-management contract.

Bargaining Deadlocks

Few negotiations progress smoothly through all the bargaining steps. On some issues, neither party is willing to budge. After contracts are rati-

fied, disagreements sometimes arise over interpretations. When the deadlocks seem insoluble, management and labor face alternatives of conciliation and mediation, strikes, lockouts, boycotts, arbitration, and government intervention.

Conciliation and mediation. When the two teams stall during negotiations, they can invite an independent third party to help them reconcile their differences. A **conciliator** serves as a catalyst to nudge both parties into movement. Usually, calling in a conciliator is a face-saving technique.

Both management and labor can adopt the conciliator's suggestions without appearing to give in. A **mediator** plays a stronger role by offering compromise solutions, but neither side is bound by the mediator's suggestions. In practice, the conciliator and mediator roles usually overlap.

Mediators are often helpful in bringing two sides of a labor dispute together after they reach an impasse and just quit talking with each other. When the National Basketball Association (NBA) and its referees could not reach agreement on a new contract at the beginning of the 1983 season,

Figure 11.3
The process of collective bargaining.

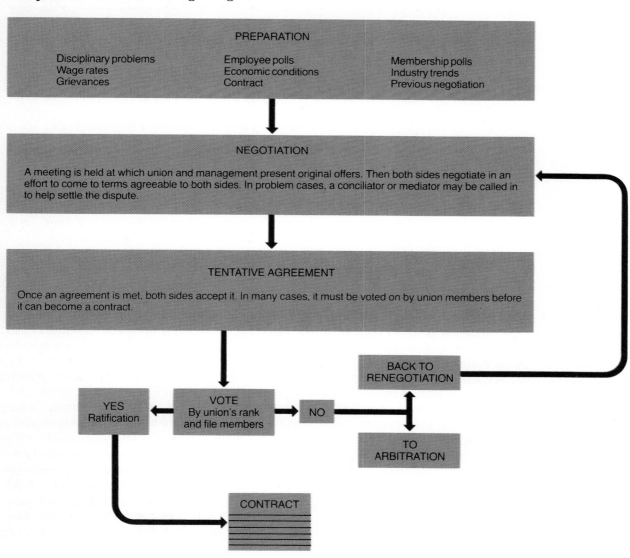

TABLE 11.2 ■ SOME FACTORS COVERED IN LABOR-MANAGEMENT CONTRACTS

Wages and Working Conditions	Employee Benefits	Promotions and Transfers	Discipline Policies
Wage rates for regular hours	Sick-leave benefits	Policies on promotions	Discipline procedures
How overtime is allocated and paid	Vacations, how they are accumulated and scheduled	Policies on transfers	Grievance procedures for employees
Shift differentials, if any	Pension program and retirement	Job evaluations	Employee rights
Cost of living adjustments (COLA)	Medical and life insurance	Employee performance	Management rights
Time for breaks, lunch periods, starting and stopping times	Unemployment benefits		
Work environment and other working conditions	Holidays and other days off		

the NBA locked out the referees and would not allow them to officiate games. Negotiations between NBA representatives and the referees' union, the National Association of Basketball Referees, sputtered along for a while and then broke off. Both sides refused to talk with each other until federal mediator Ed McMahon was able to bring them together. Two days and two nights of intensive negotiations resulted in a three-year agreement.

Union strategies. **Strikes,** outright refusals of the employees to continue working, have been declining in recent years. In 1983 there were only 81 work stoppages involving 1000 or more workers, while in 1974 there were 424 strikes involving 1000 or more workers. **Wildcat strikes,** which employees sometimes engage in on their own, are walkouts not duly sanctioned by the union. Employees may also resort to a halfway measure called a **slowdown.** During slowdown strikes, employees show up but work at a decidedly slower pace, causing significant production drops. Sometimes, during a strike, some employees may choose to continue to come to work, or persons not previously working for the company may take jobs left vacant by union members on strike. Unions contemptuously refer to such employees as **strikebreakers** or **scabs.**

A strike may occur at any time, but 90% happen during contract negotiations.

A strike may occur at any time, but 90% happen during contract negotiations. The Bureau of Labor Statistics estimates that less than 4% of contract negotiations result in strikes, but strikes are usually quite expensive to management, employees, and the surrounding community.

During strikes, the union may **picket** the employer by placing employees around the work premises with signs and placards announcing that the employees are on strike against the company. Friction sometimes develops when a number of employees form picket lines across entrances to discourage others from coming to work or prevent the delivery of goods and supplies.

Less intense than strikes are boycotts, which result when union members refuse to buy a company's product. If the union membership is nationwide, this can have a serious economic effect on the firm. Boycotts against the company with which the union is in disagreement are called **primary boycotts,** and most are legal. Attempts by unions to include third parties such as suppliers and customers to quit buying from a particular company are called **secondary boycotts,** and they are illegal in most states. In the 1970s the agricultural workers in California, with sympathy from Attorney General Robert Kennedy, conducted a successful boycott against lettuce. By encouraging people to stop buying lettuce, workers were able to pressure producers into giving higher wages.

More recently in western Pennsylvania, steelworkers and other unions urged members to withdraw their deposits from the Mellon Bank. Union leaders claimed that Mellon had invested too heavily in foreign industry while neglecting locally depressed businesses, thus depriving people of jobs at home. Currently, the AFL-CIO is telling its almost 14 million members to quit buying products from firms it accuses of antiunion activities. Some of the firms on the AFL-CIO's boycott list are Coors brewery, Procter & Gamble, R. J. Reynolds, Faberge, and Equitable Life Assurance Society.

Management strategies. Since companies are aware that they could find themselves beset by a strike, some develop strike contingency plans.

Lockouts are seldom used because of lost revenue to the company.

During strikes or boycotts, companies have the alternative of continuing operations as best they can (Phelps Dodge, despite a strike and scattered violence, kept their facility open by using replacements and nonstriking workers) or of taking more severe action such as a **lockout.** (The Metropolitan Opera Company a few years ago locked out — that is, refused to allow to come to work — their orchestra employees, members of Local 802.) Because of lost revenue to the company, lockouts are seldom used. What's more, there is evidence that

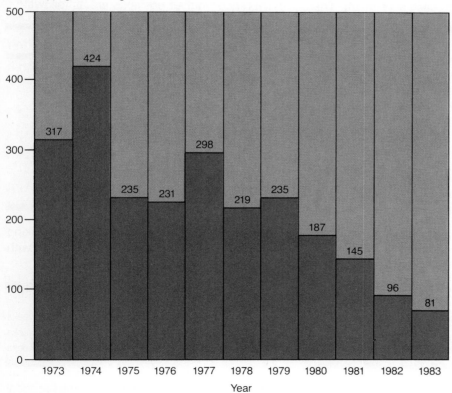

Work stoppages involving 1000 or more workers

**Figure 11.4
How strikes have declined in recent years.**
Source: U.S. Department of Labor.

they build bad public relations and could possibly result in lawsuits against the firm.

Managers of competing companies may also form **employers' associations** to help them combat or negotiate with unions. Sometimes the associations collect money from members to help a company if its employees strike.

Arbitration. **Arbitration,** the last means of dissolving a deadlock, means that the two dissonant parties bring in an independent expert to make judgments that are binding to both sides. Both union and management must agree upon the arbitrator. The arbitrator begins by holding hearings on the positions and supporting evidence of each side. Operating something like a judge, the arbitrator asks questions, listens to witnesses, and studies the documents to get a fair picture. After the hearings, the adjudicator writes the decision, called the arbitration award, which is binding to both parties. Losers have taken their cases to the courts, but the arbitration decision has always been upheld. Contract interpretation is the most common dispute that goes to arbitration, and employee discipline is second.

Arbitration may be voluntary or imposed. **Voluntary arbitration** occurs when both sides agree to use the services of an impartial third

Worker Ownership of Companies

In the past few years, there have been several instances where workers took over the ownership of their company. Employee ownership, as you might expect, creates new relationships between managers and employees. And these new relationships apparently are having a profound impact upon the company's operations and profits.

In 1981, the employees of Hyatt Clark, a manufacturer of bearings, bought the company from General Motors. Since then, the employees have cut costs, including their own wages, and reduced the break-even point from $12 million in sales to below $6.5 million. Productivity has increased, and scrappage is down by a third.

The Hyatt Clark Company holds frequent meetings between managers and workers. Manufacturing superintendents hold problem-solving sessions each week and keep employees informed about the company's finances. Officers' salaries are posted in a public place. Experts believe these efforts are paying off. A money-loser when owned by GM, the company broke even in the second half of 1982 and expects to make a profit in 1983. The accompanying table shows the current list of companies that are 100% employee owned. Other companies are expected to be added to the list in the near future.

Employee-Owned Companies	Headquarters	Number of Employees
Weirton (steel)	Weirton, West Virginia	7000
Southern Medical Services (nursing homes)	Birmingham, Alabama	3500
The Okonite Company (cable manufacturing)	Ramsey, New Jersey	1850
Hyatt Clark Industries (roller bearings)	Clark, New Jersey	1400
Katz Communications (broadcasting, ad sales)	New York	1100
Bates Fabrics (bedspreads, construction textiles)	Lewiston, Maine	950
South Bend Lathe (machine tools)	South Bend, Indiana	230

Source: "When Workers Take Over the Plant," *U.S. News & World Report*, April 18, 1983, pp. 89–90.

party to help them settle their dispute. In some cases, the federal government may force the disputing parties to seek arbitration; this is **compulsory arbitration.** The government usually does not intervene unless it thinks national security is at stake.

HANDLING EMPLOYEE GRIEVANCES

Labor contracts provide specific **grievance** steps for employees who feel supervisors have violated their rights. Many nonunion companies also have formal grievance procedures. Effective managers attempt to prevent grievances because they are costly and disruptive, but even under the best of conditions, an occasional grievance will work its way through the formal channels.

The grievance procedure varies according to the union contract and company size, but a typical procedure contains a sequence of steps from the original filing to the ultimate arbitration. Many grievances are settled before they get to arbitration, and middle-sized and smaller companies have fewer steps. The general purpose is to move successively upward in both union and management structure until there is a settlement. Figure 11.5 shows the possible steps in grievance procedures. Most contracts specify that aggrieved employees communicate their complaints in writing. If the supervisor has open communications, the

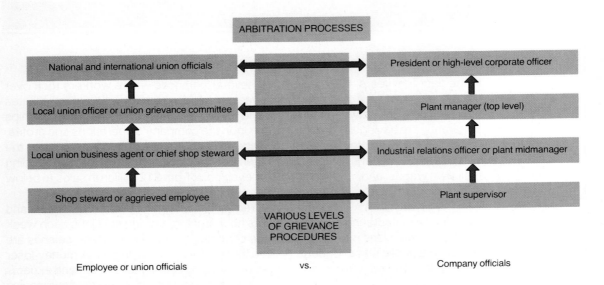

ARBITRATION PROCESSES

National and international union officials ↔ President or high-level corporate officer

Local union officer or union grievance committee ↔ Plant manager (top level)

Local union business agent or chief shop steward ↔ Industrial relations officer or plant midmanager

Shop steward or aggrieved employee ↔ Plant supervisor

VARIOUS LEVELS OF GRIEVANCE PROCEDURES

Employee or union officials   vs.   Company officials

Figure 11.5
Levels in the settling of a grievance.

disagreement may be settled at this point; otherwise, the grievance enters the formal machinery. Typically, when employees file grievances, they meet with their supervisor and shop steward.

CURRENT AND FUTURE STATUS OF UNIONS

Unions today are facing their toughest challenge. Union membership as a percentage of the work force has declined from 28.4% in 1965 to about 20% in 1983. (Figure 11.6 shows the increasing percentage of workers who do not belong to unions since 1965.) Further, unions won only 30% of certification elections in 1981, down from 60% in 1965. (Figure 11.7 pictures this declining trend.) And there is evidence that union members are not as united among themselves as they once were. For instance, 44% of union families voted for Ronald Reagan in 1980, compared to the average of about 35% that normally vote for the Republican candidates. For another example, on August 12, 1983, the International Association of Machinists and Aerospace Workers walked out on Continental Air Lines. But just a few days after the strike began, Continental reported that 50% of the 1200 employees were reporting back to work. As Don Thomas, president of United Steel Workers Local

1219 in Braddock, Pennsylvania, explains it, "There's no spirit of 'we're all in it together' any more. There are no John L. Lewises, no spirit of solidarity."

There may be several reasons why unions are not as powerful as they once were. The recent economic recession surely had something to do with it. When workers are worried about losing their jobs, they are less likely to band together for higher wages or benefits. What is more, unions are being confronted by increasing skepticism from potential new members as the spread of concessionary bargaining raises questions about the value of union membership. Second, the nature of the work force has been changing. There are relatively fewer blue-collar jobs available, as the composition of workers changes to service, professional, and informational employees. Typically, the so-called white-collar workers have been less supportive of unions than have blue-collar workers. Third, robotics and office automation have begun to erode the strength of labor unions and service unions alike. Fourth, much of industry is moving to the South and Midwest, and unions have typically been weaker in these areas than in the North and West. Finally, there is some evidence that management is trying harder to keep unions out or to get rid of those that are already in. This attitude seemed to be condoned

Percentage

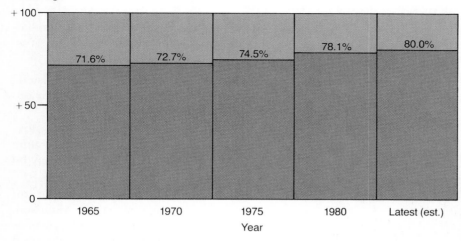

Figure 11.6
Percentage of workers who do not belong to unions. *Source: U.S. Department of Labor.*

by Ronald Reagan's breaking of the Professional Air Traffic Controllers Organization (PATCO) in 1981.

Union leaders argue that there is a conspiracy by big business to eliminate them. Labor has recently suffered setbacks in Congress, rebuffs from factories, and defeats at the voting booths. Many leaders say there is a conspiracy of business and right-wing forces to destroy their movement.

Social, economic, and business issues will determine the role of unions in the future. Unions will no doubt continue to exist, but their status will surely be determined by how well they can react to current, changing conditions.

Percentage

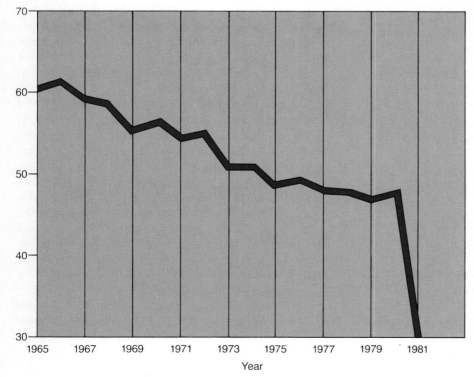

Figure 11.7
Percentage of elections won by unions. *Source: National Labor Relations Board.*

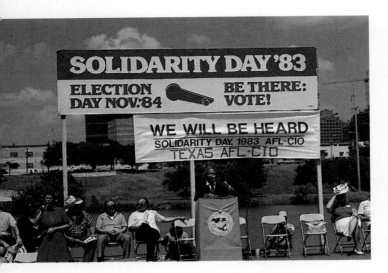

This Solidarity Day rally in 1983 is emblematic of renewed union efforts to reverse their declining influence in the work force.

In Support of Unions

Most union leaders believe that their role in equalizing management and employees remains essential. Union supporters feel that, even with existing legislation, companies could take advantage of their employees should unions fail to exist. Those in support of today's unions mention the following benefits of unions:

1. Unions, acting as a bargaining agent for employees, helped overcome abuses of corporate power.

2. Unions give employees a collective voice in negotiating working conditions with management.

3. Unions do much to upgrade pay levels, improve safety, and increase job security for employees.

4. Unions protect future earnings by negotiating automatic cost-of-living allowances (COLA) built into their pay contracts.

5. Unions increase the quality of working life for employees by pressuring for more democratic and pleasant working environments.

6. Unions provide a balance of power between employees and large businesses.

Criticism of Unions

Many people feel that unions have tilted the balance of power too far in employees' favor. Four major criticisms of today's unions are:

1. Unions, with their seniority rules, provisions for rewards, and rigid pay levels, stifle flexibility and creativity in a company.

2. Unions are too costly. The costs of strikes, luxury wage and benefit packages, and the time and staff needed to deal with unions may be too high in today's competitive markets.

3. Unions overprotect underachieving employees. As stated by critic H. L. Mencken, "Unionism seldom, if ever, uses such power as it has to insure better work; almost always it devotes a large part of that power to safeguarding back work."

4. Unions are unnecessary. "A progressive, well-managed company — one that can make it in today's competitive world — will watch out for and provide for its employees," stated a corporation president. "Failure to do so would be poor management."

SUMMARY

Labor relations cover the activities of preventing and settling management/employee differences in both unionized and nonunionized companies. Unions have emerged as a powerful force since the 1930s. The AFL-CIO is the largest federation of unions in the United States.

Unions grew in size and influence because of legal changes insuring their rights to organize and bargain collectively. Unions serve their membership with the following functions: collective representation, political lobbying, and need satisfaction. National organizations employ full-time administrators and specialists such as lawyers, engineers, and tacticians. Locals have the day-to-day responsibility of protecting members' contractual rights; their officers include president, vice-president, secretary-treasurer, business representative, and stewards. Unions can be classified as craft, industrial, or independent.

The first major labor law was the Railway Labor Act of 1926, which gave railroad employees the right to organize and bargain collectively. The

Wagner Act of 1935 established the National Labor Relations Board and obliged the federal government to protect employees in the process of organizing. In 1948, the Fair Labor Standards Act helped labor by establishing minimum wages. The Labor-Management Relations Act of 1947 streamlined collective bargaining by pointing out unfair employer and union practices. The 1959 Landrum-Griffin Act regulated internal union affairs with a members' bill of rights and detailed reporting requirements. Under Section 14-B of the Taft-Hartley Act, twenty-one states have passed laws making the union shop illegal.

Collective bargaining is the process of negotiating the labor contract and identifying working relationships between employees and employer. Both union and company representatives begin detailed preparations immediately after a contract has been negotiated. Negotiating usually centers around management rights, union rights, working conditions, contract coverage, contract duration, fringe benefits, and of course, wage rates. Distributive bargaining strategies describe win-lose confrontations. Integrative strategies assume both union and company officials work together toward improving relationships. Bargaining deadlocks may be handled by conciliation, mediation, strikes, lockouts, boycotts, arbitration, and government intervention.

Most contracts identify specific grievance steps for employees who feel their rights have been violated. Employees begin by submitting grievances in writing. Depending on the situation and the size of the company, a typical grievance moves through several steps: (1) steward and aggrieved employee meet with supervisor, (2) business agent meets with industrial-relations personnel, (3) local union officers meet with plant superintendent, (4) international officers meet with president, and (5) arbitration.

In recent years, unions have lost both elections and membership. Undoubtedly, unions will continue to exist, but they are not likely to maintain the strength and success they had earlier.

MIND YOUR BUSINESS

Instructions. In many cases, there is an adversary relationship between labor and management. Which of the following do you think favor unions? Management?

A = favors unions   B = favors management
C = favors neither

_____ 1. The National Labor Relations Act (Wagner Act) of 1935

_____ 2. The Labor-Management Relations Act (Taft-Hartley Act) of 1947

_____ 3. Union shop

_____ 4. Right-to-work laws

_____ 5. Collective bargaining

_____ 6. A mediator

_____ 7. The right of "lockout"

_____ 8. The right to strike

_____ 9. Arbitration

_____ 10. Grievance procedures

See answers at the back of the book.

KEY TERMS

labor union, 266

Knights of Labor, 267

blacklist, 268

yellow-dog contract, 268

conspiracy doctrine, 268

American Federation of Labor (AFL), 268

Congress of Industrial Organizations (CIO), 268

craft unions, 269

industrial unions, 270

independent unions, 270

associations, 271

Railway Labor Act of 1926, 271

Norris-LaGuardia Act of 1932, 272

National Labor Relations Act (Wagner Act), 1935, 272

National Labor Relations Board (NLRB), 273

Fair Labor Standards Act (Minimum Wage Law), 1938, 273

Labor-Management Relations Act (Taft-Hartley Act), 1947, 274

REVIEW QUESTIONS

1. What are unions? Sketch their beginnings in the United States. Outline the role of the AFL and the CIO in early union development.

2. What do unions do for their members?

3. Distinguish between craft unions, industrials, independents, and employee associations.

4. Outline the major provisions of the following acts: Wagner Act, Fair Labor Standards Act, Taft-Hartley Act, and Landrum-Griffin Act.

5. What are right-to-work laws?

6. Define collective bargaining. Identify four reasons why companies might lose a collective bargaining election.

7. How do union and management teams prepare for bargaining a contract?

8. Briefly identify major bargaining strategies between unions and managements. What is concession bargaining? Define givebacks, getbacks.

9. Give examples of items that union contracts usually cover.

10. What alternatives are available for working through bargaining deadlocks? Explain each alternative.

11. What are the typical steps in the grievance procedure for employees who feel they have been wronged under the contract?

12. Assess the current status of unions in the United States.

CASES

**Case 11.1: Orientation toward
Unions or Management?**

Two employees, Helen and Wilbert, were discussing their feelings toward their union. Helen said that she did not think they needed the union. She said, "If employees do their best, if they are successful in their jobs, and if they complete their work properly and on time, management would take care of them. They do not need the union to do their bidding for them." Wilbert disagreed. He said, "I know many employees who are working hard, doing a good job, but they are not particularly recognized. And I know that all of us would have lower salaries, fewer fringes, and less vacation time if we did not have a union."

Helen responded, "You know, the difference between us is that I want to do the work. I want to be left alone, and I want to carry on my own battles. If I disagree with my supervisor, I'll work it out with him face-to-face. If I can't get it worked out, I'll leave. But you like a lot of extra attention and sympathy. You want the company to pat you on the head and treat us as a family. But we're not family. I have a job to do. I do it and they reward me."

Wilbert agreed, "We *are* different. I do want more attachment to my work than just doing a job and getting rewarded for it. I want to improve our conditions for all of us, employees and management. Your problem is that you do not care about anyone else but yourself. You are a good worker, highly motivated, and management will probably treat you well so long as they have the hidden pressure of the union. But without the union, you would see that management would just treat you like a workhorse."

Questions

1. With which employee do you tend to agree? Why?

2. Do you think that prounion employees have different personality traits than procompany employees? Explain.

Case 11.2: Codetermination

For 25 years, the labor force in West Germany has had a minority voice in company plans. For the past 6 years, they have been seeking parity (equal representation) under the concept of codetermination, whereby workers will be represented on corporate supervisory boards. Workers have been demanding an equal, or controlling, voice in company operations. Business leaders have been happy with minority representation of the past 25 years, but they are intensely opposed to increasing the unions' board power. Managers fear that parity would put them in a position of demanding the union for their jobs. West German workers have had a voice in management, and unions and management have worked together quite well, managing to avoid major strikes. At present, because of a combination of apathetic workers and government fears that parity would lengthen a recession, laborers' demand for equal voice has been turned back.

Questions

1. What are your feelings about having unions share equally in the management of companies? How is this similar to union-management relations in the United States?

2. If unions were to share equally with management in controlling companies, what changes do you think would occur?

3. How do you feel about the balance of union-management power in the United States? Which side has the most power? Why? Which side should have the most power? Why? What changes do you think should be made, if any?

THE MANAGING OF BUSINESS

The following list includes a variety of activities, personality characteristics, career goals and objectives, and skills and aptitudes. All have special relevance to careers in business management. Put a check mark in front of those statements that apply to you.

____ I like to plan and direct the activities of others.

____ I do not object to defending my position to others once I have spoken my mind.

____ I plan to take as many courses as possible in business administration.

____ I have served successfully as president of a club or other organization.

____ I feel I could withstand the pressures of negotiating a multimillion dollar contract.

____ I have the ability to lead others.

____ I would like to take a course in organizational psychology to learn how people function in large companies.

____ I am often able to persuade others to adopt my plans and way of thinking.

____ I have the ability to get the most out of those who work with me.

____ Job security is less important to me than having the opportunity to be a leader.

____ I have planned and directed programs for a school, church, or community organization.

____ It is important to me to gain prestige and the recognition of others.

____ When I am with others, they tend to see me as their leader.

____ I have served as captain of a school team.

____ I look forward to a job in which I have the responsibility to make the final decision.

____ I have the ability to represent a company as a public speaker.

____ I want a job in which I closely supervise the work of others.

____ People have told me that I have good organizational skills.

____ It is important to me to find a career in which I can develop creative solutions to problems.

____ I want a job in which I have as much control of my duties as possible.

____ People see me as a logical, decisive, commonsense thinker.

____ I have a lot of confidence in myself and look forward to a job with heavy responsibilities.

____ I enjoy influencing the opinions and decisions of others.

____ I have strong social skills, so that in a group I tend to be the center of attention.

____ I have been told that I am an effective communicator and write clearly.

There is no single set of personality characteristics, skills, and aptitudes that fits a particular job. Generally speaking, the more activities and self-descriptors you checked in this list, the more satisfaction you may find in this major and its related jobs.

Job Title	Job Description	Suggested Education and Training	Personality Traits	Average Pay	Outlook through 1990
Human resources manager	Personnel (or human resources) managers supervise the hiring and firing of company employees. Personnel policies and regulations are planned and carried out by them, as is the preparation of employee performance evaluations. Workmen's compensation, employee benefits, salaries and wages, labor negotiations and training fall under the personnel manager's jurisdiction.	A college degree is required for most beginning positions in this field. Prospective personnel managers have a wide choice of undergraduate majors, for a number of disciplines provide a suitable background. Some employers look for individuals who have majored in personnel administration or industrial and labor relations, while others prefer college graduates with a general business background. Still other employers feel that a well-rounded liberal arts education is best; many personnel managers have degrees in psychology, sociology, counseling, or education. A master's in business administration (M.B.A.) also provides suitable preparation for a job in the field.	Human resources managers need supervisory abilities and must be able to accept responsibility. Integrity, fair-mindedness, and a persuasive congenial personality are all important qualities.	Starting salaries range between $20,000 and $50,000 a year, depending upon a person's experience.	Great demand
Employment interviewer	Employment interviewers help people evaluate themselves and their work potential. They help clients identify their interests and abilities; make them aware of career opportunities and alternatives; help them set goals; and assist them in planning the steps they need to take to reach their goals.	All states require interviewers in public employment offices to meet civil service or merit system requirements. However, state standards setting minimum education and experience vary widely. The majority of interviewers in state employment agencies have a bachelor's degree plus additional courses in guidance and counseling. Experience in counseling, interviewing, and job placement also may be required, particularly in the case of those without advanced degrees.	Persons aspiring to be employment interviewers should have a strong interest in helping others make and carry out vocational decisions. They should be able to work independently and to keep detailed records.	Average starting salaries are likely to be between $13,500 and $19,000 a year.	Moderate demand

Job Title	Job Description	Suggested Education and Training	Personality Traits	Average Pay	Outlook through 1990
Credit manager	A credit manager has final authority to accept or reject a credit application. In extending credit to a business (commercial credit), the credit manager analyzes detailed financial reports, interviews a company representative, and reviews credit agency reports. The manager also checks at banks where the company has deposits or previously was granted credit. In extending credit to individuals (consumer credit), the credit manager must rely more on personal interviews and credit bureau and bank reports.	A college degree is becoming increasingly important for entry level jobs in credit management. Employers usually seek persons who have a degree in business administration, but they may also hire graduates holding liberal arts degrees. Courses in accounting, economics, finance, computer programming, statistics, and psychology all are valuable in preparing for a career in credit management.	Credit managers should be able to analyze detailed information and draw valid conclusions based on this analysis. Because it is necessary to maintain good customer relationships, a pleasant personality and the ability to speak and write effectively also are characteristics of the successful credit manager.	Credit manager trainees who have a college degree earn annual salaries that range from about $13,000 to $15,000. Salaries of experienced credit managers average about $22,000 to $27,000 annually.	Moderate demand
Blue-collar worker supervisor	Blue-collar worker supervisors direct the activities of other employees and ensure that millions of dollars worth of equipment and materials are used properly and efficiently. They make work schedules and keep production and employee records, plan employees' activities and must allow for absent workers and machine breakdowns. Supervisors train new employees, explain company plans and policies, recommend wage increases or promotions, and issue warnings or recommend that poor performers be disciplined or fired.	Completion of high school often is the minimum educational requirement, and 1 or 2 years of college or technical school can be very helpful. Most supervisors rise through the ranks — they are promoted from jobs where they operated a machine or worked on an assembly line. This gives them the advantage of knowing how jobs should be done and what problems may arise and provides them with insight into management policies and employee attitudes. Although few supervisors are college graduates, a growing number of employers are hiring trainees with a college or technical school background.	When choosing supervisors, employers generally look for experience, skill, and leadership qualities. Employers place emphasis on the ability to motivate employees, maintain high morale, command respect, and get along with people.	Average annual earnings of blue-collar worker supervisors are about $23,000. Supervisors usually are salaried, and their salaries generally are determined by the wage rates of the highest paid workers they supervise. For example, some companies keep wages of supervisors about 10 to 30% higher than those of their subordinates.	Moderate demand

Job Title	Job Description	Suggested Education and Training	Personality Traits	Average Pay	Outlook through 1990
Labor relations specialist	Labor relations specialists advise management on union-management relations. When a collective bargaining agreement is up for negotiation, they provide background information for management's negotiation position, a job that requires familiarity with sources of economic and wage data as well as extensive knowledge of labor law and collective bargaining trends. Labor relations specialists might work with the union on seniority rights under the layoff procedure set forth in the contract or meet with the union steward about a grievance.	Courses in labor law, collective bargaining, labor economics, labor history, and industrial psychology provide a valuable background. Graduate study in industrial or labor relations may be required. A law degree seldom is required for entry level jobs, but most of the people responsible for contract negotiations are lawyers, and a combination of industrial relations courses and a law degree is highly desirable. Although a growing number of people enter the labor relations field directly, some begin in personnel work and move into a labor relations job.	Labor relations specialists should speak and write effectively and be able to work with people of all levels of education and experience. They also must be able to see both the employee's and the employer's points of view. What's more, they should be able to work as part of a team.	Average salaries for labor relations specialists employed by state governments range from $13,700 to $18,500. Specialists with supervisory responsibilities average from $19,500 to $27,000.	Moderate demand
Community recreation director	Recreation directors manage recreation programs. They are responsible for the operation of playgrounds and community centers, as well as for program planning, budget, and personnel.	A college degree with a major in parks and recreation is increasingly important for those seeking full-time career positions in this field. A bachelor's degree and experience are minimum requirements for directors. However, increasing numbers are obtaining master's degrees in parks and recreation as well as in related disciplines. Many persons with backgrounds in other disciplines including social work, forestry, and resource management, pursue graduate degrees in recreation.	Persons planning recreation careers must be good at motivating people and sensitive to their needs. Good health and physical stamina are required. Activity planning calls for creativity and resourcefulness. Willingness to accept responsibility and the ability to exercise judgment are important qualities since recreation personnel often work alone.	The average salary for recreation directors in public park and recreation agencies is about $25,000 and ranges as high as $50,000.	Moderate demand

Job Title	Job Description	Suggested Education and Training	Personality Traits	Average Pay	Outlook through 1990
City manager	Although duties vary by city size, city managers generally administer and coordinate the day-to-day operations of the city. They are responsible for functions such as tax collection and disbursement, law enforcement, and public works. They also hire department heads and their staffs and prepare the annual budget to be approved by elected officials. In addition, they study current problems, such as housing, traffic congestion, or crime, and report their findings to the elected council.	A master's degree, preferably in public or business administration, is essential for those seeking a career in city management. Although some applicants with only a bachelor's degree may find employment, strong competition for positions, even among master's degree recipients, makes the graduate degree a requirement for most entry level jobs. In some cases, employers may hire a person with a graduate or professional degree in a field related to public administration, such as political science, planning, or law.	Persons who plan a career in city management should like to work with detail and to be a part of a team. They must have sound judgment, self-confidence, and the ability to perform well under stress. To handle emergencies, city managers must quickly isolate problems, identify their causes, and provide a number of possible solutions. City managers should be tactful and able to communicate and work well with people.	Salaries of city managers vary according to experience, job responsibility, and city size. The average annual salary for all managers is more than $34,000. Average annual salaries of city managers ranged from about $28,000 in small cities of 5,000 to 10,000 inhabitants to about $49,000 in medium-sized cities of 50,000 to 100,000 inhabitants.	Moderate demand
Medical record administrator	Medical record administrators direct the activities of the medical record department and develop systems for documenting, storing, and retrieving medical information. They supervise the medical record staff, which processes and analyzes records and reports on patients' illnesses and treatment. They train the medical record staff for specialized jobs, compile medical statistics for state or national health agencies, and assist the medical staff in evaluations of patient care or research studies. Medical record administrators serving as department heads are a part of the hospital management staff and participate fully in management activities.	Preparation for a career in this field is available through college and university programs that lead to a bachelor's degree in medical record administration. Medical schools offer many of these programs. Since concentration in medical record administration begins in the third or fourth year of study, transfer from a community or junior college is possible. One-year certificate programs are open to those who already have a bachelor's degree and required courses in the liberal arts and biological sciences.	Medical record administrators must be accurate and interested in detail, and must be able to speak and write clearly. Because medical records are confidential, medical record administrators must be discreet in processing and releasing information. Supervisors must be able to organize, analyze, and direct work procedures and to work effectively with other hospital personnel.	The average starting salary for medical record administrators in hospitals is about $20,000 a year. Experienced record administrators in hospitals average about $23,600 a year, with some earning well over $30,000.	Stable demand

Job Title	Job Description	Suggested Education and Training	Personality Traits	Average Pay	Outlook through 1990
Bank officer	Practically every bank has a president who directs operations; one or more vice presidents who act as general managers or who are in charge of bank departments; and a comptroller or cashier responsible for all bank property. Loan officers may handle installment, commercial, real estate, or agricultural loans. Bank officers in trust management require knowledge of financial planning and investments. Operations officers direct the workflow and update systems. A correspondent bank officer is responsible for relations with other banks; a branch manager, for all functions of a branch office; and an international officer, for advising customers with financial dealings abroad.	Bank officer and management positions are filled by management trainees, and by promoting outstanding bank clerks or tellers. College graduation usually is required for management trainees. A business administration major in finance or a liberal arts curriculum, including accounting, economics, commercial law, political science, and statistics, serves as excellent preparation for officer trainee positions. A Master of Business Administration (MBA) in addition to a social science bachelor's degree, which some employers prefer, may provide an even stronger educational foundation.	Persons interested in becoming bank officers should like to work independently and to analyze detailed information. The ability to communicate, both orally and in writing, is important. They also need tact and good judgment to counsel customers and supervise employees.	Officer trainees at the bachelor's level generally earn between $1200 and $1600 a month. Those with master's degrees generally start at between $1400 and $2100 a month. Graduates with an MBA are usually offered starting salaries of $1500 to $2800 a month.	Great demand
Hotel manager	Hotel managers are responsible for operating their establishments profitably, and satisfying hotel guests. They determine room rates and credit policy, direct the operation of the food service operation, and manage the housekeeping, accounting, security, and maintenance departments of the hotel. Handling problems and coping with the unexpected are important parts of the job.	Experience generally is the most important consideration in selecting managers. However, employers increasingly are emphasizing college education. A bachelor's degree in hotel and restaurant administration provides particularly strong preparation for a career in hotel management. Included in many college programs in hotel management are courses in hotel administration, accounting, economics, data processing, housekeeping, food service management and catering, and hotel maintenance engineering.	Managers should have initiative, self-discipline, and the ability to organize and direct the work of others. They must be able to solve problems and concentrate on details.	Hotel manager trainees who are graduates of specialized college programs may start at around $15,500 a year. Experienced managers may earn several times as much as beginners. For example, salaries of hotel general managers range from about $20,000 to $80,000 a year.	Moderate demand

THE MARKETING OF BUSINESS

After completing this chapter, you will be able to:

■   Identify eight marketing functions.

■   Explain the marketing concept.

■   Describe the four elements of the marketing mix.

■   Define market target.

■   Explain four types of market segmentation.

■   Identify marketing research and describe its
     purposes.

■   Discuss buying motives and how our culture
     influences buying decisions.

■   Diagram and explain a consumer decision model.

12

THE MARKETING
PROCESS

John Sculley, newly hired president of Apple Computer, Inc., is a highly regarded consumer goods marketer who, just a short time ago, was working in that capacity at Pepsi Co, Inc. Apple's recruitment of Sculley is just one of many signs that marketing is becoming the new number 1 priority of corporations. In the past, Apple, like a number of other companies, has concentrated more on developing new technologies than on understanding the intricacies of the marketing process, and has suffered for its oversight. According to James McManus, head of a marketing consulting firm, "Today, companies realize that their raw material, labor, and physical-resource costs are all screwed down and that the only option for dramatic improvement will come from doing a better marketing job."

An excellent example of the marketing process is southern fried chicken. Years ago, fried chicken was popular primarily in the South. Today, however, so many people nationwide like fried chicken that restaurants specializing in this product ring up $4 billion annually in sales. Can you imagine the marketing phenomenon that happened over the years to allow people to casually drive up to a national chain restaurant like Kentucky Fried Chicken and order "chicken and biscuits to go"?

Marketing includes all the activities of getting products or services from the producer to the consumer. It starts with finding out what consumers want or need, and then assessing whether the product can be made or sold at a profit. A **market** is any segment of the overall population that will be interested in purchasing a particular product or service.

This chapter helps explain the marketing process by describing marketing functions, the marketing concept, the marketing mix, market targets, marketing research, and buyer behavior.

MARKETING FUNCTIONS

Businesses perform marketing functions to create **utility** — the ability of a product or service to satisfy needs and wants — for consumers.

Eight Marketing Functions

To deliver fried chicken or any other product or service to consumers in a desirable form, businesses must perform eight marketing functions. These functions are:

1. *Buying.* Typically, businesses buy many items to get a product to the consumer. Restaurants must buy chicken before they can cook it, and they must purchase hundreds of other items, ranging from spices to tableware.

2. *Selling.* Businesses must also sell. Chicken producers sell their chicken to large restaurants, who in turn, sell the finished product to consumers.

3. *Storing.* For chicken to be available when consumers want it, someone must store it until they are ready to buy it. For most fast food items, the storage may be for only a short period. McDonald's, for instance, keeps french fries only a few minutes after they cook them, but businesses may store products such as clothes for a longer period.

4. *Transporting.* Very few consumers go to a poultry farm to buy chickens for fried chicken. Businesses transport the product to consumers so that most of them only drive a mile or two to get the product they want. In fact, Kentucky Fried Chicken, the largest chicken restaurant, had 6640 outlets in 1983. And they were only 1 of 192 chains that specialized in fried chicken.

5. *Financing.* Chicken producers typically borrow money to build facilities, buy feed, and raise the chickens. Transportation also requires financing; and restaurants typically engage in high finance to be able to provide consumers with what they want.

6. *Risk bearing.* Many people in the marketing process have to take risks, sometimes high risks. Suppose the producers produce more product than consumers buy, or perhaps they prepare a new item that consumers do not like, and therefore do not buy. In such cases, people lose money — perhaps a lot of it.

7. *Securing information.* Chicken restaurants find out what kind of product consumers want and how they want it prepared. They also try to find out how many people will buy their food, where they should locate, and how they should promote. Church's Fried Chicken, number 2 behind Kentucky Fried Chicken, has many outlets in black neighborhoods because research showed blacks on the average ate seven times more chicken than whites.

8. *Standardization and grading.* Finally, the marketing process standardizes and grades products. The chicken legs consumers eat are easily identifiable because the leg has become a standard serving. Likewise, government inspectors grade foods for quality and safety.

Whether purchases be product or service, businesses perform these marketing functions to bring them to us. In some cases, the functions may be minor; in other cases, they may be major, but all the functions are important and necessary.

Utility Creation

Marketing, through these eight functions, adds to consumer satisfaction by creating four forms of utility. Moving goods from site or production to a place that is convenient to consumers is called **place utility. Time utility** is getting the goods or services to people when they want them. The legal arrangement that transfers the title from seller to purchaser at the time of the purchase is **possession utility.** The fourth type of utility, combining materials and labor to create the finished product, is called **form utility.**

THE MARKETING CONCEPT

Since the industrial revolution, marketing has evolved from a production to a consumer orientation.

Production-Oriented Marketing

At the beginning of the industrial revolution, companies concentrated on production. Producers believed that consumers would open their arms and pocketbooks to buy whatever they produced. In the early 1900s, the Pillsbury Company's philosophy said, in part, "Our basic function is to mill high-quality flour, and of course [and almost incidentally], we must hire salesmen to sell it." This production orientation worked for a while because people had been unable to satisfy all of their demands. Eventually, however, inventories built up as firms began producing more than enough to satisfy consumer demands. This led companies to think more about selling their products and services.

Sales-Oriented Marketing

Since businesses had a lot of inventory, they decided they should try harder to get consumers to buy what they had. The good, quality product no longer sold itself. Many marketers believed that a good sales force could sell almost anything. After a few years, though, customers began to resist the sales effort. Customers wanted some input into what was produced and what services were to be created for them. Wagon manufacturers went broke building and promoting "superior" wagons when the customers really wanted faster, more efficient transportation means—the automobile. Later, developers of fancy, downtown hotels lost money because the public wanted convenient motels on the outskirts.

Consumer-Oriented Marketing

While there are still companies that emphasize product or sales, many have adopted a more consumer-oriented marketing concept. The purpose of the **marketing concept** is to find out what consumers want and then to produce it for them at a profit. The marketing concept rests on the importance of customers to a firm and states that: (1) all company policies and activities should be aimed at satisfying customer needs, and (2) profitable sales volume is a better company goal than maximum sales volume. Companies use research to identify customer needs, and then work backward to develop and deliver a product that satisfies those needs.

More specifically, the marketing concept emphasizes the following:

1. Research departments try to find out what consumers really want.

2. Marketing research departments communicate to production departments what the consumers need.

3. Distribution channels are evolved to deliver consumer products at the place and time desired by customers (see Chapter 14).

4. Marketing activities are integrated and coordinated with all the firm's functions—financing, production, engineering, design, and personnel—to yield an overall approach to consumer satisfaction.

CROSS FIRE

Do Most Firms Practice the Marketing Concept?

Some people debate whether the majority of today's firms actually practice the marketing concept.

People who contend that most firms do practice the marketing concept point to all the research that firms conduct before they introduce a new product or service into the market. For example, P&G tests most of its products for months and even years before they enter the market. Further, there is evidence that firms adjust quickly to market demands. For instance, when people became interested in small home computers, existing, as well as many new, firms began designing these products to fit customers' needs. And many argue that if a firm does not pay close attention to what customers really want, their competitors will bankrupt them.

On the other side, some argue that companies would not make as many mistakes if they were sincere about customers' needs. They cite the auto industry for continuing to build and promote large, expensive cars when consumers clearly wanted more economical autos. Further, they say firms would not have to spend so much money promoting their products and services if they truly fulfilled a need. Finally, critics point to cases where companies apparently try to deceive the public by misrepresenting their products or services.

Do you think that the majority of today's firms practice the marketing concept? Why?

___ Yes   ___ No

This consumer orientation broadens company missions. For example, Revlon defines its business as "the creation of hope" rather than the production of cosmetics. Oil companies see themselves as being in the "energy business." Xerox is in the "automated office business," and IBM is "a problem solver."

In sum, the marketing concept changes the orientation from "take what we produce and sell it" to "find out what they want and make it." All roads lead to consumer satisfaction. If all marketers fully practiced the marketing concept, there would be little cause for consumer criticism. However, legislators have passed hundreds of laws, consumer protection agencies have sprouted nationwide, and communication media are engaging in consumer education programs. But the greatest potential for reducing consumer complaints is an expanded version of the marketing concept referred to as **enlightened marketing.** Enlightened marketing emphasizes long-run improvement for the entire system; according to marketing authority Professor Philip Kotler, it embodies five principles:

1. *Consumer-oriented marketing.* Under enlightened marketing, consumer orientation goes beyond trying to discover what the customer wants; it means looking at the world through consumers' eyes.

2. *Innovative marketing.* The marketing system can be justly criticized for adding a development here and a change there without creating integrative systems for more efficient distribution. Marketers need to research the depth of people's need and put together systems that serve both company and society interests.

3. *Value marketing.* Value marketing emphasizes promotional programs that put real values into products rather than creating imagined benefits. It exchanges hard-sell, gimmicky, emotional appeals that deliver transparent excitement for better products, more educational promotion, and increased customer services.

4. *Sense-of-mission marketing.* Kotler believes that companies should devote more energy toward developing social goals to give a company and its customers a sense of dignity and fulfillment that comes from pursuing a worthwhile destiny. Sales growth, market

Practicing "enlightened marketing" even before the term was coined, Seagram has run ads promoting moderate consumption of its products since 1934.

share, and investment returns are still important, but they are too narrow to be the ultimate goals.

5. *Societal marketing.* Marketers should develop wide appeals that balance three sometimes conflicting forces: consumer needs, company profits, and societal benefits. The indiscriminate satisfaction of customer needs and company profits places too weighty a burden on society's efficient use of natural resources such as clean water, fresh air, and healthy foods.

Enlightened marketing is really a broad interpretation of the marketing concept. It would be naive to expect its adoption by companies who ignore the marketing concept. Enlightened firms must replace short-run, selfish interests with long-run systems interests, and legislators need to clarify problems and establish guidelines for enlightened marketing practices. But the greatest force rests in consumers' hands; there is little doubt that the marketing system responds with lightning speed to consumer purchasing habits. In fact, today, all types of companies — airlines like Eastern, financial concerns like Visa, and high-tech firms like Hewlett-Packard — are trying hard to shape their products and services to changing consumer needs. Kroger Co., for example, inter-views 250,000 consumers a year to define their demands morè precisely.

Companies that do not respond to changes in their consumers' tastes and desires run the risk of failure. For years, Safeway Stores catered to the family of four where 85% of the shopping was

BUSINESS BULLETIN

The Consumer Is Important

From the earliest days, Procter & Gamble's founding fathers always had an eye clearly fixed on what might be important to customers. One morning in 1851, William Procter noticed that a wharfhand was painting black crosses on P&G's candle boxes. Asking why this was done, Procter learned that the crosses allowed illiterate wharfhands to distinguish the candle boxes from the soap boxes. Another artistic wharfhand soon changed the black cross to a circled star. Another replaced the single star with a cluster of stars. And then a quarter moon with a human profile was added. Finally, P&G printed the moon and stars emblem on all boxes of their candles.

At some later date, P&G decided that the "man in the moon" was unnecessary so they dropped it from their boxes. Immediately P&G received a message from New Orleans that a jobber had refused delivery of an entire shipment of P&G candles: Since these boxes lacked the full moon and stars design, the jobber thought they were imitations. P&G quickly recognized the value of the moon and stars emblem and brought it back into use by registering it as a trademark. It was the beginning of brand name identification for P&G and the first of many times that P&G listened to its customers.

P&G paid attention to customers because over the years they learned that the more they did so, the greater the payoff to the company. Certainly, customers discovered and launched Ivory soap. Soon after it was introduced, P&G learned from its customers that Ivory floated. Initially, P&G managers were so surprised by this they assumed it was an accident in the production of the soap. So it was, but customers kept asking for the "floating soap" so P&G incorporated the "mistake" into their regular production.

P&G continued listening to customers, who helped them develop all of their major products. Their experience through the years has taught them step-by-step that such attention always pays off. P&G calls this mania "consumerism: a response, after comprehensive market research, to what consumers need and want." Over the company's history, consumerism has taken many forms, from testing kitchens for Crisco shortening in 1912, to hiring housewives to provide consumer feedback on liquid dish detergents in 1922; to large-scale, door-to-door sampling efforts for Camay soap in the 1920s. Today, P&G conducts over 1.5 million telephone inter-views annually. That's the equivalent of 1000 Gallup polls each year.

In short, P&G is a company that glories in listening and listening well to con-sumers. Furthermore, they have developed more ways to listen to customers than anyone else. And why wouldn't they? They've spent years learning how.

Source: Terrence E. Deal and Allan A. Kennedy, *Corporate Cultures,* Reading, Mass.: Addison-Wesley Publishing Co., Inc., 1982, pp. 27 – 28.

done by women. However, the market changed to smaller households, two-income households, and more and younger men in the grocery stores. Safeway had to change to accommodate what they called the "jogging generation." They began to stay open longer, added bakeries, delis, pharmacies, and placed automated teller machines in many stores. Their new motto, "Fresh and Full at 5," stresses their appeal to consumers who have eclectic tastes and little shopping time. A spokesperson for Safeway says, "Marketing is our prime focus. In the past, we ran our business by giving the consumers what we thought they wanted. Now we've got to find out what they want and then develop the products."

THE MARKETING MIX

To operate a marketing program effectively, firms have to balance all the factors involved in reaching their market segment. The total package of these elements is the **marketing mix,** often referred to as the 4 Ps of marketing (see Fig. 12.1):

- Product planning.
- Pricing decisions.
- Placement channels (distribution).
- Promotional strategies.

Product Planning

Product planning includes deciding what products to produce; and it also covers package design, trademarks, guarantees, new product development, and product mix. Procter and Gamble (P&G), a company that likes to bring out new products, introduced six varieties of chocolate chip cookies under the brand name Duncan Hines in their Kansas City test market in 1983. In a few weeks, they had 25% of the area's packaged cookie market. A year earlier, PepsiCo, Inc., through its Frito-Lay subsidiary, had similar success with its Grandma's cookies. But since most new products are not successful, companies usually spend a lot of money in research and development (R&D) before deciding to enter the market.

Pricing Decisions

Pricing decisions aim at setting prices and credit policies that are reasonable to the consumer while

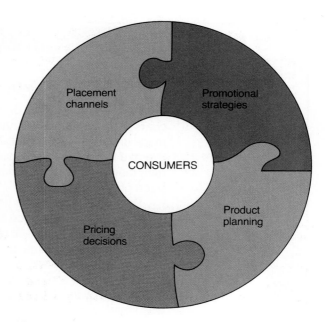

Figure 12.1
Variables in the marketing mix.

affording the firm a profit, Bissell, Inc., sells a disposable toothbrush (with paste already applied) for 39 cents. You use it once and throw it away. However, many discount stores sell regular toothbrushes for 39 cents, and for another 39 cents, you could get a tube of toothpaste. Although the product would seem to be overpriced, Bissell says that its tests have been very successful. A lot of people apparently like to keep their mouths fresh by brushing frequently, and they worry that the brush they have in their drawer is gathering germs. "Pricing decisions are critical," says a marketing manager. "If we get them too high we lose the market, if we get them too low we lose our shirt." (Chapter 13 discusses product planning and pricing in more detail.)

Placement Channels (Distribution)

Placement channels describe the routes and stops that products make from production to consumption. Firms try to select the channel that will get the product to the user in the most efficient manner. Some companies promote their channel usage. For example, Fuller Brush will sell their products only through a direct channel, from the manufacturer to the consumer, via door-to-door sales. (Chapter 14 discusses distribution channels in more detail.)

The Collapsible Umbrella Company

Bradford Phillips, owner of Totes, Inc., which makes boots, umbrellas, hats, raincoats, and bags, has a knack for making ordinary products handier. "Totes has made umbrellas into something people want rather than just need," says an executive of a large department store. Totes umbrellas, for example, don't just block the rain; they telescope to fit inside a briefcase. Totes shoulder bags fold into pocket-sized pouches.

Stores who buy Totes items also praise them for their quality and for the attentiveness of their sales force. Retailers say that Totes products sell well because they are well designed and well made. Stores have fewer returns of their merchandise.

And salespeople stop by retail stores regularly to help straighten up displays and check inventories. Margot Hebert, a buyer for Krauss Co., says, "That sounds like a little thing, but it's important to me."

The company sold only boots until 1970, then Mr. Phillips decided that, ". . . it was time to protect the head as well as the feet." He designed a collapsible umbrella, but it failed; later, he bought a company that had a patent on one. Totes wants to add a new product each year. The firm has recently added women's raincoats, and it is test marketing socks that have cushioned bottoms.

Totes profits have quadrupled in the past 10 years, and their sales are estimated to run between $50 and $100 million annually.

Source: Maryann Mrowca, "Weather-Gear Firm Prospers on Idea on Handier Products, *The Wall Street Journal.*

Promotional Strategies

Promotional strategies indicate the advertising, selling, and promotional programs designed to educate and persuade consumers to use products and services. Procter & Gamble introduced its new chocolate chip cookies by advertising heavily in the area, offering coupons for cents off the price, and even by mailing cookies to homes. Shortly after the campaign started, customers began pouring into the stores looking for the new cookies. (Chapter 15 discusses promotion in more detail.)

TARGETING A MARKET

Yuppies, YAPs, and yumpies are the latest labels to describe an important group for marketers. (Yuppies are young urban professionals; YAPs are young aspiring professionals; and Yumpies are young upwardly mobile professionals.) The labels describe fast-track middle managers and professionals in their 20s to early 40s. Their work uniforms include pinstripe suits (no polyester, please) and wingtips or dark pumps. Yuppies, according to marketers, have an insatiable appetite for designer clothes, computers, video recorders, pasta makers, phone-answering devices, espresso machines, pagers, and other gadgets.

Marketing strategy entails identifying customer groups that a business can effectively serve and tailoring its product offerings, prices, distribution, and promotional efforts and services toward those particular market segments. A good strategy recognizes that a business cannot be all things to all groups of people and that successful marketing programs appeal to specific groups of potential customers. Lloyd E. Reuss, general manager of General Motors Corp.'s Buick motor division, agrees: "We've treated the car market as a mass one, but I'm now convinced that concept is dead." Reuss now believes in target marketing — specific products and ads aimed at specific groups.

Market Segmentation

Market segmentation is the process of dividing markets into groups with similar characteristics. "We have to take the whole and divide it into smaller circles and squares, until we can get an idea of the nature of our audience," is the way a marketing manager explained it. He added, "Rather than trying to produce a swimsuit for the total market, we divide our customers into segments such as youth, older people, jet setters, and pregnant women. Then we can design and promote our products differently for each group." Campbell Soup, which recently reversed a market share decline, believes that they have to build and promote different products for different market segments. R. Gordon McGovern, Campbell's CEO, says, "My 83-year-old doesn't eat like my son, and my daughters eat differently from their parents, and," he adds, "we eat differently from the people around the corner." Campbell's is trying to gear their products and ads to specific groups. For example, they sell their spicy Ranchero Beans only in the South and Southwest.

Of the many bases for segmenting markets, the most popular are:

Geographic segmentation. This approach develops a loyal group of consumers in a known geographical territory. Coors Beer for many years concentrated on markets in the West, primarily California. This allowed the company to develop

"The following show is aimed at the 18–35 age group. If you don't fit into that category, you're not *supposed* to like it."

its distribution and promotional programs for the tastes and life-styles of one particular region.

Demographic segmentation. Perhaps the most common segment, demographic segmentation groups customers according to common characteristics such as age, sex, race, or income. Many companies still gear their products and ads to the 18-to-35 year olds who dominated the marketplace of the 1970s, but it is the 25-to-45 year olds

Figure 12.2
A psychographic segmentation. *Source: Arnold Mitchell,* The Nine American Lifestyles. *New York: Macmillan Publishing Company, 1983.*

1. *Survivors.* The depressed and poor. They tend toward decaffeinated coffee and gelatin desserts and do not have much fun in their lives. About 4% of the population.

2. *Sustainers.* Better off than survivors, but still anxious, combative, and often feeling left out. They eat breakfast out a lot, make overseas phone calls, and read condensed books. About 7% of the population.

3. *Belongers.* Traditionalists who follow the rules. Gardening and daytime television are popular with these people. Many own cats, tend to live in the same place for more than ten years, and are against extramarital sex. About 35% of the population.

4. *Emulators.* The young and ambitious. They tend to lead hollow lives. They play poker, collect tropical fish, and like to go to parties. About 10% of the population.

5. *Achievers.* Diverse, gifted, hard working. These are people who have built the system and still run it. They like California wines, own racing bicycles, tend to be Republican, and are committed to the free enterprise system. About 23% of the population.

6. *I-Am-Me.* Students and younger people. They are typically into waterskiing and cashew nuts. Surprisingly, they have a good deal of confidence in the military. About 5% of the population.

7. *Experientials.* Sophisticated and politically effective. They prefer natural to synthetic products, enjoy backpacking and chess, take a holistic view of health, and embrace left-leaning political views. About 7% of the population.

8. *Societally conscious.* Very similar to experientials. About 9% of the population.

9. *Integrateds.* Truly trustworthy and likable. They are quick with laughter and generous with tears. Alas, only about 2% of the population.

Percentage

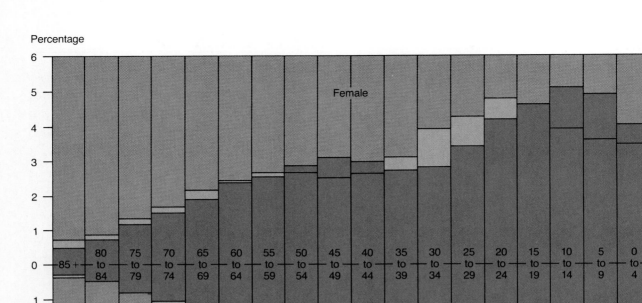

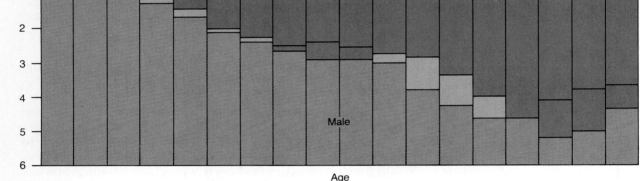

| 1970 | 1980 |

(a)

Figure 12.3
Segments of our population.
(a) Distribution of population by age and sex, April 1, 1970 and April 1, 1980.
(b) Distribution of population by region, 1950–1980. (c) Distribution of population by urban
and rural areas, 1900–1980. *Source: U.S. Department of Commerce.*

who today have the power and the size. Petticord
Swimwear sells a line of swimwear specifically for
women between the ages of 25 and 45. Realizing
that most women in this age group do not look like
Cheryl Tiegs, Petticord's suits have a mitered pattern for a slimming effect, and they include ruffles
and torso wraps for softening.

Psychographic segmentation. This rather recent method of segmentation identifies groups of
people by personality, life-style, or values. A recent study by sociologist Arnold Mitchell identifies nine life-style categories. The study's 800

questions focused on values people hold and life-
styles they pursue. Figure 12.2 identifies Mitchell's psychographic segmentations.

Product segmentation. Product segmentation
identifies existing best-selling products and services and promotes them. When Mercedes Benz
introduced its Model 190E (sedan) to the United
States, it was relying on an existing reputation and
demand for its products.

Figure 12.3 identifies some segments of the
United States population and shows how they
have been changing.

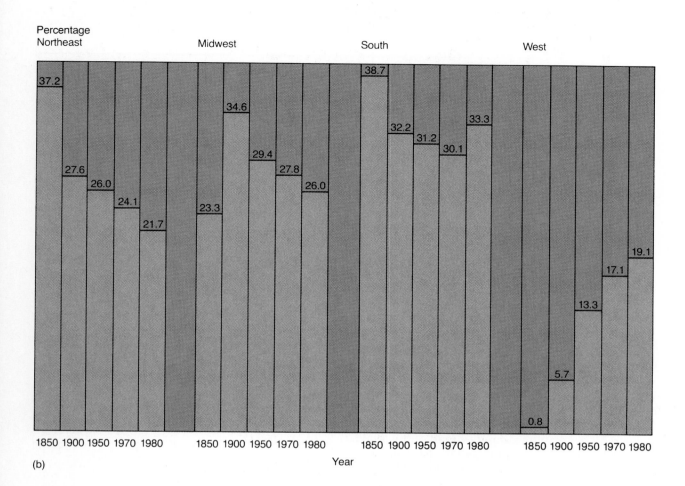

Percentage

Northeast   Midwest   South   West

37.2

27.6

26.0

34.6

24.1

23.3

29.4

38.7

21.7

27.8

26.0

32.2

31.2

30.1

33.3

19.1

17.1

13.3

5.7

0.8

1850 1900 1950 1970 1980   1850 1900 1950 1970 1980   1850 1900 1950 1970 1980   1850 1900 1950 1970 1980

(b)   Year

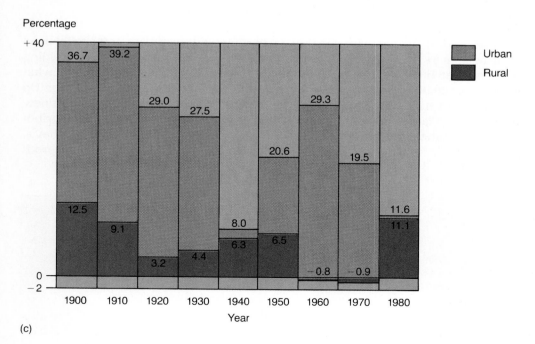

Percentage

+40

36.7

39.2

29.0

27.5

12.5

9.1

3.2

4.4

20.6

8.0

6.3

6.5

29.3

19.5

−0.8

−0.9

11.6

11.1

0

−2

1900 1910 1920 1930 1940 1950 1960 1970 1980

Year

(c)

☐ Urban
■ Rural

Market segment	Family income level			
	Less than $12,000	$12,000 to 17,999	$18,000 to 26,000	More than $26,000
Youth		░░	░░	
Teenage		░░	░░	
Young adult				
Middle age				
Mature				
Senior citizen				

Figure 12.4
An example of a market grid.

░░ = Market target

Choosing a Market Target

Out of numerous alternatives, marketers select well-defined marketing targets for their products. We define a **market target** as the characteristics of the specialized consumer group the firm is trying to reach. Market targets can be defined and isolated by developing a **market grid** of the total market. Figure 12.4 illustrates a record-producing company that aims its promotion at the teenage and youth markets in families whose income ranges from $12,000 to $26,000. In this way, the firm segments and precisely pinpoints its marketing target. From the market grid, managers can develop a profile of their customers. Figure 12.5 shows how Chevrolet has profiled buyers of Corvettes. In developing their marketing program, Corvette promoters know that they have appeal to younger car buyers, mostly male, a large percentage of whom are single and of higher-than-average income and education.

Chrysler is also trying to target its markets more precisely. Because pickup truck drivers are concentrated in Texas and Louisiana and like to listen to country and western music, Chrysler buys radio time on C&W stations in these areas to promote its trucks. "It's like a rifle taking aim at a direct target versus a shotgun that's fired in a 360-degree arc," says Campana, Chrysler's vice-president of marketing.

MARKETING RESEARCH

Why on earth would a company test a toilet bowl cleanser for as much as two years before deciding whether to produce it full scale? That is what Procter & Gamble did with its Brigade cleaner. Up to seven years may lapse between the time a new product is proposed and its nationwide distribution. Vice-president of marketing at Hershey's, Gary W. McQuaid, says, "Developing a new prod-

Figure 12.5
Profile of Corvette buyers.

Age	30	Quite a bit younger than the average age of all new car buyers, which is about 40.
Sex	Male	About 80% of purchasers are male.
Marital status	43% single	Since only 20% of the total new-car buyers are single, Corvette appeals to singles.
Income	More than $23,000	Considerably higher than the median income of all new-car buyers.
Education	College and above	Higher than average for new-car buyers.

uct is like shooting a duck. You can't shoot it where it is; you've got to shoot it where it's going to be.'' One reason companies take so long is they want to be sure, or as sure as they can be, that the product will be a success because it takes so much money to bring the product to national distribution. Procter & Gamble spent almost $100 million to roll out Citrus Hill orange juice, and outlays of $50 million are typical to bring new products to national distribution. Still, there is an urgency to get products from proposal to distribution more quickly. Aiming too far into the future is just too risky. Market testing is only one type of **market research,** the systematic gathering, recording, and analysis of data about products and services.

What Marketing Research Does

Basically, marketing research tries to provide answers to a firm's questions about such concerns as consumer likes and dislikes and the cost and effectiveness of various marketing activities. Specifically, research tries to answer such questions as:

- Who are our customers and what are they like?
- Why do people buy or refrain from buying our products or services?
- How do potential customers respond to our quality, prices, distribution methods, and promotions?
- Why do our customers want what we are not providing?
- How do we compare to our competitors?

Although it is not an exact science, firms that conduct good market research are better able to satisfy consumers' needs. Management Analysis Center, Inc. (MAC), an international consulting firm, helped a community hospital find ways to increase its occupancy rate through marketing research. They mailed surveys to 800 consumers in the hospital's area to find what kinds of care potential hospital users liked. Additionally, MAC surveyed 80 area doctors by telephone to find out what they preferred in hospitals. After analyzing the information, the hospital focused on improv-

ing its capabilities to better provide what patients and doctors wanted.

How to Conduct Market Research

Research, in reality, provides information, and conducting research is really looking for information. There are many ways and places to look.

Information from internal records. Records often contain a wealth of information. Companies might check through records to see who buys from them, how often they buy, and what types of goods or services they buy. Also, companies look at credit records, which frequently contain data on customers' jobs, income levels, marital status, and so on.

Also companies ask their employees questions about customers. They may hear a lot of minor gripes and complaints, which can give cues on what customers like and dislike.

Secondary research. Although information gathered internally is usually very good, firms may not be able to find out everything they want to know. Secondary research (which is done before undertaking any primary research) is information that has already been gathered and published in books, magazines, trade publications, government reports, and the like. For instance, if a company sells major appliances, it might keep a check on the housing starts in the area. While secondary research can provide a lot of information, it may not always relate as specifically to production as companies would like.

Primary research. Primary research is collecting data for the first time, usually by the user or by research firms hired by the user. While this research is often helpful and specific, it can also be quite expensive. A group of seventy-three corporations paid $2 million for the research to identify the psychographic information mentioned in Fig. 12.6.

Mail surveys and personal interviews are common ways of collecting primary data. Of course, test marketing products also provides good primary data. A somewhat creative approach to personal interviewing, which firms seem to be relying upon more, is the **focus group,** where a group of people, usually community leaders, are led by a skilled professional to

Middle class	Lower class
1. Pointed to the future.	1. Pointed to the present and past.
2. Viewpoint embraces a long expanse in time.	2. Lives and thinks in short expanse of time.
3. More urban identification.	3. More rural in identification.
4. Stresses rationality.	4. Essentially nonrational.
5. Has well-structured sense of the universe.	5. Has vague, unclear, and unstructured sense of the world.
6. Horizons vastly extended or not limited.	6. Horizons sharply defined and limited.
7. Greater sense of choice making.	7. Limited sense of choice making.
8. Self-confident, willing to take risks.	8. Very much concerned with security.
9. Thinking is immaterial and abstract.	9. Thinking is concrete and perceptive.
10. Sees self as tied to national happenings.	10. World revolves around family and self.

Figure 12.6
Psychological differences between middle- and lower-class buyers. *Source: Pierre D. Martineau, "Social Classes and Spending Behavior," Journal of Marketing, Vol. 23 (October 1958), p. 129.*

discuss some topic in which researchers are interested. The group typically does not know the identity of the firm doing the research, and executives might even watch the discussion through one-way mirrors or via videotape. A newspaper of the Knight-Ridder Chain used focus groups to help it develop a supplement for its paper. The paper hired a moderator who invited about two dozen community leaders, in two groups of twelve, to discuss types of information they would like the local media to provide about local business conditions. The participants did not know that the paper was involved; they were told that a local communication medium was interested in finding ways to improve their service by offering more information on local business. From the discussion, the paper designed a "Business Monday" supplement, which proved to be quite successful.*

BUYER BEHAVIOR

Why do we buy products and services? This question is the subject of much research for marketers, and it often haunts the customer. Research shows us how we spend our money. In 1983, buying everything from toy rockets to his-and-her dirigibles, we spent more than $2 trillion on goods and services. Although taking a smaller percentage bite than in the past, food still claims the largest expenditure in the family budget. We are also spending less on clothes and home expenses (with the exception of utilities) than in the past. By contrast, housing, utilities, and health costs have increased and form a larger percentage of our expenditures.

But the record of our expenses does not answer the questions of why we buy a Ford instead of a Chevrolet. Nor do the records nail down all the reasons for our spending patterns. We try to give some insight into these questions by examining buying motives and cultural influences.

Surveying a market population by telephone is one method of generating primary research data.

---

* Enrichment Chapter C, "The Use of Statistical Methods," provides more information on research methods.

Why People Buy

Basically, we buy to fulfill some need. When needs are aroused to our conscious levels, we classify them as motives because they activate our behavior. Thus, we say that our motives cause us to buy, and we can classify these as rational motives and emotional motives. **Consumer behavior** is that aspect of marketing that studies people's motives for purchasing certain products.

Rational buying motives. **Rational motives** are objective; they are based on the logic of why we should or should not buy a particular item. For example, a person may buy a new small car because her old gas guzzler was in need of repairs. Though the small car is not as prestigious or quite as comfortable, it is much more economical. It will save her a lot in gas and repair bills, and it is dependable. Decisions on price and quality are examples of rational motives.

1. *Price*. If we find two items of equal quality that perform the same function, a rational decision would be to buy the lower-priced item. That is why many people search for after-holiday sales and the less-popular brand names. Marketers appeal to this rational motive by advertising specials offering coupons for discounts and by cutting service and packaging frills in favor of lowering the price.
2. *Quality*. Some people search for quality to be sure that they are getting their money's worth. The item's construction and materials, the quality of workmanship, and its durability become important in buying decisions where quality is a motive.

Emotional buying motives. From our own fickle experiences, we know that not all of our purchases are rational. Fancy labels do not mean that jeans will last longer, but they create a lot of attention, and many people like that. **Emotional motives** are rarely logical or rational; they are subjective, and we may not be able to explain them with logical soundness. There are many emotional buying motives; we offer a few as illustrations.

1. *Status*. We see people in sports, politics, entertainment, and government who get a lot of publicity. From media reports, it looks as though they live storybook lives. We may

Seeking to emulate the status of the famous may motivate the purchase of a luxury fur or an item from a celebrity-endorsed line of clothing.

envy them and try to capture some of their glow. We often see these people wearing expensive items such as Gucci shoes, Piaget watches, and Lucchase boots. While people may not actually need or be able to afford a Mercedes, sable mink, or hand-tailored Italian suits, some buy them in reaching for the status of the stars.

2. *Getting a bargain.* Some buyers simply cannot refuse to take advantage of a bargain. Although their closets are filled with shoes, many of which they seldom wear, they just have to buy a new pair of shoes at the "ridiculous sale price." The feeling of getting a good buy or taking advantage of the seller is a powerful enough motive to stimulate the purchase.

3. *Reducing depression.* Have you ever wondered why so many people crowd into the stores on overcast, rainy, winter weekend days? Psychologists tell us that many people buy to help them overcome boredom and depression. Feeling bad? Go out and buy a new suit. Frank Sinatra once said, "When I feel down, I go buy a half-dozen new suits, and I feel better." If it works for Frank, it might work for us. While the purchase might give us a temporary boost, it is not likely to do anything to help remove the underlying causes of our dreary feelings.

4. *Fear.* We buy some things out of fear. The encyclopedia salesperson tells us that our kids may grow up ignorant if we do not buy the books. Insurance companies appeal to our fear of dying, and manufacturers of hair-care products often take advantage of our fears of being rejected by the opposite sex. Manipulation of the fear of losing our health, being unable to take care of our families, losing our social status, or being rejected is the powerful motive behind much of our buyer behavior.

How Our Culture Influences Buying Decisions

How the buying motives affect us also depends on cultural influences. Cultural influences vary between and within societies. For example, the color green represents coolness and outdoor feelings in the United States, but it connotes sickness and dis-ease in Malaysia. Blue is warm and feminine in Holland but cold and masculine in Sweden.

Social class. We can understand a lot about cultural influences in the United States by looking at characteristics of different social classes. Six class levels have been identified.

1. *Upper-upper class.* Prominent families with third- and fourth-generation wealth compose this class: Blue bloods, professionals, merchants, and financiers abound. They often use their wealth to travel extensively. The upper-upper class represents 1.5% of our population.

2. *Lower-upper class.* This class consists of the new rich: top executives, successful doctors, lawyers, and founders of large businesses who are not yet accepted by the upper-upper class. These people represent 1.5% of our population.

3. *Upper-middle class.* Reasonably successful business and professional people, middle managers, and owners of medium-sized companies are grouped here. They are status-oriented, family conscious, and associate with each other. Ten percent of our population is included in the upper-middle class.

4. *Lower-middle class.* This class consists of white-collar office workers, salespeople, small business owners, and skilled blue-collar workers. This class is conservative, respected, and strives for self-betterment; it represents 33% of our population.

5. *Upper-lower class.* Here are these semiskilled and blue-collar factory workers with reasonably high incomes. They often hold a short-run view of life and their surroundings. Thirty-eight percent of our population resides in this class.

6. *Lower-lower class.* This group encompasses the unskilled, unemployed welfare recipients and slum dwellers who are often apathetic or rebellious. This class comprises 16% of our population.

Class membership in these groups is dictated by education, family background, occupation, and earnings. Their purchasing habits differ. Even in the same income bracket, families in different social classes spend their incomes differently; they are attracted by different products and promotional methods. Pierre Martineau distinguishes ten psychological differences that affect buying patterns between the middle- and lower-class families. These appear in Fig. 12.6.

Reference groups. Each of us has certain reference groups, groups that we relate to because of special interests, that affect our buying decisions. We may identify with groups through our work, hobbies, geographical location, or other means. For instance, the National Rifleman's Association may serve as a reference group for sportspeople who like hunting. The Sierra Club may be an identity for many environmentalists.

Family influences. All of us are influenced, at least to some extent, by our family habits, traditions, and values. Pork may not sell well in traditional Jewish communities, but New York style delicatessens may thrive. The market for alcoholic beverages, because of the influence of Mormon families, is much less than average in Utah. Chinese neighborhoods have unique grocery needs.

In these and other cases, family influences help determine our tastes and buying decisions.

Consumer Decision Model

Analysts have developed **consumer decision models** to help analyze the influences on the buyer. Figure 12.7 is an adaptation of several decision models. Buyers receive information about products through promotion, advertising, sales presentations, and word of mouth.

Driven by aroused motive, consumers select a goal or goals they think will lead to need satisfaction. Then the potential customer usually faces several alternative actions (buying decisions) that can meet the goal. Eventually, one alternative may lead to purchasing a product. If the purchase does indeed satisfy the consumer's needs, this becomes reinforcing feedback. Dissatisfaction, however, is likely to move us backward to the selected goal, and we begin anew our search for alternatives that lead to need satisfaction.

**Figure 12.7
Example of a consumer
decision model.**

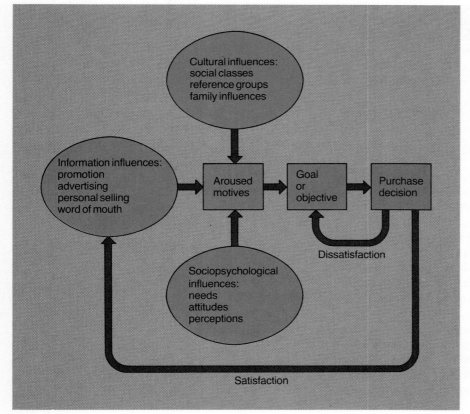

For example, suppose new-car commercials perk your need for status and recognition to the point of arousing a buying motive, and you select for yourself the goal of purchasing a new car. To satisfy your goal, you face many alternatives in price, luxury, size, weight, color, and model. Finally, you decide that a new two-tone blue convertible with a luxury interior, racing stripes, and enlarged tires fits your image of status and recognition. So you sign on the dotted line, which commits you to 36 equal payments. If this action satisfies your needs, you will remember it favorably on your next purchase decision. But if the action leaves you dissatisfied, you will seek additional alternatives, such as a trade-in as soon as you can afford it.

SUMMARY

The real purpose of production is consumption, and marketing engages in eight functions to move goods or services from production to consumers. At the turn of the century, manufacturers stressed production quality, efficiency, and improvement of the production process. Later, as firms found they were building excess inventory, they developed a more aggressive marketing program. Finally, a consumer orientation emerged as the marketing concept: firms find out what customers want and try to deliver it.

At the same time that the marketing concept gained prominence, consumers began demanding more consideration in product planning and distribution. In developing marketing plans, managers consider market segments and mixes. Segmentation divides markets into smaller groupings of people with similar characteristics. Three popular means of market segmentation are geographic location, age, and expenditure patterns. After segmentation, planners identify a specific market target — the specialized characteristics of the consumer group the firm is trying to reach. The total package of variables balanced in a program is called the marketing mix and consists of: (1) product planning, (2) pricing decisions, (3) distribution channels, and (4) promotional strategies. Marketing research is the process of recording and analyzing information about customers' reactions to firms' products and services. The study of buyer behavior identifies both rational and emotional motives for buying, both of which are sub-

ject to cultural influences. Consumer decision models help to explain the interrelatedness of buying variables.

MIND YOUR BUSINESS

Instructions. Answer each of the following questions by writing Y for yes or N for no in the blanks at the left.

____ 1. Are grading and standardizing products and services considered part of the marketing process?

____ 2. Does the marketing concept emphasize the notion of "Take what we produce and sell it"?

____ 3. Are pricing decisions considered part of the marketing mix?

____ 4. Is promotion considered part of the marketing mix?

____ 5. Does market segmentation mean "store products until there is a need for them"?

____ 6. Does marketing research try to find out what customers want that the firm is not providing them?

____ 7. Do people buy for purely rational motives?

____ 8. Does our culture influence our buying decisions?

____ 9. Do lower social classes have different buying habits from higher social classes?

____ 10. Is concern for getting the best price an emotional buying motive?

See answers at the back of the book.

KEY TERMS

marketing, 300
market, 300
utility, 300
place utility, 301
time utility, 301
possession utility, 301
form utility, 301
marketing concept, 302
enlightened marketing, 303

REVIEW QUESTIONS

1. Discuss the eight major functions of the marketing process.

2. What is the marketing concept? What is the opposite of the marketing concept?

3. Briefly describe production-, sales-, and consumer-oriented marketing.

4. What is the marketing mix? Describe the four Ps of marketing.

5. What is involved in choosing a target market? Identify four means of market segmentation. What would be the target market of detergents? Sports cars? Vacation tours?

6. What is the relationship between target markets and market segmentation?

7. What is marketing research? Describe several ways of conducting marketing research.

8. What is consumer behavior? Why is it practiced?

9. Describe rational motives and emotional motives involved in buying a new car.

10. How does culture affect buying decisions? What are the three major cultural influences with regard to purchase decisions?

11. Describe the consumer decision model.

CASES

Case 12.1: The Marketing Process

Martina Cross is director of marketing for a new radio station, KROX. They feature hard rock music exclusively. Their goal is to become the most popular hard rock station within a large, metropolitan area. Having just started her new job, Martina is most concerned with reaching the potential audience.

Questions

1. Which of the basic functions of marketing will be her first and greatest concern?

2. In what ways will the station create utility?

3. Which of the four Ps of the marketing mix will receive the most of Martina's attention at the beginning?

4. Prepare a marketing grid for Martina. Which qualities of the potential audience will she be most interested in? Detail her target market.

5. What motives will the listeners of KROX be using as they decide which radio station to listen to? What cultural influences will be involved?

Case 12.2: The Problem of Customer Wants

Jose Wiley is director of marketing for a small greeting card company. So far, store accounts have gone very well, and they have a proper supply of inventory. However, the company has a serious problem. Stores seem to be running out of some cards, while being overstocked with others. The loss of sales, especially for most big holidays, is hurting both the company and the stores it supplies. Jose needs to solve the problem of providing the stores with a more appropriate selection of greeting cards.

Questions

1. If you were Jose, using only topics presented within the chapter, how would you solve the problem? Propose some cultural influences that may be causing the shortages of the proper cards.

2. How could Jose more fully utilize the marketing concept?

3. Prepare a target market profile for the following occasions: Thanksgiving, Hanukkah, Easter, and graduation.

4. Discuss changes in target market and influences in purchasing decisions for card retail stores located in each of the following: (a) Inner city, (b) Wealthy suburban community, (c) Heavily ethnic neighborhood, and (d) Small rural neighborhood.

STRATEGIC
MARKETING

In the late 1970s, high school rings and yearbooks accounted for two-thirds of The Jostens Company's sales. But because of changes in their environment — student population was expected to decline almost 3% annually — the company had to develop a new strategy for dealing with this environment or face declining sales and profits. To counter the trend of their diminishing market, Jostens refocused their marketing effort to appeal to junior high students and to students in the sun belt. They projected sun belt enrollments to remain relatively stable; most of the student decline was in the north. Jostens also advertised more in executive periodicals to reach graduates who might not have purchased a ring when they graduated. And they made an attempt to get into traditional jewelry markets. These were strategic responses to environmental shifts.

Today virtually all large organizations have strategic plans. Many medium-size firms also have them. A strategic plan sets forth long-range objectives that the firm intends to pursue. Typical examples include return on investment, growth, and market share. These objectives help the organization compare its own performance with that of the competition.

The two primary considerations in every strategic plan are marketing and finance.

In contrast to many other types of plans, a strategic plan is external in orientation. It focuses on helping the organization get ahead of the competition. There are two primary considerations in every strategic plan: marketing and finance. Both have one thing in common: the firm lacks total control over them. For example, a company can design the most up-to-date products possible and market them via a vigorous promotion campaign; however, it cannot make people buy the new goods. Likewise, when a firm has to go to the bank to raise money, it can negotiate with the banker; but in the final analysis, it will end up paying the going rate for money. So unlike areas such as production or personnel, where the organization has a great deal of control regarding what to do and when to do it, in marketing and finance the firm is in the position of having to respond to the market.

At the heart of every strategic plan is the marketing area. Even finance is secondary when one stops to consider the fact that banks will lend a firm money if they feel it is a good risk. For this reason, many organizations today spend a great deal of time developing the strategic marketing part of their overall plan. They know that if they are successful in the marketplace, they will be able to attain their desired goals of return on investment, growth, and market share.

The **strategic marketing plan** has six basic steps or phases: (1) evaluation of the corporate strategic plan, (2) analysis of the product-market situation, (3) formulation of a target market strategy, (4) setting objectives, (5) development of a positioning strategy, and (6) the implementation and control of the marketing plan. We will examine each of these six steps in detail.

EVALUATION OF THE CORPORATE STRATEGIC PLAN

Strategic marketing activities must be tied to the organization's overall plan. Thus the process begins with a review of the corporation's strategic plan. In this evaluation, the company's basic mission must be examined. This requires the planners to answer the question: What business is the firm in? Figure B.1 provides a statement of purpose or basic mission for a family-owned regional firm. Notice that the purpose spells out what the company does and where the firm intends to be heading. This statement is very well developed and offers important direction for the marketing plan. Particularly, it focuses on two key marketing-related areas: new business direction and new product development. With information like this,

it is possible for the marketing people to link their plan into that of the strategic plan.

Large firms that have many different divisions and product lines offer even more guidelines than those proffered in Figure B.1. However, too much input can be detrimental to the formulation of a viable strategic marketing plan. For this reason, it is common for marketing people to merely seek out the overall, general direction of the firm and tie their plan to that focus. In this process, the planners will try very hard to stay within the basic expertise of the firm. For example, if we are dealing with IBM, the marketing people will develop a plan that draws on the company's two major strengths: strong research and development and effective service. In the case of Sears Roebuck, the strategic marketing people will develop a plan that concentrates on the firm's ability to offer a wide array of consumer goods at very reasonable prices. Marketing does not lead the strategic plan; it meshes with it.

Consolidated Distributors is a family-owned regional distributor of industrial lubricants and solvents. It prides itself on product knowledge, customer counsel, and promptness in filling orders. Within the Northeast region that it serves, it is recognized and respected as a company that is competitive and will stand behind its products.

The principals recognize that the market served is shrinking — customers are slowly but steadily relocating to the Sunbelt. Remaining customers are not modernizing and are losing their competitive positions. Further, the principals themselves are aging and new family members may or may not wish to pursue the business. The principals note a weakness in their middle management.

The principals are watching closely the development of industrial "robots." While unsure about the extent of their application, they feel that robots will replace at least 40 percent of the workers on production lines by the year 2000. They believe that robots will require special care and a new line of lubricant products.

Based on the company's existing position, and the expectation that the cost of their products will generally go up faster than prices overall (because many of the products are petroleum based), the principals have established the following goals:

1. Expand Consolidated's territory to the Sunbelt states, starting with those areas where old customers have relocated.

2. Seek alternative products that will meet the requirements of existing customers but that are not petroleum-based or contain a minimum quantity of petroleum and, thus, are not totally subject to the turbulence of the petro markets.

3. Study closely the further development of robots and develop a complete product line to serve this growing market.

4. Build middle management by selective hiring, primarily to coincide with expansion into the Sunbelt region.

5. Prepare the company so that it can be taken over either by junior family members or so that it will be attractive as an acquisition by a company with stock traded on the New York or American Stock Exchanges.

Figure B.1
An example of basic mission. *Source: Bruce M. Bradway, Robert E. Pritchard, Mary Anne Frenzel,* Strategic Marketing: A Handbook for Managers, Business Owners & Entrepreneurs, © *1982, Addison-Wesley, Reading, Massachusetts. P. 4. Reprinted with permission.*

ANALYSIS OF THE PRODUCT-MARKET SITUATION

The first real action step in strategic marketing is the analysis of the situation. In this step, marketing people scan the environment for the purpose of identifying customers and competitors. Customers represent opportunities; competitors represent threats. The firm wants to take advantage of these opportunities but not at the price of costly retaliation by the competition. During this phase, marketing people also draw conclusions regarding the likelihood of customers buying the firm's current and proposed products and the strategies likely to be employed in these markets by the competition.

If a firm makes a serious marketing error, it usually does so as a result of incorrect product-market situation analysis. For example, in 1981, Adam Osborne introduced the first portable personal computer. He was convinced that people would be willing to pay $1800 for a machine that they could take to the office, bring home, and carry on trips. The convenience of having a computer so close at hand, he believed, would be recognized by millions. For the first couple of years, his machine sold well. For example, in 1982, the firm grossed $100 million. Unfortunately, in that same year, the company just managed to break even. Why? Because fifty other firms also were in the personal computer (PC) market and many of them were offering portable PCs that had larger video screens (making it easier to see what was being displayed) and software that was IBM-compatible (meaning that if the firm already had the IBM PC, staff could take the work they did on the road and at home, and throw it into an office computer to finish the job). Osborne overlooked the large number of competitors that would enter the market with better-quality machines. Additionally, the firm seemed to lack a general understanding of how to plan. Confronted with complaints that its screen was too small and the machine was not IBM-compatible, Osborne announced that it would soon be coming out with a machine to correct these problems. Result? Customers who were thinking of buying an Osborne decided to wait and see what the new machine looked like. Cash flow dried up, machines sat collecting dust on dealers' shelves, and the firm filed Chapter 11 bankruptcy in late 1983.

IBM refused to say a word about their PC Jr. before it was released, realizing that if customers believed the PC Jr. was a better buy than their PC, sales of the latter would dry up.

Meanwhile, IBM continued to dominate the market because it did understand the product-market situation. As its PC gained market share, the firm let it be known that it had a smaller version that would sell for less money than the original and would be called the PC Jr. When would this machine hit the market? What would it look like? What would it be able to do? IBM refused to say, realizing that if customers believed the PC Jr. was a better buy than their PC, sales of the latter would dry up until the PC Jr. was released. Instead, IBM kept everyone in the dark. The firm knew better than to follow Osborn's example.

The two specific types of product-market analysis conducted during this phase relate to customers and competitors. Some of the typical questions that the marketing staff attempt to answer in their **customer analysis** of new products include: How many of these units will we sell in a year's time? What is the annual growth of this market likely to be over the next 5 years? What kinds of people are likely to buy this product (income level, education level, geographic region, occupation, etc.)? Where are they likely to want to go to buy it? How much would they be willing to pay for it? Responses to such questions are used to construct a detailed customer analysis.

Key competitor analysis questions focus on the activities, present and projected, of other firms in the market. Some of the most common queries include: How many firms are there in this market and how many more can be expected within the next 2 to 3 years? What share of the market does each of these current competitors now have, and how will this change, given the expected entry (or exit) of additional firms? What is the financial strength of each competitor? What other strengths, crucial to success in this market, do each of the competitors have? What market strategy is each likely to pursue during the next 2 to 3 years in terms of product, price, distribution, and promotion?

Target marketing means deciding which specific products should be marketed and what particular groups of people should be pursued.

These questions give the market planning team the general type of information it needs in order to proceed. Now planners must decide which specific products should be marketed and what particular groups of customers should be pursued. This is done with target marketing.

FORMULATION OF A TARGET MARKET STRATEGY

In formulating a **target market** strategy, planners answer the question: To whom do we want to sell our product(s)? In some cases, although these are rare, the answer is: Just about everyone. For example, to whom does McDonald's want to

---

sell hamburgers? Their potential market is just about everybody from 6-year-old kids to teenagers to adults. On the other hand, most firms do not have products that appeal to everyone. Consider automobiles. To whom does General Motors want to sell a Cadillac? Realistically, the market is people who are looking for status, want a good quality car, and can afford to pay more than the average buyer. Chevrolet comes closer to McDonald's strategy than does Cadillac, although it too realizes that not everyone will be interested in buying its car. At the other extreme is Rolls Royce, which targets itself toward a very narrow, exclusive segment of the auto market. While the quality and reliability of the car is very high, so is the price. So what we have here are three different cars that attempt to capture specific niches in the overall automobile market.

Most target strategies are similar to our auto example; they focus on a limited market niche. Consider the PC market. There are a number of different niches here. One is for business PCs that have bubble memory and color graphics. The cost of these machines can range up toward $10,000. Companies that need a good, efficient, rugged PC are attracted to this type of machine. The average executive or homeowner does not need anything this sophisticated. The IBM PC, Apple II, and similar machines suffice. Then there are the very limited home computers that offer word processing and some calculation power. These typically cost $1000 or less and are particularly attractive to families who want computers that can be used by their children for educational assignments or can help them balance their budgets or do financial forecasts. Commodore and Coleco offer products for this market niche. Finally, there are the portable PCs that are so useful to executives who want to conduct financial analysis or write memos or reports while away from the office. Depending on the desired size of the machine (the smaller ones cost more), there are a number of competitors in this market niche including Compaq, Corona, Gavilan, and Zorba.

Unfortunately, it is not very easy to identify specific niches in these markets because there is a great deal of blurring caused by machines that offer characteristics desired by customers in more than one niche. For example, the Compaq portable is really not so much a portable as it is a comportable, meaning that it can be moved from place to place but it is fairly bulky. On the other hand, Compaq is IBM-compatible and many firms like it better than the IBM. Its price is also less than that of the IBM PC. So while its original niche was in the portable computer market, it has also invaded the

BUSINESS BULLETIN

Find a Market Niche

Rather than trying to conquer the world with marketing, it is better to find a small niche and then branch out. As entrepreneurship professor Frederick Wiersema says, ''Pick your area. Than try to preempt others from coming in. Once you have control, you can branch out.''

The software firm Finreport Systems Inc. did just that. Massachusetts has 110 general acute care hospitals. The president of Finreport was a former assistant controller of a large Massachusetts hospital. He believed that existing software was aimed at a more widespread market, so he set out to develop file programs, management programs, and a programming language just for these 110 hospitals. Because his product fit the niche so uniquely, he got 90% of the market, which totals $3 to $4 million annually. Now, Finreport is branching out into New York to attempt the same thing.

Source: ''Gaining Market Share,'' Venture, Aug., 1983, pp. 81–84.

By offering both self-sufficiency and the capability of interacting with larger systems, portable computers appeal to customers in several market niches.

desk-top market. On the other end of the portable market niche are lightweight, liquid crystal, calculator/typewriters that offer the user many of the same features as do portable PCs. They can be used to write memos and make financial calculations. They have memory capacity and, when hooked up to a printer, can provide a copy of the material that has been put into memory. They do have limited capabilities and are currently fairly expensive ($700 to $1000), but they can fit easily into a small attache case and operate off batteries so executives can even use them while on a plane or in a taxi. As their prices come down and their capabilities increase, we are likely to see some of the demand for portable PCs being taken away by these smaller, lighter machines, especially among those who want the machines for word processing only.

SETTING OBJECTIVES

Market objectives are goals toward which the strategic plan is geared. Large firms today place **return on investment (ROI)** (profits/assets) very high on this list and with good reason. By measuring the amount of profit they are able to achieve with the assets they have committed to this product line, they are able to judge their effectiveness in the marketplace. After all, even though a large firm makes $10 million from one of its product

lines, this may not be a very significant accomplishment; we need to know how much money they put into plant, equipment, marketing effort, etc., in order to judge their overall success. This is one of the primary reasons why ROI is so important to these firms. A second reason is that the computation allows the firm to compare its effectiveness with that of other major competitors quickly. Rather than looking at profit, the company can compare ROI. Small firms, on the other hand, tend to be much more interested in profit as a strategic objective. They know that if they compete with larger firms, they will have to offer lower prices or extra service. So they cannot hope to match the giants in terms of ROI.

Market share is another major objective of many strategic marketing plans. Consider the big TV networks: ABC, NBC, and CBS. Every week, the Nielsen ratings indicate which shows were the most popular and which did not do well. Based on these ratings, the networks renew or cancel their offerings. Market share is important on a week-to-week basis in this industry. Another group that pays close attention to market share is the automobile industry. Every week, the number of cars sold by the big four American producers (General Motors, Ford, Chrysler, and American Motors) is reported in the financial press. Executives at these firms closely monitor how well their companies are doing against the competition.

Protecting your market share is often harder than building a market.

Protecting market share is often harder than building a market. If a company has a good idea and a unique product or service, they might start with 100% of the market. But when others see the company's results, successful competitors will move in.

Firms try to preserve their market shares in a variety of ways, including:

- Creating a unique character for the company.
- Advertising to build a specific image.
- Creating and holding onto customer representative (dealer) networks.

- Protecting the product's or service's distinctiveness by going to court if necessary.

Growth is a third major objective. Every strategic marketing plan is designed to help product lines grow (or at least stop them from shrinking). Naturally, since products go through life cycles, there comes a time when growth stabilizes and then begins to decline. This is when new product offerings are brought on to the market and promoted as substitutes. At the same time, the marketing plan encourages those who are buying the old product to continue doing so. Since this latter strategy is often only a holding action, it is common to find businesses reducing the amount of promotion they are putting behind their fading product lines and attempting to milk as much profit from them as possible. These products have become "cash cows" and as long as they remain, the marketing strategy will be one of minimum promotional expenditures and maximum ROI.

ROI, market share, and growth are the three most common strategic marketing objectives.

While ROI, market share, and growth are the three most common strategic marketing objectives, there are others ranging from promotion

CROSS FIRE

Tracking Strategic Changes at CBS

CBS, by comparison to ABC and NBC, has earned unimpressive profits in recent years. And they have made two strategic changes to try to better themselves.

In mid-1982, CBS economists told their market planners that the recession would soon be over. Thus, the network wanted to sell fewer commercials up front, that is, before the fall season began. They wanted to hold off and sell commercials later — scatter sales, as they are called — hoping to get higher prices. However, scatter sales went soft and CBS had lots of prime time on its hands with few commercials to cover them; this ploy cost them about $50 million in revenues. This year, CBS went strong for the up-front market.

CBS also had a policy of demographic guarantees. That is, they would guarantee their client that certain programs would deliver viewers with specified demographic characteristics — say women between the ages of 18 and 49. If the viewers did not fit these characteristics, CBS would offer clients free commercials, called "make-goods," to get the desired number of viewers. CBS has offered such guarantees for several years, but the network's previously stable demographics suddenly turned widely unstable. And although many of their programs rated well, they could not predict the demographics of the audience very well. So they had to offer a lot of make-goods. Last year, they changed their policy, but clients were soon hollering, so hooked were they on the guarantees. Today, CBS is again offering their clients demographic guarantees.

Do you think the effort to sell more up-front commercial time will prove to be a good idea for CBS? Why?

___ Yes   ___ No

Do you think the change back to demographic guarantees was a sound decision? Why?

___ Yes   ___ No

efforts to sales force activities. Yet all objectives will have five common characteristics:

1. They help the organization achieve effective overall results.
2. Each is consistent with the other objectives being pursued.
3. Each provides a clear guide to accomplishment; progress can be measured clearly.
4. Each is realistic; it can be accomplished within the time, cost, quality, and quantity parameters assigned.
5. The individuals responsible for each objective know their tasks, and if there is joint responsibility, this is spelled out clearly.

Multiple brands manufactured by a single firm allow growth through different market segments.

DEVELOPMENT OF A POSITIONING STRATEGY

A **positioning strategy** fine tunes the marketing plan. At this point, the planners determine how product, price, distribution, and promotion strategies can be combined to market the company's goods and services effectively.

Product Strategy

Product strategy is the core of strategic planning for the organization. This strategy plays the central role in shaping the company's marketing effort. One group of authors explained its significance by noting that:

> In the 1980s, one of the most important "Ps" in the marketing mix could well be positioning. For most packaged goods—and for many other products and services as well—positioning (product, service, or corporate stance) will probably be more critical to success than product, pricing, promotion, packaging, place, or any other element in the marketing mix. You can make many mistakes in other areas and survive, if your position is right. For many products and services, if it's wrong, nothing on earth will assure success for your product or service.*

In its product strategy, the firm decides what it will offer to the customers. This decision will cut

---

* Bruce M. Bradway, Robert E. Pritchard, Mary Anne Frenzel, *Strategic Marketing: A Handbook for Managers, Business Owners & Entrepreneurs,* © 1982, Addison-Wesley, Reading, Massachusetts. P. 41. Reprinted by permission.

across every functional area of operations: distribution, advertising, pricing, sales force activities, etc. The firm's objective is to place a brand in that part of the market where it will have the most favorable reception vis à vis the competition. (See Chapter 13 for additional information on brands.)

There are a number of reasons why firms introduce multiple brands. One of the most common is to offset competitive threats to their single brand. A second reason is to seek growth through different market segments. When a firm offers something that is similar to its present product, to some degree it cannibalizes on this product line. For example, if a company selling 1 million digital watches a year comes out with a liquid crystal watch, some of those who would have bought their digital may now buy their liquid crystal offering. Is the new product line a wise decision? The answer may well be yes because those who were attracted to the liquid crystal may well have bought a similar watch from the competition. Multiple brand strategy is a little like flooding the zone in football. By sending two or more pass receivers into the same area, the quarterback hopes that if one of them is too well guarded by the defense, the other(s) will be open for the catch.

Sometimes a product needs to be repositioned. This is particularly true when a competitor has entered the market, positioned its product next to the firm's, and begun to erode the latter's market share. What else can the firm do but move to another market niche? Another reason for repositioning is when consumer preferences have undergone a change and the firm needs to alter its product niche to keep up with the customers. A third reason is when new customer preference clusters with promising opportunities have been discovered, and the firm wants to take advantage of this newly discovered market. One of the most interesting examples is provided by General Foods, which repositioned Jell-O by promoting it as a base for salads. A similar strategy was used by the 3M Company when it introduced a new line of colored, invisible, waterproof, and write-on Scotch tapes that could be used for gift wrapping. A third example is provided by the orange juice industry that used to advertise its product as an excellent breakfast drink but has now adopted the jingle, "Orange Juice — it's not just for breakfast anymore." This ad campaign has been particularly successful in getting people to drink more orange juice. In other cases, firms have attempted to reposition their product for new users. For example, Miller Beer's promotional campaign built around the slogan "If you've got the time, we've got the beer" was tremendously successful in attracting new customers to their product. Finally, there are times when a company will want to reposition its product for new uses. Nylon is an excellent illustration. When DuPont first introduced the product, it was used to make parachutes. Then

---

If new uses had not been found for nylon, it would have disappeared from the market years ago.

---

it was used for varied types of hosiery such as stretch stockings and stretch socks. Today, it is used in tires, textured yarns, and carpeting. If new uses had not been found for nylon, it would have disappeared from the market years ago. Thanks to research and development and repositioning strategies, it has remained with us for decades.

Price Strategy

Price strategies vary, depending on whether or not the product is new. New product pricing strategies tend to be of two types: skimming or penetration. As you will learn in Chapter 13, **skimming pricing** is a strategy of establishing a high initial price for a product, with the intent of "skimming the cream" off this segment of the market. Quite often, a new product that has required a lot of research and development or will soon encounter strong competition will be introduced with a skimming strategy. One of the best examples has been video game cassettes. When these cassettes first hit the market, it was not uncommon to pay $20 to $60 for them. However, as other firms began to offer games and the market started to soften, the manufacturers realized that they could not keep their prices high. Strong competition, coupled with limited market demand, dictated lower prices.

Penetration pricing is the strategy of entering a market with a low initial price so as to capture as large a share of the market as possible. There are two typical reasons for this approach. One is to discourage competition. The other is that customers will be indifferent or negative toward the product if it is offered at a high price. One of the most recent examples is Coleco's Adam, a home computer. Originally offered at $700, including a printer, the company's objective was to deeply penetrate the home computer market.

Established product pricing follows a different approach. The most common approaches are to maintain price, reduce price, or increase price. Firms that maintain price tend to have strong buyer loyalty. For example, in very few cases does IBM discount its products to the general public. If you want an IBM, you have to pay the established price.

Distribution Strategy

Distribution strategies are concerned with the channels employed in making goods and services available to customers. (Chapter 14 covers channels in more detail.) The most common types of distribution are exclusive, selective, and intensive. Exclusive distribution means that one particular retailer in a given area is granted the right to carry the product. It is not uncommon to find Hart, Schaffner & Marx suits distributed through only one store in a town. Manufacturers looking to have their goods distributed through national chains often agree to give exclusive rights to just one chain in return for the latter's promise to vigorously market the product.

An intensive distribution strategy makes a product available at as many outlets as possible. Convenience goods are often marketed this way. If a retailer is willing to carry them, the manufacturer is prepared to use outlets. Consider all the items you see near the supermarket checkout counter, from razor blades to magazines. These are all marketed via an intensive distribution strategy.

Selective distribution is a strategy in which some, but not all, outlets in a locale are given the right to distribute the product. The best example is found in the marketing of shopping goods like refrigerators, ovens, ranges, and TVs. Retailers do not want to carry a product that can be purchased at every other competitor; they want some degree of exclusivity. So it is common to find manufacturers limiting their choice of outlets. Additionally, some manufacturers do not want just any retailer selling their product line. They may want to rely only on salespeople who know or are specifically trained in their product's features. When Head skis first hit the market, the company would market only through select stores and insisted that only skiers be allowed to sell the product.

We have explained the way in which a great many distribution strategies are carried out. However, there are other combination approaches. Most of these fit under the heading of multiple-channel strategies, which refer to situations in which two or more different channels are employed for the distribution of goods or services. The most common example of a multiple-channel strategy is the complementary channel. Complementary channels exist when each channel handles a different noncompeting product or noncompeting marketing segment. For example, except for some cosmetic changes, American Tourister sells the same type of luggage to discount stores that it sells to retailers.

Promotion Strategy

Promotion strategies are used to inform customers about product offerings or persuade them to purchase the goods or services. (See Chapter 15 for information on promotion.) There are three basic types of promotion strategies: advertising, personal selling, and sales promotion. Advertising strategies are geared toward choosing the most effective media for conveying the message(s) and writing the most effective advertising copy. Countless rules and guidelines can be cited regarding how to carry out these strategies. Those drawing up the strategic marketing plan will know which are of most value to the organization and implement them accordingly. Personal selling strategies are designed to ensure the greatest amount of efficiency and effectiveness from the sales force. All other forms of promotion, including demonstrations, contests, sampling, cents off, etc., are collectively known as sales promotion strategies.

IMPLEMENTATION AND CONTROL OF THE PLAN

The last step in the strategic marketing process is implementing and controlling the plan. Whenever something goes wrong, it is usually because some part of the plan was incorrect. Perhaps the competition came out with a new and unexpected product. Or the company raised its prices but no one else followed. Or thanks to superior research and development, competitors were able to reduce their costs and consequently their selling prices dramatically.

The firm must continually assess how well it is doing and be prepared to take necessary correc-

Effective strategic marketing plans require constant input and assessment from the sales and marketing staff.

A Successful Strategy for Gerber

Gerber's share of the baby food market has grown to an all-time high of 71%. They did it by "selling more to the same mothers." Gerber has long dominated the baby food market (they had a 69% share in 1978), but the declining birth rate made it hard for them to continue growing.

Gerber tried to improve its sales by venturing into other markets. They tried to market adult foods, but they failed. They even dipped into investing in mail-order insurance and day-care centers, but these were at best modest successes. Then they decided to go back to what they knew best, selling baby foods and related products to mothers. In 1983, their profits totaled $39 million, up 63% from 1978.

Gerber's planners do not expect their 71% share to increase very much, but they think the market will expand at about 3% a year as babies eat more prepared foods. In 1976, the average baby ate twenty-seven cases of baby food before going on solids. This eventually dropped to twenty-two cases as mothers used more infant formulas and prolonged breast feeding. Now, planners believe that the market will expand slowly, and Gerber hopes to sell a little more each year to a few more mothers.

Source: "Gerber: Concentrating on Babies Again for Slow Steady Growth," *Business Week,* Aug. 22, 1983.

Perhaps the most important thing to keep in mind is that few plans work as intended; without fine tuning, desired ROI, market share, and growth are usually not possible.

tive action. Perhaps the most important thing to keep in mind is that few plans work as intended. Even the most successful plan must be changed in some way. Without this fine tuning, desired ROI, market share, and growth are usually not possible. Additionally, since most markets are in a state of flux, strategic marketing efforts must be periodically evaluated. The longer the plan's time horizon, the more likely it is that things will not work out as anticipated. Yet this need not be fatal to the firm's effort, just as long as it is willing to revise its plans and adjust to these external conditions. Successful strategic marketing is less a matter of willingness to plan as it is a matter of willingness to change.

SUMMARY

Strategic marketing is a six-step process. Its purpose is to help the organization achieve desired ROI, capture market share, and attain growth. The first step in this process is an evaluation of the corporate strategic plan. The reason for this evaluation is to ensure that the strategic marketing plan is properly linked to the overall efforts of the organization.

The second step is an analysis of the product-market situation. At this point, marketing people scan the environment for the purpose of identifying customers and competitors. Some of the most important questions that are raised at this point include: What do people want from our product? Who is likely to buy it? What forms of competition will we encounter both now and over the next 3 to 5 years?

The third step in this process is the formulation of a target market strategy. At this point, the objective is to identify the desired market niche. Specifically, the company wants to know as much as it can learn about the customer: How much does the individual earn? Where does the person live? What is the individual's background? Where does the person go to buy the company's product? How much is the individual willing to pay? Answers to these types of questions help the company clearly pinpoint its target group.

The fourth step in this process is setting objectives. The three most common strategic marketing objectives relate to ROI, market share, and growth. These objectives also have common characteristics, including helping the organization to achieve effective overall results, being consistent with each other, providing a clear guide to accomplishment, and being realistic.

The fifth step in this process is the development of a positioning strategy. The purpose of this step is to fine tune the marketing plan. This is when the planners determine how product, price, distribution, and promotion strategies can be combined so as to market the company's goods and services effectively. Each of these four is developed in sufficient detail to ensure effective implementation of the plan.

The sixth and last step in the strategic marketing process is the implementation and control of the plan. Quite often, something in the plan goes wrong. Even under the best conditions, plans need fine tuning. The most important thing for the management to remember is that a willingness to change direction and alter the plan is often the factor that turns failure into success.

MIND YOUR BUSINESS

Instructions. Check your knowledge of strategic marketing by designating the following statements as true (T) or false (F).

____ 1. The two primary considerations for strategic planning are marketing and finance.

____ 2. The organization's overall plan must be tied to its strategic marketing plan.

____ 3. The product-market analysis focuses on internal production capabilities.

____ 4. It is often hard to identify specific market niches of products or services.

____ 5. Return on investment is an example of a marketing objective.

____ 6. Price strategy is the core strategy for planning for the organization.

____ 7. Companies introduce multiple brands to counter competitive threats and to seek growth in different market segments.

____ 8. When a competitor enters the market and erodes market share, it may be necessary to reposition the product.

____ 9. Pricing strategies are usually different for new and established products.

____ 10. Distribution strategies are concerned with getting the product promoted in the right physical locations.

See answers at the back of the book.

KEY TERMS

strategic marketing plan, 320

customer analysis, 322

key competitor analysis, 322

target market, 323

market objectives, 325

return on investment (ROI), 325

positioning strategy, 327

product strategy, 327

price strategy, 328

skimming pricing, 328

penetration pricing, 328

distribution strategy, 328

promotion strategy, 329

REVIEW QUESTIONS

1. Strategic marketing activities must be tied to the organization's overall plan. What does this statement mean?

2. What is a statement of purpose or a basic mission? What does it contain? What is its relevance to strategic marketing?

3. In conducting a customer analysis, what types of questions are commonly asked? What does the organization hope to learn from the answers?

4. In conducting a key competitor analysis, what types of questions are commonly asked? What

does the organization hope to learn from the answers?

5. When formulating a target market, what specific types of questions does the market planner hope to answer? Identify two and discuss each.

6. In a strategic marketing plan, what are three of the most common objectives? Identify and describe each.

7. What are some common characteristics possessed by all good objectives? Identify and describe four.

8. What is the objective of the market planner when developing a position strategy? Explain.

9. How do each of the following help the market planner develop a positioning strategy: product strategy, price strategy, distribution strategy, promotion strategy?

10. When would a company be likely to use a skimming pricing strategy? A penetration pricing strategy? When would it be likely to price above the average market price? With the average? Below the average? Give an example of each of your answers.

11. What is the most important thing a company should keep in mind regarding control of the marketing plan? Be complete in your answer.

CASES

Case B.1: Gil's Challenge

Until recently, Gil McCarthy was in charge of the East Coast marketing division for a large computer firm. Gil was highly regarded as a marketing expert, and much of the company's success has been attributed to his advertising and sales promotion ideas.

Last month Gil was offered a job by a home computer manufacturing firm. This company is located in California and in the process of developing a computer that appeals to children and family members. The machine will do word processing, mathematical calculations, and spread sheets. The company is also developing educational material for use with the machine. Current plans call for programs to help people read faster, spell better,

and learn basic high school and college courses such as math, physics, and chemistry. The firm hopes to bypass the competitive market niche being dominated by the IBM PC and Apple II and go head-to-head with Coleco's Adam. Initial estimates by the firm reveal that there are approximately 15 million homes in this market niche. At an average price of $500, this translates to $9 billion just for the hardware. Software packages are expected to sell for about $25 each.

Gil has decided to accept the new offer to become head of the company's entire marketing division. His first job will be to develop an effective strategic marketing plan to get the new product off the ground. The president of the firm has indicated that he would like to see the company capture 4% of this market within the first year and 18% within the first 3 years. Although Gil has not made any promises to the president, he believes that these market share estimates are indeed realistic.

Questions

1. In your own words, what does a strategic marketing plan involve? Provide a thumbnail sketch.

2. What specific analysis will Gil have to conduct in making an evaluation of the product-market situation? Be complete in your answer.

3. What recommendations would you give to Gil regarding implementing and controlling the plan? Be as realistic as possible.

Base B.2: A New Way to Travel

The Claiborne Company's research and development department recently patented a new process that can be used in making a long-lasting auto tire. This tire, if production estimates are correct, can be manufactured for less than $35 and will have a life span of between 45,000 and 50,000 miles. Although Claiborne is best known for its consumer products, the firm believes that this new product is too important to sell to another company. The firm wants to develop and sell these new tires personally.

Last week there was a meeting of top management staff in the boardroom. During the meeting, the head of R&D gave a brief report on the proposed tire. There were a half dozen samples for the managers to look at. There were also four tires that had been road-tested. "It took us two months, but we drove a car up and down the state, changing drivers every four hours," reported the head of R&D, "We put 1000 miles a day on this car for almost 50 days. When we got to 47,477 miles, we decided to stop. The right rear tire was too worn to continue. The other three, however, could probably have gone another 1500 to 3500 miles, depending on road conditions."

The management staff all believe that Claiborne will make a great deal of money if it develops this tire. The biggest challenge will be convincing the public that this tire is better than anything else on the market. This will require a very effective marketing plan.

The head of marketing, Janice Ramirez, believes that the company's product is so superior to anything on the road that it will literally sell itself. "We've already conducted preliminary analysis on the product quality and marketing approaches of Goodrich, Goodyear, and the other top tire manufacturers," she told the group, "and there is no reason why we can't bring out this tire and dominate the market. It's all a matter of effective marketing. We've never tried selling a product of this nature before, but we do know what strategic marketing is all about. On that score, we have a lot of experience. I'm really looking forward to promoting and selling this tire."

The chairman of the board was delighted with her comments. "We've allocated $20 million to developing a strategic marketing plan and introducing the tire to the general public," he told her. "You've got 90 days to get everything going. Let's see your stuff."

As they left the boardroom, Janice was all smiles. "I can't wait to see the competition's faces when we make our first announcement," she told her assistant.

Questions

1. How should the company go about formulating a target market strategy? Explain.

2. In what way will Janice use product, price, distribution, and promotion to develop a position strategy? Be complete in your answer.

3. What is the biggest threat that Janice's company has to look out for? Explain.

After completing this chapter, you will be able to:

■ Define a product.

■ Classify products into consumer and industrial goods.

■ Identify seven levels in the product hierarchy.

■ Describe four stages of the product life cycle.

■ Identify six steps in new-product development.

■ Explain the functions of product brands, packaging, and labeling.

■ Explain alternative pricing policies for new products.

■ Describe product pricing strategies.

13

PRODUCT
PLANNING AND
PRICING

Remember TV dinners? Most customers have quit buying these low-quality, frozen dinners in tin trays. But consumers still spend $1.6 billion a year for frozen entrees, purchased primarily in supermarkets. Frozen food giants dominate this highly competitive market, the major brands being Nestle's Stouffer, Pillsbury's Green Giant, and Campbell's Swanson and Mrs. Paul's Kitchens.

How does a smaller company like Van de Kamp compete in product and pricing with these larger firms? President Steven H. Porkress, in the 1970s, believing that most frozen fish dinners were undistinguished, introduced a high-quality, light-tasting line of batter-fried fish. Today, they hold 16% of this market. A competitor said, "Van de Kamp's was smart. They spotted a category that had a history of quality problems and filled a void."

In the 1980s, Porkress decided to introduce another higher-quality and higher-priced line of frozen dinners—Mexican Classics. Later, the company added Chinese Classics and Italian Classics. To compete with the giants, the company is offering better meats, spicier foods, and unusual flavors. They are also charging higher prices. Van de Kamp management believes that these high-quality ethnic frozen foods, even though they are higher priced, will be the right recipe for success in this crowded market.

Product planning and product pricing are two critical management decisions. How do companies decide what products or services customers want? And how do they price their product or service? This chapter addresses how managers make these decisions.

PRODUCT PLANNING

Decisions about products depend on many factors, including: What do customers want? What do owners like to make? How much money is available? Do we have the technology? Do employees have the skills? How creative is the company? This section classifies different types of products, examines the product life cycle, describes the steps in new product development, reports methods of product identification, and discusses the importance of product differentiation.

What Is a Product?

Your first thought might be, "Why waste time with the definition of a product?" We know what they are: cameras, airplanes, shoes, candies, breakfast cereals, watches, pianos, electric shavers, rakes, and helium-filled balloons. You might even add sophistication to your answer and say that services are also products: razor haircuts, shoe shines, auto repairs, counseling, legal advice, and medical checkups. But these products and services exist beyond their physical characteristics. A hand-painted tie is certainly more than a neck napkin, platform shoes do more than cover feet, movies provide more than celluloid experiences, and cars are surely more than mere transportation. Thus, marketers identify three aspects of a product. The **tangible product** is the physical item or visible service a company offers to a buyer. You can touch fine underwear, smell freshly ground coffee, and taste juicy steak, to name a few examples. The **extended product** is a broader conception that includes packaging, services, financing arrangements, delivery alternatives, branding, labeling, and other things that customers value. The **generic product** comprises the intangible social and mental benefits that satisfy needs beyond the product's tangible functions. Perfumes are sex appeal, razor cuts are uptown, and steaks are status food.

Product Classifications

We can group products from chocolate-coated crickets to Smith and Wesson pistols into different classifications, according to consumer attitudes toward them. Since the products have varied features and appeal, special strategies are necessary for selling each. The two major groupings are consumer and industrial goods.

Consumer goods. Items purchased by the ultimate buyer are called **consumer goods.** We classify goods according to consumer buying habits into convenience, shopping, and specialty categories. **Convenience goods** are purchased quickly and often with minimal effort. Examples are magazines, milk, beer, cigarettes, candy, and most other items near checkout counters or in vending machines. Because they are inexpensive, conveniently located, often duplicated, and often bought on impulse, companies try to establish brand loyalties for convenience goods. **Shopping goods,** in contrast, generate much effort in comparing prices, quality, style, design, and service. Shopping goods include dresses, suits, shoes, and furniture. Buyers seek more product information because cost is greater. They meticulously go from store to store, noting prices, quality, and services. Shopping goods usually locate centrally because traveling a long distance deters shoppers. Brands are influential, certainly more so than they are for convenience goods; physical attributes of pricing and styling receive more attention. For **specialty goods,** the consumer knows exactly what he or she wants and makes every effort to find it. Examples are expensive cameras, shotguns, art objects, and some brands of clothing. The consumer acquires exhaustive information about the product and may travel miles to make a purchase. There are fewer retail outlets for higher-priced, brand-designated specialty goods. But price, effort, and shopping distance are secondary to distinguishing characteristics and particular brand preferences.

All products do not fit neatly into one of these three categories. What is a shopping good for one person might be a specialty good for another. Many items fit somewhere in between. Some buyers scrutinize all twelve eggs in a dozen, while others pick up the front carton.

Industrial goods. **Industrial goods** are items that companies purchase to make something else, which they will then sell. Unlike consumer goods, we classify industrial goods on the basis of use rather than buying habits. Raw materials include farm and natural products such as wheat, corn, cotton, lumber, silver, and coal. These become part of final products. Supplies are necessary for daily operations, but they do not become part of the finished product. Supplies include paper, typewriter ribbons, light bulbs, lubrication oil, brooms, and pencil sharpeners. Installations cover capital equipment that is instrumental in producing the final product, such as machinery, trucks, and production lines. Fabricated parts are partial or complete items that become part of the final product. Flour for cake mix, tires for automobiles, and leather for shoes are end products for some firms; for others these items are used to make the final product.

Convenience goods are purchased quickly, almost impulsively; offering such goods with other quick services is one outlet.

Product Hierarchy

Each product or service can also be related in hierarchical fashion to many other products. Professor Philip Kotler, in his *Marketing Management* text, identifies seven levels of the **product hierarchy.** Definitions and illustrations of this hierarchy are as follows:

1. *Item.* The distinct unit, product, or service that we can identify by size, shape, color, etc.: a personal computer.

2. *Brand.* The name that we associate with items in this line of products: IBM, Apple, Commodore.

3. *Product type.* The range of items that share similar characteristics: personal computers.

4. *Product line.* A group of products that are closely related and serve similar functions: microprocessors.

5. *Product class.* A larger group of products that serve the same basic functions: computers.

6. *Product family.* All the product families that tend to perform similar functions: information processing equipment.

7. *Need family.* The core needs that this line of product appeals to: efficiency, status, fulfillment.

Product Life Cycle

Like physical organisms, products pass through several distinct life stages, each of which produces unique problems and opportunities, calling for special strategies. Figure 13.1 depicts a **product life cycle,** the total sales from a product over a period of time. Both sales and profits move along a growth pattern of early struggle, rapid growth, stabilization, and decline. Of course, all products

**Figure 13.1
Characteristics of each stage of the product life cycle.**

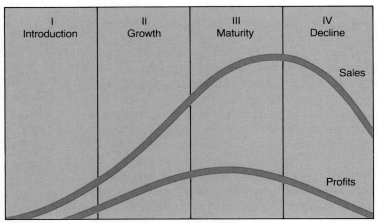

Sales and profits

Characteristic	Stage I	Stage II	Stage III	Stage IV
Sales	Low	Rising fast	Level	Declining
Promotional costs	High	Rising	Stable	Minimum
Profits	Lowest	Average	Too high peaks and declines	Average or below average
Cash	Starved	Hungry	Rich	Fair
Price	High	Declining	Lower and stable	Low, but may rise

do not follow this precise movement and some will continue to recycle through the steps, but it is a good model for developing marketing strategies.

Introduction. During its introduction, the product is new to the public, and sales falter while the company loses money. Customers have established purchasing habits and do not quickly change. The company meanwhile takes time to gear up to production capacity and devise distribution channels. Since the public is unfamiliar with the product, promotional expenditures are often very high. The company has to indicate the market with information to potential consumers and middlemen on product benefits. Prices are also high because of heavy development costs; sales overhead has to be spread over few products; production bugaboos mysteriously appear; and high promotion costs have to be borne. When Texas Instruments brought out their first hand-held calculator, prices were very high, running more than $100 for many models. Losses are common during the introduction period while the company gambles that its product will eventually be accepted. Mead Corporation spent more than $27 million over 6 years on its computerized information service, Lexis (which provides legal information), before finally making money in 1977. Three years later, Mead introduced Nexis (which provides general news) and expected it to be profitable by 1984.

Growth. If the product is accepted, it usually enters a rapid growth stage. Persuaded by advertising, word of mouth, and acceptance by opinion leaders, many individuals give the product a try. Because of greater sales, promotion costs per product sold become much less significant. Prices remain high in the beginning of the growth stage to recoup heavy introduction losses. During later growth, prices decline to fend off competitors who enter the field in a mad rush. Improvements are usually developed, and the firm vigorously penetrates its market targets. Because profits are rising, it is to the firm's advantage to prolong the growth period as much as possible.

The personal computer industry was in a growth stage during the early 1980s. IBM, Apple, and Radio Shack were holding strong; but many

Like most products in the introduction stage, Mead Data Central's Nexis, which provides computerized access to these publications, required time and extensive investment to establish itself as a profitable venture.

new competitors—Compaq Computer, Kaypro, Convergent Technologies—were flailing away at the market with differing strategies. Some old standbys like Osborne Computer bit the dust. Companies spent millions, $500 million in 1983 alone, on advertising and promotion. And prices began dropping as much as 20 to 40%, as specials and advertised sales became more widespread.

Maturity. Growth rates stabilize and eventually decline during maturity. Competition is intense, and pressure to reduce prices persuades some producers to get out. The maturity stage usually lasts longer than the introduction or growth stages. Customer loyalty to certain brands be-

comes well established, and sales are limited to repeat purchases by satisfied customers. Most competitors, fearing counteractions, spend about the same amount on promotions. They search for new messages, catchy phrases, and bright personalities. American Home Products Corporation is trying to establish a bond between some of its products and the persons advertising them. In 1983, it hired actress Patricia Neal to promote its well-known Anacin. The company believes that Neal, who recovered from a series of strokes, is associated with fighting pain. Another product, newer and not so well known, is Youth Garde, a beauty lotion. For good reason, American Home has hired actress Catherine Deneuve to promote this lotion.

TAKING STOCK

Time for NutraSweet

Aspartame is a natural sweetener that the Food and Drug Administration has recently approved for inclusion in consumer products. Although at $90 a pound, it costs thirty times as much as saccharine, it has the potential for taking much of saccharine's market share because the FDA still considers saccharine a potential health hazard. What's more, consumers, if not disturbed by the threat of saccharine's possibly causing cancer, dislike its bitter aftertaste.

Aspartame, better known by its brand name, NutraSweet, was already being used in hundreds of products in twenty-two countries by 1983. It has been approved for such American products as cereals, desserts, and table-top sweeteners. But the major market potential is the diet soft-drink area, which accounts for 23% of all soft-drink sales.

This sweetener, serendipitously discovered in 1966 by a researcher for G. D. Searle Company, might be the salvation for this old-line company that has had a lot of problems. In 1982, Searle sold $74 million worth of NutraSweet and they estimate that sales will go as high as $900 million by 1984 and account for about half of the company's total sales by 1985.

Searle's aspartame patent does not run out until 1992; and while there are competing sweeteners in the lab, they are years away from the marketplace. Robert Shapiro, president of Searle's aspartame operation, says, "The real test is are American consumers going to like this product? All implications are that the answer is emphatically yes."

Recent research, however, suggests that NutraSweet may chemically break down in warm climates to form methanol, a toxic substance. Equally disturbing are the reports of dizziness, menstrual irregularity, and convulsions suffered by people who have heavily used the product. Whether NutraSweet is the cause of these inauspicious side effects or not may take some time to discern. Meanwhile, Searle's NutraSweet is savoring sweet success.

Prices during the maturity stage are lower and relatively stable among competitors. After hand-held calculators entered the maturity stage, customers could buy one for less than $20 that would perform many more functions than the earlier, higher-priced models. Furthermore, attempts are frequently made to increase sales by adding slight improvements, developing new uses of the product, and concentrating on different market segments. This stage may experience cyclical spurts and declines as improvements take hold, quickly become imitated, and are improved again.

Decline. In the decline stage, the product fades as something new takes its place. Fewer firms produce the product. Businesses withdraw from smaller market segments and reduce promotion costs as they begin to accept the product's fate. Automobiles outpaced horse carriages, color television bedazzled black and white, and denims faded to prewashes. Companies differ in handling this period: some scurry off in a rush; others cling to a dead horse. Firms with strong brand loyalties are able to eke out a profit for some time, while less identified products drop quickly out of existence.

Some products move through the life cycle rapidly, others more slowly. CB radios for automobiles, now in the decline stage, enjoyed only 2 or 3 years in the maturity stage, whereas Coke has served many years in the maturity stage. Remember hula hoops? They spun through the cycle about as quickly as they spun around the torsos of those who bought them.

Some experts claim that the product life cycle concept is not much help because prediction is extremely difficult. But most say it is useful because the general model aids management in preparing competitive marketing strategies and planning for anticipated stages. Several products have been able to extend the maturity stage by making adjustments. Jell-O found new users for its products in salad molds and all types of diets. Jell-O also gained new users—especially among youth—with colorful displays and dressed-up advertising and packaging designs. Yet the basic product has remained unchanged for many years.

Marketers modify products to try to extend their life cycles in some of the following ways:

- Longer warranties
- Change the color
- Trademarks
- Change design
- Change advertising media
- Alter accessories
- Add accessories
- Change the size
- Change the package
- Different advertising
- Alter taste
- Lower price
- Relate to other products
- Extend credit

Stages in New Product Development

Because products eventually decline, companies are interested in creating new products. Researchers have identified six stages of product development or modification. At each stage, management decides whether to maintain or abandon the idea.

1. *New idea generation.* Every new product begins as an idea. Ideas flow from research departments, managers, salespeople, employees, customers, and the average person on the street. General Foods receives more than 80,000 spontaneous letters from consumers each year. To encourage idea generation, companies have to establish ways of stimulating and rewarding ingenious ideas.

2. *Screening.* While generation multiplies ideas, screening reduces them. Screening is the first decision stage and can be very costly. Some-

Prototypes of a new product (such as this interactive home videotex service) are often tested by experts as part of its development.

for safety, a new tea mix is tasted, and the fragrance of a new perfume is sniffed. Experts also look at the functional design, packaging, and possible brand or labeling aspects of their new product.

5. *Test marketing*. Next comes the adrenalin-producing, market-testing phase. For the first time, the company tests the idea by asking a selected group of consumers to pay money for it. The real test, then, comes when a company produces a limited number of the product, chooses a representative sample for its test market, and observes how the product sells. If sales justify their hopes, managers stand ready to jump into full-scale production. Some larger firms introduce products at a rapid rate. From mid-1982 to mid-1983, Procter & Gamble unveiled eleven test products. And at one point in 1983, they had twenty-two products in the testing phase.

6. *Commercialization*. Even with testing, new product failure is astonishingly high. Two out of three products still fail, about the same percentage as in the 1960s. For that small handful of products that do survive to this point, managers busily project sales, expand facilities, recruit needed labor, and search for capital to gear up for mass production and distribution.

In late 1983, after years of development and testing, Hattori Seiko Company entered the commercialization stage with the first wristwatch-type computer system. The system can calculate, retain memo data, carry out basic programs, and print out data. The watch unit, along with providing time, has a calendar, an alarm, and a chronograph. The price: $230.

Martin Friedman of the ad agency Dancer Fitzgerald Sample estimates a new brand must log first-year sales of at least $25 million to be considered a success. Only about 1% of new products that he tracts meets this qualification. Manufacturers, however, give themselves higher marks. In a recent Association of National Advertisers survey of 138 major marketers, 92 claim that at least 50% of their new products meet "key business objectives."

Not every new product traverses all these stages. A few managers prefer to reduce expenses by shortcutting one or more of the development steps. Some skip testing for fear they will tip off their competitors. The development cycle varies

times managers lack vision to see an idea's potential, or a company sends a bad idea into the analysis or production stage. Production managers or committees screen out ideas that do not fit company objectives, skills, and capabilities, or that would flop in the marketplace.

3. *Market research*. Market research is the systematic gathering of data regarding the market of a potential product. The information may include any or all of the following: (1) past sales of similar or competing products, (2) sales and industry trends of similar or competing products, (3) consumer tastes and buying motives of current products on the market, and (4) testing of new product features.

4. *Limited development*. The very few products that survive business analysis enter development on a limited scale. Products move from the idea stage or crude model phase to an actual, concrete product. A few sample products called prototypes are created for expert examination. For example, ski poles are tested

from a few weeks to several years. Figure 13.2 diagrams the product decay curve for new product ideas.

Product Liability

Rely, a superabsorbent tampon, was taken off the market in 1980 after it had been linked to toxic-shock, a sometimes fatal reaction to the product. Although different experts argued about whether or not the company was liable for the product, the manufacturer did, without admitting guilt, agree to settlements with some families of victims. In 1982, someone put cyanide poisoning into Extra-Strength Tylenol capsules in Chicago, resulting in several deaths. Though Johnson and Johnson, the parent company of the makers of Tylenol, still have lawsuits against them totaling $40.1 million claiming négligence, evidence may eventually prove that the company was not negligent. Still, product liability is becoming an increasingly important issue.

Just to what extent is a producer responsible for injury or damage caused by a product's use? Traditionally, most states have said that a manufacturer generally was not liable for defective products. However, this has changed in the past 10 years; today, courts are holding manufacturers and sellers responsible for injury or damage due to a product determined to be defective or unsafe, when the product was used as intended. Even if the product functions as intended, the producer may still be responsible if it appears that they overlooked problems in the design and testing of the item. And if misleading advertising causes damage or injury, this, in most cases, is a liable activity.

Product Rejuvenation

Because of the feeble chances of scoring a hit with a new product, many companies try to breathe new life into dying brands. Chester Kane, president of Kane, Bortee & Associates, a new-product consulting group, says, "There are dozens of older brands lying around that have been neglected over the years. Companies must discover ways to make them viable for today's consumer." Gillette is trying just that. Its Right Guard deodorant, which in the mid-1960s enjoyed 25% of the market, has today plummeted to a mere 8% of the market share. For the past 2 years, Gillette's marketing, R&D, manufacturing, sales, and finance departments have been meeting monthly to discuss a strategy for rejuvenating Right Guard. So far, they have settled on a boldly striped container and a huge $28 million ad campaign.

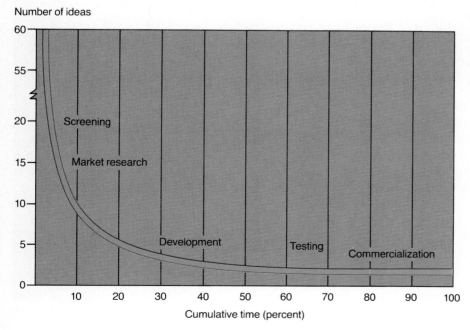

**Figure 13.2
Product decay curve for new product ideas.**
Source: Management of New Products, *New York: Booz, Allen, and Hamilton, 1968, p. 2.*

Product Identification

Because so many items vie for consumer attention, producers must create a means of identifying their products among countless others that share the shelves in shopping centers. Companies go to tremendous trouble to create worldwide identities; even a kindergartener can distinguish Coke from other soft drinks, spot a Sunkist at a fruitstand, or spy the distant red roof of Kentucky Fried Chicken. Indeed, identification decisions may be as important to product development as the actual product. Companies rely primarily on three means to identify and maintain product recognition: brands, packaging, and labeling.

Brands.   A brand name can be a name, song, symbol, design, or combination thereof to distinguish a product from other similar offerings. The **brand name** is the words or letters that identify the product. Xerox, Scotch tape, Coke, Kleenex, and Band-Aid are brand names. In fact, these particular names are so well known that they are rather close to becoming generic designations; that is, many people say Xerox when what they actually mean is photocopy, or Kleenex when they mean tissue (see Fig. 13.3).

The brand name becomes a **trademark** when the company gains legal protection as the only user. This allows companies to spend millions on promotion without worrying that someone else is copying the brand and taking advantage of promotional buildups. There are some 500,000 active trademarks registered at the U.S. Patent Office. And 25,000 new ones are added every year. Companies use brands to reach the following objectives:

1. *Standardization in the eyes of the customer.* From a customer: "I know that all Smucker's jellies are cooked to certain specifications. When I buy Smucker's, I know it will taste like Smucker's."

2. *Build brand loyalty.* From a marketing manager: "If we can get customers to identify and become loyal to our brand, we don't have to worry quite as much when the competition lowers its price." Familiar brands of aspirin like Bayer typically sell at higher prices than lesser-known brands such as Certified.

3. *Quick recognition.* From an advertising agency: "We try to develop instant recognition through sight and sound." For this reason, brand names are usually short, catchy, and easy to say. How many of the brand names can you match to the product in Fig. 13.4?

**Figure 13.3
Brand names — preserved and spoilt.** Source: "The Name of the Game," Donna Sammons, Inc., September 1983, p. 89.

Many companies have successfully preserved their trademarks, despite the fact that their brand names have become virtually synonymous with an entire product category and are often incorrectly applied to products made by other manufacturers.

Band-Aid (Johnson & Johnson)	**Q-tips, Vaseline** (Chesebrough Ponds Inc.)
Coke (The Coca-Cola Co.)	**Ritz crackers** (Nabisco Brands Inc.)
Formica (American Cyanamid Co.)	**Scotch tape** (3M)
Jeep (Jeep Corp.)	**Styrofoam** (Dow Chemical Co.)
Jell-O (General Foods Corp.)	**Technicolor** (Technicolor Inc.)
Kleenex (Kimberly-Clark Corp.)	**Teflon, Orlon** (E. I. Du Pont de Nemours & Co.)
Magic Marker (Berol Corp.)	**Windbreaker** (Men's Wear International Inc.)
Ping-Pong (Parker Bros.)	**Xerox** (Xerox Corp.)

Some of the most common nouns in the English language started out as brand names before going generic.

aspirin	escalator	**shredded wheat**
cellophane	kerosene	**thermos**
celluloid	lanolin	**yo-yo**
cola	milk of magnesia	**zipper**

Brand name	Product	Brand name	Product
Swiss Miss	_____	Mellow Yellow	_____
Gulden's	_____	Keebler	_____
Oscar Mayer	_____	Kretchmer	_____
Mueller's	_____	Era	_____
Mattel	_____	Trojans	_____
Jif	_____	Craftsman	_____
Jhirmack	_____	Technics	_____
Reunite	_____	L'Air du Temps	_____
Glidden	_____	Commodore	_____
Kohler	_____	L'Eggs	_____

Figure 13.4
How many of these brand names can you match to the product?

A **family brand** covers several products of the same company such as Hunt foods and Johnson & Johnson baby products. This helps reduce promotional costs by spreading expenses over a variety of products, and new products are cradled by promotion of previous products. **Individual brands** cover only one product, and a single company may have several. Individual brands can be used when a company chooses to market dissimilar products or goods of varying quality and cost. A company can separate its discount product from its more prestigious item via individual brands. **National brands** or manufacturer's brands are identified by the company that makes the product, and they are usually promoted nationally or worldwide. But large wholesalers and retailers put their own **private brand** on products they sell. The wholesaler or retailer buys the manufacturer's product and places its brand on them to develop store loyalty. More typically, the manufacturer produces the item to retailer specifications and identifies it as the retailer's product. Sears, Roebuck and J.C. Penney are two organizations that have developed their own brands. National brands of washing machines can be found in many stores, but you can buy a Kenmore only at Sears.

Packaging. The package does more than protect the product; it announces the contents with color, shape, and design. The package is considered a part of the product by producers. Package development may require many months, and more than $20 billion is spent annually on packaging, which makes it approximately as large as the automobile industry.

Since Henry Heinz meant for ketchup to be poured when he first introduced it in 1876, he packaged it in a tall, narrow-necked bottle. But in the 1960s, when consumers complained about how hard it was to get the ketchup out of the bottle, Heinz introduced a short, squat, wide-mouthed, 12-ounce bottle. It was not popular; the bottle never made it. People still wanted to pour ketchup over their food. But Heinz is trying again. They have agreed to buy from American Can Company six-layer, plastic, squeezable bottles for their ketchup. American Can says it is the perfect ketchup bottle. Consumers will be the judge of that.

About 65% of consumers' buying decisions are made at the store; thus product packaging is very important. The package must catch the consumer's attention and, as they say in the trade, "walk off the shelf." L'Eggs pantyhose, for instance, hit upon a very novel and successful idea when they packaged their hose in an egg-shaped plastic container with the brand name L'Eggs.

Philip Morris, the nation's biggest tobacco company, has launched a new brand of cigarettes called Players, packaged in an elegant black box. By deciding on black, the company is breaking a long-standing taboo against using what, for the tobacco industry especially, is regarded as a morose color. "The American brands are finally waking up to elegance in packaging," says Jerry Nestos of England's Dunhill cigarettes. Or, as one ad executive remarked, "They're creating extra value through the beautiful black box."

Still another innovation in packaging occurred when the Tylenol tampering case signifi-

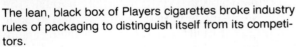

The lean, black box of Players cigarettes broke industry rules of packaging to distinguish itself from its competitors.

cantly altered packaging habits for over-the-counter medications. The Food and Drug Administration now requires that all capsules and liquid medications be placed in tamper-resistant containers. The package for Tylenol has triple safety seals: outer boxes with all flaps glued shut, plastic bands sealing bottle caps to necks, and inner foil seals over the mouths.

Even more recently food companies are packaging products in "retort pouches," sometimes called "flexible cans." The retort pouch is made of aluminum and polypropylene. After pouring food into these pouches, machines seal them airtight and heat them at very high temperatures. Kraft currently markets such products as sweet-and-sour pork, beef burgundy, and chicken milanese in retort pouches. The consumer can store the products on the shelf rather than in a refrigerator and simply pop them into a microwave for a few minutes when preparing them for serving.

Because packaging changes are very expensive to develop and easy to copy once developed, many packages remain the same for years. Since 1892, toothpaste has been sold in a tube, and the

6.5-ounce Coke bottle has been around since 1915.

Labeling. Labels are usually an integral part of the package and perform promotion and informing functions. Because promotional programs confused consumers with their vague use of "giant, king-sized, family-sized, and economy-sized," the **Fair Packaging and Labeling Act** was passed in 1966 to require that descriptions and package size be easily comparable among competitors. Several industries developed voluntary packaging and labeling standards: Toothpaste companies reduced their variety of sizes from fifty-seven to five. Federal legislation requires many clothing, drug, and food packagers to label fabric, chemicals, calorie count, and ingredients accurately. For example, the label on McCormick's Pure Vanilla Extract lists the ingredients as: vanilla bean extractives in water, alcohol 35%, and corn syrup. The label on Target's enriched skin care lotion is a little more complex, listing such ingredients as water, glycerin, mineral oil, stearic acid, glycol stearate, and twenty additional items.

Product Differentiation

Product differentiation includes all the ways that producers try to make their product different from others on the market. Differences may appear in product design, quality, packaging, labeling, pricing, or promotion. To differentiate themselves, McDonald's restaurants have a distinctive golden arch, what's more, they emphasize the freshness of their hamburgers and fries and the speed of their service. Even a city dweller can tell the difference between John Deere and International Harvester products at a distance: John Deere's tractors are green; International Harvester's are red. At one point, Irwin Publishing Company published all of their textbooks in a blue color. On a bookshelf with hundreds of books, the Irwin publications stood out.

Through product differentiation, sellers can develop recognition and loyalty for their products. Often, promotional programs contain a theme that highlights a product's distinctiveness from those of competitors. When Bounty paper towels wanted to stress that their product was more absorbent than competitors, their advertising showed pictures of their paper towel absorb-

ing more liquid than others. And they often repeated the catchy phrase, "the quicker picker
upper."

PRODUCT PRICING

After product development, managers face the
pricing decision. Economic theorists have long argued the ramifications of pricing and price
changes. Marketing managers treat pricing as a
decision commensurate with product planning,
distribution channels, and promotion. One study
of 135 successful firms ranked pricing decisions
sixth in importance behind research develop-

ment, sales research and planning, sales management, advertising, and service. **Price** is the value
given up in exchange for the item purchased.

So how should the price be set? To try to answer this question, we will examine some of the
pricing policies of firms and then observe how the
prices are quoted.

Pricing Policies

Even with an uncertain basis for understanding
and justifying prices, managers have to establish
policies for pricing decisions. Pricing policies
must be set for new products, promotions, product lines, odd pricing, flexibility, and markup.

CROSS FIRE

Competition in the Coin-Operated Telephone?

The breakup of AT&T has caused a lot of uncertainty in the phone business. One of
Ma Bell's few remaining strongholds, the coin-operated telephone, is also currently
under seige. Robert Albertson, president of Tonk-a-Phones, Inc., is selling alternative pay phones called Tonk-a-Phones.

The phones are mechanically a little different from Bell phones. But the biggest
difference is cost and possible benefits to owners. If, for example, someone owned
an apartment house and installed a Bell phone, the owner would have to pay to have
the line installed. When phone users dropped their coins into the phone to make calls,
the Bell system would collect the money. However, with the Tonk-a-Phone, the
customer would pay for the phone, the installation, and the hookup — a cost of about
$650 — but the revenues and profits would go to the phone's owner. In other words,
the apartment owner could make a profit off the phone much like he or she might
make a profit off coin-operated washers and dryers in the complex.

As you might expect, local phone companies are fighting this approach. Phone
companies argue that the pay phone is a public service and it could deteriorate under
deregulation. And some companies have pulled the plug on business lines connected
to non-Bell pay phones. President Albertson says that allowing his and other companies to sell pay phones where the owner keeps the revenue is just good free enterprise. And he adds that service will get better rather than deteriorate.

Do you favor the position taken by local phone companies or the position taken
by Albertson of Tonk-a-Phone?

____ A. Local phone companies   ____ B. Tonk-a-Phone

Do you think the government will eventually force local phone companies to
maintain business lines to non-Bell pay phones? Why?

____ Yes   ____ No

New products. One of the toughest pricing decisions concerns new products because the price has so much to do with their success or failure. And the lowest price is not necessarily the best price. Companies face two types of new product pricing decisions: penetration pricing or skimming pricing. With **penetration pricing,** the product usually comes out with a lower price than the firm maintains for the long run. A lower price may mean better market acceptance. After promotion establishes some brand loyalty, prices may be raised. The low price has the advantage of discouraging early competition, but brand loyalty must be strong if it is to overcome dissatisfaction with later price increases. Customers are particularly enraged by large price hikes.

The opposite policy is to set a **skimming price,** a high price, and capture just a small share of the market. This policy assumes that the firm will later have to reduce the price in the face of competition. Ballpoint pens first came out at about $20 each; the top seller now goes for around 19 cents. Mercedes Benz introduced its Model 190E to the U.S. market at a price of $24,000. This is more than double the $10,601 price tag for the same model sold in West Germany. Mercedes Benz, practicing a skimming philosophy, continues to price their products using a high-margin strategy because, as they say, it has produced "profits that have got to be phenomenal." Table 13.1 shows other German and U.S. automobile price comparisons. Market skimming prices hold several advantages. They allow the company to recover its investment more quickly and acknowledge that price reductions are better received than increases. The major problem with skimming is flocking competition, which may force the firm to drop its price before it planned to.

TABLE 13.1 ■ EXAMPLE OF A SKIMMING STRATEGY

Make and Model	German Price	U.S. Price
Mercedes Benz 190E (sedan)	$10,601	$24,000
Mercedes Benz 300TD (stationwagon)	$13,157	$33,850
Mercedes Benz 380SL (sports car)	$23,620	$43,822
BMW 318i (sedan)	$ 8,483	$16,430
Audi 4000 (sedan)	$ 6,062	$10,205
Audi Coupe	$ 8,313	$13,105

Promotional pricing. **Promotional pricing** is similar to new-product pricing. It may be used to introduce a new product, regenerate interest in an old product, or focus on a good seller. Promotional prices are lower for the sake of advertising one product or another in the company's line. This approach is often used at retail levels; a store will price some items very low to entice customers into the store, hoping they will buy other items at regular prices. This strategy is based on the fact that customers can only remember a limited number of prices on widely advertised staples like coffee, sugar, and milk. The philosophy used is that keeping these prices low will develop customer loyalty. Although promotional pricing can have the advantage of drawing attention to a product, it may violate fair trade laws in some states. Also, the artificially lower price may become so fixed in the customer's mind as to prevent a company from ever raising it without undue resistance.

Product-line pricing. Most firms sell several products and their aim is to develop a pricing mix for their total merchandise that helps them achieve company goals. This approach is superior to pricing each product in isolation. **Price lining** identifies a limited number of prices for merchandise. A shoe manufacturer sells one style of shoe at $19.95, another type at $24.95, and a still fancier shoe at $49.95. There are no prices between these lines. This simplifies pricing decisions and adds consistency because each product does not require the agony of a completely separate decision. The major problem is again the difficulty of adjusting established price lines in the face of consumer awareness. Price lines may be a prime factor in creating a company's image; to change it by adjusting several prices upward simultaneously hampers the entire product line's reputation.

Odd pricing. Some companies quote their merchandise at various prices for psychological purposes. **Odd pricing** (also called **psychological pricing**) is quoting just under the next highest dollar figure. For instance, $19.99 sounds like a savings compared to $20. There is an even more sophisticated concept: Since prices ending in .95, .98, or .99 are the custom, some retailers end prices with threes and sevens, such as $8.93 or $6.97, because they believe the customer thinks these are discount or bargain prices. There is little research to indicate just what impact odd pricing has on consumers, but it has become a tradition in the last few years. One of the original purposes of odd pricing was to force clerks to be conscious of giving correct change. But the additional record keeping, working with odd figures, and totaling the numbers might more than offset any advantage.

Flexible pricing. What is the policy on price flexibility? Will the product be sold at one price to all markets, or will variable pricing develop as the result of individual or retail bargaining? In U.S. retailing, one price is common because of mass markets and mass purchasing; the customer either takes or leaves the quoted price. For some items such as automobiles, furniture, and expensive jewelry, where customer outlay is great, prices may vary according to size of purchase, inventory level at the moment, or the customer's bargaining ability. Flexible pricing is more common in the large-scale consumption of industrial markets. Industrial customers usually make large purchases, but some buy smaller; some are long-time customers, others newly arrived. These factors affect the price. Flexible pricing allows the company more latitude; it can show concern and feeling for the consumer. But some purchasers will be angry when they find that another buyer negotiated a better price.

Gasoline wholesalers, as noted in this Exxon TV ad, have been providing cash discounts directly to customers of their retail outlets to discourage use of credit.

Markup pricing. **Markup pricing** adds a certain percentage to the actual cost of the product. This method is popular in retailing. For instance, a firm might decide to mark up its jeans 50%. Thus, if the store paid $16 for the jeans, they would sell them for $24 (50% $\times$ $16 = $8, and $16 + $8 = $24). Some restaurants mark up canned soft drinks as much as 100%.

Price Quotations

Describing prices is an art and depends upon many factors. Price quotations become part of the information about the product, a portion of the promotional package, and must be understood for intelligent, competitive purchasing.

List prices. Prices normally quoted to purchasers, listed in catalogs and on invoices, or shown on price tags in the store are list prices. This is the beginning stage of price identification and for many items remains the final purchase price.

Price discounts. When buying from wholesalers or manufacturers, purchasers sometimes pay a discounted price that is lower than the catalog price. Retailers are given **cash discounts** when the purchaser buys on terms and pays promptly. Terms such as 2/10, net 30 mean that the purchaser has 30 days to pay the bill but receives a 2% discount for paying within 10 days. These discounts normally occur between suppliers and manufacturers or between wholesalers and retailers. Such terms are not usually available for the ultimate consumer. The **trade discounts** are unique in that they are given to buyers who perform some of the functions the manufacturer normally performs. The list price might be 100%, but when the manufacturer sells to wholesalers, asking price may be 40% of the list price to pay for the wholesaler's services.

Transportation pricing. Part of the product's price rests in transportation. If the items are enormous and bulky, the transportation charges are likely to be considerable. For most volume purchases in retail outlets, the price reflects transportation costs. But for large, hard-to-handle items, various alternatives exist. **F.O.B.** factory or F.O.B. origin indicates that the buyer will pay all freight charges and the seller will load the merchandise, but the price reflects what the item costs at the manufacturer's location. This allows buyers the choice of how they cover their transportation. If they are a long distance from the origin, transportation costs may prohibit the purchase. Opposite to F.O.B. is **uniform delivered price** where the buyer pays the same price, which includes transportation, regardless of how far products are shipped. Buyers who are a long distance from the origin pay less freight cost per mile, but this is averaged out by purchasers located closer to the origin who pay a "phantom freight" — or higher freight cost per mile. Uniform delivered price is used mostly for small items or where a market is concentrated. **Zone pricing,** a modification of uniform delivered price, means producers divide their market into geographic zones and establish the same charge within each zone. Mail-order houses usually vary their price in different sections of the country to absorb relative freight charges. This flexibility makes transportation costs more equitable.

SUMMARY

Effective marketing departments concentrate on systematic product planning and pricing. All products can be classed into consumer goods or industrial goods. Consumer goods are purchased by the ultimate consumer, and producers buy industrial goods to make their products. Each product also can be related to other products in hierarchical fashion.

Product sales and profits follow an S-shaped life cycle growth pattern. After the introduction stage, products typically, if they are successes, begin to sell very rapidly—the growth stage. Next, in the maturity stage, growth rates decline. Finally, in the decline stage, sales and profits begin to drop off. Profits are usually highest toward the end of the growth stage and in the maturity stage. Advertising and promotion strategies also differ as the stages change.

As new products develop, they pass through stages of new-idea generation, screening, business analysis, limited development, test marketing, and commercialization. Courts are holding product manufacturers and sometimes sellers liable for damage or injury when the product was used as intended by the consumer.

Firms try to identify their products with brands—names, songs, symbols, designs, etc.—that distinguish the product from similar offerings. Brands help standardize the product, build consumer loyalty, and offer quick recognition.

In packaging, a $20 billion plus industry, firms protect the product and try to announce the contents with color, shape, and design. Product labels may help in promotion as well as in describing the contents of the product. Pricing policies serve as guidelines for consistency and work with other factors of the marketing mix. Policies usually address such concerns as pricing new products, promotional pricing, product-line pricing, odd pricing, flexible pricing, and markup pricing. Actual price quotations take the form of list prices, price discounts, and transportation considerations.

MIND YOUR BUSINESS

Instructions. Test your knowledge of product planning and pricing by designating the following statements true (T) or false (F).

____ 1. Marketing people consider packaging, services, and intangible aspects to be a part of the product.

____ 2. Magazines, candy, and milk are examples of specialty goods.

____ 3. Profits are highest during the introductory stage of the product life cycle.

____ 4. Price is usually highest during the maturity stage of the product life cycle.

____ 5. All new products pass through six stages of development.

____ 6. Both manufacturers and sellers of a product can be held liable for injury or damage when the product is used as intended.

____ 7. Strong brand loyalty allows producers to charge a higher price for their products.

____ 8. The sole purpose of packaging is to protect the product.

____ 9. Most managers follow the same policy when pricing new products.

____ 10. Product-line pricing and odd pricing are the same thing.

See answers at the back of the book.

KEY TERMS

REVIEW QUESTIONS

1. What, specifically, is a product? What is not a product?

2. Discuss the two major classifications of products. How do they differ?

3. Identify and give an example of the seven levels in a product hierarchy.

4. What are the four major aspects of a product life cycle? Explain how sales, promotional costs, profits, cash requirements, and prices vary at each stage.

5. Explain each of the stages in new product development.

6. Describe product liability. What are its implications for producers and sellers?

7. What are the four major methods used in product identification?

8. How do the pricing policies of new products differ from those of existing products?

9. What is product-line pricing?

10. Give some examples of odd pricing. Is it common in your area? If so, present some specific examples from your local newspaper.

11. The chapter presents three major types of price quotation. Discuss each and give some examples where each may be used.

CASES

Case 13.1: Price versus Taste

For the past 10 years, Dr. Pepper has been a major seller in the soft drink market, rising out of towns in the South and Midwest to compete in major markets across the country. Until recently, the giants — Coca-Cola and Pepsi, who control 55% of the soft drink market — ignored the small company based in Dallas. But now the big two are fighting back. Coca-Cola is particularly upset because about 25% of its bottlers have opted to distribute Dr. Pepper instead of its own cherry soda, Mr. Pibb. Still, W. W. Clements, the chairman of Dr. Pepper, believes that the company can double its profits and earnings every 4 years for the immediate future.

Questions

1. What is the importance of pricing for soft drink products?

2. How do soft drink manufacturers differentiate their products?

3. If you were going to develop a new soft drink, outline how you would go about it.

Case 13.2: The Pricing Decision

A mobile home manufacturer produces a single model, the Streamline. It sells this line through dealers at a retail price of $12,000. Because of the company's reputation for quality, dealers have been asking them to produce a higher-priced mobile home. The company decided to produce the line and is trying to decide what price range to target for.

It will take about $150,000 to get set up to produce the new line, and they can produce the product at about $8000 per unit. Their plant capacity allows them to produce only about 800 additional units per year; if they produced more, they would have to expand their plant. The company showed their new model at a mobile home fair, and visitors expressed a strong preference for the design over all other competitors.

Preliminary market testing suggests that retailers could sell the product at a retail price of about $16,000, about 10% above the major competitor's model. Managers in the firm are arguing about the pricing policy they should take. The marketing manager wants to price the model to their dealers at about $15,000. He says they have a good product and they should try to get as much profit as they can while their design is new. The general manager is afraid that this strategy would alienate some of the dealers, and she believes it is a good idea to maintain dealer loyalty. She argues for a price to dealers of about $13,000. This would allow the dealers to make a little more profit, and they could lower the price a bit if they needed to. While the manufacturer would not make as much profit per unit, the general manager believes that dealer loyalty is more important than quick profits.

Questions

1. Do you tend to agree with the marketing manager or the general manager? Why?

2. In general, do you think it is best to price high when you have a design advantage, or do you think you should price lower and try to build long-term commitment from dealers and consumers? Why?

3. What other things should be considered in the pricing decision?

After completing this chapter, you will be able to:

■ **Diagram four marketing channel alternatives.**

■ **Identify five kinds of channel flows.**

■ **Explain four factors that managers should consider when making a channel selection.**

■ **Describe three kinds of direct marketing channels.**

■ **Explain the functions of middlemen.**

■ **Explain vertical marketing systems.**

■ **Comment on horizontal marketing, multichannel marketing, and channel conflicts.**

■ **Explain the objectives of physical distribution.**

14

DISTRIBUTION
CHANNELS

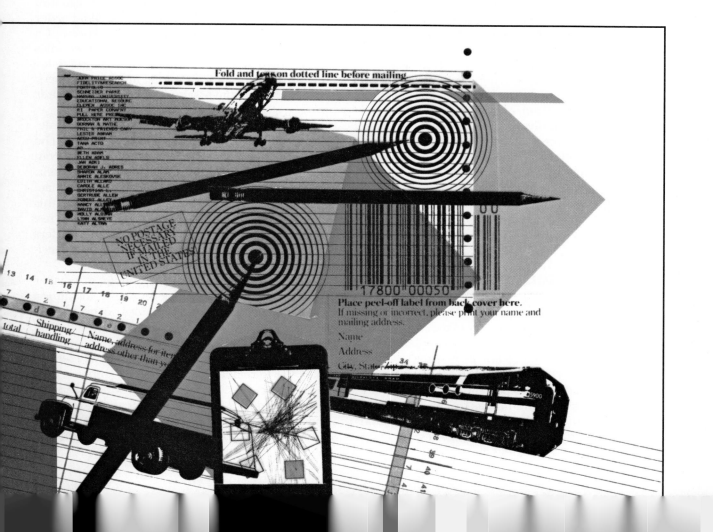

**W**hoever controls the channels of distribution controls the market," says James Lally, partner in a high-tech venture capital firm. In the first half of the 1980s, there were as many as 150 personal-computer manufacturers, each trying to get their 10% of the market. However, there were not enough dealers to handle the products from all these manufacturers.

With any mass consumer product, marketing and distribution becomes as important as research and development. As the sheer volume of personal computers began to clog the market, it was not enough to have a better product at a lower cost. Dealers could only handle, at most, three or four different brands and still know something about them. Although IBM was not the first to introduce a personal computer, they became the top seller in 1983. Of course IBM had a good product, but their mastery of distributing and marketing is what gave them their key advantage.

Today, instead of relying solely on their legendary direct-to-the-customer sales force, IBM is selling more and more small systems through new channels: industrial middlemen, independent retailers (ComputerLand, Sears), and its own retail outlets (IBM has more than forty stores and will build at least as many more by the end of 1983).

Getting the product from the producer to the user (that is, creating place utility) involves channels, middlemen, and physical distribution.

CHANNEL DECISIONS

A **distribution channel** is all the institutions that perform the activities necessary to move the product and its title from producer to consumer. Channel decisions are important to marketing managers because: (1) they affect all other decisions once the channel is fixed, and (2) they usually imply long-term commitments to a particular distribution method. Normally, it takes years to build a channel and, once built, it is not easy to alter.

Effective marketers evaluate channel alternatives to achieve the best results for their firm.

Channel Alternatives

The simplest channel flows goods from producer to consumer; this direct channel, or zero-stage channel, has no intermediaries. Some vacuum cleaners, encyclopedias, cosmetics, mail-order items, or roadside vegetable stands represent a direct channel. Less than 5% of consumer sales travel this route, but it is the most popular for industrial goods. For example, heavy machinery manufacturers have salespeople who visit user firms.

A one-stage channel contains one intermediary, usually a retailer in consumer goods. The most-used process is a two-stage channel from producer to wholesaler to retailer to consumer. Thousands of small and medium-sized manufacturers who produce limited lines feel that this channel best suits them. Smaller producers use the expertise and financial support of wholesalers to find their markets and take specialized distribution functions off their hands.

When there are a great number of smaller companies, they might use an agent, forming a three-stage channel. An agent does not take title to the goods but finds a wholesaler for them. The meat packing industry uses another three-stage channel, which goes from producer to wholesaler to jobber to retailer to consumer. A jobber orders from wholesalers, accumulates products, and distributes them to retailers not accommodated by the regular wholesaler. In the industrial market, the three-stage channel might be termed manufacturer to agent to wholesaler to industrial user. Figure 14.1 diagrams these channels.

Forms of Channel Flows

In addition to moving the physical product through channels to the consumer, a firm must also move title, payment, information, and promotion materials through the channels.

Physical flows. Physical flows refer to ways the physical products move from producer to user. For large items such as automobiles, manufacturers usually ship the cars via truck to dealers who then sell to the user.

Title flows. The actual passage of the title from one marketing institution to another is the title flow. In some cases, the manufacturer holds the title even though the product is in the hands of a retailer. In other cases, the title may pass to the dealer and then to the user when he or she buys from the dealer.

Payment flows. How does the payment get from the ultimate purchaser back to the pro-

ducer? This is called payment flow, and it may take several forms. For instance, when a customer buys an automobile, he or she might borrow money from a credit union. Thus, the payment flow would be from the customer to the credit union, to the dealer, to the manufacturer.

Information flows. Information flows describe the way information is exchanged between the marketing institutions in the channel.

Promotion flows. The promotion flow pictures how advertising, personal selling, and the like move through the channels. (Promotion is covered in more detail in the next chapter.) In some cases, the manufacturer might advertise to channel institutions or promote directly to the ultimate purchaser.

Channels for Services

Although not exactly the same, sellers of services must also create place utility for the user. Unless the service is provided at the right place, consumers will not buy the service. For example, banks provide a service. As people moved away

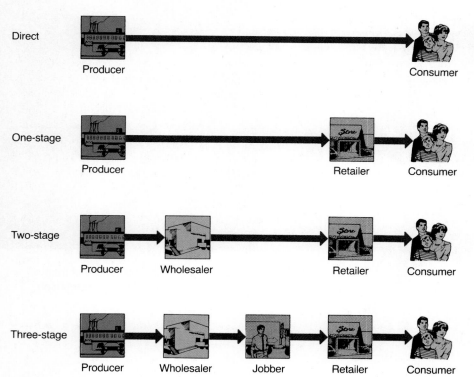

**Figure 14.1
Examples of channel
alternatives.**

Direct — Producer → Consumer

One-stage — Producer → Retailer → Consumer

Two-stage — Producer → Wholesaler → Retailer → Consumer

Three-stage — Producer → Wholesaler → Jobber → Retailer → Consumer from downtown areas, banks began to build branches in outlying neighborhoods so their service would be convenient.

Selecting Channels

Although it is hard to change channels, managers do not select only one channel and stay with it forever. As conditions change, they have to adjust.

Goods often travel through several channels simultaneously.

Often, their goods travel through several channels simultaneously. Newer or smaller companies nearly always rely upon middlemen. As companies grow and markets expand, they face a diversity of methods for moving their products. Channel selection involves characteristics of the consumer, product, company, and middlemen.

1. *Consumer.* Of foremost concern is the consumer. Channels will be long if there are large numbers of customers, if customers are geographically scattered, and if they purchase goods in small quantities. It becomes very costly for a producer to perform all the functions in a long channel, so he or she calls on channel intermediaries, specialists in transportation, storage, and handling who operate more efficiently. When consumers are clustered and buy in volume, channels shorten.

2. *Product characteristics.* Many product characteristics directly affect the channel-selecting decision. Perishable products, such as fresh fruits, live lobsters, and jelly rolls, dictate direct channels by their nature. Custom-made products usually go from manufacturer to user because of design specifications communicated between them. Items needing special service or maintenance, such as technical machines and equipment, typically have shorter channels. Companies producing goods of high unit value often hire their own salespeople to move these products; control is thus maintained over handling, and individual attention can be given in training. Standardized

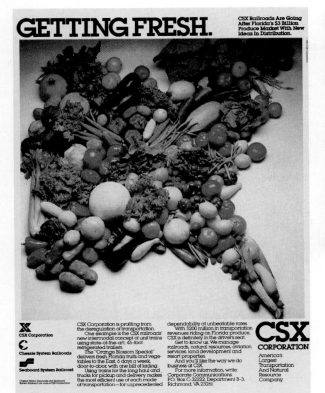

As this ad suggests, the perishable nature of fresh fruits and vegetables helps dictate a rail distribution channel.

products require less individual attention and travel longer channels.

3. *Company characteristics.* Financially strong companies can more easily develop their own sales forces for shorter channels. Weaker companies rely on commission payments to intermediaries who are better able to absorb inventory costs and customer services such as credit. Middlemen can combine deliveries for several companies that produce only one product. If a company manufactures a large variety of products, it can market directly and spread distribution costs. Increased service and individual attention require more direct channels of middlemen willing to represent company policy to customers.

4. *Middlemen characteristics.* The middleman is involved in many ways: the number of locations, transportation methods, facilities, customer services, transactions, and cost of delivery. Middlemen must be able to perform these functions more cheaply than the manufacturer. Producers also consider middlemen's attitudes toward sharing part of the advertising burden. Will they allow the company to train their salespeople? How interested are they in the company's product? What standing does the company's product assume in relation to other items they handle? Most important, will they do a good job with the company's product?

DIRECT MARKETING

Direct marketing is moving the product from producer to consumer through direct channels. Although most producers use multistage channels, direct marketing is increasing. The most common forms are mail-order, telephone, and door-to-door. Television marketing is on the way.

Mail-Order Marketing

In 1983, direct marketers bombarded consumers with nearly 6 billion copies of 5000 catalogs. But unlike the thick, general-purpose, traditional Sears and Montgomery Ward catalogs, most of today's models are sleek and specialized.

The *Epicurean Delights* catalog from Neiman Marcus is thirty-two pages of food as an art form.

A chile wreath, plum pudding, Italian flat bread, and chocolate popcorn are among the items you can order. The *Aztech* catalog from Aztech Electronics, Inc., in Springfield, Missouri, lists over 150 electronic items, ranging from stereos to Mickey Mouse telephones. Another catalog offers nothing but weather vanes and sundials — 14, four-color pages of them, and another offers only nuts — pecans, peanuts, and mixed varieties.

The more traditional department stores have also gone to specialty catalogs. Spiegel, the nation's fourth-largest mail-order retailer, offered its first speciality catalog in the spring of 1983. A test issue, specializing in lingerie, went to 300,000 homes. The result: 7500 orders, averaging $80 each. Sears, Roebuck has issued twenty-four specialty catalogs, and Bloomingdale's issued fourteen in 1983 alone.

Specialty-catalog publishers use computers to advantage. If a customer buys a bathing suit at Saks Fifth Avenue, she is likely, in a short time, to receive a catalog of bathing suits. The computer tracks purchases, puts customers' names on the proper lists, and addresses the labels. Soon, the catalog is in the mail. Some companies also purchase mailing lists from other sources. Sears bought names of pregnant women from doctors and hospitals to mail catalogs for infants.

Companies also shower tons of direct-mail pieces on consumers each year. Some direct mail may promote a particular item such as a book or a training workshop. Other direct-mail pieces fold out in several directions and actually resemble small catalogs.

Why the increased emphasis on this form of direct marketing? There are several reasons. As John Shea, vice-president of Spiegel, puts it, "You don't want to waste time running from store to store on Saturday to find they don't have your color or size." Direct marketing is easy for the consumer, who simply flips through the catalogs at leisure, perhaps while visiting with a friend, and makes an order — either by returning the order blank or calling an 800 number and charging items. Another reason direct marketing is becoming more important is the larger number of women working at paid jobs who have less time to shop. Third, people buy from catalogs when there is no local store in the area: Most people do not live near a Bloomingdale's or a Saks. The catalog creates a form of place utility. Finally, marketing through direct mail is sometimes cheaper. The specialty catalogs aim for a well-defined target market and reach a lot of people at a low cost per person. According to the Direct Mail/Marketing Association, the use of direct marketing methods will become even more important in the future.

Telephone Marketing

In a recent report issued by the Distribution Research and Education Foundation (DREF), the ratio of field salespeople to inside telephone salespeople is shifting. By 1990, the report concludes, telephone salespeople will amount to 50% of the average wholesale distributor's sales force. In 1980, the figure was 30%. At Louisiana Oil & Tire Co., all ten of the traveling salespeople were brought inside and put at a bank of phones. Since then, the company's phone bill has increased by $6000 a month, but other sales expenses have de-

clined by $15,000 a month. More important, says Gregory Martin, sales manager, is that sales have doubled.

Firms shied away from telephone marketing for awhile, and public sentiment was also against it. In fact, some groups, claiming that it was an invasion of privacy, proposed laws to ban or limit it. However, firms are finding they can establish the same rapport over the phone as they did with eyeball-to-eyeball selling.

"Telemarketing isn't just how to talk on the phone," says a telephone consultant. It may take 3 to 6 months before a program starts to pay off. Success depends upon: (1) an analysis of which accounts can best be sold by telephone and which accounts require hand-holding, (2) knowledge of company policies and product lines, (3) extensive training in telephone techniques, and (4) a good personality. The phone seller must be enthusiastic

---

TAKING STOCK

Trouble in the Direct-Marketing Industry?

During the first six months of 1983, Mary Kay Cosmetics' stock price plunged 65% in value. The main problem at Mary Kay, and for the whole direct marketing industry, is the inability to attract new recruits.

Much of the success of Mary Kay and similar direct sales companies comes from hiring new recruits. The new recruits typically have good sales for awhile; then sales drop off, and many of the recruits quit. So, without a successful recruiting program, direct marketing firms like Mary Kay, Avon Products, Inc., Dart & Kraft, and Tupperware face stagnant sales. A sales director for Mary Kay in Dallas says that she is attracting only about five recruits a month, compared to ten a month a year ago.

There may be several reasons why these direct-marketing efforts are having trouble. More women are working full-time; thus fewer are available to work in direct marketing. Also, because of divorce and changing life-styles, the extended family of relatives and friends is not as stable as it was to provide day-care. And direct sales jobs are less attractive during economic recoveries when more salaried jobs become available.

However, according to a spokesperson, Mary Kay is planning "to fly right in the face of the problem" by quadrupling the 1984 recruiting budget. The firm planned to take all of its 1984 promotional and advertising budget and pour it into recruiting. Part of the money will provide greater financial incentives to people who bring new recruits on board. No doubt, this effort will help; but a long-term problem for direct-marketing companies is the increasing number of steadier jobs available in other fields for women.

Source: Dean Rotbart and Laurie P. Cohen, "The Party at Mary Kay Isn't Quite So Lively, as Recruiting Falls Off," *The Wall Street Journal*, Friday, Oct. 28, 1983, pp. 1, 12.

enough to create interest and thick-skinned enough to handle dozens of rejections per day.

Door-to-Door Marketing

Perhaps the oldest form of direct marketing is door-to-door, or on-the-premise, selling. Here, a manufacturer's representative visits customers at their homes. Historically, we have associated this form of direct marketing with World Book Encyclopedias, Fuller Brush, Avon cosmetics, and Tupperware parties. All these companies have used this channel to great advantage. More recently, Amway and Mary Kay Cosmetics have made millions of dollars through door-to-door sales.

Currently, **multilevel marketing,** a process that uses levels of people with each person moving a small amount of product, is in vogue for door-to-door selling. In multilevel selling, salespeople get commissions for the products they sell. And if they hire others to sell products for them, they also get a small commission on what the people they hired sell. When people they hired hire someone else, the salespeople get a part of their commission also. Thus, there is a strong incentive to hire people to sell under your supervision and to encourage them to hire people to sell under them.

Salespeople for Mary Kay Cosmetics, called "beauty consultants," pay $20.75 for their beauty kits, and they sell them for $41.50 — a 100% markup. However, the big incentive comes from recruiting other consultants. If a consultant recruits eight others, Mary Kay pays the original consultant 8% of the sales of all of his or her recruits. If the original consultant finds as many as twelve recruits, he or she achieves the title of "director," and gets 9 to 12% of recruits' sales. If a director and her recruits exceed $72,000 in sales in a 6-month period, the director gets the use of a pink Cadillac.

Although multilevel marketing has been around since 1944, it did not achieve acceptability until 1979. In that year, the Federal Trade Commission challenged Amway Corporation, saying their multilevel marketing operation was illegal. Amway won. Now, this rapidly growing field has about 1000 companies with annual sales between $5 and $7 billion. Rick Walsh, copublisher of *Multilevel Marketing News* magazine, says, "It is the fastest growing merchandising industry in the U.S." One consultant says that several of the Fortune 500 companies are looking into it.

Television Marketing

After years of study, companies are beginning to offer sales and services through a combination of a telephone line, television set, and computer. Videotex systems offer consumers home access to shopping, banking, and a wide variety of computer information. Viewtron, a system developed by the Knight-Ridder newspaper chain, allows subscribers to shop electronically at more than 100 South Florida retailers. A purchaser simply looks through the color pages of an electronic catalog, displayed on the TV screen, and presses buttons to order something. The fee to the subscriber is $12 per month plus $1 in telephone charges for each hour of use. Initially, the subscriber must purchase a special terminal made by AT&T, called Spectre; the cost is $600.

To boost their catalog sales, J. C. Penney has already made arrangements with Knight-Ridder to link into the Viewtron system. Viewtron users, in addition to shopping, can also view the national news or get scores from a local little league, plus lots of other information. They can check the money in their bank accounts, transfer funds from one account to another, and pay bills.

Experts predict the revenues from television marketing will range between $4 and $30 billion by 1990.

Knight-Ridder plans to sweep the country with this technology if Viewtron does well in its test in the Miami area. Other firms, including Field Enterprises, The Times Mirror Co., and Chemical Bank, are poised in the wings ready to go. And in early 1984, three corporate powerhouses — IBM, Sears, and CBS — announced a joint venture to develop a nationwide commercial videotex service for households with personal and home computers. Albert Gillen, president of Knight-Ridder's Viewtron, called the venture "a vote of confidence in the videotex market." No one knows what the television marketing industry will amount to, of course; but experts predict that revenues will range between $4 and $30 billion by 1990.

Combined Methods of Direct Marketing

Some firms apparently are combining direct marketing methods. Telephone salespeople may make calls to prospects and follow up with direct mail. Or before a company tries to sell via telephone, they may send direct mail to a client, which might include the salesperson's picture along with catalogs and brochures.

And more companies now provide salespeople with computer terminals. From the terminal, the salesperson can get a wealth of information, such as inventory available, price, order status,

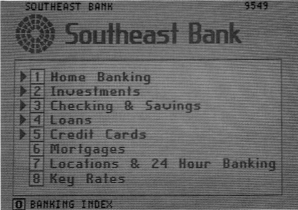

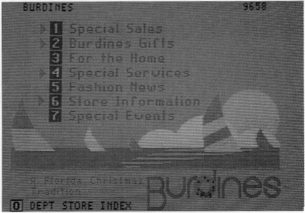

Knight-Ridder's Viewtron offers a number of services, as is shown by these photos of a terminal screen.

Electronic Shopping

Electronic shop-at-home services, where customers look at video screens and make their purchases by punching keyboards, is another form of direct marketing. Publishers, banks, and retailers are about to begin selling services that enable people to make purchases, check bank balances, and even buy and sell stocks — all without leaving home or talking to a human. The consulting firm of Booz, Allen, and Hamilton ran a two-year test on electronic shopping and concluded that electronic retail sales will total $50 billion by 1995.

Others are not so euphoric. An executive for a large video shopping system says, "The number of people who are going to change their behavior because of a technological change is small. To say that technology is going to make dinosaurs of retail stores is a little silly."

Although most are expecting electronic sales to grow, it does have some drawbacks:

1. Many shoppers enjoy the social interaction of a purchase. Video purchasing eliminates this.

2. Although video technology may present pretty good descriptions and in some cases images of the product customers are about to buy, it is not like seeing the product.

3. The systems require capital investments. For example, Knight-Ridder's system, called Viewtron, uses a special terminal that costs $600.

4. It is harder to shop around for the best deal.

The biggest problem, however, as James Holly, head of the Times Mirror system, laments, is that "the cost of providing this service to the consumer far exceeds what you can get from subscribers." So, despite the optimism of some, electronic shopping still has a few glitches.

Source: "Electronic Shopping Is Called Imminent, but Doubts Persist," *The Wall Street Journal*, June 23, 1983, and "Coming Fast: Services Through the TV Set," *Fortune*, November 14, 1983, pp. 5–56.

characteristics of the customer, previous customer activity, and perhaps the customer's nickname. With a handy terminal, a telephone salesperson can provide a lot more information to the client and get it there quicker.

FUNCTIONS OF CHANNEL MIDDLEMEN

Marketing channels are the province of **middlemen,** those institutions that handle goods between the producer and ultimate consumer. Middlemen are very important since well over 90% of goods move through their hands. Often the comment arises, "Middlemen drive up the prices. Why do we need them?" Middlemen aid in distributing products by performing the following functions:

1. They undertake many storage costs, assume the risk of price changes in storage, and provide a convenient means of storage.

2. They assume some of the financing burden by selling on credit and financing inventories while they hold items in storage.

3. They transport items.

4. They gain efficiency through volume transactions.

Figure 14.2
How your meat dollar is spread between rancher and middleman. *Source: U.S. Department of Agriculture.*

Rancher gets 58¢   Retailer keeps 28¢   Packer/transporters keep 8¢   Wholesaler keeps 6¢

5. They gather information from the marketplace.

6. They search out and communicate with prospective buyers.

Such services cost money. According to the U.S. Department of Agriculture, the rancher gets only 58 cents of a dollar from sale of beef; the remaining 42 cents goes to middlemen to perform the functions just described. Figure 14.2 shows how the middlemen divide the 42 cents. Studies show that middlemen are often responsible for 40 to 59% of the markup. But, does eliminating the middlemen reduce the cost to the purchaser? Not necessarily.

If producers eliminated middlemen, then producers would have to perform these channel functions. If Wrigley chewing gum were not sold through channel middlemen, the company would have to establish its own gum stores throughout the country, or else they would have to sell door-to-door or via direct mail. Either of these methods would no doubt drive up the price of gum. If General Motors decided to eliminate middlemen, they would have to build more storage facilities, buy delivery trucks, hire more laborers, build or buy dealerships, and add to their sales force. Middlemen are specialists in what they do, and they typically can perform these functions more efficiently than a producer. Two major channel institutions are wholesalers and retailers.

Wholesalers

Wholesalers market products between producers and retailers or between producers and other wholesalers. They ordinarily do not sell directly to the ultimate consumer. Over 300,000 wholesale establishments exist with sales totaling over $500 billion annually. Some manufacturers with huge volumes operate their own wholesale facilities. Others have branch outlets and sales offices far from the central office to provide many wholesale functions. Some smaller firms developing new territories use independently owned public warehouses as storage facilities. Independent wholesalers operate as a separate business entity and account for some 55% of the wholesale establishments and almost 70% of the wholesale sales in this country. Two categories of independent wholesalers are merchant wholesalers and agent wholesalers.

Merchant wholesalers actually take title to the goods. **Full-function merchant wholesalers** offer a full complement of functions to the producer: They store goods, maintain a sales force, make deliveries, and extend credit. Costs may go as high as 20% of sales. They are especially helpful to small retailers who carry inexpensive items such as hardware, drugs, and some groceries. **Specialist wholesalers,** known as rack jobbers, emerged with supermarket development to provide their own racks, stock merchandise, and deliver to retail outlets. **Limited-function merchant wholesalers** do not offer a full array of wholesale functions. **Cash-and-carry wholesalers** developed during the depression to try to reduce costs. Retailers pick up goods at wholesale warehouses and pay cash for the items. Several specialists have emerged among merchant wholesalers.

Agent wholesalers never take title to their goods, although they may assume possession. They are usually more specialized than merchant wholesalers, with an emphasis on bringing together buyers and sellers. Three major categories of agent wholesalers include brokers, selling agents, and manufacturers' agents.

Brokers bring buyers and sellers together; they represent either the buyer or seller, but not both, and collect a fee from their client. Brokers perform very few services because they operate on a less stable basis. They are effective in industries with a large number of small suppliers and purchasers, like real estate or frozen foods. **Selling agents** are usually responsible for the total marketing program of a firm with full authority over pricing and promotions. They may have exclusive rights to a company's products. They exist as independent marketing departments and provide their expertise to the small manufacturer. Selling agents thrive in textile, coal, and lumber industries. **Manufacturer's agents** are independent salespeople working on a commission. They may represent several companies. This agent develops efficiency by combining a list of many non-competing items and spreading the distribution costs over several of these items.

Retailers

A **retailer** sells the product directly to the end user. About 97% of all consumer sales take place in retail stores. The general store became the first important retail institution although it was preceded by traveling peddlers who sold their wares or remedies across the country. The general store included truly one-stop shopping, handling everything from beans, drugs, and candy, to feed, rakes, cloth, and guns. A few survive today, primarily in rural areas. A few major examples of retail outlets consist of department stores, specialty shops, chain stores, and discount stores.

Somewhat like their general-store ancestors, the **department store** handles everything. Macy's in New York City has over 400,000 items in 168 departments to serve 150,000 customers per day. Most shopping centers include department stores. Some of the most famous are Marshall Field, Rich's, and Neiman Marcus. **Specialty shops,** or limited-line stores, stand opposite department stores and zero in on a special marketing segment. They offer great choice but within a limited category of products. Specialty shops concentrate on shoes, cameras, sporting goods,

Sears, Roebuck is currently the largest retail outlet in the world; their sales exceed the gross national product of many countries.

cheeses, stationery, or books, to name a few. **Chain stores** consist of two or more commonly owned and managed stores handling similar products. They try to gain the advantages of volume sales. Even though chain stores make up only 10% of all stores, they account for about one-third of retail sales. Chains dominate in variety stores (80% of sales), department stores (75%), and shoe stores (50%). The Mitsui was a chain store operated in Japan as early as the 1600s. Sears, Roebuck is currently the largest retail outlet in the world; its

BUSINESS BULLETIN

K Mart's New Image

K Mart Corporation, the nation's number 2 retailer with 2160 stores, is trying hard to upgrade its polyester-palace image. While older shoppers are still buying from K Mart, management is worried that they are not getting enough action from 25- to 44-year-old shoppers.

Like Sears, Roebuck and Co., J. C. Penney Co. Inc., and Montgomery Ward & Co., K Mart has embarked upon a major remodeling and image-building campaign. Their purpose is to get their share of the younger customers who want quality products and are willing to pay a little more to get them.

Management has allocated $2 billion to create in-store "boutique" layouts. The company has already added 500 Kitchen Korners with shiny molds and butcher-block cutting boards. Additionally, the stores are adding home electronic centers, home care centers, clothing boutiques, and bed and bath shops. More designer goods and name brands are also appearing in K Mart stores, including such well known names as Wrangler, Sasson, Black & Decker, and Copco. And, finally, management is experimenting with some financial services. Its Florida stores are already selling certificates of deposit and money market funds, and the stores in Texas and Florida sell insurance.

K Mart was very successful in appealing to the lower-income shopper, and the company does not want to give up this market. They simply want to add lines that will appeal to the shoppers looking for higher-quality items.

Summarized from Lorraine Cichowski, "No. 2 Retailer Putting on New Image," *USA Today*, Friday, April 20, 1984, p. 1B.

sales exceed the gross national product of many countries. After World War II, a number of **discount stores** emerged when marketers believed that customers would gladly sacrifice some store services in order to pay less for goods. So discount stores opened with reduced prices but no delivery services or credit, and with fewer sales clerks. As discount stores attracted attention and grew to over 10% of all retail stores, they added some of the previously cut features and services such as carpet and credit, moving toward full service. They now tend to deemphasize the discount trademark and carry as many services as possible.

Catalog showrooms allow customers to come to a showroom where they can see sample items of the products advertised in the catalog displayed. After selecting the products they wish to buy, customers wait only a few moments while store employees retrieve the product from a back-room warehouse. Safeway, Kroger, and A&P are examples of **supermarkets** — large departmentalized stores that offer a wide variety of food and food-related products. Supermarkets have, in recent years, expanded into other items such as delicatessens, computer sales, books, and even clothing items. Smaller stores located at easy-access locations that offer basic food and food-related items are called **convenience stores.** Examples include 7-Eleven and Quik-Trip. Finally, **factory outlets** offer merchandise to the consumer directly from the factory. Customers can buy items such as furniture, food, and housewares directly from factory-owned outlets usually for a cheaper price.

A few changes are occurring in the retailing system. There has been a decentralization from downtown and movement toward suburban centers, commensurate with population shifts. To counter this, downtown construction in such cities as Minneapolis, Houston, and Kansas City is again attracting retailers. Some predict that moves to shopping centers may be slowing and even turning around.

The clear-cut lines of retail distinction are being muddied by the concept of **scrambled merchandising** — stores adding products they normally do not carry: Drugstores sell milk, gasoline stations offer food, and food stores carry automobile accessories.

Retail trade has become concentrated in a few large-scale retailers. Countering this trend is the growth of specialty and subspecialty shops.

Specialty shops, like the Bell System's Phone Stores, offer a wide choice within a limited product category.

Vertical Marketing Systems

Traditionally, channel members emerge and negotiate agreements without an overall plan. However, **vertical marketing systems (VMS),** well-planned and coordinated distribution networks, have emerged to become a force in the channels. In fact, they are the most common means of distribution in the consumer goods area. Three types of VMS are popular.

Corporate VMS. **Corporate vertical marketing systems** combine stages of production and distribution under single ownership. Kroger, the supermarket, owns thirty-three manufacturing plants and a fleet of trucks. They make over 15% of all the prepared food they sell through their supermarkets. Sears owns many of the producers that supply its stores, and Sherwin-Williams operates thousands of retail outlets.

Administered VMS. Members in an **administered vertical marketing system** are able to achieve cooperation in the production and distribution stages because of the strength of one of its members. Because they are so large and powerful, companies like General Electric and Procter & Gamble can get unusual cooperation from channel members on such issues as shelf space, pricing policies, promotion, and the like.

Contractual VMS. In a **contractual vertical marketing system,** independent firms are able to achieve cooperation at different production and distribution levels via contractual agreements. Sometimes a wholesaler will make an agreement with a group of retailers to cooperate on promotion, pricing, and the like. These are called **wholesaler-sponsored voluntary chains.** Other times, a group of retailers will get together and organize themselves to form **retailer cooperatives.** Franchising agreements also link together various production and distribution stages.

Horizontal Marketing Systems

Horizontal marketing systems (HMS) occur when two or more companies agree to pool their efforts to take advantage of a marketing opportunity. Neither organization may have the know-how, capital, or connections to get the product to the user efficiently. However, between them, they might be able to do it. When Pillsbury Company developed its refrigerated doughs for biscuits and cookies, they realized that they did not know enough about the special, refrigerated displays that these products required. Since Kraft Foods had experience with refrigerated displays in marketing their cheeses, Pillsbury reached an agreement with Kraft to distribute their product.

Multichannel Marketing

Some companies try to reach the same or different markets with more than one channel system, called **multichannel marketing.** J. C. Penney operates three types of retail outlets: department stores, mass-merchandising stores, and specialty stores. Levi Strauss & Company sells its jeans through traditional department stores, specialty stores, Sears, and J. C. Penney's, and the prices may not be the same in each of these outlets.

Channel Conflict

As you might expect, there is often conflict between channel units. When Levi Strauss began selling their jeans to Sears and J. C. Penney's, Macy's discontinued handling them. Gap Stores, Inc., another group of retail stores, severely reduced their Levi product line. Some producers who depend heavily upon dealers also sell directly to the consumer through catalogs or via telephone. Thus, customers might use a dealer to educate themselves about the product and then order the item directly from the manufacturer at a lower price. Of course, dealers bridle at such producer practices.

Producers also create conflicts with channel members when the producer disapproves of dealer practices. An auto manufacturer might drop a dealer if the dealer does not follow the manufacturer's guidelines on service and promotion.

PHYSICAL DISTRIBUTION

After the channels are set, marketers must move the product from the producer to the user. The objectives of physical distribution are to get the product to the right place at the right time at the least cost. Physical distribution is important because the cost of storing and handling the product may run as much as 20% or more of their net sales.

In selecting carriers, companies consider cost, speed, convenience, product safety, storage facilities, and reliability. Table 14.1 identifies the advantages and disadvantages of the major types of transportation.

Air is the fastest and, as you might expect, the most expensive. Rail is usually cheapest, but rail

TABLE 14.1 ■ ADVANTAGES AND DISADVANTAGES OF VARIOUS SHIPPING METHODS

Mode of Transportation	Speed	Cost	Product Safety	Convenience	Storage Requirements
Plane	Best	Most	Best	Fair	Few
Truck	Fair	Moderate	Poor	Best	Many
Ship	Poor	Low	Poor	Poor	Many
Train	Poor	Low	Poor	Poor	Many
Pipeline	Good	Moderate	Good	Poor	Many

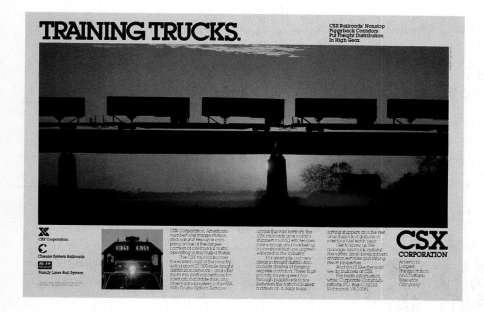

"Piggyback" combinations
exploit the relatively low cost
of rail and the convenience
and flexibility of trucking.

does not always go to the buyer's location. Many
times, shippers use a combination of methods for
convenience and reduced costs. But most shipments today go by truck, at least for some part of
their journey.

Many shipments combine two or more means
of physical distribution. For example, a canned
goods factory may load crates into a trailer for
Safeway. A crane lifts the trailer onto a railroad
flatcar. After the train carries the Safeway trailer
to a regional destination, the trailer will be un-
loaded, and a truck will haul the trailer to distribution stores. Such a combination is called **piggyback. Fishyback** is a similar combination of
truck and water service, and **birdyback** combines air and ground travel service.

Containerization, packaging of products by
the producer in large-bulk containers that can be
moved easily by heavy equipment, is a new trend
in physical distribution. This method reduces
manual labor costs, provides flexibility in shipping methods, increases speed of delivery, and
reduces damage.

SUMMARY

Effective channel management is necessary to get
goods and services to the user effectively. A distribution channel consists of all of the institutions
that perform activities that move the product and
title from producer to user. Some channels are
direct from producer to consumer, but the most
popular is a two-stage channel including a wholesaler and retailer. In selecting channels, firms consider customer needs, product characteristics,
company characteristics, and middlemen characteristics.

Direct marketing is moving the product directly from the producer to the user. The most
common forms are mail-order, telephone marketing, and door-to-door sales.

Channel middlemen perform specific functions, including storing, financing, transporting,
volume transactions, information gathering, and
seeking prospective buyers. Usually, the middlemen, because they are specialists, can perform
these functions more efficiently than the producer.

Wholesalers market products between producers and retailers or between producers and
other wholesalers. There are many different
types of wholesalers, each performing different
middlemen functions. Retailers sell the product to
the ultimate user. Vertical marketing occurs when
firms plan and organize their distribution functions in systematic ways. Horizontal marketing
occurs when two or more firms agree to combine
their efforts to exploit an opportunity. Many firms
use many different channels, and there is often
conflict between channel members.

Physical distribution involves all of the activities needed to physically move the product from producer to user.

MIND YOUR BUSINESS

Instructions. Respond to the following questions by answering yes or no in the blanks at the left.

_____ 1. Is the most widely used distribution channel a direct channel?

_____ 2. Is the passage of title to goods part of the channel flow?

_____ 3. Do characteristics of the product influence the channel-selecting decision?

_____ 4. Are catalogs becoming more general than they were in the past?

_____ 5. Is telephone marketing decreasing in volume?

_____ 6. Do middlemen sell directly to the ultimate consumer?

_____ 7. Do agent wholesalers take title to goods?

_____ 8. Does the sale of most goods take place in retail stores?

_____ 9. Do administered vertical marketing systems achieve cooperation in the marketing channels because of the strength of a member?

_____ 10. Is distribution by plane the most convenient mode of physical distribution?

See answers at the back of the book.

KEY TERMS

REVIEW QUESTIONS

1. What is a distribution channel? Describe the alternative channels available to marketers.

2. Identify five forms of channel flows.

3. Briefly comment on the channel for services.

4. Explain four factors firms consider when making decisions on what channels to use.

5. Define direct marketing. Discuss three common forms of direct marketing.

6. Define middlemen. Describe the functions middlemen perform.

7. Define wholesalers. Identify the various types of wholesalers.

8. Define retailers. Identify the various types of retailers.

9. Define vertical marketing systems and describe three types.

10. What is horizontal marketing? Multichannel marketing?

11. Explain the nature of channel conflict.

12. What are the objectives of physical distribution?

CASES

Case 14.1: American Can's Direct Marketing Strategy

American Can, in addition to its packaging operations, is engaged in specialty retailing and financial services. They signed a letter of intent to purchase Michigan Bulb Company, a mail-order garden supply firm, in 1984. Management of American Can said they wanted to move more into the service side of the economy and particularly into specialty retailing. Their people think that is where continued growth in the economy will be.

American Can, under their specialty retailing sector, already owns Fingerhut and Figi's, a specialty food and gift marketer, and Musicland, the retail stores that sell records, albums, and tapes. Michigan Bulb, which sells 120 garden and nursery products through the mail, will join these firms as part of American Can's specialty retailing.

Questions

1. What are the advantages and disadvantages of American Can diversifying into specialty retailing?

2. Do you think American Can's strategy of getting into specialty retailing is wise? Why?

    ___ Yes   ___ No

3. Do you think American Can's purchase of Michigan Bulb Company will prove to be a wise decision? Why?

    ___ Yes   ___ No

Case 14.2: Practices of a Large Retailer

In 1982, Kroger purchased Dillon's supermarket chain and became the largest supermarket chain in the United States. Sales totaled about $14 billion that year.

Kroger does not hesitate to close down stores that are not profitable; in fact, they have already closed 1237 supermarkets. They operate 1199 food stores in 19 states, plus another 560 drugstores. Last year alone, Kroger closed 65 stores in its Market Basket division in Southern California.

Kroger is also going for large size and additional volume. They have added 12 million square feet of supermarket floor space in the last 10 years, and the average-size Kroger store is 11% bigger than Safeway and 38% bigger than A&P.

Kroger can also be tough on unions. In Pittsburgh, a local chain won wage rollbacks from its union. Kroger demanded the same from its union; when they balked, Kroger threatened to close seven stores and stop construction on five others. Earlier, Kroger's union had refused similar demands in another state, and they sold their twenty-one stores in that state.

Questions

1. Do you agree with Kroger's policy of closing stores that are not profitable? Why?

    ___ Yes   ___ No

2. What do you think about Kroger's emphasis on large-sized stores?

3. How do you feel about their strategies for dealing with the union? Why?

    ___ Strongly agree   ___ Agree

    ___ Disagree   ___ Strongly disagree

After completing this chapter, you will be able to:

■ **Identify five objectives of promotion.**

■ **Identify how firms try to measure promotional effectiveness.**

■ **Explain how firms determine their promotional budgets.**

■ **List and describe the seven steps of personal selling.**

■ **Explain eight advertising strategies.**

■ **Analyze six common forms of advertising media.**

■ **Discuss three criticisms of advertising.**

■ **Describe six sales promotion techniques.**

15

PROMOTION, ADVERTISING, AND PERSONAL SELLING

Soft-drink producers are waging a promotion, advertising, and selling war to gain part of the soft-drink consumption market. Coca-Cola, introduced in 1886, was the first successful soft drink. And for many years, consumers could choose only Coke. Now Coca-Cola company offers Tab, Diet Coke, Caffeine-Free Coke, Caffeine-Free Diet Coke, and Caffeine-Free Tab. In addition, competitors offer a variety of other brands: Pepsi Free, Sugar-Free Pepsi, Dr. Pepper Free, Sugar-Free Dr. Pepper, Salt-Free Diet Rite Cola, Like, Pepsi Lite, and on and on. Figure 15.1 identifies the cola family tree.

According to a bottler, the soft-drink explosion happened because we live in a society where "people want a lot of different things." Because of the large market (Americans drank an average of 419.5, 12-ounce servings in 1982), the wide variety of products available, and differences in consumer preferences, the success or failure of a new cola depends heavily upon promotion, advertising, and selling techniques. As a promotional manager described it, "We try to instill in consumers' minds images that will make them want to buy the product."

To better understand how managers communicate their images to consumers, we examine in this chapter promotional mix, personal selling, advertising, promotional devices, and public relations.

PROMOTIONAL MIX

Promotion is any activity that encourages the purchase of a good or service. Managers must determine how much they are going to invest in promotion and what tools they will use. The **promotional mix,** or plan, utilizes personal selling, advertising, and sales promotion to deliver the message. Public relations and all types of publicity that attract customer attention to the product also become part of the mix. The mix depends upon the product, the life cycle stage, and how the product is sold. The more alike the products, the more promotions differentiate among them in the early life cycle stages. Promotion is most important in the product's introduction and maturity stages. In introduction, the market is unaware of the product and therefore uninterested; promotion must overcome ignorance and generate interest. In the maturity stage, competition is stiff, and the promotion must show how a product is different or unique. Promotional mix policies are affected by promotional program objectives, implementation strategies, evaluation of program effectiveness, and the promotional budget.

The Objectives of Promotion

The key objectives of promotion are to:

Provide information. Promotion must inform the market about what is available, the characteristics of the product or service, and how to use it. For instance, Panasonic's ad for their voice-activated microcassette recorder tells customers that their product starts recording automatically when someone starts talking. And it also stops when they stop. Further, they claim, its playback is 30% faster than others; and because it has two tape speeds, owners can record for two hours on a one-hour microcassette.

Stimulate sales. Obviously, companies want to stimulate customers to buy their products and services. Promotion tries to get consumers to recognize, look for, examine, try, and purchase the product. In advertising their personal computer,

TeleVideo Systems, Inc., begins an ad with, "Here's what makes it irresistible. . . ." Then they stress the product's easy-to-use features to entice you to try it; and to stimulate you to purchase it, they close their ad with, "So why resist?"

Highlight values. Status-oriented advertising to highlight values makes sure customers are aware of what the company considers to be a real value. Canon, the first company to produce a low-priced personal copier, stressed the high-quality copy

that people could make conveniently in their homes. They also showed buyers how to produce color copies and described their removable cartridge, which made it unnecessary for the user to worry about adding fluids.

Differentiate between products. Somewhat related to highlighting values is product differentiation—letting consumers know how a product or service is different from that of competitors'. Few consumers can differentiate be-

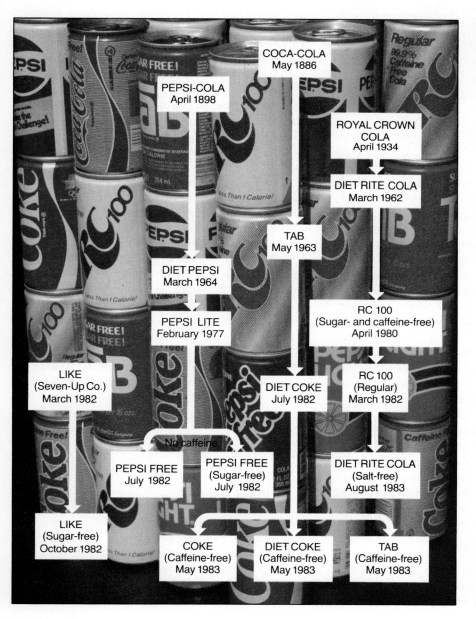

Figure 15.1
The cola family tree.
Source: Copyright Wichita Eagle-Beacon, reprinted with permission.

Eye-catching colors and the status of a designer's name can be effective in differentiating a product line from that of the competition.

tween the effectiveness of many similar products or services. Digital, trying to differentiate itself from IBM in the personal computer market, began offering a free, one-year, on-site maintenance contract to anyone who purchased a Digital personal computer through a retail outlet. Digital also announced a 30-day cash guarantee for all of its equipment. A spokesperson said they could have tried to differentiate by lowering the price; instead, they chose to add enhancements and customer protection. Similarly, since most consumers cannot distinguish between the effectiveness of many soaps, perfumes, shampoos, and the like, promoters try to make these different with color, shape, and packaging.

Stabilize sales. Since consistent sales will help to smooth production output, some promotion attempts to create sales stabilization. In the middle of the summer, Gragg's Furs, an independent retail store, advertised their furs at prices reduced up to 40%.

Implementation Strategies

The promotional program pulls the product through the channels by stimulating ultimate consumer use. Customers shop for and request products and otherwise pressure retail outlets, who in turn pressure wholesale institutions to deliver the products. This **pull strategy** relies heavily upon advertising and public relations. Early in Elvis Presley's career, backers effectively used a pull strategy to sell his records. After he became known, he would appear on television and sing a number not yet released. Avid fans would look for the record, request it, sign waiting lists, and give their orders well in advance. This sent retail record stores scurrying to make sure they could pull the record through the channels from the producers.

The reverse, or **push strategy,** happens when producers work on channel members rather than the final user. With heavy emphasis on personal selling, producers try to make wholesalers and retailers aware of their product's benefits and how successful it will be. Producers stimulate interest in the channel with sales persuasion, dealer supports, trade discounts, and advertising allowances; channel members then take the incentive to convince the ultimate consumer of the product's value.

Federated Department Stores, Inc., is struggling with product differentiation. The store has added a lot of designer labels and discount items, and management fears that they are losing their unique identity. Their solution is to develop high-quality merchandise that carries a higher profit margin and is different from competitors'. For example, they brought out a line of sheets and towels under the brand name "Home Concept." Through their ads, they will try to promote the differences between their stores and others.

These strategies represent two ends of the continuum. Actually, most promotional plans use both pull and push pressures, although one may be highly featured.

Measuring Promotional Effectiveness

A haunting question for promotional experts is how well does the program work? Is it causing people to buy the product? Promotion research is costly and cannot isolate the variables well enough to be positive of the results. Still, managers have to measure effectiveness so they can decide whether or not to continue. The direct-sales approach is the most desired and addresses the question of how much the promotion increased sales. Suppose the company undertakes a $3 million advertising campaign over a 2-year period, and sales increase by 30%. Because of multiple variables, we will never know for sure how much sales would have increased without the program, or whether the direct-sales approach actually caused increased sales. Perhaps the price, competitors' actions, economic conditions, or change in consumer tastes had a greater impact than the promotional plan.

Other evaluation points use indirect methods. Some research tries to measure potential customer **readership;** how many people actually saw the promotion and were aware of it? Researchers test **recall** by interviewing or sending questionnaires to people to see what they can remember about the advertising program: the brand name, the price, how it is used. While research can measure these variables reliably, companies still do not know if recall and readership translate into sales. Customers can be informed and impressed with advertisements and still not purchase the product.

The Promotional Budget

There is no definitive answer to the question, "Just how much should we spend on promotion?" Several methods are used to determine

---

The most common way of allocating a promotional budget is percentage of sales.

budgets, and industries have developed guidelines for using each method. The most common way of allocating a promotional budget is percentage of sales. Managers may take last year's sales or next year's projections and designate promotion to be 5% of either figure. Others set aside a fixed sum for advertising, which does not vary directly with sales. Producers of high-cost items, such as cars or appliances, tend to use this fixed-sum method. Another promotional budget strategy is to keep up with the competition: Try to estimate what the competition is doing and match it. While this keeps competition from getting too far ahead, it is a passive strategy and probably does not relate to promotional objectives. The more recent task-objective method identifies program goals and estimates how much must be spent to accomplish these goals. Using this method, Pizza Hut spent several million dollars developing, testing, and promoting their very successful "5-minute" pizza. While this is more analytical and objective, it fails to project just how much must be spent to reach the objective. Suppose a promotional objec-

CROSS FIRE

Trade Promotions

Often, producers give wholesalers and retailers special discounts for promoting their products extra hard, to encourage them to provide desirable shelf space, and the like.

A supermarket may carry fifty different soft drinks. A single display at the front of the store can increase a product's sales by sixfold. So supermarkets may entertain bids from different producers to see who will give them the best price discount.

When a manufacturer gives a retailer a discount, the producer usually requires special treatment in return for the discount. For example, they might require the retailer to pass along some of the discount to customers, feature the product in local newspaper ads, or place the product in a special place within the store. Producers then follow up to see if the retailers kept their part of the deal.

Currently, there is a debate going on between manufacturers and retailers over trade discounts. Retailers say that manufacturers are trying to reduce their trade discounts and increase their profits at the expense of retailers. Manufacturers say that retailers often refuse to pass along the discounts to customers, and retailers have fattened their own profits at the expense of the manufacturer and the customer. Further, because competition is so fierce among producers, they may offer huge trade discounts without getting much benefit from them. Retailers tend to overstock during the discount period; thus, many months pass before they have to start buying at list price. Still, there will likely be little drop-off in this type of promotion in the near future. Do you believe trade promotions benefit the consumer? Why?

____ Yes   ____ No

Do you think manufacturers should increase or decrease the use of trade promotions? Why?

____ A. Increase   ____ B. Decrease

Source: Monci Jo Williams, "The No-Win Game of Price Promotion," *Fortune,* July 11, 1983, pp. 92–102.

tive is to increase sales by 10% during the year. We do not know how much to spend to generate this increase. Also, some promotional expenditures create proportionately larger shares of revenue than others.

While the last method is more objective and more active than the others, most decisions rely upon considerations of all these. The budget is still largely a matter of subjective judgment. It boils down to what someone in power thinks is appropriate.

PERSONAL SELLING

Nothing much happens in business until someone sells something. In our society, salespeople comprise more than 6 million employees, and selling costs average between 10 and 15 cents of each sales dollar. **Personal selling** occurs when a person interacts with one or more people with the purpose of promoting a good or a service.

Much of the stigma attached to the selling profession originated with nineteenth-century pitchmen who hawked novelties and medicines on street corners and in bare barns.

Much of the stigma attached to the selling profession originated with nineteenth-century pitchmen who hawked novelties and medicines on street corners and in bare barns. With magic, music, and jokes, they drummed up attention and attracted crowds for the pitch. They also used animals, monkeys, lizards, and burning money. One ingenious method developed by a pitchman called for a rope, the Bible, and a human skull. He would lay out these strange props and, with care and concentration, begin to rearrange them until a fascinated crowd gathered around him. This continued for a half hour or so after the crowd gathered until he felt his audience was ready. Then he launched into a lecture on his "medicines," never once mentioning the rope, skull, or Bible.

Pitchmen were able to hypnotize a crowd with oratory, giving their explications the intensity of a mystic. Many items they sold had no function, and some were harmful. The epitome of the pitchman was shown in the delightful musical *Music Man*. But there were a number of legitimate sales travelers or drummers in this era. Modern sales, composed primarily of professional salespeople, emerged in the late forties as the economy returned to normalcy after the war. As Arthur Miller's play *Death of a Salesman* depicts, we have turned the corner from the days of riding the smile and the flamboyant orator to the professional, knowledgeable salesperson who knows the product, consults buyers, helps with ordering, and advises on service calls.

Professional Selling

Professional salespeople know their companies, their products, competitors, customers, and themselves; they are professional communicators. Professional selling is an educational process. Salespeople have four primary responsibilities: creative selling, missionary selling, order receiving, and feedback.

Creative selling perhaps draws upon the energy of the old-time drummers in making the product come alive to the prospect. The purpose is to dramatize product appeal, product uses, and customer benefits. Professional salespeople stop short of the pitchman's final phrase, "If it doesn't cure you, prepare to meet your Maker!" But creative selling does appeal to intangible needs and buying motives. When selling to industrial users, a more logical approach is in order.

Missionary selling is indirect; it focuses on building goodwill and a positive company image. Follow-ups with customers, extra efforts to be sure they are satisfied, special attention to service, and technical and expert assistance on the continuing use of goods are classified as missionary selling.

Many wholesalers and retailers emphasize order receiving. Much catalog selling is order receiving in person or over the telephone. Salespeople who primarily receive orders also take positive action by identifying and inventorying stock and recommending order sizes. They can be especially helpful in smaller retail outlets by advising how much to order, how best to display the goods, and even recommending markups. In this way, missionary selling combines with order receiving.

Finally, professional salespeople are an excellent source of feedback for the company. Using their close relationship with the purchaser, they can relate feelings, emotions, and hunches on how the market is moving, which even well-designed research may not unearth. Although some salespeople tend to operate in one mode or another, most professional sellers employ all these activities.

Selling Steps

The actual selling process has been discussed and researched for some time. While authorities vary their models slightly, there are several identifiable activities or subprocesses in the personal-selling process. These activities — prospecting, qualifying, presentation, product demonstration, objections, closing, and follow-up — overlap, and some are omitted in certain situations.

Prospecting. Prospecting for customers, like panning for gold, means putting in time, sweat, and a lot of heart. **Cold canvassing** is going out prospecting without leads to interest people in the product. Likely prospect sources are current customers' friends, other vendors, social contacts, professional contacts, and systematic referral systems. Commercial real estate firms estimate that more than half their sales come from referrals after 2 years in the business.

Qualifying. Customers without the need or financial ability to purchase the product may be pursued fruitlessly. Insightful selling requires directed questions and an attentive listener to sense buying motives, purchasing ability, and need for the product. Many people wander into a furniture store to look around, compare prices, or "ooh and ah" over children's furniture though their children are grown. As one salesman quipped, "It is hard to tell the interested people from those with a few minutes to spare on the way to the airport."

Presentation. After qualification, the salesperson makes the presentation, emphasizing product advantages and uses, superiority to other products, research reports, customer satisfaction, and answering customers' questions. Some

Sales representatives for Mary Kay Cosmetics bring their presentations into the homes of prospective customers.

"canned" approaches consist of a script that the salesperson memorizes, practicing wording, voice inflections, and effective pauses. Flexible presentations are favored and no doubt are the most effective because they tailor the presentation to the circumstance.

Product demonstration. When possible, sales approaches try to incorporate product demonstrations: a new car ride, a vacuum cleaner sweeping up dirt, or a cleaning fluid removing a spot. This visual approach often convinces the customer. Television commercials simulate demonstrations.

Objections. Responding to objections is a skillful art in personal selling. Objections should be viewed as clues to concern rather than obstacles to the selling process. Sometimes the more direct denials and arduous arguments fail to overcome the objection, but stressing the positive points, turning the objection into an advantage, and explaining the facts with a soft sell are persuasive.

Closing. Tension rises, adrenalin flows, and perspiration surfaces on closing the sale. This is the salesperson's last spurt and determines whether the sale will be consummated. As strange as it sounds, one mistake in closing is failing to ask for the order. At some point, the salesperson has to put his or her ego on the line and accept the possibility of a "no." Just before closing, the salesperson builds to a peak in trying to destroy any wavering doubts.

Follow-up. After the purchase, salespeople should follow up to reinforce the buying decision, increase customer satisfaction, and check on product usage. They can share the customer's excitement about the new purchase. Good repeat customers are invaluable and often provide leads to new customers.

ADVERTISING

Unlike personal selling, **advertising** is a paid nonpersonal appeal to customers. The power of advertising is debated and has many critics. Nonetheless, advertising keeps booming along, setting new records each year. In 1985, the money spent on advertising is expected to hover around $70 billion.

Product Advertising

The nonpersonal selling of a product is **product advertising.** Ads try to point out features of the product or a service. When Sharp Electronics Corporation, the leading seller of small copiers during the last 2 years, advertises its Sharp SF-755 model copier, it is engaging in product advertising. The same is true when Sears advertises its Budget Rent-A-Car and when Time, Inc., promotes *Sports Illustrated.* Product advertising concentrates on the personal attributes of the product, its brand, style, and type.

Institutional Advertising

Institutional advertising promotes a philosophy or a company image, such as Avis's successful motto, "We are second — we have to try harder." Other examples include, "Get your favorite NFL team shirt," the Dairy Association's promotions to get people to drink more milk, the state of Florida's ads to visit Florida on vacation, and the life insurance industry's efforts to educate consumers about life insurance. When engaging in institutional advertising, firms try to build an overall positive image of the company or of their industry.

Advertising Strategies

As the head of an ad agency commented, "We try to communicate, persuade, and reinforce customers to buy selected products and services. And

Although there is some doubt about its effectiveness, positioning, an advertising strategy that compares products to competitors, now makes up about 10% of all advertising.

in doing this, we are always looking for newer strategies, ones that work even better than what we have." These advertising strategies differ and have changed over time.

Positioning. **Positioning,** one of the newer strategies, compares products to competitors. "In the old days, we avoided naming competitors' products like they were painful plagues," said an elderly advertising executive. "But now," he added, "we put the competitor right up there beside our product so the customer can see the difference." Sometimes called **comparative advertising,** positioning tries to establish a relative market position for the product or service. Al-

A positioning ad

THE DAY THE IBM PC BECAME OBSOLETE.

though there is still some doubt about its effectiveness, positioning now makes up about 10% of advertising. It is more widely used where a few brands dominate the market.

Pulsating. Another recent concept that does not claim many followers is **pulsating**—hitting the advertising hard for a period, then slacking off. Ipana was dropped as a brand name for toothpaste several years ago, but a couple of years ago, a company started using the Ipana label again without any advertising and found many sales still lingering from the advertising of earlier years. A beer distributor's research indicated that its advertising had a lingering effect. This distributor flooded the market with advertising for a few months, then stopped for several months, repeating the cycle in pulsating fashion.

A persuasive ad

Persuasive advertising. **Persuasive advertising** tries to improve the competitive status of the product or service, and it is usually used when the product or service has been around for a while. An example of persuasive advertising is the Army Reserve's, "Join an army you don't have to leave home for," and, "Army reserve. Be all you can be." Another example is the state of Oklahoma's appeal to tourists, "Visit our green country."

Informative advertising. When the primary purpose of advertising is to provide information to the potential consumer, it is **informative advertising.** Many times, the ad asks viewers to write or call for additional information, perhaps a brochure or a catalog describing the products or service in more detail. Other times, informational ad-

An informative ad

Criteria for the ad were that it contain thinkers who are deceased, from a variety of disciplines and encompassing a chronological span from ancient to modern times. After the eight were chosen from among 15 to 20 well-researched possibilities, their accomplishments were rechecked with historical societies.

If you weren't able to identify all eight of the world's great thinkers, or would like to check your answers, please don't reach for the telephone. Corporate Advertising isn't staffed to handle 107,000 employee inquiries. (*Answer key:* Aristotle, DaVinci, Shakespeare, Newton, Jefferson, Darwin, Curie, and Einstein.)

Source: Reprinted with permission from the December 1983 issue of *Update*, the Allied Corporation employee publication.

vertising describes what a company can do or perhaps where their locations are. An ad on Xerox service centers says, in part, "Come to one of our Xerox Service Centers. We have eighty-two nationwide. And we're multiplying faster than software programs." The ad then lists twenty-one personal computers the service centers are equipped to work on and gives the addresses of its eighty-two service centers. Ernest Gray, an advertising consultant, considers informational advertising to be far superior to pointless boasts. Examples of messages that do not sell are: "The best your money can buy," "The best on the market," and "The top value around." A furniture ad makes this mistake with, "The finest furniture around." A competitor does better with an informational slogan, "Old-fashioned furniture at old-fashioned prices."

Reminder advertising. Reminder advertising tries to reinforce a message or an image from previous advertisements. Firms typically use this strategy when their product or service has been

An advocacy ad

around for a long time and sales are beginning to drop. Sometimes coupons that allow you a discount on the price of the item accompany reminder advertising. An ad for Mazola margarine contained their oft-repeated slogan, "Made from 100% corn oil," and contained a clip-out coupon that customers could return for a 25-cent savings.

Advocacy advertising. In advocacy advertising, a firm takes a stand on a controversial issue or makes a proposal to solve some societal problem. Mobil Oil Company spends millions of dollars per year on advocacy advertising, most of which they aim at what is good about our private enterprise system. One of their recent ads included, "The U.S., with only one-twentieth of the world's population, accounts for fully one-fourth of its

A reminder ad

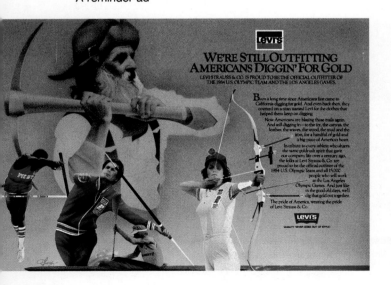

Gross National Product." Another part of the ad read, "Well then, to the list of freedoms — of religion, of speech, of the press, and more — that make America *great*, let us add thanks for economic freedom: It makes America *work*."

Westinghouse provides another example of advocacy advertising with their emphasis on quality family entertainment on television. Their advocacy ads say they take the social responsibility of broadcasting very seriously. One ad says, in part, "We won't produce or distribute anything we wouldn't want our own families to watch." The ad goes on to say that they support the arts in Boston, crime prevention programs in Baltimore, and the Children's Hospital in Pittsburgh.

Pioneering advertising. The purpose of **pioneering advertising** is to stimulate demand for a new product or service. Last year, Coca-Cola launched their new product, Diet Coke, with Hollywood-style hype. The company rented Radio

A personality ad

City Music Hall and invited 4000 people to attend entertainment by the Rockettes and a forty-piece orchestra. Coca-Cola, after the event, took guests to a West Side pier where they feasted on hot dogs, ethnic delicacies, and, of course, Diet Coke. After the fireworks display, guests took home 4000 six-packs of the diet drink. Although this event cost $100,000, Coca-Cola spent at least an additional $50 million promoting the product across the country. As a result, Diet Coke was an instant success, moving to number 4 in soft drink sales shortly after its introduction.

Use of personalities. Using well-known personalities is another way companies try to build trusting images of their products and services. Some of these ads make a long-term commitment; some examples: Joe Namath signed a 10-year contract with Brut, O. J. Simpson and Arnold Palmer have become closely identified with Hertz Rent-A-Car, Bill Cosby and Coca-Cola, Bjorn Borg and the Concord Centurion Sportswatch, Bob Hope and Texaco Oil Company, and many years ago, Dinah Shore and Chevrolet.

However, there is some doubt about the effectiveness of using celebrities in ads. *Advertising Age* polled 1250 adults across the country. Fifty-four percent of the respondents said that using celebrities in ads made "no difference" in believability. Thirty-three percent said that a celebrity who plugs several products is actually less believable. And 64 percent said that they did not believe the celebrity spokesperson used the products or ser-

A pioneering ad

Starting in July, 1984, color will come to the Life and Money sections of USA TODAY. That will make a total of 16 color pages, and give our advertisers the opportunity to run their color ads in all four sections.

vices they represented. The pollsters concluded that today's consumer is probably too sophisticated to place too much credence on advertised recommendations of hired celebrities.

How Advertisers Select Media

Advertisers have many choices on what media they are going to use to get their message to the public. In making their decisions, advertising managers consider three questions:

1. What is the size of the product's (or service's) market appeal?
2. How effective is the medium in reaching this market?
3. What does the medium cost?

A brief analysis of the more popular media for advertising follows.

Newspapers. Newspapers, receiving almost a third of all advertising revenues, are the most popular of all advertising media. In a 1982 survey that asked respondents to identify what they considered the "most believable" advertising media to be, 42% said newspapers had the most believable advertising. Twenty-six percent selected television, 11% chose radio, and 5% said direct mail.

Of course, experts perceive some newspapers to be better media than others. *Advertising Age* in 1983 polled 110 journalism faculty members from schools in 39 states. They concluded that the *New York Times*, which has a Sunday circulation of more than 1.5 million, was the country's number 1 newspaper. The *Washington Post* was second, the *Los Angeles Times* third, and *The Wall Street Journal* was fourth.

Firms like to advertise in newspapers because they are low-cost, require little lead time, and they can selectively penetrate market segments. The biggest negative: newspaper life is short, usually just a few minutes as readers scan the paper.

Television. Television advertising represents the fastest-growing media. Via television, commercials zoom to millions of viewers in a flash; their color and movement give an added glow to the message, and they can be repeated for lasting effect. However, the cost is prohibitive for many. Many commercials for sporting events, the highest priced of all, cost more than half a million dol-

In the 1983–1984 season, ABC TV's hunk-and-centerfold show "Dynasty" sold commercials at $179,000 for 30 seconds.

lars a minute (yes, that amounts to over $8000 per second). In the 1983–1984 season, ABC TV's hunk-and-centerfold show "Dynasty" sold commercials at $179,000 for 30 seconds. A half-minute on an average prime-time program went for $75,000. However, because of increased competition among the networks and from cable, executives are unable to raise the prices as much as they once did. Figure 15.2 shows the percentage change in TV commercial rates during the past 10 years.

Purchasers buy many of their commercials "up front," that is, before the season actually begins. Commercials sold after the season begins are called scatter sales. One of the largest up-front buyers, Ralston Purina, spends about $70 million annually advertising pet foods and cereals on network TV.

Also on the negative side, TV commercials carry only brief messages, and some research indicates that a lot of people leave the screen during the inevitable commercial break.

Direct mail. Chapter 14 covered direct mail as a distribution channel. But direct mail is also an advertising media. Companies can buy mailing lists from list brokers that identify market targets by zip code, profession, earnings, location, attendance at meetings, membership in organizations, family size, and the like. For instance, if an agency wanted to promote a training seminar to people in the Southwest, they could buy from a broker names of executives who had a title of mid-level manager or higher. If you wanted to, you could also specify that the list contain people who had attended at least one other training program during the last 3 years. Mailing lists sell between $175 and $300 for a list of 5000 names, which is usually a minimum order.

Often, direct mail advertising offers free samples or trial offers to would-be purchasers. According to Kobs and Brady Advertising in Chicago, 10 to 15% of the people who accept a trial offer will return the merchandise. Still, trial offers produce about twice as many orders as money-back guarantees.

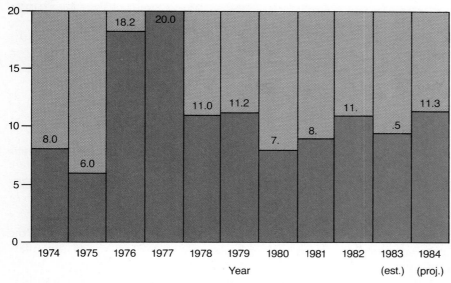

Percentage

Year										
1974	1975	1976	1977	1978	1979	1980	1981	1982	1983 (est.)	1984 (proj.)

18.2 20.0 11.0 11.2 11. 11.3 8.0 6.0 7. 8. .5

Figure 15.2
Percentage of increase in TV commercial rates.
Source: McCann-Erickson.

While direct mail offers maximum selectivity and flexibility, it suffers from a negative image; many receivers ignore direct mail advertising, regarding it as "junk mail." Also, increased postage rates make mass mail-outs more costly than in the past.

Radio. Much like newspapers, radio stations blanket the country. There are more than 7000 and they send everything over the airwaves, from talk shows to news to hard rock. Radio broadcasting stations typically have a profile of their listeners, and this allows advertisers to make appeal to select market targets. The rates are reasonable, especially when compared to television, but like newspaper and television ads, the message appears for only a few seconds. The most effective stations for radio advertising develop a clear image of what they are. For example, The Great Empire, Inc., a chain of stations in the midwest, presents a country image by playing country music and building country images of their disk jockeys and station personnel. As they say, "We are country and we are selling it."

Magazine. Although there are a few general purpose magazines like *Reader's Digest, U.S. News, Time,* and *Newsweek,* most appeal to very specialized readers. There are magazines for practically every type of interest imaginable — from home computer users to hunters to gar-

deners. Because of this specialization, magazine advertising can appeal to special audiences. They also last longer than newspaper, television, and radio because people keep them around for days and maybe even weeks or years. Many people collect their special magazines, keeping them for 10 years or more. They do, however, require a long lead time; preparation sometimes takes several weeks before the publication goes to print. And elaborate ads in prestigious journals are quite expensive.

Of late, companies have begun creating their own publications that look and sound very much like magazines. They send the publications to potential buyers at no charge. These often slick and polished periodicals strive to convey the message that the corporate sponsor is concerned and helpful. Webb Co. of St. Paul, Minnesota, publishes for Farmers Insurance Group, Inc. a magazine called *Friendly Exchange.* Although *Friendly Exchange* goes to the 4 million policyholders of Farmers Insurance Group, the magazine rarely mentions the company or its policies. According to Jack Klobucar, communications director for Webb Co., the magazine "works almost subliminally."

This method of advertising is apparently effective. Younkers, an Iowa department store chain, mails *You,* a fashion magazine, to its 205,000 credit-card customers. A questionnaire survey of its readers concluded that not only did they keep the magazine around, many bought clothes fea-

TABLE 15.1 ■ ADVANTAGES AND DISADVANTAGES OF ADVERTISING MEDIA

Factor	Media					
	Television	Newspaper	Direct Mail	Radio	Magazines	Outdoor
Media cost	Most costly	Low	High per contact	Low	High	Low
Preparation cost	Most	Moderate	Low	Very low	High	Very high
Life span	Short	Short	Average	Short	Long	Longest
Lead time	Most	Little	Little	Little	Much	Much
Impact	Moderate	Highest	Low	Less	Moderate	Low to moderate
Selectivity	Slight	Slight	Excellent	Good	Excellent	Slight

tured in the publication. Not everyone is convinced, however. A Sears executive says that free magazines may benefit some groups such as insurance companies, but they probably would not benefit merchandisers that much.

Outdoor techniques. Billboards; inflatables; beetleboards; messages on buses, taxis, and subway trains; signs in the outfield at a ballpark; overhead streamers from a biplane; and T-shirt advertising are all examples of outdoor advertisements.

A few years ago, an enterprising entrepreneur made thousands of dollars by leasing space on the side of Volkswagen Beetles. About 6 years ago, Robert Vicino tried leasing space on the side of a hot-air balloon. On his first venture he floated over a cow pasture rather than over the busy highway he was aiming for. Now, however, he is apparently doing quite well by making inflatable advertising pieces in the shape of corporate products and characters. Resembling the helium-filled balloons used in a lot of parades, Vicino's company has produced giant soda pop and beer cans, liquor bottles, and cigarette packs that float over

---

As an outdoor advertisement, an inflatable, giant King Kong cost $35,000, and even though it collapsed when climbing the Empire State Building, it got the company a lot of publicity.

---

beaches, trade shows, and grand openings. You might remember, a couple of years ago, the inflatable giant King Kong that collapsed when mounted on the Empire State Building. This inflatable Kong cost $35,000, but it got the company a lot of publicity, even though it collapsed. Most inflatables cost the advertiser between $3000 and $10,000.

Outdoor advertising is very flexible and seems to be effective in metropolitan areas where there is a lot of traffic. These ads also last a relatively long time. However, the public sensitivity toward the cluttering effect of signs and billboards may limit the growth of outdoor advertising. Table 15.1 shows advantages and disadvantages of various advertising media.

Advertising Agencies

Typically, advertising agencies perform many advertising functions for companies. Employing about 160,000 people, ad agencies bill clients more than $28 billion annually for their services. Typically, the agencies collect a 15% commission on their billings. Agencies are under immense pressure to produce new clients and to keep current clients satisfied.

Agency-client relationships. A full-service agency typically offers five services to clients, including: (1) creative services—art, writing; (2) media services—media analysis, selection, and space purchasing; (3) research—surveys to help identify customer profiles and ad effectiveness; (4) merchandising advice—what mixes of products and services to offer and to what types of clients; and (5) campaign design and planning — overall theme, timing, and placement of ads.

Agency switching. With all the high pressure and the demands for creative freshness, both advertisers and agencies occasionally switch their loyalties. One advertising executive said, "You must always keep new accounts coming in the door. It is not a matter of whether you will lose an account, it is a matter of when you will lose the account." In any given year, hundreds of large accounts may change agencies.

And although it does not happen as often, the agency itself might drop an account to pick up a

Some large firms maintain an in-house agency to provide advertising services.

competing account. Young & Rubicam, Inc., did just that when they dropped Procter & Gamble to pick up $120 million in annual billings from Colgate-Palmolive Co. Understandably, P&G was miffed. A spokesperson said, ". . . our principal disappointment is that the agency has chosen to be employed by a direct competitor of P&G working on brands directly competitive to those it handled for us." Young & Rubicam said that Colgate approached them and they decided to go with them because "the best possibilities for long-term growth are with Colgate."

Criticisms of Advertising

Critics of advertising focus on truth, price, and material values.

Is advertising misleading? In a recent Harris poll, 85% of those questioned said they believed that TV advertising was misleading, and 80% felt the same way about newspaper and magazine ads. Of course, some commercials, like some ministers, are dishonest. And the Federal Trade Commission (FTC), the government watchdog, has taken on some of the largest companies. For instance, the FTC stopped Colgate-Palmolive commercials that said Rapid Shave creme enabled razors to scrape clean "tough, dry sandpaper." The sandpaper was really plastic sprinkled with sand. Campbell Soup Company had to stop showing ads that used marbles in bowls of soup to make solid ingredients rise to the top. Warner-Lambert Company had to stop claiming that Listerine mouthwash cured colds and sore throats. And the FTC stopped STP from claiming that its oil additive was equal to an engine tune-up.

Outright fraudulent practices can be caught and usually are, but sometimes it is hard to tell the difference between deception and trade puffery. Some advertisers argue that many products would go down the drain if promotions did not contain a little fluff because they claim purchasers do not make decisions strictly for functional reasons. Looking for subtle forms of deception such as half-truths and unsubstantiated claims requires enough effort.

But the FTC is also concerned about psychological manipulation. For instance, they are asking the advertising industry to defend itself on such questions as:

- Is it misleading to use adults to plug children's products because children tend to trust grown-ups?
- Is it misleading to link beautiful, clean, sunlit meadows with cigarette smoking?
- Is it misleading to imply that mouthwash, deodorant, shampoo, toothpaste, and chewing gum will make you sexy?

There may be some evidence, however, that the FTC is easing its rules requiring firms to support their ad claims. FTC Chairman James Miller began questioning some of the FTC rulings when he took office in 1981, and as a result, many firms are appealing the agency's new sympathies. In a recent ruling, the FTC ordered Bristol-Myers Co. and Sterling Drug, Inc., to drop ads saying tests show their Excedrin, Bufferin, and Bayer aspirin brands are better than others unless they have clinical studies to back up the claims. But the ruling said that the company might rely upon other kinds of scientific evidence. This changed a previous ruling that said that if an ad does not mention test data, superiority claims must be backed up by two clinical studies. In short, the FTC seems to be making it easier for sellers to make claims about their products' capabilities.

Just what is a reasonable accurate impression? The Supreme Court has tried to draw the fine line by saying, "Advertising as a whole must not create a misleading impression." It is not enough for each line, taken separately, to be literally true. The Supreme Court further adds that advertising must not conceal material facts or distract attention away from the true nature of the conditions. Because of the difficulty of this issue, more advertisers will probably find themselves trying to keep their wits as they struggle through stormy court cases. On the face of it, many modern commercials do seem to make claims that are at least somewhat exaggerated.

Does advertising increase the price? Critics charge that advertising costs run prices up higher than necessary. And economists add that since advertising does not create value, it fails to create new demand but merely switches buyers from one brand to another. Pointing to multimillion-dollar advertising budgets of larger companies, critics complain that as much as 40 to 60% of the price of products such as cosmetics, soaps, and toiletries result from advertising and packaging.

Likewise, stamps, games, contests, and other advertising gimmicks add significantly to the cost of the product without improving its tangible or psychological benefits. Companies spend millions of dollars packaging and promoting products to create brand loyalty. Yet studies indicate that most users cannot identify their favorite brand among all brands in blind tests.

On the other side, advertising serves a needed educational function by making consumers aware of prices, quality, and ingredients. With this information, consumers become better shoppers, selecting the most efficiently priced goods and leaving overpriced, poor-quality items to gather dust on the shelves. Some states prevent advertising of selected products or services. For instance, a few states prevent advertising by optometrists, and surveys show that eye examinations are more expensive in these states. There is little doubt that some advertising is wasteful, but the answer is surely not withdrawal of all advertising. Rather, businesses must plan promotional budgets more carefully. Also, consumers should be selective in their choices because unpurchased brands are quickly dropped.

Does advertising encourage excessive materialism? Critics accuse marketers of overstimulating demands for goods, especially those that return high profits, while ignoring more spiritual needs. Professor and author Vance Packard, in his best-selling book *The Hidden Persuaders,* accuses promoters of using psychiatry and social science findings to shape, mold, and alter our purchasing decisions beyond our ability to control them. Economist and social critic John Kenneth Galbraith adds that demand is managed through a network of communications, promotions, merchandising, selling, advertising, and related services.

Faultfinders add that our emphasis on materialism paints success as a large house in the suburbs, two cars in the garage, three color television sets, and a swimming pool in the backyard.

Achievers are disillusioned when they find that happiness did not accompany their material acquisitions. Others suffer emotional and physical damage through frustration because their best efforts get them only part way up the slippery treadmill. Some slide into an apathetic existence, feeling that they never had a chance.

This criticism probably exaggerates the power of promoters because consumers are not easily brainwashed. They receive information from many sources, including government, religion, education, and a host of social critics and protection groups. Media are quick to publicize information on malpractice and research findings that discount advertising claims, and competitors also watchdog improprieties that might hurt their industry's reputation. Advertising is only one ingredient in this wide information flow. Perhaps people are more easily persuaded to buy when a desire already exists, but dissatisfied buyers are not likely to repeat their purchases. They have too many other choices. The stark reality is that most new products fail. If companies were capable of manipulating the membranes of the brain with millions of promotional dollars, advertising managers would be able to reduce their failures substantially.

PROMOTIONAL DEVICES AND PUBLIC RELATIONS

In addition to advertising, sales promotion and public relations help firms create demand for their products and services.

Sales Promotion

Sales promotion devices, usually supplementing other forms of advertising, encourage the purchaser to buy now. A few popular sales promotion techniques include:

Trade shows, fairs, and conventions. Close to 100 million people attend trade shows, fairs, and conventions in any given year. Many industries organize trade fairs in conjunction with their conventions. They invite producers to display

A trade-show demonstration of new products — such as this industrial robot — is an effective sales promotion technique.

their products so that potential buyers or middlemen can view a large number of competing products. At the American Society for Training Directors' (ASTD) annual meeting in Dallas in 1983, more than 100 producers of training equipment and material rented booths to display their latest products and services.

Samples. Samples contain free products, usually in a small quantity, given or mailed to the consumer. They are most widely used in calling attention to new products or pinpointing modifications of existing products. This approach expresses the belief that the product itself is the best communication available. Beecham Products mailed thousands of 1.4-ounce samples when introducing their fluoride Aqua-fresh toothpaste with a see-through tube.

Premiums. Premiums offer the buyer a gift or a prize, at little or no extra cost, as an incentive for purchasing a product or service. A local bank gave free toasters to people who opened a new account in excess of $500. For a period, manufacturers of the Maxell minifloppy disk offered a premium of four felt-tipped marking pens with the purchase of a box of ten disks. Zenith Corporation gave away Wordstar and Multiplan, two popular software packages, with the purchase of their Z-100 model personal computer.

Coupons. Unlike premiums, coupons actually offer a price reduction. Coupons are in effect bargains; buyers can clip them from newspapers,

FUNNY BUSINESS

packages, or direct mail, and return them for a discount. Return rates average from 4% in newspapers to more than 20% for coupons on the package. An advertising supplement in a recent Sunday newspaper contained more than eighty-five coupons, some of which were: $1 to $2 refunds for sending proofs of purchase on Mazola corn oil, Hellmann's real mayonnaise, Skippy creamy peanut butter, and Mazola margarine. Last year, industry offered 119.5 billion coupons on practically everything — shoes, flying lessons, baby food, etc. Coupons are also changing. Burger King, on their TV ads, instructed buyers to say a few words about the advantages of the Whopper over the Big Mac. Customers who went to Burger King and did this received a free Whopper. What's more, coupons are turning up in the most unlikely places — shopping bags, cash register tapes, and phone books. Coke is even coming out with a coupon on its cans of soda that are sold through vending machines.

Contests. Some firms create interest with contests offering cash prizes, merchandise, or trips for winners. Among the more widely known contests are the Publishers Clearing House Sweepstakes and the Reader's Digest Sweepstakes, both of which offer hundreds of thousands of dollars in prizes and prize money to the lucky winners. However, many contests have come under legal fire because they did not offer the amount of prizes they said or they may have had contests where there were no winners.

Trading stamps. Trading stamps, a very old form of sales promotion, gives customers stamps on purchases, which can be redeemed for additional merchandise. Green Stamps, one of the most popular brands, were usually given at the rate of one stamp for a 10-cent purchase. The customer collected the stamps in books and then returned them for merchandise. Critics contend that stamps add to the price of the original purchase, and some states have made trading stamps illegal.

Point-of-purchase displays. Point-of-purchase (POP) consists of in-store promotions,

TAKING STOCK

How Gillette Got into Trouble with Premiums

In 1978, Gillette offered a premium of a lucite table lighter stand for Cricket disposable lighters at a nominal price. All customers had to do was send in 50 cents and two proof-of-purchase seals from Gillette's Cricket disposable lighters.

So what was the problem? Simply, Gillette, far from estimating the response, ran out of lucite table stands and left 180,000 customers holding the Cricket, so to speak. Steven Miner, a disgruntled customer and a law student, brought a class action case against Gillette, charging that the company continued to promote its offer extensively after supplies were running low. The suit also charged that Gillette made no effort to get new stands. A company spokesperson said that it would have taken several weeks to reactivate the molds and produce the lucite stands. They thought the delay and the additional costs would be prohibitive. So, Gillette refunded the 50 cents and sent a disposable Cricket lighter with a form letter explaining.

However, Miner's lawsuit says that Gillette owes 180,000 customers $7.95 for the stand they did not get and he is asking punitive damages. The premium industry is watching the outcome closely because it obviously has wide implications. Regardless of the outcome, one attorney in the case offered some good advice, "When you offer a premium, make damn sure you can fill the demand."

Source: Gary Levin, "The Accent Is on Having Enough Premiums," *Advertising Age*, Aug. 22, 1983, pp. 18–19.

using small cardboard displays, signs, loud-speakers, and the like, to call attention to a product. The POP often repeats a theme or trademark that has been widely advertised as a final reinforcer to encourage the product to jump into the shopper's basket. Business volume in the point-of-purchase topped $5.8 billion in 1982. According to a Consumer Buying Habits Study by POPAI/Du-Pont, consumers make almost two-thirds of their buying decisions in the store. Another study showed that one-third of all purchases in drug stores were unplanned. POP is most effective when tied into overall advertising and promotion schemes. When graphically tied to a TV commercial, for instance, POP can increase sales by more than 500%.

7-Up used POP effectively when they introduced their caffeine-free promotions. Reinforcing television that stressed that 7-Up did not have caffeine, the POP message said, "No caffeine. Never had it. Never will." After testing window banners, shelf talkers, and bottle hangers, 7-Up sent out 50 million pieces of POP. During the 12 months of this promotion, 7-Up was the only soft-drink company to increase market share.

Specialties. Giveaways of pins, bags, glasses, ashtrays, letter openers, and bottle openers sporting company names are specialty advertising. Tourists toting home Harrah's ashtrays from Lake Tahoe are participating in specialty promotions. Holiday Inn towels for sunbathing boast the trade name for neighbors to see.

Public Relations

Public relations represents any activity that increases public awareness of a company or a product or service that the company does not directly pay for. Usually, public relations is some form of legitimate news such as the company sponsoring a public event like a road race or a community fund drive. For instance, Pepsi sponsors a series of road races throughout the country.

Of course, firms get publicity whether they want it or not. When a utility company, for instance, announces a request for a rate increase, the news media cover it. But most firms have departments that strive to get them favorable publicity. One goal of the local publications department of the Kansas Gas and Electric Company is to have

---

BUSINESS BULLETIN

How Manufacturers Hanover Promotes Corporate Road Racing

Manufacturers Hanover Trust Co. has joined hands with the running boom to sponsor corporate challenge road races. According to a Hanover official, it costs only about $30,000 to sponsor a race, and, "It is the biggest bang for our buck in our whole marketing effort."

When people enter a MHT-sponsored race, their names and job titles go into the computer. Later, MHT officials go over the lists and screen out people who are already customers or too closely tied to other banking institutions; the remaining names are prospects. In a recent corporate challenge race in Houston, the company turned up twelve companies they consider to be active prospects. Additionally, the race was a morale booster for MHT's own people. Hanover has many subsidiaries scattered all over Houston, and the race brought them together, giving them pride in the company they work for.

Source: "What Makes Manny Hanny Run," *Business Week,* Aug. 29, 1983, p. 55.

at least one newspaper article or television story each month that is favorable to the utility industry. Dunkin' Donuts got an unusual amount of free publicity through human interest stories on the number of doughnuts consumed each month in their stores and on the "romance" of the doughnut: how the idea was born, the history of the hole in the middle, and how adults are now eating more doughnuts than children.

SUMMARY

Promoting the product to potential consumers includes personal selling, advertising, and miscellaneous sales promotion devices. Promotional objectives are to provide information, stimulate sales, highlight values, differentiate products, and stabilize sales. Pull strategies create forces within consumers to pull products through the channels, while push strategies stimulate middlemen to push products through to consumers. Promotional effectiveness is measured by several methods: direct sales, readership surveys, and recall interviews. Approaches to determining the promotional budget include percentage of sales, fixed sums, match competition, and task objective.

Professional salespeople know their companies, products, competitors, customers, and themselves. They engage in creative selling, missionary selling, order receiving, and information feedback. Steps in the selling process cover: (1) prospecting, (2) qualifying, (3) presentation, (4) product demonstration, (5) objections, (6) closing, and (7) follow-up.

Advertising, unlike personal selling, appeals to customers through impersonal media. Advertising is a paid nonpersonal appeal to customers. Two major forms of advertising are: (1) product advertising and (2) institutional advertising. Advertising strategies include: positioning, pulsating, persuasive advertising, informative advertising, reminder advertising, advocacy advertising, pioneering advertising, and use of personalities. In selecting media, advertisers choose from newspapers, television, direct mail, radio, magazines, and outdoor techniques. Many firms turn their advertising tasks over to advertising agencies. Critics of advertising say that advertising (1) is

often misleading, (2) causes prices to be higher, and (3) encourages excessive materialism. Sales promotion devices and public relations efforts often supplement advertising programs.

MIND YOUR BUSINESS

Instructions. Designate each of the following questions true (T) or false (F).

_____ 1. One key objective of promotional programs is to provide information.

_____ 2. A pull promotional strategy tries to sell middlemen on the product's benefits.

_____ 3. Percentage of sales is the most common way of determining the promotional budget.

_____ 4. Missionary selling focuses on building goodwill and a positive company image.

_____ 5. Closing the sale is the last step in personal selling.

_____ 6. When using a positioning advertising strategy, a firm would very likely compare its product or service directly to competitors' products.

_____ 7. Advocacy advertising offers a precise incentive for the customer to buy the product now.

_____ 8. More money is spent on television advertising than in any other form of media.

_____ 9. Advertising agencies typically receive a 15% commission on their billings.

_____ 10. There is clear evidence that advertising increases the prices of products and services.

See answers at the back of the book.

KEY TERMS

REVIEW QUESTIONS

1. What is meant by a promotional mix? Give some examples.

2. Discuss the five major objectives of promotion.

3. What is the difference between the push and the pull advertising strategy? Give at least one obvious example of each.

4. Give at least four different methods of figuring a promotional budget.

5. What is the difference between personal and professional selling?

6. Describe missionary selling and give an example.

7. The text presents seven major steps in personal selling. Discuss each step and give an example of each.

8. Distinguish between product and institutional advertising.

9. Describe eight advertising strategies and give examples other than those used in the text.

10. Describe the six major advertising media. Give advantages and disadvantages of each.

11. What do advertising agencies do for clients? Describe agency switching.

12. Analyze three criticisms of advertising.

13. Identify six sales promotion devices.

14. Explain public relations.

CASES

Case 15.1: Advertising by Doctors?

In January 1976, The Federal Trade Commission (FTC) filed an antitrust complaint against the American Medical Association (AMA) for illegally restraining competition by refusing to let doctors advertise and engage in price competition. The complaint reads that the AMA's position leads to fixing of prices, restraint of competition, and withholding of information pertinent to selection of a physician. The FTC claims that physician advertising could lead to lower prices and better information for patients about doctors' services.

But the AMA and most physicians are opposed to advertising, saying that advertising is unprofessional for them. Further, physicians say that pricing information can be provided simply by calling their offices. Physicians also think that the patient might be the loser in an advertising campaign because doctors cannot advertise competence and quality of work. One doctor said, ''I don't believe people should shop for health care. It's dangerous to go to a physician because he charges less or more.''

Questions

1. What advantages would there be to the patient if doctors were to engage in advertising? Disadvantages?

2. What are the advantages and disadvantages of advertising for the physician?

3. Do you think physicians should advertise or not? Justify your answer.

Case 15.2: Promotion or Communication?

The managers of a large company were debating over the approach the company should take in promoting their product lines. Several managers wanted to hire promotional specialists to develop promotional and advertising campaigns for making the products known to customers. Another smaller group wanted to hire total communicators seasoned in every facet of communications. They argued that it was not enough to have an advertising manager, sales promotion manager, or marketing manager. Rather, they needed a marketing communicator who thoroughly understood the internal aspects of the business, as well as promotion and all other types of communication, including writing and speaking. Such an approach could give consistency through service uniforms, company identification, interiors, trucks, and the like. These skilled personnel would be a great help with internal organizational communication and would make it mesh with the external promotional program.

Questions

1. What are the advantages of the total communication approach? Disadvantages?

2. Which approach do you think would be most effective? Why?

3. What impact does the total communication approach have on costs?

CAREER SCOPE

THE MARKETING OF BUSINESS

The following list includes a variety of activities, personality characteristics, career goals and objectives, and skills and aptitudes. All have special relevance to careers in business marketing. Put a check mark in front of those statements that apply to you.

____ I would like to plan a sales campaign for a company.

____ I would like to take a course in merchandising.

____ People have told me that I am good at selling.

____ Traveling frequently and being away from home for several days at a time would not bother me.

____ I would like to study people's buying habits.

____ I would enjoy taking an advertising course.

____ I would enjoy attending a trade exhibition and displaying merchandise.

____ I would like to compete with others in buying merchandise.

____ People have often asked me how to go about selling something that they own.

____ I have enjoyed working in a sales position.

____ I would like conducting market research.

____ I want to buy and sell commodities.

____ I have sold door to door or telephoned people to persuade them to buy something.

____ I would like to train a group of new salespersons.

____ I feel that I can create an attractive merchandise display in a retail store.

____ I have sold advertisements for a school or community group's newsletter or publication.

____ I would like to explain to others the services that a company performs.

____ I am confident that I can influence others to make their purchases from me.

____ I have strong social skills so that it is easy for me to meet all kinds of people.

____ I would enjoy marketing a new product.

____ I would enjoy doing competitive purchasing for a large industry.

____ In the past, I have been able to accept other people rejecting my suggesting a product to use and not feel badly about it.

____ I do not easily accept no for an answer.

____ I would welcome the challenge of meeting large sales quotas.

____ I don't turn people off when I try to convince them to do something.

____ I have strong social skills so that in a group I tend to be the center of attention.

____ I have been told by my teachers that I am a very effective communicator and write clearly.

There is no single set of personality characteristics, skills, and aptitudes that fits a particular job. Generally speaking, the more activities and self-descriptors you checked in this list, the more satisfaction you may find in this major and its related jobs.

Job Title	Job Description	Suggested Education and Training	Personality Traits	Average Pay	Outlook through 1990
Public relations representative	Public relations workers help businesses, governments, universities, and other organizations build and maintain a positive public reputation. They may handle press, community, or consumer relations, political campaigning, interest-group representation, fundraising, or employee recruitment. Understanding the attitudes and concerns of customers and employees and communicating this information for management to help formulate policy is also an important part of the job.	A college education combined with public relations experience is excellent preparation for public relations work. Although most beginners have a college degree in journalism, communications, or public relations, some employers prefer a background in a field related to the firm's business — science, finance, or engineering, for example.	Creativity, initiative, and the ability to express thoughts clearly and simply are important to the public relations worker. Fresh ideas are so vital in public relations that some experts spend all their time developing new ideas. People who choose public relations as a career need an outgoing personality, self-confidence, and an understanding of human psychology. They should have the enthusiasm to motivate people. The ability to be competitive but function as part of a team are important qualifications.	Starting salaries for college graduates beginning in public relations work generally range between $12,000 and $15,000. The median annual salary of top level public relations workers is $39,000.	Moderate demand
Radio-TV announcer	At radio stations, most announcers are disc jockeys. They introduce recorded music; present news, sports, weather, and commercials; interview guests, and report on community activities and other matters of interest to the audience. Announcers at television stations often specialize in a particular kind of programming, such as sports events, general news broadcasts, or weather reports.	Though formal training in a college or technical school is valuable, station officials pay particular attention to taped auditions that present samples of an applicant's delivery and, in television, appearance and style on commercials, news, interviews, and other copy.	Announcers must have a pleasant and well-controlled voice, good timing, and excellent pronunciation. Good judgment and the ability to react quickly in emergencies are important because announcers may be required to "ad-lib" all or part of a show. A neat, pleasing appearance is essential, of course, for television announcers and news broadcasters. The most successful announcers combine an appealing personality with poise to win the following of large audiences.	Announcers generally start at around $10,000 to $15,000 a year. Earnings among experienced announcers are much higher, and some well-known personalities in major metropolitan areas earn extremely high salaries.	Slight demand (Competition for beginning jobs as announcers will be very keen through the 1980s. The broadcasting field will attract many more seekers than there are jobs.)
Market researcher	Market researchers analyze the buying public and its wants and needs, thus providing the information on which these marketing decisions can be based. Researchers plan, design, implement, and analyze the results of surveys. Most marketing research starts with a collection of data and information about products or services and the people who are likely to buy the product or service.	Although a bachelor's degree usually is sufficient for trainees, graduate education is necessary for many specialized positions in market research. Graduate study usually is required for advancement, and a sizable number of market researchers have a master's degree in business administration or some other graduate degree in addition to a bachelor's degree in marketing.	Market researchers must be able to analyze problems objectively and apply various techniques to their solution. Creativity is essential in formulating new ideas. Patience and perseverance are necessary to complete long research projects. As advisers to management, market researchers should be skilled in both written and verbal communication.	Salaries of beginning market researchers range from about $13,000 to $19,000 a year. Persons with master's degrees in business administration usually start with salaries of about $22,700 a year.	Stable demand

Job Title	Job Description	Suggested Education and Training	Personality Traits	Average Pay	Outlook through 1990
Advertising copywriter	Companies hire advertising agencies to create the general idea for an advertising campaign, prepare the ads, and arrange for them to be printed, broadcast, or televised. Agencies produce almost all national newspaper, magazine, radio, and TV ads. Copywriters write the text of ads, called copy, and scripts for radio and TV ads.	A college degree in journalism, English, or another liberal arts major is the usual background of advertising copywriters. Certainly, copywriters must be able to write persuasively and should have an excellent command of English.	According to David Ogilvy, founder of the Ogilvy and Mather advertising agency, the hallmarks of a potentially successful copywriter include: 1) obsessive curiosity about products, people, and advertising; 2) a sense of humor; 3) a habit of hard work; 4) the ability to write interesting prose and natural dialogue; 4) the ability to think visually; and 5) the ambition to write better campaigns than anyone has ever written before.*	Starting salaries hover between $14,000 and $17,000. Experienced, successful copywriters may earn as much as $50,000.	Moderate demand
Advertising account executive	Advertising account executives are in charge of coordinating the advertising for each of the agency's clients, or accounts. Account executives determine the nature of the advertising to be produced for their clients, coordinate and review all the agency's activities involved in producing it, and maintain good relations between the agency and the client. Account executives usually handle one large account or several smaller accounts.	A 4-year degree in liberal arts or business is a good start to becoming an account executive. A master's degree in business administration or advertising is, of course, better preparation for the job. David Ogilvy says that if he wanted to become an account executive he would first spend a couple of years at Procter & Gamble in brand management, followed by a year in a consumer research company, learning what makes people tick.*	Hardworking and knowledgeable are the principal traits of a successful account executive. The ability to make good presentations to clients is an indispensable trait. Maintaining friendly relations with clients and colleagues at once is also necessary.	Salaries range between $16,000 and $60,000, depending on the person's depth of experience.	Stable demand
Product manager	The product manager oversees the marketing of a manufacturer's product or products and is responsible for meeting profit objectives. By determining and managing the strategies for distribution, market research, promotion and advertising, and pricing, product managers decide on the proper marketing mix for a product.	A college degree in liberal arts or business administration is the best beginning for becoming a product manager. Sales and marketing experience and familiarity with the product are hugely helpful.	Product managers should be creative enough to think of ways to effectively promote their products. They should have initiative and be good at planning and organizing. They also need good oral and written communications skills.	Starting salaries are typically around $16,000 for product managers, though a newly hired manager with experience not in product management but a related area may earn as much as $30,000. Experienced product managers may earn as much as $60,000.	Moderate demand

* David Ogilvy, *Ogilvy on Advertising,* Crown Publishers, Inc., New York, 1983, p. 32.

Job Title	Job Description	Suggested Education and Training	Personality Traits	Average Pay	Outlook through 1990
Buyer	The job of retail buyer often brings to mind the glamour of high fashion; indeed, many fashion buyers do lead exciting, fast-paced lives. Not every buyer, however, travels abroad or deals in fashion. All merchandise sold in a retail store — garden furniture, automobile tires, toys, aluminum pots, and canned soups — appears there on the decision of a buyer. Buyers seek goods that satisfy their stores' customers and sell at a profit. The kind and variety of goods they purchase depend on the store.	An increasing number of employers prefer applicants who have a college degree. Many colleges and universities offer associate degree or bachelor's degree programs in marketing and purchasing. Postsecondary training also is offered in vocational schools or technical institutes that prepare students for careers in fashion merchandising. While courses in merchandising or marketing may help in getting started in retailing, they are not essential. Most employers accept college graduates in any field of study and train them on the job.	Buyers should be good at planning and decision making and have an interest in merchandising. They need leadership ability and communications skills to supervise sales workers and assist buyers and to deal effectively with manufacturers' representatives and store executives. Because of the fast pace and pressure of their work, buyers need physical stamina and emotional stability.	Buyers for discount department stores and other mass merchandisers are among the most highly paid. On the average, buyers earn between $20,000 and $30,000.	Moderate demand
Manufacturers' sales worker	Practically all manufacturers employ sales workers. They sell mainly to other businesses — factories, banks, wholesalers, and retailers. They also sell to hospitals, schools, libraries, and other institutions. Manufacturers' sales workers visit prospective buyers in their territory to inform them about the products they sell, analyze the buyers' needs, suggest how their products can meet these needs, and take orders. They also prepare reports on sales prospects or credit ratings, plan schedules, make appointments, handle correspondence, and study products literature.	A college degree is increasingly desirable for this job. Manufacturers of nontechnical products usually seek graduates with degrees in liberal arts or business; manufacturers of technical products, degrees in science or engineering. Many companies have formal training programs that last 2 years or longer for beginning sales workers. Trainees may rotate among jobs in plants and offices to learn all phases of production, installation, and distribution of the product; or take formal classroom instruction at the plant, followed by on-the-job training in a branch office under the supervision of a field sales manager.	A pleasant personality and appearance and the ability to get along well with people are important. Because sales workers may have to walk, stand for long periods, or carry product samples, some physical stamina is necessary. As in most selling jobs, arithmetic skills are an asset.	Some manufacturers pay experienced sales workers a straight commission, based on the dollar amount of their sales; others pay a fixed salary. Most use a combination of salary and commission, salary and bonus, or salary, commission, and bonus. Salaries for inexperienced sales workers generally range between $14,900 and $17,400 a year. Experienced sales workers generally earn between $17,400 and $32,000 a year.	Stable demand

Job Title	Job Description	Suggested Education and Training	Personality Traits	Average Pay	Outlook through 1990
Retail trade sales worker	Whether selling furniture, electrical appliances, or clothing, a sales worker's primary job is to interest customers in merchandise — by describing its construction, demonstrating its use, and showing various models and colors. For some jobs, special knowledge or skills are needed. In addition to selling, most retail sales workers make out sales checks, receive cash payments, and give change and receipts. They also handle returns and exchanges of merchandise and keep their work areas neat. In small stores, they may help order merchandise, stock shelves or racks, mark price tags, take inventory, and prepare displays.	Employers generally prefer high school graduates for sales jobs, but also hire those with less education. Traditionally, capable sales workers without college degrees could advance to management positions. However, a college education is now becoming increasingly important for advancement. Large retail businesses generally prefer to hire college graduates as management trainees. Despite this trend, capable employees with less than a college degree should still be able to advance to administrative or supervisory work in large stores.	Employers prefer those who enjoy working with people and have the tact to deal with difficult customers. Among other desirable characteristics are an interest in sales work, a pleasant personality, a neat appearance, and the ability to communicate clearly.	Median earnings generally range from $9000 to $15,000 a year for full-time sales workers. Some sales workers receive salary plus commissions; others are paid only commissions.	Moderate demand

Job Title	Job Description	Suggested Education and Training	Personality Traits	Average Pay	Outlook through 1990
Wholesale trade sales worker	Sales workers in wholesale trade represent wholesalers who distribute from the factory to stores selling directly to the consumer. Sales workers visit buyers for retail, industrial, and commercial firms, and institutions such as schools and hospitals. They show samples, pictures, or catalogs that list items their company stocks and may show how their products can save money or improve productivity. Other services they perform are to: check the store's stock and order items needed before the next visit; keep sales records; forward orders to wholesale houses; prepare reports and expense accounts; plan schedules; list prospects; make appointments; study product literature; and collect money.	The background needed for sales jobs varies by product line and market. Complex products require technical backgrounds. Drug wholesalers, for example, seek people with a college degree in chemistry, biology, or pharmacy as trainees. Wholesalers provide training on characteristics of their products and how to sell them. For non-technical products such as food, sales ability and familiarity with manufacturers and brands are more important than knowledge about the product itself. Most wholesale sales workers get their jobs by working up the ladder or by transferring in with the appropriate background.	As with the retail sales worker, desirable personality traits include an interest in sales, an agreeable manner, neatness, and an enjoyment in being with and talking to people.	Compensation plans differ among firms. One plan is salary plus a commission based on sales; others are straight commission or straight salary. Some include a bonus. Beginning sales workers average around $19,000 a year. Experienced sales workers may earn as much as $55,000 a year.	Moderate demand

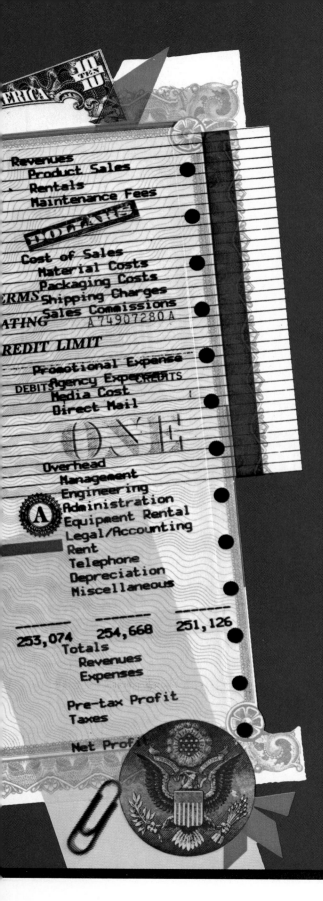

THE FINANCING OF BUSINESS

After completing this chapter, you will be able to:

■ Describe four characteristics of money.

■ Explain how banks create money.

■ Describe electronic banking.

■ Identify seven banking trends.

■ Explain the organization of the Federal Reserve System.

■ Describe three ways the FRS increases or decreases the money supply.

■ Explain three services of the FRS.

■ Identify five financial institutions other than banks.

16

MONEY, BANKING, AND FINANCIAL INSTITUTIONS

All people know about money is that they don't have enough," the late congressman from Texas, Wright Patman, was supposed to have said. Whether people have a little or a lot, they do not seem to have enough. When one very wealthy person was asked, "How much money would it take to make you happy?" he supposedly responded, "Just a little bit more." What is it about money that fascinates people so? What does it do for people? It cannot buy health, and many people proclaim that it will not buy happiness either. We know that we need money to live in our society, but it is more than that. The writer William McFee wrote, "It is extraordinary how many emotional storms one may weather in safety if one is ballasted with ever so little gold." Another writer, Jean Giraudous, said, "To have money is to be virtuous, honest, beautiful and witty. And to be without is to be ugly and boring and stupid and useless."

Perhaps it is not money itself that is harmful or good, but people's attitudes toward it. What does money mean to you? In our society, we have to have it to live: Money buys food, clothing, shelter, as well as entertainment. Even though it is so necessary, it is remarkable how little people know about it.

Money is the essence of financing. Like people, firms need money to exist. Banks, with the aid of our Federal Reserve System, play a vital role in creating, protecting, and moving money through our system.

WHAT IS MONEY?

The government has taken great pains to develop a secret method of making money so that counterfeiters cannot easily reproduce it. Still, we know that paper and metal currency have only symbolic value. In truth, **money** is a medium of exchange; it exists in many forms with identifiable

characteristics. Money performs unique and necessary functions in our business system. Money serves us in three primary ways.

A Medium of Exchange

Money is symbolic. Although inherently worthless, it gains meaning by representing something of value. The government has declared paper money to be legal tender acceptable for payment of debts and taxes. Money may also be used to purchase goods and services. People work for money only because with it they can pay the landlord rent, the grocer for food, the bartender for beer, or purchase any commodity they can afford. Money is valuable only so long as we agree to use it as a basis of exchange.

A Means of Storing Purchasing Power

Money is a convenient way of storing purchasing power. Butter sours, potatoes rot, and milk curdles; but we can exchange these for money and hold the money indefinitely. Of course, how well money stores depends upon inflation rates; if inflation is high, the value of money that we hold decreases correspondingly. Thus, as an actual practice, we typically buy something with our money—stocks, bonds, real estate, gold—that we hope increases in value more than the inflation rate.

A Measure of the Value of Things

Money is a yardstick by which we express the value of things. We express goods, services, and other items in terms of dollars and cents to communicate how much they are worth. When a retail jeweler advertises, "You can buy this quartz, digital, dual-chronography watch for only $195.98," we know exactly what the exchange means.

The Forms of Money

We designate many things as money. A quarter is money and a five-dollar bill is money, but so is a checking account, a savings account, and credit.

Paper and metal money. Most of U.S. currency is token money. Citizens resisted the use of coins and paper money for years because they lacked confidence in the government. The government issued greenbacks during the Civil War, but people did not like them. The first paper money was in the form of certificates that could be redeemed for gold. But the government withdrew gold certificates and gold coins in 1933 when the United States went off the gold standard. It became legal for citizens to own gold again in 1975, and we have rekindled a romance with gold. For a while, the government issued silver certificates, which were backed by actual silver on deposit. But it issued more certificates than there was silver. If everyone had tried to redeem their silver at the same time, many would have been left holding worthless paper. As people gained more confidence in the government, silver certificates were replaced by promissory notes from the U.S. government. Then we went to notes issued by the Federal Reserve system. These notes constitute about 90% of our paper money today. Federal Reserve banks promise to redeem their notes with money, but the money can be other Federal Reserve notes. The government has also taken most of the valuable metal from our coins. Both coins and paper

Whether represented by paper currency or electronic signals, money serves as a medium of exchange, a measure of value.

1. Individual opens tandem checking and savings accounts at bank.
2. Depositor puts money in interest-paying savings account, keeps little or nothing in checking.
3. Checks to pay bills are written against checking account.
4. Bank automatically transfers money from savings to checking as needed to cover drafts.
5. Individual collects up to 5% interest on funds in savings account and pays any fees that may be required on either account.

Figure 16.1
How banks pay interest on checking accounts.

money are only tokens—IOUs in which people have confidence.

Checking accounts. The most widely used form of money is **demand deposits,** that is, **checking account.** People deposit coins or paper money (or more likely checks drawn on other demand deposits) in the bank. To pay bills, people write checks instructing the bank to give their money to others. The payees deposit the checks in their bank accounts and write checks. Behind the scenes, banks merely keep records of these transactions. In this way, demand deposits serve the same function as paper money—IOUs on a larger scale.

Interest-paying checking (NOW) accounts. One recent change is the form of interest-paying checking accounts, technically known as **negotiable order of withdrawal (NOW) accounts.** Since 1933, by law, depositors have been unable to earn interest on idle funds in their checking accounts. But now, under the 1980 Depository Institutions Deregulation and Monetary Control Act, banks can offer interest on checking account money.

But, as Fig. 16.1 illustrates, the process is rather complicated. An individual has to open both a checking and a savings account. Most of the money is deposited in the savings account, which draws interest. Then checks are written on the checking account. As the checking account becomes overdrawn, the bank automatically transfers money from savings to checking to cover the overdraft. Interest is drawn on funds in savings accounts.

Most all large banks and many medium-size ones are offering this service. But depositors are not flocking to the new service. Why? For one

thing, most banks charge fees for the new service, some of which might outweigh the advantages. For another, interest on savings these days is quite low. And to the average customer, the automatic transfer plan seems complicated and confusing. In explaining why he did not feel a need to use it in his bank, a small bank owner said, "We have been covering overdrafts for our good customers for years on an informal basis. We often pay the check and talk with them about how they want to cover it." However, for the depositor who normally has several hundred dollars in a checking account, the new service can provide a good deal.

Savings accounts. Time deposits, popularly called **savings accounts,** are a modification of demand deposits. Depositors may have to give the bank a notice 30 days to 6 months in advance to withdraw their money. The bank pays the depositor interest on money in time deposits. Time deposits are sometimes referred to as "near money" because of the restrictions on withdrawals. Money deposited in money market accounts (see Chapter 18 for a discussion of these) may also be near monies. The depositor can typically get money from these accounts, often in just a day or so, but it is not quite as quick as writing a check at the bank. Some of the money market accounts do allow check writing, but the person who accepts the check may not agree to give credit for the payment for a few days, that is, until the process clears the account.

Credit. Credit has emerged as a popular form of money in recent years. Credit is money because the seller takes a customer's word, usually backed by collateral, that the customer will pay the debt later.

The Characteristics of Money

Whatever form money takes, it remains usable in our business world only while it is acceptable, stable, easy to handle, and difficult to counterfeit.

Acceptability. Because money has no intrinsic value, its worth comes from its acceptability. As a businessman commented, "I know that money itself is of no value; but I will accept it for merchandise, because I know my creditors will accept it from me." Historically, when governments have issued large amounts of paper money during rampant inflation, people have become disillusioned and refused to accept the currency as a method of payment. Mass rejection renders the money system useless.

Stability. Stability is also a criterion of a successful monetary system. A wide variation in what money will buy from month to month causes an undercurrent of skepticism. If a $10,000 auto in 1980 costs $20,000 in 1985, the value of a dollar has been reduced by half. Inflation rates soaring over 10% during parts of the 1980s caused an agonizing alarm over the value of money.

Convenience. Money must be convenient. Dividing it into smaller denominations lets us discriminate minutely on pricing. But it must not be so tiny that we are in constant danger of misplacing it or so bulky we cannot carry it.

Difficulty of counterfeiting. Money is of little value if it can be counterfeited easily. Most countries go to great lengths to make it hard to counterfeit paper money by including silk threads and using special plates in printing. Other forms of money, checking accounts, etc., require strict identification procedures to prevent fraud.

BUSINESS BULLETIN

A Cashless, Checkless Society

Computers have made it technically possible to go to an all-computerized monetary system, and some banks are already preparing to do so. A computerized system could theoretically produce a cashless, checkless society that works as follows.

A customer, armed with a magnetized identity card, enters a store and buys a basket of groceries. The clerk records the sale by pressing buttons connected to the customer's account at the bank. The bank's computer deducts the amount from the customer's account and adds it to the store's account. When the store's owner buys produce from wholesalers, pays its employees, or takes out profit for himself, the appropriate buttons are pushed to adjust the records accordingly.

By adding a microchip to the plastic card, a **smart card** is created, allowing information to be stored directly on the card—amount of deposit, withdrawal, balance, and the like—to be printed out later. J.C. Penney is already experimenting with chip cards, and General Electric runs several gas stations in Phoenix with them. A home banking experimental project is also going on in North Dakota.

Smart cards are hard to forge because it takes sophisticated, exotic equipment to read the cards. Casio Computer Co. has developed a smart card that not only could be used with electronic terminals but also would give the user a calculator keyboard.

Still another development, the **Drexon laser card,** is capable of storing millions of bits of data directly on the card. While it does not qualify as a smart card, it has the advantage of being able to store much more data directly on the card. Because the equipment to read and write on the card will be quite expensive, the market will probably not include normal banking customers.

COMMERCIAL BANKING

Commercial banks are the department stores of our financial system. "We are the middlemen in the monetary transactions among all segments of our society," is the way a banker described his bank.

Just like giant companies and small, mom-and-pop stores, commercial banks are privately owned businesses that operate to make a profit. And when they organize, they incorporate by requesting a charter, just like other corporations. Of the approximately 15,000 banks in the United States, about 30% receive their charters from the federal government. The remaining 70% get their charters from state governments. Federally char-tered banks are called **national banks;** state-chartered banks are called **state banks.** Table 16.1 lists the ten largest commercial banks in the United States.

How Banks Facilitate Financing

The major purpose of commercial banks is to facilitate financial flows by holding and loaning money. About half of the money going into commercial banks enters in the form of demand deposits (checking accounts). Banks obtain other money from time deposits (savings accounts), profits, and loans from the Federal Reserve system or other banks. A bank's primary source of revenue comes from interest on money loaned out.

TABLE 16.1 ■ THE TEN LARGEST COMMERCIAL BANKS IN THE UNITED STATES (RANKED BY ASSETS)

Company	Rank 1982	Rank 1981	Assets $ Thousands	Deposits $ Thousands	Rank	Loans $ Thousands	Rank	Employees Number	Rank
Citicorp (New York)	1	2	129,997,000	76,538,000	2	87,692,000	1	60,600	2
BankAmerica Corp. (San Francisco)	2	1	122,220,806	94,341,795	1	75,846,022	2	85,266	1
Chase Manhattan Corp. (New York)	3	3	80,862,903	56,857,847	3	54,973,264	3	36,810	3
Manufacturers Hanover Corp. (New York)	4	4	64,040,552	43,824,670	4	45,293,124	4	27,870	5
J.P. Morgan & Co. (New York)	5	5	58,597,000	37,910,000	5	31,477,000	6	12,711	13
Chemical New York Corp.	6	7	48,274,842	27,998,414	8	30,597,660	7	19,535	7
Continental Illinois Corp. (Chicago)	7	6	42,899,424	28,175,021	7	33,339,165	5	12,930	12
First Interstate Bancorp. (Los Angeles)	8	8	40,884,296	30,542,067	6	23,394,941	9	31,903	4
Bankers Trust New York Corp.	9	9	40,427,059	24,492,559	11	21,098,591	11	11,906	14
Security Pacific Corp. (Los Angeles)	10	11	36,991,034	25,848,489	10	26,094,632	8	27,058	6

Source: "The Fortune Directory of the Largest U.S. Non-Industrial Corporations," *Fortune,* June 13, 1983, p. 158.

The Ups and Downs of Chase Manhattan Bank

About 10 years ago, the Chase Manhattan Bank, dominated by the Rockefellers, stood at the top of the banking pyramid of influence. But the mighty Chase suffered embarrassment and humiliation and eventually became fodder for jokes.

After Chase lost millions of dollars in bonds and kept poor records regarding these losses, the U.S. Comptroller of the Currency said the Chase was running out of control in 1975. Yet, a few years later, the bank took devastating losses in real estate, got better for awhile, and then lost millions more to a suspect government securities dealer — Drysdale Government Securities, Inc. To add to their already considerable embarrassment, Chase lost hundreds of millions more through participation in energy-related loans with Penn Square Bank in Oklahoma. Loss write-offs for these two ventures finally totaled $192 million.

Reacting to such pitfalls, Chase today operates under the tightest internal controls in American banking. Of course, the strict controls offer disadvantages. A lending officer says, "I know other banks can act faster than we can or at least without the difficulty. If we try to do something innovative, we must knock ourselves out to get it through internally."

Not content to sit on their hands, the Chase people are trying to return to glory with a definite marketing strategy — reduce the percentage of business with smaller individual and corporate customer accounts and increase their business with the top half of the individual and corporate markets. Time will tell whether their strategy will work for them.

Source: Priscilla S. Meyer, "Burdens of the Past," *Forbes,* July 18, 1983, pp. 32–34.

The loan rate for the very best grade of customer is called the **prime rate.** It is a common practice to loan money to good risks at prime rate. Others may have to pay two or three points above the prime rate. Between 1969 and mid-1976, the prime rate fluctuated between 4.5 and 12%. But since 1976, it rose steadily upward to an all-time high of over 21% in the late 1970s. In the early 1980s, the prime rate fluctuated between 17 and 10%. Figure 16.2 shows the prime rate movement from January 1982 to March 1984.

How Banks Protect Money

You may be wondering, "What happens if I discover that the bank has loaned my money to someone else?" Even worse, "What happens if the bank has loaned it to someone who goes bankrupt and cannot repay it?" Do not worry excessively; you are protected in four ways. (1) The bank has to

About 99% of all banks belong to the FDIC, a government-sponsored program that insures accounts up to $100,000.

keep a certain percentage of cash reserve at all times; the reserve may range from 10 to 20%. (2) In the unlikely event that a lot of people try to withdraw their money at the same time, the bank could borrow short-term funds to cover the cash outlays. (3) About 99% of all banks belong to the **Federal Deposit Insurance Corporation (FDIC),** a government sponsored program that insures an account up to $100,000. That is, if the bank fails, a customer can recover deposits up to a maximum of $100,000. (4) The FDIC establishes guidelines that banks must follow to be insured.

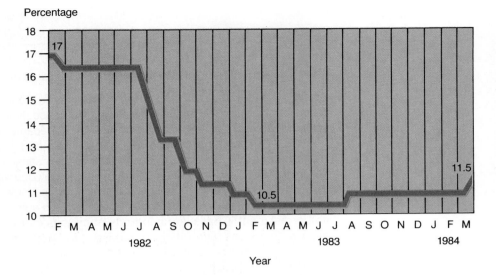

**Figure 16.2
How the prime rate changed from January 1982 to March 1984.**
Source: Federal Reserve Board.

The FDIC uses surprise audits to be sure that their guidelines are followed. A spokesperson for the FDIC says that 48 federally-insured banks failed in 1983, the most since 1939 when there were 60 failures. No depositor has ever lost money in a bank backed by the FDIC.

During the depression of 1932–1933, many people rushed to the banks to withdraw their money. But since much of the money was out on loan, the banks could not pay off and many had to close their doors. Thousands of people simply lost their deposits. Chastened by this adversity, the government created the FDIC in 1935.

How Banks Create Money

Banks create money by making loans on the money that people deposit in their checking and savings accounts. Here is the way it works. Suppose a person deposits $10,000 in a savings account (or checking account). The bank will loan most of the $10,000 but they have to keep a certain amount of reserve. If the bank loans out $8000, it has actually created money of $8000. The person or business who borrows the money will have $8000 to use or deposit in the bank. Thus, the original $10,000 now becomes $18,000. The depositor still has the $10,000 to draw interest on, show as part of net worth, or even withdraw. And the person or business that borrowed the $8000 can use it for investing, buying inventory, purchasing material, or whatever. But the money continues to expand. When the person who bor-

rowed the $8000 deposits it in a bank, the bank might be able to loan out as much as $6000 of that money. In this way, the money continues expanding until there is no more to lend.

A customer enters a personal identification number to initiate a debit-card electronic payment for a purchase at a Mobil service station in Norfolk, Virginia.

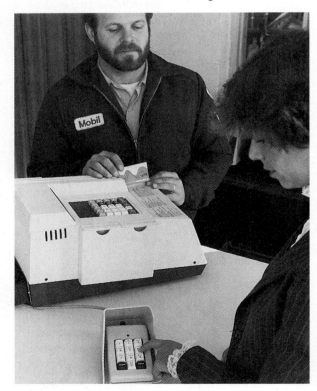

Electronic Banking

To lower the costs of processing the 30 billion-plus checks the U.S. banking system handles each year, banks are increasing their use of electronic means. It costs a bank between $150 and $200 per year to serve an average individual customer. Most analysts believe that banks must cut this by at least a third to cover the higher costs of deposits. One of the key challenges of banking is to move customers from traditional teller lines and brick-and-mortar services to electronic banking.

Automated teller machines (ATMs) allow people to get cash and make deposits by inserting a plastic card into specially equipped banking machines. A customer can place his or her card in the slot, the machine will quickly check the account balance; and if there is enough to cover the withdrawal, the machine will dispense the precise number of crisp, new bills. Today, about 40% of

CROSS FIRE

Are Banks Greedy?

At a time when banks are making large profits, many customers are unhappy with bank services. Thousands of borrowers say that banks are keeping interest rates too high. Cambridge Reports, a Massachusetts opinion research firm, in a 1982 survey, found that 50% of their respondents believed that banks' profit motives were at least partly the cause of high loan costs. Many consumers and some politicians are actively trying to pass laws setting limits on what borrowers must pay for loans.

Loans to foreign countries also do not set well with customers. People do not understand why banks charge hometown folks sky-high interest rates while at the same time making risky loans to foreign countries such as Mexico, Venezuela, and other developing countries.

Finally, many customers feel that they get poor service and too many hassles. For instance, people posing as Citibank employees bilked 485 customers out of thousands of dollars using the banks' ATMs. Citibank initially balked at paying the customers for the con-artist-imposed losses. But when the state attorney general filed suit, Citibank agreed to pay $135,000 to the 485 customers.

In their behalf, spokespeople for the banking industry say that much of the public outcry is based on the old-time distrustful feelings that borrowers naturally hold toward lenders. As John Collins, counsel for the House Banking Committee, puts it, "Bankers are in the business of having to say no to people. They have control over people's lives and people resent it." Bankers also quote economists who tend to agree that higher interest rates are the result of market forces, not bankers' profit motives. Regarding service, bankers say they have spent millions of dollars installing 24-hour teller machines, extending hours at their branch offices, and trying to make their services more friendly.

How do you rate the service provided by banks to their customers? Why?

____ A. Excellent   ____ D. Below average

____ B. Above average   ____ E. Poor

____ C. Average

Do you think banks tend to be greedy? Why?

____ A. Definitely, yes   ____ C. Probably, no

____ B. Probably, yes   ____ D. Definitely, no

the routine transactions at Wells Fargo banks are done by machine. They project the figure to reach 75% in the next few years. Customers of the Chase Manhattan Bank can withdraw cash from any of 2,000 ATMs located in 47 states. Citicorp estimates that a machine transaction costs 55 cents as compared to $1.27 for a teller transaction.

Electronic funds transfer systems (EFTS) also automate many transactions. Bank customers can, with their plastic cards, pay bills and make purchases automatically. A centralized computer system handles the transactions. Some merchants use a **point-of-sale (POS)** machine which allows customers to pay for purchases on the spot. A customer simply enters his or her plastic card, called a debit card, into the POS, which automatically transfers funds from the buyer's bank into the seller's account. In Norfolk, Virginia, customers can buy gas at Mobil service stations with plastic cards that deduct the cost from their checking accounts. And Florida shoppers can conduct banking business with robot tellers located outside public supermarkets. Within 10 years, many people predict, machines will handle the majority of consumer purchases; say goodbye to cash- and credit-card-filled wallets. See Fig. 16.3 for a diagram of this process.

Sears, offering investment, insurance, and real-estate services at their stores, is one of several new, nontraditional sources of financial services.

Trends in Banking

For years, banking has been a rich and powerful industry. With total assets soaring over $2 trillion, total deposits amounting to $1.5 trillion, and almost 300 billion accounts, banks have an enormous influence. But at a time when their size, profits, and growth over the past decades have been enough to make any board member proud, they are undergoing some pressure and public ridicule, and they are experiencing rapid change.

Increased competition. During the early and middle 1980s, the entire financial community became less regulated by the government. Savings and loan associations, money market funds, and others began offering the equivalent of checking accounts. And laws governing the amount of interest financial institutions could pay and charge became much less restrictive. Whereas in the past banks had a virtual monopoly on financial services, today they have to compete with other financial institutions for the customer's deposit.

Heavy profits. Even with the increased competition, banks are still experiencing profit growth. In 1972, the net, after-tax income of banks was $5.6 billion and that soared to $15.0 billion by 1982. They have been able to maintain this profit growth because of the difference between the interest they pay to depositors and the interest they charge to borrowers. In late 1983, banks were charging prime borrowers about 10.5%, but bank credit card plans returned 21% and new-car loans 16%. At the time, banks were paying less than 8% interest to their depositors. Further, they paid an effective income tax rate of only 2.3%, the lowest of all industries except railroads and paper.

Charges for services. Claiming that they can no longer provide free, or almost free, services for checking, savings, and other transactions, banks have started charging for more of their services. In other cases, they are raising prices on their services. Nearly 56% of all banks now charge fees, averaging $15 per year, on credit cards. This practice was almost unheard of before 1980. Some banks now charge as much as $75 a year for rental of large deposit boxes. And almost half of the banks charge at least $10 or more for a bounced

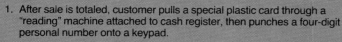

1. After sale is totaled, customer pulls a special plastic card through a "reading" machine attached to cash register, then punches a four-digit personal number onto a keypad.
2. Via a central processing center, the cash register electronically contacts a computer at customer's bank.
3. Bank computer is asked to transfer purchase amount from customer's bank account to merchant's account, even if at another bank. If customer's funds are sufficient, transfer is made.
4. Bank's computer notifies processing center that transaction has occurred.
5. Processing center relays word of transaction back to cash register, which prints receipt for customer. Entire process should take a few seconds.

METROBANK CARD

**Figure 16.3
How purchases with
plastic cards work.**

check. Table 16.2 shows how average service charges surged between 1979 and 1983.

Broadening services. Banks are also adding more services. In addition to offering a full range of financial services, banks are handling more re-tirement accounts and serving as brokerage offices for people who want to buy stocks and bonds. A bank president commented about his local bank, "We would like to see the day when a customer could come to us for everything that in any way relates to finances."

BUSINESS BULLETIN

How Visa Angered the Big Banks

Visa was created by financial institutions to market credit cards and to facilitate payments between businesses, banks, and cardholders. However, the current president of Visa, Dee Ward Hock, is planning to develop a worldwide network of automated teller machines (ATM) that would allow Visa cardholders to get cash from machines located far from the banks that issued the plastic cards.

Visa's automatic teller network is scheduled to have 8000 machines in dozens of countries by 1986. The initial purpose is to allow people to get cash from the machines, but eventually Hock would like to use the equipment to move a step closer to a cashless and checkless society.

Many larger banks are upset because they have competing ATM networks. These banks, most of which happen to be Visa participants, think it is unfair for Visa to compete with them via ATMs. For example, thirty-four banks, all Visa members, have invested up to $150,000 apiece to build an exclusive ATM system, based in Denver, called Plus System, Inc. More than 950 financial institutions take Plus cards. These banks are hardly happy with the idea of Visa's setting up competing machines in their territory.

Source: Arthur M. Louis, "Visa Stirs up the Big Banks—Again," *Fortune,* Oct. 3, 1983, pp. 196–203.

TABLE 16.2 ■ HOW AVERAGE SERVICE CHARGES INCREASED BETWEEN 1979 AND 1983

Service	Average Bank Fees		
	1979	1983	Percentage Change
Bounced check	$5.07	$ 9.46	86.6
Overdraft covered by bank	$4.72	$ 9.01	90.9
Annual rental for small safe-deposit box	$6.96	$11.37	63.4
Monthly checking fee	$1.17	$ 2.51	114.5
Cashing noncustomer's check	$ .40	$ 1.87	367.5
Balance inquiry	$1.20	$ 1.28	6.7
Credit card — annual fee*	—	$16.16	—

* Few if any banks charged such fees in 1979.

Source: Sheshunoff & Company.

Growth of interstate banking. In 1976, Congress agreed to let states nullify the federal ban on interstate banking. This gave states the right to decide for themselves whether they wanted to let out-of-state banks buy or start subsidiaries within their borders. Because of competition from other financial companies, many large banks are moving rapidly to increase their size by buying banks, particularly successful ones, in other states. Pittsburgh's Mellon Bank purchased Girard Bank in Philadelphia and another in Delaware. Bank of Boston merged with Casco-Northern Corp. of Maine and is making plans for further expansion. There are many other deals in process, some of which are quite large.

Increased mergers. Besides buying in other states, banks are also increasing their size by buying banks in their own states. A strategy of many banks seems to be, "Buy the biggest banks in the biggest markets you are not in, and then move to smaller local markets in the same area." Some experts believe that the optimal size of a bank for efficiency purposes is $15 billion in assets. Only

TABLE 16.3 ■ THE BIGGEST BANK MERGERS, 1982–1983

Price* (millions)	Announcement Date	Acquirer Headquarters	Assets** (billions)	Acquiree Headquarters	Assets** (billions)
$515	6/21/83	Mercantile Texas, Dallas	$10.2	Southwest Bancshares, Houston	$6.9
$334	5/9/83	Sun Banks of Florida, Orlando	$5.0	Flagship Banks, Miami	$3.1
$288	7/26/83	First City Bancorp of Texas, Houston	$16.6	Cullen/Frost Bankers, San Antonio	$3.0
$282	4/30/82	Interfirst, Dallas	$17.3	First United Bancorp, Fort Worth	$2.4
$275	8/9/83	First Chicago, Chicago	$35.9	American National, Chicago	$3.2
$269	7/14/83	CBT, Hartford	$5.1	Bank of New England, Boston	$5.1
$244	4/19/82	Pittsburgh National, Pittsburgh	$6.9	Provident National, Philadelphia	$3.3
$220	8/2/82	Mellon National, Pittsburgh	$18.4	Girard, Philadelphia	$4.8
$203	7/25/83	First National State Bancorp, Newark	$4.9	Fidelity Union Bancorp, Newark	$3.4
$175	2/25/83	Virginia National Bankshares, Norfolk	$3.9	First & Merchants, Richmond, Va.	$2.8

* Cash or stock being received by smaller of the two merger partners.
** Year-end prior to announcement.

Source: Merrill Lynch Capital Markets.

Three Strategies for Growth among Banks

As banks try to expand through mergers, three growth strategies are evolving.

1. *The brick-and-mortar strategy.* The first, and most common, strategy among merging banks is to pay big premiums for consumer-oriented banks. Then, they try to go after the most profitable market segments such as more affluent customers. This strategy encourages selling off unprofitable branches and pricing their loans and services according to their true costs. They will try to do this with their current brick-and-mortar system of bank buildings and branches.

2. *The ATM strategy.* Banks attempting growth through this strategy, like the brick-and-mortar group, will go after the mass market through acquisitions of other banks. Then they would try to convert the customers to use their ATMs. Sun Banks, for instance, is buying many banks in Florida, but they are reducing brick-and-mortar branches. Instead, they are blanketing the state with ATMs.

3. *The near-bank strategy.* A third approach is to go after the nearest thing to banks available, usually savings and loan associations. Citicorp, following this strategy, bought Fidelity Savings of San Francisco and is bidding for other S&Ls. S&Ls have lower operating costs than most banks, and Citicorp believes the S&Ls provide an excellent vehicle for reaching the mass markets.

Source: Orin Kramer, "Winning Strategies for Interstate Banking," *Fortune,* Sept. 19, 1983, pp. 104–120.

twenty-three banks met that requirement in 1983. Table 16.3 lists the largest bank mergers in 1982–1983.

Loss of status with customers. Partly because of size and large profits, perhaps, bank customers no longer automatically trust and patronize their local banks. People feel uncomfortable with the notion that bankers seem to always have the upper hand. John Cuddington of Stanford University observes, "There is a presumption that bankers have too much power."

Customers also feel that they get poor-quality and impersonal service. They complain of waiting in long teller lines, rude treatment from tellers, and bookkeeping mistakes in their records. In a nationwide survey by a Miami-based research firm, 68% of the respondents said banks offered "lousy" service. People complain particularly about the "we don't need your business" attitude projected by many bank workers. Bank of America had to pay out $150,000 to a customer because the bank kept dunning the customer for unautho-

rized charges on a stolen Visa card. The customer reported the stolen card promptly, but the bank kept trying to collect from her. She sued and won. Another customer of a large bank tells of an experience trying to open a checking account for her 14-year-old daughter. The bank officer said, "Your daughter is too young to have an account of her own. It would be inappropriate." The customer asked, "Is there a law against it?" "No, she is just too young," replied the officer. The officer finally agreed to open the account but misspelled the name, and after several requests still did not get the correct spelling.

HOW THE FEDERAL RESERVE SYSTEM WORKS

The government established the **Federal Reserve System (FRS)** in 1913 to stabilize the banking system. Let's look at the organization of the Federal Reserve system, often called the Fed, and analyze its powers and services.

Paul Volker, Chairman of the Federal Reserve System Board of Directors, confers with congressional leaders concerning federal monetary policy.

The Federal Reserve system has twelve Federal Reserve banks, each serving a Federal Reserve district. Figure 16.4 shows the location of each district bank and the boundaries of each Federal Reserve district. A seven-member **board of governors** directs the twelve district banks. The president of the United States appoints the directors and the Senate confirms them. They serve 14-year terms and cannot be reappointed. Each of the Federal Reserve district banks has a nine-member board of directors that administers the operating policies of the bank. Member banks of the district elect six of the directors, and the board of governors appoints the remaining three. To ensure a diversity of representation, only three members of the board can be bankers. Of the six

Figure 16.4
Federal reserve districts and bank cities. *Source:* Federal Reserve Bulletin.

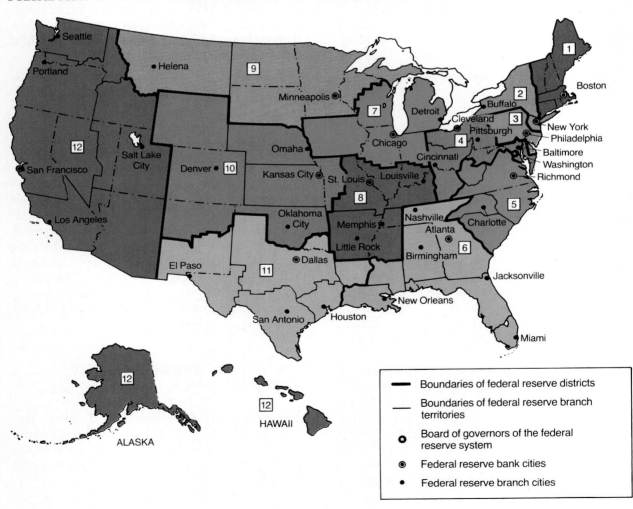

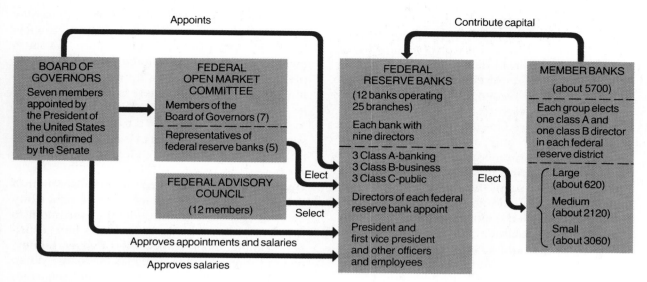

Figure 16.5
Organization of the Federal Reserve System. *Source: Board of Governors of the Federal Reserve System.*

directors outside the banking system, three must represent borrowers and three, the general public. The board of governors appoints the general public representatives. Figure 16.5 shows the organization of the Federal Reserve system. The Federal Reserve also has an **Open Market Committee,** whose membership includes the board of governors plus five representatives from the twelve district banks. This committee has the power to require Federal Reserve banks to buy or sell government securities.

How the FRS Increases and Decreases the Money Supply

Money supply is the total amount of money in our economy. Economists use several terms to indicate money supply. **M1** measures the money that regularly circulates through people, companies, and financial institutions. In mid-1982, M1 amounted to about $450 billion, and about 90% of M1 is typically in checkbook deposits. **M2** is M1 plus savings, small-denomination time deposits, and other near-liquid accounts. **M3** equals M2 plus large-denomination time deposits and other less liquid accounts. Because M1 circulates more freely, economists consider this to be the more crucial measure. For the past several years, the money supply has been increasing at a rate aver-

aging just over 6% a year. The amount of money in circulation is important; if we get too much, we encourage inflation, while too little makes the interest rates go up, which could nudge us toward a recession.

A major purpose of the FRS is to create sta-

bility in our economy, and it tries to do that

by influencing the total money supply.

A major purpose of the FRS is to create stability in our economy, and it tries to do that by influencing the total money supply. The FRS uses three techniques to increase or decrease the money supply: (1) reserve requirement, (2) rediscount rate, and (3) purchase and sale of securities in the open market.

Reserve requirement. The **reserve requirement** is the percentage of deposits that banks must hold in cash reserve. It is the system's most powerful tool. An increase in the reserve requirement reduces the amount of money that banks can lend and thereby tightens the money supply. A decrease in the reserve requirement has the opposite effect. The directors can vary the reserve requirement of demand deposits between 10 and 22% for large banks and 7 and 14% for smaller banks. To illustrate how this works, assume that a bank has $1 million in demand deposits and its current reserve requirement is 15%. It has $850,000 available for lending, and it must hold $150,000 (15%) in cash reserve. If the reserve requirement is lowered to 10%, the bank has to hold cash reserves of only $100,000. It now has $900,000 to loan. This increases the money supply by $50,000. Applying this to the approximately 7000 member banks of the Federal Reserve system, we see that a minute change in reserve requirements can tilt the money supply by millions of dollars. To illustrate, the Federal Reserve's Board of Directors in 1974 lowered the reserve requirement by 0.5%, and the supply of money increased by $760 million. For this reason, the reserve requirement remains relatively stable.

Rediscount rate. If banks wish to borrow money for additional loans or to cover their reserve requirement, they can borrow from the district reserve bank. However, the member banks must pay interest on the borrowed money in advance. This interest rate is the **rediscount rate** (or discount rate). Therefore, the FRS can raise the rediscount rate to discourage banks from borrowing money—leaving them less to lend. By contrast, the FRS can lower the rediscount rate and encourage member banks to borrow money— giving them more to lend. As a practical matter, the FRS uses the rediscount rate more as a statement of policy than to influence the money supply. By raising the rediscount rate, the FRS communicates that it thinks there is too much money in the economy. By lowering it, the Fed tells member banks that money is too tight (the money supply is too low), and that more money should be put into circulation through loans.

Open market operation. At the discretion of the Open Market Committee, reserve banks buy and sell securities of the federal government to member banks. When reserve banks buy securities from member banks, they deliver money, making more money available for loans. When district reserve banks sell government securities to member banks, money flows from member banks to the reserve bank. The Open Market Committee also buys and sells securities in different sections of the country. By moving plentiful money to an area of scarce money, it can help keep the interest rate in equilibrium for the country.

Buying and selling in the open market is now more widely used as a means of controlling the money supply because the Fed can make minor adjustments easily. This also avoids most of the negative psychological effects from news reports

Figure 16.6
An example of how the Federal Reserve creates money. *Source:* U.S. News & World Report, *May 1, 1978, p. 51.*

STEP 1	The Federal Reserve System's Open Market Committee decides to expand the money supply. It sends instructions to the open-market desk at the Federal Reserve Bank of New York.
STEP 2	Officials of the New York Federal Reserve Bank buy $100 million in Treasury bills from a securities dealer and pay with a check.
STEP 3	The dealer deposits the check in Bank A. Result: $100 million is added to the dealer's account and to the money supply.
STEP 4	Bank A puts 15 percent, or $15 million, into reserves and lends the rest to XYZ Auto Company, thus increasing the company's account and the nation's money supply by $85 million.
STEP 5	XYZ Auto buys $85 million worth of steel with a check, which the steel company deposits in Bank B.
STEP 6	Bank B puts 15 percent of the $85 million, or $13 million, into reserves and lends out the rest, thereby creating still more money.
STEP 7	Process of withholding 15 percent and lending the rest goes on until all the $100 million has been added to reserves. By then, the money supply has expanded by about $600 million.

Note: Under Federal Reserve rules, a bank that receives new funds must put a portion—currently averaging about 15 percent—in its district Federal Reserve Bank and can lend or invest the rest.

An increase in reserve requirement ——————→ Decreases the money supply
A decrease in reserve requirement ——————→ Increases the money supply
An increase in rediscount rate ——————→ Decreases the money supply
A decrease in rediscount rate ——————→ Increases the money supply
The sale of government securities ——————→ Decreases the money supply
The purchase of government securities ——————→ Increases the money supply

**Figure 16.7
How actions by the
Federal Reserve affect
the money supply.**

of changes in reserve requirements of rediscount rates. Figure 16.6 shows an example of how the federal reserve system creates additional money through its Open Market Committee. To decrease the money supply, they work in reverse, but the same chain reaction occurs. Figure 16.7 summarizes the federal reserve actions on the money supply.

Services of the Federal Reserve System

In addition to its controlling activities, the Federal Reserve system provides banking services for the government, clears checks, and distributes coins and paper money to banks.

Government banking services. The government uses Federal Reserve banks much like citizens use commercial banks. The postal service and Internal Revenue Service have accounts in Federal Reserve banks, and all checks drawn on the Treasury of the United States are payable at any Federal Reserve bank. The reserve banks also take care of the clerical work when the government borrows money. This involves keeping track of savings bonds, treasury bills, or certificates of indebtedness, which the government sells to investors. Some of the borrowing may be for 91 days; other borrowing may be for a 25-year period. Each loan carries a fixed interest rate, and the investor cashes in the loan when it matures.

Check-clearing services. Reserve banks clear checks in some cases. We write somewhere between 40 and 60 million checks daily, and about 90% of them are business transactions. Suppose an employer issues a payroll check to an employee who deposits it in a different bank from the employer's. To set the record straight, money has to be recorded in the employee's account and deducted from the employer's account in the other bank. Commercial banks develop their own system for clearing these checks within the same city. When checks are drawn on banks in various parts of the country, Federal Reserve banks handle the clearing operation. Figure 16.8 illustrates the check-clearing operation.

Coin and paper money services. District reserve banks physically house much of the cash in circulation. If member banks need dollar bills, quarters, or dimes, they can order them from their reserve bank. Likewise, if member banks have too many coins or bills, they deposit them with the reserve bank where they become available for distribution to other banks. In this way, Federal Reserve banks physically move coins and paper money throughout the country.

OTHER SPECIALIZED FINANCIAL INSTITUTIONS

Several specialized institutions have developed to facilitate handling finances. Some specialized institutions are savings banks, savings and loan associations, credit unions, pension funds, and insurance companies.

Savings Banks

Savings banks, operating a no-frills, specialized service, pool small investors' savings to create larger capital. They pay interest to depositors and then lend the money at higher interest rates. In this way, they make a profit. Savings banks typically invest their money by lending to the government, that is, buying government securities and lending for real estate purchases.

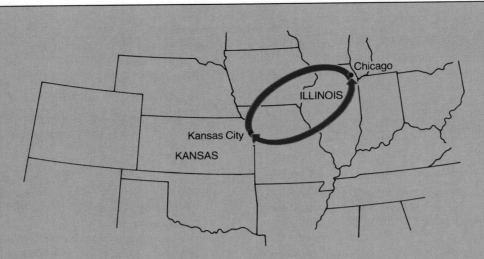

To illustrate how the check-clearing system works, suppose Hugh Hutchins, from Kansas City, mailed a check to Chicago for a subscription to *Sports Illustrated* magazine. Here is how the system would work:

1. Hugh mails check, along with subscription card, to *Sports Illustrated* in Chicago.
2. *Sports Illustrated* deposits the check in its Chicago bank.
3. The Chicago bank deposits Hugh's check for credit at the Federal Reserve Bank in Chicago.
4. The Federal Reserve Bank of Chicago sends Hugh's check to the Federal Reserve Bank of Kansas City for collection.
5. The Federal Reserve Bank in Kansas City forwards the check to The First National Bank (Hugh's bank), which deducts the amount from Hugh's account.
6. The First National Bank in Kansas City instructs the Federal Reserve Bank in Kansas City to deduct the amount of the check from the bank's account.
7. The amount of Hugh's check is shifted by the Federal Reserve Bank in Kansas City to the Federal Reserve Bank in Chicago.
8. The Federal Reserve Bank in Chicago credits *Sports Illustrated*'s Chicago bank, which then credits *Sports Illustrated*'s account.
9. Meanwhile, Hugh receives his cancelled check in his statement from the First National Bank in Kansas City.

Of course, the banks do not actually send these checks and authorizations round the country by mail. This would take entirely too long and too many records would be lost. The additions and subtractions to the accounts take place via the Fed's electronic transfer system – a computerized means of moving data.

Figure 16.8
An example of a check-clearing operation.

Most savings banks are organized as mutual banks, meaning that the depositors are actually the bank's owners. The depositor-owners elect a board of trustees who invest their money. Owners do not receive a fixed interest rate on their investment; rather, the bank divides net earnings from investments among depositors in proportion to their investment. Stock savings banks, operating like any corporation, are owned by stockholders who may or may not be depositors. Depositors in stock savings banks receive interest for their deposits, and owners receive profits in the form of dividends.

Savings and Loan Associations (S&Ls)

Savings and loan associations (S&Ls) accumulate money and redistribute it through loans on real estate, primarily residential mortgages. Most savings and loans are members of the Federal Home Loan Bank System, which operates much like the Federal Reserve System. Deposits up to $100,000 are also insured by the federally backed Federal Savings and Loan Insurance Corporation (FSLIC), which operates much like the FDIC. Originally, S&Ls specialized only in seeking investors and lending for real estate purchases. However, many went broke when interest rates climbed so high in the late 1970s and early 1980s. They had long-term loans at a fixed interest rate, say 12%. Thus, to make money, they had to attract depositors at an interest rate around 8 or 9%. However, depositors quit putting their money in the S&Ls because they could get higher interest rates in government securities, money market funds, and other places. Some went to variable-rate loans, allowing the interest rates on their loans to move up and down as actual interest rates changed, but this has not yet gained widespread acceptance.

In January, 1983, California liberalized regulation of S&Ls by significantly relaxing investment restrictions. Basically, the law frees S&Ls from ceilings on interest rates they can pay to investors and eliminates many restrictions on ownership. In the past, real estate developers were not allowed to sit on S&L boards; people feared they would use the S&L to their personal benefit. And an S&L had to have at least 400 shareholders. The new California law eliminates these requirements. Now it is easier to form S&Ls and to attract money. People are willing to invest, at least up to $100,000, if the interest rates are high because of the FSLIC insurance.

Although financing homes is still their number 1 business, many S&Ls now offer financing for short-term purchases.

S&Ls are also moving rapidly into other types of financial services. Although financing homes is still their number 1 business, many S&Ls now offer financing for short-term purchases (thanks to a 1982 law that allows them to do so). Paul Prior, president of Henry County Savings & Loan Association in New Castle, Indiana, says he will consider a loan on "most anything that rolls, floats, or flies." Mid-Kansas Federal Savings in Wichita, Kansas, now offers three-year loans to finance home computers. Others sell stocks and bonds and provide investment counseling. Some even offer insurance, including life insurance, annuities, and homeowner's protection policies. Because of these changes, S&Ls seem to be getting healthy again, as Fig. 16.9 illustrates.

Figure 16.9
Turnaround for S&Ls. *Source: Federal Home Loan Bank Board.*

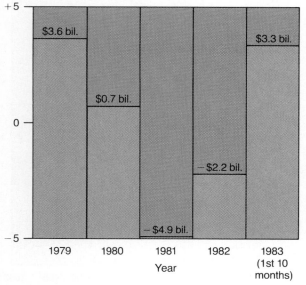

Earnings of savings and loan associations

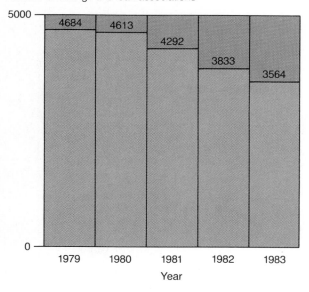

Number of savings and loan associations

Credit Unions

Credit unions are actually savings co-ops. Members usually have something in common, for example, they work for the same company. Credit unions pay interest to members for their savings, and because they are a co-op, they distribute additional profits in the form of dividends to the members at the end of the year. To borrow money, one has to become a member; this may mean depositing as little as $25 to buy a share. Deposits up to $100,000 are insured by the National Credit Union Administration (NCUA).

Because they have been much less regulated than other financial institutions, credit unions have been able to offer investors higher returns. And because some of their help was volunteer and companies often contributed space and other resources, credit unions had lower overhead costs. This allowed them to grant credit at lower rates, even though they were paying investors higher returns on their investments. Credit unions also serve members in other ways: For example, they offer checking accounts and may automatically deposit members' checks in their banks.

There are more than 20,000 credit unions, with 46 million members, and with assets in excess of $80 billion, but they will grow less rapidly in the future.

Although credit unions are still very important — there are more than 20,000 credit unions, with 46 million members, and with assets in excess of $80 billion — they will probably grow less rapidly in the future. Deregulation and additional customer services of other financial institutions reduces the favored position credit unions enjoyed during the 1970s. Figure 16.10 graphs membership growth of credit unions since 1970.

Pension Funds

Pension funds vary, but they usually collect savings from employees on a monthly contribution basis. They redistribute these funds by investing

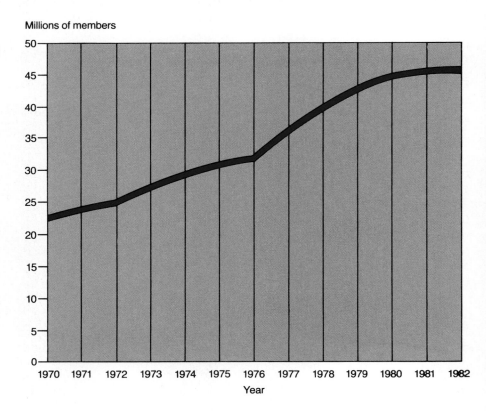

**Figure 16.10
Credit Union growth since 1970.** *Source: Credit Union National Association.*

Millions of members

in stocks and bonds. The funds guarantee employees a regular monthly income at retirement. Most of the pension funds are managed by employers, government departments, or unions as fringe benefits to the employees. A major incentive is the tax advantage. Employees can have their contributions withheld in the form of an annuity, which is not taxable at the time it is earned. Taxes have to be paid on the money when it is withdrawn, but this usually occurs after retirement when earnings are less and the taxpayer gets the benefit of a double exemption for being over 65. Pension plans hold over $400 billion in assets.

Insurance Companies

The 2500-plus life insurance companies in the United States hold more personal savings than any other type of financial institution—more than $300 billion. Individual policyholders pay regular premiums to companies. In return, the company pays a lump sum to beneficiaries when the insured policyholder dies. Life insurance policies also accumulate cash benefits that the policyholder may borrow against or cash in. Insurance companies return the money to the economy by investing in corporate bonds and stocks and, to a limited extent, home mortgages. They occasionally make loans to businesses. Most of their money goes into conservative, long-term investments that provide predictable returns.

SUMMARY

Money is a medium of exchange. It has little inherent worth but gains value because everyone accepts it as payment. Both coins and paper money are tokens. At one time, they could be redeemed for gold, but today they are backed by nothing more or less than the people's confidence in government. Checking accounts (demand deposits), NOW accounts, and savings accounts (time deposits) also represent money.

Money has remained useful in our economy because it retains the following characteristics: it is acceptable as legal tender, relatively stable in value, easy to handle, and difficult to counterfeit. Money not only serves as a medium of exchange; it allows us to store value and serves as a standard for communicating worth.

In recent years, banks have undergone several changes, including more competition, stronger profits, extra charges for services, more services, more interstate banking, increased mergers, and loss of status among customers.

Banks provide a wide variety of financial services, from storing cash to loaning money, which keeps the community growing. About 99% of all commercial banks belong to the FDIC, which insures each account up to $100,000.

In 1913, the government organized the Federal Reserve system. There are twelve Federal Reserve banks, each serving a federal district. Each district bank is governed by a board of directors. The Fed stabilizes the banking system and economy through the reserve requirement, rediscount rate, and purchase and sale of securities in the open market. Federal Reserve banks perform many banking activities for the federal government; they also clear checks for their member banks, and they physically circulate cash through the banks.

Several specialized financial institutions have evolved. The more popular ones are: savings banks, savings and loan associations, credit unions, pension funds, and insurance companies.

MIND YOUR BUSINESS

Instructions. Check your knowledge of money and banking by selecting the correct choice for each of the following questions:

_____ 1. Money serves in all the following ways except:
    a. As a medium of exchange
    b. As a means of storing purchasing power
    c. As a way of increasing the value of goods
    d. As a measure of the value of things

_____ 2. Money is protected in banks by all of the following except:
    a. Cash reserves
    b. Backing by silver holdings of banks
    c. Ability to borrow short-term funds quickly
    d. Federal Deposit Insurance Corporation

_____ 3. The text identified all of the following as trends in banking except:
    a. Heavy profits

b. Growth of interstate banking
c. Move toward smaller banks
d. Reduced status in customers' eyes

____ 4. The Federal Reserve System provides all the following services except:
a. Banking services for the federal government
b. Free check-clearing services for member banks
c. Housing and distributing coins
d. Housing and distributing paper money

____ 5. Which of the following financial institutions has benefitted from more liberalized laws in California?
a. Savings banks
b. Savings and loan associations
c. Credit unions
d. Life insurance companies

See answers at the back of the book.

KEY TERMS

money, 408
checking account (demand deposit), 410
negotiable order of withdrawal (NOW) account, 410
savings account (time deposit), 410
smart card, 411
Drexon laser card, 411
national bank, 412
state bank, 412
prime rate, 413
Federal Deposit Insurance Corporation (FDIC), 413
automated teller machine (ATM), 415
electronic funds transfer system (EFTS), 416
point-of-sale (POS), 416
Federal Reserve System (FRS), 419
board of governors, 420
Open Market Committee, 421
money supply, 421
M1, 421
M2, 421

M3, 421
reserve requirement, 421
rediscount rate, 422
savings bank, 423
savings and loan association (S&L), 424
credit union, 426
pension fund, 426

REVIEW QUESTIONS

1. What is money? What does it mean to say money is a medium of exchange?
2. Describe the most common forms of money. What characteristics should money have to be usable in the business world?
3. What is a NOW account? How does it work?
4. How does money serve us?
5. Where does money come from?
6. Describe the purpose of commercial banks.
7. How is money protected while in the custody of commercial banks?
8. Describe some of the recent trends in banking.
9. Describe the Federal Reserve System. How is it organized?
10. How do banks create money?
11. Explain how the Federal Reserve System increases and decreases the money supply.
12. Define M1; M2; M3.
13. Describe the major services of the Federal Reserve System.
14. Identify other major financial institutions and briefly describe them.

CASES

Case 16.1: Where to Put Cash?

Suppose you had $5000 in cash that you would not need for a couple of years. Where could you put it so that it would be available at the end of 2 years and still earn a respectable interest for you during the 2-year period? Consider the following alternatives: money market mutual funds, savings and loan associations, mutual savings banks, savings account, treasury bills, common stock, gold.

Questions

1. Analyze the advantages and disadvantages of each of these possibilities.

2. Select the best source for your cash and tell why.

Case 16.2: The Float as a Means of Money

Float is the amount of time that it takes a check to go through the commercial banking system's check-clearing process and to be debited to the appropriate account. It might work this way. If a company pays a supplier in Atlanta with a $500,000 check drawn on a bank in Dallas, about 2 days elapse between when the supplier deposits it and the time it reaches the company's account in Dallas. But if the company draws their check on a remote branch bank in Utah, the check has to go through one or more Federal Reserve banks, and the float may be extended to 5 days. During the float period, the company is using the Federal Reserve money interest-free while leaving their own cash in an account, investing it in inventory, or providing it for compensating balances. For a large company, the returns from float could amount to many thousands of dollars per year.

Questions

1. As a Federal Reserve banker, what attitude would you take toward the float?

2. Does the float increase or decrease the money supply? What impact does this have on the Federal Reserve system?

3. If you were an officer in a company, what would be your attitude toward the float?

After completing this chapter, you will be able to:

■ Describe the objectives and the role of the financial manager.

■ Analyze four short-term sources of capital.

■ Analyze six long-term sources of capital.

■ Explain how companies sell stocks and bonds to raise money.

■ Compare stocks and bonds as capital sources.

■ Explain three ways the firms use capital.

17

BUSINESS FINANCE: RAISING AND INVESTING CAPITAL

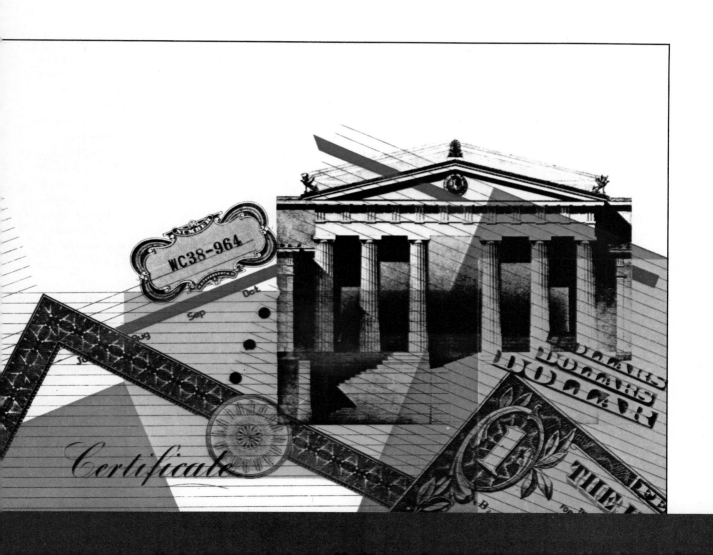

Metro-Goldwyn-Mayer Film Co. (MGM) bought United Artists in 1981, but most of their new film releases were failures. The new company ran up a debt of $675 million; interest alone was $107 million per year. Obviously, the company needed capital badly. To raise capital, Chairman Frank Rothman: 1) sold the company's music publishing division to CBS, Inc., for $68 million; 2) spun off a new company, Home Entertainment Group, Co., and sold 15% of its stock to the public for $50 million; 3) issued $400 million worth of senior notes. These moves slashed the company debt from $526 million to $46 million and cut interest payments to $53 million annually. And the company started producing hit movies, including "A Christmas Story," and "Yentl."

It seems that businesses always need capital, even large and profitable businesses. In larger businesses, expertly trained specialists, fortressed by reams of computer printouts, make recommendations to management on raising and investing capital. Small business owners shoulder this responsibility by themselves or with the aid of an accountant or friendly banker. After describing the role of the financial manager, this chapter deals with sources of short-term and long-term capital and uses of funds.

THE FINANCIAL MANAGER

One of the more powerful positions in most organizations is usually that of the financial manager. Typically holding the title of vice-president of finance, he or she is responsible for the overall financial planning of the firm. Not only must he or she be skilled in financial matters, the financial manager must be able to plan well and coordinate the efforts of production, marketing, research and development, and other units within the firm. A *Wall Street Journal* ad for a financial manager listed as some of the requirements: solid corporate-level cash management experience, supervisory experience, excellent communication skills, and excellent presentation skills, as well as the need for proficiency in financial matters.

Financial managers have been so powerful in recent years that about one in five company presidents have financial backgrounds. (See Fig. 17.1 for the backgrounds of the chief executive officers.) Recently, there has been some criticism of companies relying too much on "the numbers," (that is, financial data) in decision making. However, there is little doubt that financial managers still have, and will continue to have, a lot of influence in their organizations.

Objective of Financial Management

The financial manager's aim is to increase the worth of the firm. To do this, the financial manager, with diligence and energy, must develop policies and strategies to increase the profits and market value of the business. If the firm's stock is traded on one of the major exchanges, increase in price over a long period of time is usually a strong indicator that the financial manager is doing a good job.

In 1979, Boise Cascade offered twice the market price of the stock ($120 million) in a takeover bid for Stone Container Corp., a paperboard company. Roger Stone, CEO, refused the offer and set about rebuilding the company. Stone used long-term debt of $220 million over a 5-year period to build new plant and equipment. He also recently acquired three other mills. His moves paid off. During the summer of 1983, Stone Container Corp. stock was selling at $28 per share, three times more than the Boise Cascade offer.

Of course, a firm's success depends upon many things: having a good product or service, marketing products and services effectively, managing people well, and the like. But all this requires effective financial planning. As one analyst put it, "Finance represents the oxygen of a business. Without effective utilization of finances, you will not exist for long."

Role of the Financial Manager

More specifically, the financial manager must provide the answers to questions such as:

- How much financing will the company need?
- What is the best source of short-term funds?
- What is the best source of long-term funds?
- What is the best short-term and long-term use of these funds?
- Do we have funds available, at the cheapest cost, when we need them?
- Are we managing our cash in the most effective way?

These are the major areas. Financial managers, especially in larger firms, might also oversee most other financial matters, including credit and collections, the budgeting process, stock and

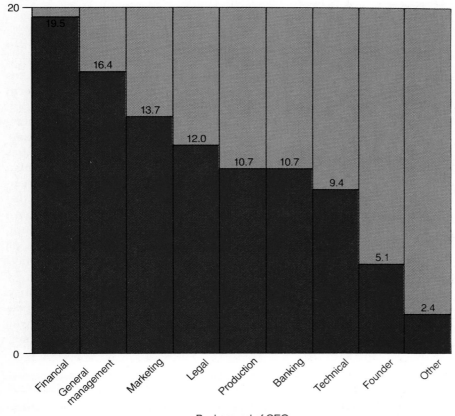

Percentage of total

Figure 17.1
Backgrounds of chief executive officers. *Source: Louis E. Boone and James C. Johnson, "The 801 Men (and One Woman) at the Top: A Profile of the CEOs of the Largest U.S. Corporations," Business Horizons, Feb. 1980, p. 50, copyright 1980 by the Foundation of the School of Business at Indiana University, reprinted by permission.*

Background of CEO

How Financial Management Contributes to USAir's Success

Last year, USAir was the most profitable airline in the Western world. And the firm has been consistently profitable at a time when airlines skyrocket during boom periods and drop like a rock during busts. During the last 3 years, USAir's profits have been $60 million, $51 million, and $59 million.

Sound financial management contributes mightily to their success. With deregulation, airlines lost the protection of their routes. Edwin Colodny, president of USAir, said that airlines had to operate more conservatively without the protection of regulation. "They can't become dependent on debt financing. It exposes a company to very difficult times in a recession," Colodny explained.

In 1976, USAir's debt was 85% of total capital. Now, it is 38%. Colodny reduced the debt load by selling common and preferred stock or convertible debentures eight times since 1978. These long-term capital sources raised $370 million. The light debt load allowed Colodny to keep buying new, more efficient airliners, even when the economy was not expanding so rapidly.

Source: Howard Banks, "Cruising Speed," *Forbes,* Nov. 21, 1983, p. 95.

---

bond issues, and even purchasing and inventory policies.

In a program to enhance the long-term value of its assets, Gulf Oil Company announced that they had made the following financial decisions:

- Invested $500 million to modernize its refineries.
- Started a cost reduction program expected to reduce overhead expenses $100 million a year.
- Sold $2 billion worth of marginal assets.
- Reduced its debt by more than $300 million.
- Increased its dividend to $3.00 per share.

Gulf further stated that they had the financial strength to spend $3 to $3.5 billion over the next few years on capital expenditures without extensive new borrowing.

SOURCES OF SHORT-TERM CAPITAL

Short-term or working capital is necessary to meet the daily operational needs of the business. Firms may need small change for a few days, or they may require large sums for several months. In either case, **short-term financing** is for a period less than a year. A successful business generates money, some of which can be used for short-term needs in its normal course of operations. But, sometimes firms feel the need to secure short-term funds from other sources. There may be several reasons for this. (1) Almost every business has seasonal peaks of activity, and a company may borrow short-term money to meet seasonal financial demands. (2) Many suppliers offer cash discounts for early payment. When firms do not have the money to take advantage of the cash discount, they may borrow it on a short-term basis. (3) Sometimes managers are not able to collect their credit sales on time. It is common to borrow money while they try to collect. (4) Occasionally, a brief and shining opportunity emerges unexpectedly, and managers may go to the short-term well to take advantage. (5) Likewise, evil-looking emer-

---

The most widely used sources of short-term credit are trade credit, bank credit, commercial paper, and finance companies.

---

gencies pop up without warning, creating capital needs for a brief period. The most widely used sources of short-term credit are trade credit, bank credit, commercial paper, and finance companies.

Trade Credit

Trade credit is credit extended to the buyer by the seller, and it is the most popular form of short-term financing. Suppose a supplier sells a customer inventory worth $5000 and allows 60 days for payment. The customer might be able to sell some or all of the inventory before having to pay the supplier. Thus, the customer has the use of the money that otherwise would have had to be spent on inventory. In this way, trade credit counts as a source of capital. As an owner of a small parts supply company expressed, "I try to get as much of my inventory on credit as I can. I don't have to come up with the cash when it is delivered."

Open-account credit. **Open-account credit,** sometimes called **open-book,** is the sale of something from one company to another, with payment expected at a later date. It is unsecured, simple, and based on the good faith of both the seller and the buyer. A buyer can order goods from a supplier with a purchase order. The supplier ships the goods and bills the buyer with an invoice listing the items shipped and stating the credit terms. The supplier has a copy of the purchase order, a duplicate of the invoice, and an entry in his books showing that the items were sold to the buyer on credit. About 80% of the total volume of wholesale and retail sales are open account. Open-account credit is usually accompanied by credit terms which express the period of time the firm has to pay its bill and any cash discount for early payment. Payment periods may range from 10 to more than 90 days, but 30 days is most common. Most suppliers allow a discount if payment is made within a specified period. An example of credit terms is 2/10, net 30. This means that full payment is due in 30 days, but the buyer would receive a 2% discount by paying within 10 days. Companies like to take advantage of the cash discount and often borrow money to do so if necessary. On the 2/10, net 30 terms, the advantage is figured as follows:

- It would cost 2% interest to use the money for the additional 20 days.

- There are approximately eighteen 20-day periods in a year (360 divided by 20).

- Two percent times 18 equals 35% interest rate (the cost of ignoring the discount).

Sellers offer cash discounts to reduce billing expenses and bad debts and so they can get, and use, the money quicker.

Open-account credit is widely used because it is economical, easy to get, flexible, and convenient. If the purchaser takes advantage of the cash discount, there is no obvious cost for the credit. The cost of credit may be buried in the price, but it is difficult to find a supplier who would reduce the price for a cash payment. Suppliers, eager to sell their merchandise, often sell on credit to firms that do not have the financial stability to borrow from a bank. A firm can adjust its use of trade credit to fit the demands of the times. Inventory may accumulate prior to the busy season; the company can do this handily by expanding its use of trade credit. During the slack season when there is less need for inventory, the business can reduce its trade credit accordingly. Finally, the purchaser can get trade credit conveniently: no lengthy investigations, no rigid payment schedules, and no paperwork rituals.

Promissory notes. A **promissory note** is a written promise by one person (the **maker**) to pay another (the **bearer**) a certain amount at a particular time or upon demand. Promissory notes are customary in a few businesses, such as wholesale jewelry and furs. If an open account is overdue, a supplier may request a promissory note to give the credit stronger documentation. However, the promissory note gives no more security than the open account; it merely reduces arguments over the terms.

Promissory notes are usually negotiable; that is, the holder of the note, the bearer, can sell the note to someone else. Suppose a wholesaler sells $10,000 worth of goods on credit to a retailer, to be paid in 90 days. The wholesaler could ask for a promissory note from the retailer. If, at the end of 30 days the wholesaler needs the money, she might be able to sell the note (at a discount) to a bank. She would get the money sooner, and when the note became due, the retailer would repay the bank.

Drafts (bills of exchange). A **trade draft,** also called **bill of exchange,** is a written instrument made by Person A ordering Person B to pay a sum of money to Person C on demand or at some future date. If payable on demand, it is a **sight draft;** if payable at a future date, it is a **time draft.** Differing from a promissory note, it is drawn by a creditor, rather than a borrower, and it is an order, not a promise, to pay.

Bills of exchange are common in foreign trade. Company A may sell goods to Company B in another country on credit. Company A requests Company B to pay their account with a bill of exchange. Company B goes to its bank and buys a bill of exchange drawn on a bank in Company A's city. Company B then sends this draft to Company A. This gives Company A quicker use of the money because they can take it directly to their bank and get immediate payment. If Company B had sent an ordinary check, the check would have had to clear Company B's home bank before the account was legally paid. Figure 17.2 diagrams this process.

A time draft may also be called a **trade acceptance,** especially when used in domestic trade. When a supplier (seller) ships goods, he may ship a trade acceptance and shipping documents to a local bank. The trade acceptance is an order for the buyer to pay. When the buyer signs it, she formally acknowledges the debt. The bank returns the trade acceptance to the supplier and turns over the shipping documents to the buyer,

who uses them to pick up the goods from the shipper. When the draft is due, the bank notifies the buyer, who pays the supplier. This paperwork produces a legal document stating the debt terms on which the supplier may collect accounts or borrow money.

A draft always involves three parties, but, as strange as it sounds, two parties may be the same person.

A draft always involves three parties, but, as strange as it sounds, two parties may be the same person. For instance, a firm can order itself to pay itself $10,000 in 6 months. Then the firm can give this order to the bank and borrow money on it for 6 months.

Bank Credit

Commercial banks have changed their image from the days of barred windows, brass spitoons, and conservative bank officers who begrudgingly made loans. In recent years, modern-thinking officers in space-age banks have so successfully marketed their services that bank credit has

Figure 17.2
Example of how a bill of exchange enhances financing.

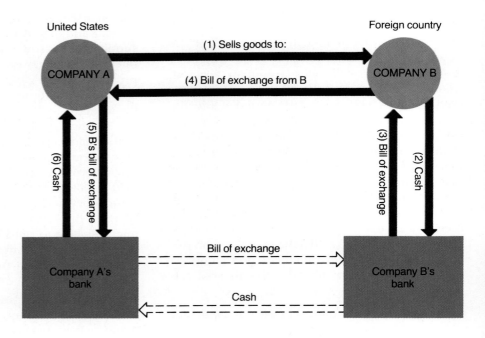

vaulted into second place among short-term funding sources.

Most companies borrow short-term funds from banks by establishing a **line of credit,** an informal agreement between the bank and the customer that establishes a maximum amount the bank will loan. Thus, the customer does not have to renegotiate each new loan. If a company has a $100,000 line of credit and owes the bank $30,000, the company can borrow an additional $70,000 just by instructing the bank to credit its account. Though the agreement is informal and the bank is not legally obligated, the bank would rather honor its agreement than develop a reputation for being quirky and unreliable. Banks customarily require that companies pay their accounts off completely at least once a year. Banks review the financial status of their borrowers at least yearly but may do so monthly as well. If borrowers use their credit line as a long-term loan, the bank may request that they convert their loan to a long-term commitment.

A **revolving-credit agreement** is much like a line of credit but the agreement extends for 2 years or longer. Also, since the funds have to be available upon request, the bank, or banks, agreeing to supply the funds typically charge 0.5% a year on the average amount of unused funds.

Clevepak, which makes heating, air conditioning, and plumbing products, negotiated a 5-year, $100-million, revolving-credit agreement with four major commercial banks — Manufacturers Hanover Trust, Bank of New York, Continental Illinois National Bank & Trust Company, and Chase Manhattan Bank. According to Clevepak, this arrangement will significantly reduce their borrowing costs.

For borrowers who want money only occasionally, the bank handles each request separately. Suppose a company experiences an unexpected sales decline that puts it into a gasp for cash. Company officers may approach the bank for a loan of, say, $50,000 to get them over the hump. The bank considers the loan a one-shot deal. If the bank makes the loan, the borrower usually signs a promissory note to repay the loan plus interest within a specified time. A **single-payment note** is a loan that is repaid in a single lump sum. Such notes are normally for a short period, 3 to 6 months. Banks also expect to handle the checking accounts of their loan customers.

They often require their borrowers to maintain some minimum deposit or **compensating balance.** Suppose a company borrows $30,000. If the bank requires a 10% compensating balance, the company will have to maintain $3000 in its account. The company has use of only $27,000 but pays interest on $30,000. This effectively increases the interest rate.

Unsecured bank loans. Bank loans may be secured or unsecured. An **unsecured loan,** also called **signature loan,** has nothing of tangible value pledged to back it up. An officer of the borrowing company merely signs her name to a note and the bank agrees to loan the money. Of course, a bank must feel confident that the borrower is financially sound and of high integrity before it would make such a loan.

Secured bank loans. Most bank loans of any size are **secured loans,** that is, they require some form of collateral in addition to the signed promissory note. **Collateral** is property, or something else of tangible worth, that the borrower pledges to support the loan. If, for some reason, the borrower cannot repay, the bank takes the collateral, sells it, and applies the cash to the loan. Banks normally accept many forms of collateral for short-term loans, including:

1. *Stocks and bonds.* This usually means **stocks and bonds** owned by the company of other well-known companies listed on the major stock exchanges.

2. *Accounts receivable.* **Accounts receivable** is money that other people owe a company for things sold to them on credit. Most banks will take a certain percentage, say 80%, of total credit sales as collateral for a loan.

3. *Warehouse receipt.* One of the most common types of collateral for short-term loans, **a warehouse receipt** is a contract for possession of goods that have been both received and stored by a warehouse. Title to the goods is described in the receipt. It works like this. A company has an excess of goods. It stores them in a public warehouse for a storage fee. The warehouse issues a warehouse receipt to the business which can present the receipt to a bank as collateral for a loan.

4. *Bills of lading.* When a company ships goods, it receives a **bill of lading** as a receipt (see Fig. 17.3). A **straight bill of lading** states that the order is being shipped to a specific person. It is nonnegotiable. If the receipt does not specify that the shipment be received by a specific person, it is an **order bill of lading,** which is negotiable. Since the bill of lading represents title to the goods, the holder of either type can use it as collateral.
5. *Chattel mortgages.* A **chattel mortgage** gives the holder right to reclaim an item if a loan is not paid. Such mortgages are used as security on personal property that is movable. Suppose a florist wants to purchase a delivery truck for his business. He can make a down payment and borrow the remainder of the purchase price from the bank (or other lending agencies, for that matter). He receives both the truck and the title; the bank retains a chattel mortgage on the truck.
6. *Floor planning.* When retailers handle tangible, expensive items such as cars and appliances, they usually assign their title to this inventory to banks, or other lending agencies, for short-term loans. This arrangement is called **floor planning.** Automobile dealers use floor planning extensively. When a car

Figure 17.3
An example of a straight bill of lading.

† The fibre boxes used for this shipment conform to the specifications set forth in the box maker's certificate thereon, and all other requirements of Consolidated Freight Classification.

† (Shipper's imprint in lieu of stamp; not a part of bill of lading approved by the Interstate Commerce Commission.)

STRAIGHT BILL OF LADING—SHORT FORM

ORIGINAL — NOT NEGOTIABLE

Shipper's No. ____________

CARRIER: Carrier's No. ____________

RECEIVED, subject to the classifications and tariffs in effect on the date of the issue of this Bill of Lading,

At ____________ 19 ____ From ____________

the property described below, in apparent good order, except as noted (contents and condition of contents of packages unknown), marked, consigned, and destined as indicated below, which said carrier (the word carrier being understood throughout this contract as meaning any person or corporation in possession of the property under the contract) agrees to carry to its usual place of delivery at said destination, if on its route, otherwise to deliver to another carrier on the route to said destination. It is mutually agreed, as to each carrier of all or any of said property over all or any portion of said route to destination, and as to each party at any time interested in all or any of said property, that every service to be performed hereunder shall be subject to all the terms and conditions of the Uniform Domestic Straight Bill of Lading set forth (1) in Official, Southern, Western and Illinois Freight Classifications in effect on the date hereof, if this is a rail or a rail-water shipment, or (2) in the applicable motor carrier classification or tariff if this is a motor carrier shipment.

Shipper hereby certifies that he is familiar with all the terms and conditions of the said bill of lading, including those on the back thereof, set forth in the classification or tariff which governs the transportation of this shipment, and the said terms and conditions are hereby agreed to by the shipper and accepted for himself and his assigns.

Consigned to ____________
(Mail or street address of consignee—For purposes of notification only.)

Destination ____________ State ____________ County ____________ Delivery Address* ____________
(★ To be filled in only when shipper desires and governing tariffs provide for delivery thereat.)

Route ____________

Delivering Carrier ____________ Car or Vehicle Initials ____________ No. ____________

No. Packages	KIND OF PACKAGE, DESCRIPTION OF ARTICLES, SPECIAL MARKS, AND EXCEPTIONS	*WEIGHT (Sub. to Cor.)	Class or Rate	EXTENSION
	CARTONS TEXTBOOKS NOIBN			
	PALLETS TEXTBOOKS NOIBN			
	CARTONS FORMS, RULED W/O HEADINGS			
	CUSTOMER'S ORDER NO.			

Subject to Section 7 of Conditions of applicable bill of lading, if this shipment is to be delivered to the consignee without recourse on the consignor, the consignor shall sign the following statement:
The carrier shall not make delivery of this shipment without payment of freight and all other lawful charges.

(Signature of consignor.)

If charges are to be prepaid, write or stamp here, "To be Prepaid."

Received $ ____________
to apply in prepayment of the charges on the property described hereon.

Agent or Cashier.

Per ____________
(The signature here acknowledges only the amount prepaid.)

Charges advanced: $ ____________

*If the shipment moves between two ports by a carrier by water, the law requires that the bill of lading shall state whether it is carrier's or shipper's weight.
NOTE—Where the rate is dependent on value, shippers are required to state specifically in writing the agreed or declared value of the property.
The agreed or declared value of the property is hereby specifically stated by the shipper to be not exceeding ____________ per ____________

Shipper Per ____________ Agent ____________ Per ____________

Permanent post-office-address of shipper:

1

ORIGINAL

Commercial paper may be bought and sold through dealers monitoring current interest rates and other money market indicators.

dealer receives a shipment of new cars, the dealer will keep the cars but will assign title of the cars to the bank. In turn, the bank makes the dealer a loan so that he or she can pay the manufacturer for the inventory. The dealer hopes to sell the new cars before the short-term note comes due at the bank. Then, when the dealer receives payment for a car, the bank loan will be repaid.

Commercial Paper

Commercial paper consists of unsecured promissory notes issued by large, well-established companies on the open market. The notes usually vary from 4 to 6 months. They are frequently issued in multiples of $5000, from a minimum of $25,000, $100,000, or even $1,000,000. Commercial paper may be sold through dealers to the public or placed directly with a lending institution. Traditionally, rate of interest on commercial paper is lower than average. Commercial banks are heavy purchasers, along with mutual funds, insurance companies, and pension funds. This method of borrowing allows companies with good credit ratings to borrow more money at a lower rate of interest than they can get through traditional bank loans.

Finance Companies

A number of finance companies specialize in providing short-term money for businesses and individuals. **Commercial finance companies** buy accounts receivable at a discount. The business gets cash immediately and the finance company has to collect the receivable. But if the receivable turns bad, the business is still obligated to pay the finance company. Finance companies may also make direct loans on inventory, machinery, or equipment. Interest rates are usually high, and the lender often places restrictions on management. Because of this, most firms consider direct loans to be a last resort. Finance companies buy accounts receivable outright at a discount. This is also called **factoring.** The receivable makes payments directly to the factor, which assumes all the risks of collecting. This allows the business to reassign the risks and costs of running a credit department to a specialist. Most factor users are small companies who do not have the wherewithal to operate their own credit departments.

Indirectly, a company can create short-term funds by encouraging customers to pay cash for their merchandise and borrow from other sources. **Consumer and sales finance companies** make small personal loans ($1000 to $4000)

FUNNY BUSINESS

"We need two hundred million bucks by Friday — any ideas?"

directly to customers. Interest rates are excessive, sometimes going over 25%. They may also loan directly to customers who wish to buy durable goods such as cars, television sets, appliances, and furniture. The lender secures the loan with a chattel mortgage, whereby the item is pledged as security. Again, interest rates are high, ranging between 18 and 30%. General Motors Acceptance Corporation (GMAC), with over $15 million in assets, is one of the largest sales finance companies.

SOURCES OF LONG-TERM FINANCING

Companies may try to get long-term money from internal sources by planning how they spend their cash and profits, but most also have to go to external sources from time to time. The most common sources of long-term capital are sale of stocks, sale of bonds, term loans, leasing, and retained earnings.

Selling Stocks (Equity Capital)

As we described in Chapter 4, stock represents ownership in the company. When a company raises money by selling stocks, whoever buys the stock actually becomes part owner of the company. Because of this, money raised from sale of stocks is called **equity capital.** Companies usually hire specialists called investment bankers to help them sell their stocks. (The same method is also used to sell bonds. We use the term **securities** to refer to stocks and bonds.)

Investment bankers are specialists in the placement of securities. They help design the pricing, special provisions, and timing of a company's offering. "Going public" refers to the process of attempting to sell a large number of shares to a large number of investors. During the first half of 1983, 317 companies offered stock shares to the public for the first time, raising a record $5.5 billion. Many investors like new public offerings because the price often jumps within a few days or weeks after the public offering. Trak Auto, an auto-parts firm, sold its stock to the public at $22 per share; within weeks, the price had soared to $48.75 before trailing off.

The negotiation and agreement on terms between the investment banker and the company is

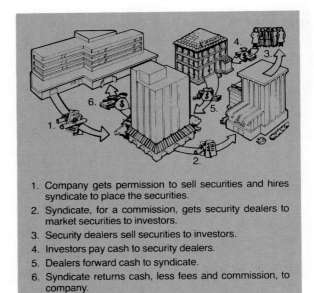

1. Company gets permission to sell securities and hires syndicate to place the securities.
2. Syndicate, for a commission, gets security dealers to market securities to investors.
3. Security dealers sell securities to investors.
4. Investors pay cash to security dealers.
5. Dealers forward cash to syndicate.
6. Syndicate returns cash, less fees and commission, to company.

Figure 17.4
How a business raises capital by selling stock (a public placement).

called **origination. Underwriting** is the purchase of the issue or the guarantee of its sale at a specific price. A number of banks agree to pool their efforts, in an arrangement called a **syndicate,** to share in the underwriting because issues of several million dollars are too much for one bank to handle. As many as fifty to one hundred separate security dealers may assist the syndicate in selling the issues. The syndicate pays the security dealers for the number of issues sold. The underwriting syndicate may take the securities on a firm-commitment or best-effort basis. On a firm commitment, the syndicate pays the company the offering price, less a discount. The company receives full payment when the offering date arrives, regardless of how many securities are sold. The underwriter or the company may decide to place the issue privately with insurance companies, pension funds, or mutual funds. Private placements are attractive because they avoid many of the fees and costs. Most private placements are bonds.

American Motors, after accruing substantial product development costs, needed long-term funds. Working with Lehman Brothers Kuhn Loeb, an underwriting firm, American Motors decided to raise money by selling common stock to the public. Eventually, they sold 10 million shares. Figure 17.4 shows how businesses raise capital by selling stock.

Authorized, issued, and unissued stock. When a company originally incorporates, its charter identifies the number of shares it can issue, called **authorized stock.** If management wishes to issue more than was authorized, they have to get their stockholders' approval. A company may not sell all the stock its charter authorizes. **Unissued stock** is that portion of authorized stock that has not been sold, and **issued** stock is the portion of authorized stock that has been sold.

Stock ledger. By law, a corporation must keep a record of who owns its stock. Such records are kept in a ledger which usually includes:

■ Each owner's name and address.

■ The date the owner bought the shares.

■ How many shares each owner has.

In smaller corporations, the secretary keeps these records, but larger companies may hire specialists such as banks to do it.

Examples of Public and Private Offerings

Public offerings

Public issues have to be registered with the Securities Exchange Commission and they are typically offered to large numbers of buyers through investment banks and brokerage houses.

1. Thermedics, Inc., in Waltham, Massachusetts, offered 650,000 shares of common stock at $9.50 per share. The company makes polyurethane plastics and is developing artificial heart systems. They planned to use the proceeds for product development and testing and to expand manufacturing.

2. Applied Circuit Technology, Inc., in Anaheim, California, offered 2,150,000 shares at $11 per share. ACT builds test equipment used in making and testing disk and tape drives. They planned to use the proceeds to pay debts and expand operations.

3. Kaypro Corp., Solana Beach, California, offered 4 million shares at $10 per share. Kaypro manufactures portable microcomputer systems for both business and personal use. They used the proceeds for working capital.

Private placements

Private placements do not have to be registered with the Securities Exchange Commission, and they are not distributed in large volume to public investors.

1. Pat's International, Inc., Philadelphia, Pennsylvania, got local investors to pay $300,000 for stock in a private placement. Pat's developed the Philadelphia cheesesteak sandwich, and they plan to try serving their steaks nationwide. They also planned to go public with another offering in 1984.

2. American Sharecom, Inc., of Minneapolis, Minnesota, raised $1,650,000 from local individuals and two institutions that agreed to purchase common stock at $1 per share. The company provides long-distance telephone service to Minneapolis-St. Paul.

3. Biskets, Jacksonville, Florida, obtained $7,250,000 from a private placement to overseas investors. Biskets is a chain of 30 fast-food restaurants in Florida.

Stock values. When companies originally issue stock, they may assign it a par value or they may issue it as no-par value. **Par value** is the dollar amount actually printed on the stock certificates. Originally, par value was the price of the sale of the stock, but today people usually pay more for stock than its par value. In no case does par value guarantee an actual price that the stock is worth. To avoid confusion over par value, most stock today is issued as **no-par value stock;** that is, they do not print a price on the certificate.

If you are not confused yet, consider that stock also has a market value and a book value. **Market value** is the actual price at which the stock is bought and sold. This is often the most important value to owners because it tells them what their stock is really worth. **Book value** is the value recorded on the company's accounting records. To determine book value, divide the net worth of the company by the shares of stock outstanding. This gives owners some idea of the dollars per share their stock is worth according to the company financial records.

Preemptive rights. Suppose a corporation decides to issue more stock for sale so they can raise additional capital. Current owners may have a right, called **preemptive right,** to purchase a proportionate share of the new stock issue. This right protects them from losing their share of ownership, and perhaps control, in the corporation. To illustrate, assume that you own 20,000 shares of a company that has issued 100,000 shares of stock. (You own 20% — 100,000 ÷ 20,000 — of the company.) If the company sells another 100,000 shares, your ownership has now dropped to 10% (200,000 ÷ 20,000) unless you buy a proportionate share of the new offering. Preemptive rights exist only when the company provides for them in their incorporation certificate or when state law requires them.

Stock option. A **stock option** is an agreement to buy stock under certain conditions or at a certain time, usually at a pegged price. Options are usually given to corporate executives as incentives for them to help make the company successful. As a board member explains, "We offer our key executives an option to buy 10,000 shares of the company's stock at a price of $50 per share,

the current market price. Although there is no advantage to exercising the option immediately, it spurs the executive to crusade for the company's success." As the company became successful, the stock, let us hope, would rise in price, say, to $80 per share. Executives could exercise their option to buy at $50 and have a tidy profit.

In 1971, Jerome W. Robbins became president of HMW Industries, the old Hamilton Watch Company. The company was in bad trouble, having just lost $23 million. To entice Robbins to become president, the board of directors provided him with options to buy 100,000 shares at $4 per share. Robbins began selling off the watches and other unprofitable products and concentrated on industrial fasteners, silver flatware, and electronic fuses for the military. Eventually, the company became profitable, and in 1983 the Clabir Corporation bought HMW Industries for $45 per share. Robbins exercised his options and made a pretax profit of about $2.4 million.

Stock splits. A **stock split** is dividing outstanding shares into additional units. Suppose you own 100 shares of stock that splits 2 for 1, and the market price is $100 per share ($10,000 total). After the split, you would have 200 shares of stock, but it would be worth approximately $50 per share ($10,000 total). Companies usually split the stock to bring the price down to a lower range so that more people will buy and sell it.

Dividends. **Dividends** are the profits of the company that are paid to the stock owners. Periodically, usually quarterly, the board of directors meets and decides whether to distribute any of the profits. Although they are under no requirement to do so, most companies like to distribute some of the profits as a return to the owners for investing their money in the company. Some companies will keep most or all of their earnings to reinvest in future growth. Eastern Airlines, which reported a record net loss of $183.7 million for 1983, voted in January 1984 not to pay quarterly dividends on three of the company's preferred stock issues. The payouts were the airline's second consecutive missed dividend.

Common stock. **Common stock,** the most common kind, represents ownership in a com-

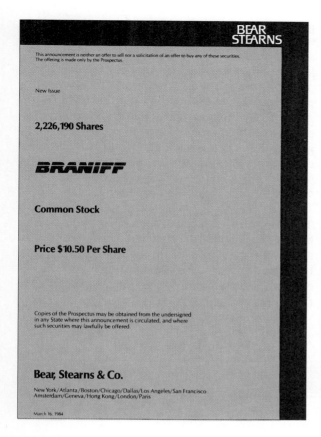

Common stock offerings, available through numerous dealers, are announced to prospective buyers by such advertisements.

pany. But it does not guarantee the owner a specific rate of return or even that dividends will be declared. Often referred to as residual owners, common stockholders receive no dividends until interest is paid on bonds and other debts and money is distributed to preferred stockholders (if there are any). If the company goes broke, common stockholders likewise get last claim on whatever is left over.

But all is not negative for common stock owners. Remember, they do have voting rights, at one vote per share, to elect the board of directors. The board of directors makes a lot of decisions, such as when and if dividends will be declared. There is no fixed limit to the amount of dividends that can be paid to common stockholders, so during favorable times, they may receive very high rates. Also, their stock tends to increase in price if the company is successful.

Preferred stock. Another type of stock, **preferred stock,** has certain preferences over common stock. Typically, preferred stockholders have a right to:

- Receive their dividends before common stockholders.
- Expect a dividend at a stated rate, such as 8%.
- Prior claim on assets (ahead of common stock owners) if the company goes broke.

The board of directors does not have the choice of eliminating dividends to preferred owners and granting them to common owners. The preferred must get theirs first, and they get it at a known, predetermined rate.

Dividends to preferred stock may be cumulative or noncumulative. **Cumulative preferred stock** maintains its claim to dividends even if the company decides not to pay them. For instance, if the company had a bad year in 1983, they might decide not to pay dividends. But if they had a good year in 1984 and declared dividends, cumulative preferred owners would get their share, at the specified rate, both for 1983 and 1984. **Noncumulative preferred stock** dividends do not accumulate. If dividends are not declared, noncumulative owners lose their claim to the profits of that period.

Participating preferred stock has the advantage of receiving its regular dividends, plus sharing with common stockholders in the division of whatever earnings are remaining. **Nonparticipating preferred stock,** the most widely used, claims only its specified rate of return. If shipping crates of profits are left for the common owners, nonparticipating preferred does not share.

To offset some of these advantages, preferred stock normally has some restrictions on voting privileges. Typically, preferred owners may vote only on selected company matters, usually decisions that directly affect the value of their stock, such as changing some of the agreements of the preferred stock. Rarely will preferred stock carry no voting rights, and equally rarely will it carry full voting rights. United States Steel Corporation recently raised $250 million through a preferred stock sale.

Comparison of common and preferred stock. In short, common stock usually has:

- More control through voting privileges.
- Greater chance for high returns.
- More risk.

Whereas preferred stock usually has:

- Less control.
- Fixed returns.
- Less risk.
- Less chance for big gains.

Selling Bonds (Debt Capital)

A **bond** is merely a certificate stating that the company owes money to the bondholder. Unlike stocks, bonds do not mean ownership in the company. When people buy bonds, they make a loan to the company. Thus, money raised through the sale of bonds is called **debt capital.** "When we issue bonds," says a company spokesperson, "we promise to pay the exact amount borrowed, the **principal,** at some future time **(maturity date).** And we pay interest yearly to the bondholder for the use of the money." Since these are fixed obligations of the company, debt capital is more risky than equity capital. But firms are wise to borrow money if they can earn more with it than is involved in the expense of borrowing it.

The bond indenture. When corporations issue bonds, they prepare a detailed agreement of the rights and privileges of the bondholder, called a **bond indenture** or a **trust indenture.** The indenture usually includes information on: (1) why the bonds are being issued, (2) at what price they will be issued, (3) how many bonds are issued, (4)

CROSS FIRE

How Important Are Dividends Versus Debt Reduction?

Warner Communications Inc.'s stock price fell from a high of almost $60 per share to $20 per share. The reasons: Warner had a loss of $425 million in the first 9 months of the year, and they borrowed $445 million. On September 30, 1983, two-thirds of Warner's capitalization was financed by debt and only one-third by equity. Put differently, the company was heavily in debt — too heavily by most financial management standards.

Warner had been paying a 25-cent, quarterly dividend to its stockholders. However, there was some discussion on whether they should cancel the dividend. Some experts said they should cancel to avoid paying out cash; cancellation would save $65 million each quarter. But others pointed out that the stock price had already fallen to $20 per share and a dividend cancellation would drive it down even further. How best can companies like this serve their stockholders?

Should the company pay the 25-cent stock dividend? Why?

____ Yes ____ No

If you held 1000 shares of Warner stock, would you be more concerned about the dividend or the stock price? Why?

____ A. Dividend ____ B. Stock price

If you held 10,000 shares of Warner stock, would you be more concerned about the dividend or the stock price? Why?

____ A. Dividend ____ B. Stock price

what secures the bonds, if anything, (5) interest rate, (6) what happens if the company goes broke, and (7) the responsibilities of the trustee.

Trustee. The **trustee,** most often a bank or other financial institution, is a third party charged with protecting the rights of the bondholders. Since most bonds are sold far and wide, it would be impossible for each holder to check to see if the company was legitimate. Among other things, the trustee checks the indenture, sees that the corporation carries out its obligations, communicates with the bondholder, and brings action against the corporation if it does not live up to agreements.

Denomination. The **denomination** is the amount of the bond. The most popular denomination is $1000; if you buy a bond from a company, you pay (actually loan) them $1000. Some companies also issue $5000 and $10,000 bonds. Firms do not like to issue bonds of small denominations because they create additional paperwork and expense.

Interest. The amount the company pays bondholders for using their money is **bond interest,** and it is expressed as a percentage, (for example, 8% or 9½%). If you bought a $1000 bond with a 9% interest rate, the company would pay you $90 per year. The rate of interest a bond pays depends on two things: (1) the reputation of the business and (2) the amount of money available for lending. A financially stable business with a long history of success could probably sell its bonds with a lower interest rate because buyers would perceive less risk. Newer or unstable companies may have to pay higher rates because of the increased risk. If a lot of money is available for lending, rates will be lower, while a shortage of money will drive the rates up. It is simply a matter of supply and demand.

Interest is usually paid twice a year, and it is due regardless of whether the company makes money or can afford it. If people hold **registered bonds,** the company must record their names and addresses on their records; and they send interest by check. If people hold **coupon bonds,** the bond will have a coupon attached which bondholders must tear off, when the time is due,

and take to a bank for payment. The company that issued the bonds repays the bank.

Maturity. People buy bonds for a specified period, usually from 2 to 50 or more years. At the end of the period, the company has to repay the principal.

How companies retire bonds. To help protect investors, companies have to show one or more plans for repaying the bonds in the indenture. Common repayment plans are:

1. *Sinking fund.* Periodically, the company has to make cash deposits with the trustee to insure that money will be available when the bonds mature.

2. *Serial plan.* Rather than wait and retire all the bonds at the same time, this method retires a few bonds each year, according to their numbers. Low-numbered bonds will be retired in earlier years, and higher-number bonds will be retired in later years.

3. *Call option.* Bonds with a call option give the company the right to retire bonds at any time before maturity date. Such securities are referred to as **callable bonds.**

Kinds of bonds. As you have probably guessed, there are many kinds of bonds. Unsecured bonds do not identify specific assets of the company as collateral. There are **debenture bonds,** which are backed only by the company's promise to pay. Secured bonds (**mortgage bonds**) backed by specific, tangible assets are understandably more popular. If the company fails to pay interest when due or to redeem the bond at maturity, it can be forced to sell the assets used for security to pay these obligations. **Collateral trust bonds** are secured by stocks or bonds that the company owns. **Income bonds** pay interest only if the company's earnings are sufficient to justify payment. The holder can still collect the face value when due, but the company can vary the amount of interest paid, according to its earnings. A holder of **convertible bonds** can exchange them for common stock at a pegged price. If the company's stock prices decrease, stockholders have the certainty of the bonds' specified rate of return. If the stock prices increase, they can convert bonds to stocks and sell them at a profit.

Stocks versus Bonds

Most companies use both. When trying to decide which method to use at a particular time, management considers their current financial mix, going interest rates, whether the market will accept stocks or bonds better, and their concern with control. Figure 17.5 highlights the advantages and disadvantages of each method.

Long-Term Loans

Companies may borrow long-term money in other ways than through the use of bonds. A **term loan** is a formal agreement to borrow and repay a sum of money at a given interest rate for periods longer than 1 year. It may be repaid in a lump sum or by installments. The term-loan agreement states the amount of the loan, interest rates, repayment dates, and security. Also, it often contains covenants, which are restrictions placed on the borrower to help ensure repayment. Such covenants include maintenance of a specified amount of cash, insurance of key management people, restrictions on cash dividends, upper salary limits for officers, limitations on other long-

term debt, and controlled expansion plans. Other than the length of the loan and special covenants, term loans are quite similar to short-term bank loans.

Retained Earnings

An internal source of funds, **retained earnings** are profits a company does not pay out in dividends. More and more companies are plowing their earnings back into fixed needs. However, retained earnings are limited because few companies have sufficient capital left after paying dividends to their owners. Rapid-growth companies like to use retained earnings and debt funds to feed their expansion desires. Godfather's Pizza, Inc., which franchises and operates a national network of pizza restaurants, says that the company has never paid a cash dividend on its common stock and presently intends to retain its earnings for use in the development of its business. Almost $5 million of retained earnings was available for distribution to owners in 1982, but management chose to use the money for expansion instead of paying dividends. If stockholders want the security of stable, predictable dividends, their compa-

Figure 17.5
Comparison of raising capital with stocks and bonds.

RAISING CAPITAL BY SELLING STOCKS

Advantages	Disadvantages
1. No interest charges	1. Sharing ownership, and perhaps control
2. Does not affect short-term borrowing	2. Dividends are not a company expense and cannot be deducted from taxes
3. Equity capital never needs to be repaid	3. The public is less interested than in the past in buying new shares
4. More flexibility; there are no fixed dividends (except in the case of preferred stock)	4. Dividends paid reduce money available for company expansion and other needs.

RAISING CAPITAL BY SELLING BONDS

Advantages	Disadvantages
1. No dissolution of ownership or control	1. Money must be repaid at a specified future date
2. The company's obligation is known and fixed	2. Interest rates must be paid at regular intervals (except with income bonds)
3. Interest payments are tax-deductible	3. Interest rates can be high if the company is in weak financial position
4. Many large lenders, such as pension funds and life insurance companies, prefer bonds because of less risk	4. Bonds are a debt and can adversely affect short-term borrowing

nies have to rely less on retained earnings as a funds source.

How leases make money available. A **lease** is an agreement between two parties to use property for a specified period of time at a certain cost.

There is an advantage to land leasing: A company can charge off lease payments as an expense and save on federal income taxes; if the company bought the land, it could not save on taxes.

For instance, Black Giant Oil Company, of Cisco, Texas, leases land in several states and many foreign countries that it feels may produce shallow oil or natural gas. The owner of the property (**lessor**) agrees to let another party (**lessee**) use it in return for rental payments. A lease is a source of funds to the lessee to use elsewhere. With land, there is a unique advantage to leasing. A company can charge off lease payments as an expense and save on federal income taxes. But if the company bought the land, it could not depreciate it against earnings to save on taxes. There are two major disadvantages to leasing. The lessee has nothing left at the end of the lease period; residue value, or appreciation, accrues to the owner. Leasing costs are usually higher than interest costs on the debt necessary to finance the property. Since the leasing company desires to make a profit, the total outflow of funds from the lessee is greater than they would be if the company purchased the property. Some leasing agreements, called **lease-purchases,** allow the lessee to buy the property, usually for a nominal fee, at the end of the leasing period.

Nonprofit organizations also use leasing and lease-purchase agreements as a source of funds. In 1982, states and cities bought $2 billion worth of typewriters, computers, fire trucks, and other fixed assets through lease-purchase agreements. Anaheim, California, got $54 million in parking facilities, and San Diego obtained use of a $34 million telephone system through lease-purchase arrangements.

USES OF FUNDS

Thus far, we have described how and where businesses get their money. Equally important is how they use it once they get it. We can divide the uses of funds into two broad categories: (1) working capital and (2) fixed capital.

Working Capital (Short-Term Uses)

For our purposes, **working capital** is the value of assets that the company can turn into cash in less than a year, minus the company's liabilities (bills) that have to be paid within a year. Or, as the accountants put it, "Working capital is the excess of current assets over current liabilities." An **asset** is anything that the company owns, while a **liability** is anything that the company owes. A **current asset** is one that normally turns into cash within less than a year, and a **current liability** is one that the company has to pay within a year.

"The main purpose of working capital," according to a financial manager, "is to provide money to pay current bills as they come due." Working capital, then, flows through the firm. For instance, the firm uses cash to buy inventories. Inventories are sold, returning cash to the firm. If the firm sells on credit, it exchanges inventories for accounts receivables; then when accounts receivable are collected, cash flows back into the firm. (See Fig. 17.6 for a diagram of this flow.) Several kinds of assets are typically used as working capital.

Cash. The purpose of cash management is to maintain liquidity, that is, to have enough cash to pay bills when they come due. At the same time, financial managers do not like idle cash surpluses.

Excess cash means that the firm is not using its working capital properly; the cash just sits around, not earning anything.

Excess cash means that the firm is not using its working capital properly; the cash just sits around, not earning anything. Cash flows into the business from sales, collecting accounts, sale of

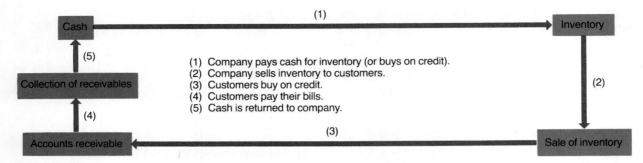

Figure 17.6
How working capital flows.

short-term securities, and short-term borrowing. Cash flows out of the business for such items as purchase of inventory, supplies, wages, selling expenses, overhead, and paying debts.

Marketable securities. As a hedge against cash shortages, some firms convert part of their cash into short-term marketable securities. The money is not idle. It earns interest, yet the business can easily convert these securities into cash if it needs to. As a guideline, some businesses invest two or three times their cash balances in short-term securities. Examples of popular short-term securities are U.S. Treasury bills, treasury certificates, treasury notes, and treasury bonds. All these are forms of government borrowing; thus, most managers consider them safe investments.

Accounts receivable. Accounts receivables represent money that customers owe on credit purchases. Accounts receivable managers weigh the risk of bad losses against sales. As a manager explained, "We can increase our accounts receivables by extending easier credit terms or by selling on credit to marginal customers. We know that we will lose a little money because we will not be able to collect. However, if we tighten up our credit requirements too much, we lose sales."

Inventory. Companies also tie up their short-term money in inventories. And should they decide to build up inventory, as a lot of businesses do prior to the Christmas season, they will need additional funds. A manager of Target Stores says that about 40% of their sales occur during No-

vember and December, and this is typical of most retail outlets. For most firms, inventory comprises a large use of working capital. Again, there is a balance of risks; a large inventory might increase sales, but this ties up capital; and there is a danger that the inventory might not sell. Additionally, inventory might lose its value through obsolescence or damage. (Refer to Chapter 8 for additional discussion on inventory concerns.)

For manufacturing firms, the inventory process is a little more complex. They have goods waiting to be sold — **finished goods inventory.** General Motors' finished cars on their lot waiting to be sold to dealers is an example. Manufacturers also have products that are partly completed — **work-in-process inventory** — such as automobile frames as they move down the assembly line. What's more, they have **raw materials inventories** — materials and parts that go into the production process, such as stacks of metal that will be shaped into doors, hoods, and trunks.

Fixed Capital (Long-Term Uses)

Money invested in fixed assets for a period longer than a year is **fixed capital.** To get the best return on their money, companies usually investigate several alternatives when investing fixed capital. Items bought with fixed capital are **fixed assets** — assets that usually take longer, and frequently much longer, than a year to convert into cash. Some examples of fixed capital uses are land, buildings, equipment, research programs, and new product development. Mediplex Group, Inc., of Newton, Massachusetts, operates a network of inpatient and outpatient alcohol abuse facilities and nursing facilities. Because their business was expanding, they needed, and acquired, $15 million to buy and build additional health related facilities—a long-term capital commitment.

Fixed capital needs vary. For instance, large firms need more fixed capital than smaller firms, and service firms need less than manufacturing firms. Since fixed capital represents the largest investments for most firms, analysts usually study opportunities very thoroughly before committing to them.

Capital budgeting. **Capital budgeting** is the process of making decisions on long-term investment alternatives. It includes the following:

- Recognizing investment opportunities.
- Estimating cash flows from the alternatives.
- Evaluating alternative cash flows.

Construction of new facilities represents the beginning of a long-term, fixed-term capital investment.

- Selecting one or more projects.
- Continually evaluating the projects.

Most firms face many long-term investment opportunities, and monies available are scarce. **Cash flow,** the amount of net cash that the investment project returns over a period of time, is critical because only cash returns can be used by firms to reinvest, pay dividends, pay bills, or whatever.

Selection and follow-up. In selecting long-term uses of funds, a firm makes two decisions: (1) Is the projected return from the commitment high enough to be worthwhile? and (2) What is the best long-term alternative? Most firms have more long-term potential uses than they have long-term capital available, so they typically rank their alternatives according to expected returns. Since this decision might commit millions or billions of dollars over a 20- or 30-year period, financial managers may ensure continued success or plant seeds of failure with their decisions.

After committing to a long-term investment, financial managers continuously monitor the project. They make yearly, quarterly, and sometimes monthly evaluations to ensure that the investment is returning cash according to its projections. If a long-term project goes bad, the firm might decide to stop or get out even if it means taking losses to do so.

Converting Short-Term Debt to Long-Term Debt

Another reason to acquire long-term funds is to pay off short-term debt. When interest rates were so high in the late 1970s and early 1980s, many firms refused to seek long-term debt. It was too expensive and they did not want to commit themselves to 20 years at interest rates of 16 to 20%, so they borrowed more short-term funds than normal. When interest rates fell, these firms sought long-term funds via the bond market to pay off their short-term debt. Ingersoll-Rand Company, located in Woodcliff Lake, New Jersey, had $171 million of short-term debt in October, 1981. In late 1983, they had raised long-term money in the bond market and used most of it to get their short-term debt down almost to zero. The result was a $12 million annual savings in interest costs.

Trouble at Charter Company over Cash Flow

Charter Company engages in oil refining and sells insurance. During the first 9 months of 1983, the company, according to securities analysts, had a negative cash flow of at least $10 million and possibly as much as $70 million. Cash flow is the difference between the cash received and cash paid out during a period. And according to Samuel R. Sapienza, chairman of the accounting department at the Wharton School of Finance, cash flow "is a vital measure that would give you a clue as to whether this company is going to continue to function."

However, Charter Company officials argue that physical cash received is actually positive. Experts agree that actual cash received during the 9-month period was positive, but accounting experts argue that many of the cash payments to the firm should be subtracted because they will not be regularly recurring. For instance, Charter received one-time payments of $9.8 million from Iran for oil-related claims, $10.7 million from reduction in oil inventories, and $4.9 million reduced operating fees through an agreement with the Bahamian government.

In addition to the squabbles over cash flow, Charter also appears to have other problems, specifically high inventory and mounting debt. Both stem from the purchase of Northeast Petroleum Industries, Inc., which sells fuel oil and gasoline. Charter bought Northeast by increasing its short-term debt to almost $120 million, up from $3.3 million a year ago. Since Northeast had a lot of petroleum inventories, this acquisition drove up inventories for Charter. Whether Charter will survive may not be known for months or years, but the company is currently squirming under their financial burdens.

Source: David B. Hilder, "Studies See Negative Cash Flow at Charter, Showing Troubles Beyond Insurance Lines," *Wall Street Journal*, Nov. 23, 1983, p. 33.

SUMMARY

Financial managers are responsible for the overall financial planning of the firm, and their key objective is to increase the worth of the firm. To do this, financial managers try to determine the most economical way of obtaining and using funds.

Popular short-term fund sources — funds that have to be repaid within a year — are: trade credit, bank credit, commercial paper, and finance companies. Trade credit, the most popular short-term source, occurs when a supplier sells inventory or supplies to a purchaser and allows a certain period, usually 30, 60, or 90 days, to pay. The short-term bank loan — bank credit — is also a popular source. Commercial paper consists of unsecured promissory notes issued by large, well-established companies. Finance companies specialize in providing short-term money to businesses and individuals.

Long-term financing lasts for more than a year. Common stocks, preferred stocks, and bonds are the most popular sources of long-term monies. Companies may also obtain term loans for longer than a year. Banks are willing to make term loans, but they usually place some restrictions on management for the duration of the loan. Retained earnings — profits that companies do not pay in dividends — are being used more and more as a funds source. Lease arrangements are considered a source of funds because the lessee has use of funds that would otherwise have been spent to purchase property.

Firms need money for working capital and fixed capital. Working capital is the value of assets that the company can turn into cash in less than a year, minus the company's liabilities that have to be paid within a year. Fixed capital is money invested in assets that last longer than a year. Some firms also use long-term funds to convert high-interest, short-term debt into lower-interest, long-term debt.

MIND YOUR BUSINESS

Instructions. Indicate whether each of the following statements is true (T) or false (F).

When raising capital by selling stocks:

___ 1. There are no interest charges.

___ 2. There is no effect on short-term borrowing.

___ 3. The money never needs to be repaid.

___ 4. There is a sharing of ownership and possibly control.

___ 5. Dividends paid to owners can be deducted from taxes.

___ 6. Dividends paid to owners reduce money available for expansion.

When raising capital by selling bonds:

___ 7. There is a dissolution of ownership.

___ 8. The company's obligation is known and fixed.

___ 9. Interest payments are not tax deductible.

___10. Money does not have to be repaid by a specific date.

___11. Interest payments must be paid at regular intervals.

___12. There can be a negative impact on short-term borrowing.

See answers at the back of the book.

KEY TERMS

short-term financing, 434

trade credit, 435

open-account credit (open-book credit), 435

promissory note, 435

maker, 435

bearer, 435

trade draft, 435

bill of exchange, 435

sight draft, 436

time draft, 436

trade acceptance, 436

line of credit, 437

revolving-credit agreement, 437

single-payment note, 437

compensating balance, 437

unsecured loan (signature loan), 437

secured loan, 437

collateral, 437

stocks and bonds, 437

accounts receivable, 437

warehouse receipt, 437

bill of lading, 438

straight bill of lading, 438

order bill of lading, 438

chattel mortgage, 438

floor planning, 438

commercial paper, 439

commercial finance company, 439

factoring, 439

consumer and sales finance company, 439

equity capital, 440

security, 440

origination, 440

underwriting, 440

syndicate, 440

authorized stock, 441

unissued stock, 441

issued stock, 441

par value, 442

no-par value, 442

market value, 442

book value, 442

preemptive right, 442

stock option, 442

stock split, 442

dividend, 442

common stock, 442

preferred stock, 443

cumulative preferred stock, 443

noncumulative preferred stock, 443

participating preferred stock, 443

nonparticipating preferred stock, 443

bond, 444

debt capital, 444

principal, 444

REVIEW QUESTIONS

1. What is the objective of financial management?

2. What is the role of the financial manager?

3. What is trade credit? What are the characteristics of trade credit? How does it serve as a short-term source of funds?

4. What is bank credit? How do companies attain it? How does it operate?

5. What is commercial paper? How does it differ from trade credit?

6. How do finance companies serve short-term financial needs?

7. What is the process by which most firms sell securities?

8. What is stock? Distinguish between authorized, issued, and unissued stock.

9. How do common stock and preferred stock differ?

10. What are bonds? Describe their major features.

11. What are the major companies' plans to retire their bonds? Describe the various kinds of bonds.

12. Compare stocks and bonds as a means of raising long-term capital.

13. Analyze term loans, retained earnings, and leasing as means of raising long-term capital.

14. What are major short-term and long-term uses of funds?

15. Explain the major components of working capital.

16. What is fixed capital? Capital budgeting?

17. Why would a firm exchange long-term for short-term debt?

CASES

Case 17.1: Paying the Bills

Harcort Company is a middle-sized retail hardware outlet. They handle all types of merchandise commonly found in hardware stores, from paints to tools to small appliances. The company has been doing reasonably well for several years, but the downturn in the economy during 1982 and 1983 caused them to have financial problems. Their business appeared to be sound because sales were not dropping much, but, as the owner commented, ''For some reason, we seem to have a lot of trouble paying the bills.'' Cash was not coming in fast enough for them to pay what they owed. Profits have fallen off, but the financial reports show that the company is still making about 60% of the profits they were showing a couple of years earlier.

Mr. Harcort has asked you to help him with his situation, and with further investigation you discover the following. Most inventory is bought on 30-, 60-, or 90-day accounts. Mr. Harcort has been very concerned about his financial ratings, and he has always tried to pay his accounts on time. In fact, he often takes advantage of the cash discounts offered by many suppliers for early payment. In the past few months, he has slipped a little, but his accounts are averaging only about 5 days past due. Harcort has also maintained that a well-supplied store helps sales. You think that perhaps he has too much inventory. He has too many items and too much of many items, but Harcort insists that this is good for business. He has tried to keep a ready supply of cash, but has never used certificates of deposit or other means of short-term investments. In fact, you think that he might have carried too much cash in the past. Now, however, his cash is very low, but you think Harcort may be more worried than necessary because he has carried so much cash in the past. Finally, many of the sales are credit, and Harcort has been very lenient, in your opinion. A quick calculation shows that his customers are averaging over 30 days past due, and a few are as much as 6 months past. When you mention this, he is aware of it but says this is good for business in the long run.

Questions

1. From this information, where do you think Harcort might look for short-term funds? List his alternatives and evaluate each one.

2. How would you go about determining whether Harcort is carrying too much inventory?

3. Lay out a detailed set of recommendations that would get Harcort out of the current cash crisis and help avoid such future problems.

4. What arguments would you use to persuade Harcort to accept your recommendations? Be specific.

Case 17.2: Funds Usage at Netword, Inc.

Diana Guetzkow is president and CEO of Netword, Inc., of Riverdale, Maryland. Netword, Inc., is certified by the Postal Service as a carrier company to tie into its electronic mail system. Much like Western Union, Netword transmits other people's messages for a fee. During the first 10 months of 1983, Netword transmitted 270,000 letters at an average fee of 60 cents a letter.

To start the company, Diana Guetzkow, who has a doctorate in foreign policy, went to private investors to raise $100,000. She used this money, over a two-year period, for development expenses. In June, she went public and sold 3 million shares of stock at $1 per share, netting her, after investment bank fees and commissions, $2.7 million.

Questions

1. Why do you think Dr. Guetzkow raised the money through sale of stock rather than trying to sell bonds?

2. Evaluate other potential long-term sources of funds for the company.

After completing this chapter, you will be able to:

- Explain how the securities exchanges work.

- Describe the various ways you can buy and sell securities.

- Describe how commodity markets work.

- Read newspaper stock and bond quotations.

- Interpret the Dow Jones and other market indexes.

- Explain the major state and federal laws that regulate securities exchanges.

- Develop your own investment strategy.

18

DEALING IN
THE SECURITIES
MARKETS

You hear wild and exciting stories of people getting rich in the stock market, and some people actually do get very rich investing in the market; others become very poor. From August, 1982, to July, 1983, David Packard's stock increased in value by $1.2 billion (that's billion). During the same period, William R. Hewlett's stock increased by more than $500 million. However, these gentlemen just happen to be the co-founders of the very successful Hewlett-Packard Corporation. On the other hand, Morley P. Thompson, former chairman of Baldwin-United Co., the piano company, lost $6.9 million when his company ousted him.

What are the chances of a private investor making a bundle in the market? Very slim indeed. If you were smart enough or lucky enough, however, you could increase your financial worth with prudent investments. For instance, Chrysler Corporation's stock was selling for $6.75 per share in August, 1982; a year later, the price was $31.75. If you had invested, say, $6750 and held the stock for a year, you could have sold it for $31,750. Your profit would have been $25,000, less commissions.

But if you want to dream, assume that you inherited just 100 shares of the old Standard Oil Trust at its 1911 price of $675 per share. Today, you would be worth about $7 million. But do not forget that prices can move both ways. One day in June, 1983, Texas Instruments' stock plunged $39.50 per share—just in one day. Knowledgeable people who invest in stocks and bonds realize that it requires a lot of analysis and patience to be successful.

Stock markets, technically called securities and exchange commissions, are where investors buy and sell corporate stocks and bonds. However, companies cannot sell their stocks and bonds initially through these markets; they exist only for outstanding securities. But companies are interested in the value of their securities on the markets because this affects their ability to raise money through additional security sales. To help us gain a better understanding of securities markets, this chapter discusses: (1) security exchanges, (2) commodity exchanges, (3) information for analysis, (4) regulation of exchanges, and (5) investment strategies.

SECURITY EXCHANGES AND MARKETS

Security exchanges are marketplaces where buyers and sellers bid for each other's stocks and bonds. The New York Stock Exchange (NYSE), which lists stocks from more than 2000 companies, is by far the largest and most prestigious exchange. Stocks like IBM, Exxon, and General Motors are traded on the NYSE. The American Stock Exchange (AMEX) is also well known. Regional exchanges are located outside New York. The Midwest Stock Exchange, the Pacific Coast Stock Exchange, and the Salt Lake Stock Exchange are three of the largest regional exchanges. Some exchanges are also located in other countries. The Amsterdam Stock Exchange, founded in 1611, is the world's oldest.

Exchanges do not do the actual buying and selling; members who purchase seats (memberships) on the exchange serve as brokers for their clients. There are 1366 seats on the NYSE owned by such firms as E. F. Hutton, Paine Webber, Smith Barney, Dean Witter Reynolds, and the largest,

Merrill Lynch. The price for one of these seats has ranged from below $30,000 to more than a half-million dollars. A seat on the exchange simply gives the member a right to buy and sell listed securities.

A board of governors elected by the members manages the exchange. The board appoints the president and officers of the exchange and assesses dues from the members to cover the expenses of operating the exchange.

Listed Securities

Listed securities are those traded on the securities exchanges. A company must pay a fee to have its stocks listed. Requirements for listing securities on the exchanges are exacting. Exchanges want their securities traded, and listing requirements are a way to ensure that stocks remain stable and widely held so that investors will buy and sell them. Exchanges also have financial disclosure and auditing requirements. Table 18.1 shows typical listing requirements of the New York and American exchanges.

Listing requirements on the regional exchanges are less stringent. In fact, the Pacific Stock Exchange, in the fall of 1983, was trading stock of thirteen companies that went bankrupt. Braniff Airlines, one of the most recognizable bankrupt companies, had traded as high as $6.50 per share. In one day of trading, when it became known that

The stockbroker, reading the latest price information, advises on the selected stock . . .

Hyatt Corp. was trying to bail out the airline, over 1.8 million shares changed hands. At the time, people still held 20 million shares of Braniff. (Table 18.2 lists the bankrupt companies trading on the Pacific Stock Exchange.) Because people have become so interested in trading shares of bankrupt companies, even the NYSE started listing them; in the fall of 1983, they listed four.

Buying and Selling on the Exchanges

How can people buy or sell stocks and bonds on the exchanges? The process seems complex, but it

TABLE 18.1 ■ MINIMAL LISTING REQUIREMENTS FOR NEW YORK AND AMERICAN STOCK EXCHANGES

	New York	American
Publicly held shares	800,000 out of 1,000,000 must be outstanding	300,000 shares outstanding
Shareholders	1800 out of 2000 must be public	600 out of 900 must be public
Market value of public shares	$14 million	$2 million
Net tangible assets	$14 million	$3 million
Earning power	$2.5 million before taxes for most recent year; $2 million in each of the two previous years	$500,000 before taxes in most recent year

. . . before the order to buy goes to the floor of either a regional exchange (such as the Midwest Stock Exchange in Chicago) . . .

is actually quite simple. Members of the exchanges operate through brokers. There are a number of stockbrokers in most cities. They are as close as the telephone book. The procedure for buying a stock listed on the NYSE is as follows:

1. Call a stockbroker and ask the latest sale price of your selected stock.
2. The broker presses a couple of buttons and gives you the most recent sale price, how many shares were traded, the current offering price, and the current bid price.
3. You can put in your bid at a certain price and tell the broker how many shares you want to purchase.

TABLE 18.2 ■ BANKRUPT STOCKS TRADING ON THE PACIFIC STOCK EXCHANGE IN 1983

Company/Business	Bankruptcy Filed	Outstanding Shares (mil)	Recent Price	—52-Week— High	Low
AM International/ business equipment	1982	10.2	$5\frac{1}{2}$	7	1
Berven Carpets/ carpets	1982	3.7	$\frac{5}{8}$	$1\frac{1}{2}$	$\frac{5}{32}$
Braniff International/ airline	1982	20.0	$1\frac{5}{8}$	$6\frac{1}{2}$	$\frac{7}{32}$
Dant & Russell/forest products	1982	0.8	$2\frac{1}{2}$	$4\frac{1}{2}$	$1\frac{1}{8}$
Gilman Services/ wholesale drugs	1982	3.2	$\frac{11}{16}$	3	$\frac{3}{8}$
Itel/transportation equipment leasing, services	1981	12.1	$1\frac{5}{8}$	$2\frac{13}{16}$	$\frac{3}{8}$
KDT Industries/retail	1982	7.3	$\frac{3}{8}$	$1\frac{5}{8}$	$\frac{13}{32}$
Lionel/electronics, toys	1982	7.1	$4\frac{7}{8}$	$7\frac{3}{4}$	$2\frac{1}{4}$
Sambo's Restaurants/ restaurants	1981	12.8	$2\frac{1}{2}$	$4\frac{3}{4}$	$1\frac{1}{16}$
Saxon Industries/ business equipment	1982	7.8	$1\frac{7}{8}$	3	$\frac{7}{16}$
Seatrain Lines/tankers, chartering	1981	14.5	$1\frac{5}{16}$	$2\frac{7}{8}$	$\frac{1}{4}$
White Motor/ automotive	1980	9.4	$\frac{3}{4}$	$1\frac{15}{16}$	$\frac{5}{32}$
Wickes Cos/retail	1982	14.4	$6\frac{1}{4}$	$8\frac{1}{8}$	$2\frac{7}{16}$

Source: Pacific Stock Exchange.

4. The broker instantly teletypes the information to the firm's member partner on the floor of the exchange.

5. The member goes to a particular post where the stock is traded and announces a bid to buy so many shares at a certain price.

6. There will be other members at the post, with orders from their clients to sell.

7. The two members get together, make the transaction, record the sale, and relay the information back to their brokers.

8. Your broker contacts you and tells you that the purchase has been made.

9. You will be billed for the amount of the purchase, and you have 5 business days to pay the bill plus the broker's commission.

A sale works the same way. You can get information about prices and other data in seconds, and an entire transaction may take only minutes. During the first half of 1983, more than 20 billion shares were traded on the major exchanges.

In early 1984, Occidental Petroleum Co. set a record for the largest exchange in history when the company paid $333.4 million for 3 million shares of its own preferred stock.

. . . where the transaction is made and the sale recorded.

In one 51-day period, the NYSE trading topped 100 million shares each day. Figure 18.1 shows the volume of shares traded on the NYSE each year since 1976, and Fig. 18.2 shows record volumes for trading in one day!

Figure 18.1
Number of shares traded annually on the New York stock exchange. *Source: New York Stock Exchange.*

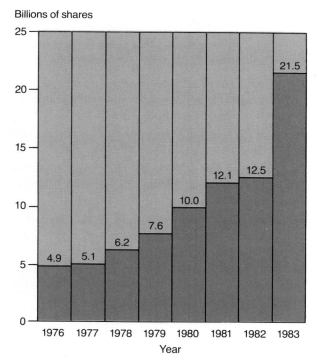

Billions of shares

Year	Billions of shares
1976	4.9
1977	5.1
1978	6.2
1979	7.6
1980	10.0
1981	12.1
1982	12.5
1983	21.5

. . . or the national New York Stock Exchange, where the brokerage firm's representative goes to the post where the stock is being traded . . .

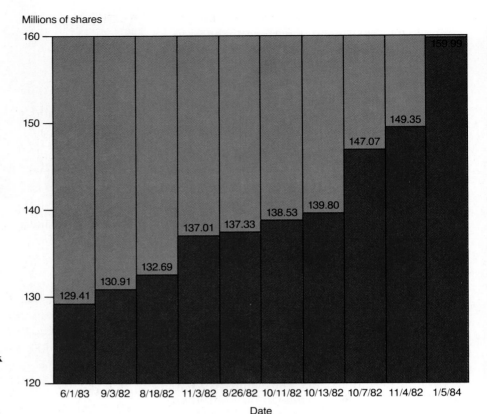

Millions of shares

Date	Value
6/1/83	129.41
9/3/82	130.91
8/18/82	132.69
11/3/82	137.01
8/26/82	137.33
10/11/82	138.53
10/13/82	139.80
10/7/82	147.07
11/4/82	149.35
1/5/84	159.99

Figure 18.2
Record volume days of trading on the New York stock exchange. *Source: New York Stock Exchange.*

Types of Buy and Sell Orders

Of course, investors may place various types of orders when buying stocks, for example:

1. **Round lot.** An order to buy or sell in 100-share multiples (that is, 100 shares, 200 shares, 300 shares, and so on).

2. **Odd lot.** An order to buy or sell less than 100 shares.

3. **Market order.** An order to buy or sell at the best price available at the time the order reaches the floor of the exchange.

4. **Limit order.** An order that specifies the price at which the stock is to be bought or sold (for example, "buy at $20 per share").

5. **Fill or kill order.** A limit order that is cancelled if it cannot be executed when the order is placed.

6. **Good-till-cancelled order.** A limit order that stays open until the purchaser decides to cancel.

7. **Stop order.** An order to sell at a specific price. For example, a person who buys stock may fear that the price might drop unexpectedly and quickly. By placing a stop order, an investor can limit losses or protect profits.

Brokers' Commissions

When you buy or sell on the exchanges, you must go through a broker. And they will charge you commissions. Before 1975, all commissions were the same, but a new law in that year made it possible for brokerage firms to compete. So, like many other things, you should shop around for commission rates. Also like other purchases, you should not select your broker simply on the basis of which one has the lowest interest rates. They offer variety in services as well. **Full-service brokers** offer a wide variety of services, including research done by their own people. By contrast, **discount brokers** typically provide only one service and that is to buy or sell your stock.

They do not provide suggestions or supply you with independent research on securities. Charles Schwab, the largest discount brokerage firm, advertises that you can save substantially on commissions when you trade with them as compared to full commission brokers. If a commission broker gets too busy, they will sometimes allow independent brokers to execute their trades. **Independent brokers,** sometimes called "two-dollar" brokers because they were originally paid $2 per hundred shares traded, hold seats on the exchanges and execute orders for other brokers during busy times.

Generally, you can expect brokerage fees to range from less than 2 to more than 10% of the total purchase price.

Generally, the fees will be less, as a percentage of price, for larger purchases and higher for smaller purchases. Also, commissions are likely to be less for round lots than for odd lots. Depending upon the size and nature of your transaction, you can expect fees to range from less than 2 to more than 10% of the total purchase price. On the average, individual brokers keep about 41% of their commissions; the remainder goes to the firms. Remember you have to pay your fees when you buy and when you sell.

Buying on Margin

When you **buy on margin,** you put up some money for purchasing the stock but not the total price; your broker loans you the difference. You might put forth $5000 toward a purchase of $10,000 and your broker would loan you the remaining $5,000. To secure their loan, the brokerage firm will hold the stocks for you. If the price of the stock falls below a certain point, the firm will call to ask you to put up more money (a **margin call**). By law, brokers have to keep their margin at certain percentages, which vary from time to time; for the last few years, the margin requirement has been 50%. If you do not come up with the extra margin, the broker will sell your stock, repay himself for the loan, and return the remaining money to you.

Selling Short

Selling short is selling shares that you do not own, with the agreement to deliver them at some future date. Why would you do this? Because you expect the price of the stock to drop before you have to buy them.

Several months prior to this writing, Mattel Inc., the Barbie doll company, was selling at $30 per share. However, Mattel had gone heavily into the video games and low-cost computer markets; alas, these markets virtually collapsed in 1983. Had you been an astute, risk-taking investor, you could, by putting up some collateral, have sold Mattel short for $30 per share. To do this, your broker would have "borrowed" Mattel stock, possibly from the account of another client, for you to deliver to the buyer that you sold to. At some future point, you would have to buy the stock to replace the broker's loan. In 1983, Mattel stock fell to $6 per share. Thus, you could have bought at $6 to cover your short sale and profited $24 per share, less commissions of course. But what if you had guessed wrong and the price had increased to $50 per share? As the price increased, your broker would have been calling to ask for more collateral. Eventually, if you sold at the higher price, you would have lost, in this case, $20 per share ($50 less $30), plus commissions. The SEC also regulates short selling.

Puts and Calls (The Option Markets)

Puts and calls are option contracts to buy and sell stock at a specific price. These stock options are traded on option exchanges, the first of which was the Chicago Board Options Exchange, organized in 1973. Options trading is more limited than securities trading, with fewer companies and fewer exchanges participating.

A **call** is an option to buy stock at a set price, called the "exercise price," or "striking price." The striking price is set near the current market price in multiples of $5 or $10. For instance, if the current price of a stock is $28 per share, the exercise price would probably be set at $30. Options typically expire quarterly, ending on the third Sunday of the month. Working the same way, a **put** is an option to sell at a fixed price within a specified period of time.

By using the option markets, individuals can make large profits or losses with small cash outlays. Suppose you had $1000 in cash and you wanted to speculate in the options markets. Assume ABC stock was selling at $20 per share. Further assume that you could purchase a call for $1.25 to buy ABC stock at $20 per share on the options markets. With your $1000 investment, you could buy options for 800 shares of ABC stock ($1000 divided by $1.25 per share). This means that you have the right to buy 800 shares of ABC stock at $20 per share until the expiration date of your option. What do you hope will happen? Of course, you want the price of ABC stock to rise.

Though the options markets are very risky, the number of shares bought and sold on the options exchanges daily exceeds trading on all stock exchanges except the NYSE.

Suppose you get lucky: The price of ABC stock goes up $5 per share to $25. Since you have the right to buy at $20, you could exercise your call and make a profit. However, the market value of your call option has now increased as well, and you could just sell your call options on the options market. Since the profit on 800 shares would be $4000 ($5 × 800), you could sell your options for $4000, giving you a profit of $4000, less the $1000 cost of your calls, less brokerage fees. However, what would happen if the price of the stock declined and your option expired? You would not exercise your option; therefore, you would lose your $1000 investment. Even though the options markets are very risky, the number of shares bought and sold on the options exchanges daily exceeds trading on all stock exchanges except the New York Stock Exchange.

Stock-Index Futures

Stock-index futures is a mechanism that allows you to buy an index of stock values to be delivered at some future date. Some of the indexes you can buy are the Value Line Composite Index which covers 1700 stocks, Standard & Poor's 100, Standard & Poor's 500, and the NYSE Index which covers the 1500-plus stocks listed on the NYSE.

Here is the way it works. Suppose you believed that in June, 1983, stock prices, in general, were going to rise. You could have bought a Standard & Poor's 500 contract for $82,000, which was 500 times the current S&P Index of 164. But, at the time of purchase, you would have to put up only 7 to 10% of the contract value. Thus, you could have entered into the $82,000 contract for only $6000. Further, assume that your contract said that you would deliver the contract in September. If the S&P Index had risen 16 points by September, your contract would have been worth $90,000 (164 + 16 × $500) or a gain of $8000 ($90,000 − $82,000) less a commission of about $100. Of course, if your bet had been wrong (if the S&P Index had fallen), you would have lost money.

By buying the indexes, you do not have to pick the right stock to make a gain. If you believe that most prices are going up, you simply buy the index. You do not have to go to all the trouble necessary to evaluate many stocks, trying to find the right one. Also, you do not have to put up as much money as you would if you bought actual stocks. Even if you bought stocks on the margin, you would have to put up 50% of their value, but you can buy indexes and put up only 7 to 10% of their value. This means you can take a bigger gamble. Since there is more risk in stock-index futures trading, Dean Witter and other brokerage firms will accept your index futures contract only if you have a net worth of $100,000 and agree to leave at least $10,000 on deposit. Figure 18.3 shows the increasing number of stock-index futures contracts being traded.

Buying and Selling outside the Exchanges

Although most all transactions of listed stocks occur through stock exchanges, it is not necessary to buy or sell through organized exchanges. You can sell your shares of stock to anyone so long as you let the company know who owns the stock. The obvious advantage to this type of exchange is that it saves the brokers' commissions. In fact, some large security dealers, who are not members of the exchanges, offer their services to companies that buy and sell large blocks of securities. These

Number traded (millions)

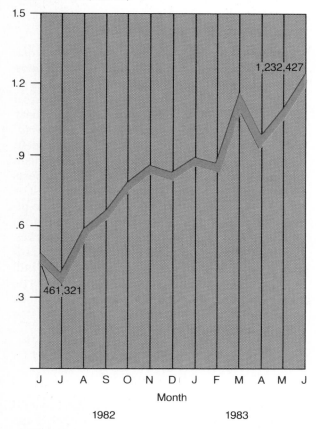

Figure 18.3
Number of stock-index futures contracts traded. *Source: Futures Industry Association.*

dealers willingly accept smaller commissions than dealers who trade through exchanges.

Trading Warrants

A **warrant** allows a person to buy a certain number of shares of stock of the issuing company at a stated price for a given time period. Some Chrysler warrants allow the holder to buy one share of Chrysler common stock for $13 until 1990. Warrants, like stocks, are traded on the exchanges. Typically, warrants come into being when a company is in financial trouble. When a troubled company tries to raise capital by selling stocks, it might also give prospective buyers warrants to entice them to buy the stock. Companies may also give warrants to banks when things are going badly to get them to extend their loans.

When Chrysler was in financial trouble, the

---

company gave the government warrants in

---

return for the guaranteed loans.

When Chrysler was in financial trouble, the company gave the government warrants in return for the guaranteed loans. Other companies that had outstanding warrants in recent years are American Airlines, TWA, Eastern Airlines, Mattel, Charter Companies, and Golden Nugget.

When Chrysler common stock was trading at $30, Chrysler warrants were trading at $17. Remember, the warrant allows a holder to buy the Chrysler stock at $13. Thus, the warrant bought on the exchange would appear to be of equal value to the $30 stock ($17 purchase price allowed you to buy a $30 stock for $13). But suppose Chrysler common went up to $40. You would have made $10 on a $30 investment (33% increase) if you had bought the common stock at $30. However, if you had bought the warranty for $17, you would have made $10 ($40 minus the $13 warranty = a gain of $27; but remember you paid $17 for the warranty, thus reducing your gain to $10) on a $17 investment, a 59% increase. Trading in warranties, then, gives you bigger, and more risky, chances for gain or loss.

Over-the-Counter Markets

More than 50,000 securities, the vast majority, are not listed on organized exchanges. Securities not listed on the organized exchanges are called **unlisted securities,** and investors can trade them through a network of some 5000 dealers. Because the trades are made outside the stock exchanges, this market is called **over-the-counter (OTC).**

Securities dealers buy and sell OTC much as they would on the organized exchanges. However, the brokers do not meet face to face as they would on the floor of the exchanges. For this reason, if you wish to buy an OTC stock, you would make an offer, called **bid price,** that you would be willing to pay for the stock. And if you wished to sell an OTC stock, you would make an offer, called the **asked price.** In the past, many investors shied away from OTC markets because they feared they could not get good information about prices. Today, however, OTC dealers accumulate and distribute a lot of information on OTC securities. The National Association of Security Dealers (NASD) is a self-governing body that regulates the OTC. In 1971, NASD began publishing Automated Quotations (called *NASDAQ*) of securities traded OTC. To be included in *NASDAQ*, a company must meet the following standards:

- At least $1 million in assets.
- At least 500 stockholders.
- At least 100,000 shares outstanding.
- At least two brokers who deal in the stock.

Bull Markets and Bear Markets

A **bull market** describes a market where stock prices are increasing rapidly. Conversely, a **bear market** depicts falling prices. But since prices go up and down all the time, there is no universal agreement on just what constitutes a bull or bear market. A bull market, according to the *Encyclopedia of Banking and Finance*, is ". . . a market in which the 'bulls' are in ascendancy and optimism and rising prices prevail." Although the experts do not agree on precise definitions of how fast or how far prices have to rise to be a bull, a rule-of-thumb is that a 20% price rise over a 12-month period would probably consist of a bull market. Reverse the numbers to get a bear. The NYSE says that since World War II, we have had nine bull markets, counting the one in 1982–1983. The average bull market lasted 37 months, and stock prices rose by an average of 78%. Figure 18.4 shows the bull market of 1982–1983.

COMMODITY EXCHANGES

In addition to securities, people can also buy and sell such products as wheat, sugar, livestock, some vegetables, gold, and silver in organized markets. **Commodity exchanges** are organized markets for trading selected lists of commodities. The actual buying and selling on commodity exchanges is similar to trading on a stock exchange. However, there are futures markets, which allow investors to engage in hedging.

FUNNY BUSINESS

Drawings by Saxon. © 1983. The New Yorker Magazine, Inc

"Mrs. Liscombe? We are from the S.E.C. As you undoubtedly know, the stock market dropped 21.5 points last Thursday because of a rumor that interest rates are going up. We have traced that rumor to you, Mrs. Liscombe, and we are here to request that you keep your perceptions to yourself."

Spot and Futures Markets

The **spot market** is the current cash market for the commodity. If you buy on the spot market, you normally expect the seller to deliver the commodities to you. However, the **futures market** allows you to buy and sell now, but the delivery is to be made at some point, maybe months, in the future. In reality, few deliveries actually occur. The buyer in a futures market will most likely sell her contract before the time of delivery.

To illustrate the futures market, suppose that in May you believe wheat, which is selling at $4.00 a bushel, is underpriced. You ask your broker to

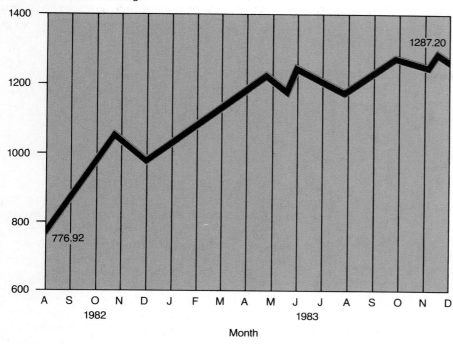

Dow Jones industrial average

1287.20

776.92

A S O N D J F M A M J J A S O N D
　　1982　　　　　　　　　1983

Month

**Figure 18.4
The 1982–1983 bull
market.** *Source: Dow Jones
& Company.*

buy 50,000 bushels of wheat for August delivery. If you have analyzed the market conditions correctly, you might find in July that August wheat is selling at $4.60 a bushel. Now, you instruct your broker to sell your August futures, and you mark up a 60 cents per bushel gain (less broker's fees). But suppose the price had gone down to $3.50 a bushel. You have two options: You can sell your futures and take the loss, or you can let them deliver the 50,000 bushels of wheat to your door in August.

Hedging

With some commodities, wheat for example, the selling price of the finished product (in this case, flour) tends to follow closely the price of the raw material (wheat). Thus, a flour producer might buy wheat in March, but the flour may not be ready for sale until June. Should the price of wheat go down, the flour producer could take a loss because the price of flour would also go down in June. To protect the expected profit from producing flour, the producer might engage in **hedging,** that is, selling in the futures market while simultaneously buying in the spot market.

Here is the way it works. Suppose, as a flour producer, you buy 50,000 bushels of wheat on March 1 at $4.00 a bushel—total cost $200,000 ($4 × 50,000). Assume that it takes $70,000 to convert the wheat into flour, and you would like to make a $50,000 profit. When converted into flour, this wheat becomes worth $320,000 to you (cost of the wheat—$200,000—plus cost of converting wheat into flour—$70,000—plus profit—$50,000).

As a hedge, on March 1, you might sell a futures contract to be delivered in June. This gives you time to convert your wheat into flour. And you protect your profit with the hedge. To illustrate, assume that in June the price of wheat drops to $3.00 a bushel. The price of your flour would also drop and you might be able to sell it for only $270,000. Without the hedge, you would make no profit. By using your hedge, you can buy wheat in the spot market at $3.00 a bushel. Since you have already sold June wheat at $4.00 a bushel, you make a $1 per bushel profit. And you had 50,000 bushels; therefore, you make $50,000 ($1 × 50,000 bushels) on the futures contract. And this is what you expected to make from processing the wheat into flour (see Fig. 18.5).

March 1:

Buy 50,000 bu @ $4 = $200,000
Conversion costs = 70,000
Expected profit = 50,000
Worth of processed wheat $320,000 (A)
$1 per bu price drop = 50,000
(50,000 × $1)
Actual worth of processed wheat 270,000 (B)
"Loss" A − B = $ 50,000

March 1:

Sell 50,000 bu June futures
@ $4 = $200,000

June 1:

Buy 50,000 bu @ $3 = 150,000
Profit on futures contract = $ 50,000

INFORMATION FOR ANALYSIS

Investors can look to many sources of information about securities and commodities. The financial section of most daily newspapers carries up-to-the-minute prices and other information about individual securities. Most papers also report indexes about the market movement.

How to Read Newspaper Stock Quotations

Figure 18.6 shows a portion of the daily NYSE transactions for November 25, 1983. The descrip-

The Wall Street Journal carries the most complete listing of stock information.

tions explain the meaning of each of the columns. As you can see, there is a lot of information available in just the daily listing of stock prices. *The Wall Street Journal* carries the most complete listing of stock information, but all but the smallest daily papers will carry some stock information. In just a quick glance, you can check the highest and lowest price the stock sold for during the previous 52 weeks; the amount of dividend the stock is pay-

Figure 18.6
How to read newspaper stock quotations (data for Friday, November 25, 1983).

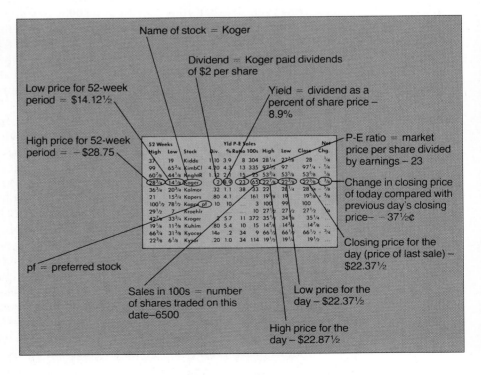

Name of stock = Koger

Dividend = Koger paid dividends of $2 per share

Yield = dividend as a percent of share price – 8.9%

Low price for 52-week period = $14.12½

High price for 52-week period = –$28.75

P-E ratio = market price per share divided by earnings – 23

Change in closing price of today compared with previous day's closing price– –37½¢

Closing price for the day (price of last sale) – $22.37½

pf = preferred stock

Sales in 100s = number of shares traded on this date–6500

Low price for the day – $22.37½

High price for the day – $22.87½

ing, if any; how much the stock is yielding (dividend as a percent of price); price-earnings (P-E) ratios; high, low, and closing price for the day; and the net change in closing price as compared to the previous day.

Since the NYSE is closed on Saturdays and Sundays and most holidays, papers following the weekends and holidays usually do not have stock listings. Frequently, the stock listings will be a composite, including quotations of several exchanges. For instance, the NYSE composite transactions usually include listings from the American, Midwest, Pacific, Philadelphia, Boston, and Cincinnati Exchanges, as well as from the NYSE.

How to Read Over-the-Counter Listings

As you recall, most stocks are not listed on the major exchanges, and a large number are not listed on any exchanges. Stocks not listed trade in over-the-counter markets. Most newspapers print the daily bid and asked prices for over-the-counter stocks. Bid price, you will remember, is the price at which a buyer is willing to buy the stock, and asked price is the price that a seller would be willing to sell at. Thus, over-the-counter listings do not list actual trades; rather, they show what a person is offering to buy or to sell at a

BUSINESS BULLETIN

Changes in Price-Earnings

The **price-earnings ratio** is price of the stock divided by its earnings. For a stock priced at $50 with earnings of $5 per share, the P-E ratio would be 10.1 ($50 divided by $5). A lower P-E ratio suggests that investors are willing to pay less for the earnings of the company. They may pay less because they believe the earnings are short-term; they think other factors are too risky; or the stock might simply be undervalued.

The chart below shows how P-E ratios for S&P 500 stocks have varied since 1968.

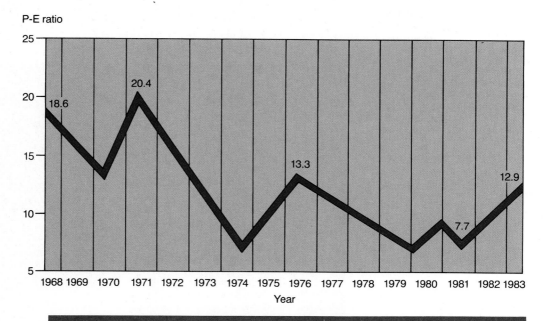

Source: Standard & Poor's Corporation.

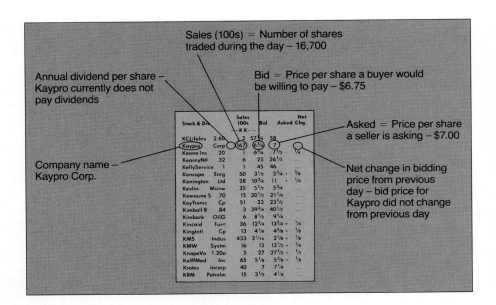

Figure 18.7
How to read over-the-counter newspaper listings (data for Friday, November 25, 1983).

moment in time. Figure 18.7 contains a portion of the over-the-counter listings for November 25, 1983.

How to Read Newspaper Bond Price Quotations

The financial pages show bond prices in much the same way they show stock prices, but there are a few slight changes. Figure 18.8 shows a portion of bond quotations for November, 15, 1983. The left column lists the company name, followed by the interest rate and due date. The "current yield" column shows the bond's interest rate based on its present value. The price quotation is based on 100, even though most of the bonds have a $1000 face value. Thus, a quote of 108 means that the bond actually sells for $1080, and a quote of 86 means the bond sells for $860. Of course, one company may issue several different bonds. Notice in Fig. 18.7 that Texaco has four different bond issues, with maturity dates ranging from 1997 to 2006.

Bonds traded among investors will vary in price to reflect current changes in interest rates.

Figure 18.8
How to read bond quotations in the newspaper.

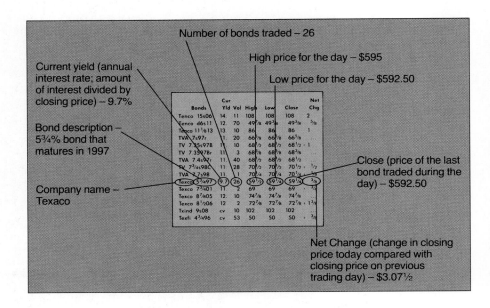

The company sells the bonds at a fixed rate that it cannot change. The following example shows how bond prices fluctuate to reflect changing interest rates.

In 1960, Ann Wertz inherited a $1000 6% bond from her mother, who bought the bond in 1955 from the Cromwell Company. Its maturity date was 2005. Ann received $60 (.06 × $1000) in interest payments each year from the Cromwell Company. In 1974, Ann had financial troubles and decided to sell her bond. Although the company would not redeem the bond until the year 2005, Ann knew that the bonds were traded on a regional security exchange. Ann called her broker.

Broker: Ann, inflation and tight money have caused interest rates to go up.

Ann: What has that got to do with my bond? It still pays $60 a year, doesn't it?

Broker: Yes, but investors can buy bonds being issued by other companies that pay 9% ($90 per year on a $1000 face value bond). They are not going to give you $1000 for a bond that pays them only $60. That would be an unwise decision for them.

Ann: Well, how can I get my money?

Broker: You can sell the bond if you are willing to take less than $1000.

Ann: How much less?

Broker: 1955 Cromwell bonds are now trading at about $700.

Ann: Why are they priced so low? The bond cost $1000 in 1955.

Broker: Because the interest payment is only $60 a year. If an investor pays $700 for the bond, the effective rate of return will be 8.5% ($700 divided into $60). Cromwell is a stable company and investors are willing to take 8.5% return on their bonds.

Ann: What can I do? I need the money!

Broker: Well, you have several alternatives. You can sell the bond and get $700, or you can hold the bond until 2005 when the Cromwell Company will give you $1000 for it. You could also hold onto the bond for a while and see if the price will go back up. It looks like money will be more plentiful in a few months; interest rates are already beginning to fall.

Ann: I guess I'll have to think about it for a few days.

Summary of Market Activity

The Wall Street Journal carries many summary statistics of market activity; Figure 18.9 provides a few of these summaries. Notice there is a listing of the shares traded in major markets (a). Total shares traded on the NYSE on this date was 57,820,000. The "Most Active Stocks" (b) listing includes the stocks that had the highest volume of trades during the day. The "Market Diary" (c) shows the number of stocks that advanced in price, the number that declined in price, those that remained unchanged from the previous day, the number of stocks that reached new highs and the number that reached new lows. "New Highs and Lows" (d) identifies the names of the stock that traded at new highs and new lows on this trading date. And, finally, the stocks that had the greatest percentage increases and decreases over the previous day appear in "Daily Percentage Leaders" (e).

The Dow Jones and Other Market Indexes

In addition to particular security prices and earnings, total stock market averages weave zigzag lines across analysts' charts. We present five common barometers of stocks' ups and downs.

Dow Jones. The **Dow Jones averages** represent a complicated indexing of the price movements of sixty-five stocks listed on the New York Stock Exchange. The sixty-five stocks in the DJ averages are divided as follows: thirty industrial stocks that account for 20% of the value of all common shares on the NYSE, fifteen stocks of utilities (gas and electric companies), and twenty transportation stocks (airlines, railroads, and trucking companies). These averages are the oldest indexes, having begun in 1884. Because of their small selection, critics say they are not as representative of the market today as they were in the past. Still, they remain popularly quoted. In 1973, the DJ averages touched nothing but history, soaring above the 1000 mark for the first time ever. They topped that, however, in 1983, peaking at 1285 on October 10.

Standard & Poor's 500. The **Standard & Poor's 500** index is based on the total value of shares of major firms, with each stock's price weighted by the number of shares outstanding.

TRADING BY MARKETS

New York Exchange	57,820,000
Midwest Exchange	4,942,500
Pacific Exchange	2,202,900
Nat'l Assoc. of Securities Dealers	1,670,600
Philadelphia Exchange	850,700
Boston Exchange	495,200
Cincinnati Exchange	237,100
Instinet System	59,100

(a) Total number of shares traded on the NYSE

MOST ACTIVE STOCKS

	Open	High	Low	Close	Chg.	Volume
Amer T&T wi	20½	20⅞	20	20⅞	+ 1⅜	6,803,700
Amer T&T	65½	66⅜	65½	66⅛	+ 1⅛	2,938,000
LL&E Rlty n	11⅛	11½	11	11½	+ ¼	1,346,800
East Kodak	73	73⅞	72⅞	73½	+ ¾	1,139,300
SuperOil	35¼	35½	34¼	35⅛	1¾	1,127,400
Exxon	37⅞	38	37⅝	37⅞	⅛	784,300
WarnrCom	21⅛	23¼	21⅛	23	+ 1¾	648,800
MidSouUt	15⅝	15¾	15½	15⅝	⅛	621,100
Gen Motors	76¾	76¾	75½	75⅞	⅝	598,400
IBM	121⅛	121¾	120⅞	121	+ ⅛	548,800
Celanese	71	73	71	73	+ 1¼	535,900
HewletPk s	40¾	40¾	40	40½	...	511,600
GouldInc	31⅞	31⅞	30¾	31	1	476,400
LIL Co	13	13⅛	12¾	13	+ ⅛	459,300
Xerox Cp	48⅜	49⅛	48¼	49	+ ½	445,400

(b) Most actively traded stocks on this date

MARKET DIARY

	Fri.	Thur.	Wed.	Tues.	Mon.	(a)
Advances	841	810	998	903	874	1,218
Declines	601	820	658	683	707	763
Unchanged	451	402	375	431	409	230
New highs	67	74	99	66	48	180
New lows	9	33	32	14	13	63

(a)-Summary for the week ended November 25, 1983.

(c) Summary of trading events

New Highs and Lows of NYSE-Listed Issues

Friday, November 25, 1983

NEW HIGHS – 67

Airbn Frt	CaroPwLt	Firestone	NevadaPwr
AmGenlCp s	CenLaElec	Gen Banc	Nwstind
AmGenl pfB	ChrisC prpf	GnDynam	ParkHan
AmGn3.25jpf	CollinFd s	GnDyn 4.25pf	PhilVanH
Ameritech wi	ConeMills	GenSignal	Piedmt NGs
AmShipB	Con Frght	GulfUtdCp	Pillsbury
Amer T&T wi	Contl Group	Humana2.50pf	PioneerEl
AmericPrm wi	Cooperln	IowaIll GE	PyroEngy
AmerTrSc wi	Copwld	IowaResrcs	RCA
AmerTrUn wi	Copwld pf	Laclede Gas	RCA cv4pf
AMP Inc	CrayRsch	Lear Siegler	SouPac s
AntaCorp	DanaCp s	LibertyCp	TxPacLd
BellCda g	EatonCp	Linc Nat	WendysInt
BethSt 2.50pf	FMC	Louisv GE	WestPtPep
Boston Ed	FMCCp pf	Matsush El	WhiteCons
Bklyn UGas	FaysDrug s	McLean n	WitcoChm s
CSX Cp pf	FedExpress s	Mont Pow	

NEW LOWS – 9

BellSouth wi	LIL CopfE	LIL CopfK	NCPipe adj pf
CnPw4.50pf	LIL CopfJ	LIL CopfT	TolEd 3.47pf
IUIntCp wi			

s-Split or stock dividend of 25 per cent or more in the past 52 weeks. High-low range is adjusted from old stock. n-New issue in past 52 weeks and does not cover the entire 52 week period.

(d) Stocks that reached a new high or a new low on this date

Daily Percentage Leaders of NYSE-Listed Issues

The following list shows the New York Stock Exchange-listed stocks and warrants that sell for more than $2 that have gone up the most and down the most based on the percent of change regardless of volume for Friday. Rights are excluded. Net and percentage changes are the difference between Friday's last price and the previous closing price.

UPS

Name	Sales(hds)	High	Low	Last	Chg.	Pct.
1 Marcade	281	3⅛	2⅝	3⅛	+ ½ Up	19.0
2 BancTexas	1712	6⅜	5⅝	6⅜	+ ⅞ Up	15.9
3 RecognEq	1613	13⅝	11⅞	13⅝	+ 1⅝ Up	13.5
4 CharterCo wt	152	4⅜	4	4⅜	+ ½ Up	12.9
5 LehValInd	125	2½	2⅜	2½	+ ¼ Up	11.1
6 Copwld	250	21¼	19½	21¼	+ 1⅞ Up	9.7
7 CharterCo	1390	8⅞	8¼	8⅞	+ ¾ Up	9.2
8 ElMemMg	295	8⅞	8¼	8⅞	+ ¾ Up	9.2
9 AmShipB	478	14¼	13⅛	14⅛	+ 1⅛ Up	8.7
10 FlowGenl	478	11⅜	10½	11¼	+ ⅞ Up	8.4

DOWNS

Name	Sales(hds)	High	Low	Last	Chg.	Pct.
1 UnitInd s	223	25½	23½	23⅝	1½ Off	6.0
2 GenGwth wt	95	4⅜	4	4	¼ Off	5.9
3 MesaOffsh n	223	2¼	2⅛	2⅛	⅛ Off	5.6
4 ToysRUs s	1484	41⅛	38⅞	39¾	2¼ Off	5.4
5 AmAgro	155	2⅜	2¼	2¼	⅛ Off	5.3
6 SuperOil	11274	35½	34¼	35⅛	1¾ Off	4.7
7 NwCnPipe adj pf	16	43	43	43	2 Off	4.4
8 DetE 3.13pf	14	22⅞	22⅝	22⅝	1 Off	4.2
9 ScieAtl	803	16½	16	16	⅝ Off	3.8
10 SthwstEnr	57	19¾	19¼	19¼	¾ Off	3.8

z-Actual sales

(e) Stocks that gained or lost the greatest percentage on this date

Figure 18.9
Summary of activity on the NYSE for Monday, November 28, 1983.

The averages include 500 stocks listed on the NYSE, comprised as follows: 425 industrials, 50 utilities, 25 railroads. Because S&P's 500 is broader based than the Dow, many people think it represents the market more accurately. As Fig. 18.9 shows, this index rested at 167.18 on November 25, 1983.

New York Stock Exchange Composite Index. The **New York Stock Exchange Composite Index** is a weighted price index of all the common shares listed on this, the largest exchange. This index was 96.55 on November 25, 1983.

American Exchange Market Value Index. Like the NYSE Composite Index, the **American Exchange Market Value Index,** for the American Stock Exchange, averages prices for all common shares on the exchange. This index usually includes smaller companies than those listed on the NYSE; it was 222.57 on November 25, 1983.

NASDAQ OTC Composite Index. The **NAS-DAQ OTC Composite Index** (National Association of Securities Dealers Automated Quotations) provides a weighted average of more than 2000 common stocks traded on OTC markets. This index on November 25, 1983, was 285.49. Figure 18.10 lists these stock market indicators.

Other Information Sources

Because investors are so hungry for all types of information about stocks and the stock markets, many sources provide this information.

News publications. In addition to daily quotations and averages, *The Wall Street Journal* gives

**Figure 18.10
Information about Dow Jones averages and other market indicators for Friday, November 25, 1983.**

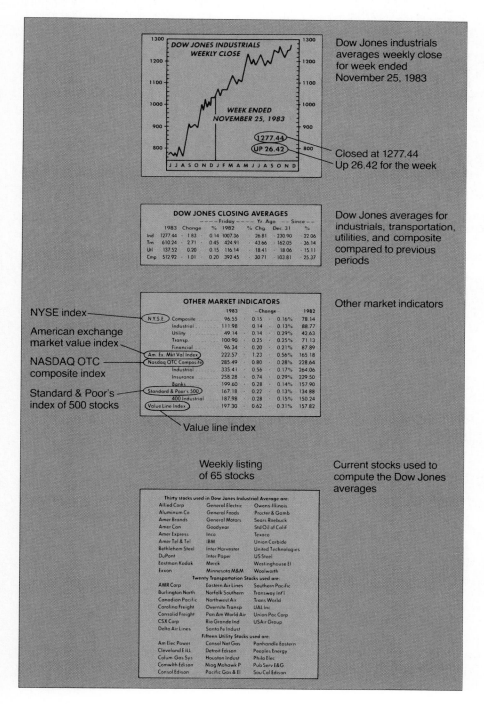

Dow Jones industrials averages weekly close for week ended November 25, 1983

Closed at 1277.44
Up 26.42 for the week

Dow Jones averages for industrials, transportation, utilities, and composite compared to previous periods

Other market indicators

NYSE index

American exchange market value index

NASDAQ OTC composite index

Standard & Poor's index of 500 stocks

Value line index

Weekly listing of 65 stocks

Current stocks used to compute the Dow Jones averages

Worldwide commodity price quotes and other trading information go out from the communications center of Commodity News Service and are received via telephone lines or with a satellite dish antenna.

comprehensive daily financial information, including stories, tidbits, trends, and significant happenings in the world. Periodicals such as *Business Week, Barrons, Dun's Review, Forbes*, and *U.S. News & World Report* publish a lot of market information. Numerous services specialize in publishing statistics about security prices, the two most popular being Moody's *Investor's Service* and Standard & Poor's *Industrial Surveys*.

Research by brokerage firms. Most of the large brokerage firms maintain a research staff that investigates and analyzes opportunities. The firms use the results of their research to aid investors who buy and sell through them. Sometimes local branches of the large firms will do their own research on local securities and make recommendations to their clients.

Market letters. Many firms and professional advisors produce periodic newsletters to tell investors what they ought to buy, sell, and hold on to. An investor subscribes to these market letters for a fee, ranging from $35 to almost $400 per year. The *Value Line Investment Survey*, one of the highest-priced market letters at $365, weekly rates 1700 stocks for probable market performance during the next 12 months. In addition to their ratings, Value Line issues new, comprehensive reports on 130 stocks every week. The reports include, for each stock, monthly price ranges for the past 15 years, the company's capital structure, sales, earnings, dividends, summary of the company's business, and much more.

The Zweig Forecast. Another higher priced market letter gives specific buy-and-sell recommendations about every three weeks. The Zweig Forecast typically lists about twenty stocks that it has recommended, along with the percentage of gain or loss on each recommendation. Subscribers also get a unique service; by calling a hotline, which is updated two or three times a week, they can get up-to-the-second, buy-and-sell recommendations.

Some of the market letters have a good record of finding good investments, but few of them, year in and year out, are able to maintain an outstanding list of recommendations. Ironically, as a group, the advisory services tend to be most optimistic when stocks are on the verge of dropping and most pessimistic when a price rise impends.

> **When a majority of advisory services are bullish, investors look for a bear market.**

And, in this way, they become a market predictor. When a majority of the advisory services are bullish, investors look for a bear market.

REGULATION OF EXCHANGES AND TRADING

We have all heard that the stock market collapsed in 1929, leaving millions of people burdened, broke, and beat. Abuses, opportunists, and speculations no doubt contributed mightily to the downfall. Because stock markets house the financial futures of millions of people, both state and federal laws regulate securities trading.

State Laws

Kansas became the first state, in 1911, to pass a law regulating security sales within a state. Today, all states have laws governing security sales. Because a member of a state legislature said "Some promoters would sell stock in the 'blue sky' itself," these state laws have become known as blue-sky laws. Although they vary, **blue-sky laws** typically require:

- Registration of security issues with a state official.

CROSS FIRE

Financial Trends

Interest rates have a lot of influence on the price of stocks as well as most other aspects of the financial community. As interest rates increase, stocks normally decline in price and vice versa. Most experts predict that interest rates will decline, at least somewhat, in the next few years. However, the large budget deficits, according to some economists, might hold rates up.

Do you think interest rates will increase or decrease in the next five years? Why?

___ A. Increase   ___ B. Decrease

The FDIC, on October 12, 1983, loaned $100 million to the First National Bank of Midland, Texas. The bank had suffered losses on loans made to oil and gas companies, and depositors began withdrawing their funds. The loan is one of the largest ever made by the FDIC, which contends they are trying to keep the bank afloat while trying to find another institution to buy it. Some argue that such large loans encourage bank managers to take unwise risks because they know the FDIC will bail them out. Others say that FDIC loans reduce the disruptions caused by bank failures.

Do you think that the FDIC should loan money to banks in trouble? Why?

___ A. Yes   ___ B. No

Banking regulators have the responsibility for checking banks to see that they are being reasonably wise in protecting the money of their depositors. However, the Securities and Exchange Commission says that publicly owned banks ought to have to reveal more data to them, especially about shaky loans. The SEC maintains that regulators are sometimes hesitant to disclose such data.

Do you think publicly owned banks should be required to disclose complete information about their loans to the SEC? Why?

___ A. Yes   ___ B. No

TABLE 18.3 ■ A SUMMARY OF THE MAJOR LAWS REGULATING SECURITIES TRADING

1933 Securities Act	Requires full disclosure of financial information about new securities given in a registration statement and a prospectus.
1934 Securities Exchange Act	Established and gave regulatory powers to the Securities Exchange Commission (SEC).
1938 Maloney Act	Allows investment bankers to form associations for self-regulation. The National Association of Security Dealers (NASD) came into being under this act to regulate OTC trading.
1940 Investment Company Act	Requires investment trust companies (mutual funds) to register with the SEC.
1940 Investment Advisors Act	Requires security advisors to register with the SEC.
1964 Securities Act Amendments	Requires dealers and brokers selling OTC to register with the SEC.
1970 Securities Investor Protection Act	Created the Securities Investor Protection Corporation (SIPC) to protect individual accounts with brokers that become insolvent, up to $100,000. The SIPC, of course, does not protect against losses due to market declines.

■ Licensing for dealers, brokers, and salespersons.

■ Prosecution of individuals engaging in fraudulent sale of securities.

Federal Securities Exchange Act of 1934

Congress passed the Federal Securities Act, the first federal law dealing with securities trading, in 1933. However, the most significant federal law, the Federal Securities Exchange Act, appeared a year later in 1934. After being amended several times, the major provisions of the Securities Exchange Act are:

1. When a company lists securities to be traded, the securities must be registered with the Securities Exchange Commission (SEC) so that investors can get needed and reliable information.

2. Companies must submit periodic accounting and financial reports describing their current financial condition. Investors can study this information to give them better data for decision making.

3. Security exchanges themselves must place on file, open for public inspection, information on how they were formed, their bylaws, membership requirements, and regulations.

4. The SEC expressly prohibits the exchanges from giving out false or misleading information about commissions and prices, price fixing, and collusion in trading.

5. Brokers are subject to controls, such as how much money they can loan investors, by the SEC.

Other Security-Related Laws

Over the years, Congress has passed several laws to regulate security trading. Some of these most important laws are described briefly in Table 18.3.

INVESTMENT STRATEGIES

Although the stock market was lackluster during the latter part of the 1970s, it took off in 1983. Investors poured money into the market and prices increased. The market, of course, has a history of ups and downs. People who have predicted the market movements have done well, but

---

Remember, for every person who buys a stock thinking the price will rise, a different person sells the stock thinking the price will not rise.

---

there is no surefire formula for success in the stock market. Remember, for every person who buys a stock thinking the price will rise, a different person sells the stock thinking the price will not rise. Thus, for all stock trading, half of the people are wrong. Most people, in all probability, will eventually invest, directly or indirectly, money in stocks and other securities. It would be helpful to know something about investment strategies.

Investment versus Speculation

The first step in developing your investment strategy is to decide how much risk you wish to take with your money. The degree of risk falls into two broad categories: speculating and investing.

Speculation. Speculation is deliberately taking a risk that offers the possibility of a short-term high gain or loss. The aim is to roll high and hope for the big payoff. But the greater the opportunity for gain, the greater the probability of loss. For most of us, speculation is not the proper strategy.

Investing. Investing is the purchase of securities, based on sound analysis, that will give a reasonable chance of earnings, safety, and increase in principal over a period of time. But even before investing in securities, most authorities recommend that you have adequate life insurance coverage and enough savings to meet emergencies.

What Is Your Investment Objective?

The first step for a sane investor is to decide what you hope to accomplish. Do you want to take a risk on securities that might increase or decrease

rapidly in price? Do you want to be sure your investment is protected? Do you want to receive a high income off your current investment? "All of the above" is the answer that we would like to give to these questions. But it does not work that way.

If you are looking for safety, go for good-quality bonds and preferred stocks with respected companies. However, the interest rate on bonds will be lower, because they are safe; and your return on preferred stock will be at a fixed rate. There is little chance of either rising very much in price. If you have a relatively large amount to invest and you want to earn a high income, common stocks are probably the best bet, but you will have to look for stocks that have been paying a high dividend rate over the past few years. Typically, public utility companies have had good records in this regard. For instance, in late 1983, Gulf States Utilities was yielding 11.3%; Illinois Power, 10.7%; Long Island Lighting, 11.6%; and Carolina Power and Light, 10.8%. And up to $750 per taxpayer per year in dividends from qualified utilities are tax-free if left in a reinvestment plan.

For investors who want their money to grow fast, you have to be willing to sacrifice some immediate income and take some risks. Again, common stocks are probably the best bet. But you have to select stocks of growing firms in growing industries. This usually means sales and earnings have been increasing faster than average for the past few years and are expected to continue. If you intend to invest seriously, you should probably follow a combination of these strategies, starting with the safer investments before winging off into the more risky areas. Figure 18.11 outlines these objectives and makes some suggestions regarding them.

How to Select a Particular Stock

Remember, absolutely no one has the stock market solved. Anytime you invest, there is a chance you will lose some or all of your money. With this caution, we offer the following guidelines for selecting stocks that meet long-term growth objectives — the most popular objectives of most investors.

1. Start with a leading company in a sound industry. This gives you some security with some chance of growth.
2. Select stocks with price-earning ratios no higher than 9:1. This is only a guide. There

Figure 18.11
How to establish investment objectives.

Figure 18.12
How mutual funds have grown since 1976.
Source: Standard & Poor's Corporation and NYSE.

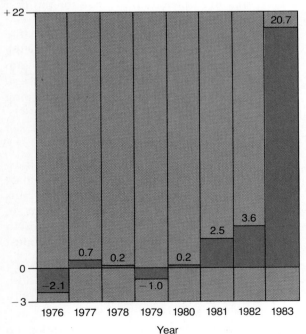

Billions of dollars

are always some good buys higher than this, and no guarantee that low ratios will pay off.

3. Check the companies' balance sheets over the past 3 to 5 years and compare them to other firms in the industry. Select companies whose balance sheets are better than average.

4. Check the earnings and dividends records for the past 5 years, and select a stock that has been steadily increasing in both.

5. Take a look at the values. They are important but do not over-stress them.

6. The best time to buy is after a long decline when the stock has fallen in price by 20% or more.

7. Spread your risk by owning stocks in equal amounts in at least five different companies in at least three different industries.

8. Relax. There are many short-term bumps and jumps in the price of most any stock. Do not look at your prices daily. Check them weekly, or better yet, monthly, to remove the temptation to speculate.

It requires effort to follow these guidelines. But you should consider this as only minimum preparation for your entry into the stock market.

Mutual Funds

If you do not have the background, time, or inclination to analyze and select stocks, you might be interested in a mutual fund. According to the Investment Company Institute, a **mutual fund** is a company which combines the investment funds of many people whose investment goals are similar, and in turn invests those funds in a wide variety of securities. Most mutual funds have several different types of portfolios to meet needs of different investors. The John Hancock mutual funds, for example, include a bond fund, a growth stock fund, a United States government securities fund, and a tax-exempt fund. As an investor, you can select which type of fund appeals to you. If you want safety, you might invest in the government securities fund; if you do not want to pay tax on the dividends or interest you earn from the funds, you can invest in the tax-exempt fund.

The approximately 550 mutual funds experienced rapid growth during 1983 (see Fig. 18.12). Mutual funds are America's fourth-largest financial force; banks, insurance companies, and pension funds are the top three forces. Mutual funds offer professional management and allow you to diversify into many securities with little investment. Some funds charge for their services, typically 7½ to 8½% of the purchase price; but **no-load funds** do not charge management fees for their services. The managers' salaries come from the earnings of the fund.

During the last 5 years, funds outperformed the market by increasing 157%. Standard & Poor's 500 stock composite index increased during the same period 129%. Because of this success, many no-load funds are beginning to charge for some of their services, thus becoming a **low-load fund** — a fund that charges low fees for its services. The Magellan Fund, with a 2% load, was the first of the no-loads to begin charging. Another large mutual fund, the Fidelity funds, charges between 2 and 3% on purchases for about a fourth of their funds.

BUSINESS BULLETIN

Where Americans Keep Their Money

From 1961 to 1981, the percentage of financial assets that Americans kept in corporate stocks declined from 44.8 to 23.2%. Most of this change represented a move from stocks to deposits of various types. See the accompanying chart for more detail on where Americans keep their holdings.

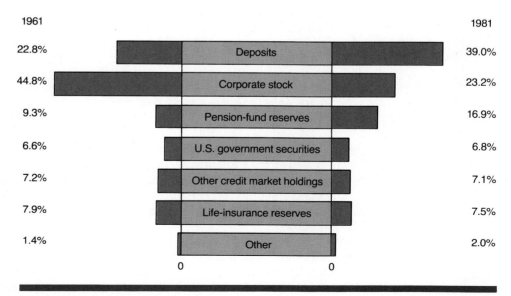

1961		1981
22.8%	Deposits	39.0%
44.8%	Corporate stock	23.2%
9.3%	Pension-fund reserves	16.9%
6.6%	U.S. government securities	6.8%
7.2%	Other credit market holdings	7.1%
7.9%	Life-insurance reserves	7.5%
1.4%	Other	2.0%

Source: Federal Reserve Board.

Because of their expertise, many sophisticated investors join with the novices to invest in these funds. By investment objectives, mutual funds tend to fall into five categories:

1. *Growth.* Oriented toward long-term capital gain.
2. *Growth and income.* Combine dividend-paying common stocks with preferred issues.
3. *Balanced.* Combine safety with some growth through common stocks and interest-paying securities.
4. *Income.* Seeks securities that produce good dividends or interest rates.
5. *Tax-exempt income.* Seeks diversified investment in municipal bonds.

Money Market Funds

Money market funds grew in popularity during the late 1970s; they were paying interest rates ranging from 12 to 17%. However, as interest rates fell, rates for the funds dropped correspondingly. **Money markets** is a term used to describe short-term debt markets. Examples of money market instruments are Treasury bills, certificates of deposit, commercial paper, banker's acceptances, and selected government securities. These are

TAKING STOCK

Ethical Investment

Ethical investing — the idea that one's dollar should be invested with regard to social consequence — has become a multimillion-dollar business. In the past 15 years, ethical investing has redirected hundreds of millions of investment dollars away from the dark side of corporate America toward "areas that address human need": consumer co-ops; inner-city redevelopment; alternative energy; small businesses; family farms; worker-owned companies; corporations with enlightened policies toward their employees, their products, and the environment.

Though the range of ethical investment may be broad, the results are impressive:

- The Lutheran Church loaned half a million dollars to the Alabama Rural Council, giving the ARC the financial leverage it needed to secure $2 million in Small Business Administration loans to build low-income housing.

- The Teachers Insurance and Annuity Association/College Retirement Equities Funds voted to screen its $9 billion in investment capital through a strict set of ethical criteria.

- The Calvert Group launched its $20 million Social Investment Fund, which went against all the rules of Wall Street by basing its money market and mutual fund portfolios on ethical considerations. It invests only in businesses that are nonnuclear, nonmilitary, proconsumer, and proenvironmental. What's more, it defies all expectations by outperforming both the Dow Jones and money market averages.

- Three manufacturers of infant formula — Nestlé's, American Home Products, and Bristol-Meyers — succumbed to shareholder pressure brought by groups affiliated with the Interfaith Center for Corporate Responsibility and agreed to conform to marketing codes that will end "baby-bottle disease" in the Third World.

short-term instruments, but many of them are sold in denominations of $100,000 to $1,000,000 — clearly outside the range of most investors. However, **money market funds,** mutual funds that trade in the money markets, are available for as little as a $1000 initial investment. The fund pools your money with thousands of other people and invests in money market instruments. The benefits of money market funds are: (1) income, (2) liquidity, and (3) safety.

Brokers have typically used money market funds as a place to park your money while you are waiting to buy stocks. If, for instance, you sold some stock and did not have an immediate alternative investment, you could put your money in money market funds and draw interest while waiting. Banks and most other financial institutions also sell money market funds.

Individual Retirement Accounts (IRAs)

In 1982, income tax laws were revised to allow wage earners to deposit up to $2000 per year in an **individual retirement account (IRA)** and delay taxes on the deposits and earnings. (For a married couple where one spouse does not work outside the home, the maximum is $2250.) The govern-

Source: ''Ethical Investment: Making Money in Good Conscience,'' *New Age Journal,* November 1983, pp. 41–44, 81–83.

ment created IRAs as a tax shelter for wage earners and to encourage greater savings for retirement. IRAs have become very popular, swelling to $80 billion in less than 2 years. Just before last April 15, Merrill Lynch alone opened 100,000 IRAs. Money in the IRAs are then invested, but you do not have to pay tax on the earnings until you retire. If you decide to withdraw your money from an IRA before you retire, you will pay taxes at the time of withdrawal, plus a penalty for early withdrawal.

Financial Planning

Because of the profusion of new financial products, most ordinary investors have a hard time determining their best investment strategy. In fact, financial planners estimate that professional people spend only about 5 hours a year planning their financial future. And many recent marketing studies indicate that 85% of those who have disposable income think they could use some kind of financial planning.

A financial planner studies your income, financial needs, investment opportunities, and tax implications, and makes recommendations on how to prepare for your financial future. Then, each year, the planner will review your situation and make adjustments if necessary. Financial planners devote their professional lives to studying complex finance packages. Thus, they are usually better qualified to recommend financial decisions than most individual investors.

One portfolio manager, Robert Zevin, handles more than $52 million in "socially sensitive" accounts for U.S. Trust, a financial consulting firm, and by 1985, he expects his accounts to total $100 million. Zevin and his associates handle U.S. Trust's social accounts (as distinct from the company's conventional accounts), and together they have developed perhaps the nation's most sophisticated system of ethical criteria. To define what a "good" company is, Zevin looks at a company's performance not just in financial terms (though this is part of the pie) but also in social terms: What kinds of products does it produce? How does it affect the environment? What are its hiring policies? How does it treat its employees? What are its

politics? These criteria automatically rule out about a third of the country's major corporations, but the vast majority of them fall into a gray area.

Although social investing has grown greatly in the past few years, it is not yet a movement with much economic clout. Still, social investing is a revolution in investment style. *Barron's* and *The Wall Street Journal* have written about it, Addison-Wesley Publishing Company is publishing a book about it, and major financial institutions like Chemical Bank, Shearson-American Express, and Franklin Management have opened departments that specialize in it.

SUMMARY

Securities exchanges are marketplaces where buyers and sellers bid for each other's stocks, bonds, and other securities. To buy or sell a listed security, you place an order with a broker who transmits the information to a representative on the floor of the exchange. Brokers charge commissions for their services. You can buy on margin, sell short, trade options with puts and calls, trade outside the exchanges, trade stock-index futures, trade stock warrants, and buy and sell unlisted securities over the counter.

Commodity exchanges allow trading of commodities such as grain, vegetables, livestock, metals, and the like. You can trade on the spot (current) market or the futures market. You can hedge by engaging in both a buy and sell transaction at the same time.

Information about securities is available in most daily newspapers; you can find daily quotations of prices, shares traded, increase or decrease in price, and much more. Five indexes of the market's movement include the Dow Jones averages, Standard & Poor's 500, the New York Stock Exchange Composite Index, the American Exchange Market Value Index, and the NASDAQ OTC Composite Index. News publications, research by brokerage firms, and market letters also report information about securities. Trading on the exchanges is regulated by state and federal laws.

Before you invest in the stock market, you should identify your investment strategy and select your investment objective. Then you should follow sound guidelines for selecting a particular stock. If you are not inclined to spend the time doing your own analysis, you might want to invest in mutual funds, money market funds, or hire a financial planner.

MIND YOUR BUSINESS

Instructions. Respond to each of the following statements by filling in the blank with the correct answer.

____ 1. On Friday, Feb. 10, 1984, IBM common stock closed at 109⅞. If you had purchased 100 shares of IBM on that date, how much profit or loss would you have made by selling it now?

____ 2. Approximately how much commission would you have paid your broker on the two transactions required to buy and sell the IBM stock?

____ 3. On February 10, 1984, the Paine Webber Money Market Fund was paying 8.86% interest on its money market fund. What is Paine Webber's money market fund paying today?

____ 4. On February 10, 1984, Sears closed at 35⅜. Suppose you had sold short 100 shares of Sears stock on that date. What would be your profit or loss if you were to buy Sears stock today to cover your short sale?

____ 5. Motorola, which closed at 116 on February 10, 1984, had a price-earnings ratio of 19. What is the price-earnings ratio of Motorola today? Considering only the P-E ratio, is Motorola likely to be a better investment today than it was on February 10, 1984?

____ 6. The Dow Jones Industrial averages closed at 1160.7 on February 10, 1984. What are the Dow Jones Industrial averages today?

____ 7. The NASDAQ index for over-the-counter stocks closed at 254.04 on February 10, 1984. What is the NASDAQ index today?

See answers at the back of the book.

KEY TERMS

REVIEW QUESTIONS

1. What is a security exchange? How do they operate?

2. What is a listed security?

3. Describe the process of buying and selling securities listed on a major exchange.

4. Explain the most common types of buy and sell orders.

5. On what do brokers base their commissions?

6. Explain and illustrate the following: buying on margin, selling short, puts and calls, stock-index futures, trading warrants, and bull and bear markets.

7. How can an investor buy and sell outside the exchanges?

8. What are over-the-counter markets?

9. What are commodities exchanges? How do they operate? Distinguish between spot and futures markets.

10. Explain and illustrate hedging.

11. Briefly describe the various types of information available on stock markets. Identify the most common kinds of market indexes.

12. Explain the major state and federal laws that regulate securities trading.

13. Distinguish between speculation and investment.

14. Identify five types of investment objectives.

15. Outline guidelines for selecting a particular stock to invest in.

16. What are mutual funds? What advantages do they offer? What is a no-load fund? A low-load fund?

17. What are money market funds? IRAs? Financial planners?

CASES

Case 18.1: Where Would You Invest?

Suppose you had $20,000 to invest. Assume that you could take an average risk with the money. You certainly would not want to lose more than 25% of the $20,000, and you want a reasonable chance of increasing your money faster than the interest rate. Taxes are not a big concern since you are in a low tax bracket at the moment. You are not an investment expert, but you do know a little something about the more common type of investment opportunities. After talking with several friends, you have narrowed your investment down to the following alternatives.

1. Place the $20,000 down to purchase $100,000, four-plex apartment building that is in good shape, requires little maintenance, and has been fully occupied for the last few years.

2. Invest the $20,000 in a combination of Treasury bills, savings accounts, and high-quality federal bonds.

3. Put $20,000 in the stock market, with about half going to high-risk common stocks and about half to blue-chip common stocks.

4. Spread the investment about equally between gold, art objects, speculative common stocks, and Treasury bills.

Questions

1. Analyze the advantages and disadvantages of each alternative.

2. Which alternative would you select? Why?

3. Should other alternatives be considered? If yes, what are they?

Case 18.2: Differing Investment Needs

People at different ages and with different investment requirements have different investment needs. For example, a young investor with only a little money to invest would certainly invest differently than would a young investor with a lot of money to invest. Consider the investment needs of the following people.

Bob Smith is 28, in a career position with a large company. He currently makes $28,000 a year, is married, and has a two-year-old son. His wife also works, making $17,000 per year. Bob is just starting his investment program and has $10,000 to invest.

Jean Smith, a single professional, is 25 years of age. Jean currently makes $30,000 per year and is very likely to receive rapid promotions in her career. Jean, also just starting her investment program, has $40,000 to invest.

Sara and Hank, a married couple in their late forties, have $75,000 to invest. Both of their children are grown; the youngest will be graduating with a master's degree within a year. The oldest is already in a career job. Hank and Sara are both healthy and have good jobs. They are looking forward to about 20 more years of working before retiring.

Helen and Jim have just retired. Jim is 67 and Helen is 63. Both are healthy and active. They own their own home, have a good medical insurance plan, and their four children are established in their careers. They have $150,000 to invest.

Questions

1. Briefly identify the major investment concerns of each of these four situations.

2. How do you think each of these investors should invest his or her money? Make your recommendations by completing the accompanying chart. (Consider only the investment opportunities listed. Suggest the percentage of the total investment that each investor should put into each type of security.

3. Explain why you allocated the investment funds as you did.

Securities	Bob Smith ($10,000)	Jean Smith ($40,000)	Sara and Hank ($75,000)	Helen and Jim ($150,000)
Corporate or U.S. bonds	_____	_____	_____	_____
Mutual fund of growth stocks	_____	_____	_____	_____
Tax-exempt bonds	_____	_____	_____	_____
Growth stocks	_____	_____	_____	_____
Mutual fund of growth stocks	_____	_____	_____	_____
IRA or Keough account	_____	_____	_____	_____
	100%	100%	100%	100%

After completing this chapter, you will be able to:

■ Explain the four steps to risk management.

■ Describe four kinds of life insurance coverage.

■ Explain four ways that businesses use life insurance.

■ Explain five ways to insure against losses due to accidents and health problems.

■ Describe three categories of insurance against liabilities.

■ Discuss the four common types of automobile insurance coverage.

■ Explain assigned risks and no-fault insurance.

■ Identify two trends in insurance coverage.

19

RISK
MANAGEMENT
AND INSURANCE

In 1981, the world-famous racehorse, Shergar, won both the English and Irish Derbies. In 1983, valued as high as $15 million, Shergar was retired to the Ballmany stud farm in County Kildare. On February 8, 1983, four gunmen entered Ballmany, kidnaped the horse, and the next day demanded $4.5 million ransom money. However, officials agreed not to pay the ransom money; and four months later, insurance underwriters Lloyds of London agreed to pay the theft insurance claim filed by the 34-member syndicate that owned Shergar.

Owning racehorses is surely a risky business. But every business is risky. In fact, every time an owner puts money into a business, he or she stands to lose all or part of it. **Risk** is the danger of loss. Business risks occur in all sizes and shapes: Consumers may not buy new products; purchasers who buy on credit may not pay; a newly hired employee may be a dud; a building may burn down; shoplifters may steal merchandise; a key person in the company might die.

We cannot eliminate risks from business, but we can and should reduce the danger of loss when possible. In this chapter, we identify ways of dealing with risks, explain how insurance works, and show how companies share risks involving property, earnings losses, liabilities, and automobiles. Finally, we look at new trends in insurance coverage.

RISK MANAGEMENT

Risk management represents a company's efforts to deal with risks before they occur. In today's complex world, risk management is very difficult, requiring knowledge of the company's business, finance, loss control, and insurance. The risk management process typically involves four rather simple steps.

Identify the Risk

A firm cannot measure its risks unless it identifies each chance of loss. Companies must look beyond the obvious into the intangible "what ifs" and "maybes." Some risks are obvious: If you own a building, there is a risk of fire or storm; if you have inventory, there is a risk of theft; and of course, there is always the risk of death. But other risks are less obvious. For instance, Congress recently passed two laws, the Resources and Recover Con-

Most insurance companies manage a variety of clearly identifiable risks, as well as related financial service.

servation Act and the Superfund legislation, that deal with hazardous wastes. Since the laws are new and rather complex, it is uncertain just what risks these laws impose upon businesses. Suppose a farmer, carrying chemicals in his farm truck, wrecks and spills the chemicals into a creek. Will he be liable for pollution? Will printers and paint distributors, who spill chemicals, be in the same position? To identify all risks clearly, management must look beyond the obvious into the bizarre "what ifs" and the murky "maybes."

Measure the Risk

After identifying the risk, management should measure the risk by figuring the likelihood of loss and the size of the potential loss. Again, this may not be as easy as it seems. Insurance people are pretty good at determining the cost of tangible items, but how do you arrive at the value of a racehorse like Shergar? Or, how do you determine your loss if your business burns during a peak selling season? You might be able to determine the value of your building easily enough, but what about the potential sales that you lost? There are procedures for estimating the value for practically any type of loss, and good risk management identifies the potential costs of losses before they occur.

Control the Risk

The goal of risk control is to do what is financially feasible to prevent the loss and to reduce the impact if the loss does occur. Companies can control risks by trying to avoid them or by reducing them.

Avoiding risk. A company might try to avoid a risk by selecting different alternatives. A company could choose to avoid the risks of expansion by choosing not to expand. An executive could avoid the risk of dying in a plane crash by taking the train. An owner can avoid the risk of bad-debt losses by requiring customers to pay cash. A manager of the Jeffery Company, a small janitorial firm, explains how he decided to avoid a risk. "We felt that a cleaning compound that we were using contained some chemicals that might possibly be dangerous if inhaled. After some investigating, we found another cleaning substance that did not

Inspection of the interior of a refinery tank for structural soundness helps reduce the risk of accident.

contain the dangerous compounds. The substance we chose was slightly less effective than the one we were using, but we decided to opt for the less effective cleaning solution to avoid the risk of injury to our people."

Reducing risk. In some cases, companies realize that it is impossible to avoid risks, so they take measures to reduce them. Sprinkling systems, electronic surveillance, fireproofing, automatic locks, guards, and inspections are examples of attempts to reduce risks. While these methods are costly, they are better than no buffer at all.

Diversification into different product lines is often an attempt to reduce risks: If a product's sales drop off, the firm has another product to rely on.

Astute risk managers also find ways to reduce the blow from failure of particular projects. Diversification into different product lines is often an attempt to reduce risks. If a certain product's sales drop off, the firm has another product line to rely upon. Accurate forecasting and economic analysis are also ways that companies try to reduce their risks.

Finance the Risk

Companies may finance risks by assuming the cost of the risk or by transferring the risk to another party — typically, an insurance company.

Assuming the risk. Companies may choose to assume some of their risks by anticipating losses and setting aside money for them. This type of self-insurance is more appropriate for large organizations than for most smaller ones. For example, a big company with 500 stores in different parts of the country can anticipate that some of its buildings will receive damage each year. If it expects losses of $50,000 per year, the organization can save funds for this purpose. When the damage occurs, it merely rebuilds the structure from its resource pool. Smaller companies, however, cannot do this. If a company owns a single warehouse worth $250,000, the owners would be foolhardy to try to save enough to take care of such a loss; it would take 25 years to cover the current cost of replacement if the firm saves $10,000 a year.

BUSINESS BULLETIN

Insurance Agents and Insurance Companies

A variety of insurance agents and companies have emerged to handle insurance needs.

- *Insurance agents (brokers).* Agents sell insurance policies. Most also offer consulting and advising services as well.

- *Independent agents.* Independent agents often represent more than one insuring company. They are in business for themselves, but they have agreements with several insurance companies to sell their policies.

- *Insurance company agents.* Salespeople work for one insurance company, and they can sell only the policies of that firm.

- *Underwriter.* Underwriters study applications for insurance and decide whether the insuring company should sell an insurance policy to the applicant.

- *Chartered Life Underwriter (CLU).* A designation that a life insurance agent has passed a rigorous and comprehensive examination given by the American College of Life Underwriters.

- *Chartered Property and Casualty Underwriter (CPCU).* A designation that an agent has passed a rigorous and comprehensive examination covering property and casualty insurance.

- *Stock companies.* Insurance companies organized as corporations and owned by stockholders. The stockholders, by buying shares of stock in the company, put up money that serves as a reserve against any losses that may exceed premiums collected. Stockholders also receive profits (if the company is profitable) in the form of dividends.

- *Mutual companies.* Insurance companies organized as nonprofit corporations. Policyholders become the owners of the company. If losses exceed premiums, policyholders are assessed additional premiums to make up the difference. If surpluses accumulate, the company returns the surplus to the policyholders in the form of premium reductions.

Transferring the risk. The most popular method of covering risks is to transfer them to insurance companies. **Insurance** shifts the responsibility of loss to a specialist who handles the risk by spreading it over a large number of incidents. Insurance, then, does not avoid the loss; it merely transfers the danger of loss (risk) to an insurance company.

HOW INSURANCE WORKS

Insurance works because companies can spread their potential losses over a large number of incidents. Still, a risk must meet certain requirements to be insurable.

The Law of Large Numbers

Insuring companies assume risks for relatively small premiums because of the law of averages. Mathematical logic explains that if we group a large number of similar risks, only a small number of losses will actually occur. By studying historical records, mathematicians can accurately project how many buildings are going to burn, what theft losses will be, and how many people in an age group are going to die each year. With losses predicted, insurance companies can determine how much they have to collect to cover losses, pay for their expenses, and leave a profit. Let's illustrate this principle.

Suppose an insurance company agrees to assume the storm risk for 10,000 similar buildings. If it determines that annual storm damages will occur to 150 of the buildings, with an average loss per building of $5000, it would have to pay out total losses of $750,000 (150 × $5000). Allowing $100,000 for operating expenses and profit, it would have to collect $850,000. This would convert to a surprisingly small annual premium of $85 per building ($850,000 ÷ 10,000).

By combining items of value from thousands of different businesses under the roof of one insurance company, the law of large numbers works for everyone's benefit.

Insurable and Uninsurable Risks

An **uninsurable risk** is one that cannot be shifted to an insuring company. For instance, companies run the risks of not making a profit, hiring irresponsible employees, and promoting incompetent managers. Yet they cannot buy insurance for these risks.

Generally, pure risks are insurable; speculative risks are not.

What then is an **insurable risk?** Generally, pure risks are insurable; speculative risks are not. A **pure risk** has no chance of gain; there is only a chance of loss. A **speculative risk** has the potential for gain or loss. Risks of theft, fire, and storm damage can only result in losses, and they are insurable. Price changes, managerial promotions, or betting on a sure thing in the fifth can return either a profit or loss; these risks are not insurable. Insurance merely offsets risks that are already present; it does not prevent them.

More specifically, insurable risks must meet the following specifications.

1. *The insured must have a measurable, insurable interest.* The person or company that purchases the insurance must be the party to lose financially on a claim. For instance, suppose a neighbor insured your house—in which he had absolutely no investment—for $100,000 against fire. Then one moonlit night, he crept over and set it aflame to collect the money. He would be raking in 100 grand on something which cost him zero to lose! Second, the insurance company has to be able to attach some financial value to the loss. Objects that carry high sentimental value but low dollar worth can only be insured for their cash value.

2. *Losses must be accidental.* There is little need to insure against something that you know is going to happen at a certain time. Premiums on such occurrences would be excessive. Insurance companies also balk at paying on losses caused purposely. If they can show that an owner set fire to his own building, they will not pay. Also, the owner is subject to arrest.

3. *Risks must be selected.* Insurance companies select their risks to make the law of averages work. They will not insure only people who have had several automobile accidents or only

employees in hazardous occupations. The company usually has the right to reject applicants who do not meet its selection standards.

4. *Losses must be predictable.* In addition to large numbers, insured projects must be spread geographically. Flood coverage may not be available to residences near storm-battered coasts; a fire insurance company would not cover all the buildings in one city.

5. *The loss cannot be catastrophic.* A massive loss to all the clients of a particular insurance company violates the principle of sharing. Insurance works because only a few losses actually occur. Most property insurance becomes invalid if there is a war or riot.

You have probably heard of insurance covering Jimmy Durante's nose, Mikhail Baryshnikov's legs, and Liberace's hands. Yet these physical assets do not meet the requisites of an insurable risk. These policies are carried by Lloyd's of London, who will underwrite any hazard if the client will pay its fee. Although Lloyd's has become publicly visible with its exotic risk-bearing schemes, most of its business is in marine insurance.

Reinsurance

Reinsurance occurs when an insurance company shares the risk of a particular coverage by passing along part of the risk to other insurance entities. For instance, ships delivering oil from one nation to another may be worth billions of dollars. It would be unwise, if not impossible, for any single insurance company to write a policy covering the risk of such a potential loss. Thus, the company that writes the policy will enter into an agreement with other insurance companies and share both the proceeds from the policy and the risk. Reinsurance represents a large percentage of the insurance marketplace.

INSURANCE AGAINST PROPERTY LOSS

Property insurance covers financial losses due to destruction of the insured's property. Losses to property can occur in many ways including: (1) fire, (2) transportation, and (3) criminal losses.

Fire Insurance

Fire insurance is one of the oldest and most popular forms of insurance coverage. Companies buy fire insurance for stores, factories, and offices; and individuals insure homes, barns, and almost any other type of structure against fire. Fire insurance can also be expanded to cover the contents of the building, whether they are sofas, television sets, clothes, shoes, office equipment, filing cabinets, inventory, or work in process. Most policies have very similar wording and usually cover a one-, three-, or five-year period. Rates are reasonable, ranging from a few cents per $100 of coverage on fireproof constructions near fire stations to a few dollars per $100 for frame buildings located long distances from a fire hydrant. By attaching additions to a policy, called riders or endorsements, companies expand their coverage to losses from smoke, wind, hail, explosion, riot, aircraft, or vehicle damage.

Few fires result in complete loss of the building. So there is a tendency for a firm to insure for less than the total value. If a building is worth $300,000, it might appear to be good business to insure for only $200,000 and take a chance on the remaining $100,000. This represents a much lower premium income for insurance companies, so they have countered with a **coinsurance clause.** Coinsurance stipulates that the firm must insure a certain percentage of the value of the building, commonly 80%, to get full coverage. If insurance is for less than 80%, the insurance company pays only a portion of the loss. To illustrate:

The Mixture Company has an office building valued at $1,000,000 that is insured for $500,000. Mixture's policy contains an 80% coinsurance clause. A fire causes $100,000 damage to the building. (Coverage of $800,000 would have been required to get full payment of the $100,000 actual loss.) So the insurance would pay only $62,500 of the $100,000:

$$\frac{\text{insured amount}}{80\% \text{ of total}} = \frac{\$500,000}{\$800,000}$$

$$5/8 \times \text{actual loss of } \$100,000 = \$62,500$$

In most states, policies on residential property do not contain coinsurance clauses.

An insurance official jokingly remarked to a fellow agent, "The Lord always seems to help out

Marine insurance covers both the vessel and its contents, protecting against nearly all possible perils.

Marine insurance covers the vessel and its contents while at sea or in port against almost all possible perils, from sinking to theft. Time policies cover shipments made on a regular basis, and single-voyage policies cover a designated shipment. Rates are based on such variables as route, season, type of ship, and nature of the cargo. In 1975, the U.S. Supreme Court overturned a 120-year precedent when it ruled that vessels in a collision at sea shared damages according to degree of fault. Previously, insuring companies shared damages equally, regardless of fault.

Inland marine insurance applies to the inland movement of goods over lakes and rivers. It covers nearly every conceivable loss, such as fire, flood, wind, hail, theft, wrecks, and earthquake. When a company ships goods by rail, truck, air, barge, inland or coastal shipping, it almost always protects its risks with inland marine insurance. Many companies ship merchandise by parcel post, and they may obtain a blanket insurance policy that covers all of their shipments. Or they can purchase a coupon book and insert a coupon in each individual package. Either of these methods is cheaper than insuring every package in each shipment.

The Insurance Information Institute esti-

mates that billions of dollars of fire losses

result from professional arsonists.

---

some marginal businesses with a fire during recessions." In bad times, fire losses increase. The Insurance Information Institute estimates that billions of dollars of fire losses result from professional arsonists—colloquially known as "torches." The Institute calls it "selling to the insurance company."

Marine Insurance

Transportation insurance is often called marine insurance because it originated with ships and cargoes at sea.

Criminal Losses

It is impossible to completely check the character or financial standing of every person a company trusts or does business with. Businesses can transfer the unreliability of others to bonding companies.

Fidelity bonds. When an employee has jurisdiction over funds, it is in the best interest of the company to shift the risk of employee dishonesty. **Fidelity bonds** guarantee the employer against losses caused by deceitful employees. The bond may cover a certain individual, a group, or a particular position in the company. Bonds can be purchased for any amount up to the maximum value of property or money to which an employee has access. Suppose the company buys a fidelity bond to cover the post of treasurer for $100,000. If the company hires a treasurer who embezzles $80,000 over a period of 5 years, the bonding company reimburses the company in full.

Surety bonds. **Surety bonds** insure against fraudulent acts and failures of another party to live up to its contractual obligations. If you hire a building contractor to erect a warehouse, you would probably ask him to post a surety bond. If the warehouse were not completed according to contractual specifications within the time allowed, the bonding company would pay you the amount denoted in the bond.

Burglary insurance. Companies also seek protection against burglars and robbers. **Burglary**

insurance covers the forcible and unlawful taking of property from businesses that are closed. Forcible entry — jimmied locks, cracked doors, or shattered windows — usually has to be evident before the insurance pays. Shoplifting, one of the most common types of store theft, is not covered by most burglary insurance because it occurs during open hours. There is no evidence of entry through force. Burglary insurance covers losses of merchandise, money, equipment, and securities.

A robbery occurs when a thief uses force or threat of force to take something of value that belongs to someone else. The use of guards and armored trucks helps to lower this risk. But a company usually wants insurance to protect it if a stocking-covered bandit breaks in, points a gun at the cashier, and demands, "Put all of your money in this bag!" Robbery insurance covers such losses. Small companies can buy a comprehensive burglary and robbery policy that encompasses everything from inventory theft to kidnapping the president.

Business Interruption Insurance

Whereas fire insurance, for example, primarily covers property lost in a fire, **business interruption insurance** covers the loss of anticipated profits, the salaries of key personnel, rent, and other continuing expenses such as real estate taxes. A $300,000 business interruption claim helped Nortronics, Co., a Minneapolis recording devices manufacturer, get back on its feet after a blaze destroyed one of its factories.

While companies usually have insurance that covers replacing damaged assets, losses due to disruption of business are often costlier than the repairs. During repairs, many firms have to continue paying interest; if they do not pay employees, they will lose them; the profits that would have been made are lost; customers have to be served or their business may be lost. Business interruption insurance covers these losses, even though Jolyon Stern, president of DeWitt, Stern, Gutmann & Co., a New York-based insurance company, says business interruption losses are generally the most difficult losses to settle.

Similarly, companies can also buy **extra-expense insurance,** which covers additional costs of operating in temporary quarters while the building is being repaired. And you can cover potential losses due to interruption of the delivery of essential supplies with **contingent business interruption insurance.** For instance, suppose a paper mill gets pulp from one source. A fire closes the pulp mill. The paper mill might very well have to close also. The wide variety of coverages, deductibles, and degrees of coverage makes the forms of business interruption insurance very complex. William D. O'Connel, of the accounting firm of Touche Ross & Co., says, "My experience is that underwriting mistakes are the rule rather than the exception." Typically, disruption insurance is inadequate for many firms.

INSURANCE AGAINST LOSS OF EARNING POWER

Many types of insurance cover loss of earning power, including: (1) life insurance, (2) accident and health insurance, and (3) disability insurance.

Life Insurance

Life insurance covers financial losses resulting from a person's death. Like other forms of insurance, life insurance is based on shifting individual risks to large numbers. The first life insurance company in the United States was formed in 1859. It carried the awkward name of The Corporation for Relief of Poor and Distressed Presbyterian Ministers and of The Poor and Distressed Widows and Children of Presbyterian Ministers. It is still in existence. By 1946, there were 473 life insurance companies in the United States, and they have mushroomed to more than 2000 today. Five of six families own life insurance, with an average coverage of approximately $50,000 per family.

Persons purchase life insurance for the specific purpose of offering financial protection to dependents when the insured dies. It is most common for the income earner to buy a policy of a certain amount. If he or she dies, the insurance company pays the policy amount to the individuals (beneficiaries) named in the policy.

Insurance company statisticians develop mortality tables that predict the number of deaths that will occur in each age level each year. Table 19.1 shows part of the Commissioner's 1958 Standard Mortality Table, currently the official table. By checking the table, we can determine that 17,300

TABLE 19.1 ■ EXPECTATION OF LIFE AND EXPECTED DEATHS, BY RACE, AGE, AND SEX

Age in 1979 (years)	Expectation of Life in Years					Expected Deaths per 1000 Alive at Specified Age				
	Total	White		Black		Total	White		Black	
		Male	Female	Male	Female		Male	Female	Male	Female
At birth	73.7	70.6	78.2	64.0	72.7	13.15	12.90	10.00	23.84	19.98
1	73.7	70.5	78.0	64.6	73.1	.88	.93	.69	1.29	1.15
2	72.8	69.6	77.1	63.6	72.2	.68	.68	.54	1.08	.95
3	71.8	68.6	76.1	62.7	71.3	.55	.53	.44	.91	.77
4	70.9	67.6	75.2	61.8	70.4	.45	.45	.36	.77	.62
5	69.9	66.7	74.2	60.8	69.4	.39	.41	.30	.66	.49
6	68.9	65.7	73.2	59.9	68.4	.35	.38	.27	.57	.40
7	68.0	64.7	72.2	58.9	67.5	.32	.36	.24	.50	.32
8	67.0	63.8	71.2	57.9	66.5	.28	.32	.21	.43	.27
9	66.0	62.8	70.3	56.9	65.5	.24	.27	.19	.38	.24
10	65.0	61.8	69.3	56.0	64.5	.21	.22	.18	.35	.23
11	64.0	60.8	68.3	55.0	63.5	.21	.22	.18	.35	.23
12	63.0	59.8	67.3	54.0	62.6	.26	.29	.20	.40	.25
13	62.1	58.8	66.3	53.0	61.6	.38	.48	.26	.51	.29
14	61.1	57.9	65.3	52.1	60.6	.54	.75	.33	.68	.33
15	60.1	56.9	64.3	51.1	59.6	.72	1.04	.42	.86	.38
16	59.2	56.0	63.4	50.1	58.6	.90	1.31	.50	1.06	.44
17	58.2	55.0	62.4	49.2	57.7	1.04	1.53	.56	1.30	.52
18	57.3	54.1	61.4	48.3	56.7	1.13	1.68	.58	1.57	.59
19	56.3	53.2	60.5	47.3	55.7	1.19	1.76	.59	1.86	.68
20	55.4	52.3	59.5	46.4	54.8	1.24	1.83	.58	2.16	.77
21	54.5	51.4	58.5	45.5	53.8	1.30	1.89	.58	2.47	.86
22	53.6	50.5	57.6	44.7	52.9	1.33	1.93	.58	2.74	.94
23	52.6	49.6	56.6	43.8	51.9	1.35	1.91	.58	2.99	1.01
24	51.7	48.7	55.6	42.9	51.0	1.34	1.86	.58	3.20	1.08
25	50.8	47.8	54.7	42.1	50.0	1.33	1.80	.58	3.41	1.14
30	46.1	43.2	49.8	37.9	45.3	1.29	1.58	.64	4.05	1.48
35	41.4	38.5	45.0	33.7	40.7	1.53	1.72	.87	4.72	2.11
40	36.8	33.9	40.2	29.6	36.2	2.21	2.43	1.38	6.34	3.03
45	32.2	29.4	35.6	25.8	31.9	3.46	3.96	2.23	8.19	4.62
50	27.9	25.1	31.0	22.1	27.8	5.47	6.48	3.60	11.40	7.10
55	23.9	21.2	26.7	18.8	24.0	8.00	9.66	5.39	15.24	9.57
60	20.0	17.5	22.6	15.9	20.4	11.96	14.70	8.27	19.28	13.51
65	16.6	14.2	18.7	13.3	17.2	15.81	19.97	11.44	19.32	14.28
70	13.4	11.3	15.0	10.7	13.9	20.38	25.05	15.82	21.78	19.24
75	10.6	8.8	11.7	8.6	11.5	27.04	30.03	24.07	27.11	31.97
80	8.4	6.9	9.0	7.8	10.7	30.71	30.56	32.13	23.64	31.41
85 and over	6.7	5.5	7.0	6.8	9.2	269.17	177.73	376.75	115.63	252.57

Source: U.S. National Center for Health Statistics, *Vital Statistics of the United States,* annual.

twenty-year-old men will die each year in the United States. Mortality tables are revised periodically as medicine and improved health habits increase life expectancies. However, in figuring payouts, it is advantageous to the insurance industry to use older mortality tables.

The purpose of mortality tables is to compute the premiums for policyholders. Insurance companies can note the age of their policyholders and predict how many are going to die each year. By noting the amount of the policies in force, they can figure the claims they will have to pay. To this sum, they add operating expenses (clerical, administrative, selling, printing) and profit. Since the insurance company invests the premiums, mostly in stable common stocks, the premium rates might be slightly less than the total costs estimated by the company.

Premiums may follow a natural-premium plan or a level-premium plan. Under the natural-premium plan, the insured pay an increasing rate each year because death statistically increases with age. An individual would be paying a higher premium for her policy at age 70 than at 30. Unfortunately, this method charges people more after they have passed their earning peak. Under the more popular level-premium plan, the insured pays the same rates each year, and rates are averaged. In earlier years, costs will be higher than the natural-premium plan, but the insured will pay less as they get older. Overall, total payments average to the same amount. There are four major types of life insurance coverage: term, whole-life, limited-payment, and endowment.

Term insurance. The earliest known record of a life insurance policy was a 12-month term insurance policy on William Gybbons issued on June 18, 1583. Ironically, the insured died on May 28, 1584, and the insurer contested the payment on grounds that the coverage was intended for 12 lunar months of 23 days each. But the courts dis-

agreed and the first beneficiary payment was made. As late as the 1700s, many term policies were written for 6-month periods.

Term insurance policies pay off only if the insured dies during the period of coverage. Policies usually cover specified periods such as 5, 10, or 20 years. Most have a provision that they can be renewed without medical examination but at a higher premium rate. Term insurance provides the maximum amount of coverage per premium dollar at a young age, but premiums are very high for older persons. Term policies appeal primarily to wage earners with young children. When earnings are low and protection needs are great, they can obtain maximum protection for lower rates. However, over the long haul, insurance companies argue that term is expensive because it does not have the savings element. Term policies can also be convertible. This allows a person to purchase term and pay low premiums for a number of years. Then she can convert the term into a more permanent form of insurance to take advantage of the savings element.

Whole-life policies. Whole-life policies (sometimes called straight-life or ordinary-life), by far the most popular, require premium payments from the date the policyholder takes out insurance until he or she dies. Upon the insured's death, the insurance company pays the total amount of the policy to the beneficiaries. Rates are based on the age at the time of the purchase. Because of shorter life expectancies, older persons pay higher rates than younger people. After a few years, whole-life policies accumulate a **cash-surrender value.** If the insured decides to stop making premium payments, the insurance company will pay cash or offer a paid-up policy based on the cash-surrender value. The company may also loan the policyholder money up to the amount of the cash-surrender value.

At age 34, Karen Wilson bought a $30,000 straight-life policy. Her premium payments were $600 per year. At 45, Karen had some unexpected bills and felt that she could no longer make premium payments. The policy had accumulated a cash-surrender value of approximately $3000. Karen had the option of borrowing, at a very favorable interest rate, up to the amount of the surrender value, stopping payments and taking a

TABLE 19.2 ■ A COMPARISON OF 1984 PREMIUM RATES FOR $1000 OF COVERAGE BY A LEADING INSURER (YEARLY RATES)

Age	5-Year Term	Whole-Life Life	Paid-Up at 65	20-Pay Life	Endowment at 65	20-Year Endowment
25	$4.00	$8.73	$12.21	$17.05	$22.32	$47.23
35	4.87	13.85	18.74	22.80	32.79	48.77
45	8.48	22.93	31.81	31.81	53.15	53.15
55	18.20	36.92	69.31	44.11	114.30	62.75

paid-up policy worth $8000, or canceling the policy and taking the $3000 in cash.

Limited-payment policies. Limited-payment policies allow the purchaser to buy straight-life and pay all the premiums in a designated period, say 20 or 30 years. At the end of the period, the policy is completely paid up, and the insured is covered for life without having to make any more premium payments. Of course, the premiums are a little higher than straight-life. Another form of limited payment allows you to pay premiums until a certain age, for example, paid-up at 65. The extreme form of limited payment is a single payment policy where the policyholder pays the entire premium in one lump sum when he or she purchases the insurance.

Figure 19.1
How life insurance policies vary in savings and protection.

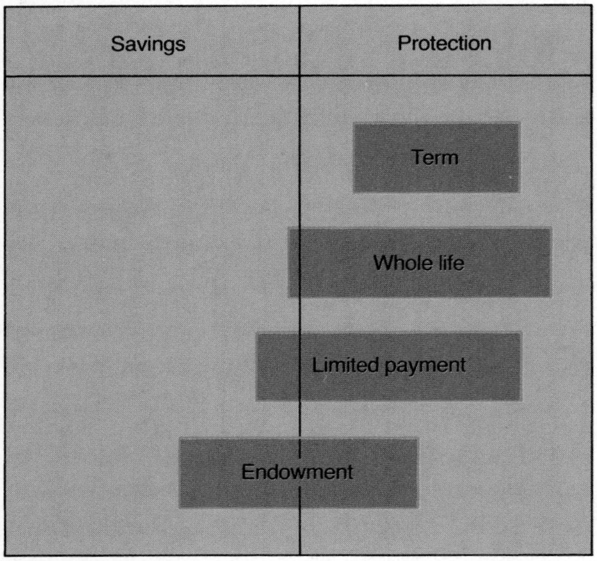

Endowment policies. Endowment policies combine savings and protection features by paying the full value of the policy after a specified number of years. If the insured dies before the maturity of the policy, the beneficiaries receive full value. To illustrate, assume that you bought a $20,000 twenty-year endowment policy at age 30.

Annual premiums are much higher on endowment policies than any other form of insurance.

At 50, the insurance company will pay you the full $20,000. If you die before age 50, your beneficiary would receive $20,000. Endowment policies may be written to cover almost any number of years, or they may endow at a certain age, say 65. Annual premiums are much higher on endowment policies than any other form of life insurance, but this type of insurance appeals to individuals who want to include savings in their coverage. Table 19.2 compares 1984 premium rates for $1000 of coverage by a leading insurer. Figure 19.1 diagrams how savings and protection vary among the different policies.

New types of life insurance. Many people have criticized the life insurance industry's high cost for policies and low interest rates on cash values. The industry has responded by offering some innovative policies, including:

- *Adjustable life.* Allows you to raise or lower the amount of the policy, increase or decrease premiums, and lengthen the protection period almost at will.

- *Universal life.* Allows you to change the amount of the policy from time to time and vary the amount or timing of your premium payments.

- *Variable life.* Benefits paid out under this policy relate directly to the value of investments that the insurance company makes with your premium payments. The death benefit is never less than the amount specified in the policy.

- *Improved whole-life and term.* Improved versions of both of these policies sometimes reduce premiums by as much as 20%.

Business Uses of Life Insurance

Key-executive insurance. What would happen if the founder of a young company were to unexpectedly die in a plane crash, in an auto accident, or of a heart attack? For most young companies, this would likely mean the end of the company because the key people keep so much of the business in their heads. **Key-executive insurance** is a policy purchased by the company on one or more of its key executives, and whereby the company is the sole beneficiary. Thus, if a key executive should die, the company would have the benefit of the proceeds while trying to replace the key person. "The purpose of key-employee insurance is to keep the business in business," says Michael I. Abruzzo, a New York Life Insurance Co. vice-president.

During the first few years of a new company, one or two high horsepower executives are usually critical to the company's success. So venture capitalists who invest in new companies almost always insist on key-executive insurance for the entrepreneur. Jim Liautaud, a Chicago investor, founded American Antenna in 1977 — manufacturer of CB antennas and other electronic products. The 24-year-old president, Doug Mele, was critical to the company's success, so the company purchased a $1 million term policy on Mele.

Management of pensions, annuities, and other employee benefits is a specialized service provided by some insurance companies.

Premiums amounted to $4500 per year. By 1983, American Antenna's sales had grown to $15 million and the management staff included several vice-presidents. Since Mele was now less critical to the firm's success, they cut the key-executive policy to $400,000 and saved 50% of the premium.

In a partnership, the company dissolves when a partner dies. To prevent closing the company's doors, a partnership often buys insurance on each partner and makes the surviving partners the beneficiaries. This provides money for survivors to buy out the deceased partner's interest and continue operating the business.

Credit life insurance. **Credit life insurance** pays amounts due on loans if the debtor dies. Lenders and credit sellers usually buy credit life on the debtor and make themselves beneficiaries. But the premium cost is transferred to the individual in loan costs. The insurance is written for the

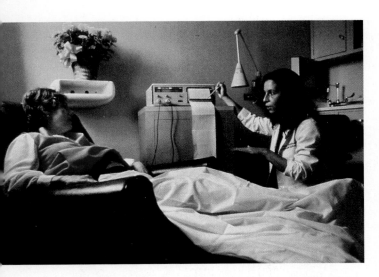

New diagnostic instrumentation (such as this fetal heart monitor) contributes to higher health care costs that must be covered by major medical insurance.

amount of debt and continues until the debt is repaid.

Group life insurance. In recent years, companies have used group life insurance quite extensively as a fringe benefit for their employees. Typically, a company buys a **group life insurance** plan that covers all of its employees for a certain amount, perhaps $10,000. Or each employee may be insured according to earnings, with employees in higher income brackets receiving more coverage. Most group policies are term, and the company renegotiates them each year. Medical examinations are usually not required unless there are only a few employees because companies do not tend to hire unhealthy people. Group rates are lower because there are no medical fees; the company pays the premiums once each year, reducing the collection costs, and commissions are lower. Some companies pay the entire cost of the premium, others share with employees, and a few require that the employees pick up the total tab. Group life insurance amounts to more than 40% of all life insurance plans in force.

Pensions and annuities. Finally, companies use pension and retirement plans to supplement employee retirement benefits beyond social secu-

rity. Small firms often have a pension trust plan that purchases a life insurance policy for each covered employee. Larger firms set up a single fund with an insurance company to cover all of their employees. When a person retires, the insurance company takes a lump sum from the pension plan and buys an annuity for the employee. An **annuity** (insurance in reverse) takes a lump sum payment and divides it into periodic payments, usually monthly, that continue for as long as the employee lives. Mortality tables are used to predict the life expectancy and thus the amount of payments the lump sum will provide.

Accident and Health Insurance

Accident and health insurance repays the injured for expenses and lost earnings resulting from accidents or sickness. Accident policies usually specify a certain amount of payment for each type of disability. For example, the insurance policy might pay $20,000 for amputation of a leg or $100,000 for the loss of an eye. Payments may be made in a lump sum over a period of time.

Medical insurance. Most companies offer accident and health coverage to their employees under a group plan. The company enrolls everyone in the plan, thereby getting reduced rates for each employee. Sometimes the employer pays the total cost of the plan, and in other situations, the cost is shared with the employee.

Major-medical insurance. Health insurance covers expenses and loss of income associated with almost any type of illness. Recently, companies have offered a **major-medical** provision to cover high-cost illnesses such as cancer. Major-medical policies usually have a deductible of $100 to $500 so that premiums can be lower. Individuals can get complete health and accident coverage by combining a regular policy with a major-medical policy. Their regular policies might cover smaller expenses, and at some point, say $300, the major-medical kicks in for the rest.

Workmen's compensation insurance. Most states require that employers purchase **workmen's compensation insurance,** which guarantees medical expenses and salary payments to employees injured on the job. If employees injure themselves purposefully or are drunk or otherwise negligent, they are not covered. Very small companies with a minimum number of employees are not required to purchase this insurance. In some states, employers must buy workmen's compensation from the state; other states allow private insurance companies to compete with the state plan; and a few states let private insurance companies handle the program. In any case, rates are geared to the danger of the work and the accident record of the firm. To discourage

What are Medigap Policies?

Many people over 65 either have to buy health insurance or risk being financially ruined by a serious illness. More than two-thirds of the people who qualify for Medicare supplement their coverage with policies referred to as "medigap policies." These are policies bought from private insurance companies to provide a supplement to Medicare in case of illness. Medigap policies, offered by many companies, differ widely in their coverage, costs, terms, and benefit limits.

It is almost impossible to rate all these policies, but they have come up with a "loss ratio" to get an indication of the economic value of the policies. The loss ratio is the percentage of premium returned to policyholders in the form of benefits. For instance, if a company pays back 70 cents on the dollar in benefits, it has a loss ratio of 70. Several states do not allow policies with loss ratios under 60 to be sold to people over 60 years of age. The accompanying chart shows loss ratios of thirty-eight companies for group and individual medigap insurance.

LOSS RATIOS FOR GROUP AND INDIVIDUAL MEDIGAP INSURANCE

Company	0%–50%	Company	50%–100%
Mutual Protective Ins.	22%	Aid to Lutherans	50%
Medico Life	25	All American Casualty	52
MONY	28	CNA	55
New York Life	29	Bankers Life and Casualty	57
American United Life	29	Guarantee Reserve Life	57
National Casualty Co.	30	American National	58
American Progressive	33	American Variable Annuity	63
National Security Ins.	35	Chesapeake Life	65
Reliable Life and Casualty	36	Guardian	66
Constitution Life	37	Rural Mutual	69
Old American	38	Mutual Benefit Life	70
Pioneer Life of Illinois	39	Banker's (Iowa)	75
Liberty National Life	40	Home Life	77
Pacific Mutual	40	Nationwide	78
Businessmen's Assurance	43	Durhan Life	79
American Exchange Life	44	Life of Virginia	82
Commercial State Life	47	Metropolitan	83
Union Bankers	48	National Life and Accident	85
Country Life	49	Provident Mutual	86

Source: House Select Committee on Aging, summarized from "New Guides to Picking a Medigap Policy," *Changing Times,* February, 1980, pp. 45–48.

Even though more than 180 million people are covered by some type of health insurance, nearly 50 million of them do not have enough coverage for large medical bills.

minor claims, most laws require that injured persons wait from several days to a few weeks before they can collect. A policy might pay up to two-thirds of an employee's salary for an injury resulting in total disability.

Medicare and Medicaid. The cost of medical care has been increasing over the past few years, and people have become more concerned. To combat these costs, they have turned more and more to health insurance. In fact, more than 180 million people are now covered by some type of health insurance. Yet authorities say that 46 million Americans do not have enough coverage for large medical bills, and 19 million do not have proper coverage for ordinary hospital and physicians' charges. Many of the people in these groups are either older, or in low income groups, or both.

From time to time, Congress and political leaders debate the merits and costs of a national health insurance program. National health insurance would cover practically everyone, either under private or government plans. Public plans would probably be restricted to the poor and elderly. Proponents of national health insurance argue that all citizens should receive proper health care, regardless of their economic circumstances. Opponents argue that Medicare and Medicaid are already doing this, and it would be too expensive to broaden the coverage. Medicare pays a lot of hospital expenses for people over 65. For doctors' fees, outpatient charges, and certain other health bills, Medicare provides insurance to help out. Medicaid does much the same thing for people who are too poor to pay for proper medical services.

Health maintenance organizations. Health maintenance organizations (HMOs) allow you to prepay a set amount for medical expenses, usually a monthly fee, and you get almost unlimited medical service at no charge or at a nominal charge. Many HMOs own their own hospitals and hire their own doctors. HMOs are in direct competition with traditional health insurance, and many people are switching to them. The largest HMO, Kaiser Foundation Health Plan Inc., has 4.3 million members.

Historically, HMOs began as local or regional units but they have now created national networks, enabling them to serve national corporations and hold down health costs. The concept of HMOs also stresses preventive care more than conventional policies. Since you pay a monthly fee whether or not you use medical services, it is to the advantage of the doctor to stress preventive medicine so that you will have to visit less often. Because the costs of HMOs have been rising more slowly than the cost of health insurance plans, many believe that they will continue to make dramatic gains against conventional health insurance. HMO enrollment was 12 million at the beginning of 1984; it is expected to grow to 40 million by 1990. Table 19.3 shows how HMOs have grown.

INSURANCE AGAINST LIABILITY

Liability insurance protects a company against damages to others due to the company's negligence or mistakes. Three common types of coverage include injury liability, product liability, and malpractice.

Injury Liability

If a customer stumbles on a loose board in your store, slips on wet steps entering your apartment building, or bangs her head on your low-hanging flower pots, you can be held liable for these injuries. The injured person has to show that the injury was due to neglect by the owner, but this is an illusory concept open to broad legal interpretation.

Product-Liability Insurance

Product-liability insurance covers manufacturers when a user sues for injuries occurring during the use of a product. For example, if a person breaks a tooth on a pebble in a can of beans, the producer might be found liable for the cost of replacing the tooth.

"The pedestrian had no idea what direction to go, so I ran over him"

Thousands of drivers nationwide have been involved in automobile accidents and the insurance rigamarole that follows afterwards. Filling out the myriad and often confusing insurance claim forms can befuddle even the most stalwart semanticist. The following are actual excerpts culled from various auto insurance company files in northern and southern California:

- Coming home, I drove into the wrong house and collided with a tree I don't have.

- The other car collided with mine without giving warning of its intentions.

- I thought my window was down but I found out it was up when I put my hand through it.

- I collided with a stationary truck coming the other way.

- A truck backed through my windshield into my wife's face.

- A pedestrian hit me and went under my car.

- The guy was all over the road: I had to swerve a number of times before I hit him.

- I pulled away from the side of the road, glanced at my mother-in-law and headed over the embankment.

- In my attempt to kill a fly, I drove into a telephone pole.

- I had been shopping for plants all day, and was on my way home. As I reached an intersection a hedge sprang up obscuring my vision. I did not see the other car.

- I had been driving my car for 40 years when I fell asleep at the wheel and had an accident.

- I was on my way to the doctors with rear end trouble when my universal joint gave way causing me to have an accident.

- My car was legally parked as it backed into the other vehicle.

- To avoid hitting the bumper of the car in front of me I struck the pedestrian.

- I was unable to stop in time and my car crashed into the other vehicle. The driver and passengers then left immediately for a vacation with injuries.

- As I approached the intersection a stop sign suddenly appeared at a place where no stop signs had ever appeared before. I was unable to stop in time to avoid the accident.

- An invisible car came out of nowhere and struck my vehicle — and vanished.

- I told the police that I was not injured, but on removing my hat I found that I had a skull fracture.

- I was sure that the old fellow would never make it to the other side of the roadway when I struck him.

And you wonder why it takes weeks, sometimes months to receive restitution from automobile insurance companies? It takes them that long to decipher what their clients are trying to tell them!

Source: Neal Leavitt, *Los Angeles Herald Examiner.*

TABLE 19.3 ■ HOW HMOS HAVE GROWN

HMO	Enrollment (thousands)		States	
	1978	1982	1978	1982
Kaiser Foundation Health Plan (Oakland, Calif.)	3500	4300	6	8
Group Health Plan (St. Paul); Harvard Community Health Plan (Cambridge); Group Health Cooperative of Puget Sound (Seattle); Health Insurance Plan of Greater New York*	1200	1500	4	5
Blue Cross & Blue Shield Assn. (Chicago)	527	1200	21	26
CIGNA Healthplan (Dallas)	182	645	3	5
HMO Group (10 HMOs in East and Midwest)*	154	333	7	7
HealthAmerica (Nashville)	0	270	0	9
Maxicare Health Plans (Los Angeles)	25	227	1	4
Prudential Health Care Plan (Roseland, N.J.)	20	210	1	6
Charter Med (Minneapolis)	33	201	2	10

* Becoming national network.

Source: Reprinted from the October 24, 1983, issue of *Business Week* by special permission, © 1983 by McGraw-Hill, Inc.

CROSS FIRE

Should Insurance Rates Be the Same for Both Sexes?

The Supreme Court, in July 1983, said that men and women should be treated equally in pension plans. That is, pension funds could no longer pay women lower monthly payments on the premise that women outlive men. This decision set off quite a stir about whether women and men should pay the same insurance rates. Currently, women tend to pay less for a car and life insurance than do men, but women pay more than men for health and pension coverage. At this writing, several bills requiring unisex rates were pending in Congress.

Arguments for unisex insurance rates include:

1. In most other areas — education, employment, credit, and housing — legislation requires that men and women receive equal treatment. Insurance is one of the last areas that permits discrimination in rates. It would be fairer to spread the risks over everybody.

2. Car insurance rates should be based on average number of miles driven and driving experience, not on whether the driver is male or female. Most women have fewer accidents than men because they drive far fewer miles.

3. Some insurance rates are actually higher for women; for example, a woman who opened her own business and wanted to buy disability insurance would find rates prohibitive.

Arguments against unisex insurance rates include:

1. Typically, companies base their rates on costs of providing insurance. When women cost less to insure, as in automobile insurance for young women and life

Malpractice Insurance

Professionals such as doctors and lawyers can be held responsible for negligence of their practices. For these risks, malpractice insurance will cover the insured person up to the policy amount. So many patients have been suing doctors that the cost of physician premiums has doubled and tripled. Doctors' have become agitated about increasing malpractice insurance rates, the inability of some doctors to qualify for coverage, and the trend of some insurance companies to pull out of the business. Doctors in several states, feeling gravely wronged, went on strike over these issues in 1975.

Liability insurance usually covers the cost of the injury and of defending the insured. Because of the publicity surrounding six-figure settlements and the inability to define negligence specifically, insurance companies keep a constant vigil against false claims and faked injuries.

AUTOMOBILE INSURANCE

Businesses that own executive Cadillacs, truck fleets, or company cars want to shift their risk of loss. Since automobile coverage includes aspects of property loss, earnings loss, and liability, we cover automobile insurance separately.

Bodily Injury Liability

Bodily injury liability covers injuries to other persons injured by the insured vehicle. If the driver of a company truck is at fault when colliding with a school bus and injuring several children, the insurance company will pay the damage up to the amount of the policy. Common coverages identify a maximum payment for individual or group deaths or disabilities. Coverage earmarked as $50/100$ means that the insurance will pay a maximum of $50,000 for the death of one person and a maxi-

insurance for all women, rates are cheaper. When women cost more to insure, as in health and pensions, rates are higher.

2. Women, on the average, outlive men by about 8 years; their life insurance rates should be cheaper.

3. If Congress were to pass a unisex insurance law, women as a group, according to the American Academy of Actuaries estimates, would have to pay $700 million a year more for auto insurance.

4. Under unisex rates, women would subsidize men for life and auto insurance, and men would subsidize women for pensions and health insurance.

5. Under a unisex law, some women would have to pay as much as $800 a year more for auto insurance and $2500 more for $50,000 of life insurance over 20 years.

Should men and women be charged the same rates for the same coverage? Why?

____ A. Definitely, yes   ____ C. Probably, no
____ B. Probably, yes   ____ D. Definitely, no

Do you think current insurance rates:

____ A. Discriminate against men   ____ C. Are probably pretty fair
____ B. Discriminate against women

Why?

mum of $100,000 for the death of more than one person. If the courts award more than these maximums, the company is liable for the remainder. The company can add a medical-payments endorsement to cover medical bills up to a specified amount for the persons, including the driver, in the insured car.

Property Damage Liability

Property damage liability covers damage to property caused by the insured car. If an insured car crashes into another vehicle, shatters a plate glass window, or nicks the gate of a neighbor's fence, the insurance company will pay damages up to the amount of the policy.

Collision Insurance

If you want insurance for damages to your car, you must purchase collision insurance. Most collision policies carry a deduction allowance from $50 to $200 per accident. If an insured car with a $200 deductible were to sustain $2000 worth of damage in an accident, you would have to pay the first $200; the insurance company would pay $1800.

Comprehensive Insurance

In addition to the major costs of collision, a lot of other things can happen to automobiles. If you want protection against losses caused by fire, storm, flood, theft (of the vehicle and things in it), flying rocks, riots, and the like, you need to purchase comprehensive coverage.

Assigned Risks

If you have two or three accidents within a short period of time, or if you are a male under 25 years old, companies may not sell you insurance. To take care of these groups, most states have a plan that assigns these people, on a fair basis, to the insurance companies. Such policies are called assigned risks, and companies are permitted to charge a much higher premium.

No-Fault Automobile Insurance

Until 1967, when Massachusetts adopted the first no-fault automobile insurance law, awards to victims of automobile accidents were determined on the basis of, "Whose fault was it?" If two people crashed into each other in a darkly lit parking lot, both parties, after snarling at each other, would run to their lawyers to prove the other was wrong. But this procedure began to be very expensive, it took a lot of time, and many people could not afford a lawyer. One study showed that 40% of the settlements were going not to the victims, but to their lawyers. Other critics argued that, "The system favors people who can afford the best lawyers and those who can attract the most cooperative witnesses."

No-fault insurance, trying to take the venom out of these inefficiencies, does away with assessing penalties based on fault. Although the requirements differ from state to state, no-fault usually provides:

- Laws that require all drivers to be covered by automobile insurance.

- For injured persons to receive payments regardless of blame. You do not have to prove the other driver was at fault.

- One person cannot sue another unless the loss is above a specified amount, say $5000.

NEW TRENDS IN INSURANCE COVERAGE

Although the insurance industry has typically been stable and staid, it is offering adaptive innovations to keep up with our work and life-style changes. Inflation, higher interest rates, changing life-styles, consumer demands, and increases in working women dictate different insurance needs, and companies are responding by offering broader and more flexible coverage.

Broader Coverage

Not only are companies broadening their coverage on traditional types of insurance, they are surging forward with new off-beat policies to meet the demands of the 1980s. Bragging to his friends, a college student claimed, "I just bought an insurance policy to cover my new water bed in case it springs a leak." A newly married young man admitted, "I bought divorce insurance to cover legal expenses just in case it does not last."

More Flexibility

Companies are allowing for more variations in the insureds. For instance, they are making allowances for health habits, income changes, and inflation.

Adjustable rates. On the premise that individuals' insurance needs change as they get older, **adjustable life insurance** allows people to change both their amount of coverage and premium payments throughout their lives. It combines a mixture of whole-life and term, and policy-holders can change them from time to time. CNA Insurance Company has developed a policy called the Optimiser that lets people buy large amounts of permanent insurance at a beginning low premium. The premium increases by 20% each year for 10 years; then it stays level. This lets people buy more permanent earlier in life, when their earnings are lower but their need is greater.

Allowing for inflation. Because of rapid inflation, if you insured your home in 1975, you would not have nearly enough coverage today. People are not likely to have the insurance coverage adjusted each year, so companies are trying to help with inflation protection policies. One such policy has a feature that automatically adjusts both the coverage and the premium rates each year. Neither the holder nor the company has to do anything. Other policies offer replacement-cost endorsements that insure household items for the

TAKING STOCK

Divorce Insurance: A Business Opportunity?

Because about half of all divorced women do not receive the alimony or child support due them, Richard Saitow of New Rochelle, New York, started a firm called Family Support Systems that sells alimony and child support insurance.

Family Support Systems only markets and administers the policies; the Republic Insurance Group and Old Republic Insurance Co. actually issues the policies. The coverage to the divorced spouse will be for only 3 years, but may be renewed in some cases. Premium costs about 6% of the amount due over the 3-year period. Saitow needs to keep the divorce payment default rate below 7% to earn a profit, and the national default rate is about 30% in actual dollar volume. Saitow says his company will take only good credit risks and get in touch quickly when payments lag.

Saitow, with his $150,000 annual salary, lives on a 50-foot yawl, sports a beard, and wears jeans to work. He was an account executive for Johnson & Higgins for ten years and also worked for Alexander & Alexander. Saitow, himself divorced, admits that he too has sometimes been late with support payments to his ex-wife.

A month after opening, Family Support System's staff of twenty-two received more than 700 calls from attorneys. Although they did not sell a single policy in the first month, the company believes that this insurance will someday be a standard part of divorce settlements.

Source: "Divorce Insurance," *Forbes*, July 18, 1983, p. 144.

full replacement value rather than the cost of the item.

Adjustments for health habits. While the standard mortality tables predict quite accurately the likelihood of large groups of people dying at certain ages, it does not account for wide variations within groups. For example, an insurance executive pointed out, "It is time that we stopped penalizing nonsmokers for the shorter life expectancy of smokers." Many companies now offer substantial discounts to nonsmokers and nondrinkers as well. Likewise, joggers often get a break in premiums because it is assumed that they are in better physical condition. And women are arguing that they should pay lower rates because they outlive their male counterparts.

There is also a trend to accept more kinds of people for coverage. About 89% of all the people who apply for life insurance now get accepted as standard risks, and insurance officials predict the rate will increase to about 95% in the mid-1980s. It is now possible for individuals who have had open heart surgery to get life coverage for only slightly higher rates. All these adjustments are attempts by the insurance companies to offer more individualized and better protection plans. Of course, their spreading umbrella coverages also increase their sales potential.

SUMMARY

Risk is the danger of loss. Any time an investor puts money into a business, there is a chance of losing it. Risk management involves identifying risks, measuring risks, controlling risks, and managing risks. Insurance companies spread the danger of loss over a large number of claims.

Insurance against property losses includes fire insurance, transportation insurance, criminal coverages, and business interruption insurance. Most commercial fire insurance has a coinsurance clause which stipulates that the firm must insure a certain percentage of the value to get full coverage. Transportation insurance covers almost all losses at sea or inland. Theft, or burglary, insurance covers forcible and unlawful taking of property. Fidelity and surety bonds also cover against criminal losses. Fidelity bonds guarantee the employer against losses caused by deceitful employees. Surety bonds insure against fraudulent acts and failure of another party to live up to contractual obligations. Business interruption insurance covers fixed expenses and lost profits when businesses are shut down due to property damage.

Life, accident, and health insurance cover against loss of earning power. Life insurance offers financial protection to dependents when the insured dies. Term policies usually cover 5, 10, or 20 years; they pay off only if the person dies during the insured period. Straight-life policies require premium payments from the date the policyholder takes out insurance until he or she dies. After a few years, straight-life policies accumulate a cash-surrender value. Limited-payment policies eliminate the necessity of lifetime payments by limiting premium payments to a specified number of years. Endowment policies combine savings and protection by paying the full value of the policy after a specified number of years. Businesses use life insurance to cover losses due to death of key executives, death of a creditor, and as fringe benefits in the form of group life coverage and pension plans.

Examples of accident and health insurance include medical insurance, major-medical insurance, workmen's compensation, and Medicare and Medicaid. These policies pay when the holder is sick or injured. Health maintenance organizations allow you to prepay a set fee and get almost unlimited medical services.

Injury liability, product liability, and malpractice insurance cover against things that a business might become liable for through negligence or incorrect performance. Injury liability covers an owner when another person is injured on insured's property. Product liability covers manufacturers when a user sues for injuries sustained during the use of a product, and malpractice coverage insures the policyholder against a negligence suit.

Automobile insurance may be written to include injuries to other persons, damage to property caused by the insured's vehicle, damage to the insured's vehicle, and medical payments for passengers in the insured's car.

New trends in insurance coverage include policies covering new users, more flexible coverage, and more flexible premium rates.

MIND YOUR BUSINESS

Instructions: Read the following examples and decide whether or not you think the claims should be paid.

Yes   No

—— —— 1. A woman decided to try her new portable whirlpool bath one day without bothering to put on the drain cover. As a result, the suction caused her to stick fast to the bottom of the pool. Several strong-armed men, including the insurance adjuster, yanked her out. She sued the manufacturer. Was her claim paid?

—— —— 2. At 1 A.M. a man crashed his car into a startled couple's kitchen sink. He wished the pair good morning, backed out, and left. The collision knocked the woman's birth-control pills into a garbage disposal. She made a claim for both the pills and the disposal unit. Was she paid?

—— —— 3. A woman, tired after shopping all day, decided to sit astride an "up" escalator to take the load off her feet. When she arrived at the top, her dress was torn off and she suffered minor abrasions. Did the insurance company pay off?

—— —— 4. After a long separation, two lovers were reunited. The man gave his true love a hug and cracked two of her ribs. He tried to collect for damages under his homeowners policy. Was he successful?

—— —— 5. A man left his poodle in the car with the engine running. The dog leaned on the gear shift and pushed it into reverse. After backing into a light pole, the runaway car made about twenty-five round trips in a tight circle with the dog calmly at the wheel. Finally, a local fire chief shot a hole in one of the tires. The man filed a claim for the car and the light pole. Did the insurance company pay?

See answers at the back of the book.

Source: Lee Mitgang, "He Who Laughs Last, Often Pays for the Joke," *The Wichita Eagle and Beacon,* August 13, 1978, p. 19A.

KEY TERMS

risk, 486
risk management, 486
insurance, 489
uninsurable risk, 489
insurable risk, 489
pure risk, 489
speculative risk, 489
reinsurance, 490
property insurance, 490
coinsurance clause, 490
marine insurance, 491
inland marine insurance, 491
fidelity bond, 491
surety bond, 492
burglary insurance, 492–493
business interruption insurance, 493
extra-expense insurance, 493
contingent business interruption insurance, 493
life insurance, 493
term insurance, 495
whole-life policy, 495
cash-surrender value, 495
limited-payment policy, 496
endowment policy, 496
key-executive insurance, 497
credit life insurance, 497
group life insurance, 498
annuity, 498
accident and health insurance, 498
major-medical insurance, 498
workmen's compensation insurance, 498
health maintenance organization (HMO), 500
liability insurance, 500
no-fault insurance, 504
adjustable life insurance, 505

REVIEW QUESTIONS

1. What is a business risk? Give some examples. What is risk management?

2. Discuss the four steps of risk management.

3. Explain the law of large numbers. How does it work for insurance?

4. Distinguish between pure and speculative risks. Identify and explain the characteristics of an insurable risk. Define uninsurable risk; reinsurance.

5. What are insurance agents? Brokers? BLUs? CPCUs? Stock companies? Mutual companies?

6. Explain the characteristics of fire insurance. What are riders? Explain the coinsurance clause.

7. Identify and explain the two major types of marine insurance.

8. How do businesses insure against criminal losses? Distinguish between fidelity bonds, surety bonds, and burglary insurance.

9. Explain how business interruption insurance works.

10. What is life insurance?

11. What is the difference between the natural-premium and the level-premium plans?

12. What is term insurance? Explain its advantages. Disadvantages.

13. Describe straight-life policies. What are their advantages? Disadvantages?

14. How do limited-payment policies differ from straight-life?

15. Explain endowment policies.

16. Identify four recent types of life insurance policies.

17. How do businesses use life insurance?

18. Explain how accident and health insurance serve as a means of protection.

19. What is national health insurance? Medicaid? Medicare? Major-medical? Workmen's compensation?

20. What are health maintenance organizations (HMOs)?

21. Explain the various forms of liability insurance.

22. How do businesses use automobile insurance? Explain the following: bodily injury liability, medical payments endorsement, property damage liability, and collision insurance.

23. What is no-fault insurance?

24. Briefly explain the new trends in insurance coverage.

CASES

Case 19.1: The Cost of Insurance

Assume that the Madrid Company is a manufacturer of small appliances, located in your community. The company is a corporation with several hundred stockholders, and it has been in existence for about 6 years. The organization employs 1200 people including their sales and office personnel. Sales run between $5 and $10 million per year and Madrid has two large manufacturing plants located in your community, each of which is modern and equipped with expensive, modern machines. They store some of their finished inventory for short periods, but most of their products are shipped off the production lines. They own six trucks, which they use for deliveries within a 150-mile radius. Madrid believes they are paying too much for insurance, and they have proposed a committee to study their company and make recommendations.

Questions

1. Make a list of the items that you think would require coverage.

2. Make a list of the items that might be a good idea to cover but could be left uninsured if management wanted to take some risks.

3. What other suggestions do you have for reducing the cost of insurance for such a company as Madrid?

Case 19.2: No-Fault

Because automobile insurance premiums have increased so rapidly and delays for settling claims have lengthened, many states have looked to the no-fault plan for covering automobiles. Approximately half of the states now have some version of a no-fault plan. Briefly, no-fault tries to accomplish the following:

1. Eliminate the need for determining who is at fault so that expensive and lengthy court cases can be reduced.

2. Require all drivers to carry a certain amount of insurance on their cars.

3. Require the insurance company of the policyholder to pay claims without regard to who is at fault.

4. Bar lawsuits, except when expenses exceed a set amount.

Supporters say that no-fault allows claims to be paid promptly and inexpensively, resulting in lower premiums. Further, service is provided more humanely and with less waste. Opponents claim that costs will not necessarily be reduced, and they quote figures to show how costs have risen. There will be more expensive lawsuits, and no-fault is a threat to private enterprise.

Questions

1. Seek out the advantages and disadvantages of no-fault insurance in your state.

2. Suppose you have been asked to testify before a state legislative committee on no-fault. Prepare your testimony. What questions would you anticipate? How would you respond?

THE FINANCING OF BUSINESS

The following list includes a variety of activities, personality characteristics, career goals and objectives, and skills and aptitudes. All have special relevance to careers in finance. Put a check mark in front of those statements that apply to you.

____ I would like to manage a brokerage office directing the buying and selling of commodities, mutual funds, or securities for clients.

____ I am very accurate in keeping records.

____ I think I would be successful as a real estate agent for a company, negotiating the acquisition and disposition of its properties.

____ I plan to take courses in financial management.

____ I would enjoy working in a bank.

____ I often check stock market results in the newspaper.

____ I have helped friends and relatives prepare their tax reports.

____ I work well with numbers.

____ I would enjoy the work of an underwriter, reviewing applications for insurance to evaluate the degree of risk involved.

____ I would like a job in which I examine a company's records and prepare its financial reports.

____ At times, I have invested money in stocks or bonds.

____ I would enjoy the work of a treasurer of a financial institution, directing the receipt and expenditure of money or other capital assets.

____ I would enjoy working as a trader in the stock market.

____ I look forward to taking courses in economics.

____ I would enjoy the work of a loan officer, evaluating and authorizing customer loans or credit for a bank or insurance company.

____ I have been in charge of the budget of a school club or other organization.

____ I would enjoy studying and analyzing a company to determine if it would make a good investment.

____ I can spend long hours working with figures and records without losing interest.

____ I enjoy reading the financial section in newspapers and magazines.

____ I would like the work of an estate planner, developing an investment and insurance program that will provide maximum financial protection for a client's family.

____ I would enjoy courses in statistics.

____ I could take the pressure of being responsible for managing large sums of money.

____ I would like the work of a foreign exchange trader, protecting a bank's position in its deposits in other countries.

____ I would enjoy providing financial counseling to people in debt.

____ I have devised a personal budget that seems to work well.

There is no single set of personality characteristics, skills, and aptitudes that fits a particular job. Generally speaking, the more activities and self-descriptors you checked in this list, the more satisfaction you may find in this major and its related jobs.

Job Title	Job Description	Suggested Education and Training	Personality Traits	Average Pay	Outlook through 1990
Actuary	Actuaries design insurance and pension plans and follow their experience to make sure that they are maintained on a sound financial basis. Actuaries assemble and analyze statistics to calculate probabilities of death, sickness, injury, disability, unemployment, retirement, and property loss from accident, theft, fire, and other hazards. They use this information to determine the expected insured loss. Most actuaries specialize in either life and health insurance or property and liability (casualty) insurance.	A good educational background for a beginning job in a large life or casualty company is a bachelor's degree wth a major in mathematics or statistics; a degree in actuarial science is even better. It is essential to pass, preferably while still in school, one or more of the exams offered by professional actuarial societies.	Good reasoning skills and an all-consuming interest in numbers are the paramount traits of a successful actuary. A tolerance for working alone at a desk all day is also necessary.	New college graduates entering the life insurance field without having passed any actuarial exams average about $15,000 a year. Top actuarial executives may earn as much as $60,000 a year.	Great demand
Insurance underwriter	Underwriters approve and select the risks that insurance companies will insure. Underwriters decide whether their companies will accept risks after analyzing information in insurance applications, reports from loss control consultants, medical reports, and actuarial studies (reports that describe the probability of insured loss). Their companies may lose business to competitors if they appraise risks too conservatively or may have to pay more claims if their underwriting actions are too liberal.	For beginning underwriting jobs, most large insurance companies seek college graduates who have a degree in liberal arts or business administration, but a major in almost any field provides a good general background. Some small companies hire persons without a college degree for underwriter trainee positions.	Underwriting can be a satisfying career for persons who like working with detail and enjoy evaluating information. In addition, underwriters must be able to make prompt decisions and communicate effectively. They must also be imaginative and aggressive, especially when they have to get information from outside sources.	Insurance underwriters with some experience average about $18,000 a year. Senior underwriters average between $26,000 and $29,000.	Moderate demand
Bank teller	Bank tellers are responsible for conducting much of the daily business of the bank with its customers. Tellers spend much of their day cashing checks and processing deposits and withdrawals.	High school graduation is considered adequate preparation for most beginning teller jobs in banks. Most tellers have at least a high school education. Courses in bookkeeping, typing, business arithmetic, and office machine operation are desirable. After gaining experience, a teller in a large bank may advance to head teller; outstanding tellers who have had some college or specialized training offered by the banking industry may be promoted to officer or a managerial position.	In hiring tellers, banks seek people with these basic qualities: clerical skills, friendliness, and attentiveness. Maturity, neatness, tact, and courtesy are also important because customers deal with tellers far more frequently than with other bank employees. One should enjoy working with numbers and feel comfortable handling large amounts of money.	Most beginning tellers earn between $150 and $180 a week. In general, the greater the range of responsibilities the teller performs, the higher the salary.	Great demand

Job Title	Job Description	Suggested Education and Training	Personality Traits	Average Pay	Outlook through 1990
Stockbroker	When investors want to buy or sell stocks, bonds, shares in mutual funds, or other financial products, they call on stockbrokers. When an investor wishes to buy or sell securities, brokers may relay the order through their firms' offices to the floor of a securities exchange, such as the New York Stock Exchange. If a security is not traded on an exchange, the broker sends the order to the firm's trading department, which trades it directly with a dealer in the over-the-counter market. After the transaction has been completed, the broker notifies the customer of the final price.	Because a stockbroker must be well informed about economic conditions and trends, a college education is increasingly important. Employers seek applicants who are well groomed, able to motivate people, ambitious, mature, and able to work independently. Successful sales or managerial experience is very helpful. Stockbrokers must meet state licensing requirements. They must register as representatives of their firms according to regulations of the securities exchanges where they do business or the National Association of Securities Dealers, Inc. (NASD).	Agents and brokers should be enthusiastic, self-confident, and able to communicate effectively. They should be able to inspire customer confidence. Many employers give personality tests to prospective employees because personality attributes are important in sales work. Since agents usually work without supervision, they must be able to plan their time well and have initiative to locate new clients.	Stockbrokers average more than $42,000 a year. Trainees usually are paid a salary until they meet licensing and registration requirements. After registration, a few firms continue to pay a salary until the new representative's commissions increase to a stated amount. The salaries paid during training usually range from $900 to $1,300 a month.	Great demand
Real estate agent	People generally seek the help of a real estate agent when buying or selling a home. These workers have a thorough knowledge of the housing market in their community. They know which neighborhoods will best fit their clients' lifestyles and budgets, local zoning and tax laws, and where to obtain financing for the purchase. Agents also act as a medium for price negotiations between buyer and seller.	Real estate agents must be licensed in every state. All states require that prospective agents be high school graduates, be at least 18 years old, and be able to pass a written test. As real estate transactions have become more complex, many of the large firms have turned to college graduates to fill sales positions. A large number of agents have some college training, and the number of college graduates selling real estate has risen substantially in recent years.	Personality traits are fully as important as academic background. Brokers look for applicants who possess such characteristics as a pleasant personality, honesty, and a neat appearance. Maturity, tact, and enthusiasm for the job are required in order to motivate prospective customers in this keenly competitive field. Agents also should have a good memory for names and faces and business details, such as taxes, zoning regulations, and local land-use laws.	Commissions on sales are the main source of earnings—very few real estate agents work for a salary. The rate of commission varies according to the type of property and its value. The median income of full-time agents is about $16,000. The most successful agents earn a great deal more.	Great demand
Financial analyst*	Working for public, industrial, and financial institutions, financial analysts make statistical evaluations of economic and political trends as well as of stock and financial data that may affect an investment program. Using these analyses, analysts try to predict the yield of various investment strategies. Analysts usually specialize in bonds, stocks, and commodities.	A bachelor's degree with a major in mathematics and statistics or in business and finance is preferred by most employers for entry level jobs.	An aptitude for mathematics and for interpreting figures and an attention to detail are all indispensable traits of a good financial analyst.	Entry-level jobs average between $12,000 and $18,000 a year.	Moderate demand

* Much of this material comes from *The Career Finder,* by Lester Schwartz and Irv Brechner. New York: Ballantine, 1983, p. 302.

Job Title	Job Description	Suggested Education and Training	Personality Traits	Average Pay	Outlook through 1990
Financial planner**	In business for the middle-class investor, financial planners give advice on saving, investing, and real-estate planning. Tax shelters and money-making schemes handled by planners have included Asian TV rights, cattle feed, precious gems, and artwork — as well as the more conventional stocks, bonds, insurance policies, and other financial packages.	Financial planners pay $85 a year in dues to the International Association of Financial Planners (IAFP). That's the one requirement of setting up shop. Other than that, a general knowledge of the broad range of savings, investment, and financial investment options available to clients is desirable. College courses in business administration or liberal arts are a good background for an aspiring financial planner.	Like the stockbroker, a financial planner's personality is especially important to doing the job well. Enthusiasm, confidence, neatness, honesty, and articulateness are all part of the successful planner's personality.	Nearly 70% of a financial planner's income comes from commissions on the investments sold to clients. One-third of all financial planners earn over $80,000 a year.	Moderate demand (Only 1000 planners were practicing ten years ago; today there are more than 7000.)
Economist	Economists study the way a society uses scarce resources such as land, labor, and raw materials to provide goods and services. Most economists are concerned with practical applications of economic policy in a particular area, such as finance, labor, agriculture, transportation, energy, or health. Economists who work for business firms provide management with information to make decisions on marketing and pricing of company products; to look at the advisability of adding new lines of merchandise, opening new branches, or diversifying the company's operations; to analyze the effect of changes in the tax laws; or to prepare economic and business forecasts.	Since many beginning jobs in government and business involve the collection and compilation of data, a thorough knowledge of basic statistical procedures is required. In addition to courses in macroeconomics, microeconomics, econometrics, and business and economic statistics, training in computer science is highly recommended. A bachelor's degree with a major in economics is sufficient for many beginning research, administrative, management trainee, and business sales jobs. However, graduate training increasingly is required for advancement to more responsible positions.	Persons who consider careers as economists should be able to work accurately with detail since much time is spent on data analysis. Patience and persistence are necessary because economists may spend long hours on independent study and problem solving. Sociability enables economists to work easily with others. Economists must be objective and systematic in their work and must be able to express themselves effectively both orally and in writing. Creativity and intellectual curiosity are essential to success in this field.	The median base salary of business economists is about $40,000. By industry, the highest-paid business economists are in the securities and investment and consulting fields; the lowest are in colleges and universities and real estate.	Great demand

---

** Much of this material comes from *The American Almanac of Jobs and Salaries*, by John W. Wright. New York: Avon, 1984, pp. 723–724.

Job Title	Job Description	Suggested Education and Training	Personality Traits	Average Pay	Outlook through 1990
Claim representative	Claim reps—a group that includes claim adjusters and claim examiners—investigate insurance claims, negotiate settlement with policyholders, and authorize payment. When a property-liability (casualty) insurance company receives a claim, the *claim adjuster* determines whether the policy covers it and the amount of the loss. When their company is liable, they negotiate with the claimant and settle the case. They must ensure that settlements reflect the claimant's actual losses. In life and health insurance companies, the *claim examiner* investigates questionable claims or those exceeding a specified amount. Examiners interview medical specialists or calculate benefit payments.	Although a growing number of insurance companies prefer college graduates, many hire those without college training, particularly if they have specialized experience. No specific field of college study is recommended. Although courses in insurance, economics, or other business subjects are helpful, a major in almost any field is adequate preparation. Most large insurance companies provide on-the-job training and home study courses to beginning claim adjusters and examiners.	Because they often work closely with claimants, witnesses, and other insurance professionals, representatives must be able to adapt to many different persons and situations. They should be able to communicate effectively and gain people's respect and cooperation. For example, when adjusters' evaluations of claims differ from those of the persons who have suffered the loss, they should be able to explain their conclusions clearly and tactfully. Examiners should be adept at making mathematical calculations. Both adjusters and examiners should have a good memory and enjoy working with details.	Claim representatives earn an average of $16,000 to $18,000 a year. Senior representatives earn $23,000 to $26,000 a year. Some claim representatives are paid a percentage of the amount of the settlements they make.	Moderate demand

Job Title	Job Description	Suggested Education and Training	Personality Traits	Average Pay	Outlook through 1990
Collection worker	Collection workers, often called bill collectors or collection agents, help maintain a company's financial well-being by keeping delinquent and bad debts to a minimum. A collector's primary job is to persuade people to pay their unpaid bills. Collectors usually receive a bad debt file after normal billing methods have failed to elicit payment. They then contact the debtor by phone or mail, inquire why the bill is still unpaid, and try to get the debtor to pay or make new payment arrangements. When customers have financial emergencies or have mismanaged their money, collectors may work out new payment schedules. If customers fraudulently avoid payment of their bills, collectors may recommend that the files be turned over to an attorney.	A high school education usually is sufficient for entry into the collection field, but college courses would be a plus to any employer. Because a collector handles delinquent accounts on a person-to-person basis, courses in psychology and speech may be useful. Entry level collectors are generally given on-the-job training by a supervisory employee or experienced worker who helps them learn collection procedures and telephone techniques. Training also is available through the American Collectors Association.	A collector's most valuable asset is the ability to get along with people without antagonizing them. He or she must be alert, imaginative, and quick-witted to handle the awkward situations that are part of collection work. While collectors should be sympathetic to the billpayers' problems, they also must be persuasive, tactful, and assertive to overcome some debtors' reluctance to fulfill their financial obligations. Because a collector spends most of the day on the telephone, a pleasant speaking voice and manner are important.	Incomes of collection workers vary substantially because employers generally pay salary plus a commission or bonus based on the amount of debts collected. Beginning collectors seem to average about $11,000 a year; experienced collectors, about $13,000 to $17,000 a year.	Moderate demand

DATA PROCESSING IN BUSINESS

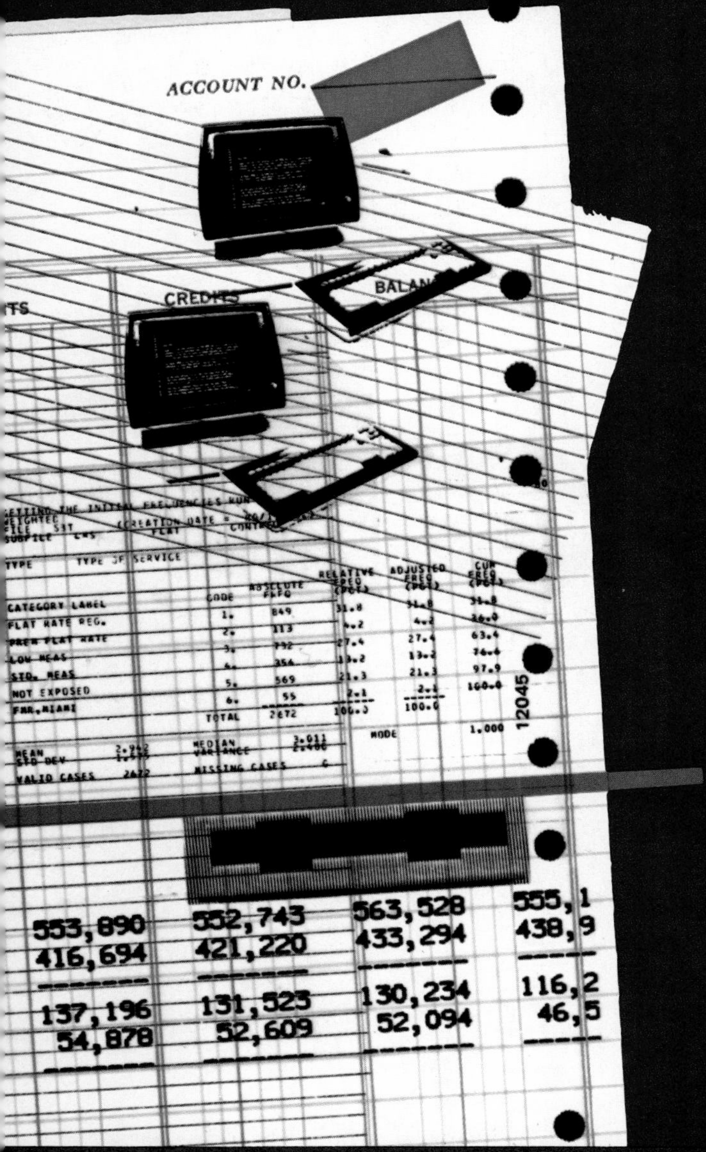

LEARNING OBJECTIVES

After studying this chapter, you will be able to:

- **Describe the accounting process.**

- **Distinguish between financial and managerial accountants.**

- **Distinguish between public, private, and government accountants.**

- **Distinguish between CPAs and CMAs.**

- **Read and understand the intent of a balance sheet.**

- **Read and understand the intent of an income statement.**

- **Calculate selected ratios of financial statements.**

ACCOUNTING
PRINCIPLES

Paine Webber Mitchell Hutchins Inc., the stockbroker and investment firm, reported their third-quarter 1983 earnings to be up 23% over the previous year. Some of these profits they distributed to stockholders as dividends, but they kept much of the profit in the company. And they used part of the profit they kept in the company to buy additional buildings and equipment they needed. Paine Webber's financial managers said that for the first time in several decades, they were able to buy equipment and buildings with money from profits they did not have to distribute to stockholders.

Republic Airlines had revenues of $1.5 billion in 1983; but their costs were even greater, and they lost $111 million for the year. Since 1980 Republic has lost $220 million, and they were $809 million in debt in early 1984. In 1983, Commodore International Ltd., the computer company, had sales of $681 million, and 1984 saw their sales exceed $1 billion.

The role of accounting is to produce financial information such as this. If you were managing a business, you would want to know a lot of information about the financial conditions of the company. Just as with your personal finances, you need to know the answers to such questions as: How much cash do I have? How much do I owe? What am I worth? How much cash am I taking in? How much cash am I spending? Do I have enough cash to meet immediate bills? Am I taking in more than I am spending? Often called the language of business, **accounting** measures and communicates information about the business's operations by recording, classifying, analyzing, summarizing, and presenting information in financial terms.

Accounting differs somewhat from **bookkeeping,** which we define as the clerical and somewhat mechanical process of keeping records. Accounting requires a higher level of knowledge and includes designing accounting systems and preparing and analyzing financial statements. Because of their financial expertise, many accountants become intimately involved in the most important decisions companies make.

After describing the accounting process, this chapter presents two basic accounting statements—the balance sheet and the income statement. Last, the chapter discusses analysis of financial statements.

UNDERSTANDING THE ACCOUNTING PROCESS

In describing the importance of the accounting process, an owner said, "I could not imagine myself making decisions without a steady flow of financial information about the company's operations." Information provided by accounting methods is crucial, not only for the managers within the company but for outsiders as well. Fortunately, because accountants have standardized methods, terms such as "profit," "assets," "equity," "sales," "expenses," and "net worth" have common meanings to managers, owners, investors, bankers, and lawyers.

The Accounting Cycle

During its long history, accounting has evolved and developed a particular way of gathering and reporting data. This sequence of recording, classifying, summarizing, and reporting transactions is called the **accounting cycle.**

Transactions. The cycle begins with transactions—any business event that is both financial and measurable. Examples of transactions include selling inventories, using supplies, writing off bad debts, cash sales, credit sales, cash receipts, cash payments, tax payments, stock sales, bond sales, loans, mergers, and the like.

Recording. To provide complete accounting records, each transaction is recorded individually. Some smaller businesses still record their transactions by hand in journals and ledgers, but many firms use computerized record-keeping devices. By punching a cash register tape, recording with electronic equipment, or making impressions on magnetic tapes, the data for every transaction is recorded and ready for retrieval. Thus, recording makes accounting statements possible. From a tally of daily sales, monthly, quarterly, and yearly sales totals can be produced.

Recall the last time you bought something in a retail store. Your description might run something like this, "I selected an item and approached the clerk at a register-like computer terminal. The clerk punched into the terminal the stock number, price, quantity, date, and department number." People and machines record hundreds or thousands of such transactions daily to help managers check on total sales, costs, theft, and profitability of items and departments.

Classifying. After recording information, accountants classify data by dividing it into various categories. For instance, all cash transactions are classified into either cash receipts or cash payments. A sale may be classified as either cash sale or credit sale (accounts receivable). Accountants further classify data into groupings such as assets, liabilities, equity, income, costs, and expenses.

Summarizing. Accounting statements summarize millions of transactions into periodic statements. The statements may be prepared yearly, quarterly, monthly, or in some cases, daily. The two most common statements are the balance sheet and the income statement. These statements tell something of the financial condition of the business. Comparing current statements to prior statements tells if the company is becoming more or less successful.

Reporting. Finally, accountants report the statements, at given periods of time, to people both within and outside the organization. These reports may be in weekly or monthly memos, or they may be printed reports to the public. Sometimes, in a larger company such as the Chrysler Corporation, a news conference will be held. And the results might be reported in the next morning's paper. Figure 20.1 illustrates the steps in the accounting process.

How Accounting Information Is Used

Accountants prepare each type of financial information for specific purposes and with particular people in mind. The plant manager may want a summary of costs. The sales manager may want the latest sales figures as soon as possible. A stockholder may want a report on how well the company is performing. To fill these needs, two categories of accounting have emerged: financial accounting (external reporting) and managerial accounting (internal reporting).

The accounting cycle for this firm might begin with the sale of its steel, here prepared for shipment to customers.

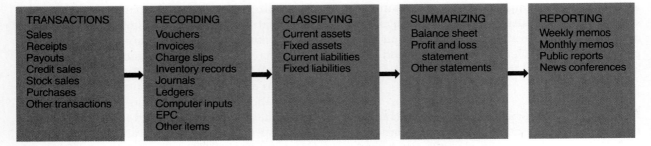

TRANSACTIONS	RECORDING	CLASSIFYING	SUMMARIZING	REPORTING
Sales	Vouchers	Current assets	Balance sheet	Weekly memos
Receipts	Invoices	Fixed assets	Profit and loss	Monthly memos
Payouts	Charge slips	Current liabilities	statement	Public reports
Credit sales	Inventory records	Fixed liabilities	Other statements	News conferences
Stock sales	Journals			
Purchases	Ledgers			
Other transactions	Computer inputs			
	EPC			
	Other items			

Figure 20.1
The accounting process.

Financial accounting. **Financial accounting** is a score card that consists of balance sheets, income statements, and supporting documents for persons outside the company, such as creditors, investors, and government officials.

Before banks and other institutions make loans, they study the applicant's balance sheets and income statements. Investments bankers, stockholders, and security analysts pore over financial statements to judge growth potential, earning ability, liquidity, and stability. Government agencies are interested in financial information for tax and regulatory purposes. The Internal Revenue Service (IRS) has set forth rigid rules on how revenue and expenses are to be determined and summarized for computing income taxes. Other agencies require accounting records for So-

cial Security payments, sales taxes, payroll, and state taxes. Regulatory agencies analyze data to see that the company is properly advertising and pricing its goods. Certain laws also regulate employee wages and control company-run pension and retirement funds. The Justice Department concerns itself with merger and antitrust regulations aimed at ensuring competition. From these uses of accounting data, we can begin to see the tremendous responsibility accountants have in developing information for internal and external uses.

Managerial accounting. **Managerial accounting** is the preparation of reports for internal decision making. These reports help in planning, budgeting, forecasting sales, controlling costs, and buying and selling assets. Amfac, Inc., a Hawaii sugarcane grower, had profits of $76.1 million in 1980. However, the company diversified into a lot of other operations and began losing money. Analysis by Amfac's managerial accountants showed that debt was climbing and they needed additional cash. So Myron DuBain, Amfac's CEO, sold some of the company's assets: its plumbing supplies division, a nursery in California, and 50% of its stake in the Waikiki Beachcomber Hotel in Honolulu.

The reports also help answer such questions as: Is the new product successful, what price should we charge, should the firm make or buy the component, are costs in line, what is the best source of funds, and how well are the departments functioning? To evaluate internal effectiveness, department heads work with accountants to prepare periodic **budgets,** estimates of costs and expenses for some future period. The budgets then become goals, and goals are compared to actual results. This helps managers identify their areas of responsibility and gives top management criteria to evaluate the efficiency of each department. Managers rely upon past accounting data and budget projections to help them decide what to do about operational problems such as: is inven-

tory shrinking, are salaries running too high, are employees working too much overtime, is the cash flow sufficient, and is credit getting out of hand? In these ways, managerial accounting provides managers with the information needed to carry out their responsibilities effectively. Figure 20.2 diagrams these accounting processes.

CPAs and CMAs

The accounting profession certifies its members who pass examinations and combine experience and education to show outstanding understanding of their fields.

Certified public accountant. A **certified public accountant (CPA)** is an accountant who has passed a rigorous examination prepared by the American Institute of Certified Public Accountants and has met certain educational and experience requirements. Requirements differ by states, but a typical set of requirements would be:

- Must be a high school graduate and, in many states, a college graduate.

- Must have from 1 to 5 years practical experience in accounting.

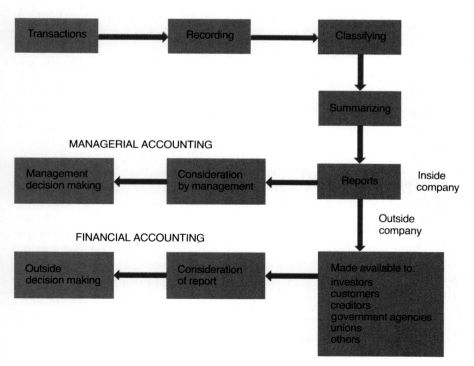

**Figure 20.2
The accounting process
for financial and
managerial accounting.**

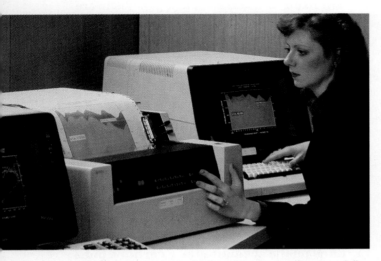

In larger companies, private accountants often specialize in a given aspect of the firm's financial information; daily petroleum prices and production costs are this accountant's focus.

■ Must take exam in the state in which he/she wishes to be certified.

■ All states require from two to five references of good moral character.

The CPA examination tests the candidate in the areas of (1) business law, (2) auditing, (3) accounting theory, and (4) accounting practice.

New York was the first state, in 1896, to pass a law making it possible to certify accountants.

Today, there are approximately one-quarter million CPAs in the United States.

Other states quickly followed suit, and all states had similar laws by 1925. Today, there are approximately one-quarter million CPAs in the United States. They are entitled to use the initials CPA after their names. Many states now require a certain number of hours in continuing education courses for CPAs to keep their designation.

Certified Management Accountant. A **certified management accountant (CMA)** has mastery in developing and analyzing information for management decision making. In 1972, the National Association of Accountants introduced the Certificate in Management program which, like the CPA program, contains rigorous examination and experience requirements. CMAs concentrate on generating and analyzing internal information to help management make better decisions. The intent of the CMA is to give the same status to management accountants as the CPA gives to public accountants.

Types of Accountants

Three broad areas make up the field of accounting — private accounting, public accounting, and government accounting.

Private accountants. Private accountants work for private businesses. They may hold titles such as accountant, financial specialist, budget officer, cost analyst, controller, or business manager. In smaller businesses, accountants deal in all areas of accounting. But in larger businesses, they may specialize in one aspect, such as taxes. An accountant for a smaller company explains her duties, saying, "I do everything. I keep all the records, prepare our taxes, make the payroll, prepare financial statements, and tell the owner when she cannot spend any more money." Accountants in private industry have seen their roles broadened by the government's requirement of more records and by the company's expanded acceptance in decision making.

Public accountants. Public accountants are firms or individuals that sell their services to private businesses. Several public accounting firms have grown so large that people refer to them as the "Big Eight" accounting firms. The largest is Peat, Marwick, Mitchell, and Company. Ernst & Whinney, Touche Ross, and Arthur Young & Co. are other Big Eight firms.

The most popular uses of public accountants are to assist in auditing financial records (checking to see if everything is according to generally accepted accounting principles) and preparing the company's tax reports. But public accounting firms, especially the larger ones, have expanded their services to include many kinds of consulting services, including:

■ Management consulting.

■ Computer systems.

Chuck E. Cheese's Annual Report for Kids

Accountants are sometimes criticized for reporting financial information only accountants can understand. However, Pizza Time Theatre, Inc., a chain of family entertainment centers that serve pizza and present musical shows, published its 1982 annual report in a form that 10-year-olds can understand.

In describing revenues, the report says, "In 1982, customers who came to the Company centers spent $82,580,391 on food, games, and merchandise. The Company also took in $16,705,677 in fees from franchise owners and from the sales of equipment to franchise owners. Together, all money taken in is called total revenues and came to $99,286,068 in 1982. This was almost three times the amount the Company took in the year before."

The publication also has coloring pages and dot-to-dot drawings to illustrate financial concepts. The report apparently made a hit, not only with youngsters, but also with grown-ups. "I've gotten letters from grown-ups saying this is the first time they've understood an annual report," commented Suzie Crocker, director of communications for Pizza Time.

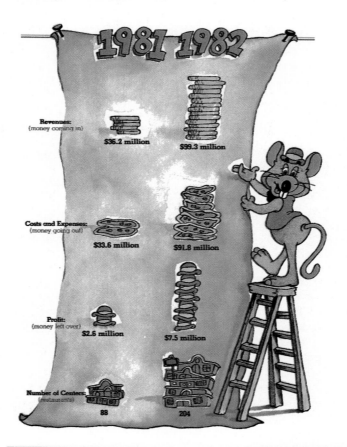

Source: Pizza Time Theatre, Inc. Reprinted by permission.

AERO CORPORATION
Balance sheet
June 30, 198X

ASSETS

Current assets:

Cash	$ 20,000	
U.S. Treasury notes	30,000	
Accounts receivable	57,400	
Notes receivable	15,000	
Merchandise inventory	122,000	
TOTAL CURRENT ASSETS		$244,400

Plant and equipment:

Land		75,400	
Equipment	$150,000		
Less: Accumulated depreciation	48,000	102,000	
Furniture and fixtures	10,000		
Less: Accumulated depreciation	3,600	6,400	
Buildings	254,000		
Less: Accumulated depreciation	76,000	178,000	
TOTAL PLANT AND EQUIPMENT			361,800

Intangible assets:

Patents	50,000	
Goodwill	69,000	
TOTAL INTANGIBLE ASSETS		119,000
TOTAL ASSETS		$725,200

LIABILITIES AND EQUITY

Current liabilities:

Accounts payable	$ 43,000	
Notes payable	34,600	
Income taxes payable	31,100	
TOTAL CURRENT LIABILITIES		$108,700

Long-term liabilities:

Mortgage on land and building	98,000	
Bonds outstanding	60,000	
TOTAL LONG-TERM LIABILITIES		158,000
TOTAL LIABILITIES		266,700

Equity:

Preferred stock	120,000	
Common stock	300,000	
Retained earnings	38,500	
TOTAL EQUITY		458,500
TOTAL LIABILITIES AND EQUITY		$725,200

Figure 20.3
Annual balance sheet, Aero Corporation.

- Market research.
- Executive hiring.
- Employee testing.
- Cash control systems.
- Employee training.
- Feasibility analysis.
- Retirement or pension program recommendations.
- Make or buy decisions.
- Merger or consolidation decisions.
- Statistical procedures.

As with private accounts, public accountants tend to specialize in one or a few of these areas.

Government accountants. **Government accountants** may do the same things as private or public accountants, but they work for a federal, state, or local government agency. In most cases, government accountants must pass a civil service exam to be considered for the job. They might work as cost accountants, auditors, budget directors, tax specialists, and so on. The Internal Revenue Service (IRS), for example, hires thousands of accountants to check the millions of tax returns that individuals and businesses file.

Accounting Standards

Because so many different people use accounting reports, it is important that accounting practices be somewhat standardized. Two national organizations help standardize accounting methods. The **American Institute of Certified Public Accountants (AICPA),** the professional organization of practicing CPAs, issues rules and guidelines regarding accounting methods. The AICPA founded the Accounting Principles Board that set standards for accounting practice from 1959 to 1973. The board helped to establish what are known as **generally accepted accounting principles (GAAP).** Since 1973, the **Financial Accounting Standards Board (FASB),** a private organization, has set standards for accounting practices. Through formal rulings and informal suggestions, these organizations have helped create a high degree of uniformity in accounting practices.

THE BALANCE SHEET

The **balance sheet,** often called the statement of financial condition, describes a company's financial position on a particular date. Many companies prepare balance sheets monthly or quarterly, and all businesses prepare a balance sheet at the end of their fiscal year. Figure 20.3 shows a sample balance sheet prepared for the Aero Corporation. The heading shows the company's name, type of statement (balance sheet), and the date. Within the body, subheadings divide data into two classifications: (1) assets, and (2) liabilities and equity. You can follow along on the balance sheet of Aero Corporation as we explain each section.

Assets

Assets, as defined in Chapter 17, are anything that the company owns. Aero, as most companies do, classifies its assets as current, plant and equipment, and intangible.

Current assets. **Current assets** are cash and items of value that can reasonably be expected to be converted into cash within 1 year. Current assets of Aero total $244,400. The $20,000 in cash includes money in the company safe, checking accounts, time deposits, and customer checks enroute to the bank. Aero has also invested $30,000 in short-term government securities which can easily be converted into cash. Customers owe the company $57,400 on open account, as shown in accounts receivable. These are goods Aero shipped to customers and allowed them 30 days to pay. For some customers of more questionable credit standings, the company required a formal document, known as a promissory note, in lieu of the open account. These notes totaled $15,000 and appear as notes receivable. A merchandise inventory account of $122,000 reflects the value of Aero's raw materials, semifinished products, and finished products not yet sold.

Plant and equipment. **Plant and equipment,** sometimes called **fixed assets,** are items of value that are typically used for longer than a year. Aero's plant and equipment accounts are re-

A firm's fixed assets, such as land and equipment, are defined by their long-term value.

corded at their cost price of $361,800. Some plant and equipment last no more than 2 or 3 years; others have a useful life of more than 20 years, and land lasts forever. For all plant and equipment other than land, there is an estimate of how much of the cost is used up; this is called **depreciation.** The Internal Revenue Service defines how quickly plant and equipment items can be depreciated. The Economic Recovery Act of 1981 contained a provision, called Accelerated Cost Recovery System, that allowed more rapid depreciation of certain types of plant and equipment. The purpose was to encourage companies to buy more long-term assets and thus help spur the economy. Accountants also adjust the balance sheet when the firm discards, sells, or trades plant and equipment items. Land, the only plant and equipment item that does not depreciate, remains on the books at $75,400, the purchase price 8 years ago. While land does increase or decrease in market value, it is not used up or worn out like buildings or machinery. The book value of these assets does not necessarily represent what the company could sell them for or what they would have to pay to replace them.

Aero's equipment (machinery and tools) with a life longer than 1 year cost $150,000. Accountants estimate that the company has used up $48,000 of this equipment's value (depreciation), leaving a book value of $102,000. The company has paid $10,000 for chairs, desks, tables, carpets,

and other furniture. Since $3600 has been depreciated, furniture and fixtures show a $6400 book value. The company owns buildings that originally cost $254,000 with a current book value of $178,000. Accountants have depreciated them $76,000.

Intangible assets. **Intangible assets** are assets of value but have no physical substance. Aero has patents worth $50,000 and customer goodwill which the accountants value at $69,000. The U.S. Patent Office grants patents, which give exclusive rights to manufacture, use, or sell an exclusive product for 17 years. Patents are usually recorded at cost. **Goodwill** results from such things as reputation, customer relations, location, efficiency, or good management. Goodwill is evident when owners sell a company at a price above the fair market value of its physical assets; the purchaser pays a premium for a business because of the goodwill a company has been able to generate. Goodwill is usually recorded on the books only when it is paid for, most often when someone buys the company. In 1969, United Brands Co. bought United Fruit Co., a banana producer. United Brands paid $300 million more than United Fruit's fair market value; the $300 million went into UB's books as goodwill. Copyrights and trademarks are other examples of intangible assets.

Liabilities and Owners' Equity

Liabilities are a company's obligation to pay cash or other economic value. They represent a claim against assets. Liabilities for Aero (total debt) amount to $266,700; some are current and others are long-term.

Current liabilities. Current liabilities— obligations to be paid within 1 year—of Aero amount to $108,700. Accounts payable of $43,000 is money the company owes to suppliers for materials and supplies bought and received, but not paid for. The company also has an outstanding 9-month note of $34,600 with a local bank. This is money it borrowed to get through a temporary cash problem when the cost of wood products increased and sales dipped.

Long-term liabilities. In addition to its current obligations, the company owes $158,000 in **long-term liabilities** to be repaid over the next several years. Aero still owes $98,000 on its land and building which are mortgaged as security for the loan. For expansion purposes, the owners sold $60,000 worth of 20-year bonds.

Equity. Owners' equity, what the company owns less what it owes, is the total value of the owners' interest in the company. On June 30, the owners had a total equity of $458,500 in the business. This is their claim against the assets. In 1966, the company sold 8000 shares of preferred stock for $120,000. Each of the five owners has 60,000 shares of common stock issued at a stated value of $1 per share. As the company has done well in recent years, the 300,000 outstanding shares probably have a market value of more than $300,000, but they remain on the books at the original value. Retained earnings of $38,500 are accumulated from previous years when owners reinvested profits back into the business. They have taken out most of the earnings in dividends, but thought it wise to retain some profits for expansion and working capital.

FUNNY BUSINESS

"Good grief! This balance-sheet won't do — why damn it, a child could understand it."

TAKING STOCK

How United Brands Improved its Balance Sheet

United Brands, a food producer and distributor, recently engaged in an accounting maneuver called a "quasi-reorganization." That is, they wrote off part of their assets, $300 million in goodwill, without reducing their profits. Normally, when writing off an asset, you would have to reduce profits by that amount. The benefit of the quasi-reorganization is a cleaner, more favorable balance sheet.

The Securities Exchange Commission rarely allows a company to go through quasi-reorganization unless the company is bankrupt. United Brands was not bankrupt, but they were in trouble. Last year, the company, because of losses and dividend payouts, suffered a $24 million deficit in its retained earnings account.

The quasi-reorganization allowed United Brands to revalue its assets and liabilities from their original cost to their fair market value. This would normally happen only if another company were to buy United Brands. Many analysts criticized the SEC for allowing the company to make this move, indicating that it would mislead investors. United Brands' accountants said the move was justifiable, though, and the SEC sided with them.

Source: "The Bookkeeping Maneuver that Cleaned up United Brands' Balance Sheet," *Business Week*, Nov. 14, 1983, p. 194.

How Inflation Affects Accounting Records

There has been much discussion about the fact that accounting records are based on original costs, but inflation causes prices to rise. Thus, a piece of land bought in 1970 for $100,000 would probably be worth three or four times that today, yet the balance sheet would still show the value of this land to be the original cost of $100,000. Some people argue that accountants should make price-level adjustments, that is, adjust the original cost to show the current or replacement costs. Others argue that this is too judgmental because there is no exact basis for determining current value of assets.

While there seems to be more acceptance of some type of price-level adjustments, this issue will probably continue to be debated for years. Indicate your feelings about this issue by responding to the following questions.

Accountants should make price-level adjustments so that their records show current or replacement costs.

___ A. Strongly agree   ___ C. Disagree somewhat

___ B. Agree somewhat   ___ D. Strongly disagree

List three reasons for your position:

A. _____ .

B. _____ .

C. _____ .

The Accounting Equation

The balance sheet is a detailed statement of the **accounting equation:**

$$\text{Assets} = \text{Liabilities} + \text{Owners' equity}$$

$$(\text{Resources}) = \begin{array}{c}(\text{Creditors'} \\ \text{claims against} \\ \text{resources)}\end{array} + \begin{array}{c}(\text{Owners'} \\ \text{claim against} \\ \text{resources)}\end{array}$$

$$\$725,200 = \$266,700 + \$458,500$$

Total assets always equal liabilities plus equity, giving the statement its name: balance sheet. There is a good reason why this statement balances. The assets list everything the company has. And the liability and equity section tells who owns those assets: creditors or owners. For example, should the company, through its operations, be able to increase its assets without increasing its debt, the increased value belongs to the owners. Naturally, this is a goal of the business. Thus, the balance sheet shows two views of the same business property.

Another reason that the equation works is an accounting concept called double-entry bookkeeping. **Double-entry bookkeeping** requires two entries for each transaction. One entry is a debit to a particular account, and the other entry is a credit. This double-entry process not only helps balance various accounts, but also helps to check on errors.

THE INCOME STATEMENT

While the balance sheet reflects a company's financial condition at a given time, the **income statement** (or profit and loss statement) depicts income or losses over a specific period of time and reflects the success or failure of a company's operations. Most firms prepare income statements monthly for management decisions, but they usually report their income position quarterly or annually to the public. To determine net income (or net loss), companies calculate the revenues received during the period. Then they calculate all the costs incurred during that period. Major cost categories are usually: (1) cost of goods sold and (2) operating expenses, including selling expenses and general operating expenses. The difference equals the net income (or net loss) from the operations. Aero's income statement for the year ending June 30 appears in Fig. 20.4.

Revenues

Revenue is the amount that a firm charges its customers for products or services. For most businesses, sales are the greatest source of revenue. Aero's cash and credit sales total $1,550,000 for the year. Notice that gross sales are reduced by $8200; this accounts for merchandise that customers returned plus price reductions because of damaged merchandise. The resulting net sales total

Figure 20.4
Annual income statement, Aero Corporation.

AERO CORPORATION Income statement for the year ended June 30, 198X			Percent of sales
Revenues:			
Gross sales		$1,550,000	
Less: Returns and allowances		8,200	
Net sales		$1,541,800	100
Cost of goods sold:			
Inventory, July 1		$ 95,000	
Net purchases		1,064,000	
Goods available for sale		$1,159,000	
Less: Inventory, June 30		83,000	
Cost of goods sold		1,076,000	69.8
GROSS PROFIT		$ 465,800	30.2
Operating expenses:			
Selling expenses:			
Sales salaries	$183,100		
Advertising	53,000		
Store supplies	6,000		
Miscellaneous selling expense	5,900		
Total selling expenses		$ 248,000	16.1
General expenses:			
Administrative salaries	$ 60,000		
Office expense	12,000		
Insurance	4,000		
Depreciation expense (equipment, furniture, and building)	26,000		
Interest expense	5,800		
Miscellaneous general expense	1,200		
Total general expenses		$ 109,000	7.1
TOTAL OPERATING EXPENSES		357,000	23.2
NET PROFIT FROM OPERATIONS (BEFORE TAXES)		$ 108,800	7.0
Less: INCOME TAXES		36,100	
NET PROFIT AFTER TAXES		72,700	4.7

$1,541,800 — the net amount charged for all merchandise Aero sold during the year.

Costs and Expenses

To determine the operating income (or loss), accountants add all costs and expenses together and deduct them from total revenues. For Aero, as for many companies, there are two categories of costs and expenses: (1) costs of goods sold and (2) operating expenses.

Costs of goods sold. Under **costs of goods sold,** for a wholesaler or retailer, we find costs directly related to purchasing the merchandise for sale. For a manufacturing firm, the cost of goods sold would represent the materials, labor, and overhead that went into producing the product. To determine cost of goods sold for Aero, we (1) determine the beginning inventory for the period, and add it to (2) the value of net purchases for the period, then (3) deduct the value of the inventory at the end of the period. For Aero, this was:

Beginning inventory + net purchases
    − Ending inventory = Cost of goods sold

or

$95,000 + $1,064,000 − $33,000 = $1,076,000

Aero sold merchandise for $1,541,800, and the cost of purchasing those goods was $1,076,000; the difference between the figures is the **gross profit,** $465,800.

Operating expenses. Costs of goods sold does not include all the expenses of the company, only those of purchasing or making the products that were sold. Aero also incurred some expenses in selling their merchandise — wages, supplies, administrative salaries, and taxes. These are **operating expenses.** Aero's total operating expenses were $357,000. We can further divide these into selling expenses and general expenses. Aero's selling expenses totaled $248,000, the largest segment being sales salaries — $183,100. The company spent $53,000 on advertising, $6000 on supplies, and $5900 for miscellaneous items. General expenses were $109,000, with $60,000 going for administrative salaries. Office expenses amounted

For most businesses, sales of products and services provide the major source of revenue.

to $12,000, and the firm paid $4000 in insurance premiums. Depreciation expenses for equipment, furniture, and building totaled $26,000. Seven thousand dollars were classified as miscellaneous.

Total operating expenses — selling plus general expenses — were $357,000. Accountants subtract operating expenses from gross profit to determine net income (profit) or net loss from operations. For Aero, net income was $108,800 ($465,800 − $357,000). If costs and expenses are greater than net revenue, the difference is a net loss.

APPRAISING OPERATIONAL RESULTS

The balance sheet and the income statement are related to each other, and both provide a wealth of information for analysis.

Relationship between Balance Sheet and Income Statement

The net income (or net loss) figures from the income statement directly affect the equity section of the balance sheet. Net income left after taxes and dividends is usually added to the owners' equity section. If there is a loss, the owners' equity is reduced by that amount. Aero paid $36,100 in federal income taxes. The tax rate graduates from 16% for the first $25,000 of taxable income up to 46% on amounts exceeding $100,000. This left an after-tax profit of $72,700. The board voted to distribute $50,000 as preferred and common stock dividends and increase retained earnings by the balance — $22,100. Thus, results in the income statement directly affect the balance sheet. Conversely, if the board should vote to pay $50,000 in dividends, there would be less assets for the business's operation and/or expansion.

Percentage of Net Sales

Notice that the far right column in the income statement (Fig. 20.4) shows selected income statement items as percentages of net sales. For instance, cost of goods sold was 69.8% of net sales, leaving a gross profit of 30.2% of net sales. Total operating expenses amounted to 23.2% of net sales, and profit before taxes was 7.0% of net sales.

These percentages help analysts compare the current income statement to previous income statements, and the comparisons might suggest some possible changes. If total operating expenses had been running about 15 to 17% of net sales in previous years, the current 23.2% might indicate the need to maintain tighter control over these expenses. Percentages also make it possible to compare financial statements with those of other firms in the industry and with industry averages.

Ratio Analysis

Financial analysts find it useful to compute ratios of various balance sheet and income statement figures. A financial ratio is simply the result of dividing one number by another. **Ratio analysis** is the comparison of financial ratios to previous periods and to industry averages. Analysts rely, at least to some extent, on dozens of financial ratios; we include a few of the most popular here, including liquidity ratios, profitability ratios, and debt ratios.

Liquidity ratios. A liquid firm is one that can meet its current obligations as they come due. Liquidity ratios measure the firm's ability to meet its cash obligations. In the case of Aero, this would be accounts payable, notes payable, and income taxes payable. Two important liquidity ratios are current ratio and acid-test ratio. Working capital, although not a ratio, is another liquidity measure.

1. *Current ratio.* The **current ratio** is current assets divided by current liabilities, and analysts use it to test a company's ability to pay short-term debts as they come due. Aero Corporation's current ratio is:

$$\frac{\text{Current assets}}{\text{Current liabilities}} = \frac{\$244,400}{\$108,700}$$
$$= 2.25 \text{ Current ratio}$$

This means that Aero has $2.25 of current assets for every dollar of short-term debt. According to its current ratio, Aero is in pretty good shape. For most industries, analysts consider a current ratio between 1.7 and 2.0 to be desirable. Put differently, Aero could probably acquire more short-term capital rather easily if they needed it.

2. *Acid-test ratio.* The **acid-test ratio** is an indicator of ability to pay current debts instantly. The acid-test ratio selects only the most liquid assets to be divided by current liabilities. Typically, the acid-test ratio does not include inventory since it normally takes a while to turn inventory into cash. The acid-test ratio for Aero is:

$$\frac{\text{Cash} + \text{Marketable securities} + \text{Notes receivable} + \text{Accounts receivable}}{\text{Current liabilities}}$$

$$= \frac{\$20,000 + \$30,000 + \$15,000 + \$57,400}{\$108,700}$$

$$= 1.13 \text{ Acid-test ratio}$$

This means that Aero has $1.13 of near-cash assets for every $1.00 of short-term debt. Again, this ratio suggests that Aero is in good shape regarding short-term debt because analysts consider an acid-test ratio of 1.0 to be a reasonable risk.

3. *Working capital.* Actually, working capital is not a ratio, but we include it here since it is an

indication of the firm's ability to meet its current obligations. **Working capital** is the difference between current assets and current liabilities. The working capital for Aero is:

Current assets − Current liabilities
= $244,400 − $108,700 = $135,700

Profitability ratios. **Profitability ratios** give an indication of how effectively management is using the company's resources.

1. *Return on investment (ROI)*. The **return on investment (ROI) ratio** measures the rate of return owners received on their investment.

This is a very important ratio because it shows the rewards returned to the owners as an incentive for taking risks with their investment. If the ROI is too low, investors will likely withdraw and place their money elsewhere. Also, it is harder to attract additional money for expansion or other purposes when the ROI is low. Aero's ROI is:

$$\text{ROI} = \frac{\text{Net profit after taxes}}{\text{Total owner's equity}} = \frac{\$72,700}{\$458,500}$$

$$= .159 = 15.9\%$$

This shows a reasonable return if the business is low risk. However, if investors considered

CONSOLIDATED BALANCE SHEET (Continued)
November 30, 1983 and 1982

Long-term debt	14,755,000	14,238,000
Deferred federal and foreign income taxes	4,021,000	5,075,000
Shareholders' equity		
Common stock, no par value:		
Class A, authorized and issued 752,682 shares	424,000	424,000
Class B, authorized 3,000,000 shares; issued		
2,217,104 and 2,119,937 shares	9,249,000	8,441,000
Retained earnings	42,594,000	38,284,000
Cumulative foreign currency translation adjustments	(175,000)	—
	52,092,000	47,149,000
Less cost of 507,945 shares of common stock in treasury	4,275,000	4,275,000
TOTAL SHAREHOLDERS' EQUITY	47,817,000	42,874,000
	$97,196,000	$89,096,000

CONSOLIDATED STATEMENT OF INCOME
Years ended November 30, 1983, 1982, and 1981

Consolidated Statements of Income	1983	1982	1981
Net sales	$114,346,000	$102,226,000	$91,476,000
Cost of sales	49,378,000	42,124,000	38,488,000
Selling and administrative expenses	50,446,000	47,237,000	42,327,000
Operating costs and expenses	99,824,000	89,361,000	80,815,000
Operating income	14,522,000	12,865,000	10,661,000
Interest expense	3,020,000	3,261,000	2,360,000
Income before income taxes	11,502,000	9,604,000	8,301,000
Provision for income taxes	5,854,000	5,048,000	4,707,000
Net income	$ 5,648,000	$ 4,556,000	$ 3,594,000
Net income per share:			
Primary	$2.26	$1.92	$1.46
Fully diluted	$2.25	$1.84	—
Number of shares outstanding:			
Primary	2,499,196	2,369,345	2,461,918
Fully diluted	2,507,319	2,477,911	—

Aero a high-risk company or if interest rates on stable securities were high, investors would probably not be satisfied with this return.

2. *Net profit margin.* The **net profit margin** measures the after-tax profits as a percentage of sales. For Aero, this figure is:

$$\text{Net profit margin} = \frac{\text{Net profit after taxes}}{\text{Sales}}$$

$$= \frac{\$72,700}{\$1,541,800}$$

$$= .047 = 4.7\%$$

For every dollar of sales, the company earns 4.7 cents. This suggests an average profit margin and indicates that the company may be pricing too low or that its costs are too high. However, low profit margins are not always a sign of low profits. If a company turns its inventory over rapidly, it can have a lower profit margin.

3. *Inventory turnover ratio.* The **inventory turnover ratio** is cost of goods sold divided by the average inventory for a period, say a year. For Aero, it is:

$$\frac{\text{Cost of goods sold}}{\dfrac{\text{Beginning inventory} + \text{Ending inventory}}{2}}$$

$$= \frac{\$1,076,000}{\dfrac{\$95,000 + \$83,000}{2}}$$

$$= 12.09 \text{ Inventory ratio}$$

This indicates that Aero sells its inventory (turns it over) about twelve times per year or about once a month, a little below average when compared to competitors. To arrive at the figure another way, divide 365 (days per year) by 12.09 (inventory turnover ratio), and you get 30.19 days. The inventory turnover ratio is important to both investors and creditors for it tells them how quickly the company is converting its inventory into cash. Because inventory turnover varies tremendously by industry, there is no universal standard, although industries do have their own standards. Typically, a shorter turnover period is better because this means less funds are tied up in inventory. And by contrast, a longer

Semiautomated operations can accelerate customer order processing and thus improve the firm's inventory turnover ratio.

turnover period suggests more trouble in turning inventory into cash.

4. *Earnings per share.* **Earnings per share (EPS)** is the average earnings per share for common stock. EPS for Aero is:

$$\text{EPS} = \frac{\text{Net profit after taxes}}{\text{Common shares outstanding}}$$

$$= \frac{\$72,700}{300,000}$$

$$= \$.24 \text{ per share}$$

Most potential investors regard EPS as the single most important factor in determining whether they will put money into a company. Higher EPS gives the company greater ability to pay dividends to stockholders or to plow back earnings into the company for growth. Both of these enhance the value of the stock and will likely drive up the stock price. Aero's $.24 per share earnings are down from $.36 the previous year. Management will probably look closely to see what they can do to perk up profits next year.

Debt ratios. Debt ratios show how much money the company has borrowed relative to other balance sheet items, and they indicate the ability of the firm to pay off its long-term obligations.

1. *Equity-to-debt ratio.* Just as short-term creditors are interested in the ability of the company to pay, long-term lenders want some indicator of how secure their long-term investments are. The owners' **equity-to-debt ratio** divides total liabilities into owners' equity. For example:

$$\frac{\text{Owners' equity}}{\text{Total liabilities}} = \frac{\$458,500}{\$266,700}$$

$$= 1.72 \text{ Owners' equity-to-debt ratio}$$

Because this ratio is a measure of the cushion against shrinkage in asset value as well as the company's ability to pay its long-term debt, it becomes one of the considerations that long-term investors look at. The 1.72 ratio for Aero means that the owners' investment is $1.72 for every $1.00 of the company's liabilities. Aero again appears to be in good shape because, as a general rule, a ratio above 1.0 is considered positive. A ratio below 1.0 suggests that the company may have too many long-term liabilities in relation to what the owners have invested.

2. *Debt-to-assets ratio.* The **debt-to-assets ratio** shows the total amount of claims that lenders have against the company's assets. For Aero, the percentage is:

$$\text{Debt-to-assets} = \frac{\text{Total liabilities}}{\text{Total assets}}$$

$$= \frac{\$266,700}{\$725,200}$$

$$= .368 = 36.8\%$$

Again, Aero appears to be in pretty good shape, with only a little over one-third of their assets being levered by creditors.

3. *Interest coverage ratio.* When interest rates get very high, management might become concerned about their ability to pay interest costs. The **interest coverage ratio** indicates the ability to pay interest charges out of earnings. To compute this ratio, we add interest and taxes back to our net profit. We do this because we deduct interest payments before figuring our income taxes.

$$\text{Interest coverage} = \frac{\text{Profits before interest and taxes}}{\text{Interest}}$$

$$= \frac{\$72,700 + 5,800 + 36,100}{\$36,100}$$

$$= \frac{\$114,600}{\$5,800} = 19.8 \text{ times}$$

This suggests that Aero is quite able to pay its interest charges as the company is earning 19.8 times the interest coming due each year.

In short, Aero seems to be financially sound. The ratios suggest that the company has the ability to meet both its short-term and long-term obligations. However, Aero's profitability might need a little boost. While profits are not bad, they do not seem to sparkle when compared to others. Of course, economic conditions would influence the interpretation of profitability ratios. During economic recessions, we might consider Aero to be very profitable; during economic growth, though, we would probably want to see a little more return on our investment.

SUMMARY

Accounting is the activity of accumulating, measuring, and communicating financial information about organizations. It includes the steps within the accounting cycle: recording, classifying, summarizing, and reporting information. Financial accounting deals with the making of reports for outside parties, while managerial accounting focuses on providing information for employees within the company. The three general types of accountants are private, public, and government. It is important that accounting methods are standardized, and today the Financial Accounting Standards Board (FASB) oversees the practice and helps standardize accounting procedures.

The two most widely used accounting statements are the balance sheet and the income statement. The balance sheet shows a company's financial condition at a given time. The income statement reveals the results of a company's operation for a given period of time. The balance sheet utilizes the accounting equation, which is: Assets = Liabilities + Owners' equity.

Ratios are used to determine information about a company. They are derived by dividing one accounting figure into another. The most popular groups of ratios are liquidity ratios, profitability ratios, and debt ratios.

MIND YOUR BUSINESS

Instructions. The balance sheet and the income statement are the two most common financial statements prepared by accountants. Check your knowledge of what goes on each statement by matching the statements in the right column with the items in the left column.

____ 1. Cash   A. Balance sheet

____ 2. Revenues   B. Income statement

____ 3. Accounts receivable

____ 4. Merchandise inventory

____ 5. Net sales

____ 6. Net purchases

____ 7. Selling expenses

____ 8. Common stock

____ 9. Net income

____ 10. Equity

____ 11. Cost of goods sold

____ 12. Advertising expenses

____ 13. Accounts payable

____ 14. Buildings

____ 15. Depreciation expense

____ 16. Mortgage on land

____ 17. Preferred stock

____ 18. Sales salaries

____ 19. Administrative salaries

____ 20. Goodwill

See answers at the back of the book.

KEY TERMS

REVIEW QUESTIONS

1. What is accounting? How do managers use accounting information?

2. Describe the standardized format by which accountants create information. Give at least

two examples for each phase of the process.

3. Identify the differences between managerial accounting and financial accounting.

4. Identify and discuss the different fields of accounting.

5. What is a certified public accountant (CPA)? Certificate in management accounting (CMA)?

6. What does the balance sheet do?

7. Distinguish between current assets and fixed assets as reported on the balance sheet.

8. How are intangible assets different from other types of assets?

9. How is the equity section of the balance sheet derived?

10. What are liabilities? Distinguish between current and long-term liabilities as defined by the balance sheet.

11. Explain the accounting equation. Why does the balance sheet always balance?

12. How does the income statement differ from the balance sheet?

13. Describe how gross profit is determined on the income statement. Is gross profit the firm's income for the year? Explain.

14. How is net income determined on the income statement? What does the net income figure mean?

15. How does net income or net loss as reported on the income statement affect the accounts on the balance sheet?

16. Define examples of liquidity ratios, profitability ratios, and debt ratios.

CASES

Case 20.1: Balance Sheet Preparation

At the end of the year, the Balox Company showed the following balances in its accounts:

Land	$3,500,000
Buildings	1,100,000
Inventories	96,000
Cash	34,000
Accounts payable	286,000
Accounts receivable	311,000
Income taxes	22,000

Bonds outstanding	64,000
Accumulated depreciation	408,000
Furniture	39,000
Prepaid insurance	21,000
Notes receivable	34,000
Notes payable	21,000
Preferred stock	310,000
Retained earnings	124,000
Common stock	_____

Questions

1. From this data, prepare a balance sheet for the Balox Company. Note that the balance in the common stock account is not given. You should be able to compute this balance by using the accounting equation.

2. What is the amount of current assets? Plant and equipment (fixed assets)? Total assets?

3. What is the amount of current liabilities? Fixed liabilities? Total liabilities? Total equity?

Case 20.2: Income Statement Preparation

For the year currently ended, the Balox Company showed the following balances in its accounts affecting the income statement:

Office expenses	$ 127,000
Cash sales	2,636,000
Credit sales	910,000
Beginning inventory	302,000
Advertising	487,000
Total depreciation expense	206,000
Estimated sales returns	24,000
Net purchases	2,118,000
Ending inventory	100,000
Other expenses	21,000
Administrative salaries	614,000
Insurance expense	22,000
Sales salaries	448,000

Questions

1. Prepare an income statement for the Balox Company. Did the company experience a net income or loss for the year? How much?

2. What were the company's total operating expenses? Cost of goods sold? Net revenue?

After completing this chapter, you will be able to:

■   Identify many government and commercial
    secondary sources of data.

■   Describe four ways organizations collect
    primary data.

■   Identify and compute basic measures of
    central tendency.

■   Describe and compute index numbers.

■   Explain the use of time series and
    correlation analysis.

■   Analyze the pros and cons of data presentation
    via bar graphs, line charts, circle graphs,
    statistical maps, and tables.

C

THE USES OF
STATISTICAL
METHODS

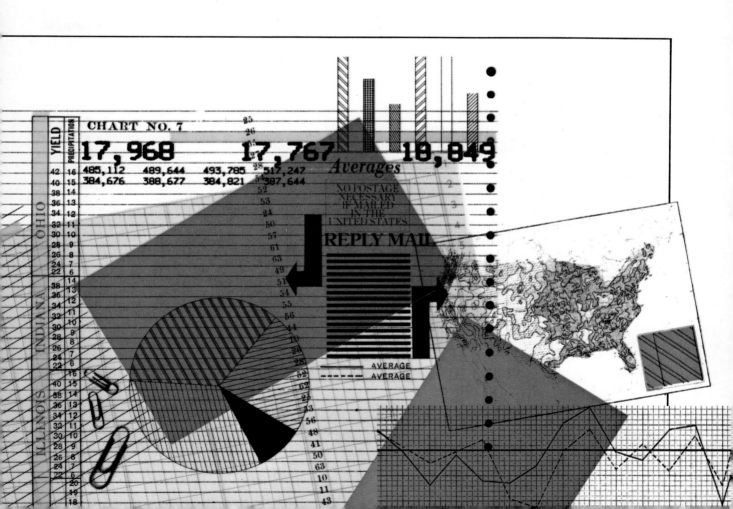

The *Statistical Abstract of the United States*, a Bureau of the Census publication, has more than 1000 pages of statistics. The 1982–1983 *Abstract* has over 1600 tables and charts offering a socioeconomic picture of the United States. For instance, the *Abstract* reports that each person in the United States uses an average of 31 gallons of water per day from public water utilities. And it reports that 18% of the men in the United States 65 and older participate in the labor force (in Japan, the figure is 41%, and in England it is 9%). In fact, the *Abstract* summarizes data on practically every aspect of social, economic, and political life in the United States: recreation, travel, national defense, welfare services, prices, immigration, health care, school enrollments, lifetime earnings, corporate philanthropy, international flow of crude oil supplies, arson arrests, and much, much more.

Statistics involves collecting, interpreting, and presenting data in numerical form. Managers are keenly aware of statistical data, apart from dollar values reported on financial statements. While accounting data centers on financial records, statistical approaches measure other fluctuating activities occurring inside and outside the firm. Statistical approaches offer a systematic way of collecting, analyzing, and presenting the volumes of information necessary for enlightened decision making.

COLLECTING DATA

Through their operations, companies generate a lot of data. Information from a company's records is called **internal data.** But even more information, called **external data,** originates outside the company.

Secondary Sources of Data

Secondary data is information already gathered and published. The volume of published data is mountainous, covering almost every possible subject. Secondary data is quick and inexpensive to gather, but it may not fit the unique data demands of a particular project. Although government agencies are the leading publishers of secondary data, commercial publications contribute to the information bank.

Government publications. Almost all government offices produce data. Perhaps the most widely known is the Bureau of the Census, which publishes the *Census of the Population* every 10 years. Not only does this thick volume count the 220 million-plus people in the United States, it also measures many other factors in our society. The Census Bureau also reports the *Census of Business* which details facts on wholesale, retail, and service businesses. In all, there are eight different censuses and countless other government publications spewing out secondary data. See Fig. C.1 for a partial listing of data sources.

Commercial publications. If government sources fail to meet your data needs, you can turn to thousands of private companies that publish for profit. The Market Research Corporation of America collects and sells data on consumers' purchasing habits, product preferences, and related demographic variables. The A. C. Nielsen Company provides information concerning retail sales of selected products and publishes the famous Nielsen ratings on television viewing audiences. Moody's Investor Service collects a wealth of data on the financial performance of stocks and

TAKING STOCK

The Census Bureau

The United States took its first census in 1790. Since that time, we have regularly counted our people, activities, products, and possessions. Today, the Census Bureau conducts numerous counts of our nation, some every 5 years and others every 10 years.

Census data has become vital to many decisions. The government uses census data to redistrict seats in the U.S. House of Representatives and state legislatures to assure equal representation. Public agencies use population and economic data to decide how to allocate services, as well as what services they should provide. Businesses use the data to identify population characteristics of their markets and potential markets, to compare sales volume with similar businesses, and to look at a host of financial and demographic changes over time.

The cost of the 1980 census was estimated to be more than 1 billion dollars. Yet, even the experts agree that they were unable to count everyone. The mobility of the population and the growing distrust of how the data are used are major reasons why it is hard to count everyone. In addition to the statistical profiles of the nation, about $50 billion of federal money is allocated yearly to state and local governments, mostly on the basis of census data. Other census facts:

- *When.* On March 28, questionnaires were received in the mail, and they were to be returned on April 1.

- *What.* The questionnaires sought data on age, education, marital status, racial and ethnic background, and other things. For most people, it would take about 15 minutes to complete the forms.

- *Who.* Everyone in the nation's 86 million housing units were counted (at least this was the hope).

- *Why.* To give a statistical profile of the nation, apportion the U.S. House of Representatives and state legislatures, and allocate federal money.

- *Personnel.* In addition to regular Census Bureau employees, about 275,000 temporary personnel were hired at $4 per hour.

The Census Bureau publishes its data in printed reports, but the data is also available on microfiche, and much of it is on computer tapes. For additional information about the Bureau of the Census, contact: Data User Services Division, Customer Services, Bureau of the Census, Washington, D.C. 20233. Phone (301) 763-4100.

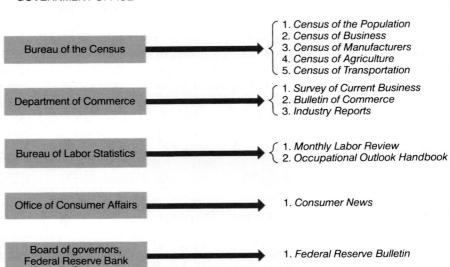

GOVERNMENT OFFICE	EXAMPLES OF REPORTS
Bureau of the Census	1. *Census of the Population* 2. *Census of Business* 3. *Census of Manufacturers* 4. *Census of Agriculture* 5. *Census of Transportation*
Department of Commerce	1. *Survey of Current Business* 2. *Bulletin of Commerce* 3. *Industry Reports*
Bureau of Labor Statistics	1. *Monthly Labor Review* 2. *Occupational Outlook Handbook*
Office of Consumer Affairs	1. *Consumer News*
Board of governors, Federal Reserve Bank	1. *Federal Reserve Bulletin*

Figure C.1
Examples of secondary information produced by government offices.

bonds. Most newspapers report business-related facts for their communities, and library shelves bulge with hundreds of journals that sell valuable data through their subscriptions.

Primary Sources of Data

In contrast to secondary sources, primary sources refer to research done for the first time. Researchers use surveys, observations, and experiments to gather new facts. All these methods use sampling.

Sampling. Regardless of the data collection method, researchers seldom try to measure everything. They draw samples from the total number of items, called the **universe** or **population,** that interests them. From the sample, analysts make inferences about the remainder of the universe. Sampling is an everyday process. You taste a bite of steak to test how well the whole steak is cooked, and you sample the sweetness of a cup of tea with only a sip. Likewise, if a firm wants information on people over 65 or families west of the Mississippi with fewer than three children, they sample the opinions of a few to make judgments about the total.

Random sampling, the simplest sampling method, assumes that every item in the universe has an equal and known chance of being selected. The sample is independent of the researcher's biases. Suppose a company wants a 20% random sample of all the people who have telephones, and the phone book lists 80,000 people. They could put the 80,000 names in a box, mix them, and draw out 16,000 (20% of 80,000). (To be technically correct, they would have to replace each name after they drew it.)

Since pure random sampling is difficult, controlled sampling is more widely used. "Convenience," "judgment," and "quota" are controlled sampling techniques. In convenience sampling, researchers measure items that are handy. If you wanted to measure the chewing gum preferences of college students, you could go to the nearest college campus and interview the first 200 students who would answer your questions. This would be very convenient, but judgments about the remaining universe could lack authority. For judgment sampling, an expert selects a typical segment of the universe. For example, a corporation might ask its store managers to run a check on credit purchasing. Quota sampling is more scientific than convenience or judgment sampling because characteristics of the universe determine the sample. If you know the family size of your customers, you might set your sample quotas to include 45 families with no children, 74 with one child, 128 with two children, and 99 with more than two.

Surveys. In surveys, researchers ask people to complete questionnaires on their habits, actions, attitudes, beliefs, or opinions. Most questionnaires use standardized questions and printed alternatives; the respondent merely checks the appropriate responses. A popular survey method is the mail questionnaire: Researchers develop questions, select respondents, and mail out questionnaires. Respondents deliver their answers by re-

> **Mail surveys are inexpensive, but the response rate is low; 10 to 15% is considered good.**

turn mail. Mail surveys are inexpensive, but the response rate is low; 10 to 15% response is considered good for many surveys. Part of a mail questionnaire appears in Fig. C.2.

Figure C.2
Excerpt from a mail questionnaire.

DEMOGRAPHIC DATA

1. Check the blank that identifies your marital status.

____ married ____ single ____ divorced ____ widowed

____ separated

2. How many children do you have?

____ none ____ one ____ two ____ three ____ four

____ five ____ more than five

3. Check the blank that includes your age.

____ below 25 ____ 25 to 35 ____ 36 to 50 ____ over 50

4. Check the blank that includes your annual salary.

____ below $5000

____ between $5000 and $8000

____ between $8000 and $12,000

____ between $12,000 and $16,000

____ between $16,000 and $20,000

____ more than $20,000

5. What type of company do you work for?

____ financial (banks, etc.)

____ construction

____ manufacturing

____ service (food)

____ service (other)

____ retail

____ other

6. Check the blank that indicates the highest formal educational experience that you have had.

____ completed nine grades

____ completed high school

____ completed some college

____ college degree

____ graduate work

____ postgraduate work

7. To what extent do you feel that your aptitudes and abilities are being used in relation to the demands placed on you by your position?

____ used to a very high degree

____ most are used

____ some are used

____ very few are used

8. How do you feel about the future opportunities for women in management?

____ very optimistic

____ somewhat optimistic

____ somewhat pessimistic

____ very pessimistic

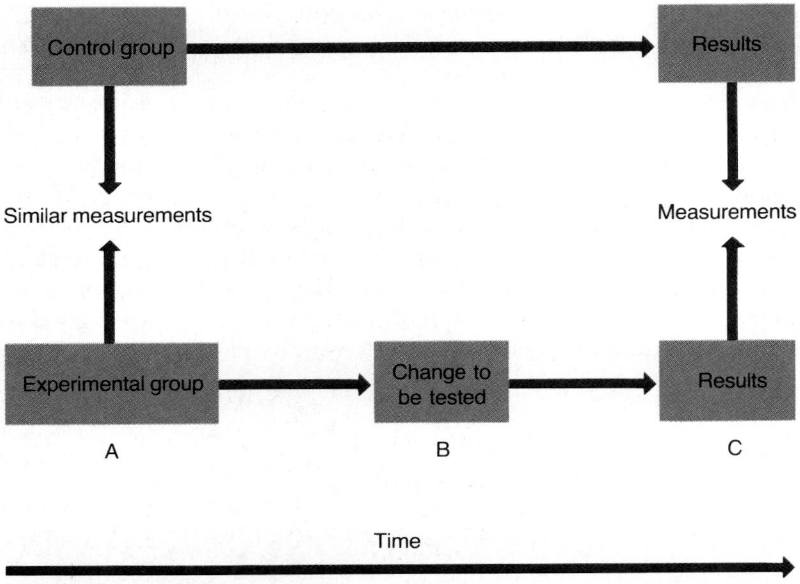

Figure C.3
Diagram of an experiment. (a) Begin with two groups that measure the same on some characteristic. (b) Inject the change to be tested in the experimental group. (c) Compare the results of experimental and control group to see if the change had any influence.

Personal interviews are more appropriate when questions are sensitive or require interpretation. Interviews can be structured or unstructured. Following a standardized format, structured interviews ask the same questions in the same way to all respondents. Unstructured interviews are open-ended. Interviewers have several points to cover but do not necessarily have a specific set of questions to ask. Personal interviews increase response rates, but interviewing costs drive expenses up. Researchers can cut costs by substituting telephone surveys for personal interviews, but people tend to distrust telephone interviews and are reluctant to divulge information.

Observation. Observation methods employ trained persons to watch events and record needed information. On a rainy day, a researcher might stand on a street corner and take notes on weather apparel — rain hats, coats, umbrellas. Professional football teams hire skilled scouts who doggedly diagram the plays of opposing teams. Mechanical counters "observe" the number of cars that pass along selected streets or the number of people going through turnstiles. Trained observers are costly, but they gather various kinds of information, whereas the less expensive mechanical devices process very limited data.

Experimentation. In an experiment, researchers begin by setting up two similar groups — an experimental and a control group. They introduce the idea to be tested in the experimental group but make no change in the control group. Later, researchers compare experimental and control groups to see if the idea caused the groups to be different (see Fig. C.3).

Experiments are very useful for testing new product ideas or advertising effectiveness. Experiments offer the advantage of identifying causal factors — what makes the results differ. But they are expensive and time-consuming, and you can never be certain you have controlled everything in the study.

ANALYZING AND INTERPRETING STATISTICAL INFORMATION

The purpose of gathering data is to improve decision making. However, as one research manager put it, "No amount of data completely takes the judgment out of decisions. After we get the data, we have to analyze it. Sometimes our computer gives us so much information, it is bewildering;

other times, we make important decisions on scanty data. We just hope that we understand the data well enough to make decisions."

Statistical techniques can add precision to data interpretation. Rather than saying, "Things are improving," or, "It looks bad from here," statisticians communicate more precisely with "up 16.8% from last year." This precision can also imperil judgment. Although statistics deal in probabilities, unwary managers tend to treat statisticians' numbers as superior to their own judgment. When data is faulty, as it sometimes is, this causes bad decisions. But when decision makers are fully aware of the dangers, statistical techniques become powerful tools. By looking at measures of central tendency, index numbers, time series, and correlations, we get a feel for what statistical techniques can do and how managers can use them.

Measures of Central Tendency

A measure of central tendency is a single summary value describing the general pattern of data. The most common measures of central tendency are mode, median, and mean. Before computing the measures of central tendency, statisticians usually arrange the raw data into an **array** — simply a list of the data arranged in increasing or decreasing order. If there are a lot of data, statisticians may develop a **frequency distribution** — a grouping of the data into broader categories.

The **mode** is the number that occurs most often in a set of data. In frequency distributions where no value occurs more than once, there is no mode. The **median** is the value that cuts the distribution in half. In 1982, the median annual income for families in the United States was about $18,400. This means that there were just as many families making above $18,400 per year as there were below that figure. The **arithmetic mean** — better known as the "average" — is by far the most widely used measure of central tendency. Figure C.4 illustrates these measures.

Index Numbers

Descriptive measures analyze data at a point in time, but **index numbers** measure change over specified periods. Index numbers are stated in percentages, and they are widely used to compare prices. A price index compares the current price to a previous base price by showing the current as a percentage of the previous. An index of 105 means that the current price is 105% of the previous price, a 5% increase. One of the most widely used indexes is the Consumer Price Index (CPI) issued monthly by the Bureau of Labor Statistics. The CPI, formerly called the Cost of Living Index, shows how retail prices change each month.

The CPI is a percentage of the average prices during the base period of 1967. Many labor con-

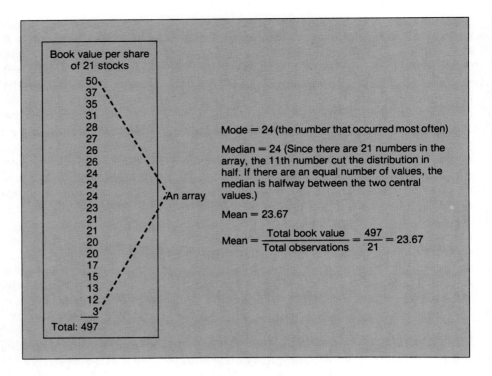

Figure C.4
Examples of measures of central tendency.

The figure shows:

Book value per share of 21 stocks
50
37
35
31
28
27
26
26
24
24
24
23
21
21
20
20
17
15
13
12
3

An array

Total: 497

Mode = 24 (the number that occurred most often)

Median = 24 (Since there are 21 numbers in the array, the 11th number cut the distribution in half. If there are an equal number of values, the median is halfway between the two central values.)

Mean = 23.67

$$\text{Mean} = \frac{\text{Total book value}}{\text{Total observations}} = \frac{497}{21} = 23.67$$

tracts adjust hourly rates according to the annual rise or fall of the CPI. Indexes are also computed on sales, production, turnover rates, and cost of raw materials.

An index is simple enough to understand, but many difficult decisions underlie its construction. A critical decision is the choice of the base period. The base period equals 100%, and it is the point against which current figures are compared. Although base-period choices are often arbitrary,

the base period should show some stability and not be too far in the past. When authorities change the base period, each index number is changed in the same way so that a series of index numbers remain comparable.

After settling on the base period, information requirements determine which items to include in the index. For instance, if a chain wanted to compute an index on its sales, they would include the products that most affect total sales.

TABLE C.1 ■ EXAMPLE OF INDEX OF PRICES FOR SELECTED ITEMS IN A RETAIL STORE

Items	Base Year, 1977	Current Year, 1985
Slacks	$15.00 ea.	$20.00 ea.
Belts	1.50 ea.	3.00 ea.
Shoes	22.00 pr.	28.00 pr.
Socks	1.50 pr.	2.50 pr.
	$40.00	$53.50

$$\text{Index} = \frac{\$53.50}{\$40.00} \times 100 = 133.8$$

TABLE C.2 ■ EXAMPLE OF A WEIGHTED INDEX OF PRICES FOR SELECTED ITEMS IN A RETAIL STORE

Items	Base Year, 1977		Current Year, 1985	
	Unit Price	Total Volume	Unit Price	Total Volume
2000 slacks	$15.00	$ 30,000	$20.00	$ 40,000
8000 belts	1.50	12,000	3.00	24,000
3000 shoes	22.00	66,000	28.00	84,000
5000 socks	1.50	7,500	2.50	12,500
		$115,500		$160,500

$$\text{Weighted index} = \frac{\$160,500}{\$115,500} \times 100 = 139.0$$

After selecting the base period and the items, either a simple aggregate index or a weighted index is constructed. A **simple aggregate index** (underweighted) compares groups of items to the base period.

$$\text{Index} = \frac{\text{Sum of the given year values}}{\text{Sum of the base year values}} \times 100$$

Rarely are companies concerned with comparing individual prices of quantities; groups of items project a composite picture. A major fault of the simple aggregate index is that it does not consider the amount of sales each item produces. The weighted aggregate index overcomes this shortcoming by assigning weights to the quantity of each item sold. Tables C.1 and C.2 show an example of these indexes for a retail store.

Time Series

Both index numbers and time series compare data over time, but **time series** aid forecasters by detecting past regularities and projecting them into the future. A time series is made from several observations at specific intervals; for example, a company might measure sales revenue of Product Z each month. If sales increased 10% this month, a 10% increase would be projected for next month. While reasonably accurate for the future, this approach is frightfully inept for the distant future. As

"An extrapolation of the trends of the 1880s would show today's cities buried under horse manure."

a British editor noted, "An extrapolation of the trends of the 1880s would show today's cities buried under horse manure."

Time-series analysts begin by collecting data and arranging them in successive time periods. Next, they examine the data for fluctuations and, by extrapolation, extend the data into the future. Four common data regularities are secular trend, seasonal variation, cyclical fluctuation, and random variation.

Secular trend data pursues a general direction over a long period. The trend may show long-term growth, such as the increase in gross national product in the United States, or may be contractionary, as the decline in the number of farm employees.

Some time series fluctuate predictably. Ice cream sales increase during the summer and decline in the winter; overshoes sales are up in the winter and down in the summer; and department store sales are highest during major holiday periods and decline in between. Regular patterns that occur within one year are called seasonal variations. For these roller coaster movements, a

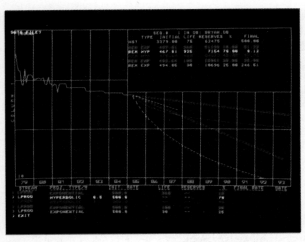

Using recent geologic and economic data and several contingency factors, a computer programmed for time-series analysis offered these projections of an oil field's performance.

25% increase in the summer and a 40% decrease in the winter does not necessarily signify expansion or decline. To project seasonal variations, analysts compare each time period's figures with an average to compute a seasonal index. Sometimes, managers want to see how sales would have been if there were no seasonal variations. Statisticians deseasonalize the data by dividing sales figures into uniform groups per time period. Managers look at deseasonalized data to determine if the actual increase was as great as might be expected for a typical seasonal pattern. Although sales increase 20% during the busy seasons, deseasonalized sales could show a 5% decline, turning an apparent growth into disappointment.

Cyclical fluctuations are up-and-down movements that occur over a long time period — usually several years. A business cycle occurs when the economy goes from stability to expansion to contraction and back to stability. Economists have developed many complex and intricate

CROSS FIRE

Is Census Data Valid?

By law, everyone must respond to all government censuses. However, since the government uses census data for very significant decisions such as redistricting members of the House of Representatives, people argue about whether the data is valid. Mayors of New York, Chicago, and Detroit, cities with a lot of blacks and other minorities, say that many of their people were not counted. Thousands of residents in these and other areas complained that they never received census forms, and the post office received many forms returned as "undeliverable." In New York, comparisons with welfare data show that the 1980 census undercounted welfare recipients by more than 8%.

The Census Bureau devises ways of estimating the undercount, but the law says that, for redistricting purposes, actual counts are necessary. The Census Bureau argues that its methods are valid and will stand up under the glare of public inspection.

Less sensitive, but also of some concern, is the bureau's reporting of other data. Since the early 1940s, the bureau has used sampling techniques for many of its surveys. For example, only a sample (19%) of all households were asked about such things as number of persons with a college education or number of homes with air conditioning. From this sample, the bureau projected results for the remaining 81% of the population.

theories to explain economic cycles, but there is little general agreement.

Despite the sophistication of statistical techniques, random or irregular variations do occur and they are unpredictable. Examples of things that cause irregular fluctuations are strikes, unusual weather conditions, and political conflicts. Rather than trying to predict random occurrences, it is better to prepare for them with contingency plans.

Some analysts assume that time series are composed exclusively of these four factors: secular, seasonal, cyclical, and random. If it were possible to measure how the components are related, time series would have more value as a predictor. But disagreements abound on whether the factors are separable or related, how they combine their influence, and whether there are other factors. On top of all this, time series assume that what has happened in the past will continue to happen in the future, and we have no guarantee of that (no city of today is mired in manure). Despite these concerns, time series are used extensively to forecast conditions for decision making.

Correlation Analysis

Correlation analysis differs from other forecasting methods because it measures the relationship between two separate sets of figures. Correlations have predictive value when one variable follows another or when one of the variables is to some degree controllable. Correlation does not imply that one set of figures causes the other to happen, merely that they occur in concert. In many cases, analysis registers correlations between births and baby food sales, high school graduates and university enrollments, advertising expenditures and sales, downtown traffic and department store sales. By pairing the data, experts can use one occurrence to predict the other. Relationships between only two sets of variables are

Finally, there is also a creeping concern about confidentiality of the data. By law, the bureau must keep all personal and business information confidential. They can publish statistics only in such a way that individual persons or firms cannot be recognized. Yet, with the magnified ability of the computer to check, cross-check, and countercheck data, some officials worry about the confidentiality of census data.

Do you believe that census data is accurate or inaccurate? Why?

___ A. Very accurate   ___ C. Somewhat inaccurate

___ B. Somewhat accurate   ___ D. Very inaccurate

Do you think that the Census Bureau should be allowed to collect some data by sampling? Why?

___ Yes   ___ No

Are you concerned about whether or not officials safeguard the confidentiality of census data well enough?

___ A. Very concerned   ___ C. Not at all concerned

___ B. Somewhat concerned

simple correlations. Sometimes we can relate several factors to the item of interest; this is called a **multiple correlation.** For instance, automobile sales might relate to employment, population, gross national product, and discretionary income.

To determine if there is a relationship, analysts plot the two variables on a graph, known as a **scattergram.** Visually, one can observe if the two items happen to occur in tandem (see Fig. C.5). Scattergram A shows a positive correlation: If y increases, x also increases, and a decrease in y accompanies a decrease in x. Scattergram B shows a negative relationship: As one of the variables increases, the other decreases; they are related but it is an inverse relationship. Through statistical techniques, we can measure the precise relationship. In some cases, it is easy to assume that one set of data caused the other set. One might reasonably expect advertising expenditures to cause a sales increase, and this assumption is probably correct.

Carefully analyzed data can either go unno-

---

ticed or have a sledgehammer effect, de-

---

pending on how it is presented.

If both increased together, statistics would register a positive correlation, but nothing in the statistical analysis guarantees that advertising caused the sales increase. Carefully analyzed data can either go unnoticed or have a sledgehammer effect,

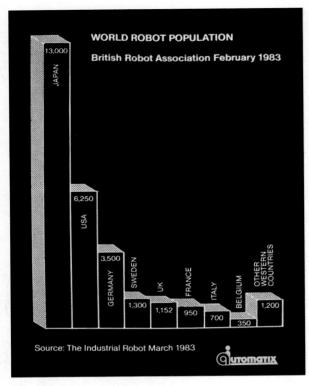

Bar graphs generally are used in presenting data for comparison.

depending on how it is presented. Information has more impact when presented in an interesting, understandable manner. Visual presentations are popular because they condense data and simplify comparison.

DATA PRESENTATION

Graphs offer several advantages in presenting data. They develop interest, they are easy to understand, comparisons are vivid, they save reading time, and their visual appearance makes the data come alive. But it takes imagination, time, and artistic skill to make graphs impressive.

Bar Graphs

Bar graphs are particularly effective for showing comparisons. Vertical bar graphs are adaptive for data comparisons at various time intervals. Dates

Figure C.5
Scattergrams showing (a) a positive and (b) a negative correlation.

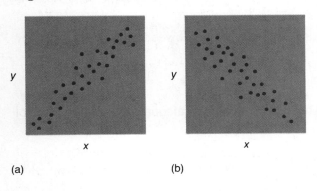

(a)   (b)

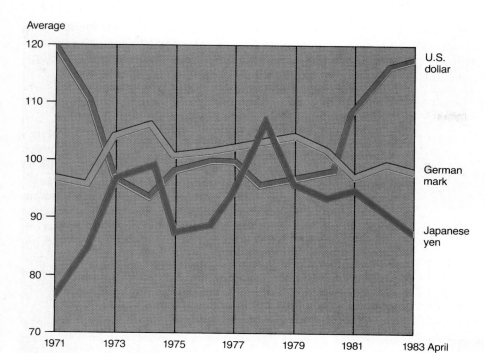

Average

Figure C.6
Example of a line chart: exchange rates, 1971 – 1983; March 1973 = 100.

appear at the bottom, and the length of the vertical bars measures the points of comparison. Horizontal bar charts are similar to vertical charts. **Pictographs** are charts that include small pictures or drawings along with the bars; their novelty probably has some attention-getting value.

This graph of variable effects of two fertilizer elements on crop yield is effectively a 3-D variation of a line graph.

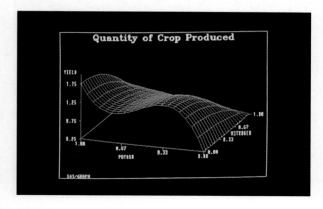

Line Charts

Line charts, also called curve charts and arithmetic line charts, are ideal for picturing trend changes. Line charts are easy to construct: the points on the chart are simply plotted and connected with lines. Several lines on the same chart make possible the comparison of trends. (See Fig. C.6.)

Circle Graphs

Circle graphs (pie diagrams) are especially suited for presenting percentage comparisons. The circle represents 100%, and the pie-shaped segments show parts of the whole. The federal government made them popular by using them to show tax receipts and expenditures, but the major reason they are widely used is they are so easy to construct.

Statistical Maps

Statistical maps present data geographically arranged by regions, states, or cities. Most daily

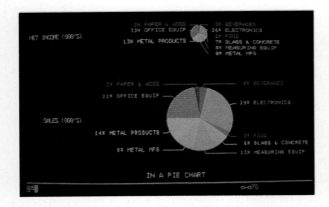

Circle graphs (pie charts) generally are used in making quick percentage comparisons.

newspapers present weather forecasts in such a form (see Fig. C.7). Companies may use colored pins, flags, and shaded areas to show store locations, sales by area, and growth plans.

Tables

When there are a large number of values involved, data are sometimes presented in tables. Tables have rows and columns, and each needs to be clearly identified. Notice that Fig. C.8 presents a lot of financial data on twenty-three separate companies. The titles across the top include "Recent Share Price," "Book Value per Share," and so on. These titles head up columns of data and describe the data in that column. For example, all the data in the first column show prices for a share of

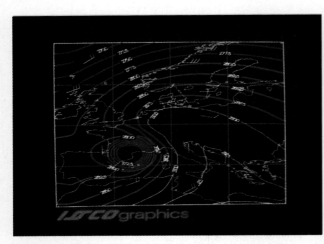

Computer color graphics can generate a variety of statistical maps to present geographic data in a clear and succinct manner.

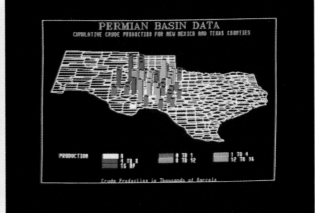

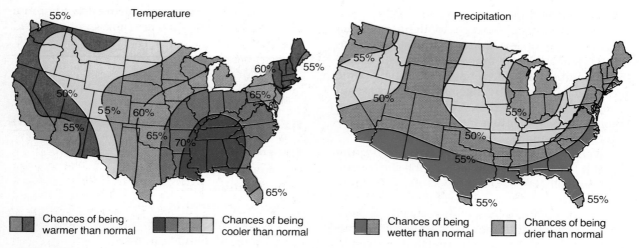

Figure C.7
Example of a statistical map.

Figure C.8
Example of a table. *Source:* Business Week, *December 26, 1983, p. 128.*

Recent share price	Book value per share	P-E ratio 1983 (est.)	1983 dividend rate	Yield (%)	Shrs. out. mils.	1983 market value change (%)	Institutional holdings	
							%	Number
45	68	12	2.36	5.23	16.6	58	55	99
44	42	10	2.76	6.31	137.0	44	45	496
28	13	16	1.15	4.05	24.4	102	38	104
22	25	NM	0.60	2.77	13.8	16	40	49
21	23	6	2.48	11.81	49.3	−7	40	246
57	27	14	1.16	2.04	12.5	46	57	68
11	15	NM	0.00	0.00	14.2	−19	73	41
50	61	NM	2.60	5.24	19.8	26	59	208
30	47	NM	0.50	1.65	24.9	28	57	136
19	15	10	0.95(d)	5.01	16.9	5	33	68
42	9	43	0.00	0.00	105.3	150	59	333
69	66	10	2.88	4.17	14.6	15	61	150
42	55	12	2.60	6.19	5.8	29	27	50
17	17	NM	1.20	7.01	66.7	−9	37	176
117	36	13	3.80	3.24	608.9	23	51	1492
32	9	16	1.04	3.30	36.6	14	43	170
14	−17	NM	0.00	0.00	35.9	272	18	52
47	39	15	2.60	5.56	26.7	47	55	161
32	25	7	1.76	5.50	8.1	5	35	48
59	66	17	2.40	4.09	49.6	22	60	369
39	38	8	2.32	6.03	44.3	44	56	232
50	28	10	1.80	3.59	5.3	19	63	65
51	83	5	3.52	6.90	8.7	24	32	83

stock. The names of the companies at the left identify rows, and each row contains data pertaining to a particular company. Tables tend to be cold and sometimes confusing, but a lot of data can be presented in a small space. They are useful as references or as detailed documentation for recommendations.

SUMMARY

Whereas accounting concentrates on financial data, statistical methods broaden analysis to include a wider variety of information. Internal data is information the company generates during its operations, and external data comes from outside the company. Secondary data sources represent data already gathered and published. Most secondary data comes from government, sources, commercial publications, and professional groups. Primary data is data gathered for the first time. Companies use surveys, observations, and experiments to provide primary information. All these methods rely heavily upon sampling.

After collection, decision makers analyze data to select a course of action. Basic statistical tools for analysis include measures of central tendency, index numbers, time series, and correlations. Statistics use summary measures to identify characteristics of a set of data. Common measures of central tendency include mode, median, and mean. Index numbers measure changes over time. Time series aid forecasters by detecting historical regularities and projecting them into the future. Correlation analysis measures the relationships between two or more sets of figures.

Well-analyzed data must be presented properly if it is to have an impact. Graphs show comparisons well, are easy to understand, and require little reading. There are several kinds of graphs. Bar graphs compare data with vertically or horizontally drawn bars. Line charts, which are points plotted over time, are widely used to show trends. Circle graphs, or pie diagrams, are popular for comparing percentages, and statistical maps use pins, flags, and shaded areas to compare geographic regions. Tables are useful for presenting a lot of information in a short space.

MIND YOUR BUSINESS

Instructions. Indicate whether the following statements are true or false.

____ 1. Secondary data is more expensive to gather than primary data.

____ 2. The *Census of the Population,* a government publication, would be an example of a secondary source of data to a company.

____ 3. Although there are various methods of sampling populations, random sampling is the simplest sampling method.

____ 4. Surveys are used to collect secondary data.

____ 5. Experimentation is especially useful to companies for testing new product ideas or advertising effectiveness.

____ 6. The mean is an example of a measure of central tendency.

____ 7. Both index numbers and time series compare data over time.

____ 8. Correlation analysis identifies causal relationships between separate sets of data.

____ 9. Bar graphs are particularly effective for showing trend changes.

____ 10. Graphs are more effective for communicating data than are tables.

See answers at the back of the book.

KEY TERMS

REVIEW QUESTIONS

1. Distinguish between internal and external data. Give an example of each.

2. Identify major sources of secondary data and explain the type of information they contain.

3. How does primary data differ from secondary data?

4. What are surveys? How are they conducted? Identify their strengths and disadvantages.

5. Distinguish between observation and experimentation as means of collecting data.

6. How is sampling employed in data collection? Explain the major means of sampling.

7. Explain how measures of central tendency assist the decision maker in analyzing data.

8. Compare index numbers to measures of central tendency. How are they similar? Different?

9. What are the major problems in constructing index numbers? How are the indexes computed?

10. What is the purpose of time series? Explain the different ways data tend to behave over time.

11. What does correlation analysis try to do that other statistical methods do not accomplish?

12. What are the characteristics of a graph? Describe the more popular kinds of graphs.

13. When should tables be used to present data?

CASES

Case C.1: Compute a Price Index

The Fluctuation Company would like to get an accurate indication of the price of their products as compared to a previous typical period. They have selected 1975 as the base year and wish to compute a price index. Relevant data are presented in the table.

Items	Part No.	Unit Price (1975)	Unit Price (1985)
3000	Part 68-A	$4.95	$10.20
8100	Part 68-C	3.17	6.75
6400	Part 68-B	1.05	2.15
3700	Part 69-A	3.75	7.20
6800	Part 69-B	2.06	4.35

Questions

1. Compute the simple aggregate index. Compute the weighted aggregate index. Analyze the differences in the two indexes.

2. List as many reasons as you can think of why they chose 1975 as their base period.

Case C.2: A Leading Research Organization

The A. C. Nielsen Company, widely known for its television ratings, is one of the largest private research organizations in the country. Nielsen employs over 8000 people who survey households throughout the United States. They provide data to companies on such topics as characteristics of television viewing audiences, recognition of advertising messages, and profiles of product users. Often the company reports on a small sample that is randomly selected. Companies pay substantial fees for this research expertise, and they make significant management decisions based on the data.

Questions

1. Why would companies be willing to pay a research organization for such information?

2. How are such research organizations able to obtain reliable data from small sample sizes?

3. Have you ever been sampled by a nationwide polling organization? Do you know anyone who has? If so, what questions were asked? What did you think of the survey?

After completing this chapter, you will be able to:

■ Define computer and identify five
computer generations.

■ Explain computer hardware, including memory,
central processing unit (CPU), and input/
output (I/O).

■ Understand three processing modes: batch
processing, on-line processing, and time-sharing.

■ Define nine key components of personal
computers.

■ Describe five kinds of business-oriented
software for personal computers, including word
processing, electronic spreadsheet, and others.

■ Discuss five ways that businesses use
computers including networking, data banks,
teleconferencing, electronic mail, and
telecommuting.

■ Discuss computer sabotage and
security measures.

■ Explain three other social implications of
computers, including privacy invasion,
depersonalization, and technical unemployment.

21

THE ROLE OF
THE COMPUTER

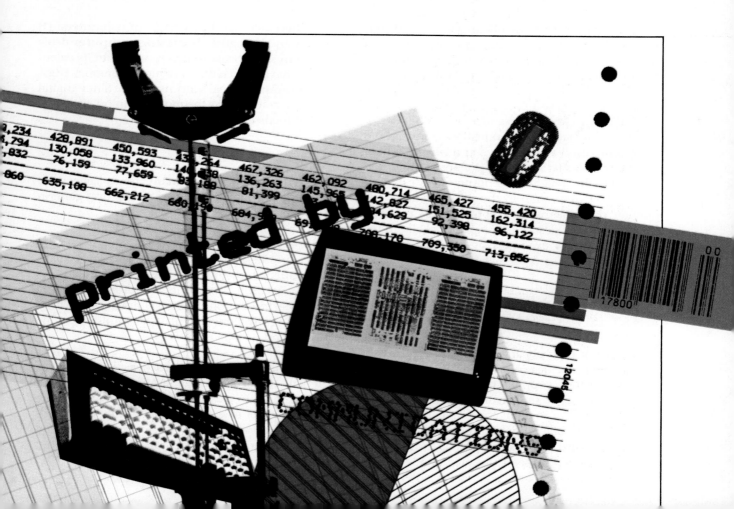

Since late 1980, Ford Motor Company has bought 2000 personal computers to help boost productivity in the office. Used mainly for financial planning, most of their personal computers pay for themselves within nine months. For example, they use the computers to prepare budgets for each area in the company; then they consolidate the individual budgets into an overall budget. The time and cost to do this manually would be prohibitive, but with the computers it is quick and easy.

San-Val Engineering, a Los Angeles-based construction company, experienced 60% growth in a short time. The payroll grew to $40,000 per week; and the company had to keep carloads of records on material costs, subcontractor costs, schedules, contract bids, inventory, accounts payable, and the like. Steve Veres, the president, said, "We were juggling scores of subcontractors and millions of dollars daily. . . . Job cost control had to be automated." Veres approached a computer dealer and asked for a complete business system. In a short time, they had most of their records on a computer and were able to provide daily information on fifty to seventy-five jobs.

"Nothing has affected industry as much as the computer," said an executive at a recent annual meeting. "But that is not all. We are likely to see even more impact of the computer on our lives in the next 10 years than in the previous 30." This chapter describes what a computer is, explains how one works, describes the personal computer impact, provides examples of business applications, and touches on social implications of the computer.

WHAT IS A COMPUTER?

A **computer** is simply an electronic machine that stores and processes information in accordance with instructions supplied to it. Charles Babbage, in 1830 at Cambridge University in England, designed the first automatic computer. He called it the "analytical machine." But Professor Howard Aiken at Harvard University designed the first successful general purpose computer in 1944. UNI-VAC I, built by Sperry Rand, was the first computer intended for commercial use. From 1951 to 1963, the United States Bureau of Census used the large and cumbersome UNIVAC I to collect and analyze census data. Today, along with the Wright brothers' plane, it is in the Smithsonian Institute.

There are two basic types of computers: (1) analog and (2) digital. An **analog computer** deals with physical measurements, and all of its calculations have to do with these measurements. **Digital computers** deal with numbers. Since digital computers are by far the more common, they will be the focus of this chapter.

Computer Generations

Modern computers are many times faster and hundreds of times smaller than the first generation computers.

First generation computers. The first generation computers of the late 1940s and early 1950s were bulky and slow by today's standards. Relying on vacuum tubes, they required about 400 cubic feet to store one million characters and they could perform only about 2000 multiplications per second.

Second generation computers. Appearing in the late 1950s, second generation computers replaced vacuum tubes with transistors, shrinking the computer's size and increasing its speed. These computers could perform about 80,000 multiplications per second and required only 150 cubic feet to store one million characters.

Third generation computers. Miniature components made the scene in the early 1960s, setting the stage for third generation equipment. A real breakthrough occurred with the development of the silicon chip. Silicon refined from sand, quartz rocks, and even clay is scientifically altered to create electronic switches for controlling electrical signals. This inert fleck is tiny, about a quarter of an inch square and flat, yet it has the calculating capacity of a room-sized computer of 25 years ago. Further, it is cheap, easy to mass produce, and infinitely versatile. Using **integrated circuits (ICs),** complete electronic circuits on a single chip of silicon, third generation machines greatly increased storage, processing speed, and reliability. They needed only 0.3 cubic feet to store one million characters, and they could perform 250,000 multiplications per second.

Fourth generation computers. Soon after the advent of ICs came **large-scale integration (LSI)** in 1970 and, in 1975 or so, **very large-scale integration (VLSI).** Respectively, thousands and hundreds of thousands of transistors were now

---

BUSINESS BULLETIN

Expert Systems

A branch of artificial intelligence that has met with sweet success is ''expert systems,'' computer programs that mimic human knowledge. General Electric needed a way to troubleshoot mechanical problems in train locomotives, so they picked the brains of their top mechanical engineers, encoded the information, and then let the computer go to it.

Expert systems combine textbook knowledge and a person's field experience. Using something called ''knowledge engineering,'' AI researchers interview one or more recognized authorities on a subject. Then they build an expert system by assembling data in thousands of logic rules. This is no small task; it's an enormously arduous, time-consuming procedure: a single program may run more than 50,000 lines and require years to compile.

So far, about fifty expert systems have been, or are being, built:

- ONCASYN is a system that helps keep doctors from making mistakes when prescribing complicated drug therapy for cancer patients.
- CADUCEUS is an expert system that diagnoses a variety of diseases.
- Teknowledge, Inc. has designed a system to diagnose oil exploration problems, such as how to salvage a shock drill bit.
- Westinghouse Corporation is designing a system for job-shop scheduling to minimize inventory and production bottlenecks in factories.
- Cognitive Systems, Inc., is developing a tax advice system that will fill out users' federal income tax forms, as well as advise users on what income must be reported.

Another thing that makes expert systems so invaluable is that they will preserve a person's expert knowledge. Such knowledge normally comes only from years of on-the-job experience and is largely lost with the loss of the person. But once the knowledge of leading authorities is encoded in an expert system, it will be available to anyone who has access to a computer terminal.

Source: Stanley N. Wellborn, ''Machines That Think,'' *U.S. News & World Report*, December 5, 1983, p. 60.

Scarcely 25 years separate these fourth-generation microprocessor and memory chips, and this first-generation computer, the IBM Mark I.

being packed onto a speck of silicon. Fourth generation computers are known for their astonishing reliability, speed, and compactness, as well as for their low cost and power consumption.

Fifth generation computers. Scientists are working hard today to extend the capabilities of fourth generation computers so that they can perform all the steps of a task at the same time.

Today's fastest computers will do 400 million calculations per second and can perform 100,000 calculations for less than a penny.

Today's fastest computers will do 400 million calculations per second and can perform 100,000 calculations for less than a penny. These machines cost between $5 and $15 million. The Boeing Company, in designing more efficient airplanes, uses a computer to simulate the nearly infinite variations in airflow around planes in flight. Will these supercomputers eventually be able to think like the human mind? That is the goal and that is the standard by which any fifth generation machine will be measured. "No reason we can't build them," says Stanford professor Dr. John McCarthy. Several experts predict that we will be able to program computers and robots with **artificial intelligence (AI),** giving them the human equivalent of intelligence, imagination, and intuition.

COMPUTER HARDWARE

Hardware refers to the actual physical equipment—the machines. All computers consist of three main parts: (1) memory, (2) the central processing unit (CPU), and (3) input/output (I/O). (See Fig. 21.1.)

Memory

The main memory (called core memory) holds all the data and processing instructions. It consists of two main sections: random access memory (RAM) and read only memory (ROM). Auxiliary or secondary storage refers to data stored on devices outside the main memory (for example, on magnetic disks and tapes).

Information stored in **random access memory (RAM)** can be changed, deleted, moved around, and added to. This is exactly what the computer does when calculating or processing information. RAM allows independent storage or retrieval of any piece of information; however, when the computer is turned off, all this information is lost. Of course, the information can be transferred to storage devices before turning the machine off.

Read only memory (ROM) consists of permanent electronic memory. It tells the computer what to do when it is first turned on. For instance, instructions stored in ROM tell the computer how to load other information. Manufacturers build instructions into ROM when they manufacture them; the user has no control over these instructions. ROM may also be used to hold instructions that are frequently used.

A **bit** is the smallest piece of information a computer can handle. Numerically, we can represent a bit as a 1 or a 0, but the computer represents a bit as high or low voltage. A **byte** is a combination of 8 bits (or 6 bits, but for our purposes, we'll stick with 8) used to record a single letter, number, or symbol. One byte of information can have 256 different combinations of ones and zeros (every possibility from 00000000 to 11111111). Put differently, a byte can identify 256 locations in the computer memory.

A **Kilo (K)** represents 1024 bytes of memory. The standard-size chip in the early 1980s was 64K, representing 65,536 bytes. (Computers can combine several chips into one computer.) Earlier, large computers had no more than 16K of memory. Personal computers today contain as much as 256K of memory. In 1983, Western Electric began marketing a fingernail-size chip containing 256K of RAM memory. The first commercial supercomputer, the Cray-1, contains 250,000 memory chips wired together with 70 miles of cable. The Cray-2, still in the design stage, by using 256K chips, will be twice as fast as the Cray-1. Large computers,

both in physical size and storage capacity, are called **mainframes.**

Central processing unit. The **central processing unit (CPU)** contains the arithmetic logic unit (ALU) and the control unit. The arithmetic logic unit adds, subtracts, multiplies, divides, and compares alternatives. This allows the computer to compare and select among alternatives as instructed. It is this process that people refer to when they say that the computer makes decisions.

The control unit coordinates all the computer's activities. It tells the memory and logic functions what to do and how to do it by providing instructions for storing, arranging, and retrieving data.

Input/output. While the CPU performs the major duties, **input/output (I/O)** devices are necessary to get data into and out of the computer. Punched cards, followed closely by faster punched paper tape, were among the earliest I/O devices, but more efficient means are now available. As computers increased their processing speed, they created a need for faster I/O devices such as magnetic tape and magnetic ink character recognition (MICR). MICR made it possible to skip the step of converting data from source documents to machine form. Special characters, like the ones on checks and deposit slips, are read directly from the imprint into a computer. Similarly, optical character readers transmit data from original documents to machine form. Optical

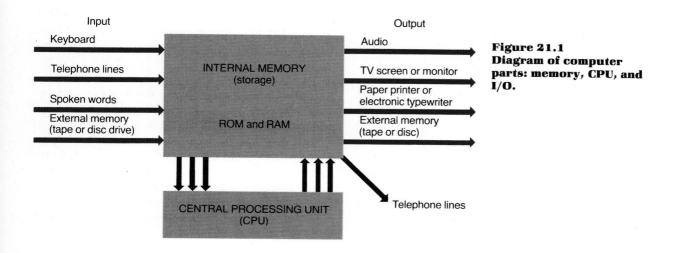

**Figure 21.1
Diagram of computer
parts: memory, CPU, and
I/O.**

readers scan data with a powerful light and special lens that distinguish between black and white patterns of reflected light. Giant Food, Inc., a grocery supermarket, cut all prices by 10% after installing computerized scanners at its checkout stands.

The typewriter keyboard is becoming one of the most common I/O devices. An operator simply types information on the keyboard, which transmits it into the computer. Most computers today have a **cathode ray tube (CRT)**, a television screen, where the operator can see the data as he or she types it in. Output also appears on the CRT. Computers can also receive and deliver information via telephone lines.

While voice recognition requires a lot of storage, researchers have achieved some success with inputs spoken carefully by individuals. And of course, computers can output voice via synthesizers that convert electrical impulses into sound. Finally, computers receive and output information previously stored on tapes and disks.

Much computer output is recorded on paper by a printer, a device that operates much like a typewriter. Major types of printers include dot matrix, daisy wheel, ink-jet, and laser printers. Printers vary in speed, cost, and quality of printout.

A **dot matrix printer** prints characters by using a matrix of ink dots. It is the fastest, easily printing 80 to several hundred characters per second (CPS); 100 CPS equals 1200 words a minute.

Laser printers, currently costing over $10,000, produce characters of typeset quality.

While the dot matrix is also the cheapest, the characters produced by it fail to meet the quality of standard typewriters. We have come to know this print as the "computer-printed" look. **Daisy wheel printers** have print elements shaped like a wheel with radial spokes and produce letter-quality characters. They are much slower and a bit more costly than dot matrix printers. **Ink-jet printers,** by spraying ink directly to the paper, also produce a letter-quality printout. And **laser printers,** using laser beam technology, produce characters of typeset quality. Laser printers currently cost something over $10,000, while a dot matrix may go for as little as $300. The faster and better quality the printer, the higher the price.

Remote terminals, typewriterlike machines located away from the mainframe and connected by telephone lines, make it possible to input and receive outputs in areas remote from the mainframe. Most remote terminals also have a CRT, allowing the operator to visualize input or output. When travellers approach a ticket counter at an airline to buy a ticket, the operator will punch in information on a terminal. The information — time of flight, destination, and the like — travels via telephone to the airline's mainframe. Within seconds, there is a response indicating whether a seat is available.

Processing Modes

There are three major ways of getting data into the computer: (1) batch processing, (2) on-line, and (3) time-sharing.

Batch processing accumulates data into similar groups and enters the data into the computer in batches. For example, a payroll program may accumulate the payroll data into groups before entering it into the computer for processing. After entering, the computer will process all of them before it starts on another program.

On-line processing means that each piece of data is transmitted into the computer as it is received. On-line is more popular than batch processing because it provides more up-to-the-second information. When a person calls a motel chain for a reservation, an operator enters the request directly into the computer. Within seconds, the person learns whether the room is available and the cost.

Time-sharing is where many different users share one central computer, each paying a fee for the time used. Users may be different departments within the same company or different companies that share facilities on rental-type agreements. If thirty users were to put data into the computer simultaneously, the computer would skip about, working on all the jobs at the same time. However, each user would get answers so fast he or she would seem to be the only one using the computer.

HOW COMPUTERS WORK

Modern computers work by switching, storing, and transforming pulses of electricity. Actually, computers are very dumb. They can only make "yes" or "no" decisions. That is, they read electrical pulse as high voltage or low voltage. A student may ask, "How can a computer accomplish so much with only two alternatives?" The answer lies in the binary system.

Binary System

Since the circuitry of a computer recognizes only two positions (low voltage and high voltage), the **binary system** uses only two numbers, 0 and 1, to represent all numbers. Humans normally use a ten-digit decimal system for counting and computing, so we have to convert the ten-digit system into a two-digit system for the computer. The accompanying conversion table shows examples of how we can represent decimal numbers in the binary code. For instance, the number 1 in decimal would be 00000001 in binary code; the number 2 would appear as 00000010.

Decimal Number	Binary Code
1	00000001
2	00000010
4	00000100
8	00001000

Notice that the rightmost column in the binary code equals decimal 1. Remembering that binary code uses only 0s and 1s, what eight-digit (byte-size) number following 00000001 would likely represent 2? The sequence 00000010 is correct. (10 is the first number after 1 that uses only 0s and 1s.) Decimal 3 is then 00000011; 4 is 00000100. To get other numbers, for example 5, you can combine the codes for 4 and 1 (or what number using only 0s and 1s follows 100?): 00000101 is right. Electrical pulses representing only two digits may seem like a thin resource for expression, but recall that telegraph operators sent Lincoln's Gettysburg Address across Civil War America using nothing more than combinations of a dot and a dash.

The binary code also allows the computer to represent letters in the alphabet and even the information in photographs and music. There is a prearranged binary code for each letter. For example, the binary code for the letter J happens to be 11000001. While this process may seem like a lot of work, remember that electrical pulses travel at the speed of light and computer circuits are so small that they can deal with thousands of characters a second.

Software

Humans must provide instructions for the computer to do everything. **Software** is a series of instructions, procedures, and rules dealing with the operation of a computer. A software **program** represents coded instructions to the computer to perform specific operations to give the user desired results. Programmers are individuals who actually write the programs. **Application programmers** write coded instructions that direct the computer through applications such as payroll, billing, cost reporting, and quality control. Since they usually work for a specific company, application programmers have to be quite familiar with the unique characteristics of their jobs. **Systems programmers** work on broader, general-use programs. Most systems programmers work for computer or software companies. Some businesses with large computers and a high volume of data processing may have in-house systems programmers, whose job might be to tailor other software to fit their particular company, implement new data processing systems, and train application programmers.

Programmers often use a **flowchart,** a graphic picture of the actions and steps required within a program, to help them plan their programming efforts. The flowchart uses symbols to represent process and equipment. Figure 21.2 uses five of these symbols in a flowchart of a program to record monthly sales. Flowcharts, by picturing the steps, improve communication between managers and computer experts.

Programming Languages

Programmers must write software in symbols, called languages, that computers can interpret. To improve program writing efficiency, experts have

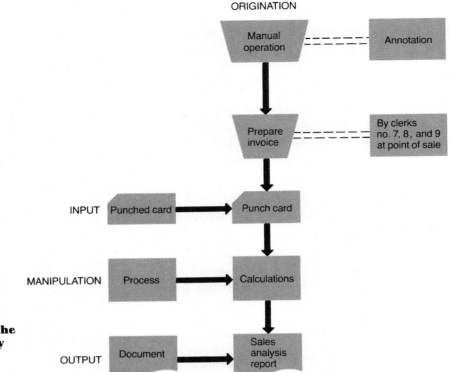

ORIGINATION

Manual operation — — — — Annotation

Prepare invoice — — — — By clerks no. 7, 8, and 9 at point of sale

INPUT — Punched card → Punch card

MANIPULATION — Process → Calculations

OUTPUT — Document → Sales analysis report

Figure 21.2
A basic flowchart for the
preparation of monthly
sales reports.

developed symbolic languages to replace the original, difficult-to-read machine languages.

Machine (low-level) languages. Early computers required programs written in languages acceptable to the computer (that is, 0s and 1s). Imagine trying to write a program where the letter J = 11000001. To make things even harder, each computer manufacturer made its computer a little different, and programmers had to learn different machine languages for each model they worked with.

Symbolic (high-level) languages. Gradually, symbolic languages evolved. Because symbolic languages were more like familiar English, programmers could write in easier-to-understand symbols. For instance, you might write PCT for percentage, A for add, and NAME for name. Since the computer cannot read the symbolic languages, **compiler programs** are used to translate the program codes into machine language.

There are many different types of symbolic languages available. **FORTRAN,** standing for Formula Translator, is the oldest symbolic language. Because it was developed for engineering and sci-

entific users, FORTRAN closely resembles ordinary mathematical notation. **COBOL,** Common Business-Oriented Language, was introduced in 1959 to meet the processing needs of growing business applications. COBOL so closely resem-

FUNNY BUSINESS

Source: From *The Wall Street Journal* — Permission, Cartoon Features Syndicate.

"Can you program the computer to cower in my presence?"

bles English that a casual reader can decipher its meaning. A typical COBOL statement is: MOVE BALANCE-FORWARD TO OLD-BALANCE. Perhaps the most popular language today, **BASIC** (Beginners' All-Purpose Symbolic Instruction Code), is very easily learned. It is especially popular for users of personal computers. Some oft-used BASIC commands include:

- CLEAR: Clears the CRT screen but does not erase information in the computer's memory.

- FOR . . . NEXT: Makes the computer do a job a specified number of times.

- PRINT: Instructs the program to write information typed into the keyboard onto the screen.

- SAVE: Tells the computer to put what is in its memory onto a tape or disk to be used later.

- END: Tells the computer that this is the last step in the program.

Figure 21.3 identifies other computer languages.

PERSONAL COMPUTERS

Designed in a garage in 1976, Apple computers paved the way for mass production of personal computers. In 1984, personal computers became a $16 billion industry. Nothing in recent years has equaled the impact of personal computers on business, government, education, and entertainment. And since the industry is still new, changes continue to occur seemingly at the speed of sound, if not light.

What Is a Personal Computer?

A personal computer (PC), sometimes called a microcomputer, operates according to the same principles of all computers; it is just smaller. Development of the **microprocessor,** an integrated circuit on one chip that functions like the CPU in a larger computer, made the PC possible. PCs are desktop computers used in both the home and businesses.

- **Assembly Language** — word abbreviations (or mnemonics) for the machine language codes. (Each CPU has its own.)

- **Ada** — a new language, designed for military computers embedded in other pieces of equipment. Similar to Pascal.

- **ALGOL** — an older math-oriented structured language. Mostly found on larger computers.

- **APL** — "A Programming Language"; an IBM invention, mostly used on their computers. Very good for mathematics.

- **C** — designed by Bell Labs; C is a general purpose language, but because it is new, it is not as easy to learn about as other languages.

- **LISP** — particularly useful for artificial intelligence and programs that deal with words and human languages.

- **LOGO** — particularly good at graphics, and designed for all ages. Originally developed at MIT, it is now used by hundreds, perhaps thousands, of preschool and elementary-school students; but it can solve "grownup" problems too. LOGO is derived from LISP, and is modular in construction, though not structured in the sense of Pascal.

- **Pascal** — a relatively new language designed to teach the proper structured approach to programming. It grew out of ALGOL, and is part of the same family as Ada and PL/1. Pascal is catching on quickly in the microcomputer market.

- **PL/1** — another IBM-designed language, patterned after ALGOL but with better ability to handle files so it can be used for business as well. Mostly used on larger computers.

- **RPG** — "Report Program Generator"; an IBM business-oriented language, only used on larger computers. It is more geared to handling files and data-bases than general programming; for most needs it has probably been superseded by newer data-base programs.

**Figure 21.3
Some examples of
computer languages.**

The IBM PC is now commonly recognized as the standard for the personal computer industry. Apple, however, is taking IBM head-on by trying to establish its Macintosh as a second industry standard (shown here with its predecessor, the Lisa).

Some companies produce very small computers like the Timex, Atari, and the Adam, sometimes called home computers, that are used primarily for entertainment and simple jobs. However, our discussion focuses on computers in the $1000 to $10,000 price range (beginning of 1984) such as the IBM PC, IBM PC jr. (once called the Peanut), Dec Rainbow, Apple Macintosh, Apple IIe, Apple Lisa, Apple IIc, H-P 150, Radio Shack 100, KayPro 10, and Zenith 100. To be sure, many consumers buy these for the home and use them both for entertainment and professional uses. But businesses also make extensive use of these PCs, and that is our focus.

In late 1983, more than 200 companies were making PCs, but IBM, Apple, and Radio Shack had most of the market.

In late 1983, more than 200 companies were making PCs, but IBM, Apple, and Radio Shack had most of the market. Osborne, once a top seller, had already gone bankrupt and Texas Instruments dropped their line after losing millions of dollars. Even though they were late getting into PC production, IBM (who else?) rather quickly wrestled

the top market share away from Apple. Figure 21.4 shows the market leaders.

Personal Computer Components

The components available for PCs are also available for larger computers, but many of these components have become closely identified with PCs.

Figure 21.4
Market share of PCs in the $1000 to $10,000 range. *Source: Future Computing, Inc.*

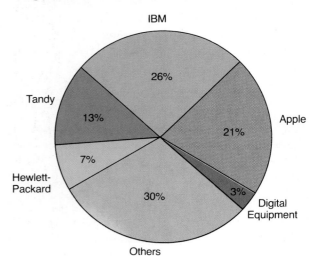

IBM 26%
Apple 21%
Digital Equipment 3%
Others 30%
Hewlett-Packard 7%
Tandy 13%

Keyboard. The keyboard is much like a typewriter, but it usually can do a few more things. Many keyboards have a ten-key adding machine pad, arranged like a ten-key adding machine, to make it easier to input numerical data into the computer. Keyboards also have **function keys** that carry out specialized instructions.

Monitor. The **monitor,** or cathode ray tube (CRT), is a televisionlike screen that allows the user to see input and output. However, PC monitors have a higher resolution than typical TV screens, that is, they can display sharper images. Because they have more image-forming dots (called pixels) within a given area, monitors may display images in color or monochrome, simply meaning one color. Monochrome colors are green, amber, and white (white lettering against a black background). Color monitors are nice for graphics, but monochrome is better for words and numbers because it displays sharper characters.

Some PCs, like the Hewlett-Packard 150, have **touchscreens** that allow users to operate the computer simply by touching the screen. They can edit a sentence, delete a line, or move a paragraph on the screen simply by touching it — yes, with their fingers.

Disks. **Disks** are thin, flexible plastic circles covered with magnetic iron oxide that record and provide access to data by computers. Cardboard envelopes with several openings and notches cover disks to protect them from dust and sticky fingers. (See Fig. 21.5.) These disks are also called **floppy disks, flexible disks,** and **diskettes.** The two most popular sizes of floppies are 5¼ or 8 inches square. A double-density, two-sided floppy can hold about thirty typed pages of manuscript.

Similar to floppy disks, **hard disks** allow the computer to store and read data; but because the magnetic material is coated onto a rigid aluminum disk, hard disks can store five to fifty times more information. The computer can access data two to ten times faster than from a floppy. Drives for hard disks, sometimes called Winchester drives, also cost more than drives for floppy disks.

Disk drives. **Disk drives** are special devices that rotate the disks and access information for the computer. **Read/write heads,** electromagnetic

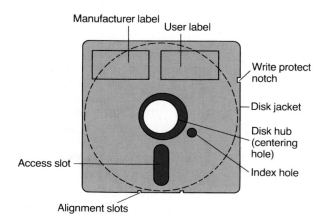

**Figure 21.5
A floppy disk.**

devices in the disk drive, read information from disks and write data onto them. Double-sided drives have two read/write heads allowing the drive to operate on either, like old-fashioned juke boxes that could play either side of a spinning 45. PCs typically come with one disk drive, but extras can be added if needed.

Disk operating system. **Disk operating system (DOS)** refers to the special programs and hardware that take care of all the details of controlling the PC system. Each type of computer has its own particular operating system. A common operating system that can be used on many different PCs is **Control Program for Microprocessors (CP/M).** With CP/M, a program can be written on one make of computer and run on another make that uses CP/M with little or no alteration in the program. Other examples of operating systems include MS-DOS (developed by Microsoft and used in the IBM PC and compatible equipment), Z-DOS (developed by Zenith and used in the Zenith 100), and UNIX (developed by Bell labs and used on a number of machines).

8-bit and 16-bit microprocessors. Most PCs operate on 8 bits of information at a time, thus the name **8-bit microprocessor.** But, more sophisticated PCs operate on 16 bits of information at a time, a **16-bit microprocessor.** Just coming out are **32-bit microprocessors,** PCs that process a string of 32 bits at a time. 16-bit and 32-bit microprocessors, since they can handle two to four times more information than an 8-bit machine, are generally faster, more accurate, and provide a wider range of options for the operator.

Modem. A **modem** is a device that connects the computer to a telephone and allows one computer to communicate with another. That is, information can flow back and forth, via telephone lines, between the computers. A **smart modem** contains its own processor and memory and is able to relieve the PC of many functions associated with its operation.

Printers. Printers can be attached to PCs that print out on typing paper or computer printout paper the information processed by the computer. Refer to the discussion on printers on page 564.

Plotters. Plotters are attachments, much like printers, except they draw graphs that the computer has constructed. Plotters can construct graphs of all sorts in black and white or in color.

TAKING STOCK

IBM's Success Story with Personal Computers

IBM entered the already-booming personal computer market in 1981 with a product put together with parts purchased from outside suppliers. Yet, within a 2-year time period, IBM PC sales captured the lead in market share. How did they do it?

To the surprise of almost everyone, IBM published its PC's technical specifications, showing exactly how the machine was built and how it operated. This strategy allowed other companies to write software for the IBM PC and to make additional products for it. As a result, software and accessories of practically every kind quickly became available for the IBM PC. And the published specifications made it possible for other companies to produce IBM-compatible machines that can use many of IBM's software programs and accessories. "The decision to publish the design was fundamental to our success," said Douglas R. LeGrande of IBM.

Before IBM entered the market, software and peripherals of one brand of computer rarely worked on another brand. But IBM's approach spanned several new companies. Lotus Development, Corp., is an example. Lotus invented the popular Lotus 1-2-3 software for IBM and quickly created annual sales of more than $30 million.

Not to rest on its laurels, IBM in 1984 came out with the PC jr. (also called the "Peanut" by practically everyone but IBM). The PC jr. comes in two modes: (1) an entry model with 64K of memory, cartridge slots for games and programs, and a detachable keyboard, and (2) an expanded model which has 128K of memory, a 360K disk drive, and other accessories.

With the PC jr., it looks as though IBM has made an ingenious market entry. The PC jr. will compete head-on with Apple IIe, another popular seller, without eating into the PC senior market. When compared to the Apple IIe, the PC jr. offers several advantages for games and education. But the PC jr. clearly is not designed as executive material, and few businesses appear to be opting for the junior over the senior model.

Interestingly, after IBM came out with their PC jr., Apple followed with its Apple IIc model. As the competition continues, customers continue to benefit from lower prices and better products.

Mouse. Apple developed a way to give commands to the computer by pointing an attachment they call a mouse. The mouse replaces typed-in computer commands. A user simply points out the command, from a list on the computer monitor, by positioning the mouse on the desk. A rotating ball inside the mouse translates moves of the mouse to the monitor. Then the user simply presses a button on the mouse to give the selected command to the computer.

Business-Oriented Software for Personal Computers

Just like large mainframes, PCs need software to make them work. Since users can program on PCs, they can write their own programs to fit their specialized needs. Or, they can hire specialists to develop customized software. But many software companies write programs for general use. Users can buy these programs off the shelf and begin immediately using them in their PCs. Off-the-shelf PC software is available for practically any business application imaginable, including payroll, accounts receivable, general ledger, forecasting, depreciation, and many more. But, the most widely used PC software programs are word processing, spreadsheet analysis, data base management, and graphics. Some integrated programs combine several of these features into one program.

Word processing. Word processing software, the most common business application of PCs, allows users to write, edit, revise, move, and format text for letters, reports, and manuscripts. Word processing software has two main functions: text editing and text formatting.

Text editing lets users write characters, via the keyboard, into the computer memory and onto the display monitor. Once users get the text into the computer, they can add or delete letters, words, lines, and paragraphs, and can move paragraphs and even pages around in the text simply by stroking a few keys. Good-bye forever to cut-and-paste efforts. With the text formatting feature, users can set margins, number pages automatically, and in some cases, select the type style for printed documents.

Many word processing programs, such as WordStar and WORD Plus, can do much more. After completing a letter or report, WORD Plus

Word-processing (WP) software has greatly enhanced document preparation capabilities in recent years.

will count the number of words written, determine how many different words were used, check spelling, and make suggestions for correct spelling of incorrect words. And it will do all this in seconds. Other special features check grammar or allow users to write and address letters to long lists of customers or prospects.

Dozens of word processing programs are available (a recent publication analyzed seventy-four different ones), and their capability and price vary tremendously. The Bank Street Writer, selling for around $70, will do simple things, while WordStar, probably the most powerful word processing program, goes for around $400 to $500. Some word processing programs will only run on certain computers: Quick Brown Fox brings word processing to the Commodore 64, Applewriter II is especially designed for the Apple IIe, and EasyWriter II is for the IBM PC. Others, like WordStar and Pie Writer, run on several different machines.

Electronic spreadsheet. Electronic spreadsheet software simulates business worksheets that have rows and columns. Users can enter column after column of related data, just as financial analysts have been doing for years with forecasts, budgets, and the like. But the difference is that with an electronic spreadsheet, when a figure in one column is changed, all other figures change automatically and instantly. This eliminates hours in figuring cost projections, and revised estimates are received in seconds, rather than days.

VisiCalc, the first electronic spreadsheet, is the best-selling computer program of all time. It was made to run on the Apple computer, and people wanted the program so badly they were willing to buy an Apple computer just so they could run the spreadsheet. VisiCalc, many people believe, contributed mightily to Apple's success. Now there are many spreadsheet software programs available, including Multiplan and a host of others. Before spreadsheets, very few people in business were doing sophisticated budgeting and forecasting because they had to use the big program on the mainframe and it was just too much trouble.

Data base. Data base software helps organize data files by many different categories such as name, size of order, zip code, birthday, last order, type of merchandise ordered, and the like. Headings or key words can easily be referenced for efficient and simple record retrieval. This replaces information that might be kept in a filing cabinet. Information can easily be added to, modified, or deleted. If a previous small customer began ordering large amounts of merchandise, by stroking a

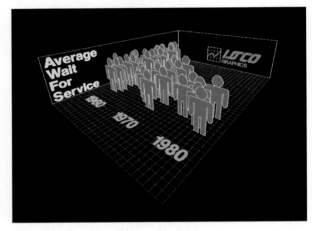

From simple bar charts to more imaginative multicolor graphs, business graphic software can produce a variety of high-quality presentation graphics.

The database capabilities of this integrated software allow data file organization by categories chosen by the user.

few keys, a company could move the customer out of the "small account" category and into the "large account" category. And data can be retrieved in many ways. Using PFS:File, for instance, users can design their own forms for storing data such as customer records, phone lists, and employee records. Every time a company wants to add, delete, or modify items on the list, they simply retrieve the form and make the change. A company can also get the names and addresses of all their customers who have a birthday this month, or a list of all the customers who have not made an order in the past year, or a list of all employees that have taken sick-leave pay within the past year. They get data in practically any form that they can think of.

Business graphics. Businesses use **business graphics software** to produce both analytical graphics and presentation graphics. Analytical graphics software helps the user analyze the data by presenting it in bar charts, pie charts, line charts, and the like. Rather than presenting a table of numbers, graphic software instructs the computer to draw pictures of the data on the screen. The computer can also be instructed to print the graph on paper if a graphics plotter is hooked up to the computer.

Presentation graphics software also produces charts and graphs, but this software produces a quality previously available only from a graphic artist. Analytical graphics have tended to sacrifice some flexibility or user control over output for speed. People making presentations want charts that look professional and they want to be able to change them quickly. Driscoll Agencies, an insurance and financial services company, uses presentation graphics when making proposals. An executive says, "Traditionally, when a proposal is made, you're looking at a ledger with columns and numbers on it which, for a lay person, is

Apple's "MacPaint" graphics software can allegedly produce any image created by the human hand.

rather confusing and difficult to understand." He adds, "We use graphics to, in effect, create a picture of that ledger." Driscoll previously used prepared slides in their proposals, but the slides were not customized. Also, presenters had to communicate what they wanted to a graphic artist, and

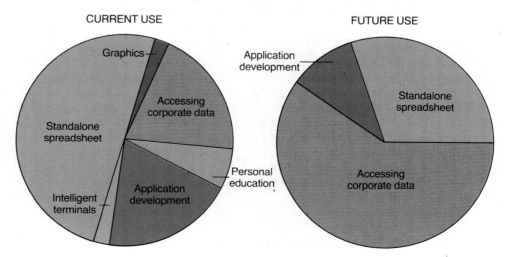

sometimes the slide did not come out as intended. In addition to the software, a plotter capable of drawing color graphics is needed. Many plotters will actually draw the graphic on acetate which can be used for overhead projection.

Integrated software. Many of the commonly used software packages once sold independently have now been integrated into single packages. For example, two top-selling integrated packages, PeachText 5000 and Lotus 1-2-3, include word processing, spreadsheet analysis, and data base management all in one package. Integration increases user convenience because users can do financial analysis, data base management, and word processing without switching the diskettes around in their PCs. Integrated software requires the capacity of at least a 16-bit machine.

HOW BUSINESSES USE COMPUTERS

Already our lives are flowing to the hum of computers in ways that we are not even aware. As *The Economist* magazine puts it, "To ask what these applications are is like asking what are the applications of electricity." Businesses use computers in thousands of ways, and it is estimated that there are at least 25,000 computer applications just

Figure 21.6
A guide to the Dow Jones data base.

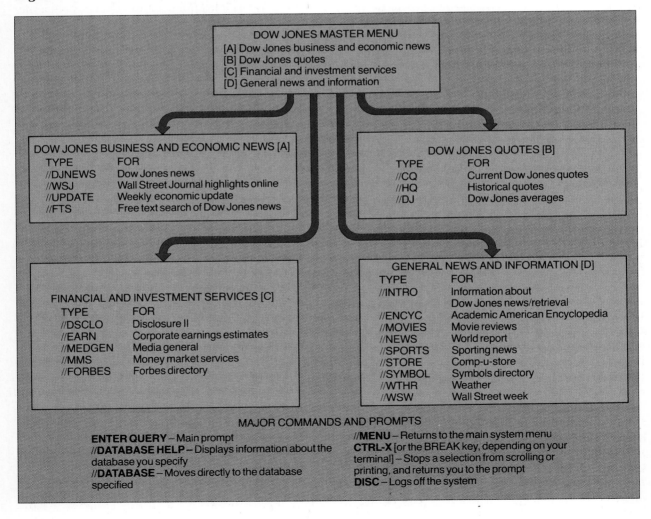

waiting to be discovered. To illustrate, here are a few of the ways businesses use computers.

Networking

A **network** is a multiple-user, multiple-function computer system of equal units. A local area network (LAN) might combine dozens of personal computers together, each identified as a **workstation,** within the same company but strung out among several buildings. Networks may also be tied into mainframes as well. Managers doing planning can transmit and receive crucial information instantly. In addition to exchanging information, a network allows sharing of files, electronic mail, and teleconferencing. Networks may also make it possible to share scarce resources such as an expensive printer or a single hard disk. Multiple users, via the network, can save money by sharing the same hardware. Ideally, local networks also combine the processing power of more than one computer for complex tasks. The Medical College of Georgia uses a local networking system to share its data base on patients among several departments. They also use it for word processing, financial modeling, and communications.

Currently, only 5% of all personal computers are connected to any type of network, but within 5 years, nearly 20% will be so arrayed. Also in the future, local area networks will be connected to other networks and will expand into larger user areas.

Data Banks

Data banks, sometimes called **data bases,** gather, store, and distribute data. Companies prepare data banks on many subjects and update them often, in some cases daily. With a computer, modem, and the proper software, companies can subscribe to a data bank and get up-to-the-minute information on practically anything. Figure 21.6 provides a guide to the Dow Jones data base, one of the more popular. Other popular data bases are Compuserve and The Source.

Encyclopedic data bases, **knowledge banks,** are actually electronic libraries, storing information on practically every subject. DIALOG, a major knowledge bank, has access to data bases containing over 55 million records. ORBIT and BSR are other knowledge bank companies. These compa-

AT&T's "Picturephone" meeting service is one of several teleconferencing systems that can link conferees from several different cities.

nies do not actually compile the information. Rather, they contract with numerous data base services which compile and update their own information.

Teleconferencing

Teleconferencing, or **telemeeting,** refers to the electronic linking of people who are located in different offices, buildings, or cities. There are as many kinds of teleconferencing systems as there are manufacturers of them. AT&T, for instance, in 1982 inaugurated in eleven cities its Picturephone meeting service. Using a digital network combination of satellite and land-based facilities, it provides two-way, full-color video, voice, and data transmissions between specially equipped meeting rooms.

Electronic Mail

Electronic mail is simply communicating with others via computers, using networking systems, modems, and phone lines. Winnie Shows of Franson and Associates, a public relations agency, says that her life changed the day her company installed an electronic mail package. Before electronic mail, it often took two days for a memo to get through to word processing, back to the writer for a signature, to the photocopy machine and

Electronic mail provides quick interoffice, intercity, or even international communication.

possible to get in touch with busy people more easily, and supervisors get status reports that people previously did not have time to do. "There is no question: Electronic mail has increased the professionalism of this agency," comments Ms. Shows. Figure 21.7 shows an example of how electronic mail works over a local network system. Users can also communicate electronically through data services with people in other states and nations.

Telecommuting

One of the newest applications of how businesses use computers is **telecommuting,** the process of commuting through the use of a computer terminal. Medical Mutual of Cleveland, Inc., for instance, allows many of its clerical workers to work at home rather than commute into the office. Each day they transmit data from their terminals to a central computer at Medical Mutual by telephone. Says claims manager Raymond Pritchett, "We've been able to reduce our in-house staff more than we expected because our home workers are pro-

back, and finally delivered by a mail person to someone's overflowing in-basket. Now, all Shows has to do is to type her message on her computer and identify the names of the people whom she wishes to receive the message. When these people sit down to their computers, the "you have mail" message greets them. Electronic mail also makes it

CROSS FIRE

The Good and Bad News of Electronic Mail

Although electronic mail, communicating via computers, is still relatively new, some criticisms are emerging. The benefits of electronic mail seem to be:

■ It is much easier to communicate notes and memos internally to several people within the organization.

■ Because people seem to be less conscious of status when talking on the computer, there is less tendency for one person to dominate in a group. The amount of communication tends to even out more than in face-to-face communication.

■ Because of feelings of anonymity, people are more likely to say what they really think and feel. There are more likely to be open, honest confrontations between levels of management.

The concerns seem to be:

■ Electronic mail does not allow users to see nonverbal cues or to hear the tone of voice of the other person; this reduces the accuracy of messages.

■ There are no social norms built around electronic mail; thus people are more likely to swear and insult others.

■ People tend to get involved with the machine, and this depersonalizes the communication event.

ducing twice as much as our people normally do inside."

Nationwide, more than thirty corporations already have work-at-home programs of this sort, involving personnel from clerical workers to pro-

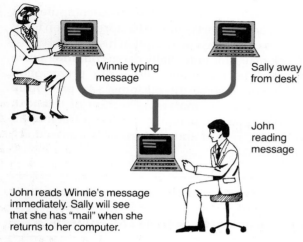

Winnie typing message

Sally away from desk

John reading message

John reads Winnie's message immediately. Sally will see that she has "mail" when she returns to her computer.

Figure 21.7
How electronic mail works over a LAN.

Telecommuting—working from home to the office via a computer terminal—can allow some working parents to balance their dual roles.

grammers. These "cottage-keyers" or "electronic home workers" frequently put in more than a 40-hour week, but it's on their own schedule. Moreover, there isn't the daily hassle of a commute. Though many cottage-keyers do not earn paid vacations or other fringe benefits, there are also no bills for office wardrobes or baby-sitters.

■ Because computers seem to be male oriented, they may work against equality of men and women at work.

Do you think that electronic mail offers more advantages or disadvantages to business organizations? Why?

___ A. Far more advantages

___ B. A few more advantages

___ C. A few more disadvantages

___ D. Far more disadvantages

What do you predict will happen to the spread of electronic mail in businesses within the next 10 years?

___ A. It will increase rapidly for a couple of years and then level off.

___ B. It will continue to increase at a rapid rate during the next 10 years.

___ C. Usage will not likely increase much more than current usage.

___ D. Ten years from now, electronic mail will actually be used less than it is now.

Examples of Specific Applications

In addition to the general computer applications just described, it might be helpful to examine a few specific ways that companies use their computers.

Manufacturing. Thirty robots, with computer chips for brains, weld new cars at Chrysler's assembly plant in Delaware. Once 30 men sweated to weld 60 cars an hour; now 30 robots handle 100 an hour and with fewer mistakes. In addition to being more efficient, the robots work more consistently than people; their work is just as good on Mondays and Fridays as it is on Wednesdays; they are never absent or late, and they never strike. In thousands of plants across the country, computers keep track of job costs, schedules, parts, supplies, labor hours, and utility usage, as well as monitoring the movement of chemicals, products, inventory of finished goods, and so on.

Office work. In probably the best-known study of its kind, the management consulting firm Booz, Allen and Hamilton, completed a study in 1982 on the impact of computer technology on white-collar productivity. The year-long study involved 300 office workers in 15 major companies and concluded that white-collar workers could realize time savings of 15 to 20% by using a more automated system.

The United Services Automobile Association (USAA) reduced its paperwork by 25% after installing an updated computer system. USAA provides auto insurance for U.S. Army officers and their families. The company processes 750,000 claims annually for its 1.3 million policyholders. The United States Forest Service uses 14,000 computer-aided workstations to keep track of mineral leasing, recreation services, timber sales, land management planning, and budget support.

Human resources. Illinois Tool Works, Inc., a Chicago-based manufacturing business, had fifty-three different forms in one division alone to handle personnel tasks. As Denny O. Wallace, Director of Management Information Systems, asked, "Isn't that an incentive to computerize?" Now, with computerization, the forms are standardized and processed much more efficiently. At Apple Computer, Inc., line managers, by using computers, maintain information on their employees. Each manager tracks salary, days missed, labor hours used, fringe benefits, and the like for employees. In this way, Apple has decentralized many of their human resource functions.

Retailing. Giant Food, Inc., uses computers in pharmacies in forty-nine of its stores to keep track of each customer's prescription history and cross-check drugs for potentially dangerous interactive effects. The computers also print prescription labels and invoice the customer. As previously discussed in the marketing section of this text, retailers also use computers to keep track of inventories, record and analyze sales transactions, and the like.

The University of Illinois uses its computer system to teach students 150 subjects, from Swahili to rocketry.

The list of computer applications is endless. The University of Illinois uses its computer system to teach students 150 subjects from Swahili to rocketry. Several U.S. hospitals are using computers to diagnose diseases. Computers help geologists pinpoint oil and mineral deposits. Researchers in England have created a computer "bionic nose" to distinguish subtle differences in fragrances—a potentially powerful aid to the perfume, brewing, and food industries.

SOCIAL IMPLICATIONS OF COMPUTERS

Because computers have touched our lives in so many ways, they have also created several social issues.

Computer Security

Within a period of just a few months, seven Milwaukee students, ranging in age from 15 to 22, illegally tapped into computers at the Los Alamos, New Mexico, government weapons research laboratory, Memorial Sloan-Kettering Cancer Center in New York, Security Pacific National Bank in Los Angeles, and many other institutions. Known as the 414 group, Milwaukee's area code, the students (or "hackers," as these computer enthusiasts are also called) met by corresponding back and forth through electronic mail. Eventually, they began meeting face to face and sharing information about their computers.

But in the summer of 1983, after seeing the movie "War Games," the group began earnestly investigating how many systems they could crack. "War Games" showed a student discovering the password of the national defense computer and almost starting World War III. The students often used a local telephone number that provided service for thousands of authorized users. Once they found a computer not in use, usually at night, they played around looking for the password. After getting inside the system, they would look around, usually finding records, files, and sometimes games.

Although this was a headline, high-interest story, the most serious computer crimes usually do not make such headlines. The more common, "dull" crimes include falsification of input, skimming payroll funds, and stealing records and money. Although no one knows for sure, security experts say computer crime ranges upward from $300 million a year. Employees have stolen millions of dollars by gaining access to the government's 16,000 computers. In one bank, the Security Pacific Bank in Los Angeles, computer thieves lifted $10.2 million before the theft was detected.

Computer sabotage. Besides stealing money and secrets, computer prowlers can also have a heyday sabotaging the system. By rearranging the software a bit, it is possible for an outsider to build a **trapdoor,** a simple code that bypasses all security devices and makes it easy to get into and out of the data base. Two programmers in Los Angeles have been charged with planting a "logic bomb" that would have destroyed payroll information for more than 400 Kentucky Fried Chicken franchises. A **logic bomb** is a piece of code that rearranges or destroys data under certain circumstances, for example, if a particular employee is terminated. Relatedly, a **Trojan horse** is a covert set of instructions that modify or replace an entire program.

Security measures. For each attack, there is a counterattack, but they cost money and make the computer a little less convenient for legitimate users. Three control measures include:

1. *Limiting telephone access.* A "call back" unit can be installed which answers the telephone for the computer and makes sure the caller is calling from an authorized number.

2. *Access control packages.* These rigidly control passwords and may also restrict the user to certain files and certain times during the day. These packages also alert security people if someone attempts to crack the system.

3. *Encryption system.* This system scrambles computer transmissions, making it impossible for an intruder to tap into the computer via telephone lines.

There are bills before Congress to make computer tampering a federal offense, and manufacturers and users are becoming more security conscious. However, illegitimate computer entry will probably remain an issue for years to come. As Dr. Phil May, a computer professor, said, "We have yet to learn of the most creative computer thieves because they are still operating."

Privacy Invasion

The powerful computer also arouses fears of government snooping into private lives of citizens. With 16,000 computers, more than 200,000 computer operators, and a cost in excess of $10 billion per year, the federal government keeps over 4 billion records on practically every person in the United States.

People can get their names on the government's records quite easily, and perhaps without knowing it. Of course, income tax records and social security records, which, between them, include most everyone, cause data to be recorded about people. But other things such as minor brushes with the law may also initiate records.

Much of this kind of information is necessary, but as the head of the Privacy Protection Study Commission asked, "What happens if this data that's being collected gets into the wrong hands? There is no reason to believe that someone won't come along at some point and abuse it." Recent action, both public and private, has moved to restrict the computer's invasion of personal privacy.

An industrial worker progresses at his own rate through an electronics course on the interactive Actioncode system.

Depersonalization

Much of science fiction portrays a future of machinelike humans and humanlike machines. Will the two, in fact, become similar? While the threat exists, it should be no more imposing than similar fears aroused by the Industrial Revolution. John Naisbitt, in his best-selling book *Megatrends,* demonstrates that as our society becomes more technically oriented, we also find ways to increase our social interaction with other humans. Naisbitt uses the phrase "high-tech" to describe this phenomenon. In fact, by eliminating jobs that are routine, boring, and dehumanizing, computers might add to the personalization and fulfillment of human beings.

Technical Unemployment

As with the Industrial Revolution, there are fears that the computer age will put many people on the unemployment rolls. And there is evidence that computers and robots *are* restructuring many of our industries—steel and automobile, for example—to reduce the need for hands-on labor. According to one estimate, intelligent robots or computers will replace more than 30 million assembly-line workers over the next 30 years, and it may be impossible, as some suggest, for these people to make the transition to computer-created jobs. "A fifty-year-old assembly-line worker will

not likely become a computer programmer, regardless of the training available," says a national training expert. The issue of how to deal with those people is expected to become one of the nation's economic problems in the years ahead. No doubt, fears of computer-induced unemployment will continue. But because of the tremendous potential of computers to increase productivity and reduce costs, these fears will likely have little impact upon their usage.

SUMMARY

A computer is simply an electronic machine that stores and processes information in accordance with instructions supplied to it. Computer hardware consists of the actual physical equipment, the machines. The computer memory, central processing unit, and input/output devices are examples of hardware.

Memory is the storage aspect of the computer, and the central processing unit contains the arithmetic and control functions. Input/output devices are necessary to get data into and out of the computer. Three major ways of getting data into the computer include batch processing, on-line, and time-sharing.

Computers work on a binary system, using combinations of two numbers 0 and 1 to represent all numbers. Software is a series of instructions, procedures, and rules that instruct the computer to perform. Programmers write software in symbols, called languages. Some examples of popular languages are FORTRAN, COBOL, PL/1, and Pascal.

Personal computers (PCs), sometimes called microprocessors, operate according to the principles of all computers; they are just smaller. PC components may include a keyboard, monitor, disk, disk drive, disk operating system (DOS), microprocessor, modem, printer, and a plotter. The most popular business-oriented software for PCs includes word processing, electronic spreadsheet, data base, graphics, and integrated software.

Networking, data banks, and electronic mail are popular general business uses of computers. More specifically, businesses use computers in practically every aspect of operations, including manufacturing, office work, human resources, retailing, and others.

Because of the widespread use of computers, society has become concerned about issues such as computer security, privacy invasion, depersonalization, and technical unemployment.

MIND YOUR BUSINESS

Instructions. Check your knowledge of computers by matching the items in the first, numbered column with the items in the second, lettered column below. Record your match by placing the appropriate letter in the blanks at the left.

____ 1. Third generation

____ 2. Computer hardware

____ 3. High-language

____ 4. 8-bit microprocessor

____ 5. Modem

____ 6. Networking

____ 7. Word processing

____ 8. Electronic mail

____ 9. Binary system

____ 10. Depersonalization

____ 11. Central processing unit

____ 12. Input/output device

____ A. Computer machines

____ B. Characterized by miniature components

____ C. 0 and 1 is an example

____ D. COBOL is an example

____ E. Operates on 8 bits of information at the time

____ F. Connects computer to a telephone

____ G. Text-writing software

____ H. Multiple-user, multiple-function computer system

____ I. Communicating via computers

____ J. Contains arithmetic and logic function

____ K. A social issue created by computers

____ L. Product scanner is an example

See answers at the back of the book.

KEY TERMS

REVIEW QUESTIONS

1. What is a computer? Distinguish between analog and digital computers.

2. Briefly explain the five generations of computers.

3. What is computer hardware? Software?

4. Explain computer memory. Distinguish between RAM and ROM, bit, byte, and K as they relate to memory.

5. What does the central processing unit (CPU) do?

6. Identify and briefly describe the input/output media for computers.

7. Explain three common processing modes.

8. What is a binary system? How does this relate to computers?

9. What is a program? Flowchart? Distinguish between application and systems programmers.

10. Discuss programming languages.

11. What is a personal computer? Microprocessor?

12. Identify and briefly describe the components of personal computers.

13. Identify and briefly describe the more common business-oriented software for personal computers.

14. Explain the following: networking, data banks, electronic mail.

15. Discuss four social implications of computers.

CASES

Case 21.1: The Computer and Privacy

As computers become faster and more widely used in business and government, the fear of invasion of privacy grows. Experts know that many of the current systems and data banks can easily be tapped by criminals or people who would use the data incorrectly. Government agencies say they take great precautions to keep their agencies from using information incorrectly. But as one authority put it: "There is no computer system made that cannot be outsmarted by somebody."

Some officials fear that many of the older systems are just waiting for someone to misuse them. The Social Security Administration is spending $500 million to modernize its computers and make them more secure, but it will be at least 5 years before the new equipment is in place. Meanwhile, an official says the system "is much too open to potential theft." In 1974, Congress passed the Privacy Act which requires, among other things, annual reports from agencies showing how their data are used and how much personal information is stored by them. The law also requires that before an agency can release personal data to another party, such as investigators or the press, they must determine that no privacy violation will occur. There are also strict restrictions on sharing personal data with other agencies or levels of government.

Yet critics say these efforts are not enough. Calls for agencies to reduce their private data have largely been ignored despite the privacy laws and Congress's concerns. Boards and panels are studying and recommending ways to protect privacy as agencies continue to collect data that is needed by them to make their decisions.

Questions

1. Do you think there is a real danger of your privacy being invaded through the use of government computers? Explain.
2. Make a list of what you think would be proper controls.

Case 21.2: A Medium-Sized Decision

A middle-sized manufacturer of parts for airplanes is using a traditional information system to keep management informed about inventory, costs, sales, expenses, accounts receivable, and the like. Several of the company's suppliers have suggested that the owner look into computer applications for his company and he has considered it. But the owner, Mr. Franke, knows practically nothing about computers, and he is afraid he will be embarrassed by showing his ignorance. He has noticed that his orders have not been going out as promptly as they should, and costs seem to be creeping up even though orders have been coming in at a steady pace for the last couple of years.

Mr. Franke's office manager is much opposed to the idea of looking at possible computer uses. Franke thinks that computers are electronic mistresses that chew up the budget and bring in a lot of experts that no one can understand. He is not at all impressed with the exotic "computerese" he has overhead at meetings where computer applications were being discussed. Mr. Franke senses that others in the company are also opposed to the installation of a computer, but he would like to consider the prospect. He thinks that his employees would be more willing to accept the idea of looking at possible computer applications if they knew more about them. He realizes that he is embarrassed by his lack of knowledge and suspects others are also.

Questions

1. Suppose Mr. Franke called you in to outline a program to explain the computer and its applications to his employees. Make a list of the topics that you would cover. Formulate an outline of the points that you would make about each topic.
2. What do you think would be hardest for the employees to understand? How would you try to approach these topics?
3. How much do you think managers should know about computers and how much should be left to computer experts?

DATA PROCESSING IN BUSINESS

The following list includes a variety of activities, personality characteristics, career goals and objectives, and skills and aptitudes. All have special relevance to careers in data processing. Put a check mark in front of those statements that apply to you.

____ I am well organized and methodical.

____ I have always been good at and enjoy math.

____ I would like to work in the computer facility of a large company, processing records and reports.

____ It does not bother me to work a long time at a task until it is completed.

____ I would enjoy investigating tax returns for any indications of fraud.

____ Working inside an office, oftentimes in a room without windows, or hearing machines constantly running would not bother me.

____ People see me as being a logical and analytical thinker with a high level of concentration.

____ I feel comfortable having to work with very large amounts of data that need to be analyzed and condensed into a report.

____ I do not mind doing clerical tasks.

____ Solving problems by using computer skills is enjoyable.

____ I have served as a treasurer of a club or organization.

____ I feel that I could convince my boss to accept my recommendation for a bookkeeping system I planned and designed.

____ I prefer making decisions based upon information that can be checked and verified.

____ Friends have come to me for help in solving their accounting problems.

____ I do not mind working by myself for a long period of time.

____ Performing statistical work is not boring.

____ I would enjoy the challenge of replacing an inadequate accounting system with an improved one.

____ I can do numerical computations quickly and accurately.

____ I feel it is important to pay close attention to details and to be orderly.

____ Figuring out the taxes that people must pay would be enjoyable work.

____ I would prefer a job where I follow established procedures.

____ I have experience keeping accurate records and maintaining an error-free checking account.

____ I am confident that I can compute costs and prepare cost estimates.

____ Writing a new computer program is exciting.

____ I want a job where I will study and advise a company about its cash flow and debits system.

There is no single set of personality characteristics, skills, and aptitudes that fits a particular job. Generally speaking, the more activities and self-descriptors you checked in this list, the more satisfaction you may find in this major and its related jobs.

Job Title	Job Description	Suggested Education and Training	Personality Traits	Average Pay	Outlook through 1990
Mathematician	Mathematical work falls into two broad classes: theoretical (pure) mathematics and applied mathematics. Theoretical mathematicians advance mathematical science by developing new principles and new relationships between existing principles of mathematics. Applied mathematicians use mathematics to develop theories, techniques, and approaches to solve practical problems in business, government, engineering, and the natural and social sciences.	Although the bachelor's degree may be adequate preparation for some jobs in private industry and government, employers usually require an advanced degree. An advanced degree is the basic requirement for beginning teaching jobs as well as for most research positions.	Mathematicians need good reasoning ability, persistence, and the ability to apply basic principles to new types of problems. They must be able to communicate well since they often need to discuss the problem to be solved with nonmathematicians.	Starting salaries for mathematicians with a bachelor's degree average about $18,000 a year. Those with a master's degree start at about $22,000 annually. Ph.D.'s average over $27,000.	Stable demand
Accountant	Accountants prepare and analyze financial reports so that managers have up-to-date financial information to make important decisions. Three major fields are public, management, and government accounting. Public accountants have their own businesses or work for accounting firms. Management accountants, also called industrial or private accountants, handle the financial records of their company. Government accountants and auditors examine the records of government agencies and audit private businesses and individuals whose dealings are subject to government regulations.	Training is available at colleges and universities, accounting and business schools, and correspondence schools. Although many graduates of business and correspondence schools are successful in landing junior accounting positions, most public accounting and business firms require applicants for accountant and internal auditor positions to have at least a bachelor's degree in accounting or a closely related field. Many employers prefer those with the master's degree in accounting. A growing number of large employers prefer applicants who are familiar with computers and their applications in accounting and internal auditing.	Persons planning a career in accounting should have an aptitude for mathematics, be able to quickly analyze, compare, and interpret facts and figures, and be able to make sound judgments based on this knowledge. They must question how and why things are done and be able to clearly communicate the results of their work to clients and management. Furthermore, accountants must be patient and able to concentrate for long periods of time. They must be good at working with systems and computers as well as with people. Accuracy and the ability to handle responsibility with limited supervision are important. Perhaps most important, accountants and auditors must have high standards of integrity.	Bachelor's degree holders in accounting average around $17,400 a year; master's degree holders average $20,200.	Great demand

Job Title	Job Description	Suggested Education and Training	Personality Traits	Average Pay	Outlook through 1990
Bookkeeper	Bookkeepers maintain systematic and up-to-date records of accounts and business transactions. They also prepare periodic financial statements showing all money received and paid out. The duties of bookkeeping workers vary with the size of the business. However, virtually all of them use calculating machines each day. Many use check-writing and bookkeeping machines.	High school graduates who have taken business arithmetic, bookkeeping, and principles of accounting meet the minimum requirements for most bookkeeping jobs. Many employers prefer applicants who have completed business courses at a community or junior college or business school. The ability to use bookkeeping machines and computers is an asset.	Bookkeeping workers need to be good at working with numbers and concentrating on details. Small mistakes can be very serious in this field, so bookkeepers need to be careful, accurate, and orderly in their work. Because they often work with others, bookkeepers should be cooperative and able to work as part of a team.	Salaries for bookkeepers are generally between $9,500 and $20,000 a year.	Great demand
Systems analyst	Many essential business functions and scientific research projects depend on systems analysts to plan efficient methods of processing data and handling the results. Analysts begin an assignment by discussing the data processing problem with managers or specialists. Once a system has been developed, analysts prepare charts and diagrams that describe its operation in terms that managers or customers can understand. If the system is accepted, systems analysts translate the logical requirements of the system into the capability of the computer.	There is no universally acceptable way of preparing for a job as a systems analyst because employers' preferences depend on the work being done. However, college graduates generally are sought for these jobs. Employers usually want analysts with a background in accounting, business management, or economics for work in a business environment, whereas a background in the physical sciences, mathematics, or engineering is preferred for work in scientifically oriented organizations. A growing number of employers seek applicants who have a degree in computer science.	Systems analysts must be able to think logically and should like working with ideas. They often deal with a number of tasks simultaneously. The ability to concentrate and pay close attention to detail also is important. Although systems analysts often work independently, they also work in teams on large projects. They must be able to communicate effectively with technical personnel, such as programmers, as well as with clients who have no computer background.	Earnings for beginning systems analysts in private industry average about $28,000. Experienced workers can earn from $28,000 to $42,000.	Great demand

Job Title	Job Description	Suggested Education and Training	Personality Traits	Average Pay	Outlook through 1990
Programmer	Programmers must write detailed instructions called programs that list in a logical order the steps the machine must follow to organize data, solve a problem, or do some other task. Programmers usually work from descriptions prepared by systems analysts who have carefully studied the task that the computer system is going to perform. These contain a detailed list of the steps the computer must follow. An applications programmer then writes the specific program for the problem, by breaking down each step into a series of coded instructions using one of the languages developed especially for computers.	There are no universal training requirements for programmers because employers' needs vary. Most programmers are college graduates; others have taken special courses in computer programming to supplement their experience in fields such as accounting or inventory control. Employers using computers for scientific or engineering applications prefer college graduates who have degrees in computer or information science, mathematics, engineering, or the physical sciences. Graduate degrees are required for some jobs. Very few scientific organizations are interested in applicants who have no college training.	In hiring programmers, employers look for people who can think logically and are capable of exacting analytical work. The job calls for patience, persistence, and the ability to work with extreme accuracy even under pressure. Ingenuity and imagination are particularly important when programmers must find new ways to solve a problem.	Starting salaries for computer programmers range from $18,000 to $24,000.	Great demand
Statistician	Statisticians devise, carry out, and interpret the numerical results of surveys and experiments. In doing so, they apply their knowledge of statistical methods to a particular subject area, such as economics, human behavior, natural science, or engineering. They may use statistical techniques to predict population growth or economic conditions, develop quality control tests for manufactured products, or help business managers and government officials make decisions and evaluate the results of new programs.	A bachelor's degree with a major in statistics or mathematics is the minimum educational requirement for many beginning jobs in statistics. For other entry level statistical jobs, however, a bachelor's degree with a major in an applied field such as economics or natural science and a minor in statistics is preferable.	A facility for keen reasoning and an attention to detail are among the qualities of a good statistician. Good communications skills are also needed.	Statisticians who have a bachelor's degree and no experience can start at $15,000 to $20,000 a year. Beginning statisticians with a master's degree may earn $19,000 to $26,000 a year. Those with a Ph.D. can command $25,000 to $30,000 a year.	Moderate demand

Job Title	Job Description	Suggested Education and Training	Personality Traits	Average Pay	Outlook through 1990
Electrical engineer	Electrical engineers design, develop, test, and supervise the manufacture of electrical and electronic equipment. Electrical engineers generally specialize in a major area—such as power distributing equipment, integrated circuits, computers, electrical equipment manufacturing, or communications. Electrical engineers design new products, write performance requirements, develop maintenance schedules, test equipment, solve operating problems, and estimate the time and cost of engineering projects. Many are employed in administration and management, technical sales, or teaching.	A bachelor's degree in engineering is generally acceptable for beginning engineering jobs. Experienced technicians with some engineering education are occasionally able to advance to some types of engineering jobs. Many colleges have 2- or 4-year programs leading to degrees in engineering technology which prepare students for practical design and production work rather than for jobs that require more theoretical scientific and mathematical knowledge. Graduates of such 4-year engineering technology programs may get jobs similar to those obtained by engineering bachelor's degree graduates. However, some employers regard them as having skills between those of a technician and an engineer.	Engineers should be able to work as part of a team and should have creativity, an analytical mind, and a capacity for detail. In addition, engineers should be able to express themselves well—both orally and in writing.	Engineering graduates with a bachelor's degree and no experience average $24,000 a year; those with a master's degree and no experience, $27,000 a year; and those with a Ph.D., $34,000.	Great demand
Technical writer	Technical writers put scientific and technical information into readily understandable language. They research, write, and edit technical materials and also may produce publications or sales or audiovisual materials. Technical writers use their knowledge of a technical subject area—laser beams or pharmacology, for example—along with their command of language and versatility of style to convey information in a way that is helpful to people who need it—scientists, engineers, technicians, and the general public. Technical writers often use their writing skills in marketing, advertising, and public relations work.	People having a variety of backgrounds find jobs as technical writers. Employers seek people who possess both writing skills and appropriate scientific or technical knowledge. Knowledge of graphics and other aspects of publication production may be helpful. An understanding of communications technology and computers is increasingly important. Many employers require a college degree and prefer degrees in science or engineering, plus a minor or an advanced degree in English, journalism, or technical communications, or degrees in journalism, English, or the liberal arts and courses or practical experience in a technical field. Others emphasize writing ability.	Technical writers should be logical and intellectually curious. They must be accurate and able to organize a mass of detailed material. Persistence and patience are important because acquiring information is not always easy. Because they often are part of a team of scientists, engineers, and technicians, they should be able to work with others; this requires tact and a cooperative attitude. Technical writers sometimes work alone with little or no supervision, so they must be self-disciplined.	Starting salaries for technical writers average about $18,000 a year. Experienced technical writers may expect salaries ranging from $25,000 to $35,000 a year.	Great demand

Job Title	Job Description	Suggested Education and Training	Personality Traits	Average Pay	Outlook through 1990
Computer operator	Information is entered into a computer system by data entry personnel in a variety of ways. The keypunch operator sits at a machine equipped with a typewriter keyboard and an electronic screen that displays the data as it is entered directly into the computer. Once the input is coded it is ready to be processed. *Console operators* examine the special instructions that the programmer has written out. To process the input, they make sure the computer has been loaded with the correct cards, magnetic tapes, or disks, and then start the computer. They watch the computer console, paying special attention to signals that could indicate a malfunction. Operators must locate the problem and solve it or terminate the program.	Most often employers recruit workers who already have the necessary skills to operate the equipment. Many high schools, public and private vocational schools, private computer schools, business schools, and community or junior colleges offer training in computer operating skills. Employers in private industry usually require a high school education, and many prefer to hire console operators who have some community or junior college training.	Keypunch and auxiliary equipment operators should be able to work under close supervision as part of a team. They also must feel comfortable working with machines and doing repetitive, organized tasks. Console oprators, however, must use independent judgment, especially when working without supervision on second and third shifts.	Weekly earnings average around $250 for beginning operators. Experienced operators earn from $275 to $400 weekly.	Keypunch operators: moderate demand. Console operators: great demand.
Computer service technician	Keeping computer equipment in good working order is the job of the computer service technician. At regular intervals, computer service technicians service machines or systems to keep them operating efficiently. They routinely adjust, oil, and clean mechanical and electromechanical parts. They also check electronic equipment for loose connections and defective components or circuits. When computer equipment breaks down, technicians must quickly find the cause of the failure and make repairs.	Most employers require applicants for technician trainee jobs to have 1 to 2 years' post-high school training in basic electronics or electrical engineering. This training may be from a public or private vocational school, a college, or a junior college.	Besides technical training, applicants for trainee jobs must have good vision and normal color perception to work with small parts and color-coded wiring. Normal hearing is needed since some breakdowns are diagnosed by sound. Because technicians usually handle jobs alone, they must have the initiative to work without close supervision. Also important are a pleasant personality and neat appearance, since the work involves frequent contact with customers. Patience is an asset, because some malfunctions occur infrequently and are very difficult to pinpoint.	Earnings of computer service technician trainees are about $300 a week. Fully trained workers may earn $450 or more a week.	Great demand

VI

331,832   345,205
79,606   82,814   344,894
52,791   57,093   83,592   348,136   369
                     61,158   82,656   81
                               62,993   66

56,62

THE FUTURE OF BUSINESS

After completing this chapter, you will be able to:

■ Discuss four ways that government regulates business.

■ Explain how the government uses financial incentives to influence business decisions.

■ Describe the implications of deregulation and responses to it.

■ Discuss the impact of three major federal taxes on business.

■ Discuss the impact of three major state and local taxes on business.

■ Explain the influence of the government acting as a customer of business.

■ Explain the role that government plays as a competitor of business.

■ Analyze the question, "Is the government too big?"

Sign here
Your signature
Spouse's signature (if join

GOVERNMENT
AND TAXES

For more than 100 years, up until about 1960, large segments of our society pushed for more government regulation of business. The Populist Party battled the banks in the 1890s; the Progressives fought for increased control over big business in the early 1900s; and the New Dealers added a lot of regulation to business in the 1930s and 1940s. In the 1960s, however, experts began to argue that excessive government regulation was leading to inefficiencies in our economy. Eventually, the argument began to take hold, and of late, government has begun to relax its control over many industries. As we move toward deregulation, as you might expect, some critics are arguing that we should reregulate. We always have debated, and probably always will debate, the relationship between government and business. But one thing is clear: To understand how our business system works, we must understand the role that government takes in business.

Complicating the relationship between government and business is the fact that **government** is a very broad term encompassing elected and appointed officials at city, state, and federal levels. The federal government includes legislative, executive, and judicial branches plus the cabinet and dozens of independent offices and agencies. Figure 22.1 shows the federal government's organizational structure. Additionally, each state has its own system, and there are thousands of city, county, and community governments, which also have a significant impact upon business. For the most part, though, we will be referring to federal government in our discussion of business-government relationships.

Over the past 200 years, the government has developed such an intricate set of relationships with business that it would be impossible to identify all of them. A few areas in which the government exerts considerable influence include pollution control, education, reforestation, weather reporting, food and drug purity, public-interest monopolies, pricing, transportation, advertising, product liabilities, employee insurance, union-management relations, and many more. After pointing out just how the government regulates business, this chapter also discusses the government's role in tax collecting, buying, and competing. Finally, we look at the size of government.

HOW THE GOVERNMENT REGULATES BUSINESS

Government exercises some control over business in four major ways: (1) laws, (2) watchdog agencies, (3) incentives, and (4) informally.

Government Regulation through Laws

In England in 1410, a schoolmaster complained that a competitor moved in with lower fees and ran him out of business. The court ruled against the schoolmaster, saying that anyone has the right to enter the market and compete in a fair way. In the early 1900s, U.S. law also built upon this principle, and it has been reinforced through several cases. Currently, however, Spray-Rite Service Corp. is suing Monsanto Co., contending that Monsanto quit supplying them with herbicides because Spray-Rite was a price cutter. Several other retailers have complained that wholesalers and producers quit selling to them when they sold their products to consumers at a discount. Eventually, the Supreme Court will rule on whether these acts are violations of our laws. This is an example of how government regulates business through law enforcement.

At first, of course, there were few laws regulating business, but the depression changed this

Today, a labyrinth of laws regulates most all business activities.

philosophy. In the famous first 100 days of President Roosevelt's term, he asked for — and Congress quickly gave him — a long list of emergency legislation which involved the government deeply in the affairs of business. Today, a labyrinth of laws regulates most all business activities. We discussed many of these laws in previous chapters, but Table 22.1 details the major acts since 1932.

The common hamburger, which we buy, carry out, and gulp down without much thought,

Figure 22.1
Organizational structure of the federal government.

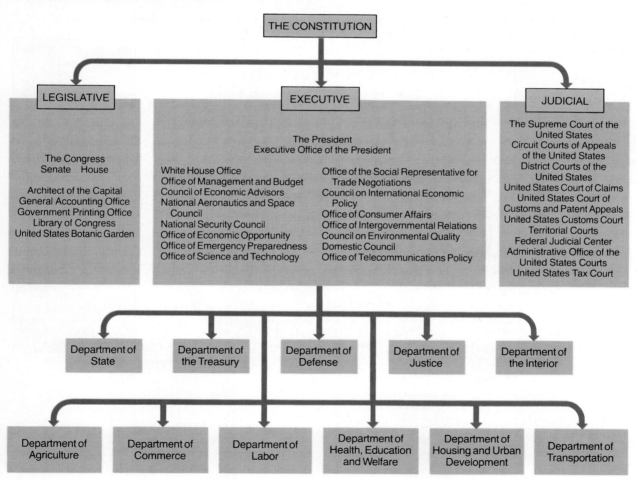

is the subject of 41,000 federal and state regulations. Many of these come from over 200 different laws and 11,000 precedent-setting court cases. Figure 22.2 gives a sample of these regulations.

Government Regulation through Agencies

Many regulatory laws have created permanent agencies that regularly monitor and regulate business activity. At latest count, the U.S. Government Manual showed 1245 such agencies. Figure 22.3 lists some of the largest agencies.

Government Regulation through Incentives

While regulatory intervention controls business directly, government incentives entice business. As a businessman described it, "The government holds out financial carrots to get us to do what they have in mind." The government offers three major types of incentives: tax credits, subsidies, and loan guarantees.

Tax credits. The government often gives businesses special tax breaks to encourage them to invest in capital. The goal is to increase jobs and

Figure 22.2
How business regulations affect the hamburger. *Source: Adapted from* U.S. News & World Report, *February 11, 1980, p. 64. Copyright 1980, U.S. News & World Report, Inc.*

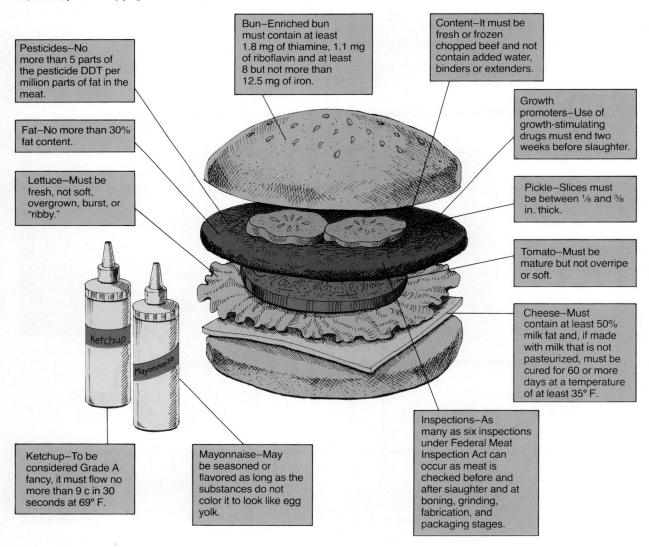

Pesticides—No more than 5 parts of the pesticide DDT per million parts of fat in the meat.

Fat—No more than 30% fat content.

Lettuce—Must be fresh, not soft, overgrown, burst, or "ribby."

Bun—Enriched bun must contain at least 1.8 mg of thiamine, 1.1 mg of riboflavin and at least 8 but not more than 12.5 mg of iron.

Content—It must be fresh or frozen chopped beef and not contain added water, binders or extenders.

Growth promoters—Use of growth-stimulating drugs must end two weeks before slaughter.

Pickle—Slices must be between ⅛ and ⅜ in. thick.

Tomato—Must be mature but not overripe or soft.

Cheese—Must contain at least 50% milk fat and, if made with milk that is not pasteurized, must be cured for 60 or more days at a temperature of at least 35° F.

Ketchup—To be considered Grade A fancy, it must flow no more than 9 c in 30 seconds at 69° F.

Mayonnaise—May be seasoned or flavored as long as the substances do not color it to look like egg yolk.

Inspections—As many as six inspections under Federal Meat Inspection Act can occur as meat is checked before and after slaughter and at boning, grinding, fabrication, and packaging stages.

TABLE 22.1 ■ EXAMPLES OF LAWS THAT REGULATE BUSINESS

Year	Name of Act	What It Did
1932	Federal Home Loan Bank	First regulation of home financing institutions
1935	National Labor Relations (Wagner Act)	Promoted collective bargaining and prohibited unfair labor practices by employers
	Social Security	Created national retirement system
1938	Fair Labor Standards	Provided for minimum wage, 40-hour week, overtime, and control of child labor
	Wheeler-Lea	Banned false and deceptive advertising
1947	Taft-Hartley	Extended prohibition of unfair labor practices to union activities
1954	Atomic Energy	Opened nuclear technology, under regulation, to private industry
1958	Federal Aviation	Centralized regulation of air safety
1963	Equal Pay	First key antidiscrimination act
1965	Medicare	First major federal regulation of health care
	Motor Vehicle Air Pollution Control	First major environmental law authorizing auto emissions standards
1966	National Traffic and Motor Vehicle Safety	Established vehicle and equipment safety standards
1970	Clean Air	Established basic standards and timetables for air pollution abatement
1971	Occupational Safety and Health	Provided for regulation of safety and health standards in work places
1972	Water Pollution Control	Established standards for federal regulation of water pollution
1974	Motor Vehicle and School Bus Safety	Established auto recall and defect notification

Figure 22.3
Some of the government's largest regulatory agencies.

Agriculture Department
(animal and plant health inspection; Forest Service; stabilization, conservation, and marketing services; commodity-credit functions)

Environmental Protection Agency

Department of Health and Human Services
(food and drug rules, medicare regulation)

Treasury Department
(tax regulation; Comptroller of the Currency; Bureau of Alcohol, Tobacco and Firearms)

Labor Department
(employment standards, occupational safety)

Commerce Department
(Maritime Administration, Patent Office)

Interior Department
(mine safety, land management)

Federal Energy Administration

Federal Deposit Insurance Corporation

National Labor Relations Board

Department of Transportation
(traffic safety, marine safety)

Equal Employment Opportunity Commission

Nuclear Regulatory Commission

Interstate Commerce Commission

Federal Communications Commission

Securities and Exchange Commission

Federal Trade Commission

Army Corps of Engineers
(inland waterways regulation)

Federal Reserve Board

Federal Home Loan Bank Board

Federal Power Commission

Consumer Product Safety Commission

Department of Housing and Urban Development
(housing regulations, federal insurance rules)

Justice Department
(Antitrust Division)

improve productivity. Currently, under the investment tax credit, businesses can deduct up to 10% of their outlays for certain equipment. For example, if a company buys $400,000 in production machinery, it can mean an immediate $40,000 tax savings. Congress also lets businesses use very rapid depreciation formulas to write off extra-large deductions during the early life of equipment. Thus, companies can deduct from their taxes as much as 58% of the cost of much new equipment in the first 3 years of use.

Subsidies. Congress also grants outright subsidies to some businesses, mostly agricultural, to influence them to do something the government desires. Usually, the subsidies to farmers are to

Figure 22.4
Farm subsidies and farm income. *Source: U.S. Department of Agriculture.*

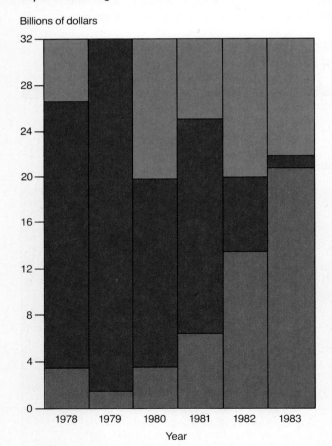

Billions of dollars

Year

■ Total government subsidies
■ Net farm income

encourage them to produce less. Very efficient U.S. farmers have created surpluses in grain, cotton, and dairy products. If the government did not intervene, the surpluses would drive the prices way down, causing many farmers to go bankrupt.

Under the Payment-in-Kind (PIK) program, the government subsidized farmers for taking some land out of production.

In the early 1980s, the government created the Payment-in-Kind (PIK) program to cut surpluses and curb production. Under this program, the government paid farmers to take some land out of production. In response, farmers idled 80 million acres. As a result, in 1983, PIK gave $21 billion to farmers, which was almost equal to the farmers' income from crops they actually produced. Figure 22.4 shows government subsidies to farmers.

Loan guarantees. In a loan guarantee, loans are made by banks or private lenders that Washington stands behind. The government, in effect, co-signs the note, agreeing to pay the entire interest and principle or a part of either in case of default. After the Chrysler Corporation teetered on the brink of bankruptcy with a $1.09 billion loss in 1979, the largest in history, Uncle Sam absorbed some of their problems by guaranteeing a $1.5 billion loan. Similarly, in 1972, the federal government guaranteed a $250 million loan to Lockheed Aircraft Corporation. In both cases, the arguments for the guarantees were that bankruptcy would cause investors to lose confidence, employees to lose their jobs, other dependent businesses to go bankrupt, and loss of taxes collected by the government. Classical economists argued that such government intervention would further threaten the principles of free enterprise.

While these two guarantees were highly publicized, they really represent only a small percentage of government-guaranteed loans. As of January, 1983, it was estimated that the government was liable for $350 billion in loan guarantees, more than double the 1972 level.

Informal Government Intervention

The government also uses its influence off-the-record. Informal intervention may be overt, such as the pressure President Kennedy put on steel prices in 1961 and 1962, or it may be covert (and sometimes illegal), as in the case of Watergate-related activities.

In 1961, President Kennedy sent telegrams to the chief executive officers of the eleven major steel companies pointing out that steel prices had risen more than 120%, while other industrial prices averaged only a 39% boost. He informed union leaders that employment costs in the steel industry had increased 85%, thus providing much of the inflationary boost that had adversely affected steel exports and the U.S. balance of payments. Government officials worked with union leaders, who agreed that the union would seek a modest 10 to 11 cents-per-hour increase in the form of a job security package. The union reached an agreement with management, and President Kennedy pronounced the contract noninflationary. The business community also commented favorably. A month later, the industry's top ten executives met and approved a 3.5% price increase. The president was so angered by the price increase that he and his advisors conducted a pressure campaign against the steel industry. Finally, Bethlehem Steel announced it had rescinded its price increase "in order to remain competitive," and the other companies quickly followed suit.

The Trend toward Deregulation

As early as the 1940s, George J. Stigler, Nobel economist at the University of Chicago, argued that government regulatory bodies eventually become captives of the industries they are supposed to regulate. And in the 1960s, many academics argued that regulation was working against us. They said regulation was subverting price competition in the markets. This, in turn, leads to production inefficiencies and higher-than-necessary costs and wages.

BUSINESS BULLETIN

The Deregulation Backlash

The Office of Management and Budgeting (OMB) says that the cost of the regulatory burden will be lightened by $150 million over the next 10 years. Regulatory agency budgets have declined 14% in the past 5 years alone, and staffing has been slashed by 16%. In 1980, regulatory agencies produced 8005 rules; in 1984, the number was down to about 6000 a year.

But there are pressures to slow deregulation, and in some cases, to tighten the noose a bit. There is a bill in Congress to reinstate the 5-mile-per-hour safety standard for auto bumpers, instead of allowing the shoddily built 2¼-mile-per-hour bumper, toughen standards for windshields, stoplights, and side body panels, and require air bags on some models by 1986. Many people believe that we need tougher regulations for hazardous waste and water pollution.

As the federal government deregulated, states upped their regulations. By the end of 1984, states had proposed 50,000 new rules, up 15% in 2 years. Companies worry that they will have to satisfy a multitude of different regulations for each state.

And of course, deregulation in the transportation, finance, and communication industries resulted in many bankruptcies and the loss of many jobs. Unions opposed this trend. Major changes such as deregulation always present controversial results, but there are signs that further deregulation will be slower and less significant as resistance builds.

Source: "Deregulation Runs into Roadblocks," U.S. News & World Report, December 12, 1983, pp. 81–82.

1968	The Supreme Court's Carterfone decision permits non-AT&T equipment to be connected to the AT&T system.
1969	The FCC gives MCI the right to hook its long-distance network into local phone systems.
1970	The Federal Reserve Board frees interest rates on bank deposits over $100,000 with maturities of less than six months.
1974	The Justice Department files antitrust suit against AT&T.
1975	The SEC orders brokers to cease fixing commissions on stock sales.
1977	Merrill Lynch offers the Cash Management Account, competing more closely with commercial banks.
1978	Congress deregulates the airlines.
1979	The FCC allows AT&T to sell nonregulated services.
1980	The Fed allows banks to pay interest on checking accounts.
1980	Congress deregulates railroads and trucking.
1981	Sears Roebuck becomes the first one-stop financial supermarket, offering brokerage services, banking, and insurance.
1982	Congress deregulates intercity bus services.
1984	AT&T divests itself of its local phone companies.

Figure 22.5
Steps toward deregulation.

Most of the deregulation, thus far, has occurred in three basic industries: finance, telecommunications, and transportation.

Further, regulation in practice was becoming a top-grade headache. Businesses complained that regulators required nightmarish reams of paperwork. Consumer groups shouted loudly that regulators were serving the regulated and not the consumers. As a result of this mounting pressure against regulation, laws and regulatory agency decisions began moving toward deregulation. Most of the deregulation, thus far, has occurred in three basic industries: finance, telecommunications, and transportation. Figure 22.5 traces the move toward deregulation since 1968.

Andres Carron of the Brookings Institution says, "The net of deregulation is that we're much better off." In real terms, long-distance airline fares are 50% lower today than they were 7 years ago. Many truckers' rates have slipped 30% or more. In 1983, the cost of standard telephones dropped by one-third. Investors, by using discount brokers, can save as much as 60% on commissions.

Labor costs in these deregulated industries are also falling. In 1982, the Teamsters signed a contract calling for pay raises at only half the inflation rate. And locals in some small trucking firms are taking 10 and 15% pay cuts. In the airline industry, unions are agreeing to more flexible working hours. And AT&T is demanding and getting concessions from its Western Electric Co. employees.

There have been some short-run adjustments, however; Braniff and a number of smaller airlines failed* and more than 300 trucking companies went bankrupt. While this is surely painful for the companies who belly up, consumers are still benefitting. Since 1978, fourteen new airline companies have sprung up to serve consumers, and 10,000 small operators have entered the trucking business. Figure 22.6 shows the impact of deregulation on air fares, truck rates, and phone bills.

Deregulation does not mean that the government will get totally out of business's hair. It just means that, for the near future, there will be less government regulation than in the past. There are some sound reasons to maintain a judicious

* Braniff, however, is flying again, having been acquired by Hyatt Corporation.

amount of government regulation, including:

- To protect individual rights.
- To strive for equality of opportunity for all people.
- To keep businesses from causing harm to the public.
- To help small businesses continue to compete with larger firms.
- To conserve our natural resources.

THE GOVERNMENT AS A TAX COLLECTOR

Federal, state, and local taxes in 1983 amounted to 35.1% of national income, but this was down from the record 36.4% of 1982. In 1950, the tax share was 27% of national income. The income of corporations, by law, is subject to tax rates of 15 to 40% of the first $100,000 of profits; the rate is 46% for profits in excess of $100,000. However, there is evidence that most corporations do not actually pay taxes at these rates.

Aside from the cost of taxes, both individuals and corporations have to maintain extensive records for accurate tax reporting. Some companies claim that they file hundreds of tax reports each year. Large corporations maintain a tax department just for that purpose. Today, there is a great clamor for simplifying and improving the complicated tax system. Some people criticize the rich and the large corporations for using loopholes to escape many tax payments. Almost everyone wants a better, more equitable tax system, but it will probably be slow in coming. This section summarizes the important federal, state, local, and miscellaneous taxes.

Federal Taxes

The federal government levies federal taxes on business and individual dealings. Major federal taxes include income, Social Security, and excise.

Income taxes. In 1909, the federal government first taxed business profits. Four years later, the government followed up with a permanent tax on personal incomes. Today, the net income of all private enterprise is subject to federal **income tax.** Personal income tax rates are progressive;

TRUCK RATES

Full truckload, rate per mi.

	1979	1983 Current dollars	1983 1976 dollars
Machinery and steel	$1.55	$1.11	$0.81
Roofing materials	1.11	0.85–1.05	0.62–0.76

HOW PHONE BILLS ARE LIKELY TO LOOK

Average monthly rate, residential

	1983	1984	1990
Local calls	$11	$20	$20
Equipment and extra features such as Touch Tone	6	3	3
Access charge	—	2	4
Long distance	18	15	11
Total	$35	$40	$38

Figure 22.6
Impact of deregulation on air fares, truck rates, and phone bills. *Source:* Reprinted from the November 28, 1983, issue of *Business Week* by special permission, © 1983 by McGraw-Hill, Inc.

AIR FARES

Lowest round-trip fare in the market

Big markets	1976	1983 Current dollars	1983 1976 dollars
New York – Los Angeles	$312	$358	$205
Los Angeles – Honolulu	240	256	146
Small markets			
Wilkes-Barre/Scranton, Pa. – Boston	74	205	117
Asheville, N.C. – Washington, D.C.	94	278	159

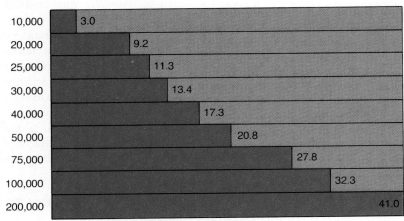

Adjusted gross income (dollars)

	Tax rate (percent)
10,000	3.0
20,000	9.2
25,000	11.3
30,000	13.4
40,000	17.3
50,000	20.8
75,000	27.8
100,000	32.3
200,000	41.0

Figure 22.7
How individual income tax rates increase with income. Figures assume a family of four filing jointly, with one wage earner and no itemized deductions, at 1983 tax rates. *Source: IRS tax tables, Department of the Treasury.*

that is, the rates increase as the income level increases. Figure 22.7 shows how personal income tax rates increase with income. For several years after World War II, the maximum bracket was taxed at more than 90%; today the maximum is 50%. But the government does not tax the income of partnerships and proprietorships as a special category. Rather, profits of partnerships and pro-

> In the past 65 years, while the population has doubled and the economy has grown eight times larger, the amount of income taxes increased 676 times.

Should Business Profits Be Taxed?

Although the government has taxed business profits since 1909, strong forces are opposed to the federal income tax on business profits. The arguments for doing away with corporate income taxes are:

1. Charles E. Walker, chairman of the American Council for Capital Formation, says, "Corporations don't pay taxes; people do." Many economists argue that corporations pass the tax burden to others: to workers through lower wages, to consumers by higher prices, and to stockholders through lower dividends.

2. Corporate profits are double taxed — once when the corporation makes a profit and again when owners receive their dividends.

Arguments for taxing corporations include:

1. Because of tax credits, corporations do not pay very much tax, only about 20% on their income, according to some estimates.

prietorships are taxed as personal income of the owners. Partnership and proprietorship owners file their tax reports on Form 1040, just as individual wage-earners do. In the past 65 years, while the population has doubled and the economy has grown eight times larger, the amount of income taxes increased 676 times.

Corporations, because they are legal entities, pay taxes on their profits. As we learned in Chapter 4, individuals also have to pay taxes on these profits when they receive them as dividends. A few years ago, corporate taxes amounted to 15% of all tax dollars collected; today, the figure is 9%. Figure 22.8 shows the variation in corporate tax rates since 1940.

Social Security taxes. **Social Security taxes,** created by the Social Security Act of 1935, provide for pensions, dependent children payments, disability benefits, dependent spouse payments, and the like. The tax is levied against company payrolls. In 1983, individuals paid 6.7% of their salaries, until they paid a maximum of $2391.90, for Social Security taxes. The employer also had to match this amount. As recently as 1970, the maximum amount of Social Security taxes was $374.40.

About 25% of all American families pay more in Social Security taxes than they do in income taxes.

Four additional increases are scheduled, pushing the rate to 7.65% by 1990. Because more people are living longer and therefore collecting more Social Security taxes, the Social Security tax burden has continued to increase. About 25% of all American families pay more in Social Security taxes than they do in income taxes. Because of this burden, many younger people are upset about forking over so much of their paycheck to go to the elderly.

Excise taxes. An **excise tax** is a sales tax placed on the manufacture, purchase, or sale of selected items. Although this tax is directed to the business, for the most part, it is passed along to the consumer in the form of higher prices. Some items covered by excise taxes are tobacco, liquor, gasoline, and automobiles. Whether or not the business is able to pass along all excise taxes to the

2. Big corporations are independent centers of wealth and power that should directly bear a tax burden.

3. If corporate income taxes were eliminated, corporations would not necessarily pass these savings along to their employees, customers, or stockholders.

Do you think that the corporate income tax should be eliminated? Why?

___ Yes   ___ No

What do you think are the probabilities of eliminating corporate income taxes in the next 10 years? Why?

___ A. Less than 20%   ___ C. More than 50%
___ B. Between 20 and 50%

Ideally, what should be the real tax rate for corporate profits? Why?

___ A. 10% or less   ___ D. 51% to 75%
___ B. 11% to 25%   ___ E. 76% to 100%
___ C. 26% to 50%

Tax rate (percent)

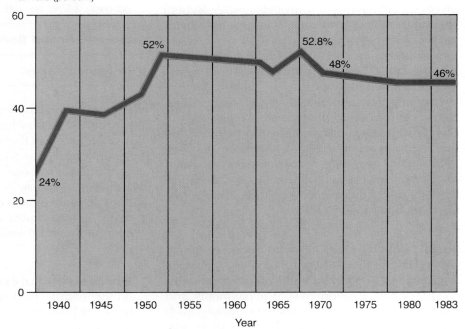

**Figure 22.8
How the maximum
bracket corporate income
tax rates have changed
since 1940.**

The trucking industry pays a variety of state and federal taxes, many of which are used to cover maintenance costs of the nation's highways.

consumer, the result is higher prices. If they pass the tax along, of course, the price is higher; but if they cannot charge all the tax to the customer, they still have additional overhead in the form of record keeping and expense for specialists. When the federal government eliminated the excise tax on tires in 1984, the big three U.S. auto makers reduced the sticker prices on their cars by an average of $10.

State and Local Taxes

Like federal taxes, state and local taxes both regulate business activities and provide a source of revenue for local government units. Although state and local units may employ corporation taxes, unemployment taxes, inheritance taxes, estate taxes, and special business taxes, the major areas include property, sales, and income.

Property taxes. **Property taxes** are placed on such items as land, buildings, equipment, and inventories. The taxes are usually based on an assessed value that is some percentage of the actual value. Real property taxes are placed on permanent, tangible property such as buildings and heavy equipment. Personal property taxes cover movable objects such as adding machines, inventories, and securities.

Sales taxes. Many state and local governments place taxes on the sale of items — a **sales tax.** All fifty states have sales taxes of some sort (either state or local), and most use a general sales tax on most goods sold at retail. The customer pays the tax, but the money is collected by the outlet selling the goods. To discourage the sale of certain items, most states place sales taxes on cigarettes, and all states place them on liquor and gasoline. Some states have a **use tax** along with their sales taxes. If people buy goods in another state to avoid local sales taxes, they will be taxed for use, consumption, or storage of such items.

Income taxes. States frequently tax income of individuals and corporations as a source of revenue. Many communities also add an income tax. State and local income taxes are levied on a graduated scale for personal incomes. But corporate taxes are figured by a simpler formula, such as a

BUSINESS BULLETIN

Taxes Lost in the "Underground Economy"

According to government estimates, $95 billion in tax money was not collected in 1981. Some private experts say the figure is much higher. Most of the lost tax money, over two-thirds, comes from underreported income. Other losses come from overstated deductions, illegal activities, and unpaid corporate taxes. The accompanying chart presents these figures graphically.

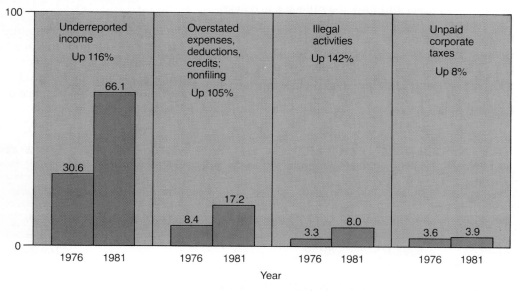

Source: U.S. Department of the Treasury.

© By permission of Johnny Hart and Field Enterprises, Inc.

rate of 6% on corporate net profit, regardless of how much profit is earned.

Miscellaneous Taxes

In addition to the obvious taxes, businesses pay other taxes as well. Some are imposed by the federal government and some by state and local governments. For example, the federal government has a use tax on heavy motor vehicles; an occupational stamp tax on some occupations, such as gambling and selling margarine; and a documentary stamp tax on some bonds, deeds, and insurance policies. State and local governments sometimes place taxes on such things as total deposits on hand in banks, and they may place a privilege tax on corporations for the right to continue doing business in a state. Of course, many professional people—doctors and lawyers, for example—have to obtain a license to practice, which is also a form of tax. Table 22.2 compares the tax sources in 1982.

THE GOVERNMENT AS A CUSTOMER

With federal expenditures of hundreds of billions of dollars, the government has become one of the hungriest customers of business. Military spending—national defense—is one of the largest government expenses. In 1982, the Defense Department alone awarded $116.7 billion in contracts to industry. General Dynamics, the top contractor in 1982, received contracts valued at more than $5.8 billion. Table 22.3 lists the top ten defense contractors for 1982. The business sector likes large defense contracts because they mean large sales, along with increased profit potential. In fact, military work accounted for 70% of the total sales of Boeing Military Aircraft Co. in 1983. Of course, the military establishment appreciates the arrangement because it allows them to obtain the weapons and other goods and services they want. Many people fear that self-serving interests are being generated because business and the mil-

TABLE 22.2 ■ A COMPARISON OF TAX SOURCES FOR 1982

	Individual Income Taxes	Social Insurance	Sales and Gross Receipts	Property	Corporation Taxes	Excises, Licenses, Others
			(Billions of Dollars)			
Federal	$297.7	$201.5	—	—	$49.2	$69.4
State	$ 45.7	—	$78.8	$ 3.1	$14.0	$21.1
Local	$ 5.5	—	$13.2	$72.0	—	$ 4.0
Total	$348.9	$201.5	$92.0	$75.1	$63.2	$94.5

Source: U.S. News & World Report, April 18, 1983, pp. 40–41.

TABLE 22.3 ■ TOP TEN DEFENSE CONTRACTORS IN 1983

Company	Value of Contracts
General Dynamics	$5,891,101,000
McDonnell Douglas	$5,630,104,000
United Technologies	$4,208,293,000
General Electric	$3,654,097,000
Lockheed	$3,498,550,000
Boeing	$3,238,796,000
Hughes Aircraft	$3,140,735,000
Rockwell International	$2,690,518,000
Raytheon	$2,262,290,000
Martin Marietta	$2,008,354,000
Grumman	$1,900,489,000

Source: Defense Department Reports.

itary are large and powerful and might unduly influence the system with their combined efforts.

Another large item, benefit payments, go for direct payments in the form of welfare, support, food programs (food stamps), and the like; but some also finance programs for education (special education programs for children with learning disabilities), medical research, and a variety of scientific projects. This category of expenditures enters the marketplace indirectly through private expenditures by recipients of government monies.

The government also spends a lot of money on education. Expenditures in this field have doubled in the last 5 or 6 years, and the rate seems to be increasing. Although inflation accounts for part of the increase, the amount is still large. Much of the federal dollar for education goes to various state and local governments to subsidize educational programs. While a significant portion goes for salaries of instructors and administrators, schools consume enormous amounts of books, supplies, desks, chairs, audiovisual and office equipment, land, and buildings.

Governments use police protection and fire control. Police expenditures include uniforms, weapons, training facilities, training equipment, office buildings, cars, radio equipment, scientific detection devices, prisons, and other rehabilita-

tion centers. For fire control, special firefighting equipment is necessary, as well as automobiles and trucks, training facilities and equipment, buildings, and communication systems.

Space exploration calls for giant research facilities that are expensively equipped, in addition to the electronic gadgetry, wire, steel, special foods, clothing, drugs, and communication equipment. We have passed the period of major emphasis on space spending generated by the man-on-the-moon program; nevertheless, space spending will continue to grow steadily as we build space labs and extend our travel to Mars and beyond.

Finally, the age of nuclear power has spurred the government to spend more on nuclear facilities. Only the federal government can own the nuclear core of our growing number of atomic power plants. This makes Uncle Sam the major purchaser of radium and other components required for nuclear construction.

These few examples illustrate the role of the government as a purchaser from our private enterprise system. Like any other large purchaser trying to serve its needs, government buyers influence businesses with the volume and nature of their purchases, as well as with their demands for changes to make purchasing more efficient for them.

Perhaps the federal government's most conspicuous consumption is its expenditures on military hardware.

The War on Federal Waste

The Reagan Administration declared war on federal waste and appointed nineteen inspectors general, referred to as "junkyard dogs," to ferret out waste. Their goal was to reduce federal spending by 10%. Although many perceive the inspectors general as qualified professionals, they have not been able to come close to the 10% goal.

The junkyard dogs do claim some savings. They recovered $44.5 million and obtained 408 indictments for bid rigging at the Department of Transportation. They have improved debt collection. In one computer match up, they found almost 200,000 persons who owed the government about $169 million. Telephone hotlines have been installed to encourage employees to report waste and fraud. One such call from an enlisted man in the Air Force produced the much-publicized incident where the government paid more than $148 for $10 rubber washers. But even this doesn't equal the recent report about the Pentagon's having paid a defense contractor $91 apiece for screws that normally retail for 3¢ apiece.

In many areas, growth of waste and fraud seems to be getting ahead of the inspectors. The Office of Management and Budget estimates that their error rate in handing out food stamps is 13%. Unreported taxable income has jumped to $250 billion annually, up from $94 billion in 1971. In December, 1982, the government was holding $40 million in overdue loans, up 35% from the prior year.

The savings thus far run to about $12 billion per year, a large sum of money indeed, but only about 1.5% of the federal budget. The accompanying chart shows the actual and targeted savings since September, 1981.

THE GOVERNMENT AS A COMPETITOR

Yes, the government actually sets up competing enterprises with the private business sector. Either directly or indirectly, the agencies of federal, state, and local governments compete with private enterprise for employees, and they offer competing services in insurance, communication, transportation, and a variety of lesser ways.

The government is a keen competitor with private enterprise for employees. As the nation's largest single employer, the federal government has become extremely competitive by offering reasonable wages, avenues for promotion, and wide-ranging benefit packages. In bidding for the bright, capable, energetic employee, businesses find they have to upgrade their salary scales, benefit packages, advancement opportunities, and security just to stay even with the Civil Service.

The government has long been a competitor with private insurance by providing special low-cost programs to such groups as veterans and government employees, and workmen's compensation. (Although most states offer private insurance to cover workmen's compensation, some states develop their own programs.) Government officials are quick to add that the reason they developed insurance programs in these areas was that private enterprise was not serving them well. Few private insurance companies wanted to insure the lives of soldiers in combat, for example. But the government kept up the insurance offerings after citizens got out of the military, and their low-cost insurance to government employees was largely an incentive to attract workers.

The U.S. Post Office offers some direct and several indirect forms of competition. It competes directly with several private businesses in the delivery of some types of mail. For instance, MCI

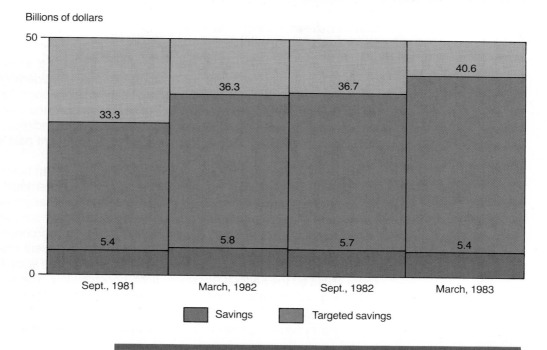

Billions of dollars

	Sept., 1981	March, 1982	Sept., 1982	March, 1983
Targeted savings	33.3	36.3	36.7	40.6
Savings	5.4	5.8	5.7	5.4

■ Savings   ■ Targeted savings

Actual and targeted savings claimed from waste, fraud, and mismanagement.
Source: U.S. Office of Management and Budget and U.S. Treasury.

Mail, an electronic mail service, calls itself "the nation's new postal system . . . one that's faster, cheaper, and more convenient." Indirectly, mail is a form of communication and as such competes with telephone companies, television, radio, and newspapers. The post office also sells money orders in competition with banks, savings and loan companies, and other business establishments.

When the rail service needed help to survive, the government chipped in and helped develop the National Railway Passenger Corporation (Amtrak), which runs the railway service in the United States via contracts with private railroads. For years, local governments have offered mass transportation with bus and subway services.

Government agencies also compete with private establishments in a number of lesser ways. Some cities offer garbage pickup in direct competition with private services. Large projects such as the Tennessee Valley Authority, developed during the administration of Franklin D. Roosevelt, are great producers of hydroelectric power. Several states own all the liquor stores in the state, which puts them in competition with nightclubs, bars, and restaurants that sell alcoholic beverages. Many city governments purchase and operate their own water systems in direct competition with private concerns, and the list continues.

IS THE GOVERNMENT TOO BIG?

The government is one of the major institutions in our society. Whether or not it is too large an influence will continue to be debated. Certainly the government has much greater influence than it did a hundred years ago. As various segments of

BULLETIN

Government Competition in the Credit Markets

Government competes head on with business for capital in the credit markets. Because the budget deficits of late have run so large, the federal government has to borrow an awful lot of money each year to keep its doors open. In 1984, Uncle Sam had to borrow over $216 billion — 42% of all borrowing in the credit markets. When you add the government's guaranteed loans and other indirect involvements, the total credit needs hit $326 billion. In 1983, the government paid interest of almost $128 billion on its borrowed money.

How does this constitute government competition with business? Businesses also borrow an awful lot of money each year. And the government has to borrow in the same credit markets as business. Many experts fear that government borrowing will swamp credit markets and drive interest rates higher for everyone. Professor Paul Craig Roberts, William E. Simon Professor of Political Economy at Georgetown University, contradicts this position. He quotes a dozen recent studies showing that large deficits do not drive up interest rates. Rather, Roberts adds, high interest rates come about by the Federal Reserve's tight money supply. The accompanying chart pictures government's borrowing relative to total borrowing in the credit markets.

Government's borrowing relative to total borrowing in credit markets.

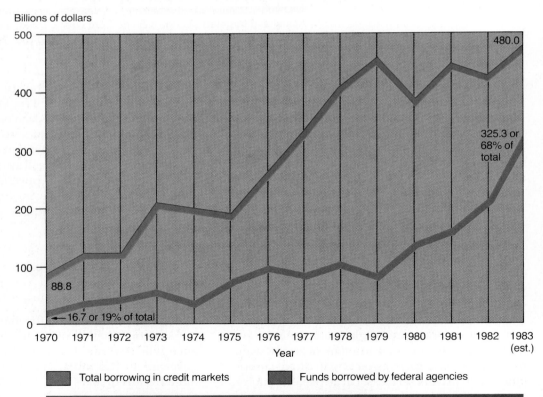

Source: Federal Reserve Board and U.S. Office of Management and Budget.

our society become more interdependent, the role of government will probably increase even more. Businesses are among the major critics of the increasing control of government over other institutions in our society. Many citizens advocate a free economy closer to the principles of capitalism in which prices and business practices are regulated by competition. This group does not like government antitrust laws, regulating agencies, and other interferences because all of these actions are restrictive.

A more liberal group feels that government is an instrument, a tool, to assist business and the other institutions to achieve the goal of well-being for all. This group contends that government is needed for its regulating power and its leadership to give greater unity to the diverse segments. They further add that history shows businesses do not regulate themselves justly with open competition; a stronger and more direct force, such as government control, is needed.

Then the question arises, how much government? Is it too big already? Do our numerous agencies overcontrol and set up stifling regulations? Do government agencies unnecessarily compete with each other? For many, the answers to these questions are a resounding "yes!" Yet, another group constantly votes for increasing regulation and control. This debate will continue far into the future. Chances are great that government controls will increase and the government will play an even greater role as a purchaser, tax collector, regulator, and competitor. No business today can afford to be unconcerned with government actions, and neither government nor business can operate effectively with old-fashioned attitudes of antagonism toward the other.

SUMMARY

Our government includes federal, state, county, and city levels. The federal government has legislative, executive, and judicial branches, plus the cabinet and dozens of independent offices and agencies. Governments exert influence on business through four primary means: (1) laws, (2) regulatory agencies, (3) incentives, and (4) informally. In recent years there has been a trend toward government deregulation of industry.

One of the more prominent roles of government is that of tax collector. Major federal taxes are income, Social Security, and excise. State and local governments also collect their share of taxes in the form of property taxes, sales taxes, and income taxes. In addition, there are hundreds of miscellaneous taxes collected by all governing agencies.

The government has become a major consumer of business goods and services. Major areas of government expenditures include: military spending, education, police and fire control, benefit payments, space exploration, and nuclear power.

As a competitor, the government has shown that it can be a significant force. In addition to competing with private enterprise for employees, government agencies compete, directly or indirectly, in insurance, communication, transportation, and other ways.

Whether or not the government is too big or has too much influence is subject to debate. The government is one of the major institutions and some critics think that it influences business too much. Others feel the government is a tool to regulate and stimulate business.

MIND YOUR BUSINESS

Instructions. Assume that you have 10 points to allocate between each of the following pairs of statements. Allocate the points according to the extent to which you agree with each statement. (For instance, if you agree strongly with statement 1A, give it 9 points and give 1B 1 point.)

1. A. There should be more government laws regulating business. ____
   B. There should be fewer government laws regulating business. ____

2. A. Government should use financial incentives more than they currently do to regulate business activities. ____
   B. Government should use financial incentives less than they currently do to regulate business activities. ____

3. A. We need to go further in deregulating business. ____
   B. We need to begin reregulating business income. ____

4. A. The government should place higher tax rates on corporations' incomes. ____

B. The government should place lower tax rates on corporations. ___

5. A. It is good for the economy when the government competes directly with private enterprise. ___

   B. It is harmful when the government competes directly with private enterprise. ___

6. A. To serve our complex society effectively, government needs to be larger. ___

   B. Our society would be served more effectively by a smaller government. ___

7. A. The government should do more to assist businesses that are in trouble. ___

   B. The government should do less than they currently do to assist businesses that are in trouble. ___

8. A. Government subsidies to agriculture, in the long run, help our economic system. ___

   B. Government subsidies to agriculture, in the long run, hinder our economic system. ___

See answers at the back of the book.

KEY TERMS

government, 594

income tax, 601

Social Security tax, 603

excise tax, 603

property tax, 604

sales tax, 605

use tax, 605

REVIEW QUESTIONS

1. Explain four ways that government intervenes in business activities.

2. How do tax credits and loan guarantees serve as incentives to business?

3. Explain why the government exerts some controls over business.

4. Explain the recent trend in government deregulation of industry.

5. What are federal income taxes? Social Security taxes? Excise taxes?

6. List and describe common examples of state and local taxes.

7. Explain the role of the government as a customer to business.

8. Explain the role of the government as a competitor with business.

9. What are the arguments for a large federal government? Smaller federal government? Which argument do you personally favor? Why?

CASES

Case 22.1: How to Handle Illegal Tax Protestors?

In 1982, over 53,000 people illegally protested against federal taxes. In 1978, the number was a little under 8000. A writer, photographer, and handyman, Ken Bush likes to stand outside the Federal Reserve Bank in St. Louis and burn his federal income tax refund. He said he stopped paying taxes in the 1970s. A service station in Indianapolis hangs a sign by the cash register proclaiming that sales taxes will not be collected. The station, says Barry Seagrave, the proprietor, owes the state $68,000 in sales taxes. The Golden Mean Society in Mesa, Arizona, charges members dues of $20 per month. For an additional $15 per month fee, they will supply a lawyer to represent tax protestors who get into trouble with the law.

Protestors offer a number of reasons for not paying taxes. One of the most popular arguments is that today's money is not legal tender since it is not backed up by silver. Another argument, repeatedly rejected in court, is that filling out the forms is testifying against yourself—a violation of the Fifth Amendment. Some groups establish a "church" and argue freedom of religion. For example, a protestor might name him- or herself as a bishop. The individual then turns over all assets and income to the church. The bishop receives no income, and the church pays all of the bills. Some established churches such as the Quakers oppose the government's use of their taxes for military purposes; they advocate a law to allow them to channel their taxes away from military projects into peace funds.

Questions

1. What are the effects of tax protestors on our business system?

2. There has been some talk of simplifying our tax system and requiring individuals and businesses to pay a flat percentage rate of their total income. What impact do you think such a measure would have on tax protestors?

3. What role should the government take toward illegal tax protestors?

Case 22.2: Dependency on Government Purchasing

Boeing Military Aircraft Co. in Wichita, Kansas, received $1.6 billion from government defense contracts in 1984. Two contracts, one for B-52 bomber modifications and another for KC-135 tanker re-engining, provide almost 39% of the jobs in the company. Their military work accounts for 70% of their total sales.

Nine of the top ten defense contract companies name the Pentagon as their principal customer. For some companies, the government is their only customer. Some companies purposefully avoid depending too much upon the government as a customer. They try to diversify into other areas so they will not be hurt too badly if government spending dramatically decreases or if they lose a contract. Others concentrate almost exclusively upon the government as a customer. They become technically specialized, attempting to ensure that the government depends upon them. Studies show that once a contract has been awarded to a single producer, competition for that sale vanishes, and the government keeps coming back to the same business for similar future projects.

Questions

1. What are the advantages and disadvantages of relying heavily upon the government as a customer?

2. If you were a top manager in a company that did work for the military, would you try to specialize in government projects, or would you try to diversify into other areas? Why?

3. If you were an employee, would you prefer to work for a company that specialized in government contracts or one that did not? Why?

LEARNING OBJECTIVES

After completing this chapter, you will be able to:

- **Diagram and describe the organization of our system of courts.**

- **Identify the three most common sources of the law.**

- **Explain the requirements of a legal contract.**

- **Describe the role of patents, copyrights, and trademarks.**

- **Describe how warranties work.**

- **Describe negotiable instruments and what makes them negotiable.**

- **Identify the rights of a property owner.**

- **Describe the intent of bankruptcy law.**

23

BUSINESS LAW

By law, ground beef in a pizza must be no more than 30 percent fat. Black olives must be treated to remove bitterness, packed in salt, and oxidized. And the crust of a pizza cannot be just any mixture of flour the pizza maker decides to use. At least 2.9 milligrams of thiamine and 24 milligrams of niacine must appear in each pound of flour.

As we saw in Chapter 22, law is one means by which government regulates businesses. Practically every type of business activity is governed by one or dozens of laws. And businesses must operate within the legal framework of their federal, state, and local governments. The laws and the legal system of the United States have emerged over a long time period, and laws continue to emerge, evolve, and change.

Law is the set of principles and standards that govern the conduct of society members. Laws are rules that societies establish to protect themselves. Many laws punish those who interfere with people's legal rights; other laws compensate people and organizations that have been wrongfully harmed. Throughout the text, we have touched on laws that concern business organization, marketing, labor relations, business finance, and the like. This chapter briefly describes how our legal system works, discusses the major sources of law, and comments on specific business laws.

LAW AND OUR LEGAL SYSTEM

Since our society is very complex, our system of law is also complex. But a brief description of laws and our legal system is necessary to understand the legal environment of business.

Types and Sources of Law

By understanding the major classifications and sources of laws, we can better understand how law fits into the overall legal scheme.

Public and private law. **Public law** is the branch of law that deals with the state or government and its relationships with individuals or other governments. International law, constitutional law, and criminal law are examples. **International law** is the body of rules that nations recognize in their dealings with each other. For instance, Revlon has a copyright on the ingredients of their "Charlie" cologne, but Taiwanese police raided forty-three cosmetic laboratories on their island and found that many were making illegal imitations of Charlie. Under international law, Apple also sued Sunrise Computer in Taiwan and forced them to quit making their Apollo II computer; they were copying too many of Apple's copyrighted features. **Constitutional law** is the specialty that deals with interpreting our Constitution. And **criminal law** is the body of law involving crime and punishment.

Private law, sometimes called **civil law,** protects the rights of individuals and governs the relationships between individuals within society. Contractual agreements and laws that protect the rights of consumers are examples. A subset of private law is **business law,** the complex system of rules, regulations, and laws that cover business practices.

Sources of the law. Since law emerges from society's norms and values, specific laws may arise from different sources. Three major sources of the law include:

1. Common law.
2. Statutory law.
3. Administrative law.

Common law or **case law** is unwritten. It emerges from society's practices. Much common law originates from the premise that most people would act morally even if there were no human-made laws to guide them. Even the most primitive societies had taboos and rituals. As a practical matter, most of our common law came into being through court decisions. Some disputes brought before courts may have no written laws to guide the decision. In such cases, the courts try to find the outcome of previous, similar disputes. Over the years, thousands of such cases have been settled, and a large body of common law has emerged.

Statutory law, by contrast, is explicitly written. Legislative bodies of various governing units develop statutory law. In the United States, city, state, and federal governments all develop statutory laws. However, a governing agency cannot make law according to whim. Statutes must be consistent with the Constitution of the United States or else they will be deemed unconstitutional and, therefore, illegal.

FUNNY BUSINESS

"I would strongly counsel against putting me on hold, Miss. Our firm has been known to sue at the slightest provocation."

Source: From The Wall Street Journal—Permission, Cartoon Features Syndicate.

BUSINESS BULLETIN

Strange and Unusual Laws

Did you know that in:

- *Alaska*, it is against the law to look at a moose out of a helicopter?
- *Alabama*, it is against the law to feed peanuts to alligators?
- *Kentucky*, it is against the law for a wife to rearrange the furniture without her husband's permission?
- *Michigan*, it is against the law to hang male and female undergarments on an outdoor clothes line at the same time?
- *Florida*, it is against the law to take a bath naked?
- *Michigan*, it is against the law to hitch crocodiles to fire hydrants?
- *Sault Ste. Marie, Michigan*, it is against the law to spit into the wind?
- *Lexington, Kentucky*, it is against the law to carry ice cream cones in your pocket?
- *Ashland, Wisconsin*, it is against the law to play marbles for keeps?
- *Logansport, Louisiana*, it is against the law to spit chewing tobacco on sidewalks?
- *Wichita, Kansas*, it is against the law for people over the age of 16 to wear masks?
- *Great Bend, Kansas*, it is against the law to drive carriages through the streets at night without someone running in front of them with a lantern?

We have heard of such silly-sounding laws, and these actually do exist. They are still on the books because no one has bothered to repeal them. They are simply not enforced. Do you know of any such laws in your community?

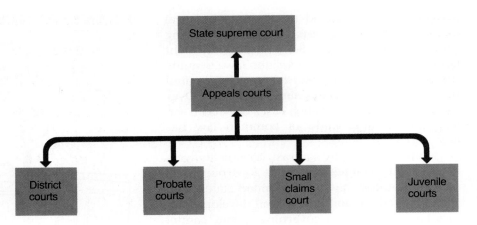

**Figure 23.1
Example of a state court
system.**

Since the UCC was a suggested model code,

each state was free to adopt its own version.

This resulted in forty-nine state versions

that are similar but not identical.

Since our fifty states all have the power to make laws relating to certain business matters within their boundaries, naturally, laws vary quite a bit from state to state. In an attempt to reduce some of the legal problems of doing business between states, the American Law Institute and the National Conference of Commissioners on Uniform State Laws conducted a study on how to achieve more uniformity among state laws. The result was a **Uniform Commercial Code (UCC),** a set of model statutes adopted by the forty-nine states. (Louisiana continues to operate under the Napoleonic code). Originally published in 1952, the UCC has been revised several times, most recently in 1978. The UCC covers such matters as sales, commercial paper, deposits, securities, contract rights, letters of credit, bulk transfers, and warehouse receipts. Since the UCC was a suggested model code, each state was free to adopt its own version. This resulted in forty-nine state versions that are similar but not identical.

Many government agencies, at all levels, have the power to hear and decide a variety of cases. These agencies develop sets of rules and regulations, called **administrative law,** to implement the provisions of statutory law. The agencies con-

duct hearings similar to trials and issue legally binding decisions based on the regulations involved. Examples of federal administrative agencies include the Federal Trade Commission (FTC), the National Labor Relations Board (NLRB), the Federal Power Commission (FPC), and the Environmental Protection Agency (EPA). Administrative laws developed by these and other government agencies carry the full force of law.

How Our Legal System Operates

Like law, we can classify the various courts within our legal system.

Using the legal system. If you have been wronged, you (the plaintiff) may initiate legal action by getting your attorney to file a complaint with the proper court against the defendant. If reasonable evidence is given, the court will issue a summons for the defendant to appear to answer your charges. Your case may be tried by a jury if your disagreement is over a point of fact. Both parties may agree to waive the privilege of being heard by a jury. In such cases, the judge makes the decision. If a business engages in a crime such as advertising and selling merchandise falsely, or if a business violates other laws, the wronged party may go to court to stop the illegal action and perhaps be awarded damages.

Organization of the court system. Our court system includes state courts and federal courts. If someone breaks a state or local law, the redress process begins in the state court system. Arguments between plaintiff and defendant usually begin in a lower court, called district courts. If either party disagrees with the district court's decision, he/she may appeal the verdict to a state appeals court. More often, another step of appeal includes the state supreme court, the highest court on state matters. In addition to district courts, many states have specialized courts that deal with such items as small claims, probate, and the like. Figure 23.1 diagrams the state court system.

Operating much the same as state courts, the federal court system becomes involved when someone breaks a federal law. Federal courts include district courts in all states, certain special courts, appeal courts, and the U.S. Supreme Court. (See Fig. 23.2.) The U.S. Supreme Court decides constitutional issues and is the highest court of appeals. Since the Supreme Court is the highest court, its decisions are final.

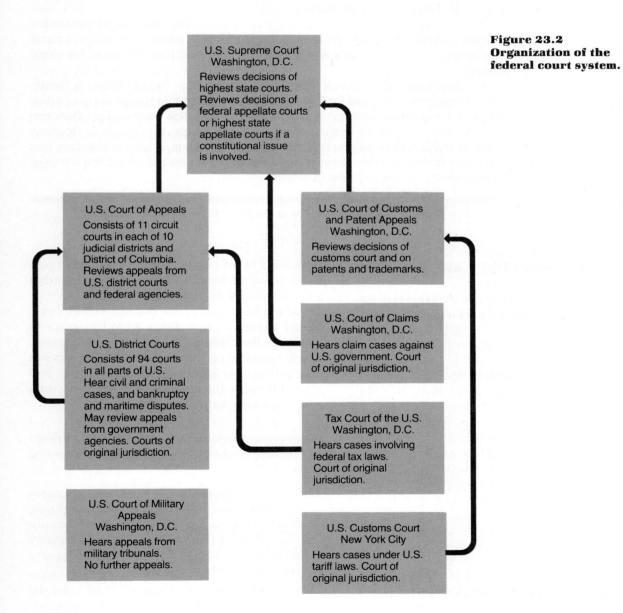

**Figure 23.2
Organization of the
federal court system.**

U.S. Supreme Court
Washington, D.C.
Reviews decisions of highest state courts. Reviews decisions of federal appellate courts or highest state appellate courts if a constitutional issue is involved.

U.S. Court of Appeals
Consists of 11 circuit courts in each of 10 judicial districts and District of Columbia. Reviews appeals from U.S. district courts and federal agencies.

U.S. Court of Customs and Patent Appeals
Washington, D.C.
Reviews decisions of customs court and on patents and trademarks.

U.S. District Courts
Consists of 94 courts in all parts of U.S. Hear civil and criminal cases, and bankruptcy and maritime disputes. May review appeals from government agencies. Courts of original jurisdiction.

U.S. Court of Claims
Washington, D.C.
Hears claim cases against U.S. government. Court of original jurisdiction.

Tax Court of the U.S.
Washington, D.C.
Hears cases involving federal tax laws. Court of original jurisdiction.

U.S. Court of Military Appeals
Washington, D.C.
Hears appeals from military tribunals. No further appeals.

U.S. Customs Court
New York City
Hears cases under U.S. tariff laws. Court of original jurisdiction.

Malpractice Against Kodak's Law Firm

In 1973, Berkey Photo, a New York-based photofinishing company, sued Kodak. Berkey claimed that Kodak was monopolizing the market for cameras, film, and developing equipment.

John Doar of the Donovan Leisure law firm led Kodak's defense. But during the trial, Doar illegally withheld a letter from Berkey, and an assistant to Doar would not turn over a suitcase of documents to Berkey, claiming that they had been destroyed when they had not. Berkey's counsel revealed these misdeeds during the latter part of the trial. The jury awarded Berkey $113 million.

Kodak fired their law firm and hired Jullivan & Cromwell. This firm got most of the charges reversed on appeal, and Kodak settled for $6.8 million. Still, Kodak's name was damaged because many speculated that they had participated in the illegal dealings.

To clear their name, Kodak hired a Philadelphia firm, Drinker Biddle & Reath, which investigated the case for 2 years. They concluded that Kodak did not participate in the misdeeds. This constituted a clear malpractice claim against Donovan Leisure. Donovan Leisure finally settled with Kodak by paying $675,000. Roughly, 5% of all lawyers face malpractice claims each year. Today, many businesses fear that if they do not hold their lawyers legally accountable, their stockholders are more likely to take action against the business.

Source: Brian Dumaine, ''Kodak's Revenge on its Law Firm,'' *Fortune,* May 30, 1983, p. 80.

TYPES OF BUSINESS LAW

This section describes some specific aspects of the following various kinds of law that especially concern business.

- Contracts.
- Patents and copyrights.
- Sales and warranties.
- Negotiable instruments.
- Property: real and personal.
- Bailments.
- Agency.
- Bankruptcy.
- Criminal law.
- Torts.

Contract Law

Most business transactions are based on the law of contracts. A **contract** is a legally enforceable agreement between two or more competent parties to do, or refrain from doing, some activity that is neither illegal nor impossible.

At the beginning of this decade, Jackie Sherill signed a contract with Texas A&M University to make him the highest-paid college football coach. Sherill agreed to provide to the university services of coaching and administering the athletic program. In return, the university agreed to pay him over $1 million for 5 years.

What contracts require. For a contract to exist and be enforceable, it must contain the following traits:

1. *Voluntary agreement.* All parties must agree to the provisions of the contract without threat, fraud, coercion, or error. Contracts require that all terms be clearly and understandably communicated to each party, and each party must have a chance to reply.

2. *Competent parties.* All parties must meet the legal definition of competency. In most states,

competency is implied for mentally capable persons of a certain age. Minimum age is 21 in most states, but many have lowered the legal age to 18 along with the right to vote. In a few states, a person becomes of legal age at marriage. Both minors and insane persons can enter into a contract for necessities and be held liable for these items. However, if a business enters an agreement for a luxury with a person who is either insane or under the legal age, the agreement will not be legally binding.

3. *Lawful purpose.* The subject of the contract must be legal as defined by federal and state laws. Promises to pay gambling debts are not legally enforceable in states whose laws prohibit gambling (however, it may not always be healthy to make a point of this issue). Businesses cannot legally enforce contracts to collect interest rates, refuse to hire certain employees, or invest their money in actions that violate state or federal laws.
4. *Consideration.* Something of value, called **consideration,** must be exchanged for the agreement to be legal; each party must give up something, such as money, which the other party receives. When a manufacturer sells a truckload of inventory for $20,000 to a wholesaler, the manufacturer gives up inventory for money. The wholesaler exchanges money for inventory.
5. *Contract form.* An oral agreement may be as binding as a written agreement, but oral contracts are difficult to prove. The law requires a written form for involved contracts or agreements pertaining to specified items. For instance, contracts must be written for sale of goods for $500 or more, agreements that cannot be performed in one calendar year, and deeds conveying title to real estate.

Figure 23.3 shows an example of a National Football League player's contract.

What happens when contracts are broken? Fortunately, most contracts are carried out by both parties. However, a contract may be broken when one party fails to perform any part of the agreement; this is called a **breach of contract.** The injured party has several alternatives. One choice, called restitution, is to do nothing, that is, to assume the contract was never made. Second, action may be brought for damages—the payment (usually money) is awarded to the party injured by a breach of contract. Third, the injured party can go to court to force the other party to perform what was agreed to in the contract. This

Figure 23.3
Example of a contract.
Source: By permission of the NFL Management Council.

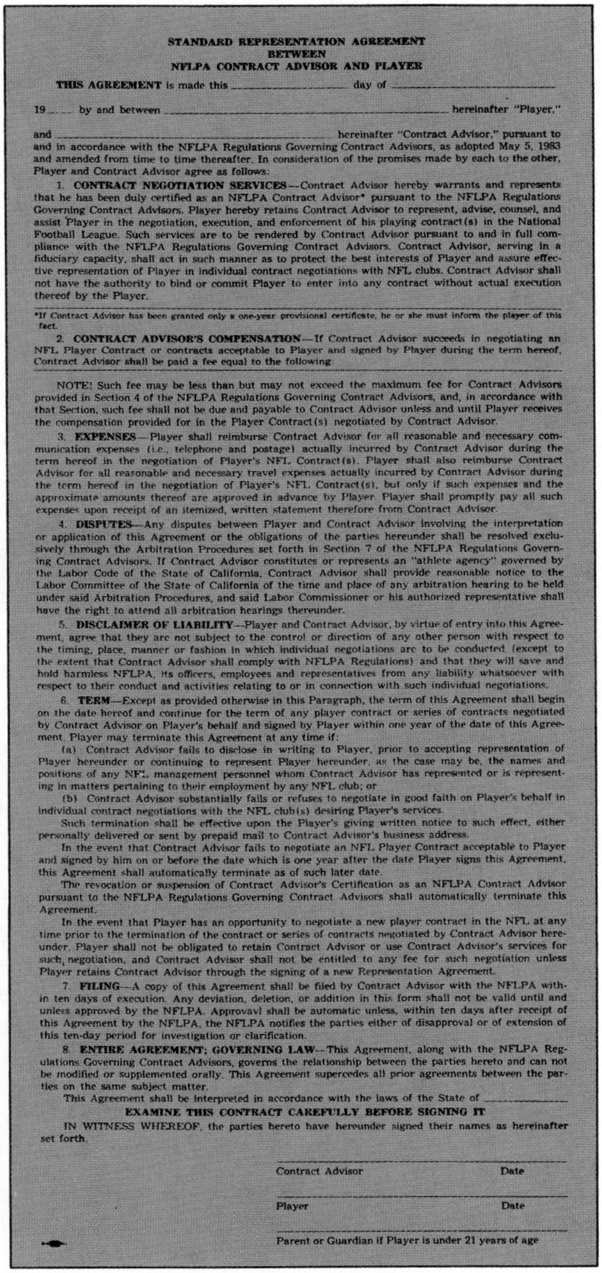

STANDARD REPRESENTATION AGREEMENT
BETWEEN
NFLPA CONTRACT ADVISOR AND PLAYER

THIS AGREEMENT is made this __________ day of __________ 19___ by and between __________ hereinafter "Player," and __________ hereinafter "Contract Advisor," pursuant to and in accordance with the NFLPA Regulations Governing Contract Advisors, as adopted May 5, 1983 and amended from time to time thereafter. In consideration of the promises made by each to the other, Player and Contract Advisor agree as follows:

1. **CONTRACT NEGOTIATION SERVICES**—Contract Advisor hereby warrants and represents that he has been duly certified as an NFLPA Contract Advisor* pursuant to the NFLPA Regulations Governing Contract Advisors. Player hereby retains Contract Advisor to represent, advise, counsel, and assist Player in the negotiation, execution, and enforcement of his playing contract(s) in the National Football League. Such services are to be rendered by Contract Advisor pursuant to and in full compliance with the NFLPA Regulations Governing Contract Advisors. Contract Advisor, serving in a fiduciary capacity, shall act in such manner as to protect the best interests of Player and assure effective representation of Player in individual contract negotiations with NFL clubs. Contract Advisor shall not have the authority to bind or commit Player to enter into any contract without actual execution thereof by the Player.

*If Contract Advisor has been granted only a one-year provisional certificate, he or she must inform the player of this fact.

2. **CONTRACT ADVISOR'S COMPENSATION**—If Contract Advisor succeeds in negotiating an NFL Player Contract or contracts acceptable to Player and signed by Player during the term hereof, Contract Advisor shall be paid a fee equal to the following:

NOTE! Such fee may be less than but may not exceed the maximum fee for Contract Advisors provided in Section 4 of the NFLPA Regulations Governing Contract Advisors, and, in accordance with that Section, such fee shall not be due and payable to Contract Advisor unless and until Player receives the compensation provided for in the Player Contract(s) negotiated by Contract Advisor.

3. **EXPENSES**—Player shall reimburse Contract Advisor for all reasonable and necessary communication expenses (i.e., telephone and postage) actually incurred by Contract Advisor during the term hereof in the negotiation of Player's NFL Contract(s). Player shall also reimburse Contract Advisor for all reasonable and necessary travel expenses actually incurred by Contract Advisor during the term hereof in the negotiation of Player's NFL Contract(s), but only if such expenses and the approximate amounts thereof are approved in advance by Player. Player shall promptly pay all such expenses upon receipt of an itemized, written statement therefore from Contract Advisor.

4. **DISPUTES**—Any disputes between Player and Contract Advisor involving the interpretation or application of this Agreement or the obligations of the parties hereunder shall be resolved exclusively through the Arbitration Procedures set forth in Section 7 of the NFLPA Regulations Governing Contract Advisors. If Contract Advisor constitutes or represents an "athlete agency" governed by the Labor Code of the State of California, Contract Advisor shall provide reasonable notice to the Labor Committee of the State of California of the time and place of any arbitration hearing to be held under said Arbitration Procedures, and said Labor Commissioner or his authorized representative shall have the right to attend all arbitration hearings thereunder.

5. **DISCLAIMER OF LIABILITY**—Player and Contract Advisor, by virtue of entry into this Agreement, agree that they are not subject to the control or direction of any other person with respect to the timing, place, manner or fashion in which individual negotiations are to be conducted (except to the extent that Contract Advisor shall comply with NFLPA Regulations) and that they will save and hold harmless NFLPA, its officers, employees and representatives from any liability whatsoever with respect to their conduct and activities relating to or in connection with such individual negotiations.

6. **TERM**—Except as provided otherwise in this Paragraph, the term of this Agreement shall begin on the date hereof and continue for the term of any player contract or series of contracts negotiated by Contract Advisor on Player's behalf and signed by Player within *one* year of the date of this Agreement. Player may terminate this Agreement at any time if:

(a) Contract Advisor fails to disclose in writing to Player, prior to accepting representation of Player hereunder or continuing to represent Player hereunder, as the case may be, the names and positions of any NFL management personnel whom Contract Advisor has represented or is representing in matters pertaining to their employment by any NFL club; or

(b) Contract Advisor substantially fails or refuses to negotiate in good faith on Player's behalf in individual contract negotiations with the NFL club(s) desiring Player's services.

Such termination shall be effective upon the Player's giving written notice to such effect, either personally delivered or sent by prepaid mail to Contract Advisor's business address.

In the event that Contract Advisor fails to negotiate an NFL Player Contract acceptable to Player and signed by him on or before the date which is one year after the date Player signs this Agreement, this Agreement shall automatically terminate as of such later date.

The revocation or suspension of Contract Advisor's Certification as an NFLPA Contract Advisor pursuant to the NFLPA Regulations Governing Contract Advisors shall automatically terminate this Agreement.

In the event that Player has an opportunity to negotiate a new player contract in the NFL at any time prior to the termination of the contract or series of contracts negotiated by Contract Advisor hereunder, Player shall not be obligated to retain Contract Advisor or use Contract Advisor's services for such negotiation, and Contract Advisor shall not be entitled to any fee for such negotiation unless Player retains Contract Advisor through the signing of a new Representation Agreement.

7. **FILING**—A copy of this Agreement shall be filed by Contract Advisor with the NFLPA within ten days of execution. Any deviation, deletion, or addition in this form shall not be valid until and unless approved by the NFLPA. Approvavl shall be automatic unless, within ten days after receipt of this Agreement by the NFLPA, the NFLPA notifies the parties either of disapproval or of extension of this ten-day period for investigation or clarification.

8. **ENTIRE AGREEMENT; GOVERNING LAW**—This Agreement, along with the NFLPA Regulations Governing Contract Advisors, governs the relationship between the parties hereto and can not be modified or supplemented orally. This Agreement supercedes all prior agreements between the parties on the same subject matter.

This Agreement shall be interpreted in accordance with the laws of the State of __________

EXAMINE THIS CONTRACT CAREFULLY BEFORE SIGNING IT

IN WITNESS WHEREOF, the parties hereto have hereunder signed their names as hereinafter set forth.

Contract Advisor Date

Player Date

Parent or Guardian if Player is under 21 years of age

is known as specific performance. Normally, people do not use this last alternative if another reasonable form of settlement can be agreed upon.

Legal reasons for breaking contracts. In the spring of 1983, Tennessee Gas Pipeline Co., a division of Tenneco, Inc., found itself with contracts for large quantities of gas it could not possibly sell. A few years earlier, when it looked like natural gas was going to be in short supply, several pipeline companies made long-term contracts with suppliers. But when the demand did not materialize, companies, including Columbia Gas Transmission and InterNorth Pipeline, wanted out of the contracts. They said that if they had to buy this gas, which they could not sell, it would bankrupt them. The suppliers, Exxon, Texaco, Amoco, Chevron, and others, said they had a contract and the pipeline companies should honor it. The suppliers sued the pipelines for breach of contract.

Pipeline companies based their case on the "force majeure"—acts-of-God—clauses in their contracts. **Force majeure** provisions excuse parties from their contracts if uncontrollable events make it impossible for them to perform to their agreement. Examples of uncontrollable events include hurricanes, pipe breaks, well blowouts, and the like. Pipeline companies argued that a combination of warm weather, recession, and unfavorable legislation had made it impossible for them to perform. Traditionally, courts have not recognized changing market conditions and "bad deals" for making contracts "commercially impractical." Some worry that these conditions might twist contract law out of shape. Gas lawyer Jeffrey M. Petrash comments, "On the one side you've got the sanctity of contract, and on the other, you've got very difficult business and policy questions." Court decisions will determine these contract interpretations.

Patents, Copyrights, and Trademarks

Fashionable Calvin Klein jeans are big sellers for Puritan Fashions Co., but companies other than Puritan Fashions produce jeans and illegally put Calvin Klein's name on them. Thus, the counterfeiters, without springing for a big advertising budget, reap the benefit of Puritan's heavy advertising. Often, the counterfeit jeans are only shoddy, cheap imitations of the real thing, thus, unsuspecting consumers are duped. Puritan estimates they lose $20 million annually to copycats. Puritan, Levi Strauss, Revlon, Inc., and Cartier Jewelers are just a few of the companies on the warpath against others who illegally copy their products. The battle is tough because many of the counterfeiters, estimated to constitute a $16 billion industry, are located in the back alleys of Brazil, Hong Kong, and Taiwan.

If a trademark becomes a commonly used term for a class of products, the registrant loses the protection.

This label outlines the provisions of the product's limited warranty.

Patents, copyrights, and trademarks protect inventors and developers from copies and cheap imitation. A **patent** guarantees inventors exclusive rights to their inventions for 17 years. **Copyrights** grant authors or their heirs exclusive rights to their published or unpublished works for as long as the author lives, plus 50 years. Companies can register words, symbols, logos, and the like, known as **trademarks,** and protect them for as long as they want. However, if a trademark becomes a commonly used term for a class of products, the registrant loses the protection. Kerosene and aspirin were once registered trademarks. And the courts recently ruled that "Monopoly," the Parker Brothers board game, had become a generic term and was no longer trademark protected.

The Law of Sales and Warranties

A **sale** is an exchange of goods or property between two people for money or other consideration. It is a contract and involves the requirements of contracts presented earlier.

When title passes. **Title** is the right of ownership. Anyone who has title to an item legally owns the item. When a person pays cash for goods, title passes immediately. But complications might arise when other arrangements are made. For instance, if a seller ships a stereo set C.O.D., title usually passes to the buyer on delivery. If the set

gets smashed during delivery, it is the responsibility of the delivery agent or the seller to replace or repair it. When an item is sold free on board (F.O.B.) factory, title passes when the seller places the item with the deliverer. Damage then is not the responsibility of the seller. When a company sells a product, say an automobile, on the installment plan, the buyer receives the car. However, the seller retains the title, for security, until it is fully paid for. Still, the buyer assumes any risk of loss as soon as he/she receives the car. If the seller is given the privilege of returning the goods (sale on approval), both title and risk of loss usually remain with the seller until the buyer approves the sale.

How warranties work. A **warranty** is a guarantee that certain conditions of the sale of goods and services are accurate as promised. Warranties may be expressed or implied.

An **express warranty** is an oral or written statement by the seller that the goods have certain features, many of which might have induced the buyer to make the purchase. The warranty for the high-priced, high-status Omega watch says in part, "Omega warrants to the owner for one full year from date of original purchase that this Omega watch is free from defects in materials and workmanship under normal use." Figure 23.4 shows a warranty.

Federal law requires warranties to be written in plain English, not legalese. Every condition

1984 JEEP LIMITED 12-MONTH/12,000-MILE WARRANTY

1. Warranty Coverage Duration: A Strong Warranty

Jeep Corporation* warrants to the original purchaser and each subsequent owner of a Jeep vehicle that the vehicle (including any replacement parts provided under this warranty) is free from defects in material and workmanship under normal use and service for the earlier of 12 months or 12,000 miles (20 000 km) from the date of delivery or first use of the vehicle, whichever comes first.

If the vehicle becomes defective under normal use and service, any authorized Jeep Dealer in the United States or Canada will, without charge and at the Dealer's place of business within a reasonable time after delivery of the vehicle to the Dealer, repair or, at Jeep's option, replace with a new or Factory reconditioned part, any part found defective.

Except for other written warranties issued by Jeep Corporation applicable to new Jeep vehicles or parts, no other express warranty is given or authorized by Jeep Corporation. Jeep Corporation disclaims any implied warranty of MERCHANTABILITY or FITNESS for any period beyond the express warranty. No authorized Jeep Dealer has authority to change or modify this warranty in any respect. EXCEPT AS MAY BE PROVIDED BELOW, JEEP CORPORATION SHALL NOT BE LIABLE FOR LOSS OF USE OF VEHICLE, LOSS OF TIME, INCONVENIENCE, TOWING, RENTAL OR SUBSTITUTE TRANSPORTATION, LODGING, LOSS OF BUSINESS OR ANY OTHER INCIDENTAL OR CONSEQUENTIAL DAMAGES. SOME STATES AND PROVINCES DO NOT ALLOW THE EXCLUSION OR LIMITATION OF INCIDENTAL OR CONSEQUENTIAL DAMAGES, SO THE ABOVE EXCLUSION MAY NOT APPLY TO YOU. This warranty gives you specific legal rights and you may also have other rights which vary from state to state or province to province.

®   Buyer Protection Plan is a registered service mark of American Motors Corporation

*   In Canada: American Motors (Canada) Inc.
    In Puerto Rico and U.S. Virgin Islands: American Motors Pan American Corporation

Figure 23.4
An example of a warranty.
Source: Publication of warranty is by permission of Jeep Corporation.

must be clearly spelled out in the writing. A **full warranty** means that a defective product will be repaired or replaced, including removal and new installation if necessary. But a **limited warranty** covers only certain things, for example, parts but not labor. If you buy a new watch that is fully covered for 12 months and it quits running after 3 weeks, you can get the watch replaced, providing you took reasonable care of it.

An **implied warranty** is implied by the law and does not necessarily have to be made explicit by the seller. For instance, laws typically imply that: (1) the title of the article purchased is clear, (2) goods purchased will perform their intended functions, and (3) articles purchased are identical to demonstration items. For example, a Goodyear automobile tire is expected to perform under normal use without blowing out. Even if the tire companies do not specifically guarantee against blow out, their advertising might imply such a warranty.

Warranties do not cover a salesperson's exclaiming, for instance, that "This is the best product on the market today." Such expressions are known as trade puffery, and the buyer should not rely on them.

The Law of Negotiable Instruments

A **negotiable instrument** is a written paper, expressing a contractual relationship, that can be transferred from one person to another. It can also be used as a substitute for money. Examples of negotiable instruments are drafts, checks, certificates of deposit, and notes. Some of these were described in more detail in Chapter 16.

What makes an instrument negotiable?   According to the Uniform Commercial Code, an instrument must meet certain conditions if it is to be negotiable, such as:

- Promise to pay must be unconditional, in writing, payable in money, and signed by the person putting it into circulation.

- The sum of money payable must be certain in amount.

- It must be payable on a specific future date or on demand.

- It must be paid to an individual who can be specified with reasonable certainty or payable "to order" or "to bearer."

Because they do not meet all these requirements, written instruments such as wills, warranties, and leases are not negotiable. Likewise, an I.O.U. cannot normally be transferred to a third party nor can a note that says, "payable when convenient."

Transferring negotiable instruments. Negotiable instruments are transferred to other parties by **endorsement**—simply signing one's name on the back of the instrument. The UCC recognizes the following four forms of endorsement.

A **blank endorsement,** the most common kind, consists of only your signature. You must sign your name in the same way that it is written on the front of the instrument. Blank endorsements are a little risky. For instance, if you endorse a check and lose it, the finder can endorse it and cash it. You have no legal recourse; it is like losing cash.

A **special endorsement** specifies a special person to whom the instrument is transferred. An example is, "pay to the order of Mary Jones." You then sign your name below it. You may restrict what the instrument can be used for by endorsing

with a **restrictive endorsement,** such as "for deposit only." Most businesses, when they receive checks from customers, routinely stamp them "for deposit only" to reduce temptation for employees or others to try to cash them. If you are not sure that the maker of the instrument will pay when presented, you can limit your liability with a **qualified endorsement,** which means that the person to whom you transferred the instrument does not have recourse to you for collection if the original maker defaults. Examples of these endorsements appear in Figure 23.5.

The Law of Property: Real and Personal

Property is something of value that is owned by an individual or group. **Real property** is land and everything affixed to the land. **Personal property** refers to easily movable objects, such as furniture, clothing, supplies, and automobiles. There are two kinds of personal property: **Tangible personal property** includes inventory, machinery, and so forth, and **intangible personal**

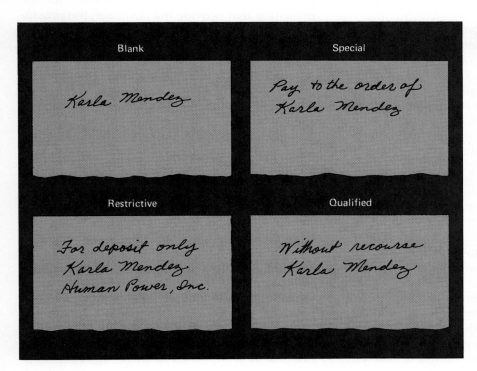

Figure 23.5 Examples of endorsements.

property includes rights and claims like trademarks, copyrights, and patents.

Property **ownership** grants persons the rights commonly attached to the property. Ownership generally means that a person can do with the property anything that does not violate the rights of others. Certain regulations do restrict ownership rights, for example:

1. Property cannot be used for purposes that violate the law. An owner cannot build a manufacturing plant on property zoned for residential purposes.

2. By the right of eminent domain, governments can take private property for public use. However, they must reimburse the owner fairly. In this way, the government acquires property for highways, parks, and public buildings.

3. If owners do not pay taxes or debts, legal action can force the sale of property to pay these obligations.

Within these broad limits, owners are free to buy, sell, keep, or use their property for profit or nonprofit. Owners may also lease their property to others for fixed time periods, during which the tenant has the right to use the property subject to lease stipulations.

Owners transfer property ownership to others through a land contract or a deed. A **land contract** is an agreement to sell the property on an extended-payment basis. There are two major types of deeds. With the **quitclaim deed,** the seller merely transfers his or her interests with no guarantees about the quality of the title. A **warranty deed** also transfers ownership, but the seller guarantees that the title is good and can be held personally liable for any title defects, liens, or encumbrances not noted in the deed.

The Law of Bailments

A **bailment** is an agreement whereby one person (an owner) leaves personal property with another person (or company). It is also understood that the property will be returned to the owner when the purpose for leaving the property has been fulfilled. The party who leaves the personal property is the **bailor,** and the **bailee** is the party to whom the property is entrusted. An example of bailment occurs when you leave your car with the dealer to be repaired. You have entrusted your personal property (your car) with another party (the dealer) for a certain purpose (to be repaired), with the understanding that it will be returned to you when the purpose is fulfilled. Other common examples occur when you place your luggage on an airline, take your clothes to be dry cleaned, leave your shoes to be shined, or have your newly bought suit altered.

Since no title passes, bailments are not sales. The bailee is required to exercise reasonable care of the property, and the bailor is usually expected to pay for the services of the bailee.

The Law of Agency

Often, people designate another person to act on their behalf. The party who represents another is called an **agent,** and the person whom the agent is representing is called the **principal.** An agency can be created via written or verbal agreement. When done in a formal, written way, it is called **power of attorney.**

Dorth Coombs, Inc., a large midwestern insurance agency, is an agent for several property and casualty and life insurance companies. Although Dorth Coombs' employees do not work for the principals that provide the coverage, the providing companies are bound by the commitments that Dorth Coombs' employees make to policyholders.

Many people in a corporation — corporate officers, service personnel, and sales people — are actually agents for their companies. To the consumer, they are the company, and the company (the principal) must honor their decisions. Very little agency law is statutory law; most has emerged out of common law.

Bankruptcy Law

In May 1982, Braniff International filed for reorganization under Chapter 11 of the Bankruptcy Act of 1978. The 1978 law, which replaced the Federal Bankruptcy Act of 1898 and the Chandler Act amendment of 1938, has two key sections: Chapter 7 and Chapter 11. Chapter 7 outlines the procedures for liquidating a firm, and Chapter 11 provides procedures for reorganizing the firm. Chapter 11 is supposed to encourage firms in financial trouble to reorganize rather than liquidate. If a firm cannot come up with an acceptable

Is the Bankruptcy Law Too Lenient?

What do Manville, Braniff, Continental, Wilson Foods, Osborne Computer, White Motor, McLouth Steel, Bobbie Brooks, United Merchants & Manufacturers, and 49,000 other businesses have in common? All have filed for bankruptcy under Chapter 11 of the 1978 Bankruptcy Act. And many of these companies are accused of using Chapter 11 to fight lawsuits, break labor contracts, and even resist the IRS.

Manville Corporation, the building materials giant, filed under Chapter 11 after 16,500 asbestosis victims brought suit against the company for damages from their disease. Although the company had a net worth of $1.1 billion, it said that it faced a potential liability of more than $2 billion in payments to asbestosis victims. The action froze all pending claims. Whether it will release the company from future liability is not settled.

Wilson Foods, the meatpacking company, also filed for bankruptcy under Chapter 11. The company said it had no choice because a contract with the United Food and Commercial Workers Union was reducing its assets by $1 million per week. Hours after they filed, Wilson slashed their meatcutters' wages by 40 to 50%. Of course, the union screamed and protested to the National Labor Relations Board. Braniff also drastically cut the wages of its employees when it filed under Chapter 11. Other companies have done the same thing, and some of the cases, at this writing, are before various state supreme courts.

A couple of years ago, the Internal Revenue Service confiscated most of the property of Whiting Pools, Inc., claiming that the company would not pay its taxes. The next day, Whiting went into Chapter 11. A district judge told the IRS to give the property back to Whiting. Since Whiting was in bankruptcy, the property was part of the company's assets to be divided among all the creditors. However, under Chapter 11, the company could continue to operate.

Vern Countryman, a bankruptcy professor at Harvard, says that Congress surely did not intend to give Manville the tools to act the way it did. Labor leaders are crying that companies are just using Chapter 11 to break union contracts.

The major argument for Chapter 11 is that it allows companies to continue operating rather than to liquidate. Some of them eventually become very profitable afterwards. Reorganization allows firms to buy time while seeking deals with creditors or looking for new money. Firms that wade through reorganization successfully are able to maintain jobs for a lot of employees, and they avoid the disrupting consequences of a failed firm.

Do you think that firms should have to prove that they are insolvent before being allowed to file under Chapter 11? Why?

___ Yes   ___ No

Do you think the current bankruptcy laws are too lenient or too restrictive?

___ A. Far too lenient   ___ D. Somewhat too restrictive

___ B. Somewhat too lenient   ___ E. Far too restrictive

___ C. About right

Why?

Sources: Anna Cifelli, "Management by Bankruptcy," *Fortune,* Oct. 31, 1983, pp. 69–71, and "Bankruptcy: An Escape Hatch for Ailing Firms," *U.S. News & World Report,* Aug. 22, 1983, pp. 66–67.

plan for reorganization, it must liquidate under Chapter 7.

While under Chapter 11, Braniff's creditors — Braniff owed them $1 billion—could not sue the company to collect. Braniff shut down for a while, but the Hyatt Corp. eventually bought them and invested $70 million in new planes and airport facilities. In March 1984, Braniff took to the skies again with 30 Boeing 727-200s. In addition to thwarting their creditors, Braniff also used the reorganization to cut their labor costs to the lowest in the industry.

The intent of bankruptcy proceedings is to provide an orderly discharge of financial obligations for honest debtors who cannot pay their commitments. However, many people argue that the liberalized 1978 law encourages companies to file for Chapter 11 bankruptcy for the purpose of reducing labor costs and eliminating other financial obligations. More than 750,000 personal and business bankruptcy cases were pending at the end of 1983.

Voluntary bankruptcy. Voluntary bankruptcy occurs when a firm files for bankruptcy on its own accord. The company recognizes that it can no longer meet its existing obligations (that is, they cannot pay the bills). During bankruptcy proceedings, the court appoints a referee who calls a meeting of the creditors to elect a trustee. The trustee's function is to guide the firm through liquidation or reorganization. However, under reorganization, the company's current management often continues to run the company. Under liquidation (Chapter 7), obligations are paid according to the following priorities.

1. Costs to preserve and operate the business while working out details.

2. Wages to employees that have been earned within a specified time prior to bankruptcy, not to exceed a set amount.

3. Reasonable expenses for creditors in proposing a bankruptcy plan.

4. Taxes to the federal, state, and city governments.

5. Debts to creditors, as determined by state and federal laws.

The trustee distributes cash from liquidation according to these priorities until it runs out. Preferred creditors, usually those who hold mortgages on the property, are paid before other creditors. If the money runs out, they settle on a percentage of their claims. Rarely do all creditors get full settlement. In fact, they may get nothing at all or they may take as little as ten cents on the dollar and write the remainder off as a bad-debt loss.

If the company can develop a sound plan for reorganization, it can continue to exist. Reorganization usually means giving the company time to seek additional funds or to work out deals with its creditors. Itel Corp. was in bankruptcy court under Chapter 11 for 32 months. The firm had $1.3 billion in debts when it filed. During reorganization, Itel persuaded its creditors to reduce their debt to $870 million which they paid with a combination of cash, stock, and notes. After these agreements, Itel emerged from bankruptcy court.

But if the reorganization phase does not resolve the underlying financial problems, the company will have to file for liquidation under Chapter 7. When MISCO Supply, an oilfield supply company, filed for bankruptcy under Chapter 11, the company owed $37 million to its 522 creditors. After several tries, it became apparent that they could not find new money or work satisfactory deals with creditors. The company then filed for liquidation under Chapter 7.

Involuntary bankruptcy. Involuntary bankruptcy occurs when creditors file the bankruptcy petition. Procedures for liquidation or reorganization are the same regardless of whether bankruptcy is voluntary or involuntary. A firm can be forced into bankruptcy if any of the following three conditions exist:

1. Past-due debts total $5000 or more.

2. If the firm has less than twelve creditors, any creditor that can prove an obligation of $5000 or more can force bankruptcy. If there are more than twelve creditors, three or more have to prove that they have aggregate unpaid claims of at least $5000 against the company.

3. The firm is insolvent, meaning (a) it is not paying debts as they come due, or (b) a third party was appointed to take control of the debtor's property within the immediately preceding 120 days.

Of course, many creditors are reluctant to force a firm into bankruptcy for fear that they will receive only a small percentage of the money owed to them. If creditors can see any hope of the firm surviving, they usually try to help by extending their credit period, allowing time to refinance the credit, and the like.

Criminal Law

Crimes are violations of specific laws that have been passed for the public good. Some examples of business crimes are public swindles, false advertising, illegal hirings, falsifying public records, counterfeiting, robbery, burglary, embezzlement, and violations of union laws. It is also a violation of the law, and therefore a criminal act, to obtain goods or services under false pretenses. For instance, if you were to write a check for $10 knowing that you had only $5 in your account, you would be committing a crime. The list of crimes relating to business could go on for many pages.

Individuals or groups who believe that their rights have been interfered with may seek relief through court action. The **plaintiff** is the person who feels wronged and takes legal action against the offender, or **defendant.** The plaintiff files a complaint in the court with jurisdiction over the matter, and the judge issues a **summons,** a statement requiring the defendant to appear in court.

The Law of Torts

Torts (the French term for "wrongs") are violations of basic rights of all citizens, that is, wrongdoing that commits an injury to another person. It is illegal for one person, either intentionally or through negligence, to interfere with the rights of another. Examples of torts include trespassing, assault and battery, libel, and fraud. It is also fraudulent for a business to advertise that a competitor sells stolen goods when it does not, or to copy trademarks, copyrights, and patents. Concerning business, there are three major categories of torts, as follows.

Negligence. **Negligence** occurs when one party's careless behavior causes injury to another person. For instance, if a store owner fails to repair an obviously defective step and a customer trips and breaks a bone, the store owner is liable for the injury. It was not intentional, yet failure to keep the premises safe would be negligent. Similarly, if a bus were to have a blowout due to excessively worn tires, passengers who were injured would have recourse against the bus company.

Product liability. **Product liability laws** hold businesses responsible for the design, manufacture, and use of their products or services. Businesses have an obligation to provide products and

---

BUSINESS BULLETIN

Bankruptcy Warning Signals

If you are an unsecured creditor of a company, you are likely to lose everything if the company goes into bankruptcy, especially if it has to liquidate. Here are a few warning signals of an impending bankruptcy:

1. A change in how quickly the company pays its bills. One of the first signs of a company in trouble is slow pay or complete failure to pay bills as they come due.
2. A very low inventory. If the shelves seem to be empty or if there is a lot of warehouse space left over, beware.
3. Very slow to get orders filled. Unless there is an industrywide short supply, this can be an indication of possible trouble.
4. A change in suppliers, especially sudden changes. This might indicate that the company is having a hard time paying others.

BULLETIN

The Lighter Side of the Law

If you think that you have neighbor problems, read the following case. Stephen Saunder was the owner of a small farm in Hamilton County, Texas. The farm had been his since the end of the second World War, and he had continually worked its lands and fished its ponds. This life-style changed abruptly in 1970, though, when the Acme Feed Company purchased an adjoining tract of land.

Acme was in the business of raising turkeys—not just a few dozen for its employees, but thousands for commercial use. In fact, Acme raised two turkey crops a year, each containing about 60,000 little gobblers. Apparently, Stephen bore these turkeys no personal grudge but rather was upset by certain biological functions that they had —like molting. There were feathers in Saunder's water tank, in his fishing areas, and on his crops. It was so bad that during certain seasons of the year, his farm looked as though it had been covered by a blanket of freshly fallen snow.

One hundred and twenty thousand little turkey feet also kick up a lot of dust which invariably seemed to blow on to Saunder's property. And with the wind came a terrible odor, thousands of flies, and the beautiful sound of 60,000 gobbling voices. It was not a very good place to live, a former neighbor testified.

Finally, Saunder could stand it no longer and sued Acme, charging it with operating a nuisance. How was the case resolved? The Texas Court of Civil Appeals decided the case in favor of Stephen and affirmed the lower court judgment which had awarded him damages for his personal inconvenience and for the loss in market value to his property. So, at least as far as Saunder was concerned, Thanksgiving came a little early.

services that are safe to use. Thus, if you break a tooth by biting a pebble found in a Crackerjack box, you can reclaim the cost of your injury. Many cases of product liability require trials because it is sometimes hard to prove whether or not the company did everything it could to design and deliver the product safely.

Strict products liability. Some states have extended the concept of torts to cover product-related injuries regardless of whether the producer was negligent. This legal concept is known as **strict products liability.** To have a valid claim, the injured party must show the following: (1) defective product, (2) defect was the proximate cause of injury, and (3) the defect caused the product to be unreasonably dangerous.

Over the years, the emphasis has shifted to holding businesses more responsible for their ac-

tions. This increases the need for business to be aware of their responsibilities under the law.

SUMMARY

Law is the set of principles and standards that govern the conduct of our society. Business law is the set of rules and regulations that cover business practices. People who have been wronged can take action through our court system.

Law has emerged in our society from three major sources: (1) common law, (2) statutory law, and (3) administrative law. Common law is unwritten; statutory is written by our legislative bodies; and administrative law arises out of rules and regulations developed by certain government agencies.

Business law covers many specific subject matters. A contract is a legally enforceable agreement between two or more competent parties to do, or refrain from doing, something. Patents, copyrights, and trademarks protect companies' investments in development. Sales and exchanges of goods and services are also covered by laws regulating such things as passage of title, and warranties. A negotiable instrument is a written paper, expressing a contractual relationship, that can be transferred from one person to another. Examples include drafts, checks, certificates of deposit, and notes.

Property is something of value that is owned by an individual or a group. Ownership of property generally means that the owner can do with the property whatever he or she wishes so long as it does not violate the basic agreement whereby one person leaves personal property with another. Law of bailments covers the responsibilities of both parties. When people designate another person to act in their behalf, the other person becomes an agent and must live within the responsibilities of the law of agency.

Bankruptcy laws cover the orderly transaction of affairs when a person or business can no longer meet its financial obligations. Criminal law covers violations of specific laws that have been passed for the public good, and torts are violations of the basic rights of all citizens.

seniority. The company terminated the employee for refusing job assignments. The woman filed a claim based on the fact that she was a divorced mother of two children and the job assignment was discriminatory. A U.S. Appeals Court decided the case. Do you think the court decided in favor of:

____ A. The employee ____ B. The company

3. A purchaser of land in Massachusetts sued the bank's attorney for failing to examine a seller's title properly. The bank claimed that it had hired the attorney to represent the bank's interest and not the purchaser's interest. Do you think the Massachusetts Supreme Judicial Court ruled in favor of:

____ A. The purchaser ____ B. The bank

4. A customer was shot by another customer in a California restaurant. A Good Samaritan, seeing the squabble develop, tried to use the restaurant's phone to call the police, but the restaurant manager would not allow the use of the phone. Survivors of the victim sued the restaurant. Do you think the California Appeals Court found in favor of the:

____ A. Restaurant ____ B. Survivors of the victim

See answers at the back of the book.

MIND YOUR BUSINESS

Instructions. Read each of the following situations and select what you think is the appropriate decision.

1. A company that produces chain saws conducted several tests and concluded that its product was the smoothest running and fastest starting on the market. Competitors disagreed, saying the company conducted the tests 3 years ago; and they had since added improvements to their products. The Federal Trade Commission investigated the claim. Do you think they found the advertising to be:

____ A. Deceptive ____ B. Not deceptive

2. A woman employee refused travel assignments that had been made to her on the basis of

KEY TERMS

REVIEW QUESTIONS

1. Define law. Define business law.
2. Explain briefly how to use our legal system if you are wronged.
3. Diagram and explain how our court systems are organized.
4. Identify and briefly explain the three major sources of the law.
5. What is the Uniform Commercial Code?
6. Define contract. What must contracts contain to be legally binding? What is a breach of contract?
7. Explain the role of patents, copyrights, and trademarks in business.
8. Define sale. Define warranty. Explain how warranties work. Identify the various kinds of warranties.
9. What is a negotiable instrument? Give examples. What conditions must an instrument meet to be negotiable?
10. Distinguish between real and personal property. Explain three regulations that restrict property ownership rights.
11. Explain how the law of bailments functions.
12. Describe how law of agency works.
13. What is bankruptcy? What is the intent of the Bankruptcy Act of 1978? Describe the priorities for paying obligations in a bankruptcy.
14. Explain criminal law.
15. Explain the law of torts.

CASES

Case 23.1: When Courts May Take Control of Your Life

Courts may take control over your money and your life under the following circumstances:

■ If you are kidnapped by foreign terrorists or held by a foreign power.

■ If you are judged seriously alcoholic or drug addicted.

- If you are unable to communicate because of an incapacitating illness or injury.

- If, in some cases, you are considered too old to manage your own affairs.

Some people think the courts have too much power, in some instances, to step in and make decisions for people. They argue that it is sometimes hard to tell when a person is seriously alcoholic or when an injury or illness has incapacitated an individual. Others say that it is necessary for the court to take over for people who cannot make decisions for themselves for the protection of the individuals' rights and the rights of others.

Questions

1. Do you feel that the court should take control of the money and the life of individuals under the four conditions just described? Why?

2. When people are unable to make decisions for themselves, what other ways, besides court intervention, can a society handle these issues?

3. Have you personally known of a case where the court took control of an individual's money affairs? If so, briefly explain.

Case 23.2: When Law Firms Investigate Their Own Clients

In the late 1970s, the Security Exchange Commission (SEC) requested investigations of several corporate practices due to concern about ethics. Southland Corp. was one of the companies the SEC wanted to investigate. Southland hired their own law firm, Arnold & Porter, for the investigation. The firm did the investigation and concluded that Southland was clean. Later, a grand jury indicted Southland for conspiring to bribe a state tax official.

Ashland Oil and Citicorp had similar experiences. After an internal investigation by their own legal firm cleared Ashland, a whistle blower exposed an arrangement with a Liechtenstein company that was rescinded. After Citicorp was cleared by its firm of any violations concerning improper foreign currency transactions, foreign governments assessed the bank $10.5 million in penalties and taxes.

There is evidence that ethical problems may exist when a firm investigates its own client. A new firm might also feel pressure to compromise its ethics to get additional business. But Kathleen A. Warwick, chairwoman of the American Bar Association Securities Subcommittee, says that the company's law firm can often get better information in internal investigations because they know the firm. Others point out that there are many examples of a company's legal firm doing a first-rate internal investigation.

Questions

1. Do you think firms should use their current legal counsel when doing internal investigations? Why?

2. Which legal firm is most likely to compromise its principles: a company's established firm or a new firm that might be trying to get a client? Why?

3. What should firms do to increase the credibility of their internal investigations?

After completing this chapter, you will be able to:

■ Identify nine ways that companies engage in international business.

■ Explain the theories of absolute and comparative advantage.

■ Define balance of payments and balance of trade.

■ Explain how countries use tariffs, quotas, embargoes, and other restrictions to reduce free trade between nations.

■ Explain four justifications for trade restrictions.

■ Identify six attempts at reducing trade barriers between nations.

■ Discuss four cultural barriers to trade.

■ Explain the nature of multinational businesses.

24

INTERNATIONAL BUSINESS

General Motors of the United States and Toyota of Japan want to jointly produce 200,000 subcompact cars annually in a GM plant in Fremont, California. Chrysler is trying to team up with Mitsubishi, which already produces almost 100,000 Dodge and Plymouth Colt subcompacts for Chrysler, for more auto production. Ford and Toyo Kogyo, maker of Mazda cars, are talking of building 200,000 subcompact cars in Mexico. About 10 years ago, Japanese-made compact cars burst onto the American market and left Detroit holding the bag with its big cars. Today, Japan, not America, leads the world in auto production. And they have a healthy 21% share of all the new-car sales in the United States.

U.S. auto makers are adapting to world competition by producing more smaller cars and by entering into partnerships with auto makers in other nations. Never again will the United States be as independent as it was after World War II. Far more than most of us realize, we depend on other nations for necessities, comforts, income, jobs, and economic security. This chapter describes important international business concepts, discusses trade restrictions between nations, and identifies the unusual conditions surrounding multinational firms.

INTERNATIONAL BUSINESS CONCEPTS

International business includes the movement of goods, services, money, knowledge, technology, and other business components across national boundaries. More than ever before, the United States is becoming dependent upon other nations for goods and services that consumers crave. We have always purchased all of our diamonds, the stones so central to our culture, from Africa. But we also buy huge quantities of stereo and electrical equipment from Japan, coffee from Brazil, bananas from Costa Rica, sugar from the Philippines, suits from Korea, razor blades from England, cameras from Germany, and watches from Switzerland. And of course, there is oil, our largest purchase of all.

On the other side, we depend upon our ability to sell a lot of things to other countries. Land-locked Kansas, for example, a state far from trading ports, sells more than half of its wheat to other nations. Japan serves Kansas beef; Coleman cookers are available in Mecca; Pizza Hut is changing the diets in Abu-Dhabi; and more than 20% of the airplanes made by Cessna, Beech, and Lear are sold to other nations. In fact, 40% of the top 200 U.S. companies sell more than one-fourth of their products in other lands. If all international dealings were to cease next week, many undeveloped countries would not notice. But countries like England would choke badly, and many nations, including the United States, Canada, Mexico, Russia, and Japan, would struggle along at a paralytic pace.

To grasp the full impact of international business, we must understand its terms and concepts. Some of these concepts involve ways of trading with other nations; others hinge on theories of comparative and absolute advantage, foreign exchange rates, and balance of payments.

How We Trade with Other Nations

Nations trade with each other in many different ways. We describe several, moving from the simple to the complex.

Exports. Perhaps the simplest strategy for entering markets in other nations is **exporting**—selling products in other countries through middlemen, company sales representatives, or branch offices. Exporting requires a minimum of investment and cultural cultivation. Very small firms with limited capital and product diversification can export quite easily. General Motors is the top exporting firm in the United States, and motor vehicles and parts are our leading export. We sell more products and services to Canada than to any other country. Japan, Mexico, West Germany, and Britain, in that order, are our next best customers. Table 24.1 lists our top fifty exporting firms in 1982.

Imports. The opposite of exporting, **importing** is the process of buying products and services from other nations. The importing company merely buys products for resale along with its regular product lines. Or the importing company may enter a contract to represent other nations in its home market. The importance of importing, like that of exporting, continues to grow. Our biggest import is petroleum. But we also import billions of dollars of motor vehicles and parts, iron and steel, electrical machinery, TVs, clothing, natural gas, chemicals, and special-purpose machinery. We buy more products from Canada than any other nation. Products from Japan, Mexico, Britain, Saudi Arabia, West Germany, and Taiwan also sell big in the United States.

Licensing. **Licensing** occurs when a producer in one country makes an agreement with a manufacturer in another country specifying the right to sell the product, on a royalty basis, to a specified market. General Motors has agreements with manufacturers in many countries to assemble and manufacture automobiles. Licensing agreements have not always worked out well because the domestic or foreign country may not live up to its agreement. And the complexities of international law make it difficult to enforce licensing agreements.

Joint ventures. McDonald's operates 350 fast-food restaurants in Japan. Hewlett-Packard sells almost $200 million worth of computers to Japan annually, and American Hospital Supply markets 3000 kinds of products there. In all these cases, the U.S. firms have created joint ventures with the Japanese firms. More recently, indeed, at the age of a mere 18 months, GM Fanuc Robotics Corp.—the offspring of a joint venture between General Motors Corporation and Fanuc Ltd., one of Japan's leading robot manufacturers—has risen to the number 3 spot among U.S. robotics vendors. And today, largely because of severe competition, the telecommunications industry is becoming increasingly enamored of joint ventures. For instance, in 1982, AT&T International reached an agreement with the highly respected Netherlands firm of N. V. Philips to form a joint venture company to market and service switching and transmission equipment outside the United States.

Because of problems with licensing, joint ventures have gained in popularity.

Because of problems with licensing, joint ventures have gained in popularity. A **joint venture** stipulates the percentage of ownership of both the foreign and domestic companies, and the ownership establishes the degree of control of each. Joint ventures are more stable than exporting, importing, or licensing, but they are less expensive than wholly owned operations. Still, there are some control problems because of required coordination across national boundaries. Several countries such as Japan and England do not allow foreign firms to own controlling interests in domestic joint ventures. This form of business is popular in developing countries, where there is a considerable market to be tapped, and foreign companies offer the product or the capital necessary to reach that potential market. In just the last 4 years, there have been 63 joint ventures formed between U.S. and Japanese companies: 21 in the U.S. and 42 in Japan. In most cases, the U.S. offered

TABLE 24.1 ■ THE TWENTY-FIVE LEADING EXPORTERS OF 1982

Rank		Company	Products	Exports	Fortune 500		Exports as Percent of Sales	
'82	'81				Sales	Rank	Percent	Rank
1	2	General Motors (Detroit)	Motor vehicles and parts, locomotives, diesel engines	4,673,800	60,025,600	2	7.79	39
2	3	General Electric (Fairfield, Conn.)	Aircraft engines, generating equipment, locomotives	3,921,000	26,500,000	11	14.80	22
3	1	Boeing (Seattle)	Aircraft	3,879,000	9,035,000	34	42.93	1
4	4	Ford Motor (Dearborn, Mich.)	Motor vehicles and parts	3,733,000	37,067,200	5	10.07	38
5	5	Caterpillar Tractor (Peoria, Ill.)	Construction equipment, engines	2,619,000	6,469,000	45	40.49	2
6	7	E. I. du Pont de Nemours (Wilmington, Del.)	Chemicals, fibers, polymer products, petroleum, coal	2,559,000	33,331,000	8	7.68	41
7	8	United Technologies (Hartford)	Aircraft engines, helicopters	2,271,721	13,577,129	20	16.73	17
8	6	McDonnell Douglas (St. Louis)	Aircraft, missiles, space systems	2,076,500	7,331,300	43	28.32	4
9	9	International Business Machines (Armonk, N.Y.)	Information-handling systems, equipment, and parts	1,875,000	34,364,000	6	5.46	45
10	10	Eastman Kodak (Rochester, N.Y.)	Photographic equipment and supplies	1,853,000	10,815,000	26	17.13	16
11	•	Chrysler (Highland Park, Mich.)	Motor vehicles and parts	1,795,900	10,044,900	29	17.88	14
12	11	Westinghouse Electric (Pittsburgh)	Generating equipment, defense systems	1,356,700	9,745,400	31	13.92	24
13	23	Occidental Petroleum (Los Angeles)	Agricultural chemical products, coal	1,205,000	18,212,226	15	6.62	44

invention and innovation, and Japan offered efficient, low-cost production.

Joint ventures sometimes encounter problems concerning percentage of ownership, amount of investments, and how much of the product will be exported. Procter & Gamble Co. proposed a joint venture with Nam Chow Chemical Industrial Co. to make P&G toothpaste, soap, and other products in Taiwan. P&G was to invest $20 million and Nam Chow, over a longer time period, was to match the investment. However, the deal stalled when local Taiwan manufacturers objected. The Taiwan government said they might require the joint venture to export at least 50% of their product. This would protect local manufacturers. But P&G objected to this require-

TABLE 24.1 ■ (Continued)

Rank '82	Rank '81	Company	Products	Exports	Fortune 500 Sales	Fortune 500 Rank	Exports as Percent of Sales Percent	Exports as Percent of Sales Rank
14	22	Philip Morris (New York)	Tobacco products	1,142,000	9,101,600	32	12.55	29
15	17	Hewlett-Packard (Palo Alto, Calif.)	Computers, electronic equipment	1,083,000	4,254,000	81	25.46	5
16	12	Signal Companies (La Jolla, Calif.)	Trucks, engines, chemicals, audio-video systems	1,075,400	4,935,600	69	21.79	10
17	14	Union Carbide (Danbury, Conn.)	Chemicals, plastics	979,000	9,061,500	33	10.80	34
18	18	Weyerhaeuser (Tacoma, Wash.)	Pulp, logs, lumber, wood products, newsprint	924,000	4,186,224	82	22.07	9
19	13	Raytheon (Lexington, Mass.)	Defense electronic systems, aircraft	917,000	5,513,370	58	16.63	18
20	20	Archer Daniels Midland (Decatur, Ill.)	Soybean meal and oil, wheat, corn	876,000	3,712,977	102	23.59	7
21	15	Monsanto (St. Louis)	Herbicides, chemicals, polymer products, fibers	864,000	6,325,000	47	13.66	26
22	•	General Dynamics (St. Louis)	Tanks, aircraft, missiles, gun systems	852,900	6,352,600	46	13.43	27
23	21	Exxon (New York)	Petroleum, chemicals	831,000	97,172,523	1	0.86	49
24	19	Dow Chemical (Midland, Mich.)	Chemicals, plastics, magnesium metal	826,000	10,618,000	27	7.78	40
25	25	Northrop (Los Angeles)	Aircraft, electronic equipment, related support services	823,700	2,472,900	158	33.31	3

ment because it would reduce their penetration of the local market. Such hitches in joint venture agreements are common.

Direct investment. If a domestic company cannot find an acceptable partner in a foreign country, the domestic company might simply buy a controlling interest in a foreign operation; that is,

they make a direct investment. This is more risky than a joint venture, but there may be fewer hassles and there is also chance of greater gain.

An easy way to make a direct investment in another country is to buy stocks in companies located there. As the stock market began to sputter in the U.S. in 1984, investors began buying foreign securities in record numbers. Primarily because

The Success of Moosehead Beer

Until 1978, Moosehead Beer was available only to loggers and fishermen in Canada's Maritime Provinces. But New York marketing consultants persuaded Philip W. Oland, the Canadian brewer, to put up $20 million for plant expansion and try to squeeze in among the American giants in the U.S. Market.

The company promoted an aggressive advertising campaign in the states, stressing Moosehead's macho outdoors image. And from nowhere, Moosehead sales quickly rocketed to the number 4 selling import beer. Other Canadian companies are currently playing on their image of lumberjacks and Mounties in hopes of tripling their 1% share of the $22 billion U.S. market.

Source: "Canadian Beer Barrels Across the Border," *Business Week,* July 4, 1983, p. 66.

of the increased U.S. interest, stock markets increased 37% in Britain, 35% in Japan, and 31% in France between January 1983 and April 1984. During the same period, the U.S. stock market increased only 11%.

Wholly owned operations. Wholly owned operations exist when a foreign firm maintains 100% ownership of a company in another nation. The wholly owned operation may be a branch office or a subsidiary. The branch office simply serves another region, similar to branch offices within the home country. However, branch offices are subject to the legal, political, and cultural norms of the country where they are located. Wholly owned subsidiaries usually have their own management staff, financial structure, and marketing programs.

The Corning Co., maker of mixing bowls, tableware, and bakeware, established an office in Japan in 1966 with only two people. Now, Japan is their number 1 export market, amounting to 25% of all Corning's export business. While Corning enters into joint ventures with some Japanese firms, it has a wholly owned distribution company in Japan. Japan manages the subsidiary, but most profits go to the United States. There are ten American credit card companies in Japan, but American Express is the only wholly owned subsidiary. Japan, of course, has also been very active in the United States. Nissan, in October 1983, dedicated its $660 million truck plant in Tennessee. And Honda has agreed to build its Accord sedans in its own factory in Ohio. Mitsubishi, which began making color television and projection sets in the United States in the early 1970s, attained $500 million in sales last year.

In 1983, Japan opened 83 factories in the U.S., bringing their total to 479. The greatest Japanese presence is in California which has 128 Japanese-owned factories. Texas is next with 35. Figure 24.1 shows the states with the most Japanese-owned factories.

Multinational companies. A series of wholly owned subsidiaries or joint ventures make up a **multinational company.** These conglomerate giants combine the intelligence, resources, and influences of many countries into an independent

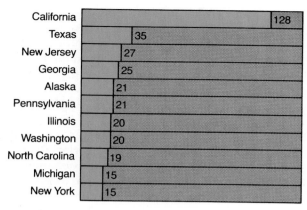

Figure 24.1
States that had the most Japanese-owned factories in 1983. *Source: Japan Economic Institute.*

entity. As a result, they are becoming somewhat like powerful nation-states. We will discuss multinational companies in more detail later in this chapter.

Contract manufacturing. Contract manufacturing occurs when a firm enters international markets by contracting with a foreign firm to manufacture its products. The foreign firm agrees

This delivery in Paris forms part of the operations of Rank Xerox, one of Xerox Corporation's several multinational units.

to produce a certain number of products according to specification, but the foreign firm puts the label of the domestic company on the products. The domestic company may distribute the products through its marketing system, or they might ask the foreign firm to distribute as well as produce the products.

Barter. As we mentioned in Chapter 1, in ancient days, most trade occurred by barter: Countries swap goods with little or no money changing hands. Today, barter, often referred to as **countertrade,** is making a comeback in international trade, amounting to 20 to 25% of all world commerce. Levi Strauss, the world's largest jeans maker, built and equipped a new plant in Hungary. In return, Hungary will give Levi Strauss 60% of their annual output of jeans for the next 10 years. Occidental Petroleum shipped 1 million tons of phosphate rock to Poland. In exchange, Poland gave Occidental half a million tons of Polish molten sulfur. Mexico sent oil and sulfur to

Brazil in return for petrochemicals, soybeans, and oil industry equipment. The deal amounted to about $2 billion. Poorer nations especially like to barter because many have heavy debts and little cash. But bartering exports also reduces the money coming into countries, and this is bad news for poor nations. Although countertrade will likely remain popular, Edwin Barber, international affairs officer at the U.S. Treasury, says "It often means higher costs, often 20 to 40% more." Figure 24.2 shows major U.S. imports from countertrade.

Countertrade typically involves straight, two-way barter deals between two countries. But, as Figure 24.3 shows, countries sometimes work out three- and four-way deals.

Theories of Absolute and Comparative Advantage

Why do nations enter into these diverse trade agreements? International trade occurs because it benefits both parties; that is, nations behave in ways that serve their own self-interests. Some nations, like Canada, have an abundance of resources; others, like many Latin American and African nations, do not. But even rich countries find that other nations can produce some things more efficiently.

A country has an **absolute advantage** when it is the only nation that can produce an item or when it can produce the item more efficiently than anyone else. Such conditions are rare. South Africa has an absolute advantage in producing diamonds because it is the only place they are found in great quantities. And the Middle East, for a time, enjoyed an absolute advantage in oil production because they could produce crude in great quantities at a low cost.

Countries that have an absolute advantage in several products tend to concentrate on those products where their advantage is greatest. This is called the theory of **comparative advantage.** A number of things—access to raw materials, cheap labor, good climate, or skilled technicians — might give a country an advantage. Although the United States is a resource-laden nation, we have a particular advantage in producing agricultural products because of rich land, good climate,

Figure 24.2
Major U.S. imports from countertrade for 1980. *Source: U.S. International Trade Commission.*

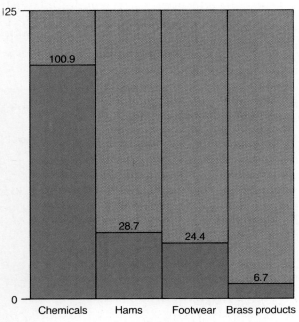

Imports (millions of dollars)

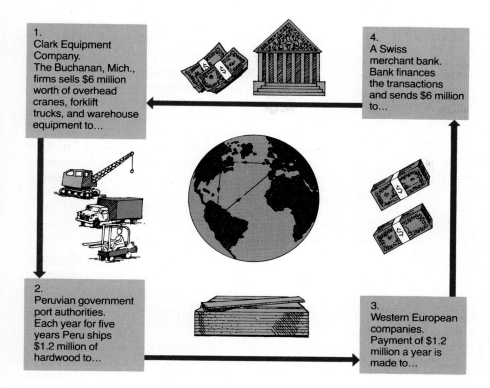

1.
Clark Equipment
Company.
The Buchanan, Mich.,
firms sells $6 million
worth of overhead
cranes, forklift
trucks, and warehouse
equipment to...

4.
A Swiss
merchant bank.
Bank finances
the transactions
and sends $6 million
to...

2.
Peruvian government
port authorities.
Each year for five
years Peru ships
$1.2 million of
hardwood to...

3.
Western European
companies.
Payment of $1.2
million a year is
made to...

and technology. We produce a lot of coal cheaply because it is so plentiful, and a skilled work force helps us produce computers efficiently. South America's climate and soil are beneficial to raising cattle and growing coffee; and Hong Kong, because of cheap labor, has an advantage in producing certain kinds of apparel.

When one country has a strong comparative advantage with a given product, it may sell the product to another country at greatly reduced prices. This process is called **dumping.** The exporting country may just break even on its sales, but makes up for the difference in selling the same product at more profitable prices domestically. A country like New Zealand, for example, may sell millions of dollars of lamb to the United States at a price that American producers cannot compete with. However, the additional business created and the resulting favorable balance of payments may well be worth the lack of profit. In this case, New Zealand may "dump" a great deal of lamb into the United States at well below the market price. But because a demand is created through

this activity, the country may benefit considerably, although the profit margin may be minimal.

The exchange rate of the American dollar is the number of dollars and cents it takes to buy currencies of other nations, for instance, an Austrian schilling, a Belgian franc, or a British pound.

Rates of exchange depend upon the world supply and demand of nations' currencies.

The rates of exchange depend upon the world supply and demand of nations' currencies. In the early 1980s, a lot of foreigners wanted American dollars to buy our goods, invest in our country, and for other purposes. Thus, the dollar was rising in value. See Fig. 24.4. To Americans, an increase in the dollar against, say, the Italian lira means that we will likely import more Italian shoes at lower costs. But, increasing the cost of U.S. goods and services to Italians will dampen demand for our products in Italy. In short, if the

Value of dollar against foreign currencies

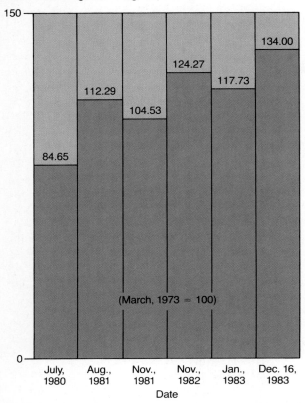

(March, 1973 = 100)

Figure 24.4
Rising value of the dollar against other currencies. *Source: Federal Reserve Board.*

dollar gains value, imports are less expensive here, but our products cost more to people in other countries. If the dollar loses value, imports become more expensive, and our products are cheaper to other nations. In large part because of the dollar's strength, the value of pianos imported by the United States rose by $15 million in 1982. Grenwill Mills' exports (a textile plant) fell more than 50% in 1983.

Foreign Exchange

For countries to trade with each other, they must work out a way of exchanging their different currencies. **Foreign exchange** is the interchange of national currencies, such as American dollars for Mexican pesos. Some communist and a few un-

derdeveloped countries still rely upon barter in international transactions, but most trade depends upon financial exchange. The mechanism for converting one currency to another is accomplished through the **foreign exchange market,** a place for trading various types of monies. The foreign exchange market allows a U.S. importer to pay U.S. dollars to a British exporter who receives payment for his goods in British pounds. The **foreign exchange rate** is the ratio of one currency to another. Table 24.2 lists examples of foreign exchange rates.

TABLE 24.2 ■ FOREIGN EXCHANGE RATES FOR $1 U.S., APRIL 1983	Two Years Ago	One Year Ago	Latest
Australian dollar	.877	.944	1.13
Austrian schilling	16.20	16.27	17.31
Belgian franc	37.39	43.67	49.17
British pound	.479	.552	.642
Canadian dollar	1.20	1.23	1.23
Danish krone	7.21	7.84	8.78
Dutch guilder	2.55	2.57	2.77
Finnish markka	4.31	4.50	5.43
French franc	5.49	6.02	7.41
W. German mark	2.29	2.31	2.46
Irish pound	.63	.67	.78
Italian lira	1,140.80	1,283.37	1,465.00
Japanese yen	220.60	237.00	232.80
Mexican peso	24.10	46.90	150.00
Norwegian krone	5.67	5.97	7.13
Portuguese escudo	60.79	70.61	99.50
Spanish peseta	91.30	102.99	137.30
Swiss franc	2.07	1.95	2.02

Source: Federal Reserve Board.

Balance of Payments

Balance of payments is the difference between what a nation receives from foreign countries and what that nation pays out to foreign countries. It comprises five major categories of expenditures and receipts:

1. Exports and imports.
2. Tourist spending.
3. Investments.
4. Military spending.
5. Foreign aid.

Balance of trade is the difference between what a country pays for imports and receives for exports. Historically, the United States has exported more than it has imported and, as a result, enjoyed a favorable balance of trade for many years. But as wage rates in the United States and our demand for oil increased, we began buying more products from other countries. And, relatively, we exported fewer items because ours

---

Except for 1975, our trade deficit has steadily deepened, amounting to $65 billion in 1983.

---

were more expensive. In mid-1971, we realized our first unfavorable trade balance since 1893. Our trade deficit, with the exception of 1975, has steadily deepened, amounting to $65 billion in red ink in 1983. The strong dollar and aggressive export policies by other nations contribute mightily to our current trade deficit. Coleman Company's exports of lanterns, ice chests, camping equipment, and sporting goods fell 40% in 1983. Coleman's kerosene lanterns are basic necessities for lighting in many parts of Southeastern Asia. However, Hong Kong and China are invading these markets with lower prices, as low as $12 per lantern. Coleman lanterns typically retail for about $30 overseas. Our greatest negative trading balance during 1983 was with Japan, a minus $19.3 billion. We also had negative balances of $13.9 billion with Canada and $7.7 billion with Mexico. Our greatest positive trade balances were with the Netherlands at $4.8 billion and Saudi Arabia with $4.3 billion. Figure 24.5 shows our balance of trade since 1973, and Figure 24.6 depicts the relationship between the value of the dollar and trade deficits.

When Americans tour other countries, they spend money, causing an outgo of payments from the United States. Foreigners visiting the United States create an income of payments. However, U.S. citizens travel extensively and therefore spend far more in other nations than we receive from foreign visitors.

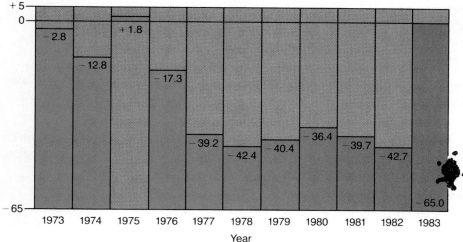

Billions of dollars

Figure 24.5
U.S. balance of trade since 1973. *Source: U.S. Department of Commerce.*

Is Japan a Good Trading Partner?

In 1982, the United States had an $18.9 billion trading deficit with Japan. That is, the value of goods imported from Japan was $18.9 billion more than the value exported to Japan. In 1983, the trading deficit was even higher at about $19.3 billion. We had a larger trading deficit with Japan than any other nation.

Many American firms complain that Japan is unfair with us. They accuse Japan of imposing unreasonable tariffs and quotas on our products. And critics add that Japan uses red tape and lengthy inspections to keep other American-made products out of their markets. Finally, Americans point out that Japan relies too heavily upon us for military support. Japanese citizens pay an average of about $97 per person each year for their military, while Americans pay $877 apiece. We maintain almost 50,000 military personnel in Japan and another 39,000 in Korea.

At the same time, the United States has kept its markets open for Japanese traders and investors. Japanese automobiles and electronic equipment, for example, impact heavily upon American markets. Labor unions say that these imports cost Americans hundreds of thousands of jobs annually.

The Japanese say they want to cooperate with the United States. They point to the fact that they voluntarily limited shipment of cars to this country. And it is a matter of record that American companies sold over $20 billion worth of goods in Japan in 1982. Consumer groups in the United States say that if we discouraged Japanese imports it would only make the prices of goods higher.

As a trading partner, do you think Japan is taking advantage of the United States? Why?

____ A. Definitely, yes   ____ C. Probably, no

____ B. Probably, yes   ____ D. Definitely, no

Do you think the United States should restrict Japanese imports into the United States? Why?

____ A. Yes, very severe restrictions   ____ C. yes, mild restrictions

____ B. yes, somewhat severe restrictions   ____ D. No, we should allow Japan open access to our markets

If the United States were to consider restricting Japanese imports, which methods should we use? Rank three of the following, with 1 being your first choice. Explain why you ranked the items as you did.

____ Tariffs   ____ Quotas

____ Embargoes   ____ Inspections

____ Red tape delays   ____ Subsidies to our industries

____ Cartels among our businesses ____ Threats

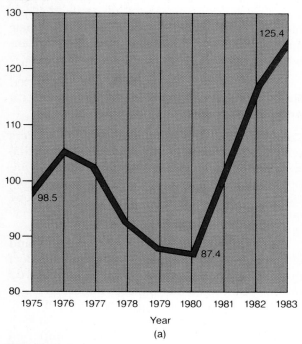

Value of dollar against foreign currencies

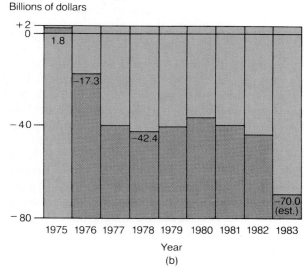

Billions of dollars

Figure 24.6
Relationship between the dollar's strength and trade deficits. (a) Annual average value of the dollar against ten foreign currencies (March 1973 = 100). (b) U.S. merchandise trade balance. *Source: U.S. Department of Commerce, Federal Reserve Board.*

Military expenditures in other countries and foreign aid also represent substantial cash outflows, further reducing our net balance of payments. In 1983, U.S. military and foreign aid to other countries totaled $14.3 billion. Israel and Egypt received the most, with each country get-

Figure 24.7
The 10 nations receiving the most military and foreign aid from the U.S. in 1983. *Source: Agency for International Development, U.S. Dept. of State.*

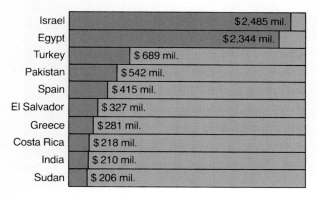

Israel	$2,485 mil.
Egypt	$2,344 mil.
Turkey	$689 mil.
Pakistan	$542 mil.
Spain	$415 mil.
El Salvador	$327 mil.
Greece	$281 mil.
Costa Rica	$218 mil.
India	$210 mil.
Sudan	$206 mil.

ting over $2 billion. Figure 24.7 shows the 10 nations receiving the most U.S. military and foreign aid in 1983. Also, many companies and citizens invest money in overseas projects. This is only partially offset by income from foreign investments in the United States. More and more foreign firms are investing in the United States and we are welcoming them. As one businessman said, "Foreign capital has built many of our railroads, ranches, farms, and machines. I'm not afraid of it. We need their capital to fuel our capitalistic machine." Other countries like to invest in the United States because we have been politically and economically stable. And, of course, we are good customers for many of their products.

TRADE BARRIERS

While the theories of absolute and comparative advantage are strong forces for encouraging world trade, other factors create trade barriers between nations. Officials estimate that about half of world trade is restricted by tariffs, quotas, and other barriers. In the mid-1950s, about 40% of trade was in some way restricted. We seem to be moving toward more rather than fewer trade restrictions.

How Tariff Barriers Restrict Trade

A **tariff** is a tax or duty levied on commodities when they cross national boundaries. It is the most common method of restricting trade. Tariffs may be placed on both exports and imports, but most nations impose tariffs only on imports because they want to encourage exports. Import tariffs can be specific, ad valorem, or a combination of the two — compound. **Specific duties** relate to some particular physical measurement such as dollars per pound, yard, or barrel. **Ad valorem taxes** are figured on the value of goods. **Compound duties** combine these approaches as a basis for taxation. Tariffs are flexible because governments can apply them to specific countries or commodities for which they think trade should be restricted. But once tariffs are established, political pressures may make them difficult to change. Tariffs almost always result in higher prices to the ultimate consumer. Many European countries, for

instance, place tariffs of 12 to 19% on fertilizer from the United States, claiming that the United States is dumping excess fertilizer in Europe. Japan, a big exporting nation, faces tariffs on their outboard motors in Australia. Australians, meanwhile, say that Japan is flooding their markets.

Restricting Trade by Quotas and Embargoes

Countries also complement their tariff barriers with quotas and embargoes. **Quotas** are quantitative restrictions on commodities that might be imported (or exported) during a period of time. Quotas may be applied to the products of one country, or they may be global and include everyone. Quotas limit goods, regardless of price.

Japan's quotas restrict the amount of beef and citrus fruits that other nations sell to them. (Beef quotas is one reason why a steak in Tokyo costs up to $35). The United States places quotas on sugar imports, adding, according to Doreen L. Brown, president of Consumers for World Trade, at least 13 cents to one 5-pound bag. Because imported steel has steadily increased in the United States during the last 8 years, we put both tariffs and quotas on imported steel in 1983.

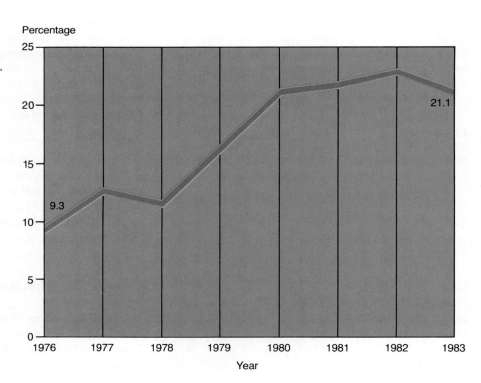

Figure 24.8 Japan's share of U.S. new-car sales. *Source: Ward's automotive reports.*

After the influx of Japanese-made cars into the United States, causing unemployment and adding to our trade deficit, we got Japan to agree to a voluntary quota. Japan, since 1981, has agreed to limit the number of cars it ships to the United States to 1.68 million per year. Figure 24.8 shows how this has reduced the growth rate of Japanese car sales in the United States. In all likelihood, this means that consumers are paying higher prices. France, also concerned about Japanese cars, limits their imports to 3% of the domestic market. Britain's quota on Japanese cars is 11% of the domestic market.

Embargoes are usually enacted for reasons of health, politics, morality, or economics.

Embargoes are simply orders prohibiting goods from entering the country. Again, embargoes may apply to particular products or to certain countries. They are usually enacted for reasons of health, politics, morality, or economics. To serve these purposes, the United States has embargoed fruit containing Mediterranean fruit fly infestation, trade with China, and pornographic material from any country. During his term, President Carter decided to use food as a weapon to punish Russia for invading Afghanistan by placing an embargo on U.S. grain moving to the Soviet Union. He stopped the sale of 17 million metric tons of grain and 1 million metric tons of soybeans.

Other Trade Restrictions

In addition to these common barriers, countries also control trade in other, more subtle ways, including lengthy inspections, red tape, restrictions, subsidies, cartels, and threats.

Japan discourages cosmetic and pharmaceutical imports by insisting on lengthy tests in Tokyo. They also set safety standards on these products that may take years to satisfy. All foreign investors in Canada must go before a time-consuming review board. The French, masters of red tape delays, require all import documents be written in French. Some nations, like Britain, simply restrict outside service companies such as insurance firms, banks, and law firms. The West German government feeds massive doses of cash to its airplane and steel industries. With these sub-

sidies, West German companies can undersell most competitors in the foreign markets and thus reduce free trade of other nations. European farmers, with about $15 billion in annual subsidies, undercut U.S. farm prices in other nations. In retaliation, the United States pushed the French out of the Egyptian wheat flour market by selling a million tons of subsidized wheat flour to Egypt.

Although illegal in the United States, cartels operate in many other countries. In a **cartel,** a group of businesses or nations agree to operate as a monopoly, thereby controlling the prices and production of certain products. When diamond prices fall too low, diamond producers in South Africa agree to cut production to keep the prices up. Finally, countries are not above threatening other nations with tariffs and quotas. Europe agreed to cut its steel exports to the United States after we threatened to put a stiff tariff on them.

Justifying Trade Restrictions

The major argument against trade restrictions is that they inhibit free trade, resulting in higher prices. However, many see tariffs and other artificial restrictions as desirable, and they base their justifications on four central themes, as follows.

Home industry. The home industry argument maintains that tariffs provide a wall to protect domestic industry. Without tariff cushions, many businesses would go broke because they could not compete with the more cheaply produced commodities from other nations. Beef and automobiles are partially protected products in the United States. Other countries tax U.S. exports.

Tariffs by one country are usually countered by tariffs in other nations, resulting in higher costs for everyone.

Tariffs by one country are usually countered by tariffs in other nations, and the result is higher costs for everyone. Further, protection of inefficient industries through tariffs reduces our ability to compete in world markets.

Infant industries. The infant industry argument says that new industries need protection until they have a chance to grow to a size that allows them to compete. The iron and steel industries in the United States grew much faster in the 1800s because they were protected from the larger, more efficient English industries by tariffs. But as industries mature, they gain more political clout and maintain the tariff long after it is needed. Again, the result is higher prices.

Wage protection. People in the textile, electronic, and shoe industries have become particularly upset with increasing imports of these products. Fearing that they are being cast adrift, they clamor for trade restrictions to protect their jobs and wages. As a spokesperson in the shoe industry put it, "We are importing eight times more shoes than we did 10 years ago. This forces more

Some are concerned about weak or absent restrictions on imports and protection of home industries.

layoffs and holds down wages, causing our employees to have to accept a lower standard of living." While this argument gets emotional support, it fails to account for the impact of skills, technology, and capital. Also, protective tariffs lower living standards because they almost always cause higher prices.

Military sufficiency. The national self-sufficiency argument has the most validity. It maintains that certain tariffs protect a nation's security. The oil crises of the mid-1970s encouraged the United States to seek ways of reducing its dependency on the oil of other countries. If oil imports were suddenly cut off, the nation would be impaired in its ability to maintain military preparedness. Unless a country maintains a supply of resources, technology, and skills for military capability, it becomes vulnerable. The United States also has policies against selling sophisticated computers and nuclear weapons to "enemy nations" such as Russia. The military argument is hard to repudiate, but it is sometimes used to perpetuate an inefficient industry.

Reducing Trade Barriers

Sometimes countries, or groups of countries, negotiate among themselves to reduce trade barriers. A few examples of such efforts follow.

International Monetary Fund. The **International Monetary Fund (IMF)** originated at the Bretton Woods conference in 1944 for the purpose of lending short-term funds to countries in temporary trouble. Today, the IMF has expanded its role to making three- to five-year loans and operating as world central bank. Many nations, including the United States, with its $8 billion-plus contribution, contribute to the IMF. Currently, the United States is balking at future contributions. But many of our commercial banks have outstanding loans to nations that are way behind in their debt payments. Countries owe foreign lenders about $700 billion, and at least twenty-five of the poorer nations are already behind in their interest payments. Mexico with $58.9 billion and Brazil with $56.0 billion are the nations with the largest debt. In 1982, U.S. banks had loans to non-OPEC countries amounting to $108 billion. We fear that if the

Trade with the Soviet Union

In late 1983, our government had stringent controls on exports of high-tech items to the Soviets, but there was no opposition by President Reagan to expanded peaceful trade. A top official said the president has no intention of "conducting economic warfare against the Soviet Union." The government argued that we could sell farm machinery and technology to Russia without negative military consequences.

In October, 1983, Moscow held an Agribusiness USA '83 trade fair, and more than 100 American agribusiness companies showed up — companies like Ralston Purina Co. and John Deer & Co. The market is apparently big. Soviets have committed $300 billion, over a 4-year period, to importing and producing foodstuffs. Still, selling to the Soviets is risky. International Harvester Co. got a license from the Commerce Department to build a $300 million combine plant in southern Russia. However, the Pentagon disrupted the dealings because they feared Russia might use the factory to build tanks.

IMF does not help debt-laden nations with cheap emergency credit, many of them will default. This so-called "debt bomb," should it explode, would create financial shockwaves throughout the world.

General Agreement on Tariffs and Trade. Originated in 1947, the **General Agreement on Tariffs and Trade (GATT)** has a goal of eliminating tariff barriers to worldwide trade. For example, in an effort to protect the cotton industry, the United States may place restrictions on the amount of cotton imported to America. However, a country like Israel, who is interested in purchasing airplanes from the United States, may suggest that they will purchase our aircraft if we allow them to export their cotton goods to us. In this case, because the United States might be interested in exporting aircraft, they may work through the GATT in removing trade barriers against Israel for cotton, so that Israel will purchase aircraft.

GATT has a set of rules for trade negotiations between nations, and its administrative staff oversees these rules. In short, GATT provides a way for disagreeing nations to negotiate trade agreements and concessions.

The Common Market. In 1950, six nations — Belgium, France, West Germany, Italy, Luxembourg, and the Netherlands — signed the European Economic Community Agreement, also known as the **Common Market.** Later, other nations, including Great Britain, Denmark, Ireland, and others, joined the original six. Members of the Common Market set up common import duties and established trade barriers between them. These agreements tended to enhance trade between the members, while controlling imports from outside nations such as the United States.

The Trade Expansion Act. The United States passed the **Trade Expansion Act** in 1962, giving the president increased authority in making tariff concessions to expand trade. The act actually allows the president to withdraw protection of domestic industries by agreeing to lower tariffs on imported products.

The Kennedy Round. With the Trade Expansion Act as his authority, President Kennedy initiated negotiations among the fifty member nations of GATT in 1963. The negotiations, which became known as the **Kennedy Round,** resulted in an average of 40% tariff cuts on 60,000 separate items.

The Ottawa Summit. Representatives from the United States, France, West Germany, Italy, Britain, Canada, and Japan met in Ottawa in 1981 to discuss ways to reduce the trend toward increased trade barriers between trading nations. But even with these and other efforts, it seems that nations insist upon erecting artificial barriers to free trade between nations.

Cultural Barriers

In addition to artificially imposed trade restrictions, companies trading internationally must overcome many cultural barriers. Of special importance are the differences in language, esthetics, religion, and values.

Language. Language is one of the most pronounced variances among countries. As a mirror of the culture, language is a key to understanding the ways and values of other peoples. To get their messages across to consumers, businesses must account for cultural meanings as well as literal translations. We do not have to look far for costly blunders caused by the language barrier. The General Motors motto of a few years ago, "body by Fisher," translates into "corpse by Fisher" in

> **A detergent company that advertised that its product was particularly suited for cleaning the really dirty parts of the wash blushingly withdrew their boasts when sales plummeted in Quebec, where words in its ads corresponded to the American idiom "private parts."**

Flemish. Pepsi's ad "come alive with Pepsi" created consternation in Germany where the literal translation was "to come alive out of the grave." A detergent company advertised that its product was particularly suited for cleaning the really dirty parts of the wash. The company blushingly withdrew their boasts when sales plummeted in Quebec, where words in its ads corresponded to the American idiom "private parts."

Esthetics. Esthetics are ideas of beauty and good taste normally expressed through the fine arts of music, art, and drama. Color and design are important media for communicating beauty. Product design, packaging, and advertising should be particularly sensitive to local esthetic pressures. The blend of colors and shapes has to appeal to the buyer's rather than the marketer's culture. While black signifies mourning in most Western countries, white is frequently the color of mourning in Eastern nations. In many regions of Southeast Asia, black teeth are a symbol of prestige because of the elite's habit of chewing betel nut; Pepsodent's question, "Wonder where the yellow went?" just did not make it.

Religion. Religious beliefs often provide enlightening insights into a local culture and help to explain why people behave as they do. Since about 90% of India's population practices Hinduism, foreign companies must understand something about Hinduism to operate there. Buddhism counts more than 350 million followers, mostly in southern and eastern Asia. Followers of Islam, numbering almost 400 million, spread across the northern half of Africa, the Middle East, Asia, and the Philippines. Shinto is Japan's principal religion, encompassing 100 million people. Most readers of this book come from countries where Christianity is the predominant religion. Religious beliefs affect international business in many ways, but particularly because of their impact on holidays, consumption patterns, the role of women, staffing considerations, and fears.

Values. Various cultures place different emphases on what is important; values refer to these differing priorities. Although international companies can have a powerful effect on changing values, tradition-oriented societies are not likely to change their ways quickly. It is only because the trade forces are so strong that international business exists on a grand scale in the face of both government restrictions and cultural barriers.

MULTINATIONAL BUSINESS

Some companies have become so invested in international trade that they have developed a multinational dimension. Although experts disagree, one widely accepted definition of a multinational company is one that operates in at least six countries and has at least 20% of its total assets, sales, or labor force in foreign subsidiaries. Multinational companies are also very large: They must boast annual sales of more than $100 million to be seriously considered as a multinational influence. Further, they usually have above-average growth and profits, tend toward high-technology industries, and spend great quantities on research and promotion. They also develop a global philosophy of production, financing, managing, and marketing.

Unilever of Britain was one of the first and most successful multinational operations. It began developing multinationally in 1929 when a major margarine producer in Holland merged with a soap manufacturer in England. Today, Unilever operates in many nations. It earned almost $660 million profits in 1982 on gross sales of $23 billion. Unilever is the largest ice cream manufacturer in the world, has more than half of the U.S. market of teabags, and owns salmon farms in Scotland, chocolate factories in Ireland, yogurt companies in France, fish restaurants in Germany, and animal food plants in Spain. Well-known Unilever brands are All laundry detergent, Lipton tea, Lifebuoy soap, and Imperial margarine. Some of the largest multinational U.S.-based firms are Exxon, General Motors, Ford Motor Company, General Electric, IBM, and Mobil Oil. (Table 24.3 ranks the world's twenty-five largest corporations.)

Multinational companies gain some unique advantages, and their management requires special skills; but they face special problems with national loyalties.

Advantages to Multinationals

Multinationals have expanded into many nations because of advantages in production and distribution. Specific advantages center around production costs, raw materials, markets, and antitrust pressures.

Lower production costs can be effected in many countries because of cheap labor. As a country becomes more industrialized, its labor costs increase because workers tend to organize and get higher wages. As the production process becomes more efficient, it is more difficult to reduce costs through improved methods. At this point, it becomes advantageous for manufacturers to seek cheaper labor sources. Korea, because of cheaper labor costs, produces many clothes purchased in the United States, and Mexico assembles many of our computers and television sets because of its cheaper labor. Primarily because of lower labor costs, Ford Motor Company is building a plant in Mexico. Qume Corporation cut 600 jobs in early 1984 when they started making computer products in Taiwan and Puerto Rico. U.S. shoemakers set up plants in Haiti and the Dominican Republic where they can hire cheap labor to stitch the upper parts of shoes. There seems to be a strong movement by American firms to shift their pro-

duction to countries with lower labor costs. Labor costs among countries may vary as much as 100%. This provides a strong incentive to move the production process where cheaper labor abides; costs of transportation, inconvenience, and the like can be more than offset.

Cheaper raw materials are also a motive for investing in other countries. Since raw materials are distributed unequally throughout the world, companies search for abundant and inexpensive sources. If firms can locate plants near critical raw materials, they will not need to transport mate-

TAKING STOCK

Matsushita Electric Industrial Co.: Profile of a Multinational Company

Matsushita Electric, the world's largest maker of consumer electronics products, earned a profit of almost $700 million in 1983. The company has 120,000 employees in 35 countries, and they make 14,000 different kinds of products. In 1982, Matsushita ranked thirty-ninth in the world in sales volume, with almost $15 billion. Its products range from vacuum cleaners to videocassette recorders selling under four popular brand names — National, Panasonic, Quasar, and Technics.

Osaka, Japan, is the company's home. Each morning, thousands of workers sing the company hymn and cite the company creed before they go to work.

Konosuke Matsushita, founder of the company, still shows up at the office two or three times a week in his cobalt blue Rolls-Royce. But at 88 years of age, his legs are a little wobbly, and he turned over the management of the company to Yamashita in 1977. Still, engineers occasionally show off their new appliances to Matsushita, and he comments on shape, weight, design, prospects, all the while bearing an incandescent smile. Matsushita is still the company's largest individual shareholder, with 2.9% of the stock.

Current president Yamashita wants to shift the company's focus away from electronics. He believes that the market is maturing, and he is looking elsewhere for continued growth. The company is planning to sell robots to outsiders. They already manufacture about 1000 robots a year, but they use them in their own factories. Yamashita also plans to move heavily into office automation, which he estimates will have five times the potential of factory automation. In a few years, Yamashita estimates that electronic products will amount to little over half of their total sales.

Matsushita will likely be a potent force in office automation. The company has an excellent reputation as a low-cost, high-quality producer. Its equity-to-debt ratio is about 1 to 1, making it a wealthy company indeed, and it has more than $4 billion in cash and other liquid assets. Matsushita's future is, to say the least, bright.

Source: Lee Smith, "Matsushita Looks Beyond Consumer Electronics," *Fortune,* Oct. 31, 1983, pp. 96–104.

TABLE 24.3 ■ THE WORLD'S TWENTY-FIVE LARGEST INTERNATIONAL CORPORATIONS

Rank '82	Rank '81	Company	Headquarters	Sales $000	Net Income $000
1	1	Exxon	New York	97,172,523	4,185,932
2	2	Royal Dutch/Shell Group	The Hague/London	83,759,375	3,486,694
3	4	General Motors	Detroit	60,025,600	962,700
4	3	Mobil	New York	59,946,000	1,380,000
5	6	British Petroleum	London	51,322,452	1,245,623
6	5	Texaco	Harrison, N.Y.	46,986,000	1,281,000
7	8	Ford Motor	Dearborn, Mich.	37,067,200	(657,800)
8	11	International Business Machines	Armonk, N.Y.	34,364,000	4,409,000
9	7	Standard Oil of California	San Francisco	34,362,000	1,377,000
10	16	E. I. du Pont de Nemours	Wilmington, Del.	33,331,000	894,000
11	12	Gulf Oil	Pittsburgh	28,427,000	900,000
12	9	Standard Oil (Ind.)	Chicago	28,073,000	1,826,000
13	10	ENI	Rome	27,505,858	(1,206,970)
14	14	General Electric	Fairfield, Conn.	26,500,000	1,817,000
15	13	Atlantic Richfield	Los Angeles	26,462,150	1,676,078
16	•	IRI	Rome	24,815,296	N.A.
17	15	Unilever	London/Rotterdam	23,120,471	659,550
18	18	Shell Oil	Houston	20,062,000	1,605,000
19	17	Française des Pétroles	Paris	20,029,197	(80,595)
20	23	Petrobrás (Petróleo Brasileiro)	Rio de Janeiro	19,004,999	579,170
21	44	U.S. Steel	Pittsburgh	18,375,000	(361,000)
22	41	Occidental Petroleum	Los Angeles	18,212,226	155,602
23	20	Elf-Aquitaine	Paris	17,785,313	536,336
24	31	Siemens	Munich	16,962,630	279,794
25	29	Nissan Motor	Yokohama (Japan)	16,465,167	444,462

Source: Reprinted by permission from *Fortune* Magazine; © 1983 Time Inc.

rials thousands of miles, nor worry about whether the country will continue selling to them.

Another advantage for multinational corporations is the potential of new markets in various countries. Domestic competition quickly stiffens for successful products, and companies begin looking elsewhere for sales. McDonald's had sales of $293 million in Japan in 1982, and IBM earned $1.5 billion in sales revenue from Japan in the same year. Applied Computer Techniques, a British computer manufacturer, was trying hard in 1983 to find a U.S. company that would build and sell their popular 16-bit Apricot personal computer. They felt they needed a local producer to

The expansion by multinationals into new markets is a direct result of their form of organization. For instance, Coca Cola has penetrated the markets of both Egypt and the People's Republic of China.

crack the U.S. market. Finally, as firms grow larger, they feel the pressure of antitrust legislation in their home countries. International expansion offers a way of growing within legal restrictions. These external advantages have caused many domestic companies to adopt a global orientation.

Organizational Structure of Multinationals

AT&T, after losing battles to sell its private branch exchanges and microwave radio systems in foreign markets, decided it had to pay more attention to global management. Today, AT&T and many other companies realize they have to develop "global managers" who understand the culture and ways of doing business in other nations. Universities are also trying to catch up with this need. Harvard University and Dartmouth College have been integrating the international dimension into their key business courses for several years. But most of the business schools have just started and have a long way to go before its graduates understand marketing, manufacturing, financing, and human resource development in the international context.

Managing a multinational firm is not just a bigger job, but a unique one. Because the firm has various global operations, managers must pay special attention to integrating systems. Since some operations are almost like independent companies, it is easier for them to suboptimize. Suboptimizing occurs when a company division does what is best for itself even if it means the company as a whole loses in the process. To counteract this tendency, management must emphasize foresight and overall direction to direct the organization's branches toward a common purpose. Second, managers must give special attention to flows of information, capital, products, material, labor skills, technology, and management expertise among subsidiaries. If branch operations restrict their flexibility according to national boundaries, companies lose many advantages of being multinational. Finally, multinationals face special problems arising from the laws and customs of each nation. Every country has different patent laws, antitrust codes, and taxation methods. Keeping abreast of this complex framework requires a major information system.

To cope with these problems in managing multinationals, companies build a world organizational structure. They maintain some centralized home office control, but decisions must reflect customs and values of the particular branch or subsidiary location.

Multinationals and Nationalism

Although multinationals face most of the same problems and opportunities offered by international trade, they face a special problem of national loyalties. The multinational enterprise directs a family of varied nationalities toward supranational corporate goals. Companies have been accused of developing corporate nation-states that do not answer to any national government unit. Each subsidiary of the company is granted a charter by the specific foreign nation, but the company is a transnational system with different goals. As each multinational and each country tries to maximize their goals, there may be conflicts between what is good for the company and what is good for the country. Further, unlike domestic companies, multinationals call upon their tremendous wealth and power to combat national leaders with whom they disagree. When a small country deals with a General Motors, with sales ($60 billion in 1982) five times greater than that country's gross national product, things get tricky. We have seen the rebirth of economic nationalism in many countries. The Canadian government still restricts foreign investment in its country, and Australia has similar regulations. Zambia, Zaire, and Chile have fully or partially nationalized major copper companies.

The conflicts between government goals and multinational company policies are far from resolved. To regulate multinational concerns, the International Chamber of Commerce drafted a "code of good behavior" for both governments and multinationals to guide their relations. Because of the precarious relationships between multinational companies and various governments throughout the world, the future form and development of multinationals remain uncertain.

SUMMARY

International business covers business activities that cross national boundaries, including movement of goods, services, capital, technology, and

Opening Zimbabwe's market to Heinz's products in 1983 required direct negotiations between the company's CEO and President and Prime Minister Robert Mugabe.

personnel. International operations typically evolve through the stages of exporting and importing, licensing, joint ventures, direct investments, wholly owned operations, and multinational companies, contract manufacturing, and barter. The theoretical basis for trade rests on the theories of absolute and comparative advantages. An absolute advantage exists when a company is the sole producer of a good or when a country can produce a good more efficiently than other countries can. A comparative advantage exists when nations enjoy several absolute comparative advantages, and they concentrate on those goods in which their advantage is greatest. Foreign exchange is the interchange of national currencies, which is necessary for trade to exist between nations. Balance of payments is the relationship between what a country pays to and receives from other countries.

Governments place restrictions on free trade with both tariff and nontariff barriers. Tariffs are taxes, or duties, placed on commodities that cross national boundaries. Nontariff restrictions are quotas and embargoes. In addition to overcoming trade barriers, companies also have to solve cultural differences between countries.

Multinational companies are those that operate in at least six countries, with foreign subsidiaries accounting for at least 20% of total assets, sales, or labor force. Multinationals take global views in organizing their production and distribution systems. They guide a family of varied national groups toward supranational corporate goals, and this causes problems in some countries. In the past, giant multinationals pushed many countries around to take advantage of their resources, labor, or markets. But recently a renewed nationalism has countered the power of multinationals.

MIND YOUR BUSINESS

Instructions. Check whether you agree or disagree with the following statements:

Agree   Disagree

_____   _____   1. We should have the right to buy cars made in Japan.

_____   _____   2. We should have the right to own factories in Canada.

_____   _____   3. We should have the right to buy diamond mines in South Africa.

_____   _____   4. We should have the right to buy bananas grown in Brazil.

_____   _____   5. Other nations should not put a tax on the products we export to sell there.

_____   _____   6. Russia should have the right to buy wheat from us.

_____   _____   7. Saudi Arabia should have the right to buy military planes from the United States.

_____   _____   8. Japan should have the right to buy farmland in the United States.

_____   _____   9. Arabs should have the right to buy banks in the United States.

_____   _____   10. We should not put a tax on items that other countries sell in the United States.

See answers at the back of the book.

KEY TERMS

international business, 636
exporting, 637
importing, 637
licensing, 637
joint venture, 637
multinational company, 641
countertrade, 642
absolute advantage, 642
comparative advantage, 642
dumping, 643
foreign exchange, 644
foreign exchange market, 644
foreign exchange rate, 644
balance of payments, 645
balance of trade, 645
tariff, 648
specific duties, 648
ad valorem taxes, 648
compound duties, 648
quotas, 648
embargoes, 649
cartel, 649
International Monetary Fund (IMF), 650
General Agreement on Tariffs and Trade (GATT), 651
Common Market, 651
Trade Expansion Act, 651
Kennedy Round, 651

REVIEW QUESTIONS

1. In what specific ways does international business contribute to the success of our economy?

2. Identify and briefly explain the methods for engaging in international business.

3. What are the differences between absolute and comparative advantage?

4. What is the foreign exchange market, how does it work, and why is it so important to international business?

5. What is a balance of payments? Balance of trade? How does the balance of trade impact upon international business?

6. Explain the concepts of dumping and give an example.

7. Explain the differences between the various trade barriers: tariff, specific duty, ad valorem tax, compound duties, quotas, embargo, cartel, and others.

8. Explain six attempts at reducing trade barriers.

9. Discuss the four major cultural barriers to international trade.

10. Discuss the major advantages and disadvantages of a multinational company.

CASES

Case 24.1: Code of Ethics for Multinationals

Governments of many industrialized countries have, from time to time, considered a voluntary code of conduct for multinational companies. Officials hope such a code would restore public confidence in multinationals, but they also fear that it might place undue restrictions on their operations. Multinational codes contain rules for corporate behavior on issues ranging from bribery to restrictive business practices and disclosure of information. Although observance of the code would be voluntary, agreement could set a precedent for laws and regulations. Most companies agree that something should be done to restore credibility, but they tend to object to any code that requires extensive disclosure of information to governments, the public, and labor unions. Companies think such disclosures would be costly, could benefit competitors, and would provide governments with data for political attacks.

Questions

1. What would be the advantages to such a code for multinationals? Disadvantages?

2. How could such a code be enforced?

3. Assume that you are assisting in developing a code for multinationals. What do you think the code should cover?

Case 24.2: Foreign Investments in the United States

Investment by foreign buyers in U.S. stocks and bonds has increased rapidly in recent months. Europeans are investing in the United States because of our economic recovery and rising costs abroad. Many of the European rich are also concerned about the safety of their holdings if communists come to power in many countries. Foreign investments are sometimes considered a threat because they draw money out of the United States; foreign buyers invest in our businesses and take the earnings and interest out of the country. Some critics think that we should not allow ourselves to be a "free lunch ticket" for European aristocrats and entrepreneurs.

Questions

1. Explain how investments in our country from foreign companies affect our balance of payments.

2. What can we gain by encouraging or allowing foreign countries to invest in the United States? What can we lose? What can we do to encourage or discourage such investment?

3. What is your opinion of foreign governments and entrepreneurs investing in the United States? Why?

LEARNING OBJECTIVES

After completing this chapter, you will be able to:

■ **Name nine industries that are likely to grow faster than the average during the 1980s.**

■ **Identify four industries that are likely to grow at slower-than-average rates during the 1980s.**

■ **Identify the occupations that are likely to add the most jobs by 1990.**

■ **Name the occupations likely to have the greatest decrease in jobs during the 1980s.**

■ **Identify jobs that will likely offer the highest starting salaries.**

■ **Discuss and apply three aspects of career planning.**

■ **Describe four psychological preparations for job hunting.**

■ **Name six job hunting strategies.**

CAREERS IN
BUSINESS

The good news is that there is no secret, hidden formula for finding an interesting, well-paying job. The bad news is that finding the right job in the right career requires extensive preparation, very hard work, persistence and time.

Jim Mullin, who earns $20,000 as an assistant account executive at Benton Bowles, a large ad agency, says, "You've got to make a job out of getting a job." Mullin prepared by working at summer positions and internships in ad agencies while still in college. In April of his junior year, he boldly took a trip to New York City and knocked on every ad agency door he could find, asking for "10 minutes of your time to help a college student with career decisions." After many calls and many call backs, Mullin got some advice and a few leads.

During his senior year, Mullin continued to search out leads and interview for jobs. He organized his effort with meticulous, up-to-date files of names, dates, and conversations. In April of his senior year, Mullin once again returned to New York, hand delivering resumes and setting up interviews. As a result of his extensive effort, he finally got an interview which eventually led to a job. He says you get a good job by making it your number 1 priority.*

Looking for a career in the 1980s will be like shooting a moving target. Many new fields will spring up: Some will last, some will not. Traditional careers will continue to change dramatically. Research programs in space, medicine, and the military will sprout new products and services not yet applied to human needs. Some industries will grow; others will decline; all will change. Unfortunately, many college graduates will have prepared themselves for jobs that have evaporated.

To increase the odds of securing the job and career that is right for you, begin your career planning now. Consider opportunities — what industries will expand, which will shrink, specific

---

* Randy Ring, "How I Got My Job," *Business Week's Guide to Careers*, Fall/Winter Edition, 1983, pp. 71–72.

jobs available, how you should choose a career, and job hunting skills.

CHANGES IN INDUSTRIES

Changes in technology and human need no doubt will continue to impact on all industries. Projections of current industries will not totally account for industry changes in the 1980s. For instance, there are about 2000 electric automobiles in use in the United States today. But the Department of Energy projects that as many as 9 million electric vehicles may be operating by the year 2000. If this projection is reasonably accurate, it will create a new industry. Still, we can, with some accuracy, project how rapidly or slowly current industries will grow in the 1980s.

Fast-Growing Industries

For the past several years, service industries have grown more rapidly than manufacturing industries. This trend will likely continue throughout the 1980s. In fact, of the 20 million jobs created in the 1980s, more than 75% are expected to be in service businesses. Advanced technology simply allows companies to manufacture more with fewer employees. The modernization of General Electric's locomotive plant will increase capacity by 33%, but they will need only 10% more workers. And because incomes have risen, we are demanding more and more services of all types. Experts predict that the following industries will likely grow faster than average during the next 10 to 20 years.

Computers. Shortly after World War II, the computer began a new industry. Rapid developments in speed along with reductions in size made it easy for businesses to use computers. The microcomputers of the 1970s and 1980s continued the explosion. Because they have applications to practically everything, the computer hardware and software industry will no doubt continue to expand.

Communications. Communications will touch more lives in the future than perhaps any other industry. You will be able to see people in living color as you talk to them via phone, even if they live on the other side of the world. Computers will diagnose problems in machines, as well as human health, in remote locations. Television and radio programming will transmit almost perfect signals, and you will be able to dial individual programs on your digital-wired network. Communication and data processing will become even more entwined. Phone companies are already rewiring the world with optical cables. AT&T and IBM are visiting each other's backyards.

Biotechnology. Few could have realized that by 1984 $2.5 billion would have been invested in starting up more than 100 new companies dedicated to discovering new products from biotechnology. Sales are mounting speedily, however, and some people are predicting billion-dollar an-

The computer, real estate, and waste management industries are among those anticipating rapid growth during the 1980s.

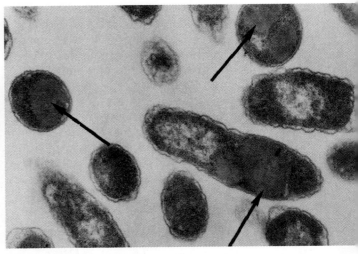

Arrows point to sites on bacteria where rennin (used in cheesemaking) is manufactured because of genetic reprogramming by scientists. Such advances in biotechnology can now produce many substances desired by medicine and industry in cost-efficient quantities.

nual revenues within the next few years. Congress's Office of Technology Assessment (OTA), for example, predicts that before the turn of the century, annual sales of chemicals and drugs produced by gene splicing could top $15 billion. And sales of products generated by gene splicing will come from virtually every area of manufacturing.

Finance and insurance. Finance and insurance created 1.4 million positions between 1973 and 1983, an increase of 34.7%. Because of the demands that firms and individuals make on capital and money management, these industries are likely to continue growing.

Retail and wholesale trade. Primarily due to rapid expansion in restaurants and food stores, retail and wholesale trade will add millions of jobs throughout the 1980s.

Real estate. Experts predict a need for 34% more real estate agents and brokers during the 1980s. Baby boomers have grown up, and, like their parents before them, they want to own their homes. Many can afford second homes or vacation retreats, even with the higher cost of real estate.

Waste management. Industries throw off 40 million metric tons of hazardous wastes each year. As the amount of waste increases, more and more environmental engineers and chemists will be needed to work in this area. People must learn to live with waste, and they will do it by recycling. Some experts predict that waste management will grow into a mammoth industry, not only collecting and processing waste but distributing products from the conversion.

Health care. Because of better methods for preventing and curing illnesses, Americans will live 10 to 20 years longer in the future than they do now. In fact, the health care industry will likely provide as much as 15% of all new jobs created by 1990. However, the industry will likely experience dramatic changes. We will rely more upon machines for diagnosis and prevention. Big companies will provide more health care services by operating their own facilities and producing drugs and medical equipment. Traditional hospital treatment will not likely grow as fast.

Mechanical repair services. Increased use of mechanical and electronic products, robots, and gadgets will increase the need for repair services. This industry will demand more auto mechanics, appliance repair people, and people who can repair business machines, including robots.

Energy. Even with conservation, energy needs will grow. Companies that now control valuable energy sources such as oil will broaden their base into mining, move more into nuclear power, eventually fusion, and finally into solar power. Some day, giant satellites circling the earth will convert the sun's rays into microwaves and transmit them to earth.

Entertainment. As more money and time become available, people seem to yearn more for entertainment. In a few years, most homes will have an electronic home entertainment center. Say goodbye to current-day movie houses and broadcast TV, but look for new forms of entertainment that stress total sensory environments.

Slower-Growing Industries

Many manufacturing industries will either shrink or grow at a very slow rate. Not only can more goods be produced with fewer workers, but largely because of cheaper labor, almost 8% of the world's manufactured goods come from developing countries such as Brazil, Korea, Singapore, Hong Kong, and Mexico. In 10 years, this figure will probably double.

Labor-intensive industries like apparel manufacturing are expected to decline because of low-wage foreign competition.

Basic metals. During the recession of the early 1980s, thousands of steelworkers lost their jobs. Many steel mills were shut down, and others were modernized. Steel imports also increased. Many

---

Many of the jobs lost in the steel industry will never return; they are gone forever.

---

of the jobs lost in the steel industry will never return; they are lost forever. The same thing is occurring in most basic metal areas.

Higher education. While more kindergarten and elementary teachers are needed, experts predict that there will be less need for professionals in secondary and university positions.

Agriculture. Although agriculture will continue to be a giant industry, it will likely experience slow growth in the future. Currently, only $\frac{1}{16}$ of U.S. land is used for crop production. Other nations who are not able to produce as efficiently as U.S. farmers will likely increase their demands for food imports. However, drug companies, food processors, chemical producers, oil companies, and conglomerates will buy and operate more farms. Advances in agricultural science and mechanization will continue to allow this country to produce more with less.

Apparel and shoe. Intense competition from abroad is already crippling U.S. apparel and shoe industries. In 20 to 40 years, they may be wiped out completely. These industries are labor intensive, and the wage rates of many other nations are simply much lower than ours. We will continue to import more and more of these items.

JOB OPENINGS AND SALARIES

While industry predictions project important trends of career opportunities, they do not detail job specifics. Many jobs cut across all industries — for example, accounting, secretarial, and janitorial. It might be helpful to know about specific job openings and salaries.

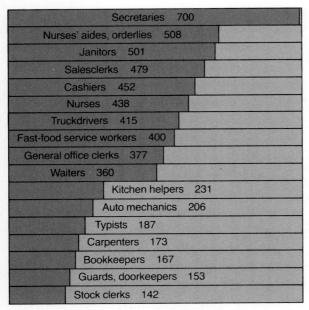

Secretaries	700
Nurses' aides, orderlies	508
Janitors	501
Salesclerks	479
Cashiers	452
Nurses	438
Truckdrivers	415
Fast-food service workers	400
General office clerks	377
Waiters	360
Kitchen helpers	231
Auto mechanics	206
Typists	187
Carpenters	173
Bookkeepers	167
Guards, doorkeepers	153
Stock clerks	142

Jobs created by 1990 (in thousands)

Figure D.1.
Projected new jobs for noncollege graduates by 1990. *Source: U.S. Department of Labor.*

Job Growth by 1990

Most of the job growth by 1990 will not necessarily require people with college degrees. Job positions will actually shrink in many occupations.

Jobs for nongrads. The U.S. Department of Labor projects that the greatest number of new jobs by 1990 will be for secretaries: Industry and government will need 700,000 more of them. However, they will not be likely to spend too much time making coffee and taking dictation; rather they will be operating computers and other machines to speed the flow of information through the office. There will also be many new jobs for nurses' aides, janitors, and sales clerks. Figure D.1 lists the projected new jobs for nongrads by 1990.

Jobs for college graduates. Leading the parade for new jobs for college graduates will be elementary school teachers. But experts also project many new openings for accountants, computer system analysts, electrical engineers, and computer programmers. Figure D.2 lists the projected new jobs for college graduates by 1990.

Job decline. Experts predict there will be 20% fewer farm laborers in 1990. Experts also predict reductions in graduate assistants, farmers, shoe-making machine attendants, secondary school teachers, and college professors. Figure D.3 outlines these declines.

Job Salaries

In 1984, electrical engineers' average starting salary was $26,643. Accountants with 1 to 3 years' experience earned between $17,000 and $25,000 per year. Doug Olson made $18,700 as a public school teacher. He says, "I wouldn't think of doing anything else. Working with young children is the most gratifying thing for me." Beth Silbergleit, a college graduate, made $11,949 as a park ranger. She liked working outdoors more than making money. Of course, salary is not the only, nor even the major, consideration when planning for a career; nevertheless, it is an important factor for many people.

Many factors influence salary. Typically, people with college degrees earn more than noncollege graduates. A man with a college degree will earn $329,000 more over his lifetime than his nongraduate counterpart. Women graduates earn $142,000 more over a lifetime than women non-

Figure D.2.
Projected new jobs for college graduates by 1990. *Source: U.S. Department of Labor.*

Elementary-school teachers	251
Accountants, auditors	221
Computer-system analysts	139
Electrical engineers	115
Computer programmers	112
Mechanical engineers	62
Aero-astronautic engineers	29
Architects	26
Psychologists	24
Dietitians	17
Physical therapists	17
Speech, hearing clinicians	16
Economists	12
Geologists	12
Veterinarians	11

Jobs created by 1990 (in thousands)

TABLE D.1 ■ AVERAGE STARTING SALARIES BY ACADEMIC FIELD FOR 1984

Bachelor's Degree in	Average Expected Starting Salary
Electrical engineering	$26,643
Chemical engineering	$26,164
Mechanical engineering	$25,888
Computer science	$25,849
Metallurgy, materials	$24,445
Physics	$22,852
Civil engineering	$21,266
Mathematics	$19,539
Accounting	$18,684
Financial administration	$18,122
Agriculture	$17,586
Marketing, sales	$17,550
Social science	$16,763
Business administration	$16,650
Personnel administration	$15,908
Communications	$15,636
Hotel, restaurant management	$15,447
Education	$14,779
Liberal arts	$14,179
Human ecology	$13,917

Source: Michigan State University survey of 617 companies.

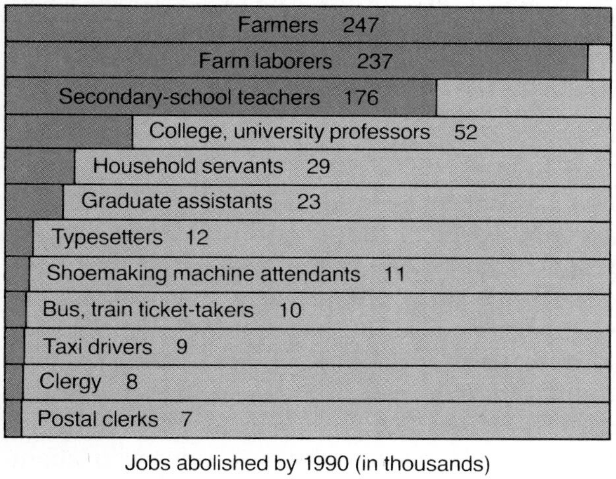

grads. Figure D.4 diagrams average starting salaries by degree in 1984.

Unionized occupations usually pay more than similar nonunion jobs. Carpenters (who are not unionized) earned an average hourly rate of $9.61 in New York City in 1983. The national average for unionized plumbers in large cities was $15.68 per hour.

Large companies usually pay better than smaller ones. Traditional female fields — nursing, for example — pay less than male-intensive occupations. Caron Macdonald says she found more money and more excitement doing a man's job; she made $31,000 last year as a locomotive engineer for Burlington Northern Railroad. But the greatest determinant of salary is simply supply and demand. Where there is a relatively short supply of applicants, companies have to bid the salaries up. That is why engineering graduates earn more than education majors. Table D.1 lists average starting salaries for 1984 by academic field, and Table D.2 projects 1990 salaries for the hottest careers. By 1990, the labor force will grow to between 122 and 128 million. Although, as we have shown, jobs will increase, competition will still be tough in many areas.

Figure D.3.
Projected decreases in jobs by 1990. *Source: U.S. Department of Labor.*

Farmers	247
Farm laborers	237
Secondary-school teachers	176
College, university professors	52
Household servants	29
Graduate assistants	23
Typesetters	12
Shoemaking machine attendants	11
Bus, train ticket-takers	10
Taxi drivers	9
Clergy	8
Postal clerks	7

Jobs abolished by 1990 (in thousands)

TABLE D.2 ■ PROJECTED AVERAGE SALARIES FOR HOT CAREERS BY 1990

Career	Projected Average Salaries by 1990
Data Processing	
Programmer	$33,000–$ 43,500
Systems analyst	$38,000–$ 52,500
Data base manager	$49,500–$ 67,000
Engineering	
Mechanical	$33,500–$ 47,000
Electronics	$35,300–$ 49,000
Energy	$44,000–$ 60,500
Accounting & Finance	
Cost accountant	$34,700–$ 46,000
Auditor	$34,900–$ 48,000
Financial V.P.	$80,000–$115,000
Human Resources/Personnel	
Technical jobs recruiter	$31,500–$ 43,800
Personnel V.P.	$70,000–$ 95,000
Marketing and Sales	
Sales engineer	$34,000–$ 47,500
Secretary	$15,100–$ 28,900

Source: Fox-Morris "1980s U.S. Job Market" Survey.

TABLE D.3 ■ PAY RANGES, NUMBER OF EMPLOYEES, AND TYPE OF WORK FOR FEDERAL WORKERS, 1982

General Schedule Grades	Number of Employees in Grade	Pay Range (Year)	Type of Work
GS-1	2,375	$ 8,676–$10,857	Messenger
GS-2	17,734	9,756– 12,278	File clerk
GS-3	81,406	10,645– 13,840	Typist
GS-4	163,802	11,949– 15,531	Senior stenographer
GS-5	191,130	13,369– 17,383	Engineering technician
GS-6	90,739	14,901– 19,374	Secretary
GS-7	132,131	16,559– 21,527	Computer operator
GS-8	28,160	18,339– 23,838	Computer operator
GS-9	142,290	20,256– 26,331	Buyer
GS-10	28,037	22,307– 29,003	Electronics technician
GS-11	159,550	24,508– 31,861	Job analyst
GS-12	164,954	29,374– 38,185	Attorney
GS-13	111,485	34,930– 45,406	Chief accountant
GS-14	56,772	41,277– 53,661	Personnel director
GS-15	28,491	48,553– 63,115	Personnel director
GS-16	739	56,945– 72,129	Super grades— supervisors, directors of bureaus
GS-17	163	66,708– 75,604	
GS-18	75	78,184– —	

Source: Federal Register.

Jobs in Government

Currently almost one out of five employed persons works for the government. While the size of government—national, state, and local—is not likely to increase at the same rate as in the past, the number of jobs will probably increase somewhat. Practically any type of job can be found in government that can be found in the private sector. In many government jobs the pay is competitive with private enterprise, and fringe benefits are just as good or better.

The federal government pays according to **general schedule (GS) grades,** a system of 18 grades for classifying salary levels. Table D.3 identifies the pay ranges, number of employees, and type of work for each of the 18 GS grades.

Figure D.4.
Average starting salary by degree for 1984.
Source: Michigan State University, based on a survey of 617 companies.

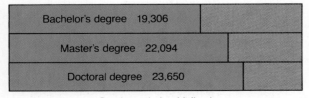

Bachelor's degree   19,306
Master's degree   22,094
Doctoral degree   23,650

Starting salaries (dollars)

CAREER PLANNING

Bob Seevers earned a degree in history, with an accounting minor. But like so many students, he really did not know what he wanted to do. He went to every campus interview, regardless of the company; he also interviewed for positions that his parents and friends lined up. Nothing seemed right. Although Seevers had been an excellent student, he could not find a job that felt right for him—mainly because he was uncertain about what he wanted. He had only a faint idea of how a company might use his skills; he did not know what type of organization he wanted to work for; and his career goals were indefinite, to say the least. Graduates who avoid Seevers's dilemma begin their career planning at the front end of their college education. Effective **career planning** includes identifying your career concept, analyzing your skills and goals, selecting an industry and a company, and staying flexible.

Identify Your Career Concept

Dr. Michael J. Driver, professor of management and organizational behavior at the University of Southern California, identifies four career concepts.

The steady-state career. The **steady-state career** centers on lifelong commitment to a profession or craft — law, medicine, engineering, and accounting, for example. Steady-state careers appeal to people with high security needs or a strong desire to steadily increase their commitment and competence. Today, such careers require periodic retraining.

Linear career. People who wish to advance steadily upward through the organizational hierarchy are following the **linear career** concept. This strategy requires an organization whose structure resembles a tall, narrow pyramid. Such ladder climbers like the power and status of the top jobs and the sense of achievement that the

---

BUSINESS BULLETIN

How to Negotiate Your Starting Salary

Many candidates feel inadequate negotiating their starting salaries. You can reduce these feelings by researching the going salaries for the type of job you are seeking. Consider the following:

■ Check with college placement offices and ask what salary range companies are offering for the type of job you are seeking.

■ Call several private personnel placement agencies and ask them the same question.

■ Find a friend who works in a job similar to the kind you seek and ask him or her about salary expectations.

■ Check the want ads: Some will include salary ranges.

Armed with the latest data on salary ranges, you are better prepared. In negotiating your starting salary, consider the following:

■ Candidates who are best prepared to show the company how they can benefit them have the best chance for higher salaries.

■ Keep your salary discussion focused on the issue of the market rate. It may be hard to show the employer why you deserve more than other candidates.

■ According to research, 80% of the candidates who refuse the first salary offer get a second offer. The second, in some cases, may be only a few dollars higher, however.

■ Ask yourself, "Are there skills that I haven't sold properly?"

■ Do not give the impression that you will work for any sum just to get a job.

Source: Marilyn Moats Kennedy, "The Fine Art of Salary Negotiations," *Business Week's Guide to Careers*, Fall/Winter Edition, 1983, pp. 62–63.

climb provides. Linear career seekers are the most common type in our society.

Transitory career. Devotees of the **transitory career** approach move erratically from job to job and from company to company. They seem to enjoy the time off between jobs and the variety this concept affords them.

Spiral career. Some people make a major career change after devoting years to something else—a **spiral career** pattern. A college president might move into insurance, or an ad executive might choose to become a psychologist. Personal growth is usually the motive of spiral types.

Know Thyself

After thinking about and selecting the type of career pattern that you think fits you best, you next have to analyze yourself. What are your goals? What skills do you like to use? What kind of organization do you want to work for?

Identify your career goals. Of course, you will not likely be able to accurately identify 40-year career goals. Things change too much. But you can look at goals 3 to 5 years ahead. Consider whether you would like to become a manager eventually? Head of a department? Vice-president? President? Do you want to own your company? Do you want to stay in sales all of your life? Do you prefer to enhance your skills, that is, do you want to become known as an expert in tax accounting, or do you want to become a generalist? How important is money? Job challenge? Do you want to travel or live in one area?

Many universities have career counselors at their placement centers to help job seekers identify their goals. And there are tests such as the Strong-Campbell Interest Inventory to help identify your interests.

What are your skills? A college education provides a lot of knowledge in many areas. And it should also enhance your skills. A skill is something you can do. Ask yourself, "Am I good with words and writing?" "Have I developed quantitative skills in, say, mathematics or accounting?" "Do I have good interpersonal skills?" "Am I persuasive?"

Do not assume that you have a good idea of your skills simply because you have spent some time developing them. Stephen Morris, an executive at Drake Beam & Morin, a placement firm, tells of an accountant who was fired from his job. Although the accountant had 20 years' experience, a battery of tests showed him to be in the lowest 10% in quantitative abilities. The accountant commented, "Gee, maybe this explains why I've been unhappy for 20 years." He had gone into accounting because a friend told him it was a good field; now he is a successful salesman.

The key to long-term career happiness is to select a job that you enjoy; good pay, status, and security wane in importance if the job is distasteful.

The key to long-term career happiness is to select a job that you enjoy. Good pay, status, and security wane in importance if the job is distasteful; the price is just too high for most of us. Richard N. Bolles, in his top-selling book *What Color Is Your Parachute?*, explains how to analyze your skills.

Choose an organization. Before you begin a serious job search, make decisions about your likes and dislikes regarding organizations. Respond to the following questions:

- Do I like a large structured organization?
- Do I prefer a smaller, more informal work group?
- Do I like to work on my own?
- Do I enjoy working with groups of people?
- Is the organization's status important to me?
- Do I prefer a high-pressure organization?
- How much emphasis does the organization place on continued training and development?
- What kind of career movement does the organization offer?
- Does the organization produce a product or service that I think is worthwhile?

Although you should make conscious decisions on these matters, you should also remain somewhat flexible. After gaining some experience, you might find that your interests change. For instance, a demanding organization might scare you a bit, but if the organization provides proper support and rewards, you might find that you prosper in such an environment.

Take a Broad Outlook

Jan Toennison, seeking a journalism degree, wanted to be a newspaper person, "doing investigative reporting," as she put it. In her senior year, she worked on a class project with a company's public relations department. The result was a 36-page report that impressed the company so much

CROSS FIRE

Is the Master of Business Administration (M.B.A.) Degree Worth the Price?

According to Thomas Peters, coauthor of *In Search of Excellence,* the rash of jokes about M.B.A.s suggest their fall from favor. Sample joke: If Thomas Edison had been working with M.B.A.s, he wouldn't have invented the light bulb; he'd have made a bigger candle. Harvard professors Robert Hayes and William Abernathy warned businesses in 1980 that they were stultifying under the influence of over-analytical managers. When John F. Welch, Jr., became chairman of General Electric in 1981, he slashed the corporate planning department, a traditional entry point for M.B.A.s.

General Electric trimmed its overall hiring in 1983 by 4%, but they cut their M.B.A. hiring by almost a third. Philip Morris reduced their hiring of M.B.A.s by 50% in recent years. Joseph E. Seagram & Sons cut the number of M.B.A.s in their management development program from 21 in 1980 to 3 last year. Xerox hires 50% fewer M.B.A.s now than in 1980. At the same time, the number of M.B.A.s has increased tremendously, from 4640 in 1960 to 62,000 in 1982. Further, companies are hiring a larger percentage of students with B.S. and B.A. degrees from liberal arts programs.

Unadorned college graduates are gaining favor for several reasons. Many top students in the humanities are underrecruited; thus, they will be happier with less salary than an M.B.A. They also have less expansive egos and are much easier to mold into the corporate image.

Corporations are not turning their backs completely on M.B.A.s. They just seem to need fewer of them. And companies are going to second-tier, but still first-rate schools for more of their M.B.A.s. Some companies feel that M.B.A.s from the top schools do not offer a good return on their investment.

Still, starting salaries for Harvard M.B.A.s in consulting firms average $50,000 per year. Production-oriented graduates get around $35,000, and salaries for investment banking M.B.A. degrees range over $40,000. And overall, the average starting salaries for people with master's degrees average almost $3000 more than starting salaries for people with a B.S. or B.A.

Do you think good undergraduate students should invest the time and money necessary to get an M.B.A. from a top-flight graduate school? Why?

____ Yes   ____ No

Do you think good undergraduate students should invest the time and money necessary to get an M.B.A. from a low-ranked graduate school? Why?

____ Yes   ____ No

Source: Susan Fraker, "Tough Times for MBAs," *Fortune*, Dec. 12, 1983, pp. 65–71.

they asked her for a job interview. Even though she thought she had her heart set on being a reporter, she interviewed for the job; the company made an offer and she took the job. A couple of years after taking the job, Jan said, "I never would have guessed that I would be working as a public relations coordinator for a large organization, but I enjoy my work very much."

Pat Malone graduated from college with a degree in education, and she taught in the public schools for several years. Later she obtained a master's degree in student personnel and guidance. Pat planned to be a public school counselor. But there were few jobs available, so she looked in industry and accepted a job in human resources at Pizza Hut where she eventually became a manager of the training and development department.

Do not define your career choice too narrowly; keep your options open.

The fact is that most people have a hard time identifying exactly what they want in the way of a career. And, because of limited experiences, they are not aware of just what is available. Even though you want to plan for a career, it is still best to keep a broad outlook. Do not define your career choice too narrowly; keep your options open. Most large organizations offer opportunities for practically any academic area.

Results of a recent study funded by the National Institute of Education (NIE) indicate that "contrary to much of the current rhetoric about the great demands for high-technology skills in the future, of the twenty occupations expected to generate the most jobs by 1990, not one is related to high technology." According to the Bureau of Labor Statistics, the high-tech occupations will account for only 7% of all new jobs between 1980 and 1990.

This is not to suggest that a college education or training in high-tech skills will not be important but, instead, reflects a need for workers to have good basic skills and a strong educational foundation to be able to respond to rapidly changing needs. One particular NIE recommendation points to the need for developing skills in life and career planning. "Since we cannot predict, with any precision, what kinds of jobs people will hold

over their 40-year working life, it is best to provide a good general education and an ability to adapt to changing jobs and careers."

JOB HUNTING

"Blood, sweat, and tears . . . literally," is the answer given by a Bryn Mawr graduate when asked how she got her job. Job hunting is neither easy nor necessarily pleasant.

Psychological Preparations

The Approach 13-30 Corporation, in its publication, *The Graduate,* outlined three psychological axioms designed to help weather job hunting experiences. We have also added a fourth suggestion: Be prepared to sell yourself.

Hang on to your ego. John Stoner, after graduating from Lawrence University in Appleton, Kansas, began beating the pavement. After 5 weeks, he had talked with nearly 100 people and received 15 interviews. Still, he managed to land only a temporary internship. Later that year, he took a job in the Congressional mail room for $15,000. He said he never dreamed that after graduation he would be in a Senate post office, hearing a supervisor say, "Stoner, sweep the floor."

Most job seekers can expect only one to five leads or interviews for every 100 resumes mailed out.

K. E. O'Neill, a career consultant in Englewood, Colorado, says that most job seekers can expect only one to five leads or interviews for every 100 resumes mailed out. Rejection is a constant companion of job hunters. But rejections do not necessarily mean that you are worthless or even that the company did not think highly of you. Rejections occur for various reasons: They already had someone else and just politely went through the interview; your personality did not match the company's expectations; the company's budget is too tight to hire but they want to keep interviewing; there may be more graduates in the field than jobs available; or maybe they feel that the job is just not right for you. Job hunting can be tough, risky, and ego deflating. Many candidates sell themselves short and take a job beneath their qualifications because of a few early rejections.

Get your fantasies in line. You must have confidence, but do not overdo it. You can quickly turn off most interviewers by making extravagant claims. Interviewers fear a candidate with unrealistically high expectations because they think the candidate will be dissatisfied when things do not turn out as expected. But if an interviewer asks what you would like to be doing 20 years from now, tell him or her your dreams — then turn to the reality of your present search and what you expect.

Hard, cold facts go farthest. Ian McCutcheon, who eventually took a job with Beckman Instruments, says it is important to cultivate a clear answer to the commonly asked question, "What do you want to do for us?" Do your homework on the company. Almost without exception, recruiters say they are impressed when a candidate can talk intelligently about particulars of their company. To research a company, use the library, seek information from professional associations, ask competing companies, talk to present and former employees, and read annual reports. By knowing about the company, you can save yourself and the interviewer a lot of time. You can also present your background more precisely to fit the position and philosophy of the potential employer.

Develop your qualifications, being especially careful to play up past work experiences, positions of responsibility (in jobs, community and school organizations, church), and personal goals.

Sell yourself. "You have to be willing to sell yourself because nobody else will," advises Amy Rowe, who took a job as trainee with the Bell Telephone Co. in Pittsburgh. She prepared herself by taking a workshop on interviewing, and even participated in a videotaped mock interview where she dressed in her job hunting suit and a career counseling specialist played the role of a Bell interviewer.

Good personal selling requires that you confidently, but realistically, present your abilities and accomplishments to the recruiter. After her third interview for an internship with IBM, Jackie Brewton received the dreaded rejection. When she received the message that IBM was not going to hire her, she asked, "Why?" The recruiter said they were hiring a very outgoing young man because they thought he would fit in well with the company. This led to further discussion where she talked about herself. A few days later, Brewton received a call reversing the bad news; the recruiter had previously felt that the candidate was too quiet. Figure D.5 offers a list of fifty questions that employers most often ask of candidates. In preparing for an interview, practice responding to these questions.

What Companies Look For

"We look at GPAs and we look at performance as it relates to outside activities and classroom work," says J. Clyde Kunkel of Owens-Illinois. "In short, we look for the total human being." Michalene G.

When considering a candidate, IBM says they evaluate work experience, academic background, extracurricular activities, and honors and awards.

Trainor of R. R. Donnelley & Sons Co. says, "We look for college graduates who demonstrate motivation and achievements in personal or academic life." "The graduate's work, school experiences, and ability to communicate" is important to J. G. Whilhite of Hughes Aircraft Co. IBM says they evaluate work experience, academic background, extracurricular activities, and honors and awards. Of course, companies look at special courses and degrees: A firm looking for an accountant would require an accounting degree, and engineering openings require engineering degrees. But in general, companies seem to seek students who have the combination of:

- Academic courses relevant to the job requirements.
- High grade point averages.
- Successful work experiences related to job requirements.

1. What are your long-range and short-range goals and objectives, when and why did you establish these goals, and how are you preparing yourself to achieve them?
2. What specific goals, other than those related to your occupation, have you established for yourself for the next ten years?
3. What do you see yourself doing five years from now?
4. What do you *really* want to do in life?
5. What are your long-range career objectives?
6. How do you plan to achieve your career goals?
7. What are the most important rewards you expect in your business career?
8. What do you expect to be earning in five years?
9. Why did you choose the career for which you are preparing?
10. Which is more important to you, the money or the type of job?
11. What do you consider to be your greatest strengths and weaknesses?
12. How would you describe yourself?
13. How do you think a friend or professor who knows you well would describe you?
14. What motivates you to put forth your greatest effort?
15. How has your college experience prepared you for a business career?
16. Why should I hire you?
17. What qualifications do you have that make you think that you will be successful in business?
18. How do you determine or evaluate success?
19. What do you think it takes to be successful in a company like ours?
20. In what ways do you think you can make a contribution to our company?
21. What qualities should a successful manager possess?
22. Describe the relationship that should exist between a supervisor and those reporting to him or her.
23. What two or three accomplishments have given you the most satisfaction? Why?
24. Describe your most rewarding college experience.
25. If you were hiring a graduate for this position, what qualities would you look for?
26. Why did you select your college or university?
27. What led you to choose your field of major study?
28. What college subjects did you like best? Why?
29. What college subjects did you like least? Why?
30. If you could do so, how would you plan your academic study differently? Why?
31. What changes would you make in your college or university? Why?
32. Do you have plans for continued study? An advanced degree?
33. Do you think that your grades are a good indication of your academic achievement?
34. What have you learned from participation in extracurricular activities?
35. In what kind of work environment are you most comfortable?
36. How do you work under pressure?
37. In what part-time or summer jobs have you been most interested? Why?
38. How would you describe the ideal job for you following graduation?
39. Why did you decide to seek a position with this company?
40. What do you know about our company?
41. What two or three things are most important to you in your job?
42. Are you seeking employment in a company of a certain size? Why?
43. What criteria are you using to evaluate the company for which you hope to work?
44. Do you have a geographical preference? Why?
45. Will you relocate? Does relocation bother you?
46. Are you willing to travel?
47. Are you willing to spend at least six months as a trainee?
48. Why do you think you might like to live in the community in which our company is located?
49. What major problem have you encountered and how did you deal with it?
50. What have you learned from your mistakes?

Figure D.5.
Fifty questions employers most often ask of candidates. *Source Frank S. Endicott, The Endicott Report: Trends in Employment of College and University Graduates in Business and Industry. Northwestern University, 1974.*

- University honors and awards such as scholarships and honor roll.
- Leadership in extracurricular activities, for example, presidency of a student organization in the student's career area.

Job Hunting Strategies

To find her job with Lutron Electronics, Denise Lee, an English major, interviewed with ten campus recruiters, contacted alumni for job hunting contacts, mailed out at least 100 letters and resumes, and made five to seven follow-up calls weekly. Like Lee, most successful job finders use a combination of search strategies.

College placement offices. Placement directors agree that their best service is giving students the chance to interview with a variety of employers. Take this opportunity by signing up for many interviews with companies of different sizes, industries, and philosophies. Many placement offices also offer other services, including testing and career counseling. Amy Rowe recommends that students take full advantage of the career services offered by their schools.

TAKING STOCK

What Has Happened to Harvard's Class of '73 Women M.B.A. Graduates?

Thirty-four women, a mere 5% of the total class, entered Harvard's M.B.A. program in 1973. *Fortune* was able to find and interview thirty-three women of the 1973 class last year. All are working full time, except for one who is working part time. Eighteen are married, and fourteen are mothers. Their median earnings is $57,000, and the top earner makes more than $200,000 per year. Four others make more than $100,000 per year. Still a survey of the 1973 class of men showed them to be earning much more than the women — 35% of the males were earning more than $100,000 per year.

It is still hard to find women who have worked their way to the top of a significant U.S. corporation. The big names, Elizabeth Arden, Helena Rubinstein, and Mary Kay Ash, started their own companies.

Discrimination no doubt accounts for some of the salary and position differentials between the Harvard women and their male counterparts. But many women also seem to have been slowed down by family responsibilities. For example, Joyce Fensterstock, vice-president in corporate finance at Blyth Eastman Paine Webber in New York, has been married twice and went through five pregnancies before producing a son. Cecilia Healy Herbert, a Morgan Guaranty vice-president, chose to stay flexible because her husband was an entrepreneur who kept moving around. By contrast, Elisabeth Spector, vice-president of Merrill Lynch Pierce Fenner & Smith, one of the highest paid of her class, is divorced and committed to work.

For many, the decision of whether to have children is a major factor. "It took me a long time to accept the fact that personal ambition conflicts with what's best for my husband, my baby, and me in the long run," says Joyce Fensterstock. Grappling with the motherhood question, Lois Juliber of General Foods, says, "I'm facing the hardest decision I've ever had to make."

The Harvard women M.B.A.s, like other businesswomen, find that older men have more trouble accepting them initially, but they eventually come around. Fensterstock describes her experiences: "Chairmen of the out-of-town banks where I make presentations are getting to know me." She added that they used to be embarrassed to introduce her.

The women at first thought that many of the pressures and the competition in business was unique to them. But later, many discovered that the business world was just tough, whether you are a woman or a man.

Source: Roy Rowan, "How Harvard's Women MBAs are Managing," *Fortune*, July 11, 1983, pp. 58–72.

Application letters. Plan to send out a hundred or more application letters and resumes. Try to make your application letter as individual as possible. It is better to aim it at a specific job in a specific company. Shotgun approaches show little preparation on your part. Remember, you may be competing with hundreds of others. Compose the letter carefully and neatly. Let the company know that you have done some prior research on them. Be able to tell them why you are applying to their firm.

Personal contacts. If you have friends who are already working, ask them to recommend you to appropriate people. Many companies encourage recommendations by employees, and in any case, it cannot hurt you. But do not rely entirely on personal contact. It will rarely land a job for you if you are not prepared and qualified.

Telephone contacts. It is usually considered unprofessional and tactless to drop in unannounced for an interview. Telephone calls are

Industry-supported career fairs are one source of information for student job-hunters.

BUSINESS BULLETIN

Early Jobs of Famous People

Traditional dead-end jobs do not necessarily have to be. Some very famous people worked, early in their careers, in what some might consider to be dead-end positions. Here are a few examples of famous people who got their start on low rungs of the ladder.

- Ronald Reagan, fortieth president of the United States, worked as a lifeguard.
- Carl Sandburg, poet, began as a dishwasher.
- Eugene O'Neill, famous playwright, began as a sailor.
- Singer Della Reese drove a taxi.
- Robert Conrad picked up dirty diapers for a diaper service.
- Abraham Lincoln, sixteenth president of the United States, worked as a farmer and as a hired hand on a flatboat.
- David Thomas, founder of Wendy's Hamburgers, began as a fast-food cook.
- Author of *Future Shock,* Alvin Toffler, drove a truck.
- Loretta Lynn picked strawberries for 25 cents a day.

If your first job is not what you had dreamed it to be, do not be discouraged. It is not where you start but where you end up that counts.

more desirable. Be brief. Tell them what you are interested in and why. Offer to follow up with a resume or personal visit. Pause occasionally to be sure the employer has a chance to ask questions. Telephone contacts do not produce a high percentage of successes, but they are economical and quick. Do them if you can handle the bruises to your ego.

Want ads. Frankly, most want ads are disappointing except for very specialized jobs such as secretary, mechanic, metal worker, waitress, and the like. But if you see an ad that grabs your interest, you may as well respond.

Computer placement. Some college placement offices and recruiting firms use computer networks to make job searches. The candidate typically provides the computer with a lot of information, something like what might appear on a resume, and the computer checks to see if it has any jobs on file that match the applicant's background. If so, the company might follow up with an invitation to the candidate to interview with them.

Sheraton Hotels recently experimented with computers in seeking applicants in Dallas. More than 1000 applicants showed up to interview for 400 jobs. The computers asked candidates about fifty questions, which they answered by pressing certain keys. Sheraton expects the process to reduce time spent in interviewing and to make hiring more rational.

SUMMARY

In looking for a career, it is helpful to know which industries are likely to expand and which likely to lose jobs. Experts predict the following industries to grow faster than the average during the next few years: computers, communications, finance and insurance, retail and wholesale trade, real estate, waste management, health care, mechanical repair services, energy, and entertainment. Slower-growing industries include: basic metals, higher education, agriculture, and apparel and shoe industries.

The greatest growth areas in new jobs during the 1980s will not necessarily require college de-grees. Secretaries, nurses' aides, and janitors lead the list. Leading the list of new jobs for college graduates are elementary school teachers, accountants, and computer system analysts. Jobs in farming, graduate assistants, and shoe making are most likely to lead the list of declining positions. Engineering graduates, followed by graduates in accounting and finance and data processing, are likely to command the highest starting salaries.

Career planning begins with identifying your career concept, for example: steady-state, linear, transitory, or spiral. Next, you should analyze yourself by: (1) identifying career goals, (2) recognizing skills, and (3) choosing among organizations.

Psychological preparations for job hunting include: hanging onto your ego, getting your fantasies in line, remembering that hard, cold facts go farthest, and selling yourself. Hiring companies typically look at academic courses, grade point average, work experiences, and university leadership and honors. To engage in a job hunt, consider using a combination of college placement office services, application letters, personal contacts, telephone contacts, and perhaps want ads and computer placement.

MIND YOUR BUSINESS

Instructions. Answer each of the following questions yes or no.

_____ 1. Do you have an ultimate career goal?

_____ 2. Are you making educational and work experience choices that are in harmony with your ultimate career goal?

_____ 3. Do you hold high expectations for your personal achievement?

_____ 4. Are you willing to take risks and experience failures in your career search?

_____ 5. Do you believe that you make your own luck?

_____ 6. Are you willing to relocate geographically?

_____ 7. Do you normally develop a strong sense of loyalty to your employer?

_____ 8. Do you actively develop contacts among your peers and in your community?

_____ 9. Do you plan to use both college recruiters and relatives and friends aggressively to find a job?

_____ 10. Are you obtaining an undergraduate business degree from a large state university?

See answers at the back of the book.

KEY TERMS

general schedule (GS) grades, 668
career planning, 669
steady-state career, 669
linear career, 669
transitory career, 670
spiral career, 670

REVIEW QUESTIONS

1. Identify the industries that are more likely to grow at faster-than-average rates during the 1980s.

2. Identify the industries that are more likely to grow at slower-than-average rates during the 1980s.

3. Where will most new jobs be created by 1990 for noncollege graduates? College graduates? What occupations are likely to lose the most jobs by 1990?

4. Compare the earnings of college and noncollege graduates. What academic areas will likely command the highest starting salaries by 1990?

5. Define career planning. When should you start career planning?

6. Identify and briefly describe Dr. Michael J. Driver's four career concepts.

7. Identify three things that you should do in analyzing yourself as a job candidate.

8. Should you take a broad or narrow outlook at possible positions and occupations? Explain.

9. Discuss four psychological preparations in looking for a job.

10. What do companies look for in a candidate?

11. Briefly describe six job hunting strategies.

CASES

Case D.1: Desire versus Opportunities

Kenny, an above-average student, always thought that he wanted to be a teacher. And he wanted to teach science at the secondary-school level. Upon graduating from high school, Kenny enrolled in a university with the intention of preparing himself to be a science teacher.

However, in one of Kenny's courses, a professor noted that there would likely be a decline in demand for secondary school teachers in the 1980s. This worried Kenny, and he consulted with a guidance counselor at the university. The counselor indicated that most job openings would occur in engineering, accounting and finance, and in elementary school education, and suggested that Kenny might change his major to elementary education.

Even though Kenny did not wish to be an elementary education teacher and felt that he had little aptitude for engineering or accounting, he was strongly considering changing his major.

Questions

1. Do you think Kenny should change his major to an area that offers more job opportunities? Why?

2. When there appear to be fewer opportunities in an area that a student likes, how much consideration should the student give to desires versus job opportunities?

3. What other factors should Kenny consider in his decision?

Case D.2: Future Jobs for Young, Minority Males?

Today, about 50% of minority teenagers are unemployed. The future does not hold much hope. Experts say the number of white youths will decline by about 30%, but the total of black and Hispanic youths will hold steady. And low-skilled, industrial jobs, which are traditional entry-level positions for many minorities, will shrink. Thus, the Bureau of Labor Statistics predicts that the unemployment rate for minority men age 16 to 24 will remain about 50% in the year 2000.

Black and white females are becoming more alike in the kinds of jobs they perform. But this does not appear to be true for black and white males. Semiskilled entry jobs, typically held by young men, are declining. Further, new plants are moving to the suburbs, making it harder for young, male minorities to find employment.

Questions

1. Why do you think it will be so much harder for young, minority males to find work by the year 2000?

2. What is the responsibility of educational institutions in preparing young, minority males for work? What is the responsibility of companies? The government? The young, minority male?

After completing this chapter, you will be able to:

■ Describe the future environment of business.

■ Analyze the perspective of social problems in the future.

■ Predict the role of the government in the future.

■ Identify population growth and trends.

■ Explain three economic challenges to our business system.

■ Predict how the work force, workers' attitudes, and jobs will likely change in the future.

THE FUTURE
OF BUSINESS

Totally electronic cars? Voice commands to start and stop your car, select a radio channel, and activate your ventilation system? Communications via video telephones on wristwatches with anyone in the world? Dams that reverse the flow of rivers? Bridges spanning the Strait of Gibraltar and the English Channel? Magnetic levitation trains traveling 250 miles per hour? Large colonies in space? These are a few of the exciting predictions that experts see in our future. But before you take these predictions too seriously, remember that economists of the 1920s did not predict the Great Depression, World War II, the computer, or even the ballpoint pen.

Prophecies have always been popular. In earlier times, kings had prophets sitting at their right hand, and they often beheaded prophets who made incorrect predictions. Today, leaders of nations still surround themselves with staffs who develop predictions to help their leaders usher the rest of us along.

Experts who busy themselves interpreting present trends and predicting future happenings do not always agree. So, from an uncertain launching pad, we blast into the future. This chapter presents the current speculations of experts, and we are reasonably confident that many of their projections will prove correct. If not, please spare us the treatment given the early prophets.

WHAT WILL THE BUSINESS ENVIRONMENT BE LIKE?

Experts believe that the U.S. economy will climb steadily for at least the balance of this century and produce a completely different country within the next 50 years. Our business system will continue to exist within the larger social environment of the nation. In the next few years, what is likely to happen to life-styles, buying power, leisure time, education, social problems, government, and our population?

Simpler Life-styles

As a professor of behavioral science explains it, we will see a more primitive return to life's basics. "Status conscious Americans are beginning to take their status from 'simpler is better.' Quality of life is overcoming the excesses of 'more and bigger is better.'" Already, people are showing less interest in big cars, big homes, big boats, and big living styles. People, including the in-crowd, are riding bicycles, sailing small boats, exercising, drinking imported water, and dieting at lunch. This trend will likely continue for several years.

As labor and material costs continue to increase, young marrieds will put off buying homes and settle for smaller houses when they do buy. Rumpus rooms, large entertainment areas, and family rooms will feel the crunch. Less space, combined with safer, more predictable birth control methods, will continue to limit family size. Many women are already abandoning their traditional homemaking roles, and this trend will continue. With fewer children and more money, couples may feel freer to take career risks. There will be more attempts at writing novels, starting businesses, shifting careers, and other midstream changes in people's lives. Sociologists also expect to see the revival of the extended family, as close relatives—especially the elderly—live with younger families to fight inflationary costs. More single people will group together to get the advantages of communal living.

Experts say that the soaring divorce rate will soon stabilize and perhaps decline as couples delay marriage until they are more able to cope with its emotional and financial demands. Singles and childless couples will look for more conveniences of big city living, thus prompting more self-contained downtown developments.

Our appetite for beef is expected to decline in the 1980s. Diets will contain other protein-rich foods and fresh vegetables — often grown in family greenhouses and backyards. Americans are in some ways adopting European habits, such as drinking more domestic wine, running short errands on foot, and establishing deeper community roots. Some studies show that already the number of families changing homes is declining as real estate prices hit the sky. Community planners will pay more attention to restoring old neighborhoods and preserving open spaces.

Within these restrictions, tensions are sure to exist. Americans are willing to give up some of their comforts. In exchange, they pursue esthetic values, personal growth, art, education, and perhaps religion. But few will accept drastic cuts in their living styles. After years of prosperity, we are unwilling to accept risks such as losing jobs, pensions, and savings. We look to government to guarantee these "rights," but at the same time distrust in government is at an all-time high. Crime is rising at record rates, and we distrust the police. Electronic devices make life easier in many areas, but we fear the loss of privacy. There is a possibility of income gaps widening; it is already happening between blacks and whites. Within these positive and negative projections, the more than 225 million Americans will have more problems and resources to cope with over the next several years.

Increased Buying Power

Economists predict that the recovery from the recent recession will last longer than usual. Forecasters at Wharton Econometric Associates in

Increased consumer buying power, as well as more leisure time, are predicted for the near future.

Megatrends for the Future

In his best-selling book, *Megatrends,* John Naisbitt predicts ten new directions that will transform our lives during the coming years.

1. *Shift from an industrial to an information society.* When President Lincoln was shot, it was 5 days before London heard of the event. When President Reagan was shot, a journalist, Henry Fairlie, working within a block of the shooting, got word by telephone from his editor in London just moments after the shooting. His editor had seen it on television. In 1956, for the first time, American white-collar workers in technical, managerial, and clerical positions outnumbered blue-collar workers. As the text predicts, the vast majority of new jobs will appear in service industries. And most service workers will be in jobs that create, process, and distribute information.

2. *Move toward high tech/high touch.* To Naisbitt, **high tech/high touch** describes what happens as we adjust to technology. He predicts that the more technology we introduce, the more people will aggregate and be with each other. Even though more people will work at home with their computers, and more people will shop from their homes, and teleconferencing might reduce some executive travel, the author believes that these activities will not be dominant. People simply need to be around other people.

3. *From a national to a world economy.* In 1960, U.S. plants produced 95% of the autos, steel, and consumer electronics sold in the United States. Today, the United States produces less than 70% of the autos, less than 80% of the steel, and less than 50% of the electronics bought by its consumers. In 1982, Japanese workers could build a car in 11 hours; U.S. workers required 31. People from other nations own more and more of the land, companies, and assets of the United States.

4. *From short term to long term.* Business executives have received a lot of criticism for taking a short-term view; in the future, we will be forced to look at the long run. Seventy-six percent of a group of 1000 executives surveyed by Hedrick and Struggles, a research firm, in 1981 said there has been a damaging emphasis on short-term financial goals.

    Changing to the long term means rethinking and asking the question, "What type of businesses are we in?" In 1981, GE said they were in the "business of creating business." Xerox announced that it was in the "automated office business." Sears wants to remain a top retailer and become the number 1 deliverer of financial services. All these require long-term commitments.

5. *From centralization to decentralization.* As centralized structures topple, we are rebuilding from the bottom up. Political change occurs more rapidly at the local than at the national level. We are moving toward an almost union-free society.

National magazines publish regional editions. States are becoming more assertive. Employees are demanding more participation in management decisions.

6. *From institutional help to self-help.* For the past few decades, we have looked to institutions for help — government, school systems, corporations, the medical establishment. The future will see us disengage our dependence upon institutions and go back to taking care of self. Parents have become interested in improving their local schools. The number of entrepreneurs creating their own businesses is exploding. From crime to consumerism, individuals are finding ways to tackle problems rather than depend upon large, organized institutions.

7. *From representative democracy to participative democracy.* "People whose lives are affected by a decision must be part of the process of arriving at the decision." National political parties have lost their unique identities; rather, many splinter groups have emerged within each party. Four movements are reshaping participation in corporate affairs: (1) increased consumerism, (2) more outside board members, (3) new shareholder activism, and (4) greater worker participation and employee rights.

8. *From hierarchies to networking.* The pyramid structure of our organizations is giving way to clusters, decentralized groups, and informal networks. Networks, according to Naisbitt, are "people talking to each other, sharing ideas, information, and resources." Networking media include conferences, phone calls, air travel, books, papers, photocopying, lecturing, workshops, parties, grapevines, mutual friends, summit meetings, tapes, and newsletters.

9. *From north to south.* The 1980 census showed that, for the first time, the South and the West had more people than the North and the East. Wealth and economic opportunity are also making this shift. Three sun belt states, California, Florida, and Texas, are the major recipients of the population and economic shifts. These three states are likely to be the economic growth centers of the future.

10. *From either/or to multiple option.* For years, we lived in an either/or nation: Ford or Chevy, chocolate or vanilla, full-time work or no work, married or single. Bathtubs were white, telephones were black, and checks were green. Today, you can choose from 752 different models of cars and trucks sold in the United States. Working hours are flexible and open to many types of sharing arrangements. You can purchase dozens of varieties of mushrooms, not to mention the dozens of flavors of popcorn, including pizza flavor. Cable television offers twenty to thirty channels in many locations. And the story continues.

Source: John Naisbitt, *Megatrends,* New York: Warner Books, Inc., 1982.

Philadelphia predict a 3.1% average annual growth rate, after inflation, through 1992. Major economic indicators—growth in total output, inflation rate, gain in personal income, and unemployment rate—all look favorable through the year 2000. (See Fig. E.1.) People are likely to remember that it took a costly recession to bring down inflation, and as a result, we may be more tolerant of unemployment rates than in the past. The combination of higher salaries, although at a slower rate of increase, smaller families, and more women in the job market will also add to the purchasing power of family units.

More Leisure Time

For years, the average workweek has steadily declined. In 1975, the average workweek for hourly employees was 36 hours, and it is expected to decline to 34 hours by 1985. (Automation, yielding more product for less work, is the major cause.) Reduced work hours mean more **leisure time,** time not required for working or sleeping. In 1900, leisure time made up about one-fourth of the average person's day. This increased to 34% by the 1950s. Leisure activities are expected to consume over 40% of a person's time by the year 2000.

In the future, many people will have the time to do things of their choosing and more money to do them with. Americans seem to have boundless energy for travel, entertainment, sports, and self-improvement. In the future, people will have even more time, and some more money, to spend on their leisure time pursuits. From 1965 to 1978, we more than doubled the amount of money spent on leisure time. And experts predict that the figure will double again during the 1980s. Sales managers of recreational items believe that ''the boom is across the board.''

But the most rapid growing leisure markets are:

- Foreign travel.
- Vacation trips, although they may be shorter and closer to home.
- Sports and all outdoor activities—exercising, picnicking, bicycling, boating, hiking, canoeing, etc.
- Home entertainment—TV, stereo, radios, home computers, books.

Figure E.1.
Projections of key economic indicators to the year 2000. *Source: Wharton Econometric Forecasting Associates.*

Projections (percentage)

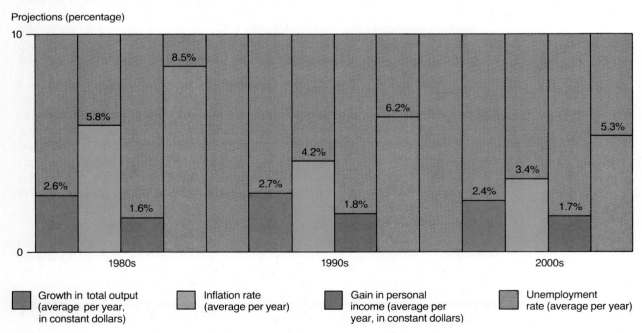

More Formal Education

Today about 30% of adults attend college; 50 years into the future, more than 60% of American adults will have attended college. Around 1960 we were spending only 3% of our gross national product on education. This amount has more than doubled and will double again in the next few years. In the late 1980s, college enrollments are expected to reach over 12 million as more adults, especially adult women, go back to college and stay longer.

Of course, the computer will bring true individualized instruction to education in every kind of setting. Desk top computers will allow students to work at their own speed and will eventually shift the focus of education to problem-solving and reasoning skills. The purposes of education will also broaden. We will see more emphasis on education for individual change and more attention to both the sciences and values.

Industry will become much more involved in education and job training. Many corporations, with state-of-the-art equipment and research methods, will grant degrees in technology, science, and engineering. In fact, businesses will pour more money into employee development of all types, from specialized welding instruction to improvement in individual/group adjustments.

Continued Social Problems

The world now generates between 500 million and a billion tons of waste each year; these figures will likely double in 15 years. Pollution and other social problems will persist because they are exceedingly complex. Environmentalists will continue to face opposition; discrimination solutions are perhaps light-years away; stiffer competition will make it hard to upgrade business ethics; and consumer complaints are likely to grow louder. Many of these problems will be compounded by the continuous accumulation of people in cities; experts predict that 74% of the population will live in 300 major metropolitan areas by the year 2000. Such congestion creates a lot of solid waste, dirty air, infested slums, and transportation troubles, which cause a host of psychological problems. Most experts believe that we have the technical know-how to solve these problems, but society will have to put hard cash into finding the solu-

tions. This will require trust and confidence in government and business—critical ingredients that are lacking at the moment. However, society is growing more impatient and insisting that government, businesses, foundations, and nonprofit organizations assume responsibility for their actions or inactions.

Larger Government

Government will continue to grow, perhaps at slower rates. We predict this simply because institutions in power almost always want more. However, the government will apply more of its time to policy determinations, and its role in implementations could be reduced. There is a growing feeling that programs can be more efficiently implemented at state and local levels. Although business leaders have resisted big government and especially government control, the 1980s seem sure to see government/business teams, especially in the "public need."

Because of social pressures, the government is likely to become more involved in setting goals. With increasing fragmentation of larger institutions, there is a growing need for guidance. The government is the most desirable mechanism for establishing national priorities, but the means for doing this are still disputed. Liberals have traditionally opted for a strong central government, while conservatives push for more state and local control. Simultaneously, liberals will probably develop more tolerance for local control, and conservatives are realizing that some federal influence is needed to stabilize our society. Among voters, independents, who are less bound by traditional political philosophies, will grow in influence.

Population Growth and Changes

There were about 1.8 billion people in the world in 1900; today, there are about 4.4 billion; in 50 years, the world population will approach 9 billion people. Within the United States, since World War II, we have seen three drastic shifts in population patterns: (1) the "baby boom," (2) the "baby bust," and (3) growth in the elderly population.

Annual births shot up to the 4 million mark between World War II and the early 1960s. After

Birth rate

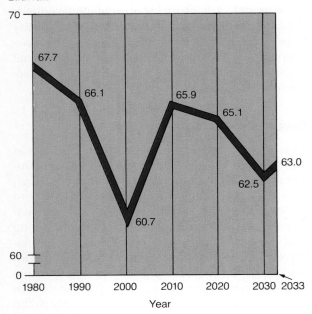

Figure E.2.
Projected decline in birth rates for the next 50 years. *Source: U.S. Department of Commerce.*

this baby boom came the baby bust, and birth rates are expected to decline into the foreseeable future. But since the 1950s, the number of people aged 65 or older has increased, to 11.3% of the population by 1980. In 50 more years, this percentage will almost double, to 21.5%. That is, more than one of every five people in the United States will be elderly. Figures E.2 and E.3 show the trends in births and the elderly.

As the population ages, the median age will move from 30.9 years to 41.1. The percentage of blacks will increase from the current 12% to about 16% in 50 years. Life expectancy for both males and females will increase, but women will still live, on the average, about 4½ years longer than men. The ratio of women to men in the population will change only slightly. Figure E.4 pictures these projections.

These **population dynamics,** changes in population characteristics, will have many implications for business and society, including:

- Slower growth in the labor force, which reduces the unemployment rate and allows the economy to grow at a more placid pace.

Figure E.3.
Percentage of people 65 or older in the population for the next 50 years. *Source: U.S. Department of Commerce.*

Percentage of people 65 and over

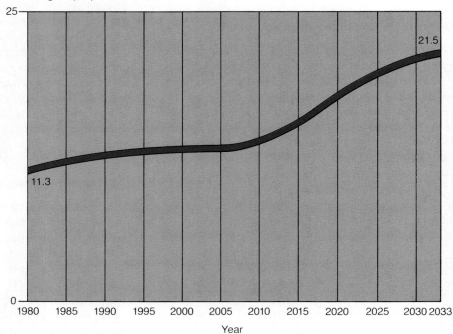

- Fewer youth-aged members, meaning less money for crime, welfare, and education, all of which are youth oriented.
- Shortage of experienced managers because of the lack of growth in the 45 to 64 age grouping.
- Fewer children and more working spouses, meaning more buying power. Some believe that the per capita income will reach record levels after a few years.

- Better entry level jobs, and faster promotions for new job seekers because of sparser numbers.
- Population stability, which is helpful in economic planning.

In short, it looks like the stabilizing population changes will contribute to a healthier economy over the next 10 to 20 years.

Figure E.4.
Projected population dynamics during the next 50 years. *Source: U.S. Department of Commerce.*

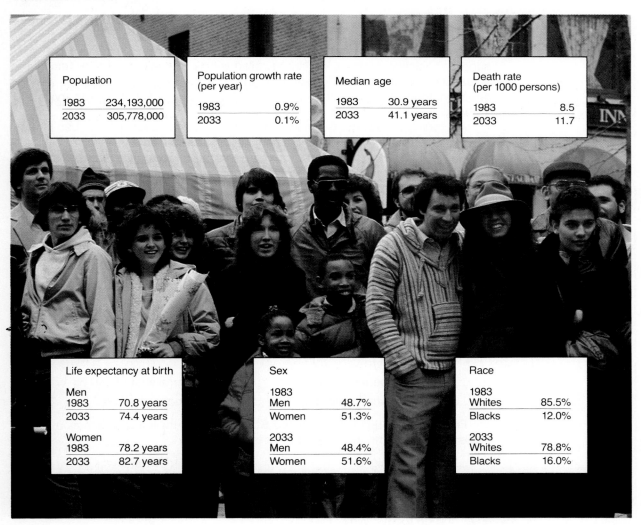

Population		Population growth rate (per year)		Median age		Death rate (per 1000 persons)	
1983	234,193,000	1983	0.9%	1983	30.9 years	1983	8.5
2033	305,778,000	2033	0.1%	2033	41.1 years	2033	11.7

Life expectancy at birth		Sex		Race	
Men		1983		1983	
1983	70.8 years	Men	48.7%	Whites	85.5%
2033	74.4 years	Women	51.3%	Blacks	12.0%
Women		2033		2033	
1983	78.2 years	Men	48.4%	Whites	78.8%
2033	82.7 years	Women	51.6%	Blacks	16.0%

ECONOMIC CHALLENGES OF THE FUTURE

Within these shifting society trends, our business system will have to stare down a few economic problems if economic health is to improve. Most of the projected problems of the 1980s were rooted in the 1970s. Specifically, the decade of the 1970s produced:

■ The worst recession since the Great Depression of the 1930s.

■ A 29% drop in the value of the dollar.

■ A doubling of consumer prices.

■ Twice as great a reliance on oil imports, as prices soared, causing very large trade deficits.

■ Productivity rates of workers increasing at less than half of the pace of the 1960s.

■ A drop in the Dow Jones average of industrial stocks of about 30% from a high of 1051 in 1973.

CROSS FIRE

Survive or Suffer?

Nine billion people in the world? Tons of waste produced annually? Inadequate water supplies? Nuclear destruction? Uncontrolled pollution? Lack of food? Waste of our valuable natural resources? Pessimists predict that we are on the road to self-destruction; they feel there is little chance that planet earth will continue to survive and do well.

According to experts, two-thirds of the world's population goes to bed hungry every night. Can we feed the world's population during the next 50 years? Scientists say they will be able to create plants that make their own fertilizer and resist pests and disease. Food production will come from farms, many of which will be in tropical countries, rain forests, and oceans.

The future will see stiff competition for water; we will need more than half of all rainfall for drinking water and mineral resource development. We use only a fraction of rainfall for these purposes today. Pessimists predict water wars, but other experts say we will be able to make sea water drinkable and even tow iceburgs to dry areas for fresh water.

Some believe that pollution will eventually bury us. Others say we will be able to recycle wastes and recover valuable chemicals. Technology will no doubt provide dramatic ways to extend our resource supplies. However, will we be prudent enough to safeguard the basics of life for future generations?

Do you think people in the world will be better off or worse off in the year 2000 than they are today?

_____ A. Much better off   _____ C. Somewhat worse off

_____ B. Somewhat better off   _____ D. Much worse off

For people working in the United States, do you think job satisfaction will be higher or lower in the year 2000 than it is today? Why?

_____ A. Much higher   _____ C. Somewhat lower

_____ B. Somewhat higher   _____ D. Much lower

Would you prefer to be entering college 50 years from now or would you prefer to enter college today? Why?

_____ A. 50 years from now   _____ B. Today

Major business problems of the remainder of the twentieth century will likely cluster around energy, capital requirements, productivity, and interest, all of which are related. (Inflation, a feared problem of the 1970s, seems to be under control.)

Energy

The skyrocketing fuel prices of the 1970s probably did the world a favor; it caused nations, including the United States, to curb wasteful habits. As a result, oil and natural gas supplies are likely to last much longer than anticipated. For the next few years, oil, gas, and coal will serve as our major energy supplies. Nuclear power will probably play a slightly bigger role. But solar and other forms of renewal energy will very likely provide less than 10% of our energy 50 years from now. Table E.1 shows where we will get our energy in the year 2000.

Capital Needs

Because of high inflation rates and corresponding drops in the stock market, companies have had a hard time raising the capital they need to keep their plants modern. As a result, many companies badly need a dose of new, more efficient technology. Because competitors in foreign markets spent more money for modern technology, we lost some ground in world markets. To get back to the head of the pack, U.S. companies not only need more capital for plant and equipment, they also need funds for research and development.

Output

From 1948 to 1968, we averaged a blistering 3.1% annual increase in output per man-hour. While we are not likely to see that again soon, everyone believes that the dismal 0.8% average during the last 5 years of the 1970s is just too low. By contrast, the first half of the 1970s was about 1.9%. Many possible reasons for the slowdown were explored in Chapter 2. Some say that the lack of new capital, partly the result of high energy prices, and an influx of younger workers and more women have helped drag the output down. There is hope that as we adjust better to the energy problem and our experience level of workers increases, we will return to the historic trend of 2.0 to 2.5% annual rate of increase. Indeed some experts predict that an-

TABLE E.1 ▮ ESTIMATES OF OUR ENERGY SUPPLY BY THE YEAR 2000

	1981 Consumption	Estimate for 2000
Oil (barrels per day)	15.9 million	13.7 million
Natural gas (cubic feet)	19.6 trillion	19.9 trillion
Coal (tons)	729 million	1,455 million
Nuclear (Btu)	2.9 quadrillion	9.2 quadrillion
Synthetics (barrels per day)	0	1.25 million
Solar, other renewable (Btu)	4.8 quadrillion	9.1 quadrillion
Total energy use (Btu)	75.7 quadrillion	97.0 quadrillion

Source: U.S. Department of Energy.

nual growth rates in output could run as high as 3% a year for the rest of this decade.

HOW WILL COMPANIES CHANGE INTERNALLY?

Future trends will surely have their impact on the organization and management of employees. Because employees are better educated and more independent than ever before, they are influencing decisions that were once considered none of their business. They are reacting against some management decisions, such as job specialization, that stunt human development. Ahead are significant changes in work force composition, worker attitudes, and job structure.

How the Work Force Will Change

Many of today's jobs will disappear as we continue to shift from a production to a service society. By the year 2000, production jobs will account for only about 11% of the labor force, down from almost 24% in 1980. We will also likely see the following shifts in the work force during the next several years:

■ More women and older workers in the work force.

■ More frequent career changes as jobs change.

- More emphasis on lifelong training and re-training.
- A shorter, more flexible workweek.
- More people working at home, with the aid of a computer.
- More union efforts to organize professional and white-collar workers.

How Worker Attitudes Will Change

Newer people coming into work places will be educated, ambitious, confident, impatient, and secure. This will have marked changes on employee attitudes. The most affluent, independent, and best-educated work force in the world simply will not accept financial and security rewards as enough. As a younger employee told a recruiting officer, "I am a very hard worker, but honestly, if you want me to come to work for your company, I must see opportunities to use my abilities and grow. That is even more important than money." A general manager from Cadillac said, "A new breed is coming into the work force with different ideas, and we have to adjust to these new thought patterns."

Employees have come to expect job security. To ensure this security, workers will insist upon some type of income maintenance. This may take a variety of shapes. Perhaps income can be fixed at

TAKING STOCK

The U.S. Will Continue to Be a Superpower

Relatively, West Germany, Japan, and Brazil will likely gain on the United States in economic and political stature during the next 50 years. Russia will likely continue to rival the United States militarily, but they will surely lose ground in other areas. In fact, experts wonder if Russia will be able to make the adjustments necessary to remain economically powerful for the future. Samuel Huntington of Harvard University says, "The United States 50 years from now clearly will still be a superpower, but there is a real question that the Soviet Union may not be." Seweryn Bialer of Columbia University believes that one of the key events of this century will be the decline of the Soviet Union.

The Western alliance will likely remain durable and continue to be more supportive of the United States, while growing more wary of the soviet bloc. Canada, a friendly neighbor and trading partner for years, will surely remain so. Central American nations face a struggle as Marxist guerrillas try to set up governments, but most experts think that the United States simply will not let that happen. Japan and the United States, even though they have some economic differences, will likely maintain good relationships.

Even though the rate of growth in the United States and North America will likely be gradual, the beginning of the twenty-first century will still feature the United States as the world's largest economy. The accompanying chart shows the estimated rates of economic growth to the year 2000.

Source: "U.S. Will Stay No. 1 Even As Superpowers Wane," *U.S. News & World Report*, May 9, 1983, pp. A34–A36.

some minimum level through negative income taxes, or companies may have to provide financial security to their workers when they are laid off. Unions will also help establish funds and pensions so that most citizens will be assured a minimum income. At the same time, workers within a company will bring pressure to lessen the differences in financial rewards between skill levels and between employees and management. Wage and salary differences between workers will grow smaller.

The security of having enough money to meet basic needs will give employees the courage to push through changes netting them more control in the organization. The youth of today worry much less about security; it was provided for them and they are developing ways to protect it. Some managers will interpret the worker's idea of an enjoyable job as playing around and not having too many demands. However, the concept of adult fun is growing and developing. Managers who offer their people challenging work and deserved recognition will get responsive employees operating at high need levels.

How Jobs Will Change

Jobs will undergo structural changes to accompany attitude changes. Younger workers and many older ones will not spend their working lives fixing the same bolts on 100 cars per hour for

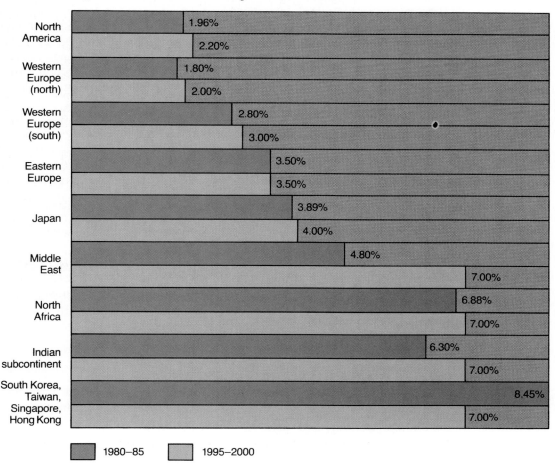

Rate of economic growth; estimates of annual averages in constant dollars

	1980–85	1995–2000
North America	1.96%	2.20%
Western Europe (north)	1.80%	2.00%
Western Europe (south)	2.80%	3.00%
Eastern Europe	3.50%	3.50%
Japan	3.89%	4.00%
Middle East	4.80%	7.00%
North Africa	6.88%	7.00%
Indian subcontinent	6.30%	7.00%
South Korea, Taiwan, Singapore, Hong Kong	8.45%	7.00%

Quality-of-life concerns, such as life-long training and retraining and a more flexible sense of the work week and environment, are some expected changes in work-force attitudes.

30 years. But much of U.S. industry is trapped by its heavy capital investment in boring jobs. A few companies in foreign countries have built new plants that allow more worker participation in jobs, and results have been favorable. As domestic companies build new plants to replace old ones, we will probably see more team-oriented work facilities.

Likewise, middle managers will clamor for the right to participate in higher-level decision making. Young managers are insisting on being involved in setting goals, and they want more freedom to implement their projects. These managers are willing to work hard, but not just because they have a job. Like blue-collar employees, they want to find meaning and growth from their contributions. Established executives realize the need to attract and hold fresh talent, but on the other hand, they feel pressure from other executives to avoid fast promotions. As with most major changes, resistance occurs. But we predict the future will see more young managers getting their way. However, when they arrive at top levels, they will probably be as fixed in their ways as are today's traditional managers.

SUMMARY

Most experts predict that the economy will steadily improve during the remainder of the twentieth century and perhaps well beyond. In the business environment, there appear to be trends toward simpler life-styles, more buying power, more leisure time, and more formal education.

Current social problems will likely continue into the future, and most people believe the government will continue to grow, although at a reduced rate. The population will grow at a slower rate, but the percentage of people 65 and older will increase dramatically.

Economic challenges of the future include providing and conserving energy sources, increasing capital spending, and improving output. The work force will change as more women and more older people hold positions. And workers will demand more say-so in management decisions.

MIND YOUR BUSINESS

Instructions. Match your predictions with those of the experts by answering the following questions true or false.

_____ 1. Divorce rates will decline.

_____ 2. People will live in smaller homes.

_____ 3. Families will have greater buying power.

_____ 4. People will work fewer hours and have more leisure time.

_____ 5. Education will become more of a lifelong process.

_____ 6. Most of our social problems will be solved.

_____ 7. Government will shrink in size.

_____ 8. Our population will become younger.

_____ 9. For energy, we will depend almost exclusively on solar sources.

_____ 10. Output per worker will drop.

_____ 11. People will change careers more often.

_____ 12. Workers will participate more in management decisions.

See answers at the back of the book.

KEY TERMS

high tech/high touch, 684
leisure time, 686
population dynamics, 688

REVIEW QUESTIONS

1. Describe how life-styles will likely change in the future.

2. Will buying power increase or decrease? Explain.

3. How will the amount of time we spend in leisure activities change?

4. Explain the role of formal education in the future.

5. How will we handle our social problems?

6. Will government continue to grow? Explain.

7. Identify how the population will likely change in the next several years.

8. Identify and describe the major economic challenges of the future.

9. Describe how the work force, worker attitudes, and jobs will change in the future.

CASES

Case E.1. Emphasis on Retraining

The decline and change of the steel and auto industries in the early 1980s displaced and dislocated hundreds of thousands of workers. Experts predict that technological change will repeat the displacement and dislocation process for other industries in the future.

Because of job complexity and technological changes, few workers will hold one job for life. Some experts predict that career changes every 10 years or so will be common. These changes will place a great demand on the need to retrain people in the work force. No longer will a few years of formal education at the beginning of an employee's career last a lifetime.

Questions

1. What is the role of the government in providing these retraining opportunities? Private industry's role? Organized labor's role?

2. What can people do to prepare themselves for the expected changes in jobs during their careers?

3. What kinds of employees are likely to have the most trouble adjusting to career changes during the next 50 years?

Case E.2. Preparing for a Long Life

Within 50 years, the Census Bureau expects males to have a life expectancy of 74.4; life expectancy for females will be 82.7. But a lot of scientists think these figures are far too conservative. Some doctors, because of discoveries in genetics and immunology, think we can reasonably expect to live to be 120 or 150 in the not-so-distant future. Dr. Roy Walford, of the medical school of the University of California at Los Angeles, believes that people who are 70 will look as if they are 35. Without doubt, people will continue to live longer and remain physically active for many years. And older people will comprise a much larger percentage of the population.

Questions

1. What implications does this trend have upon work, careers, and retirement?

2. How will the increased number of elderly people influence our marketing system? Human resources departments? Management ranks?

3. Do you think the retirement age will change in the next 50 years? Explain.

VALUES AND CAREER SATISFACTION

What do you want to get out of your career? Money? Fame? A chance to work with people? We call these things values: rewards we derive from our work, things that bring us satisfaction. Often whether or not we like a job depends on how well it satisfies our value system.

Presented here is a list of values, followed by some jobs associated with each value. Remember that values are highly personal and that different people derive different rewards from the same job. This is a partial listing of work values; not included are such values as high salary, for example, that are associated with many business careers.

Read each value, along with its definition. Check the two or three values you especially desire to gain from your work.

_____ *Travel:* Working in a job in which you take frequent trips.

Salesperson	Branch manager, international corporation
Business executive	
Import-export agent	Buyer

_____ *Public contact:* Working in a job in which you have day-to-day dealings with the public.

Pharmacist	Fashion model
Public relations representative	Travel agent
Employment interviewer	

_____ *Prestige:* Working in a job that gives you status and respect in the community.

Business executive	Lawyer
Banker	Economist
Business school professor	

_____ *Persuading:* Working in a job in which you personally convince others to take certain actions.

Lawyer	Sales manager
Account executive	Lobbyist
Labor arbitrator	

_____ *Variety:* Working in a job in which your duties change frequently.

Foreign service officer	Athletes' agent
Fashion coordinator	Sales manager
Convention manager	

_____ *Independence:* Working in a job in which you decide for yourself what work to do and how to do it.

Lawyer	Real estate developer
Retail store owner	Urban planner
Newspaper publisher	

_____ *Work with machines or equipment:* Working in a job in which you use machines or equipment.

Contractor

Computer programmer

Director, computer operations

Quality control inspector

Industrial engineer

_____ *Work with numbers:* Working in a job in which you use mathematics or statistics.

Accountant

Statistician

Loan officer

Auditor

Budget officer

_____ *Leadership:* Working in a job in which you direct, manage, or supervise the activities of others.

Business executive

Warehouse manager

Production supervisor

Farm manager

Director, industrial relations

_____ *Creativity and self-expression:* Working in a job in which you use your imagination to find new ways to do or say something.

Industrial designer

Advertising manager

Movie-TV producer

Clothes designer

Sales promotion director

_____ *Intellectual stimulation:* Working in a job that requires a considerable amount of thought and reasoning.

Systems analyst

Publications editor

Environmental analyst

Design engineer

Economist

_____ *Competition:* Working in a job in which you compete with others.

Salesperson

Purchasing agent

Fund raiser

Leasing agent

Auctioneer

_____ *Authority:* Working in a job in which you use your position to control others.

Bank examiner

Insurance commissioner

Health and safety inspector

Director of security

Internal revenue officer

Review the values you selected. The more agreement there is between your personality type (Careerscope I), your interests and activities (Careerscopes II–V), and your values (Careerscope VI), the more likely you are to find satisfaction in that field of work. The following are possible steps for you to consider if you are having trouble deciding on a career:

- Talk with people (friends, relatives, neighbors) working in the careers in which you are most interested.
- Visit them at their places of work.
- Seek the advice of career counselors.
- Read as much as possible about those careers. You will find materials in libraries and school and college career resource centers. The *Occupational Outlook Handbook,* a Department of Labor publication, is one valuable information resource.
- Arrange to go on informational interviews by calling the human resources department of companies that offer the career path that you're exploring.
- Try to find related part-time job or volunteer experiences.

Glossary

Absolute advantage (24) Situation that exists when only one country can produce a certain item, or can produce it much more efficiently than any other country.

Accident and health insurance (19) Insurance that repays injured person for expenses and lost earnings due to accidents or sicknesses.

Accountability (7) The liability of subordinates to accomplish tasks and/or goals as agreed.

Accounting (20) The activity of accumulating, measuring, and communicating financial information about organizations for the purpose of planning, controlling, and decision making.

Accounting cycle (20) The sequence of recording, classifying, summarizing, and reporting information.

Accounting equation (20) An algebraic statement that reflects the relationship of a company's assets, liabilities, and equity. It is stated as: Assets = Liabilities + Equity.

Accounts receivable (17) Money that others owe a company for things sold to them on credit.

Acid-test ratio (20) An accounting ratio used to determine a company's ability to pay its short-term debt quickly. It is found by dividing the sum of a company's cash, marketable securities, notes receivable, and accounts receivable by its current liabilities.

Active Corps of Executives (ACE) (5) An organization of actively working executives who work through the SBA in providing management counseling and advice for small business owners.

Adjustable life insurance (19) Insurance that allows policyholders to change both the amount of coverage and premium payments throughout their lives.

Administered VMS (14) Cooperation in production and distribution stages brought about because of the strength of a channel member.

Administrative law (23) Rules and regulations developed by certain governmental agencies to implement the provisions of statutory law.

Ad valorem tax (24) Tax figured on the cash value of a good.

Advertising (15) Paid nonpersonal appeal to customers.

Advertising boom (1) Factor of the consumer era where advertising suddenly became a way of business life.

Advocacy advertising (15) Advertising that takes a stand on a controversial issue or makes a proposal to solve some societal problem.

Affirmative action (9) Executive order requiring all companies with federal contracts to set targets for hiring and promoting minorities and women.

Affirmative action program (3) Program created by the federal government that requires companies with a certain number of employees and government contracts to develop a plan that encourages the hiring of minorities.

Age Discrimination in Employment Act of 1967 (9) Federal legislation that outlaws discrimination against job candidates between the ages of 40 and 65.

Agency shop (11) Work situation where all employees pay dues to support union activities, whether or not they choose to join the union.

Agent (23) Party who legally represents another party.

Agent wholesaler (14) Wholesaler who does not take title although taking possession.

Age of technology (1) Modern business era, when a boom in electronics has had impact on the running of business and consumer products; the age of the computer.

Alien corporation (4) Corporation formed in another country but allowed to do business within the United States.

American Exchange Market Value Index (18) Index of average prices for all the common shares listed on the ASE.

American Federation of Labor (AFL) (11) First major organization of labor unions. It began in 1886 and grew to its greatest strength in the 1930s.

American Institute of Certified Public Accountants (AICPA) (20) Professional organization of practicing CPAs.

Analog computer (21) Computer that deals with physical measurements.

Analytic process (8) Production process in which raw materials are broken down into one or more products.

Annuity (19) Agreement by which an investor makes a lump-sum payment to a company, and the company pays out monthly payments, determined by mortality tables, until the person dies.

Anticipation inventory (8) Purchase made in expectation of a future need.

Application programmer (21) Person who writes coded instructions that direct the computer through such applications as payroll, billing, and cost reporting.

Apprenticeship training (9) Training where an employee is given a temporary lower status until the basic skills of a job are learned.

Arbitration (11) Situation by which an unsettled dispute is forced into settlement by an outside party, usually the federal government.

Array (C) List of data arranged in increasing or decreasing order.

Articles of incorporation (4) Legal document submitted to a state government that allows a business to operate as a corporation.

Artificial intelligence (21) Programs that give computers the human equivalent of intelligence, imagination, and intuition.

Asked price (18) Offer to sell in the OTC market.

Assembly line (8) Production process used when the product moves a set route and various production processes are performed at different stages of that route.

Asset (17, 20) Anything that the company owns; resources that are owned or controlled by an organization that are expected to have future economic benefit.

Authority (7) Power given to a manager to exercise influence over others and to make decisions in the completion of tasks.

Authority delegation (7) Process of passing authority and responsibility within different levels of organization.

Authorized stock (17) Number of shares of stock, identified in the company's charter, that the company has permission to issue.

Autocratic leadership (6) Leadership style that emphasizes dogmatic leader decisions with little or no subordinate input.

Automated teller machine (ATM) (16) Machine that allows customers to get cash and make deposits by inserting a plastic card in specially equipped machines.

Automation (8) Situation in which the production process is divided in routine, standard (Automatic) functions.

Bailee (23) Party to whom the bailer entrusts property.

Bailment (23) Agreement whereby one person leaves property with another person for a specific purpose.

Bailor (23) Person who leaves personal property with another person.

Balance of payments (24) Difference between the value of goods received and accepted between two countries, or the overall value difference for one specific country.

Balance of trade (24) Difference in terms of cash value between what a country pays for imports and receives for exports.

Balance sheet (20) Accounting statement that describes a company's financial position on a particular date.

Barter (1) Business activity of trading one good for another.

BASIC (21) Beginners All-Purpose Symbolic Instruction Code, an easily learned computer language, especially popular for personal computer users.

Batch processing (21) System that accumulates data into similar groups and enters the data into the computer in batches.

Bearer (17) Person, in a promissory note, who is to receive payment from the other party.

Bear market (18) Market where stock prices are falling.

Beehive organization (7) Type of organization where varying levels of authority work throughout the company, interfacing with all employees at both the immediate upper and lower level.

Better Business Bureau (3, 5) Nonprofit local organization of business people that helps protect consumers and businesses against unfair or unethical business practices by monitoring and reporting the successful and unsatisfactory practices of local businesses.

Bet your company culture (A) Organizational culture characterized by high risk and slow feedback.

bfoq (9) *Bona fide* occupational qualifications; actual requirements, usually physical, that an applicant must have to be able to perform the job.

Bid price (18) Offer to buy in the OTC market.

Bill of exchange (17) *See* trade draft.

Bill of lading (17) Receipt from shipper to a company that has shipped goods.

Binary system (21) Numbering system using only two numbers, 0 and 1, in various combinations to represent decimal numbers and letters.

Birdyback (14) Combining air and truck transportation.

Bit (21) Smallest piece of information a computer can handle.

Blacklist (11) List circulated by employers of union activists making it hard for them to get a job.

Blue-sky laws (18) State laws that regulate securities trading.

Board of directors (4) Group of individuals elected by the stockholders and charged with the responsibility of managing a corporation.

Board of Governors (16) Seven-member board that directs the twelve federal reserve district banks.

Bond (17) Certificate stating that the company owes money to the holder.

Bond indenture (17) Detailed agreement of the rights and privileges of the bondholder; also called trust indenture.

Bond interest (17) Money, like rent, paid to lenders for the use of their money for a certain time period.

Bookkeeping (20) The mechanical process of recording and maintaining accounting information.

Book value (17) Value of the stock recorded on the company's accounting records; the net worth of the company divided by the number of shares outstanding.

Boom (2) Period of unusually prosperous business activity.

Boycott (11) Labor tactic where union members organize in refusing to buy a company's product until more satisfactory labor practices are adopted by the company.

Brand name (13) Words or letters that identify the producer of a particular product.

Breach of contract (23) Situation in which a party fails to perform any part of a contractual agreement

Broker (14) Person or business that brings the buyer and seller together and usually represents one or the other; usually collects a fee for the services provided.

Budget (6, 20) Plan for future goals or expectations expressed in numbers; a plan for the spending or distribution of an organization's resources over a period of time.

Buffer inventory (8) Purchase made in excess of actual need to be certain that adequate quantities are available.

Bull market (18) Market where stock prices are rising.

Burglary insurance (19) Insurance that covers the forcible and unlawful taking of property from businesses that are closed.

Business (1) Organization that engages in the creation and sale of goods and services with the goal of earning a profit.

Business cycle (2) Variation in the level of business activity within a country.

Business graphics software (21) Programs that create analytical and presentation graphics primarily for business use.

Business-interruption insurance (19) Insurance that covers fixed expenses and the profits that would be lost if a business were shut down due to fire or other insured perils.

Business law (23) Unwritten law that has emerged through custom and legal precedent.

Business plan (5) Paperwork prepared for the beginning of a business, including sales forecasts, a detail of all costs and cash requirements, and projected profits.

Business system (1) Composite of all business firms and their relationships.

Business trust (4) Legal form of partnership in which a trustee completely manages the business, and the owners have limited liability.

Buyer co-op (4) Cooperative that buys products, usually in volume and at low cost, for members.

Buying power (1) Money left after taxes and inflation.

Byte (21) Combination of eight bits.

CAD/CAM (8) Computer-aided manufacturing systems.

Cafeteria-style benefits (9) Program that allows employees to select their individual packages of fringe benefits from a wide range of alternatives.

Call (18) Option to buy stock at a set price.

Callable bonds (17) Type of bond that the issuing company can retire before their maturity date.

Capital (1) Monetary value of resources used in production, usually in cash and tangible assets.

Capital budgeting (17) Process of making decisions on long-term investment opportunities for a firm; relates to decisions of whether to spend money on new equipment, buildings, automobile fleet, and the like.

Capitalism (2) Economic system in which businesses and individuals are allowed to function for themselves without intervention by the government.

Cartel (24) Group of businesses or countries that agrees to operate as a monopoly.

Cash-and-carry wholesaler (14) Limited-function wholesaler to whom retailers pay cash for the items.

Cash discount (13) Discount given to purchasers of items to encourage them to pay for the merchandise within a given period of time.

Cash flow (17) Amount of net cash an investment project returns over a period of time.

Cash-surrender value (19) Amount of money that will be paid to the holder of an insurance policy should the insured decide to cancel the insurance. The insured may also choose to purchase a paid-up policy with the cash-surrender value, or borrow money against it.

Catalog showroom (14) Store where customers who receive catalogs can view samples of products, make the purchase, and receive delivery of the product.

Cathode ray tube (CRT) (21) Television screen that displays computer input/output data.

Centralization (7) Situation in which decision-making authority is held by a few people at the top levels of an organization.

Central processing unit (CPU) (21) That part of the computer that contains the logic (arithmetic) and control functions.

Certified Management Accountant (CMA) (20) Accountant who has passed an examination and other requirements indicating an ability to analyze financial information for management decisions.

Certified Public Accountant (CPA) (20) Accountant who has successfully passed a rigorous, state-administered examination and met certain educational and experience requirements.

Chain of command (7) Established relationship of authority and responsibility at different levels and among employees of an organization.

Chain stores (14) Two or more retail stores that are commonly owned and managed and sell related products.

Chattel mortgage (17) Agreement giving the holder the right to reclaim property if the buyer of the property does not repay the loan on the property.

Checking account (demand deposit) (16) Checking accounts in banks; a depositor can obtain money on demand.

Civil Rights Act of 1964 (3, 9) Federal law that prevents employment discrimination based on race, religion, national origin, or sex.

Clean Water Act of 1972 (3) Federal law that controls water pollution.

Close corporation (4) Privately held corporation, owned by family or a few individuals, whose stock is not available to the public.

Closed shop (11) Situation where an employee must join a union in order to be hired by a company (also called a union shop).

COBOL (21) Common Business-Oriented Language, a computer language oriented toward the processing needs of business applications.

Coinsurance clause (19) Clause in fire insurance coverage that stipulates that the policyholder must insure a certain percentage of the value of the building, commonly 80%, to get full coverage for the loss.

Cold canvassing (15) Personal selling, like door-to-door, where the sales persons contact people directly without a lead or reference.

Collateral (17) Property, or something of tangible worth, that the borrower pledges to offer the lending party if the borrower cannot or does not repay the loan.

Collateral trust bond (17) Bond backed by stocks and bonds of other companies.

Collective bargaining (11) Method or process of negotiating a contract between labor and management.

Combination layout (8) Plant layout that utilizes some elements of product, process, and fixed position layouts.

Commercial finance company (17) Financial institution that typically buys accounts receivables from businesses at a discount.

Commercial paper (17) Unsecured promissory notes issued by large, well-established companies on the open market.

Commodity exchange (18) Organized market for trading several kinds of listed commodities.

Common Market (24) European Economic Community Agreement encouraging trade among members while controlling imports from outside nations; made up mostly of European nations.

Common stock (17) Stock that carries full voting privileges.

Common stockholder (4) Owner of stock who has a right to vote on company issues.

Communism (2) Economic system characterized by the absence of classes and by common ownership of property.

Comparable worth (9) Idea that people should receive equal pay for work of equal value.

Comparative advantage (24) Situation that exists when a country can produce a good or service at much lower cost than any other country.

Comparative advertising (15) Type of advertising that directly compares the qualities of a product to competing products, using company or brand names.

Compensating balance (17) Minimum deposit required by a bank when making a loan to a customer.

Competition (1) Rivalry between two or more businesses striving for the same customer, market, or resources.

Compiler program (21) Program used to translate symbolic codes into machine language.

Compound duty (24) Tax charged on a particular good that combines the cash value and some physical measurement in determining the actual tax.

Computer (21) Electronic machine that stores and processes information in accordance with instructions supplied to it.

Concession bargaining (11) Process of refusing accepted wage patterns in the industry as a basis for pay and incentive packages.

Conciliator (11) Third party, meant to be unbiased, who works with both labor and management to help them come to terms agreeable to both.

Conglomerate (4) Joining of companies that offer unrelated products or services.

Congress of Industrial Organizations (CIO) (11) Organization of unions that split off from the AFL and then rejoined in 1955 to create the AFL-CIO—still the largest federation of unions.

Conspiracy doctrine (11) Doctrine stating that it was an illegal act of conspiracy for unions to bring economic pressure on employers.

Consumer Advisory Council (3) Federal agency established by President Kennedy in 1962 to protect citizens' rights.

Consumer and sales finance company (17) Financial institution that specializes in making small personal loans directly to the consumer.

Consumer behavior (12) Field of study within the discipline of marketing that analyzes the various reasons people choose to buy products.

Consumer co-op (4) Retail outlet owned by the customers.

Consumer decision model (12) Graphic illustration that specifies the influence on buying decisions.

Consumer era (1) Business era when businesses first began stressing the desires and tastes of consumers.

Consumer goods (13) Actual physical goods purchased by the ultimate consumer.

Consumerism (3) Public demand for more protection of buyer's rights.

Consumer price index (2) Index that reflects the rate of inflation, usually using a previous year as the base value.

Consumer Reports (3) A monthly magazine published by the Consumers Union that reports the quality of products.

Consumer's Bill of Rights (3) List of rules published by the Consumer Advisory Council that provide citizens the right of safety, information, choice, and hearing.

Consumers' Union (3) Nongovernment organization that tests and rates products for the benefit and information of consumers.

Containerization (14) Modern method of shipping where goods are specially packaged for shipping in large bulk containers.

Contingency leadership (6) Belief that no single leadership style is best for all situations and that the appropriate leadership style depends on the situation.

Contingent business-interruption insurance (19) Insurance that covers potential losses due to interruption of the delivery of essential supplies.

Continuous process (8) Production process that operates for long uninterrupted periods of time.

Contract (23) Legally enforceable agreement between two or more competent parties to do or refrain from doing some activity.

Contract buying (8) Type of buying, usually involving a contract, where certain quantities of goods are purchased over a period of several years.

Contractual VMS (14) Vertical marketing system in which independent channel members achieve cooperation through contractual agreements.

Control charts (8) Graphic illustrations of the production process with time required for each step.

Controlling (6) Management process of ensuring that objectives are accomplished properly and changing strategies if they are not.

Control program for microprocessors (CP/M) (21) A common operating system that can be used in many different personal computers.

Convenience goods (13) Type of consumer goods that are purchased quickly with minimal effort.

Convenience store (14) Smaller store, located at an easy-access location, that offers basic food and food-related items.

Convertible bond (17) Bond that can be exchanged for stock at a pegged price.

Cooperative (co-op) (4) Business owned and operated by the people it serves—usually for their benefit.

Corporate culture (A) Norms, beliefs, attitudes, and philosophies of the organization.

Corporate VMS (14) Vertical marketing system that combines stages of production and distribution under one ownership.

Corporation (4) Legal form of ownership that is recognized by the state through articles of incorporation; the owners hold shares of stock in the company. Legally, a corportion is able to act as a person.

Correlation analysis (C) Measures the relationship between two separate sets of figures.

Cost of goods sold (20) Cost directly related to the manufacture or acquisition of a product.

Cost of living adjustment (COLA) (11) Major issue of negotiation, by which employees are automatically given an increase in compensation equal to a raise in the cost of living (or inflation).

Countertrade (24) Form of barter arrangement between two or more countries.

Coupon bond (17) Bond with a coupon attached, which the bondholder must tear off, at stated times, and take it to the bank to receive an interest payment.

Craft union (11) Labor organization that restricts its membership to employees of a certain trade (craft), regardless of company affiliation.

Creative selling (15) Method of personal selling that appeals to the customer's intangible needs and buying motives.

Credit life insurance (19) Term policy that pays the amounts due on loans if the debtor dies.

Credit union (4, 16) Cooperative whose members loan their savings to other members for interest.

Crime (23) Violation of specific laws passed for the public good.

Critical path (8) Sequence within a particular production process that takes the longest time to complete.

Critical path method (8) Method whereby production planners use the sequence of production process that takes the longest time to complete in order to estimate production time.

Cumulative preferred stock (17) Stock that maintains its claim to dividends even if the company decides not to declare dividends during a period; dividends accumulate.

Current asset (17, 20) Asset that normally turns into cash within less than a year.

Current liability (17, 20) Obligation that the company has to pay within a year or less.

Current ratio (20) Accounting ratio used to determine a company's ability to pay its short-term debt.

Customer analysis (B) Detailed investigation of who buys the company's products and why, the purpose of which is to construct a profile of the typical customer and develop a marketing plan for attracting that person's business.

Custom manufacturing (8) Production of goods specifically to the buyer's specifications.

Daisy wheel printer (21) Printer that contains a print element shaped like a wheel with radial spokes; produces letter-quality characters.

Data banks (data bases) (21) Commercial companies or departments within an organization that gather, store, and distribute data via computers.

Data base software (21) Programs that organize data files by many different categories such as name, size of order, or zip code.

Daywork (9) System whereby an employee is paid according to the hours worked.

Debenture bonds (17) Unsecured bond.

Debt capital (17) Money raised by borrowing.

Debt-to-assets ratio (20) Total amount of claims lenders have against the company's assets.

Decentralization (7) Situation in which decision-making authority has been mostly delegated from top to lower levels of management.

Defendant (23) Person toward whom legal action is taken.

Democratic leadership (6) Leadership style that emphasizes subordinate input into leadership decisions.

Denomination (17) Amount at which the bond is sold.

Department (7) Division of employees within an organization with similar tasks and/or goals; usually a separate component of an organization chart.

Departmentation (7) Management function of creating divisions of labor within an organization.

Department store (14) Large retailing store that handles many products located in several different departments.

Depreciation (20) Assigned value of assets, usually diminished over a period of use.

Depression (2) Severe recession or downswing in the level of business activity.

Digital computer (21) Computer that deals with numbers.

Directing (6) Management process that energizes and motivates employees toward the accomplishment of the organization's objectives.

Direct marketing (14) System of moving the product directly from producer to consumer.

Disaster loan (5) Loan made to small businesses by the SBA to help the owner recover from a presidentially declared disaster.

Discount broker (18) Broker who typically provides only one service, to buy or sell stock. Commissions are lower than those of full-service brokers.

Discount store (14) Large store that sells products in high volume at lower prices and usually provides less service.

Discrimination (3) Unequal treatment of people based on race, sex, religion, age, or national origin.

Disk (floppy disk, flexible disk, diskette) (21) Thin, flexible plastic circle covered with magnetic iron oxide on which computers record, store, and access data.

Disk drive (21) Special device that rotates a disk in a personal computer and accesses information from the disks.

Disk operating system (DOS) (21) System of special programs and hardware that takes care of all the details of controlling a computer system.

Distribution channel (14) One of a wide range of alternatives given to the producer in getting goods to the ultimate consumer.

Distribution strategy (B) Strategy concerned with the channels to be employed in making the firm's goods and service available to the customer.

Distributive bargaining (11) Type of collective bargaining where one party wins advantages at the direct expense of the other party; a more highly contested type of negotiation.

Divestiture (4) Process of a larger company breaking into smaller companies by selling off some of its operations.

Dividend (4, 17) Profit paid to the owners of stock over a certain period of time.

Domestic corporation (4) Corporation doing business within the state where it was established.

Dormant partner (4) Owner within a partnership who is neither active in management nor known to the public.

Dot matrix printer (21) Printer that prints out characters using a matrix of ink dots.

Double-entry bookkeeping (20) Common accounting practice that requires two entries to be made for each transaction, helping to balance accounts and prevent errors.

Doughnut organization (7) Type of business organization in which top management is represented by a center circle, and lower staff and line levels are represented by larger, expanding circles.

Dow Jones averages (18) Index of the price movements of 65 stocks listed on the New York Stock Exchange.

Drexon laser card (16) Plastic card capable of storing millions of bits of data.

Dumping (24) Situation whereby a country sells goods or services in which it has a strong comparative advantage to another country in mass and at a greatly reduced price.

Dun & Bradstreet (5) National private organization that reports and keeps records of the credit standings of businesses.

Earnings per share (EPS) (20) Average earnings per share of common stock.

Echelon of management (7) Different levels of authority within an organization.

Economics (2) Study of the allocation of scarce resources.

Economic system (2) Combination of citizens', businesses' and government's economic activities.

8-bit microprocessor (21) Personal computer that operates on eight bits of information at one time.

Electronic funds transfer system (EFTS) (16) Automated system that handles transactions between customers, sellers, and their banks.

Electronic mail (21) Communication via computers using networking systems or modems and phone lines.

Electronic spreadsheet software (21) Programs that simulate business worksheets with rows and columns.

Embargo (24) Order prohibiting certain goods from entering a specific country.

Emotional motive (12) Reason people act to buy certain products, based on more personal, internal factors.

Employee association (11) Organization of employees, usually from the public sector and white-collar professionals, that operates much like a union.

Employer association (11) Organization of companies to control the power and abuses of unions.

Employment at will (9) Legal doctrine that says an employee or employer can terminate a relationship at will.

Endowment policy (19) Insurance policy that pays the full face value to the insured after a certain number of years. Such policies also pay the full face value to the holder's beneficiary should the holder die.

Energy (3) Power and ability to accomplish work; includes physical effort by people or the power of other harnessed sources.

Enlightened marketing (12) Extreme of the marketing concept proposed by Professor Phillip Kotler.

Entrepreneur (1, 5) Person who takes the risk of beginning and managing a business with the goal of making a profit. While the managers of large corporations are often entrepreneurs, the term is most often used with regard to the small business venture.

Entrepreneurship (1) Factor that initiates, manages, and effects production, oversees the other factors of production.

Environmentalism (3) Movement or interest in maintaining a safe, clean environment and protecting natural resources.

Environmental Protection Agency (EPA) (3) Nation's largest regulatory agency; formulates and enforces environmental laws.

Equal Employment Opportunity Commission (EEOC) (3) Federal agency created to enforce the Civil Rights Act of 1964.

Equity capital (17) Money raised from the sale of stocks.

Esteem needs (10) According to Maslow, a noted psychologist, needs that result from human interaction, but are above social needs. Examples are respect of self, respect from others, pride, and achievement.

Ethics (3) Principles of right or proper behavior.

Excise tax (22) Sales tax placed on the manufacture, purchase, or sale of selected items.

Exit interview (9) Informative meeting that takes place between a manager and an employee at the termination of the employee.

Export (24) Good or service shipped out of a country for sale or use.

Exporting (24) Business practice of selling products in a foreign country through the use of representatives in that country.

Extended product (13) Qualities beyond the actual product that include packaging, services, financing, delivery, branding, and other like methods.

External data (C) Information that originates outside the company's operations.

Extra-expense insurance (19) Insurance that covers additional costs of operating in temporary quarters while a building is being repaired.

Factoring (17) Method by which finance companies buy accounts receivables outright from a business.

Factors of production (1) Ten resources used in the production of goods and services, including natural resources, labor, capital, and entrepreneurship.

Factory outlet (14) Store that offers merchandise directly from the factory.

Fair Labor Standards Act or Minimum Wage Law of 1938 (11) Federal legislation that created the minimum wage.

Fair Packaging and Labeling Act of 1966 (13) Law requiring descriptions and package size that shoppers can easily compare with competitive products.

Family brand (13) Brand that covers several products of the same company line.

Featherbedding (11) Condition where unions force employers to keep employees on the job — to remain employed — after their work is no longer essential.

Federal Deposit Insurance Corporation (FDIC) (16) Government-sponsored program that insures a deposit in a FDIC-covered bank up to $100,000.

Federal Occupational Safety and Health Act of 1970 (3) Federal law that regulates noise levels for manufacturers in interstate commerce.

Federal reserve system (FRS) (16) Organization of directors and twelve district banks that guide our banking system, largely by influencing the supply of money available.

Fidelity bond (19) Insurance that guarantees an employer against losses caused by deceitful employees.

Fill (or kill) order (18) Limit order that is cancelled if it cannot be executed when placed.

Financial accounting (20) Area of accounting concerned with creating and reporting the financial information of an organization to outsiders on a periodic basis.

Financial Accounting Standards Board (FASB) (20) Private organization established by the AICPA that sets the standards for accounting practices.

Fishyback (14) Method of shipping combining truck and water transportation.

Fixed asset (17, 20) Asset that takes longer than a year to convert to cash; another term for plant and equipment.

Fixed capital (17) Money invested in fixed assets for longer than a year.

Fixed-position layout (8) Type of plant layout where employees, equipment, and machinery move around a stationary product.

Flat organization (7) Organization where a manager has authority over many employees, and there are relatively few levels of authority.

Flexible manufacturing system (FMS) (8) Computer-driven system that integrates all the elements in the production process.

Flextime (10) Situation in which employees have some flexibility in choosing their working hours.

Flowchart (21) Graphic picture of the actions and steps required within a program.

F.O.B. pricing (13) System whereby the buyer pays all freight charges on goods shipped to the buyer by the seller.

Focus groups (12) Market research method that encourages small groups, guided by a moderator, to provide information about a product or service.

Foreign corporation (4) Corporation formed in one state and doing business in another.

Foreign exchange (24) Interchange of national currencies, such as U.S. dollars for Mexican pesos.

Foreign exchange market (24) Established international mechanism for converting the currencies of one country into another.

Foreign exchange rate (24) Rate at which one currency is exchanged for another; usually expressed as a ratio.

Form utility (12) Combining of materials and labor in the creating of a product that can satisfy human wants and needs.

FORTRAN (21) Formula Translator; the oldest symbolic language, oriented toward scientific applications.

Forward buying (8) Buying where large orders are placed less frequently.

Franchise (5) Agreement between a manufacturer or operating company and a private owner to conduct business in a certain manner. The owner (franchisee) is allowed to use trade names, specific products, and/or marketing channels in return for payments to the original company (the franchisor).

Franchisee (5) Individual owner that operates under the franchise agreement.

Franchisor (5) Company that offers a franchising agreement to an individual owner or company.

Free Enterprise System (1) Business system of pure capitalism, where individuals are free to conduct business activity without government intervention.

Free-vein leadership (6) Leadership style whereby leaders provide very little, if any, direction to subordinates.

Frequency distribution (C) Set of data grouped into categories.

Full-function merchant wholesaler (14) Wholesaler who offers a full complement of services to the producer, such as storing, selling, transportation, and credit.

Full-service broker (18) Company licensed to buy and sell on the organized exchanges that offers a full range of services, including research on securities.

Full warranty (23) Guarantee that a defective product will be fixed or replaced.

Function key (21) Keyboard key that carries out specialized instructions for the computer.

Futures market (18) Buying and selling in the commodity markets with delivery to be made at some point in the future.

Gantt chart (8) Production control chart, developed by Henry Gantt, that uses bar graphs to compare the work completed with that planned.

General Agreement on Tariffs (GATT) (24) International organization that helps nations negotiate in an effort to remove trade barriers.

Generally accepted accounting principles (GAAP) (20) Accounting methods that, through formal rules or general practice, have become accepted as the accepted practices of accounting.

General partner (4) At least one owner within a partnership who has unlimited liability and is active in management.

General partnership (4) Partnership whereby all owners have unlimited liability, often referred to simply as a partnership.

Generic product (13) Intangible social and mental benefits that satisfy needs beyond the physical product itself.

Getback (11) Attempt by a union to get back some of the benefits it gave up during the recession-bargaining of the early 1980s.

Givebacks (11) Items (such as pay, fringes, or vacation days) won in previous negotiations given back by a union.

Good-til-cancelled order (18) Limit order that stays open until purchaser decides to cancel.

Goodwill (20) Value of a business above its asset market value.

Government (22) Elected and appointed officials at city, state, and federal levels.

Government accountant (20) Accountant who works for a federal, state, or local government.

Grapevine (7) Informal channels through which company information is passed.

Grievance (11) Formal complaint by an employee or union representative regarding a violation of the worker's rights or the union contract with the company.

Gross national product (2) Total value of goods and services produced by a country, usually within the period of a year.

Gross profit (20) Net sales less cost of goods sold.

Group incentive plan (9) Situation in which an employee is paid according to the productivity by a group of workers.

Group life insurance (19) Plan whereby a company covers all of its employees, as a group, with life insurance. Premiums are usually smaller, and there is often no need for a physical examination.

Group norms (7) Standards that a working group informally set for themselves.

Guaranteed annual wage (GAW) (9) Agreement that guarantees certain employees a minimum annual wage.

Hand-to-mouth buying (8) Buying situation in which small orders are placed frequently.

Hard disk (21) Electromagnetic device in the disk drive that reads information from disks and writes data onto them.

Hardware (21) Physical equipment of computers.

Health maintenance organization (HMO) (19) Health plan that allows a member to prepay a set amount for medical expenses in return for almost unlimited medical coverage for no charge or for a nominal charge; competes with health insurance programs.

Hedging (18) Buying and selling commodities in both the spot and the futures markets at the same time to protect against price movements.

Hero (A) Integral role model for the personnel, this individual serves to develop and reinforce the corporate culture.

Herzberg's motivation theory (10) Motivational theory presented by Daniel Herzberg whereby all human needs related to work are divided into two types: hygiene and motivational needs.

High tech/high touch (E) Increased need for people to be around people, brought on by technology.

Holding company (4) Company that buys and owns stock in another company.

Horizontal chart (7) Type of organizational chart that usually shows higher-authority positions to the left and lower positions to the right.

Horizontal marketing systems (14) Situation whereby two or more companies agree to pool their efforts to take advantage of a marketing opportunity.

Horizontal merger (4) Joining of companies with similar business activities and/or products.

Human resource management (9) Personnel management; a staff position that deals with the staffing, training, compensation, and providing services for a company.

Hygiene need (10) Need that is aside from, or peripheral to, the job itself, according to Herzberg.

Import (24) Good or service that is brought into a country for sale or use.

Importing (24) Business practice of buying products from a foreign country with the purpose of generating business activity.

Incentive (1) Reward or compensation designed to effect productive behavior.

Income bond (17) Bond that pays interest only if the company earns money.

Income statement (20) Accounting statement that reveals income or loss over a period of time, sometimes called the profit and loss statement.

Income tax (22) Tax placed on personal income.

Independent broker (18) Broker who holds seats on the exchanges and executes orders for other brokers during busy times.

Independent union (11) Labor organization that is not associated with national unions and is usually local in nature.

Index number (C) Stated as a percentage, this measures change over a period of time.

Individual brand (13) Brand that covers only one product. Typically, one company may have several individual brands.

Industrial good (13) Good purchased by companies enabling them to manufacture other products.

Industrial revolution (1) Business era that is characterized by the replacing of hand tools by power-driven machines.

Industrial union (11) Labor organization that represents employees of a wide variety of occupations involved in production.

Inflation (2) Increase in the general price level.

Inflation rate (2) Rate of increase in the general price level.

Informal organization (7) Organization of relationships between employees that develops naturally as they interact on the job.

Informative advertising (15) Advertising that has the primary purpose of providing information.

Ink-jet printer (21) Printer that produces letter-quality printouts by spraying jets in ink directly to the paper.

Inland marine insurance (19) Insurance that applies to inland movement of goods against nearly every conceivable loss while the goods are en route.

Institutional advertising (15) Type of advertising that promotes a company image or quality.

Insurable risk (19) Risk that meets the requirements of insurance coverage.

Insurance (19) Method of shifting responsibility for losses to specialists (insurance companies) who handle the risk by spreading it over a large number of incidents.

Intangible asset (20) Item that has value to an organization but no physical substance.

Intangible personal property (23) Property that is often in the form of documents or data.

Integrated circuit (21) Complete electronic circuit on a single chip of silicon; paved the way for third-generation computers.

Integrative bargaining (11) Type of collective bargaining where both labor and management work together in a cooperative manner.

Interest coverage ratio (20) Ability of the company to pay interest charges out of their earnings.

Interest rate (2) Amount paid to borrow money.

Intermittent process (8) Production process that has periodic starting and stopping points.

Internal data (C) Information from a firm's records.

International business (24) Movement of goods, services, money, know-how, technology, and other business activities across national boundaries.

Inventory turnover ratio (20) Accounting ratio used to determine how quickly a company's inventory is normally converted into cash; determined by dividing the cost of goods sold by the average inventory for the period.

Investing (18) Purchasing securities on the sound analysis that they have reasonable chances of paying acceptable returns over a period of time.

Involuntary bankruptcy (23) Result of proceedings being filed by creditors, and a federal court declaring the firm bankrupt.

Issued stock (17) Portion of authorized stock that has been sold.

Job analysis (9) Personnel process that determines the exact tasks that make up a job.

Job description (9) Written summary of a specific employee's duties and responsibilities.

Job enlargement (10) Change in the nature of a job by adding meaningless tasks to the current job, as opposed to job enrichment, which adds challenging tasks to a job to make it more interesting.

Job enrichment (10) Process of changing the job so that the work will appeal to the employee's higher needs; efforts by management to make the job more meaningful and interesting.

Job sharing (10) Situation where two employees work part-time to share the same job.

Job specifications (9) Written listing of the physical, mental, and emotional requirements of a position.

Joint venture (4) Temporary partnership for the purpose of carrying out a single project.

Junior Chamber of Commerce (5) National, professional organization with local offices that acts in promoting and aiding businesses.

Just-in-time dispatching (8) Production process that issues work orders to managers and supervisors to allow for the resources of labor and materials. Sometimes it includes a schedule for the completion of a task.

Just-in-time inventories (8) Method of ordering smaller amounts of inventory more frequently.

Kennedy Round (24) Name given to tariff negotiations with 54 countries from 1964 to 1967, reducing average tariffs on nonagricultural items by 35%. This was made possible by the Trade Expansion Act of 1962, passed during President Kennedy's administration.

Key competitor analysis (B) Detailed investigation of other firms in the market place; the purpose of this analysis is to evaluate the current strengths and future strategies likely to be implemented by these firms.

Kilo (K) (21) Unit representing 1024 bytes of memory.

Knights of Labor (11) First large union for factory workers, started in the 1870s.

Knowledge bank (21) Electronic library that gathers, stores, and distributes information on practically every subject.

Labor (1) Factor of production that utilizes human resources other than management.

The Labor-Management Relations Act or Taft-Hartley Act of 1947 (11) Federal legislation that gave management more power and defined unfair labor practices of unions as well as employers.

Labor union (11) Organization of employees legally empowered to engage in collective bargaining to help its members obtain better wages and working conditions.

Ladder organization (7) Type of business organization where staff employees are shown at the side of an organization chart at each level with which they are involved.

Laissez-faire (2) Doctrine proposed by Adam Smith that government should not interfere with commerce.

Landrum-Griffin Act of 1959 (11) Federal legislation that provided the Union Members' Bill of Rights and established reporting regulations.

Large-scale integration (LSI) (21) Silicon chip containing thousands of transistors, dramatically improving the speed and compactness of computers.

Laser printer (21) Printer that produces characters of typeset quality using laser beam technology.

Law (23) Set of principles and standards that govern the conduct of society members.

Leadership (6) Ability to inspire people to complete tasks properly and willingly.

Lease (17) Agreement between two parties to use property for a specified time period at a certain cost.

Lease-purchase (17) Agreement allowing the lessee to buy property at the end of the leasing period.

Leisure time (E) Time not required for working and sleeping; time that can be spent in leisure and recreational activities.

Lessee (17) Person who leases property from another party.

Lessor (17) Property owner who leases the property to another party.

Leveraged buyout (4) Technique of buying a company through a lot of debt financing, typically using the company's assets as collateral.

Liability (17, 20) A company's obligation to pay cash or other economic value in the future; anything that the company owes.

Liability insurance (19) Insurance that protects a company against damages to others due to the company's negligence or mistakes.

Licensing (24) Situation whereby a producer of one country makes an agreement with people within another country to provide a service; usually marketing a product in foreign countries.

Limited-function merchant wholesaler (14) Wholesaler who does not offer a full array of wholesaling functions.

Limited liability (4) Situation whereby owners of a business are responsible for losses only up to the amount of their investment.

Limited partner (4) Owner within a partnership who does not take part in management and has limited liability on personal assets.

Limited-payment policy (19) Insurance policy that limits the premium payments to a specified number of years.

Limited warranty (23) Guarantee implied by law; does not necessarily have to be made explicit by the seller.

Limit order (18) Order that specifies the price at which the stock is to be traded.

Line authority (7) Right to direct the work of others.

Line of credit (17) Informal agreement between the bank and a customer establishing the maximum amount the bank will loan.

Listed security (18) Security traded on security exchanges.

Lockout (11) Condition established by management where employees are not allowed to come to work during a labor dispute.

Logic bomb (21) Piece of code that rearranges or destroys data in a computer memory under certain circumstances.

Long-range planning (6) Planning that involves objectives to be accomplished in one year or more.

Long-term liability (20) Obligation to pay cash or other economic value beyond one year.

Low-load fund (18) Mutual fund that charges low management fees.

M1 (16) Amount of money in our economy that regularly circulates through companies and financial institutions, such as currency, demand deposits, and travelers' checks.

M2 (16) M1 plus savings, small-denomination time deposits, and other reasonably liquid accounts.

M3 (16) M2 plus large-denomination time deposits and other less liquid accounts.

Main frame (21) Large computers, both in size and capacity.

Major medical (19) Provision of health insurance policies that covers high-cost illnesses such as cancer.

Make-or-buy decision (8) Type of buying policy whereby small orders are placed frequently.

Maker (17) In a promissory note, the person who promises to pay the other party.

Management (6) Process that includes planning, organizing, directing, and controlling in an effort to accomplish an organization's goals.

Management by objectives (10) Management process whereby a worker and manager agree on goals to be accomplished over a given period of time. MBO adds to job interest by letting the employee establish the methods of meeting the objectives established.

Manager (6) Employee within an organization given the authority and responsibility to act in achieving goals through the process of management.

Managerial accounting (20) Area of accounting that deals with providing information for internal decision making.

Manufacturer's agent (14) Independent salesperson, representing a manufacturer, who works on commission.

Margin buying (18) Situation whereby the buyer puts up part of the money to buy an order of stock and borrows the remainder from a broker.

Margin call (18) Request of a broker to put up more money on a margin buy if the price of the stock falls below a certain level.

Marine insurance (19) Insurance that covers a vessel and its contents while at sea or in port.

Market (12) Segment of the overall population that will be interested in purchasing a particular product.

Market grid (12) Chart or document that shows the result of market segmentation and portrays a specific target market.

Marketing (12) Business activity that includes all of the activities of getting products from the producer to the consumer.

Marketing concept (12) Marketing approach that emphasizes the needs and wants of consumers first and then produces goods and services and makes them available to the consumer. It replaces the old approach of ''take what we produce and sell it'' with ''find out what they want and make it available.''

Marketing mix (12) Combining of the four major marketing activities, called the four Ps of marketing, into a strategy that is best for a given situation. The four Ps are product planning, pricing, promotion, and placement (distribution).

Market order (18) Order to buy or sell at the best price available.

Market research (12) Systematic gathering, recording, and analyzing data about a firm's products or services.

Market segmentation (12) Process of dividing potential customers into groups with similar characteristics.

Market target (12) Specific group with qualities that make them prime potential customers for a given product.

Market value (17) Actual price at which stock is bought and sold.

Markup pricing (13) Method of pricing where the final price is determined from a percentage markup from cost or purchase price.

Marx, Karl (2) Political theorist who first described communism; author of *Das Kapital*.

Maslow's hierarchy of needs (10) Theory of Abraham Maslow that presents five different levels of human needs: physiological, security, social, esteem, and self-realization. He believed that people behave differently in acting to satisfy each of these types of needs.

Materials inventory (8) Physical count of materials used in the manufacture of a product.

Materials requirements planning (MRP) (8) Technique used by production managers to be certain that the proper amount of goods gets to a specific place at the right time. It can be in chart, graph, or tabular form.

Matrix organization (7) Situation within an organization when an independent project is established and employees are organized to work under a separate chain of command.

Maturity date (17) Date a bondholder has to be repaid.

Mean (C) Average of a set of data.

Mechanization (8) Replacing of human labor with machines.

Median (C) Value that cuts a frequency distribution in half.

Mediator (11) Third party, meant to be unbiased, who works as a liaison between both labor and management and offers compromise suggestions that are meant to be acceptable by both parties.

Mercantilism (1) Early form of economic system whereby countries formed colonies and controlled them in order to maximize their wealth.

Merchandise inventories (8) Finished products of the manufacturing process.

Merger (4) Joining of two or more companies to operate as one.

Microprocessor (21) Integrated circuit on one chip that functions like the CPU in a computer.

Middle management (6) Managers with the authority and responsibility of carrying out more specific plans within the organization's overall objectives. They work between the top managers and the operating managers and are usually in charge of specific departments.

Middleman (14) Person or institution in the marketing channel between the producer and the consumer.

Minority Business Development Agency (MBDA) (5) Federal agency created by the Chamber of Commerce in 1969. It provides special assistance to small business ventures that are owned and managed by minority entrepreneurs.

Minority Business Opportunity Committee (MBOC) (5) Agency that operates with OMBE to help coordinate programs from over sixteen other federal agencies that serve minority businesses.

Minority enterprise (3) Business owned and operated by minorities that receive special support.

Minority Enterprise Small Business Investment Company (MESBIC) (5) Agency that works within the OMBE that provides funds for small businesses owned and operated by minority entrepreneurs.

Missionary selling (15) Indirect selling that focuses on building a good company name and positive company image.

Mode (C) Number that occurs most often in a set of data.

Modem (21) Device that connects the computer to a telephone allowing one computer to communicate with another.

Money (16) Symbolic medium of exchange that gets its value because people have faith in the government which, by law, requires money's acceptance in payment of debts.

Money market (18) Short-term debt market.

Money market fund (18) Mutual fund that trades in the money markets.

Money supply (16) Total amount of money in the economy.

Monitor (21) Televisionlike screen that allows a computer user to see input and output.

Mortgage bond (17) Bond backed by specific tangible assets of the issuing company.

Motivation (10) Inner drive or impulse that stimulates action; often an enticement to a specific behavior.

Motivational need (10) According to the Herzberg theory, need directly related to a specific job.

Multichannel marketing (14) Practice of using more than one channel to reach the same or different markets.

Multilevel marketing (14) Distribution process that uses levels of people who get commissions of the sales of the people below them.

Multinational company (24) Business organization that operates in at least six countries and has at least 20% of its total assets, sales, or labor force in foreign subsidiaries.

Multiple correlation (C) System of measuring the relationship between several sets of data.

Mutual company (4) Cooperative where the members or users are also the owners.

Mutual fund (18) Company that combines the investment funds of many people whose investment goals are similar and in turn invests those funds in a wide variety of securities.

NASDAQ OTC Composite Index (18) Weighted average of over 2000 common stocks traded by brokers in OTC markets.

National Air Quality Standards Act (3) Federal legislation that regulates air quality.

National bank (16) Bank that receives its charter from the federal government. Such banks have the word "national" in their title.

National brand (13) Brand specifically identified with the company that makes the product, usually promoted nationwide.

National Federation of Independent Businesses (5) Professional organization organized by the Chamber of Commerce in 1943 that represents small business interests in Washington.

National Labor Relations Act or Wagner Act of 1935 (11) Most prounion legislation that provided legal rights to employees with regard to union activities.

National Labor Relations Board (11) Organization created by the Wagner Act that gave unions and employees federal representation.

National Small Business Association (5) Professional organization organized by the Chamber of Commerce in 1937 that represents small business interests in Washington.

Natural resources (1) Factor of production that utilizes land or items from the land.

Need (10) State in which something necessary or desirable is required or wanted. The satisfying of needs is a motivation for certain behavior.

Negligence (23) Situation whereby one party's careless behavior causes injury to another person.

Negotiable instrument (23) Written paper, expressing a contractual relationship, that can be transferred from one person to another.

Negotiable order of withdrawal (NOW) account (16) Interest-bearing checking account.

Net profit margin (20) After-tax profits as a percentage of sales.

Network (21) Multiple-user, multiple-function computer system of equal units.

New York Stock Exchange Composite Index (18) Weighted price index of all of the common shares listed on the NYSE.

No-fault insurance (19) Insurance that does not access penalties in automobile accidents based on fault.

No-load fund (18) Mutual fund that does not charge management fees for services.

Nominal partner (4) Individual who allows, or even encourages, the public to think that he or she is a partner in a business; however, the person is not an owner.

Noncumulative preferred stock (17) Stock for which dividends do not accumulate should the company decide not to declare dividends.

Nonparticipating preferred stock (17) Stock that claims only its specified rate of return.

No-par value stock (17) Stock with no dollar amount printed on its certificates.

Norris-LaGuardia Act of 1932 (11) Legislation that provided opportunities for the organizing of employees and made the yellow-dog contract illegal.

Objective (6) Broad plan that is the end result of managers' efforts; sometimes called a goal.

Occupational Safety and Health Act (OSHA) (9) Federal legislation that sets safety standards for industry.

Odd lot (18) Order to buy or sell less than 100 shares of stock.

Odd pricing (13) Method of pricing just under the next dollar figure (also called psychological pricing).

On-line processing (21) System whereby each piece of data is transmitted into the computer as it is received.

Open-account credit (17) Sale of something from one company to another with payment expected at a later date; a form of trade credit; sometimes called open-book credit.

Open-book credit (17) *See* open-account credit.

Open corporation (4) Corporation that makes its stock available to the public.

Open Market Committee (16) Committee of the Federal Reserve System composed of the board of governors plus five representatives from district banks that has the power to buy and sell securities on the open market.

Open shop (11) Work situation in which employees have an individual right as to whether or not to join a union.

Operating expenses (20) Predetermined variety of expenses considered to be the costs of operating a business.

Operating management (6) Managers that work directly with the workers and are responsible for putting into operation the plans of middle and top management.

Operations management (8) Broader term than production management that applies the technical techniques of production in the management of the whole company.

Order bill of lading (17) Bill of lading that does not specify a specific person to receive the goods.

Organization chart (7) A diagram of an organization's departments showing their relationships to one another.

Organizing (6) The management process that designs the structure of jobs and establishes lines of authority and communication.

Orientation program (9) A program that introduces new employees to the company and explains company policies to them.

Origination (17) The agreement on terms between an investment banker and a company offering securities for sale.

Outplacement (9) Efforts by a firm to find employment in other organizations for employees they have had to lay off.

Output (1) Annual production per person, adjusted for inflation.

Over-the-counter markets (OTC) (18) Securities traded through a network of brokers rather than on one of the organized exchanges.

Owners' equity (20) The total value of the owners' investment.

Parkinson's law (7) "The number of subordinates that a manager can control reduces as one moves up the management hierarchy." This creates the need for more staff at higher management levels.

Participating preferred stock (17) Stock for which the owner receives dividends at a fixed rate and shares with common stockholders in the division of remaining earnings.

Partnership (4) Legal form of business with two or more co-owners.

Partnership agreement (4) Legal document that creates a partnership form of business ownership.

Par value (17) Dollar amount actually printed on stock certificates.

Penetration pricing (B, 13) Pricing strategy in which a low price is established so as to capture as large a share of the market as possible and discourage competition at the same time; system whereby a product is first introduced at a much lower than usual, or anticipated future, price.

Pension fund (16) Group that collects savings of employees on a regular basis and invests them to be paid out to employees upon retirement.

Performance (8) Production process where the product is actually produced by the action of machines and/or labor.

Performance evaluation (9) Formal, planned evaluation of an employee's job performance over a given period of time.

Personality trait (7) Individual way of interacting with other people.

Personal property (23) Things of value that are easy to move, such as clothing, furniture, and supplies.

Personal selling (15) System whereby a person interacts with one or more people with the purpose of promoting a good or service.

Persuasive advertising (15) Advertising that tries to improve the competitive status; usually used after the product has been around for a while.

PERT (Program Evaluation and Review Technique) (8) Graphic illustration (or control chart) that identifies each job that makes up a production project and details the time required for each step.

Physiological need (10) Need basic to survival, such as food, water, oxygen, and rest.

Picket (11) Labor tactic where employees or union workers are placed at a working area with signs or placards announcing that the employees are on strike against the company.

Pictograph (C) Chart that includes pictures or drawings along with bars.

Piecework (9) System whereby an employee is paid according to the units produced.

Piggyback (14) Method combining truck and rail transportation.

Pioneering advertising (15) Advertising that tries to stimulate demand for a new product or service.

Place utility (12) Ability of product to satisfy human needs and wants due to its physical location.

Plaintiff (23) Person who feels wronged.

Planning (6) Establishment of future objectives with the tasks and strategies necessary for their accomplishment.

Plant and equipment (20) Items of value that are typically used for a period longer than a year; also called fixed assets.

Plant capacity (8) Maximum production abilities of a particular production plant.

Point-of-purchase display (15) Promotional device used in high-traffic areas that encourages the customer to buy a product.

Point-of-sale (POS) (16) Machine that automatically transfers funds from buyer's bank to seller's bank when the customer makes a purchase.

Policy (6) Plan that creates boundaries for and guides performance; encourages consistent decisions throughout the many facets of the company.

Population (C) *See* universe.

Population dynamics (E) Changes in the characteristics of the population.

Positioning (15) Advertising a product or service by comparing features with a competing product or service; sometimes called comparative advertising.

Positioning strategy (B) Strategy used to fine-tune a marketing plan; has four basic substrategies related to product, price, distribution, and promotion.

Possession utility (12) Ability of a product to satisfy human needs and wants due to its transfer of title or ownership.

Power of attorney (23) Written document creating an agency relationship.

Preemptive right (17) Right of a current stockholder to purchase a proportionate share of newly issued stock.

Preferred stock (17) Ownership in the company, but with certain preferences over common stock, typically relating to receiving dividends.

Preferred stockholder (4) Owner of stock who does not vote and usually has first claim on the profits of the company.

Price (13) Value given up in exchange for the item purchased.

Price lining (13) Pricing method that identifies a limited number of prices for specific merchandise.

Price strategy (B) Part of the strategic marketing plan in which the firm decides how much to charge the customers for its product(s).

Priest (A) Individual in the organization who has been around a long time, knows its history, and uses advice, assistance, and guidance to support the organizational culture.

Prime rate (16) Interest rate charged by banks for their best grade of customers.

Principal (17) Exact amount borrowed with a bond.

Private accountant (20) Accountant who works for private businesses.

Private brand (13) Brand name that identifies a product but is not directly tied to a manufacturer.

Private corporation (4) Corporation that is owned by individuals rather than a government.

Private enterprise system (1) Business system, a form of capitalism, that stresses private ownership of business and individual choice with regard to business activities.

Procedure (6) Plan that specifies methods for completing specific activities; guide to specific action in the completion of tasks.

Process culture (A) Organizational culture characterized by low risk and slow feedback.

Process layout (8) Type of plant layout that clusters all functions of a particular type.

Producer co-op (4) Cooperative organized in order to sell products for its members.

Product advertising (15) Type of advertising that focuses on the qualities of a specific product.

Product differentiation (13) Combination of brand, trademark, packaging, labeling, and advertising that promotes public knowledge of a product's unique features.

Product hierarchy (13) System of relating products and services to other products and services in hierarchical fashion.

Production (8) Process of creating goods and services.

Production management (8) Application of management principles to the production process.

Productivity (1, 8) Percentage amount of increase or decline in the amount of goods and services produced in one hour of work; a measure of goods produced (output) in consideration of resources used (input). Higher productivity results in lower cost per unit manufactured.

Product layout (8) Type of plant layout in which operators and equipment are stationed in one spot and the product moves through each station.

Product liability (23) Businesses' responsibility for the design, manufacture, and use of their products and services.

Product life cycle (13) Stages in the life of a given product, including introduction, growth, maturity, and decline.

Product strategy (B) Part of the strategic marketing plan in which the firm decides what to offer to its customers.

Profit (1) Return received on business activity after all operating expenses have been met.

Profit sharing (9) System whereby an employee is paid a percentage of a company's profits over a period of time (usually a year, usually as a bonus).

Program (21) Example of software; represents coded instructions to the computer to perform specific operations.

Progress control (8) Production control process that compares scheduled to actual productivity.

Project manager (7) manager who takes charge of the matrix project team.

Promissory note (17) Written promise by one person to pay another a certain amount at a particular time, or upon demand.

Promotion (15) Any activity that encourages the selling or the purchase of a good or service.

Promotional mix (15) Combination of promotional activities planned to be used with a specific company, good, or service.

Promotional pricing (13) Special discount, similar to penetration pricing except that it also applies to existing products.

Promotion strategy (B) Strategy used to inform customers about a firm's product offerings and/or persuade them to purchase the goods and/or services.

Property (23) Something of value owned by an individual or a group.

Property insurance (19) Insurance that covers financial losses due to destruction of the insured's property.

Property tax (22) Tax placed on such items as land, building, equipment, and inventories.

Proxy (4) Legal document used to transfer voting rights from stockholders to other people.

Psychological pricing (13) Also called odd pricing; prices just under the next dollar figure.

Public accountant (20) Firm or individual who sells accounting-related services to private businesses.

Public corporation (4) Corporation owned by a governmental body.

Public relations (15) Any activity that increases the public awareness of a product or company, but that is not directly paid for by the company.

Pull strategy (15) Method of advertising that relies heavily on advertising and public relations in encouraging the customer to purchase a product.

Pulsating (15) Advertising method where much advertising is conducted over a period of time, and then slackened off.

Purchase order (8) Form that goes to a vendor, that is, in effect, a contract to buy.

Purchase requisition (8) Form showing a need for goods to be purchased; usually includes the quantities, specifications, and date required of each product.

Pure risk (19) Risk in which there is no chance of gain; there is only a chance of loss.

Push strategy (15) Method of promotion that relys on channel members—rather than the customer—to effect the sale.

Put (18) Option to sell a stock at a fixed price within a specified period of time.

Pyramid chart (7) Type of organizational chart, similar to the vertical chart, that shows higher levels toward the top of the chart, but also shows an expanding number of departments at the lower levels of authority.

Pyramid organization (7) Type of business organization, popular in sales companies, where the levels of all employees are determined by both the date they joined the firm and the number of employees hired to work under them.

Quality circle (10) Group of workers in the same area who meet together voluntarily on a regular basis to solve problems and reduce costs in their departments.

Quality control (8) Any of the various methods used in checking the quality of a manufactured product.

Quality of work life (QWL) (10) Programs designed to increase employee participation and democratic processes and improve working conditions.

Quota (24) Quantitative restriction placed on commodities that may be imported to a specific country over a given period of time.

Railway Labor Act of 1926 (11) First major legislation regarding the organization of labor; enabled railroad employees to organize unions.

Random access memory (RAM) (21) Storage space in a computer where data can be changed, deleted, moved around, and added to.

Ratification (11) Process or voting procedure where employees formally accept the conditions of a tentative agreement between labor and management.

Ratio analysis (20) System of comparing financial ratios to previous periods and to industry averages.

Rational motive (12) Reason people act to buy certain products, based on real, practical qualities such as price or quality.

Readership (15) Circulation of a given periodical; used in making media decisions for advertising.

Read only memory (ROM) (21) Permanent, electronic memory in a computer.

Real gross national product (2) Total value of goods and services produced by a country without the effect of price changes.

Real property (23) Land and everything affixed to the land.

Recall (15) Research method of testing a customer's knowledge or memory regarding specific advertising.

Recession (2) Downswing in the level of business activity.

Reciprocal buying (8) Type of buying where both buyer and vendor agree to buy and sell to each other.

Rediscount rate (16) Rate of interest that member banks must pay to borrow money from the federal reserve bank.

Registered bond (17) Bond for which the issuing company records the name and address of the holder and sends interest by check.

Reinsurance (19) Situation wherein an insurance company shares the risk of a particular coverage by passing along part of the risk to other insurance entities.

Reminder advertising (15) Advertising that tries to reinforce a message from previous advertisements.

Remote terminal (21) Typewriterlike machine, located away from the main frame and connected by telephone lines, used for input and output off the main frame.

Reserve requirement (16) Percentage of deposits that banks must hold in cash reserve.

Responsibility (7) An individual's obligation to carry out, or successfully accomplish, the goals or tasks assigned.

Retailer (14) Person or business that sells a product to the ultimate consumer.

Retailer cooperative (14) Situation in which a group of retailers organize themselves.

Retained earnings (4, 17) Profits of a corporation that are not paid out to the owners in dividends but invested back into the business.

Return on investment (ROI) (B) Amount of profits that an individual or corporation receives from investments, often expressed in terms of a percentage rate.

Return on investment (ROI) ratio (20) Ratio that measures the rate of return owners received on their investment.

Revenue (20) Money from sales of products or services.

Reverse discrimination (9) Situation in which companies give hiring and promotional preferences to women or minorities who may be less qualified than white males.

Right-to-work laws (11) State laws, permitted by a section of the Taft-Hartley Act, regarding employees' rights to choose whether or not to join a union. To date, twenty-one states have passed right-to-work laws.

Risk (19) Danger of loss.

Risk management (19) A company's efforts to deal with risks before losses occur.

Robotics (8) Use of automatic equipment to perform production activities.

Role (7) Set of expected behaviors.

Round lot (18) Order to buy or sell stock in 100-share multiples.

Routing (8) System that specifies the particular path through which a production process will take place.

Rule (6) Specific guide to action in establishing what activities may or may not take place; requires no interpretation and allows no exceptions.

Sale (23) Exchange of goods or property for money or other consideration.

Sales promotion (15) Use of promotional devices to provide greater motivation for the purchase of a certain product.

Sales tax (22) Tax placed on the retail sales price of many items; usually ranges from 3% to 7% of total price.

Savings account (time deposit) (16) Money deposited in a savings account in a bank. Ordinarily, depositors have to give the bank from 30 days to 6 months notice to withdraw their deposits.

Savings and loan association (16) Financial association that accumulates money in the form of savings and makes loans on real estate, primarily residential mortgages.

Savings bank (16) Bank that specializes in pooling the savings of small investors to create larger capital pools.

SBA direct loan (5) Loan made directly from SBA funds to small business; rare and made only in special conditions.

SBA guaranteed loan (5) Loan made to a small business by a commercial bank for which the SBA guarantees 90% repayment.

SBA participating loan (5) Loan made by the SBA for which part of the funds are made available from SBA funds and the rest is usually made by a commercial bank.

Scattergram (C) Plot of two variables on a graph.

Scheduling (8) Aspect of the production process that assigns time requirements for each function of the process.

Scrambled merchandising (14) System in which retailers carry and sell merchandise that they normally, given the type of business, would not carry.

Secret partner (4) Owner within a partnership who actively participates in management but is unknown to the public.

Secured loan (17) Loan backed up by some form of collateral.

Security (17) Stock, bond, or other financial certificate.

Security need (10) Human need, according to Maslow, that provides safety, predictability, and comfort.

Self-realization (10) Human needs dealing with self-accomplishment. Examples are personal development, growth, fulfillment, and personal pride in one's station.

Selling agent (14) Business or individual that contracts with a producer to manage and conduct a total marketing program; usually has full control over the prices and promotional campaign.

Service Corps of Retired Executives (SCORE) (5) Organization of retired executives who work through the SBA in providing management counsel and advice for small business owners.

Shopping good (13) Good purchased by a consumer after much consideration of the product's qualities by the purchaser.

Shop steward (11) Elected union representative who represents members' concerns to management.

Short-range planning (6) Planning that involves objectives to be accomplished in one year or less.

Short sell (18) System of selling shares that one does not own with an agreement to deliver the stock at some future date.

Short-term financing (17) Financing for a period less than a year.

Sight draft (17) Draft payable on demand.

Signature loan (17) *See* unsecured loan.

Silent partner (4) Owner within a partnership who takes no active part in the management of the business, but is known to the public.

Single aggregate index (C) Method of comparing groups of items to a base period.

Single-payment note (17) Loan (note) that must be repaid in one lump sum when it becomes due.

Situationalist theory (6) Concept that traits necessary for capable leadership vary with different situations.

16-bit microprocessor (21) Personal computer that operates on sixteen bits of information at one time.

Skimming price (B, 13) High price placed on a new product with the intention of reaching only a small portion of the total market.

Slowdown (11) Form of job action during which employees work at a decidedly slower pace, thereby causing productivity to drop.

Small business (5) Manufacturer with fewer than 250 employees; Retailer with annual sales of less than $1 million; or Wholesaler with annual sales of less than $5 million.

Small Business Administration (SBA) (5) Federal agency created by the Small Business Act of 1953; aids small businesses by helping to provide financing, managerial assistance, and information.

Small business investment company (SBIC) (5) Private investment firm that works under the direction of the SBA to raise money for investment into small businesses.

Smart card (16) Plastic card with a microchip that stores information regarding deposits, withdrawals, and the like directly on the card.

Smart modem (21) Modem that contains its own processor and memory and is able to perform many computer functions.

Smart terminal (21) Terminal that has its own microprocessor, allowing it to be useful when not connected to the main frame.

Smith, Adam (2) Economic theorist who first described capitalism; author of *The Wealth of Nations.*

Socialism (2) Economic system whereby political power and ownership are shared, somewhat equally, between the people and the government.

Social need (10) Human need that results in human interaction, such as love, affection, friendship, and belonging.

Social responsibility (3) Activity of business becoming involved with social issues and contributing to overall improvement of social conditions.

Social security tax (22) Federal tax placed on wages to cover such needs as pensions, dependent children, disability, and dependent spouses.

Software (21) Series of instructions, procedures, and rules that tell the computer what to do.

Sole proprietorship (4) Business that is owned by only one person.

Solid Wastes Act (3) Federal law that exercises control over disposal of solid wastes.

Span of control (7) Number of employees responsible to any one manager; a wide span of control includes many employees, while a narrow span would include only a few.

Specialist wholesaler (14) Wholesaler who specializes in providing one specific service to the producer.

Specialty good (13) Good purchased because of its very specific qualities.

Specialty shop (14) Limited-line retail store.

Specific duty (24) Tax applied to a good with regard to some specific physical measurement, such as dollars per pound, yard, or barrel.

Speculation (18) Method of taking a high risk with an investment that has a possibility of high gain or loss.

Speculative risk (19) Risk that has a potential for either a gain or a loss.

Spot market (18) Current cash market for a commodity.

Staff authority (7) Authority in a working relationship that is usually advisory and outside of direct authority channels.

Standard and Poor's 500 (18) Price index based on the total value of shares of major firms listed on the exchanges.

Standardization (8) Production of standard or interchangeable parts.

State bank (16) Bank that receives its charter from the state government; has the word ''state'' in its title.

Statistics (C) Process of collecting, interpreting, and presenting data in numerical form.

Status (7) Way in which other individuals informally perceive a person's prestige.

Statutory law (23) Written law adopted by a legislative body.

Stock (4, 17) Legal certificate that is evidence of ownership in a corporation.

Stockholder (4) Owner of a corporation.

Stock-index future (18) Method of buying an index of stock values to be delivered at some future date.

Stock option (17) Agreement to buy stock under certain conditions or at a certain time, usually at an agreed-upon price.

Stock split (17) Situation in which a company decides to divide its outstanding shares into additional units. The company may trade new shares at some ratio, say two for one, for the currently outstanding shares.

Stop order (18) Order to sell at a specific price.

Storyteller (A) Individual who has been with an organization a long time, done an outstanding job, and uses stories to convey organizational values and philosophies.

Straight bill of lading (17) Bill of lading specifying that an order has been shipped to a specific person.

Straight salary (9) Payment to an employee for employment over a given period of time.

Strategic marketing plan (B) Six-step plan designed to help an organization evaluate and analyze its current product-market situation, set objectives, formulate target market and positioning strategies, and implement and control the overall plan.

Strategic objective (B) Long-range objective that can be used to compare a company's performance with that of its competition; typical examples include ROI, market share, and growth.

Strategic planning (6) Long-term planning (typically five years) that defines the organization's mission, environmental opportunities, internal strengths and weaknesses, and key long-term objectives.

Strict products liability (23) Liability that holds a manufacturer responsible for a product or service regardless of whether the manufacturer was negligent.

Strike (11) Labor tactic where employees refuse to come to work until a new contract is negotiated.

Strikebreaker (scab) (11) Employee who crosses the picket lines to work during a union-organized strike of the company.

Style flexibility (6) Style of leadership that applies both autocratic and supportive methods according to the situation.

Subchapter S corporation (4) Corporation that qualifies to be taxed as a partnership.

Summons (23) Statement requiring the defendant to appear in court.

Supermarket (14) Large departmentalized store that offers a wide variety of food and food-related products.

Supplies inventory (8) Physical count of supplies used by a company.

Supply-side economics (2) Approach to stimulating economic growth by producing more goods and services.

Surety bond (19) Insurance that covers fraudulent acts and failures of another party to live up to its contractual obligations.

Syndicate (17) Group of banks that agree to pool their efforts to sell securities for a company.

Synthetic process (8) Production process where two or more materials are combined in the production of one final product.

Systems programmer (21) Programmer who develops broad, general-use programs.

Tactical planning (6) Short-range plans (less than a year) designed to achieve long-term goals.

Tall organization (7) Organization in which a manager has authority over a few employees and where there are many different levels of authority.

Tangible personal property (23) Physical property, such as goods and products.

Tangible product (13) Physical product or visible service that a company offers to a consumer.

Target market (B) Market niche that a firm wants to capture.

Tariff (24) Duty or tax levied on a specific commodity when it crosses national boundaries.

Termination (9) Situation in which employee leaves a company.

Term insurance (19) Life insurance policy that pays off only if the insured dies during the coverage period.

Term loan (17) Formal agreement to borrow and repay a sum of money at a given interest rate for periods longer than a year.

Theory X (6) McGregor's concept that managers view employees as lazy, irresponsible, and requiring direction.

Theory Y (6) McGregor's concept that managers view employees as wanting responsibility, liking work, and willing to work diligently for proper rewards.

Theory Z (6) Management philosophy that emphasizes trust, openness in communication, consensus decision making, strong commitment to employees, and a long-term perspective.

32-bit microprocessor (21) Personal computer that operates on thirty-two bits of information at one time.

Time draft (17) Draft payable at a future date.

Time series (C) System that considers past regularities of data and projects them into the future.

Time-sharing system (21) System whereby many different users share one central computer.

Time utility (12) Ability of a product to satisfy human needs and wants due to the timing of its availability.

Title (23) Legal right of ownership.

Top management (6) Managers given the authority and responsibility for carrying out the broad plans of the organization and making decisions that effect its long-range future.

Tort (23) Violation of the basic rights of all citizens.

Touchscreen (21) CDT that allows a user to operate the computer simply by touching the screen.

Tough-guy, macho culture (A) Organization culture characterized by high risk and fast feedback.

Trade (1) Any exchange of goods or services.

Trade acceptance (17) Time draft that is used in domestic trade.

Trade credit (17) Credit extended to the buyer of inventory by the seller.

Trade discount (13) Discount in price given to a purchaser of goods who performs certain services advantageous to the seller.

Trade draft (17) Written instrument made by one person ordering a second person to pay a sum of money to a third party upon demand, or at some future date; also called a bill of exchange.

Trade Expansion Act (24) Federal legislation that gives the president more authority in making tariff concessions to expand trade.

Trademark (13) Brand name for which the company obtains legal, exclusive rights to its use; may be a graphic of some type as well as the name itself.

Traitist theory (6) Concept that capable leaders have personality traits that differentiate them from poor leaders.

Trapdoor (21) Simple code used by computer thieves allowing them to bypass security devices and get data into and out of a computer easily.

Trojan horse (21) Covert set of computer instructions that modify or replace an entire computer program.

Trustee (17) Third party charged with protecting the rights of bondholders.

Trust indenture (17) *See* bond indenture.

Turnover (9) Rate of employees leaving a firm.

Underwriting (17) Purchase of securities, or the guarantee of their sale at a specific price, by an investment group.

Unemployment rate (2) Percentage of employable people within the work force who are unable to find work.

Uniform commercial code (23) Model statutes intended to create more uniformity among state laws.

Uniform delivered price (13) Price that includes cost of transportation regardless of how far products are shipped.

Uniform offering circular (5) Legal document, required in most states, that discloses all financial information and details the specific arrangements between the franchisor and franchisee.

Uniform Partnership Act (4) Act of Congress in 1914 that established the legal guidelines for the existence of partnerships.

Uninsurable risk (19) Risk that cannot be shifted to an insuring company.

Union contract or agreement (11) Final result of collective bargaining that is agreed on, or accepted, by both labor and management.

Union shop (11) Situation where, if workers vote to have a union, all employees of certain job descriptions must eventually join that union; also called a closed shop.

Unissued stock (17) Portion of authorized stock that has not been released.

Universe (C) Total number of possible items from which sample measures are drawn; also called population.

Unlimited liability (4) Situation in which an owner's personal wealth is vulnerable to claims against the business; owners of partnerships and proprietorships usually have unlimited liability.

Unlisted security (18) Security traded in over-the-counter markets.

Unsecured loan (17) Loan that has nothing of tangible value pledged to back it up in case the loan is not repaid; also called a signature loan.

Use tax (22) Tax on goods bought in another state to avoid local sales taxes.

Utility (8) Extent to which the production capabilities of a country satisfies the needs of its consumers.

Vendor (8) Supplier of goods or services.

Vertical chart (7) Organization chart that shows higher levels of authority above those of subordinate positions.

Vertical marketing system (VMS) (14) Well-planned and coordinated distribution network.

Vertical merger (4) Joining of companies with related but different business activities.

Very large scale integration (VLSI) (21) Hundreds of thousands of transistors packed onto a single silicon chip.

Vestibule training (9) Training conducted within a simulation of the working situation.

Visual display terminal (VDT) (21) Computer terminal that has a televisionlike screen for displaying data.

Voluntary bankruptcy (23) Situation in which a firm files for bankruptcy on its own accord.

Warehouse receipt (17) Contract for possession of goods that have been received and stored by a warehouse.

Warrant (18) Right to buy a certain number of shares of stock at a stated price for a given time period.

Warranty (23) Guarantee that certain conditions of the sale of goods or services are accurate as promised.

Whole-life policy (19) Life insurance policy that requires premium payments from the time a person takes out insurance until he or she dies. After a period, this policy accumulates a cash-surrender value.

Wholesaler (14) Person or business that (usually) buys products from a producer and sells them to a retailer at a profit. A wholesaler might also sell goods to other wholesalers.

Wholesaler sponsored voluntary chain (14) System in which wholesalers make an agreement with a group of retailers to cooperate on promotion, pricing, and the like.

Word processing software (21) Programs that allow the user to write, edit, revise, move, and format text for letters, reports, and manuscripts.

Work hard/play hard culture (A) Organizational culture characterized by low risk and fast feedback.

Working capital (17, 20) Excess of current assets over current liabilities; cash and immediate resources available to a company at a specific time.

Workmen's compensation insurance (19) Accident insurance that guarantees medical expenses and salary payments to employees injured on the job; required by law in most states.

Workstation (21) Computer work area where executives and others use a terminal or a personal computer tied to a network or to a main frame.

Yellow-dog contract (11) Agreement between a company and its employees where the employee agrees not to join a union. This type of contract was made illegal by the Norris-LaGuardia Act of 1932.

Zone price (13) Method of pricing whereby producers divide their market into zones and establish the same price within each zone.

Answers to Mind Your Business

Chapter 1: Foundations of Our Private Enterprise System

All answers are false (F). 1. They amount to about 5%. 2. The backing is the willingness of people to accept it. 3. The major cause is an increase in productivity. 4. Only about one-fourth of civilian workers belong. 5. There are far more individually owned businesses. 6. The major purpose is to make it easy for people to buy and sell their stocks and to help companies raise money. 7. It owns about one-third of all land. 8. Fringe benefits average more than 30%. 9. Most money is spent on newspapers. 10. You loan money to the company. 11. It is equal to about 33%. 12. Wages have increased faster. 13. The cost of living goes down. 14. It's not impossible, but there may be required procedures to follow. 15. Advertising usually causes prices to be lower.

Chapter 2: Business and Economic Systems

1. B 2. C 3. C 4. A 5. A 6. B 7. A 8. B 9. C 10. A
Statements 4, 5, 7, and 10 reflect characteristics of capitalism; 1, 6, and 8 describe aspects of socialism; and 2, 3, and 9 are more characteristic of socialism.

Chapter 3: Business and Society

Total your scores. Although each of these statements is open to debate, higher scores tend to reflect a more liberal view, whereas lower scores suggest a more conservative view for dealing with social issues. Compare your scores to others in the class and discuss your reasoning.

Chapter 4: Forms of Business Ownership

1. A 2. B 3. B 4. C 5. C 6. C 7. A 8. C 9. C 10. C 11. C
12. G 13. H 14. A 15. B 16. D 17. E 18. F 19. C 20. C

Chapter 5: Small Business, Entrepreneurship, and Franchising

1. True. 2. True. 3. False. They are married. 4. False. They are usually in their thirties. 5. False. It first appears when a person is in his or her teens. 6. True. 7. False. The major reason is that they do not like to work for others. 8. False. He or she typically moves from new venture to new venture. 9. True. 10. True. 11. True. 12. False. He or she frequently relies on external management professionals. 13. False. They are doers. 14. False. They are moderate risk takers. 15. False. Another necessary ingredient is customers.

Chapter 6: The Process of Management

1. False. You must have enough technical background to communicate with your people and to gain credibility. 2. True. In addition, the objectives should be in writing, be discussed regularly, and create enthusiasm. 3. False. The reverse is the case. 4. True, and other functions as well. 5. False. Theory X. 6. False. Theory Z. 7. True, according to authors Peters and Waterman. 8. True. Quality control departments, inspectors, and inspection processes require a lot of budget. 9. True, because they are more informal and spontaneous. 10. False. In fact, some evidence suggests that liberal arts majors, because of their broader interests and greater interpersonal skills, might be better.

Enrichment Chapter A: Corporate Culture

The answer to Numbers 1, 2, 4, 6, 8, 9, and 10 is Yes. The answer to Numbers 3, 5, and 7 is No.

Chapter 7: Business Organization and Structure

The following relationships, most authorities would agree, are ineffective: 1, 4, 5, 6, 7, 8, 9, 10

Chapter 8: Production and Operations Management

Numbers 2, 4, 5, and 7 are true. Numbers 1, 3, 6, 8, 9, and 10 are false.

Chapter 9: Human Resources Management

1. b   2. c   3. a   4. b   5. d   6. a

Chapter 10: Understanding and Motivating Employees

Numbers 3, 5, 6, 8, 12, 13, 16, 19, 23, 25, 26, 27, 31, and 32 are important motivations for employees (Yes). Numbers 1, 2, 4, 7, 9, 10, 11, 14, 15, 17, 18, 20, 21, 22, 24, 28, 29, and 30 are not effective motivations today (No).

Chapter 11: Management and Labor

Most authorities agree that the following are correct: 1. A   2. B   3. A   4. B   5. A   6. C   7. B   8. A   9. C   10. C

Chapter 12: The Marketing Process

The answer to Numbers 1, 3, 4, 6, 8, and 9 is Yes. The answer to Numbers 2, 5, 7, and 10 is No.

Enrichment Chapter B: Strategic Marketing

1. True. Marketing and finance are major factors, but production and human resource considerations are also important. 2. False. It is just the opposite. 3. False. It focuses on customers and the environment. 4. True. Competition often offers similar characteristics. 5. True. One of the top. 6. False. Product strategy. 7. True. Both of these strategies. 8. True. A major reason for repositioning. 9. True. Penetration pricing is often used to introduce a new product into the market. 10. False. Distribution strategies concentrate on channels of distribution, while promotion strategies consider advertising approaches.

Chapter 13: Product Planning and Pricing

1. True. All these go together to help define the product. 2. False. Convenience goods. 3. False. Typically during maturity. 4. False. Usually during introduction. 5. False. Many skip some of the stages. 6. True. Both may be held responsible. 7. True. People continue to buy the brand if the price is increased. 8. False. Packaging is also part of promotion. 9. False. There are many different policies for pricing. 10. False. Product-line pricing identifies a limited number of prices for their items, and odd pricing quotes prices just under the next highest dollar figure for psychological purposes.

Chapter 14: Distribution Channels

1. No. The two-stage which includes a wholesaler and a retailer is the most popular. 2. Yes. Title must move from producer to purchaser. 3. Yes. Perishable goods, for example, may have to travel the most direct channel. 4. No. More specialized. 5. No. Increasing. 6. No. Retailing. 7. No. Possession but not title. 8. Yes. About 97%. 9. Yes. Powerful companies can get unusual cooperation. 10. No. Truck is the most convenient.

Chapter 15: Promotion, Advertising, and Personal Selling

1. True. A very important objective of promotions. 2. False. The ultimate consumer. 3. True. Other methods include trying to keep up with the competition and allocating enough budget to accomplish the task. 4. True. It tries to make sure customers are satisfied. 5. False. Follow-up is the last step. 6. True. For the purpose of establishing a relative market position. 7. False. It expresses a position on a social issue. 8. False. Newspapers. 9. True. This is rather standard. 10. False. Although in some cases it might.

Chapter 16: Money, Banking, and Financial Institutions

1. c, does not increase value, only measures it. 2. b, money is not backed by silver, only the government's declaration that it is legal tender. 3. c, banks are getting larger, not smaller. 4. b, check-clearing services since 1980 are no longer free. 5. b, savings and loans associations have benefitted from less restrictive laws in California.

Chapter 17: Business Finance: Raising and Investing Capital

1. True. You are not loaning money. 2. True. Since selling stock does not increase your debt. 3. True. Selling stock is not making a loan. 4. True. People who buy the new stock are owners. 5. False. Companies have to pay taxes on the profits, and people who receive the dividends also have to pay taxes on the dividends. 6. True. If the firm pays part of its earnings out in dividends, this money is not available for expansion. 7. False. This is a loan, not a stock sale. 8. True. As spelled out in the bond indenture. 9. False. Payment of interest is a tax deduction. 10. False. Money has to be paid when the bond becomes due. 11. True. Perhaps quarterly or yearly. 12. True. Your ability to borrow short-term funds may be reduced because of your long-term debt (bonds).

Chapter 18: Dealing in the Securities Markets

1. Check the price of IBM common in a current paper and calculate the difference between today's price and the February 10, 1984 price. 2. Call a broker and ask how much commission would be charged on a transaction of 100 shares of IBM common. The broker may give you an approximate commission. Remember you have to calculate the commission when you buy and when you sell. 3. Look the figure up in a current paper. 4. A short sale means that you sold stock that you did not have. So the February 10 price will be the money that you received from the sale. The current price will be the figure you had to pay for the stock. Do not bother to figure the commission on this one. 5. Look up the price-earnings ratio for Motorola. A lower price earnings ratio would suggest a better investment today. A higher P-E ratio would suggest that the February 10 price was a better investment. Of course, there are many factors to consider other than just the P-E ratio when analyzing investment opportunities. 6. Check the stock pages in a current paper. 7. Check the stock pages in a current paper.

Chapter 19: Risk Management and Insurance

1. No. The judge decided that she was not using the product as intended, as the instructions clearly stated the drain must be covered. 2. Yes. Both the pills and the disposal unit as well as other damage to the house. 3. No. The accident was due to the shopper's negligence, but the shopping center did give her $100 worth of credit coupons to be used at the center. 4. No. Hugs were not covered. 5. No. The driver was negligent to leave the car running, and the dog did not have a driver's license.

Chapter 20: Accounting Principles

Balance sheet items (A) include: 1. cash, 3. accounts receivable, 4. merchandise inventory, 8. common stock, 10. equity, 13. accounts payable, 14. buildings, 16. mortgage on land, 17. preferred stock, and 20. goodwill.

Income statement items (B) include: 2. revenues, 5. net sales, 6. net purchases, 7. selling expenses, 9. net income, 11. cost of goods sold, 12. advertising expenses, 15. depreciation expense, 18. sales salaries, and 19. administrative salaries.

Enrichment Chapter C: The Uses of Statistical Methods

1. False. Primary data is more expensive. 2. True. Because the data has already been gathered by the government. 3. True. Although it may not be the easiest to perform. 4. False. Primary data. 5. True. Because you can identify causal factors. 6. True. The most widely used. 7. True. But time series tries to identify past irregularities in the data. 8. False. Only that they occur in concert. 9. False. Line charts are better. 10. True. But tables can convey a lot of data and serve as good means of documentation.

Chapter 21: The Role of the Computer

1. B, the silicon chip made it possible to make smaller computers. 2. A, most people refer to any computer machine as hardware. 3. D, language more like English. 4. E, operates on 8 bits of information at the time, as opposed to 16 bits or 32 bits. 5. F, allows one computer to communicate with another via telephone lines. 6. H, combines many computers together. 7. G, software for writing letters, manuscripts, and reports. 8. I, communicating from computer to computer with messages, memos, and the like. 9. C, a two-digit numbering system. 10. K, one of the several social issues created by computers. 11. J, CPU, the main computer component. 12. L, other examples include punched cards, magnetic-ink-character recognition, and magnetic tapes.

Chapter 22: Government and Taxes

Circle the points that you allocated to the following answers: 1. A, 2. A, 3. B, 4. A, 5. A, 6. A, 7. A, 8. A. Total your circled points. Interpretation: 51 or more = a more liberal view; 29 points or lower = a more conservative view; 30 to 50 points = a moderate view.

Chapter 23: Business Law

1. A, deceptive. The advertising did not reflect significant changes made by competitors since the test. 2. B, the company. The court ruled that even if the assignment policy effectively prevented many women from holding key jobs, the policy was legitimate and protected by law. 3. B, the bank. The purchaser was not entitled to rely on the attorney's performance because the attorney had been hired by the bank. 4. B, survivors of the victim. A business cannot deny the use of a phone in a public place to call the police in case of an emergency.

Chapter 24: International Business

By dividing your answers into two groupings, we can get a profile of your attitudes toward international trade. Check your responses in the accompanying scales.

Questions 1–5	Questions 6–10	Attitude
3 agrees	3 agrees	Favorable toward international trade
4 or more agrees	4 or more agrees	Very favorable toward international trade
3 disagrees	3 disagrees	Unfavorable toward international trade
4 or more disagrees	4 or more disagrees	Very unfavorable toward international trade
3 or more agrees	3 or more disagrees	Exploitive American
3 or more disagrees	3 or more agrees	Anti-American

Agreements with Questions 1–5 favor the benefits that the United States gets from international trade, and agreements with Questions 6–10 favor benefits that foreign nations get from trade with the United States. By agreeing with all or most of the ten statements, you show very favorable attitudes toward international trade. By disagreeing with all or most of the statements, you indicate negative attitudes toward international trade. But if you agree with 1–5 and disagree with 6–10, you may favor the United States exploiting other countries. And if you disagree with 1–5, while agreeing with 6–10, you may favor other countries exploiting the United States.

Enrichment Chapter D: Careers in Business

The more "yes" answers you can give, the more your job and career pattern matches success-inducing thoughts and actions cited by executives in the Cox Report on the American Corporation, an in-depth survey of more than 1000 executives, conducted by Allan Cox. 1. Successful people tend to be goal directed. 2. Let your ultimate career goals guide your education and work experiences. 3. High achievers have high expectations. 4. Getting a good job and having a successful career require taking risks. 5. Good breaks do not just happen; you earn them. 6. If you limit yourself geographically, you will limit your job and career choices. 7. It is hard to give your best effort if you do not feel loyalty. 8. Successful people cultivate contacts. 9. About 44% of middle and top executives get their first jobs through college recruiters, and another 43% of middle and top executives get their first jobs through relatives and friends.

Enrichment Chapter E: The Future of Business

1. True. Probably, because people are waiting longer to marry. 2. True. We are adapting to smaller homes. 3. True.

More women will continue to work, and we will realize some of the benefits of technological improvements.   4. True. Leisure time has been increasing for the past 50 years and will continue to do so.   5. True. We will continue to place more emphasis on education.   6. False. We have the technology, but social skills or the desire seem to be lacking.   7. False. Rate of growth will no doubt slow.   8. False. Population will be older because of health habits and medicine.   9. False. Oil, gas, and coal.   10. False. Output will grow.   11. True. Jobs and careers will likely change more rapidly.   12. True. Participation will increase at every level.

Photo Credits

367. Courtesy of AT&T Bell Laboratories.
369. © 1983 CSX Corporation.
375. Courtesy Sandra Johnson.
376. Sears, Roebuck and Co.
380. Photo courtesy of Mary Kay Cosmetics.
381. Advertiser: MCI Mail, Washington, D.C. Agency: Ally and Gargano, New York, N.Y.
382. Agency: Needham, Harper and Steers USA. Art Director: Paul Frahm. Copy Writer: Michael Robertson.
383. (top) Consumer Information Service, CompuServe, Inc.; (bottom) © 1983 Allied Corporation.
384. (left) Courtesy Levi Strauss & Co.; (right) Reprinted with permission of The Travelers Corporation.
385. (left) Gannett Co., Inc.; (right) © 1982 Bell Helmets, Inc. Agency: Cochrane Chase, Livingstone & Co. Inc., Newport Beach, California.
389. Gannett Co., Inc.
392. Courtesy of the Allied Corporation.
409. Courtesy of the Allied Corporation.
410. Tom Belanger.
414. Courtesy of Mobil Oil Corporation.
416. Sears, Roebuck and Co.
420. United Press International.
439. ITT Corporation.
443. Courtesy of the National Bank of Commerce, Lincoln Nebraska.
449. United States Steel Corporation.
457. Courtesy of the Allied Corporation.
458. Courtesy of the Midwest Stock Exchange.
459. Photos courtesy of the New York Stock Exchange.
472. Photos courtesy of Knight-Ridder Newspapers, Inc.
479. Courtesy of The Calvert Group.
486. Printed with the permission of Frank B. Hall & Co., Inc.
487. Courtesy of Texaco Inc.
491. United States Steel Corporation.
492. Permission granted by Cigna Corporation.
497. Fred S. James & Co., Inc.
498. Photo courtesy of Hewlett-Packard Company.
521. United States Steel Corporation.
524. Courtesy of Texaco Inc.
528. Tenneco Inc. photo.

532. E. I. du Pont de Nemours and Company, Inc.
536. Fleming Companies, Inc.
550. Photo courtesy of Ramtek Corporation.
552. Automatix Robotic Systems, Billerica MA.
553. Displays produced by SAS/GRAPH®, from SAS Institute, Inc., on a Tektronix 45105 Computer Display Terminal.
554. (top left) Slide contributed by Artificial Intelligence Corporation; (bottom left) Photo courtesy of Ramtek Corporation; (top right) Display produced by SAS/GRAPH®, from SAS Institute, Inc., on a Tektronix 45105 Computer Display Terminal; (bottom right) ISSCO.
562. Photos reprinted by permission from *Annual Report, 1979* © 1979 by International Business Machines Corporation.
568. Photos courtesy of Apple Computer, Inc.
571. Photo courtesy of Hewlett-Packard Company.
572. (top and middle) ISSCO; (bottom) Courtesy Lotus Development Corporation.
573. Courtesy of Apple Computer, Inc.
575. Reproduced with permission of AT&T.
576. Photo courtesy of Hewlett-Packard Company.
577. Photo courtesy of Hewlett-Packard Company.
580. Courtesy of ICS-Intext.
604. Fleming Companies, Inc.
607. Tenneco Inc. photo.
623. Courtesy of Raytheon.
640. Advertisement reproduced courtesy of The Moosehead Brewery, Saint John, New Brunswick, and Dartmouth, Nova Scotia.
641. Xerox Corporation.
650. United Steelworkers of America.
656. Photos courtesy of The Coca-Cola Company.
657. Courtesy of H. J. Heinz Company.
663. (top left) Courtesy Honeywell Inc.; (top right) Sears, Roebuck and Co.; (bottom) Photo courtesy of Waste Management, Inc.
664. Photo courtesy Genex Corporation, Rockville, MD.
665. Courtesy of Texaco, Inc.
676. Courtesy of Texaco, Inc.
683. Photos courtesy of Knight-Ridder Newspapers, Inc.
689. Courtesy of Sandra Johnson.

Index